RICHARD BROOME AM is Emeritus Professor of History at La Trobe University. One of Australia's most respected scholars of Aboriginal history and an award-winning writer, he is the author of more than twenty books including *Aboriginal Australians* in five editions (1982–2019), *Fighting Hard* (2015), co-author of *Mallee Country* (2019), author and co-editor of the four-volume textbook *Analysing Australian History* (2021), and a contributing author to *Failed Ambitions* (2023).

'Richard Broome is to be congratulated for writing this history in a style that is easy to read, very informative and brings the past to the present.'
Jim Berg, JP, Gunditjmara man, founder and former director of the Koorie Heritage Trust

'This finely crafted and wonderfully compassionate book deepens our understanding of the history of colonialism.'
Bain Attwood, Professor of History, Monash University

'One of the most important books written about our corner of the planet . . . It stands alongside the great Victorian histories of Margaret Kiddle, Geoffrey Serle and Graeme Davison.'
Professor Janet McCalman's review in Meanjin

'Thoroughly researched and beautifully written, without clamour or artifice . . . yet it reads like an epic.'
Judges' comments, Victorian Community History Book prize

ABORIGINAL VICTORIANS

A HISTORY SINCE 1800

Second Edition

RICHARD BROOME

ALLEN&UNWIN

SYDNEY·MELBOURNE·AUCKLAND·LONDON

This second edition published in 2024
First edition published in 2005

Published with the assistance of the Australian Academy of Humanities
This publication has been supported by La Trobe University
Internet: http://www.latrobe.edu.au

Allen & Unwin
Cammeraygal Country
83 Alexander Street
Crows Nest NSW 2065
Australia
Phone: (61 2) 8425 0100
Email: info@allenandunwin.com
Web: www.allenandunwin.com

*Allen & Unwin acknowledges the Traditional Owners of the Country on which we
live and work. We pay our respects to all Aboriginal and Torres Strait Islander
Elders, past and present.*

A catalogue record for this
book is available from the
National Library of Australia

ISBN 978 1 76087 947 1

Index by Sharon Betridge
Set in 11.5/13.5 pt Minion Pro by Midland Typesetters, Australia
Printed and bound in Australia by Pegasus Media & Logistics

10 9 8 7 6 5 4 3 2

The paper in this book is FSC® certified.
FSC® promotes environmentally responsible,
socially beneficial and economically viable
management of the world's forests.

CONTENTS

Note of warning		ix
On words		ix
Preface and Acknowledgements		xi
Reflections		xvii
Part 1	Wild Times: 1800–1850	1
1.	Meeting strangers	3
2.	Melbourne, an Aboriginal domain	15
3.	Countering civilisers	35
4.	Accommodating sheep herders	54
5.	Dangerous frontiers	69
Part 2	Transformations: 1850–1886	95
6.	Negotiating two worlds	97
7.	New communities	119
8.	Country 'wanderers'	146
9.	A 'miserable spadeful of ground'	166
Part 3	Assimilationism: 1886–1970	183
10.	Under the Acts	185
11.	'Old Lake Tyers'	217
12.	Fighting for Framlingham	235
13.	Country campers	258
14.	Melbourne and Aboriginal activism	286
15.	Assimilation and its challengers	312
Part 4	Renaissance: 1970 Onwards	339
16.	Seeking autonomy	341
17.	Being Aboriginal	375
18.	New day dawning?	398
Appendix		423
Recommended reading		429
Endnotes		435
Index		489

I dedicate this book to my parents:
my late father Cec and late mother Valma (nee Russell).
They taught me the value of family,
to search for truth and to love the past.

Note of Warning

This book, which is a history, contains many references to deceased Aboriginal people, their words, names, actions and sometimes their photographs. Their words used and actions described here are already in the public domain. Permission has been sought to use their images. Many Aboriginal people follow the custom of not using the names or images of those deceased. Individuals and communities should be warned that they may read or see things in this book that could cause distress and should therefore exercise caution when using this history.

On Words

This book will use multiple words to describe the historical actors. The traditional owners will be referred to where possible by their own local group or language names that stem from traditional times, such as Wathaurong, Woiwurrung, Boonwurrung or Gunditjmara. Also, local names will be used that have been acquired, employed and accepted by Aboriginal people since colonial contact—for instance, Lake Condah or Lake Tyers people. When the need arises to describe those in wider regions, Aboriginal names that are widely, but not universally, accepted by original owners may sometimes be used, such as Kulin, Wergaia or Gunai/Kurnai.

When all traditional owners are referred to, we must use European words, as no such Indigenous names existed in traditional times. This book will use interchangeably: Aboriginal people(s), Indigenous people(s), Aboriginal and Torres Strait Islander people(s), original owner(s), traditional owner(s), Aboriginal Victorian(s), Indigenous Australian(s) and First Nations people(s). However, in modern times an overarching Aboriginal word for people in Victoria, Koori(s), has been widely adopted. The plural of these words is indicated in brackets here, as the plural is used to denote that there are many distinct and sovereign groups.

Those who came to settle after 1788 will be called settlers, whites, non-Indigenous people, Europeans, British, and other Australians, where appropriate.

Preface and Acknowledgements

In 2005 when the first edition of this book was published it became the first and only history of how Aboriginal peoples in Victoria experienced and battled with colonisation since 1800. It remains unique in this way to this day. The first edition was well received, winning two prizes—the NSW Premier's Prize in History in 2006 and the Victorian Community History Awards Best Print Book in 2007—and selling over 5000 copies to date. I have updated it for this second edition with an additional last chapter to relate the progressive story from 2004 to the present. I have also updated the names of groups to fit with current usage, revised the section on frontier violence, updated the recommended reading and added an appendix. Sharon Betridge's new and detailed index gives greater access to this epic story.

I began researching this book in 1988 and some people expressed surprise that 'there were any Aboriginal people left in Victoria'. This both astounded me and vindicated my decision to write this book. Their view stemmed from the twin reasoning that as darker skin colour is now less in evidence in Aboriginal Victoria, and traditional dress and customs are generally not adopted, people are therefore no longer Aboriginal. I hope that a reading of this book will end such misapprehensions. My belief is that people should be defined culturally, not racially or by skin colour, and that people are free to define themselves, although communities also have a say in these self-definitions being accepted beyond the self. People do not cease to be Aboriginal due to their skin having been lightened by intermingling and intermarriage with lighter-skinned groups. Nor do people cease to be Aboriginal because they no longer use traditional tools, but laptops, power tools and credit cards to earn their living. Cultures can and do evolve, and people can and do reinvent themselves, while still retaining core cultural values that define them as distinct from other groups.

There is no denying that the European presence in this state, beginning over 200 years ago, irrevocably changed Aboriginal peoples. The

European arrival created a landed and cultural struggle that continues. We must try to imagine the depth of feeling of this contest between original owners, who saw the land as life, as their cultural essence and identity; and newcomers, who saw it as an arcadia, the reward for their uprooting from distant homes and hearths. The subsequent interactions of these groups were diverse, complex and deadly serious—too often literally so—and I have tried to portray them on the large canvas of two centuries. This book is about how Aboriginal people have been challenged by change since 1800, forging a place in Victoria, to live as Aboriginal people in an altered world.

The first edition of this book was delayed until 2005 by other projects: a background paper for the Royal Commission into Aboriginal Deaths in Custody; educational writing, including a brochure for the Aboriginal and Torres Strait Islander Commission and a textbook for Year 12. Two other books, *Sideshow Alley* (1998) on Aboriginal boxers, and *A Man of All Tribes* (2006), a biography of Alick Jackomos, who married into and worked with the Koori community, and academic papers also rescheduled the writing. I was teaching full time at La Trobe University as well. These were not really distractions, but preparations for the writing of this book, which was finished in 2004.

Books create many debts, and I must acknowledge these. My colleague Alan Frost encouraged me to apply successfully for an Australian Research Council grant. It allowed me to employ two clever and meticulous young researchers, my PhD student Corinne Manning and Antoinette Smith, my former Koori honours student. Both combed the archives, libraries and picture collections, discovering enough for three volumes, not one. They acted as my eyes, appraising quantities of material that I could never have covered alone. The ARC grant allowed me time to write in 2003, and La Trobe University also provided me study leave for which I am grateful. My history colleagues gave me much support, especially Adrian Jones and Inga Clendinnen who both inspired me to aim higher.

The first edition was published with the assistance of an Australian Academy of Humanities grant. The large number of images that inform and enhance the text of this book was only made possible by a publication grant from La Trobe University.

In 2001 I wrote to twenty Aboriginal communities across Victoria, inviting them to participate in the making of this history, by providing people willing to be interviewed. After negotiating the rigorous ethics approvals, the following agreed to work with me—the Mildura Aboriginal Cooperative; Budja Budja Aboriginal Cooperative (Halls Gap); Worn Gundidj Aboriginal Cooperative (Warrnambool); Wathaurong Aboriginal

Cooperative (Geelong); and Ramahyuck District Aboriginal Corporation (Sale).

Over six months I travelled across Victoria to interview twenty Koori people from five communities about their lives and views. These conversations, which lasted several hours, were extremely useful and humbling. Each interviewee gave freely of themselves to someone who came to them as a stranger. While only snippets of our long interviews directly appeared in the book, they all informed and shaped my ideas and writing. Once the manuscript was complete, I revisited them all for each to approve their words as they appeared in this book. They also gave permission for the corrected transcripts (so ably typed by Mandy Rooke) to be retained for the future. These are stored in the AIATSIS Library, Canberra. I extend my endless thanks (in alphabetical order) to: Glenda Austin, Lynette Bishop, Murray Bull, Tim Chatfield, Betty Clements, Ivan Couzens, Noel Couzens, Brendan Edwards, Myra Grinter, Charlotte Jackson, Daphne Lowe, Robert Lowe, Ray Marks, Mark Matthews, Albert Mullett, Sandra Neilson, Sandra Stewart, Jamie Thomas, Elizabeth Tournier and Bess Yarram.

The staff of other Aboriginal organisations also assisted me, notably: Gunditjmara Aboriginal Cooperative, Warrnambool; Bangerang Cultural Centre, Shepparton; KODE School, Mildura; Koorie Heritage Trust, Melbourne; Krowathunkoolong Keeping Place, Bairnsdale; Museum Victoria's Aboriginal Advisory Committee; Rumbalara Aboriginal Cooperative, Mooroopna; and Wathaurong Glass, Geelong. Thanks also to Julie Wilson, Daryl Rose, Mark Edwards and Trevor Abrahams.

Historians depend on archival repositories and libraries. My deepest thanks to the staff of the following institutions: Aboriginal Affairs Victoria (especially Christina Pavlides); Ararat Genealogical Society; Australian Institute of Aboriginal and Torres Strait Islander Studies, Canberra; Catholic Heritage Commission, Melbourne; Colac and District Historical Society; Echuca Historical Society; Herald and Weekly Times Library; National Archives of Australia, Victorian and Canberra Branches; Public Record Office of Victoria; Salvation Army; and the State Library of Victoria.

I must thank the following for assistance with pictures and the kind permission to publish. ATSIC (especially Giuseppe Stramandinoli); Fairfax Ltd; Herald & Weekly Times Ltd; Dixson Gallery and Mitchell Library at the State Library of NSW (special thanks to Jenny Broomhead); Museum Victoria (with great thanks to Mary Morris, Melanie Roberts, Sandra Smith and Gaye Sculthorpe); National Library of Australia; Parliamentary Library, Parliament of Victoria; Royal Historical Society of Victoria; and State Library of Victoria (particularly Diane Reilly and Fiona Jeffrey). Great thanks also for use of photographs to Richard Collopy, Ivan Couzens, Jan Critchett, Tony Garvey, Merle Jackomos and the family of the late Alick Jackomos, Amy and Robert Lowe, Bill Nicholson, Tony Garvey, Elizabeth Tournier and Margaret Donnan. Sharon Harrup supplied the map for Chapter 18.

Many unnamed families, which the privacy laws stop me from thanking by name, gave moral permission to use images found in Museum Victoria and the State Library of Victoria. I have included all the known names of individuals in the photographic captions. I do this meaning no disrespect, but on the contrary, to dignify the lives of those in the past by acknowledging their existence. A publication assistance fund at La Trobe University ensured that over a hundred images, double the number at first contemplated, inform the book. My thanks go to Debra Couzens, who drew the part title image 'Kooyoorn' (meeting place) and chapter title page image 'Thanambool Yana' (black women's path) and gave me permission for them to grace the book.

I owe an immense debt to the readers of my manuscript. Corinne Manning and Antoinette Smith provided advice and much warm support. John Hirst, long-time friend and colleague, gave fierce advice and much quiet encouragement. Bain Attwood offered many thoughtful and detailed comments on the final manuscript. The writing group at La Trobe University provided pertinent comments on Chapter 18, which improved it markedly. My publisher at Allen & Unwin, Elizabeth Weiss, extended wise thoughts about audience and presentation, for both the first and second edition. My editor Karen Gee (first edition) and Samantha Kent (second edition) meticulously guided production, and my first edition copyeditor, Edwina Preston, and my second edition copyeditor, Jessica Cox, both made my writing more precise and pleasurable.

My family gave me unfettered support. Two Burmese cats—Cocoa and Sandy—helped the hundred days I spent writing the first edition pass more easily, curled up as they often were at my elbow, occasionally strolling across the keys. Despite living to nineteen they did not make this second edition writing. My children, Kate and Matthew, tolerated my obsession with the book, asking after progress and always offering bemused encouragement and sometimes a coffee. My wife, Margaret Donnan, remains my rock through both editions, despite her own busy career. Her willingness to take more than her share of domestic life when writing became intense was unbounded. Her love sustained my belief in this project, when at times I thought the writing of the book in both editions might keep fading into the distance.

Richard Broome AM

Aboriginal Places
in Victoria

Map of major Aboriginal places, reserves and missions referred to in this book.

Yelta
Mildura
Robinvale
Lake Boga
Swan Hill
Ebenezer
Toolondo
Halls Gap
Mount William
Lake Condah
Framlingham
Elliminyt
Geelong
Ballarat
Bendigo
Mount William (Lancefield)
Mooroopna
Echuca
Cummeragunja
Wodonga
Melbourne
Corranderrk
Ramahyuck
Lake Tyers
Orbost

Reflections

The richness and beauty of the Victorian countryside is evident to any traveller. In 1835 its vista, shaped by Aboriginal burning to create fine pasture for game, moved the NSW Surveyor Major Thomas Mitchell to call it *Australia felix*—happy south land. He saw it as prize left for English-men by God. Mitchell's claim was wrong, in that Victoria was not a prize left by God, but one wrestled from Aboriginal people—the original owners and occupiers—in a fierce and determined colonial struggle.

Times long ago

Aboriginal oral traditions still relate that a formless and empty world was vitalised by great ancestors in ancient times. Many Victorian groups believe Bunjil, the eaglehawk man, brought such life. He shaped the surface of the land and made it bountiful. He carved images of people out of bark and breathed life into them. He gave the people spears and digging sticks and taught them how to hunt and gather. He also gave them a code for living. Another version of his creation powers collected from the Woiwurrung by a settler, Richard Howitt in the 1840s was that Bunjil held his hand to the sun and warmed it. He then turned it to the earth, which caused it to open and people emerged and danced a corroboree called *gayip*. The Wotjobaluk believed the great ancestors, the Bram Bram brothers, also helped Bunjil to shape and name the land and made humans out of a tree. In Gippsland, the Gunai/Kurnai believed their great father was not Bunjil but Munga-ngana, who taught the people how to live and how to act.[1]

Non-Aboriginal scientists prefer to listen to what the bones say, believing that people evolved in the cradle of humanity, now thought to be Africa, some million or more years earlier. These early people later migrated to Asia and finally Australia, at least 60,000 years ago, in a masterly feat of ancient voyaging between islands. As more bones are

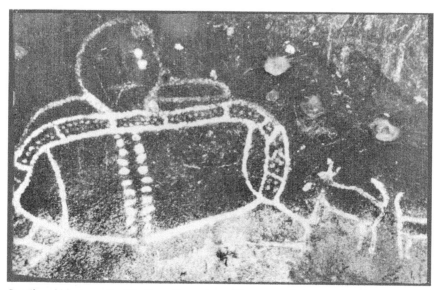

Bunjil and his dogs, Bunjil's Cave, Grampians. (Courtesy of Museum Victoria)

unearthed, the age of Aboriginal society in Australia keeps increasing. Seemingly old human remains, the 'Talgai cranium' and 'Cohuna cranium', were found in 1886 and 1925 respectively, but their age was unclear. In 1940 a cranium was found at Keilor by a quarryman, which, despite early extravagant claims, is now thought to be about 15,000 years old. In the late 1960s an avalanche of evidence about Aboriginal antiquity emerged. Skeletal material of forty individuals was found by Alan Thorne at Kow Swamp near Cohuna on the Murray River in the late 1960s and dated between 10–13,000 years old. Amidst the salt pans and searing heat of Lake Mungo, north of the Murray near Wentworth, ancient camp sites and skeletal remains were discovered by Jim Bowler in 1968 onwards. These remains were dated to at least 42,000 years before the present. Aboriginal Victoria is proving to be very old indeed.[2]

At least 1,600 generations of Aboriginal people have made a continuous life in Victoria. People experienced massive environmental changes that reshaped their lives. A cooling and drying of the world, with average temperatures 5° C lower than today, climaxed about 20,000 years ago. This made life more difficult, changed the ecology and food supply, and extinguished some species, including the giant forms of current Australian fauna. Global warming thereafter led to a rising of the seas by 100–150 metres over 15,000 years, which flooded coastlines, forming Bass Strait and Port Phillip Bay 9,000 years ago. Levels only stabilised to near current heights 6,000 years ago. The Victorian land mass was reduced by one fifth in this process, causing slow but massive alterations to tribal territories. Volcanic activity in the Colac–Port Fairy region, some of it at Tower Hill near Warrnambool as recently as 7,000 years ago, also changed the landscape.[3]

Human knowledge is cumulative and piecemeal. Over millennia a great Aboriginal cultural tradition evolved. Ideas about creation, life, death, species and people, formed in relationship to a changing land, are revealed in human remains. Burials of diverse kinds occurred: cremations, placement of remains in the ground in various positions, burials in trees and caves. Some individuals were interred with possessions, and along the Murray River, human remains were discovered wearing gypsum grave caps. This is evidence both of a sense of an after-life and of cultural diversity among early Aboriginal groups. Surviving stories of the great ancestors collected by early settlers clearly indicate a moral and imaginative life.

Artworks reveal a great tradition as well. Art seen by early settlers was painted on bodies and bark or drawn in sand and much, therefore, has not survived. However, rock art sites survive particularly in the Grampians-Gariwerd region of western Victoria, where 100 sites have been found containing animal figures, bird tracks, and stencilled hands. Recent dating by a La Trobe University archaeological team suggested the occupation of these rock shelters occurred 20,000 years ago. This art is often overlaid by other art, different in colour and style. Aboriginal art is traditionally refreshed as well. Layers upon painted layers exist, suggesting a continuous but changing tradition.[4]

Technological change over long periods reveals an adaptation to the altered climate. New tools emerged, indigenous to Australia, such as the returning boomerang, whose subtle aerodynamics indicate a long period of honing its perfection without the aid of design drawings, books or a wind tunnel. Australian tools shifted from stone to greater use of wood and bone and became smaller as the technology was refined.[5] Strategies for hunting Australian animals that jumped, ran and burrowed were devised, using stealth, diversions, hiding and disguises. Massive nets were made out of fibre to trap ducks, which hunters caused to swoop low at the end of a billabong. Baskets were woven to trap fish corralled in waterways, and fish hooks, nets and barbed spears were developed for fishing. Many of these changes encouraged Aboriginal hunters and gatherers to become semi-sedentary.

The eel fisheries of western Victoria were first sighted in early colonial times. Below Mount William in 1841, George Augustus Robinson, the Chief Aboriginal Protector, described a vast network of channels and weirs, hectares in size, dug into the soil and rock of the wetlands to connect swamps, floodways and watercourses. At strategic places, fences and baskets channelled and trapped eels. Archaeologists have since studied these waterworks, dug with sticks and wooden dishes. They revealed a massive effort which suggested an intensification of food gathering some 5,000 or so years ago, due to population pressures, a preference for a more sedentary life, or for the power that would flow from creating sufficient foodstocks to hold great meetings for the purposes of trade and ritual. Other such works exist at Toolondo, Lake Bolac, Darlot Creek and Heywood. The remarkable thing is that some of these channels purpose-fully connect the seaward and inland waterways to enlarge the range and catch of fresh water eels (*Anguilla australis*), which travel between sea and river in their life-cycle. Robinson also described groups of huts with low stone walls and wicker and turf-domed sides and roofs built beside these eel farms, which suggest a more sedentary form of living. Groups of earth mounds for houses and camps have also been found near eeling sites.[6]

New political forms emerged from this economic activity. Scientist–historian Jared Diamond and others have argued that in human history a surplus of food leads to greater complexity, socially, economically and politically, as occurred in the fertile crescent in the Middle East over 7,000 years ago.[7] New technologies, power structures and specialisations would have been needed to organise such novel food production. It has been claimed by anthropologists that power in Aboriginal society was shared by older men and was consensual in nature. Chiefs or 'big men' did not traditionally exist, but were created by Europeans seeking to negotiate with an opposite number. However, fish farming suggests a hierarchical political structure, as such a structure would have been needed to organise the immense labour involved in creating kilometres of channels. Archaeologist Harry Lourandos has argued that intensi-fication of food gathering in Aboriginal communities was for political reasons and tribal prestige.[8] James Dawson, who collected evidence from Western District Aboriginal informants in the 1870s—evidence which was 'approved of by them before being written down'—was told that 'every tribe has its chief, who is looked upon in the light of a father, and whose authority is supreme'.[9] Perhaps 'big men' existed beyond the eel and fish farms. In 1970 skeletal remains were found of a 188cm male buried 7,000 years ago at Lake Nitchie near Wentworth. The individ-ual was encircled by a necklace of 162 meticulously and laboriously chiselled Tasmanian Devils' teeth, suggesting a man of high degree.[10] The Aboriginal Protectors in the 1840s were certain there were chiefs in central Victoria as well, William Thomas remarking: 'each tribe has a chief, who directs all its movements'.[11]

When Europeans arrived, Aboriginal people enjoyed an intricate social structure, invisible to most Europeans and only recently painstakingly reconstructed by anthropologists. For instance, Billibellary, otherwise known as Jika Jika (one of the signatories of the Batman Treaty), was the leader or 'chief' of the Wurundjeri-willam clan, which owned the land from north of the Yarra River at Melbourne to Mount William near Lancefield. Clans were patrilineal descent, land-owning groups, perhaps 300–500 strong, composed of people who were all of the one totemic division (moiety), being either *bunjil* (eaglehawk) or *waa* (crow). Billibellary's people called him *ngurungaeta* (clan head or 'chief'). His clan was one of five like-minded, land-owning groups, sharing a common dialect and coalescing loosely as Woiwurrung people: *woi* being their language name and '*wurrung*' the word for 'mouth' or 'speech'. The Woiwurrung were perhaps 1,500–2,500 in number. Four other similarly sized cultural-language groups of central Victoria, the Boonwurrung (Westernport), Wathawurrung (Geelong), DjaDjawurrung (Bendigo) and Daungwurrung (Goulburn), existed in a loose confederation with the Woiwurrung. They all called themselves Kulin and shared a common language. The Kulin intermarried, but generally outside their *wurrung* to avoid marrying near kin, and always to a person of the opposite division or moiety: a *bunjil* person (eaglehawk) had to marry a *waa* (crow). Each Aboriginal person thus had multiple identities, that of their moiety, clan, language group and confederation, which most European observers found almost impossible to fathom.

This was the pattern over most of Victoria in which there were about thirty cultural–language groups formed by hundreds of clans or land-owning groups. These thirty cultural–language groups comprised perhaps 60,000 people before Europeans and their diseases arrived. Many of these cultural–language groups ('tribes' as they used to be called) interacted and intermarried with adjoining groups, but they were at enmity with those further afield, who were feared as possible enemies and sorcerers. Warfare existed with such distant groups, and even with neighbours, after disputes arose over women, trade or ritual transgressions. However, there were traditional mechanisms for containing excessive violence, especially with neighbouring groups.

Billibellary was the owner of the Mount William axe-head quarry near Lancefield, an important technological resource, still under heritage protection today. Other groups came to Mount William to exchange goods—possum-skin cloaks, ochres, specialty weapons and spears—in return for axe-head blanks, which had been worked from the volcanic quarry face. Once traded, these were either passed on in further trading or, through hours of labour, worked into a ground axe-head against a rock face, and then hafted onto a handle with fibre and tree gum to become a valuable tool. This quarry of volcanic greenstone, a most valuable early industrial site, was the centre of a vast chain of relationships that saw these axe-heads traded up to 200 kilometres over much of central and western Victoria and even across the Murray River. This has been verified by research and chemical analysis. Indeed, Victoria was dotted by trade routes as large groups— hundreds strong—met to feast on eels at Lake Bolac and elsewhere, on bogong moths in the high plains, and, at other places where seasonal food surpluses occurred, to arrange marriages, trade goods and swap ritual.[12]

It was into this world of dense relations of kinship, trade and cultural exchange, developed over millennia, that Europeans intruded with their ships, guns, livestock and, unconsciously, killer microbes, to create wild new times, in which all became uncertain and much was altered.

Victoria's distinctiveness

Aboriginal people clashed with English, Scottish, Irish and other European settlers in Australia (termed Europeans hereafter), in patterns that were common across the continent and, indeed, were reminiscent of indigenous–settler clashes across a global imperial frontier. However, Victoria, as in every other place, had its own distinctive indigenous– settler interactions, which must be briefly outlined here.

Victoria, or the Port Phillip District as it was first named by the British, was founded in a unique context of time and place. It was part of the British expansion into Australia, but one undertaken in the 1830s and 1840s (like South Australia) without significant convict labour and in a moment in which a modicum of imperial conscience prevailed. The absence of convicts meant, perhaps, that more god-fearing settlers were present to counter hard-line settler views. It also meant a greater Aboriginal participation in the early labour market of the pastoral economy. Aboriginal people were thus somewhat more valued as labourers for the first fifteen years of Victoria's settlement, before the gold rushes flooded the colony with workers.

The 1830s saw the Whigs in power in Britain, who were influenced by a pressure group of humanitarians and evangelicals. The latter group, known as the Clapham Sect, pressured the Whig Liberal Government to enact the Sect's long-held dream of emancipation for the African slaves in the British West Indies. The Clapham Sect then looked to the plight of indigenous peoples in the British Empire, forging and leading a select committee of the British House of Commons, which made stern pronouncements about British imperial practice and called for the better protection of indigenous peoples. This committee did not seek to end British colonialism, but to ameliorate its effects on indigenous peoples. Its recommendations gave rise to the Port Phillip Protectorate, a unique but failed attempt to make the frontier in Port Phillip a safer place for indigenous people. The presence of this group in London also induced land-hungry entrepreneurs in Hobart, who were seeking land in 'unexplored' Victoria to offer the Kulin people of Central Victoria a treaty in Melbourne in 1835, known as the Batman Treaty. It was the only treaty ever extended to Aboriginal people in Australia, but it was not undertaken for pure motives. It was done to persuade the humanitarian lobby in London that Aboriginal people would be protected, in the hope that they would lobby the British Government to allow settlement to take place on the southern coast, which was against the Government's wishes as it wanted to confine settlement. The absence of convicts and the presence of a humanitarian conscience made for a unique Port Phillip experience and possibly some amelioration of hardline frontier attitudes, compared to New South Wales at the time. South Australia might have been similar to Victoria, but the private nature of its settlement meant that a similar Protectorate never developed to any significant degree.

Port Phillip settlement was shaped also by the landscape. There was no barrier of mountains as around Sydney, no daunting chain of salt lakes like those that lay north of Adelaide, or forest and mountain ranges that hedged pastoral lands in Tasmania and Queensland. Instead, grasslands lay for hundreds of kilometres to the west and north of Melbourne, into which squatters and their sheep made rapid forays, as fast as any expansion in the history of European colonisation. Aboriginal people were overwhelmed by this swift challenge to their ownership of lands—it did not occur so rapidly in other colonies, or not until the Blue Mountains were breached thirty years after Sydney's foundation. Only much later was such a rapid spread possible in the far north of Australia, but more limited access to markets meant the northern pastoral industry was slow to expand. In Port Phillip, Melbourne provided easy access to the world and made surrounding pastoral lands a strong, if distant link, in the supply chain of Lancashire's woollen mills.

While the landscape encouraged the rapid overwhelming of Aboriginal groups, the Port Phillip Protectorate ameliorated the impact. So too did the fire-arms technology available on the Port Phillip frontier. Muzzle-loading, smooth-bore rifles, with gunpowder and pan, or percussion cap ignition systems, were less formidable weapons than the more accurate rapid-fire, breech-loading and rifled weapons of the post-1850s frontier. Thus spear and gun were more evenly matched on the Port Phillip frontier than on northern frontiers. *Racial thinking* was still emerging in the 1830s and 1840s, which made attitudes on the Victorian frontier less hard-lined than those that dominated on later northern frontiers. However, the intensity of the struggle over land in Port Phillip meant that the Aboriginal to European loss of life ratio, through violence on the Port Phillip frontier, was high at about twelve Aboriginal deaths to every European death.

The post-frontier world was also different in Victoria. The gold rushes brought perhaps the most educated and liberal group of migrants to Australia of the whole colonial period. These migrants forged a colonial conscience about indigenous people in Victoria in the 1850s, out of which emerged the first protective legislation enacted by a colonial government. This legislation created a unique Aboriginal administration and a network of Aboriginal reserves and missions. As Aboriginal people moved on and off reserves and missions, most experienced the Protection Board's regime. This system was replicated by NSW authorities increasingly from the 1880s.

After 1886 Victorian governments began to dismantle this reserve system out of fear of creating poor houses and permanent Aboriginal lands, and did so in the face of fierce Aboriginal opposition over more than a generation. During the 1930s an Aboriginal political movement emerged from this struggle, focused on the Kulin and Yorta Yorta people. They remained at the forefront of Aboriginal political struggles for land and rights until the 1960s.

During the period of dismantling protective administration, successive Victorian governments denied that people of 'mixed descent' were Aboriginal, and refused to attend to their special needs. This became increasingly easy to do as the Victorian Aboriginal population plunged to about 500 in the 1920s, the lowest indigenous population level of any colony, except for Tasmania. Victoria, once progressive in Aboriginal administration, fell behind other State administrations in these years, as its Protection Board went almost into hibernation. In the 1950s the Victorian Aboriginal administration was pulled into line by Aboriginal and humanitarian agitation from within the State, and Paul Hasluck's assimilation push at the federal level. By then, the Victorian story was becoming more like those of other States, a situation that increased with federal control of Aboriginal affairs from the 1970s.

However, the experience of Aboriginal Victorians remains distinctive because of the unique family and group stories they tell, and their unique struggles to be free of the colonial past. The stories they tell about the past—'in them days', to quote their Aboriginal English—form a rich account into which this history has tapped.

Part One
Wild Times
1800–1850

The meeting, clashing and entangling of cultures creates wild times—times of excitement, drama, fear, and unpredictability. So it was with Port Phillip from 1800 to 1850 as European intruders, invaders, and settlers encroached on the lands of Aboriginal Victorians.

The Europeans wielded power through the guns they brought, the sheep they grazed over Aboriginal lands, and the structures of new language, new law, new administration and new ideas—capitalism and Christianity—they introduced. They imposed their power on the land by naming it, calling it first 'Port King', then 'the Port Phillip District', and finally 'Victoria', all names of distant English governors and monarchs. Aboriginal names were generally overridden. The Europeans asserted their power over the Aboriginal people too, by calling them 'natives', 'savages', the 'lowest in the hierarchy of races', and setting down their characteristics as a people, claiming to know them. Meanwhile the Aboriginal population was being virtually decimated, falling by eighty per cent.

But these wild times were not one-sided times. The story of the Port Phillip frontier was not a story of all-powerful Europeans with guns of steel and aggressive attitudes pitted against peoples with weapons of wood, who passively gave way. All frontiers are complex places. They are robust and fragile at the same time, places where fear and power are experienced simultaneously and by both sides of the cultural divide. The Port Phillip District was no different. Aboriginal people manipulated, accommodated, imitated, and resisted the European presence. They maintained their cultural ideas, practised their rituals, and continued to seek bush tucker along with forays into the European economy. They devised ways of surviving the wild times, although the majority of them did not succeed.

This section tells stories of these wild times from European documents, both detailed and fragmentary, which recorded Aboriginal actions and, occasionally, Aboriginal voices. It is impossible for us to know what Aboriginal Victorians were really like before 1850, but we can glimpse their shadows on a wall cast by European words.

1

Meeting Strangers

Aboriginal people initially experienced the European adventure in Port Phillip (as pre-1851 Victoria was known) like puzzling fragments of a drama played out behind a translucent screen. The Gunai/Kurnai people probably spied the sails of Lt James Cook's *Endeavour* in April 1770, as he coasted off Gippsland north of Point Hicks, and were bemused by their novelty. The next generation of Gunai/Kurnai secretly watched the shipwrecked crew of the *Sydney Cove* struggling overland from Ninety Mile Beach to Sydney in 1797. They also watched George Bass's whaleboat coast Gippsland as far west as Western Port in 1798. Sealing and whaling ships wallowed past, occasionally to land and refresh. A century later, a missionary in Gippsland, Rev. John Bulmer, noted a song recording these mystical events of sails and men and guns:

mundhanna loornda kathia prappau
There are white men long way off with great noise
Muraskin mundhanna yea a main
Guns there sailing about[1]

First encounters

In 1800 the *Lady Nelson* traversed Bass Strait, the first known European ship to do so. Two more explorations by this vessel found Lt Murray and his crew surfing the rip into Port Phillip Bay in February 1801. Boonwurrung men, leaving their women and children hidden, met five crewmen on the sands near Sorrento—white-faced ghosts with strange cloaks—spirit men perhaps. The warriors were wary, but exchanged spears, an axe and a basket for shirts, mirrors, and a steel axe. Dancing followed but tensions ran high, as the British sought water, and the Boonwurrung queried the strangers' intent. Armed warriors hidden in nearby bushes alarmed the British. Panicked warnings led to spears flying and firing from muskets and the ship's cannon, wounding several Boonwurrung as they fled, the English shirts flapping on their backs. Murray termed it a 'treacherous and unprovoked attack', but the British were intruders on Boonwurrung land. In early March, the Boonwurrung met Captain Milius of the *Naturaliste* alone on the Western Port shore in a more peaceful encounter. The Frenchman stripped, sang and danced to earn their trust. The people inspected his clothes, body, even teeth (for a sign, perhaps, of initiation) before hurrying away in disbelief. Milius considered them 'great children'.[2]

The Boonwurrung faced the first large-scale invasion in 1803. A British convict settlement of 467 people under Lt David Collins disembarked at Sorrento in October 1803 to defend Bass Strait against the French. The Boonwurrung avoided the camp, which was inhabited by as many as the Boonwurrung numbered themselves. Wathawurrung warriors encountered the settlement's survey parties on the western

Sealers' huts at Western Port ('Habitation de Phoques au Port Western') by Louise Auguste de Sainson, 1833. (Courtesy of La Trobe Picture Collection, State Library of Victoria, H84.167/43)

shores of Port Phillip Bay. Nervous moments occurred at Corio Bay as warriors fingered the clothing and implements of the British. Spears, blankets and food crossed the cultural divide, but hostility also emerged. A remarkable incident occurred at the Werribee River as 200 shouting Wathawurrung, some with faces painted in red, white and yellow clays, bore down upon the surveyors, brandishing spears. Several carried between them, on their shoulders, a warrior wearing a reed necklace, a large septum bone and a massive coronet of swan's feathers. The alarmed Europeans fired. A Wathawurrung warrior fell, probably victim of a 19-mm lead ball from a 'Brown Bess' English service musket, which tore his flesh and bone. The charge halted and the Wathawurrung fled in panic at the deadly lightning from the strangers' eyes. After eight months, Lt Collins termed Sorrento an 'unpromising and unproductive country', and withdrew to establish a settlement in Tasmania at Hobart Town. The Boonwurrung picked over the camp for glass and iron and all the Bay people pondered the meaning of this visit.[3]

Several escaped convicts remained behind in Boonwurrung territory. They split up and one of them, William Buckley, headed west around the Bay and survived in the most novel of ways. Buckley, a 195-cm ex-soldier from Cheshire and a convicted thief, was dying of exposure and starvation after failing to live off the land, when the Wathawurrung found him. They believed him to be Murrangurk, a deceased relative, transformed into ghost-like whiteness and strangely bereft of his former language and customs. They took him in, tolerated his oddness and gave him a wife. His tales of the Napoleonic Wars, of armies and horses, of England and London, must have awed them as the knowledge of a spirit traveller, but Buckley always remained a novice in terms of Aboriginal ways. He was assimilated in an extraordinary tale of survival and acceptance, passed down to us in reminiscences he related in old age.[4]

The Kulin peoples of central Victoria had few contacts with Europeans for a further generation, although they picked up rare European flotsam and jetsam that floated the world's seas. Sealers and bark cutters occasionally watered in the Bay. The *Geordy*'s crew clashed with the Boonwurrung during one such visit in 1815, killing one man. Buckley recalled that Wathawurrung saw two Europeans brought ashore, tied to a tree and shot, which horrified them, as they generally punished in less fatal ways. Buckley heard that some Wathawurrung had secretly boarded another visiting vessel to steal glass and iron. When the Frenchman Dumont D'Urville sketched sealers at Western Port in 1826, he drew an Aboriginal woman attending the sealers' hut. In 1833, nine Woiwurrung and Boonwurrung women and a youth, Yonki Yonka, were

'Native Women Getting Tam Bourn Roots. 27 Ag. 1835' from John Helder Wedge's field book. (Courtesy of La Trobe Australian Manuscripts Collection, State Library of Victoria)

captured by sealers, and the women were taken as 'wives' to the Bass Strait Islands according to a story told in 1836 by Derrimut, a Boonwurrung man. Yonki Yonka made it home in 1841 via voyages to Western Australia, and two female descendants of his did so in 1854.[5]

Elsewhere coastal groups encountered or watched Europeans. The Gunditjmara observed and perhaps met bark cutters at Port Fairy as early as 1810, while whalers and sealers visited Wilson's Promontory, Western Port and Portland Bay in the decades before the 1830s. We know nothing of these interactions. Explorers and a temporary British garrison penetrated Western Port in 1826. Numerous Aboriginal groups saw or heard of Captain Charles Sturt as he voyaged the Murray in 1830, and Major Thomas Mitchell as he explored overland to Portland in 1835, leaving puzzling wagon tracks in the soil.[6] Aboriginal people pondered these events in campfire discussions, and speculated on the scraps of iron and fragments from another world that filtered from the north via three great trading routes: that of the Kulin, of the Wergaia-speaking peoples to the north-west, and the Gunai/Kurnai of Gippsland.

Other things intruded from the north: invisible viruses and bacteria. The most devastating human virus of all, smallpox (*variola major*) had been endemic in Asia, Africa and Europe for possibly 5,000 years, having killed Pharaoh Ramses V in 1,157 BC. The disease spread through riverine populations of eastern Australia. Residents of early convict Sydney witnessed an outbreak that killed half the local Aboriginal population in 1789. Historians have debated that outbreak's origin and some have blamed the convict settlement for its introduction. However, smallpox was endemic in Macassar and across the Asian region for several millennia. European contagion certainly did not cause the south-east Australian outbreak of 1830. The weight of evidence suggests that smallpox occasionally spread from Macassan fishermen, who visited northern Australia annually from about 1720 to 1900 in search of trepang (sea slug).

The Asian variety was the most virulent of the various strains of smallpox. Classically, the disease began with raging headaches and high fevers and proceeded to a rash and pustules that covered the body after a week, especially the face, hands and feet, with either a thin spread, or a confluence of lesions in the more virulent forms. Once the pustules broke, the sufferer became even more infectious, and death followed in the second week. The survivors, weak, sore and debilitated, were incapable of caring for themselves for some weeks, particularly as the hard skin on the soles of the feet carried painful scabs for up to a month. Further deaths also occurred from pulmonary and other complications, and from subsequent malnutrition. Survivors were immune to subsequent attacks. The research that assisted smallpox's global eradication in 1979 indicated that it normally killed sufferers of all ages, but was lightest by far on 10–14-year-olds, and killed more women than men, especially pregnant women. It was endemic in populations over 200,000 where survivors were immune, but could infect and re-infect societies of small, scattered groups. In the Americas, it ravaged indigenous hunting peoples sporadically over three centuries after Cortes's conquest in 1518, killing between 30 and 100 per cent of tribal populations.[7]

Smallpox leaves a unique signature by way of pitted marks upon the face. As Lt James Flemming and others observed Aboriginal people with pockmarked faces in 1803, it is likely the Kulin peoples of central and western Victoria were infected with smallpox in 1790 and then 1830 before they ever met a European.[8] William Buckley remembered a 'complaint which spread through the country, occasioning the loss of many lives, attacking generally the healthiest and strongest, whom it appeared to fix upon in preference to the more weakly. It was a dreadful swelling of the feet, so that they [sufferers] were unable to move about, being also afflicted with ulcers of a very painful kind'.[9] Indigenous skin diseases—such as yaws—could not kill. Thus Buckley's recollection of a 'loss of many lives', together with the 'ulcers' and his description of the state of the feet suggests smallpox.

Aboriginal ceremony, by William Barak about 1885.
(Courtesy of La Trobe Picture Collection, State Library of Victoria, H29640)

Many Europeans recalled meeting pock-marked Aboriginal people in the 1830s and 1840s. George Haydon, a settler, noted many in early Melbourne were 'disfigured' in this way. Dr David Thomas recorded in 1839: 'I saw several Blackfellows of the Yarra, Goulburn, Geelong, and other tribes, all of them rather advanced in years, having pits of smallpox'.[10] Settlers in central and western regions of the colony made similar comments. Only Gippsland was free of such observations, which reflected the customary sparse contact between the Gunai/Kurnai and other Victorian groups.[11] Elderly Aboriginal Murray River men with pock-marked faces told a pastoralist, Peter Beveridge, in the 1840s that a pestilence travelled the Murray sent by malevolent sorcerers from the north. So dreadful was the loss of life that after a time the people were unable to bury their dead and simply fled. Beveridge recalled the elderly spoke of it 'with such an amount of loathing horror' as the only time large numbers of people died from one cause.[12] The Wotjobaluk told John Bulmer it came down the river, and termed it *thinba micka*.[13]

William Thomas, the Aboriginal Protector who recorded Aboriginal stories in the 1840s, wrote of the *Mindye*, the great rainbow snake that lived in the northwest and was controlled by one family. The *Mindye* could hiss and spread white particles from its mouth, from which 'disease is inhaled'. Thomas added that 'when the *Mindye* is in a district the blacks run for their lives, setting the bush on fire as they proceed, and not stopping to bury their dead or attend to any seized. Many drop down dead on the road'.[14] In 1843 Europeans witnessed a *gageed* ceremony in Melbourne meant to ward off epidemics.[15] This story and ceremony suggest the memory of an horrific incident of disease.

Smallpox infected Aboriginal people, except the Gunai/Kurnai people of Gippsland, twice before Europeans arrived, perhaps halving the population each time. Women died at higher rates, impeding population recovery. It is likely that sealers, some of whom captured or bartered for Aboriginal women, introduced venereal bacteria as well. However, any infertility from syphilis was minute compared to the impact of smallpox on mortality and population recovery. Noel Butlin, an economic historian who studied smallpox and modelled its likely impact on the population of south-eastern Australia, believed a south-eastern Aboriginal population of 250,000 (perhaps 60,000 in Victoria) in 1788, was halved around 1790 and again in 1830.[16] These new diseases assisted the European conquest.

Managing the intruders

Most Aboriginal people shared the notion of a periphery,[17] an afar place, from which strange things emerged and could be explained. Campfire debates drew on this idea as Aboriginal groups contemplated recent novelties: the *Mindye* (smallpox) was sent from the northwest; Murran-gurk (Buckley) travelled back from a land of the dead; iron and cloth came from a distant place. However, in 1834, sixty-four years after the first glimpse of Cook's sails, a deluge of new things began. The Henty family permanently settled the Gunditjmara's land at Portland Bay in November 1834 with their servants, peculiar livestock and a world of farm technology. In June 1835 John Batman surveyed the future site of Melbourne on behalf of some Van Diemen's Land (Tasmanian) adventurers, who formed the Port Phillip Association. Aboriginal people struggled to explain the increasing changes and fiercely debated how to manage them. While the numbers of intruders remained small and the indigenous economy was intact, Aboriginal people exercised considerable influence, but within a few years only marginal control was possible.

The Kulin watched Batman, a Ben Lomond pastoralist from across Bass Strait, as he walked the lands around the Yarra, pronouncing them the 'most beautiful sheep pasturage I ever saw in my life'.[18] Batman came with his experience of Pallawah people in Van Diemen's Land, seven 'Sydney blacks' as mediators, a treaty to purchase land (the only one ever offered in Australia's colonisation), and a promise to protect Aboriginal people. His fourteen associates were Hobart officials and educated men: capitalists with a humanitarian streak, who genuinely sought good relations with Aboriginal people, but also knew a treaty might win favour in London for their illegal settlement on the southern coast. After a week the Kulin chose to meet with Batman, who trod their lands with a hungry eye. Through the customary gestures and shared dialects of his 'Sydney blacks', Batman communicated his desire to purchase land in exchange for blankets, steel blades, mirrors, beads and 'a tribute, or rent, yearly'. His performance was respectful of the owners. Batman's land purchase document was ritualistic, being in the ancient form of a feoffment, which involved marking the land and exchanging a handful of earth. Land purchase had no meaning to the Kulin—for how could a clan sell its religious and social birth right to strangers who did not know the country, its stories, nor how to care for it. However, the Kulin had a notion of welcome and temporary usage for strangers by way of a *tanderrum* ceremony. Eight Kulin, whom Batman called 'chiefs', signed the treaties (there were two involving land around Melbourne and Geelong).

While land soon worth £150,000 to Europeans (3,000 times a shepherd's annual wage) was 'signed' for little in return, it was a deal freely done and one which had meaning for the Kulin, not as a purchase, but as a hospitality, and perhaps as an agreement regarding the use of resources. Besides, the Kulin knew the value of iron, since Batman had found some sharpened into a blade in a woman's dilly bag. We should see the acceptance of the treaty as a Kulin political strategy (as it was for Batman), and not simply as some white trick or swindle, as five of the eight signatories were Kulin clan heads, astute men who knew what they were about with strangers and were not adverse to killing dangerous interlopers. They had gathered, debated and decided to meet Batman and deal with him, not kill him. Batman and his men with white skins, who came in ships, possessed steel and wrote on paper, were exotic and were thus treated differently to Aboriginal strangers and enemies. That night Batman's 'Sydney blacks' staged a corroboree to the delight of the Kulin, who in turn presented Batman with possum-skin cloaks and weapons on his departure. While both parties acknowledged the treaties—Batman renewed his tribute on the first anniversary and the Kulin's descendants give it a positive significance to this day—the British government rejected them immediately, in order that the Crown's claim of 1770 to own Aboriginal lands would not be questioned.[19]

The Wathawurrung observed Batman's party, led by his brother Henry and including several 'Sydney blacks', as they camped at Indented Head to guard their land deal, while John Batman hurried back to Launceston. Wathawurrung investigated the camp, with its huts and garden laid out in straight lines, as if in accordance with some ritual. Some helped with the work. Within a month of Batman's treaties, William Buckley rejoined white society, claiming he was a shipwrecked soldier. He took days to retrieve his English language.[20] When John Wedge, a former government surveyor and one of the Port Phillip Association members, visited in August 1835, he recorded the first brief ethnographic descriptions of Aboriginal Victorians, shaped more by his preconceived ideas of 'savages' and Buckley's information than by any careful observation. Wedge claimed the Wathawurrung were slaves to the food search, made their women drudges, practised cannibalism (but only after warfare), and infanticide (due to the needs of extended breast-feeding of their young).[21] Joseph Gellibrand, a barrister and another Association member, visited the following January. They traversed the 'purchased' lands with Buckley, who was made Superintendent of the Aborigines by the Association. Gellibrand was touched when Buckley met his Wathawurrung kinsfolk near Geelong, as they 'were all clinging around him and tears of joy and delight [were] running down their cheeks'.[22] Gellibrand termed the Kulin a 'fine race of men many of them handsome in their persons and all well made. They are strong and athletic very intelligent and quick in their perceptions'. The women were 'modest' in their behaviour and dress.

He was certain the Kulin could be brought to the 'habits of Industry and Civilization'.[23]

While finally unanimous in their dealings with Batman, the Kulin disagreed on how to deal with John Pascoe Fawkner, who landed at the Yarra in October 1835, with his wife, servants, farm and household stock, but without a treaty or Aboriginal intermediaries. About 300 Kulin—Woiwurrung, Boonwurrung (both from the Melbourne area), Wathawurrung (Geelong region) and Daungwurrung (Goulburn River)—came to Melbourne in October 1835, allegedly summoned by Buckley to meet John Batman whose return was imminent. Fawkner recorded in his reminiscences that some Kulin helped him unload and erect his house and in return he gave out biscuits, potatoes and clothing, but he made no mention of knives or axes. Several Kulin befriended Fawkner's workman William Watkins and they swapped words as they worked. In late October Fawkner recorded in his diary: 'the Blacks we learnt intended to murder us for our goods'.[24] Derrimut, as one of the informants was later identified, soon warned Watkins (through William Buckley) of an attack by the Wathawurrung and Daungwurrung people. In mid-December more threats were made, perhaps stirred up by Batman's 'Sydney blacks', who, playing a double game, as Fawkner recorded, 'told the natives that we, Batman and me, intended to kill them all'.[25] Derrimut again warned of an attack, Fawkner recording, with archetypal fear of the 'savage' that 'if they succeed they will kill and eat us all'. The Europeans quietly armed. They observed that the Kulin women and children were now absent, and that the warrior men were dragging spears between their toes and had weapons concealed under their cloaks. Fawkner shot into a tree and Buckley was told to order them off. The Kulin scattered. Fawkner and Batman then persuaded them to move across the river, and ferried them there under guard, burning their canoes to impede their return.[26]

What politics was evident here? Why did the up-country Kulin want to attack and the coastal Kulin to befriend? Traditionally, the Melbourne and Goulburn peoples were distrustful of each other, so to disagree on this matter was not unusual. The Europeans' different approach might have caused the split. Yet it was the up-country Kulin, the Daungwurrung and Wathawurrung who did not own the land about Melbourne—although they had rights to it through intra-Kulin marriage—who threatened attack. Unlike Batman, Fawkner had not shown respect through the right protocols and ceremony. Unlike Batman's party, Fawkner's group had not been introduced to land through dance and ceremony. And, unlike Batman, Fawkner had not exchanged steel blades, which were so desired that thefts of axes occurred from Fawkner's camp within a month. Was it anger at Fawkner's lack of respect, or at his lack of generosity as he intruded on Kulin land, that caused the attempted attack by up-country Kulin? What role did Batman's 'Sydney blacks' play, mixing as they did with the Kulin and spreading false rumours? What do we make of Derrimut's actions? Why did he warn Watkins? Derrimut was a clan head of the Boonwurrung on whose land Fawkner was building a house. To see him as a 'collaborator' seeking power, as some have, seems unlikely, since he enjoyed power in his traditional world.[27] Did he (unlike the Goulburn people) see negotiation rather than violence as the way to control these interlopers? It appears that Billibellary, one of the signatories of Batman's treaty, and Benbo, another Aboriginal elder, also shared Derrimut's desire for negotiation and warned Fawkner of an impending clash.[28]

Derrimut exchanged names with Fawkner, a key way of establishing kinship ties and of assimilating outsiders. As the historian Jan Penney wrote of similar name exchange on the Murray: 'names possessed power and indicated relationships, which in turn carried obligatory rights and duties'.[29] Derrimut was given trousers and a knife and, together with his

'Native Encampment on the Banks of the Yarra', J. Cotton, 1842.
(Courtesy the La Trobe Picture Collection, State Library of Victoria, H252)

kinsman Bait Banger, became Fawkner's huntsman, having the use of his gun, knives and boat. Fawkner in turn was bound to the Boonwurrung. In 1836 the two Aboriginal men travelled with Fawkner to Hobart and met Lieutenant Governor Arthur, who presented Derrimut with a drummer boy's uniform.[30] Benbo and his wife Kitty built a hut in John Batman's garden in a similar binding gesture, and made a four-poster bed, which Benbo placed in his hut as 'he wished to do as the white men did'.[31]

The members of the Port Phillip Association assisted initial peacemaking. One member, John Wedge, investigated violence against Boonwurrung people by sealers at Western Port, while Gellibrand sent three shepherds back to Hobart for molesting an Aboriginal woman: 'all the punishment which we had the *power* but not all that we had the *will* to inflict'.[32] While New South Wales's Governor Bourke awaited orders from England about the illegal settlement of the Port Phillip District, he sent James Simpson, a magistrate, to settle the growing unruliness among the 177 settlers and the Kulin. A town meeting in June 1836 agreed to form rules to establish law and order and pledged to protect the estimated 800 Aboriginal people in the area and to report aggressions by or against them. It was a noble sentiment, but one bound as well by fear, as the meeting also pledged not to allow Indigenous warriors to possess or know firearms.[33]

Encounters—well-meaning, confused and violent—occurred in Port Phillip over the next decade, as Aboriginal people met white strangers from other worlds and learned to deal with them. The wild times were just beginning.

2

Melbourne, an Aboriginal Domain

The Kulin and other Aboriginal people camped about the place the British called 'Melbourne' more frequently than was customary because of the European presence. As Edward Curr, a young squatter, recalled, in 1839 Aboriginal people 'constantly wandered about in large numbers, half-naked, and armed with spears in the usual way. To hear them cooeying and shouting to one another, in shrill voices and strange tongues, in the streets had a strange effect'.[1] George McCrae, a youth in 1840, described the Kulin as 'lively, loquacious, good-humoured and honest'. They walked unselfconsciously before packs of mangy dogs, cradling their boomerangs and spears, with possum-skin rugs or government blankets draped about them, fastened by a wooden toggle. Men and women wore ochre-dyed string headbands, adorned with feathers. Some had clay tobacco pipes stuck in their headbands or through their septum. The women wore necklaces of kangaroo teeth, and some had ribbons in their hair and metal rings or bracelets on their hands and wrists. McCrae thought some of the women 'well-favoured and really pretty'. Their children 'were bright-eyed, interesting and intelligent'.[2] McCrae's account reveals an Aboriginal confidence. This English town was on their domain—Boonwurrung and Woiwurrung land—and on the site of a traditional Kulin meeting place.

About the town

Melbourne's foodstuffs lured the Kulin and others from afar. Richard Howitt, an English settler and literary man, saw Aboriginal people 'loaded with sheep's head and feet' heading for the Yarra bank to bake

'Collins Street, Town of Melbourne, New South Wales, 1839' by William Knight.
(Rex Nan Kivell Collection, courtesy of the National Library of Australia, AN5695310)

them in ashes, while the squatter Edward Curr observed them at sunset 'retiring to their camps on the outskirts of the town, well supplied with bread and meat'.[3] At first they were given food, which was plentiful in a pastoral boomtown, but they were soon required to chop wood and carry water from the Yarra in return. A traveller, A. Russell, wrote in 1839 that both groups were 'on the best of terms possible, families having regular visits from some one or other of them, who perform at times little services, getting clothing, etc in return'.[4] Other Aboriginal people made claims on food and goods, by such kinship-aligning techniques as taking the names of Europeans.

These early years in Melbourne were a special period in black–white relations, for they were marked by affability, and driven by a curiosity and an openness of view and manner on both sides. Europeans were intrigued by these people who looked and acted so differently, had no permanent structures, no visible signs of government or religion, no visible use of the land, yet who appeared healthy and happy. One settler wrote to the *Launceston Chronicle* in 1836 that the men were 'fine, tall, well-made fellows, and the[ir] physiognomy and general appearance by no means disagreeable'.[5] The squatter John Cotton described their greased hair that hung in ringlets and commented: 'I have seen some of the blacks walking the streets of Melbourne who might have been termed the native dandies of the town. Their walk is usually very stately and in general they are animated and always ready to smile and laugh ... There is great beauty in the well-moulded limbs and forms of the young native'.[6]

Others like settler Richard Howitt were more ambivalent. His views were strongly ethnocentric, but not racist; that is, he believed he was culturally superior to Aboriginal people, but without subscribing to the idea of biological superiority and separateness as well. Thus Howitt believed that while the people were 'as low as human nature can descend', they were yet 'human creatures—of the same, I am convinced, origin with our race'. Howitt believed Aboriginal people were shaped not by racial attributes, but by an environment that was 'destitute' of domesticable plants and animals. They were 'very erect and dignified in the[ir] attitudes and motions', the men very 'venerable looking, with quite Roman-like nobility of contour', and some of the women 'pleasing-looking'. He penned a poem, 'The Native Woman's Lament', which ended: 'the food, the life, the land is gone / and we must perish in the wild'. However, he disliked the greased and ochred bodies of Aboriginal people, which made them the 'ugliest pieces of human nature'.[7]

Other Europeans were more tough-minded in their attitudes to Aboriginal people. Members of the middle and labouring classes, rarely recorded their thinking, so we can only know their views from their actions. Shopkeepers traded with the Kulin and employed them at times. Some who lived life rough fraternised with the 'blacks', as they termed Aboriginal people, working alongside them, drinking with them and sleeping with their women. Fights erupted in these situations as tensions developed. The term 'savages' fell easily from white lips. However, antagonisms were initially minimal, and especially so around Melbourne, where the presence of the law and mutual curiosity made relations tolerable.

Aboriginal people were also intrigued by the novelty of all before them. They stopped Europeans in the street to shake their hands and the whites responded positively. They were keen to understand the newcomers and gain access to the cargoes their ships disgorged. Aboriginal people were attracted to Melbourne in the same way that hunters and gatherers had always moved to the most accessible food sources.[8] Presents of flour were preferable to hours of gathering and grinding seed. Gifts of offal were preferable to hunting their own meat down. And Melbourne offered novel stimulants—tea, sugar, tobacco—that their own diet lacked. The Kulin expected access to European food resources in accord with their ideas of reciprocity—whereby kin shared food and goods—and also because of the privileges they felt were their due as landowners. If these strategies failed, they laboured for Europeans, some women offering sexual services. Mostly, however, the Kulin expected bounty, not as handouts, but by right of being landowners.

European actions fuelled these expectations and increased the magnetism of Melbourne. Batman first encouraged Aboriginal expectations with his treaty, which promised annual payments. In May 1836—the treaty's first anniversary—he duly issued rice, flour and sugar. Fawkner himself gave out food, usually for work in return, but bent to Kulin demands that sugar be added.[9] Others were more liberal, expecting little in return, perhaps guilty about the usurpation of land.[10] Melbourne became a place of plenty via gifts or exchanges. When Governor Bourke arrived in March 1837 to inspect the new town, he gave out blankets, clothing, and a few brass, crescent-shaped neck-plates to denote supposed Aboriginal authority. He received kangaroo meat and a corroboree in return. In late-March 1839 George Augustus Robinson arrived to become Chief Protector of the Aborigines, and the Government sponsored a feast on the north bank of the Yarra, to which all Melbourne was invited. Over 300 people each consumed or carried away a kilogram of meat and of bread or flour, as well as copious amounts of rice, tea and sugar. The white residents had wine as well, sufficient to make men drunk by nightfall. (Initially the Kulin were wary of attending, having been told by whites antagonistic to the newly-formed Protectorate that they would be kidnapped. Once there, others told the Kulin the food was poisoned, hence the people needed much convincing to begin feasting.) There followed an old English sports day, with Kulin racing for tomahawks, spearing a target for 'white money' (silver coins), climbing greasy poles for prizes of knives and handkerchiefs and watching fireworks in awe.[11] The Kulin also held their own conference in Melbourne while food was in abundance.

'Native Encampment' by John Skinner Prout.
(Courtesy of La Trobe Picture Collection, State Library of Victoria, H13545)

These things were long remembered. The Chief Protector, George Augustus Robinson, reported in May 1839 that Aboriginal people 'pressingly inquired when the big ship would come with the proffered boon of food and blankets'.[12] The following September when news emerged of Superintendent Charles La Trobe's imminent arrival to become the colony's first Superintendent, the Kulin anticipated another feast of tea, sugar, flour, meat and tobacco. In January 1840, a Daungwurrung man told Protector Thomas, who was trying to get him to leave Melbourne, that 'plenty long time ago Mereguk [Mister] Batman come here Blackfellows stop long long time all Blackfellow, plenty bread, plenty sugar, blanket, etc'.[13]

Though effective, this food-gathering strategy in Melbourne created problems. The Kulin were gradually de-skilled and pauperised once they stopped making possum-skin cloaks and catching bush foods, relying on blankets, flour, and mutton instead. With each year the number of Aboriginal campers in Melbourne increased. In April 1839 there were 300 campers by the Yarra, mostly Kulin from the Woiwurrung, Boonwurrung and Daungwurrung groups, gathered around 60 campfires. Most stayed about three months. Increasingly, other upcountry people voluntarily came to Melbourne, some travelling down on drays or with stock working for settlers, while others came to look or transact Aboriginal business. In January 1844 there were 675 Indigenous people near the town, including groups from the Campaspe and Loddon River regions and from the north-west. By mid-year, there were still 447 spread in a semi-circle in four encampments a few kilometres from Melbourne, each nearest their own country: the Goulburn and Devil's River people to the north; the Mt Macedon people to the north-west; the Yarra and Goulburn people to the north-east, and Western Port and Barrabool people to the south-east. People came and went to hunt for skins and lyre-bird (*bullen bullen*) feathers for sale in Melbourne. The four temporary camps became two and then, after a conference, became one.[14]

It is extremely difficult to assess the degree to which colonisation deprived the country of bush foods, forcing Aboriginal people to seek European food in Melbourne. By 1840 over 700,000 sheep grazed central and western Victoria and the number doubled by 1842, while the cattle numbers doubled to 100,000 in that time.[15] In mid-1844, one 'upcountry black' complained to William Thomas, an assistant Aboriginal Protector, that 'the bush big one hungry, no bellyful like it Melbourne'.[16] Certainly cloven-footed animals, unlike Australian fauna, compacted the ground and verges of waterholes. They also monopolised the native grasses on which the kangaroo thrived, and their presence caused the kangaroos, emus, bush turkeys and other fauna to retreat to unpastured regions. Some plant foods were decimated by the stock. The *murnong* or yam daisy (*Microseris scapigera*) was a staple, its turnip-like roots yielding a vast edible food. However, sheep favoured it, and ate it to the roots. Isaac Battey, who settled the Sunbury District, wrote that *murnong* gathering ceased after 1846, 'for the all-sufficient reason that livestock seemingly had eaten out that form of vegetation'.[17] An Aboriginal man agreed, saying: 'no murnong, no yam at Port Phillip, too much by one white man bullock and sheep, all gone murnong'.[18]

The question about scarcity really is: what traditional foods were becoming scarce, and what part of the country was under threat? Resource loss was greatest on Melbourne's fringe, where land use was most intense from small farming as well as grazing. A landowner near the Bolin Swamp at Bulleen complained that Kulin had stolen potatoes. Despite the fact that it was the after-harvest gleanings that were taken (which were regarded as a rural labourer's right in England), William Thomas the assistant Protector was forced to move the Kulin off. He remarked: 'I could not but feel for the poor blacks. They had till this visit an undisturbed range among the lagoons and supplied themselves for a month or 5 weeks, now one side of the Yarra is forever closed to them'.[19] Similarly, the banks of other Melbourne creeks were being denied them. By 1844 Thomas wrote: 'I do not think that of the five tribes who visit Melbourne that there is in the whole five districts enough food to feed one tribe'.[20] In the nearby ranges, by rivers still open to them, and on the more distant plains, traditional food remained available in the 1840s, but European settlement clearly reduced Aboriginal food supplies, while boosting those of Europeans.

Dependence grew on European foods or on European means of obtaining scarcer bush foods. Guns brought down game—and were fun. Aboriginal men quickly developed a love affair with the gun. Derrimut used Fawkner's within days of exchanging names with him in late 1835. By 1840 there were 26 firearms in the Kulin's Yarra camp. Perhaps one in three Kulin adult men possessed one, especially *ngurun-gaeta* (headmen), such as Billibellary. Geoffrey Blainey has claimed that 'Aboriginals who chanced to obtain firearms did not care for them'.[21] However, William Thomas observed two men at Arthur's Seat in 1839 'cleaning their guns. They had screwdrivers and took the lock to pieces, cleaning barrel and touch hole as carefully as any white man'.[22] They often left them in Thomas's care when they departed the Yarra camp. In 1840 the Chief Protector George Robinson observed Kulin men in Melbourne's gun shops, 'not only by day but even after dark'.[23] The Kulin fired guns off at night in the Yarra camp with dangerous exuberance. Guns were certainly prestigious and exciting items, but increasingly they became useful in the search for food. In 1840 Thomas asserted: 'I have known one gun to be almost the support of an encampment in the Bush'.[24]

The settlers became increasingly nervous about Aboriginal people possessing guns. In 1840 the NSW Legislative Council banned Aboriginal gun-owners except with a magistrate's permission. The Kulin were angry when their guns were confiscated without recompense. Thomas commented only half in jest that an Aboriginal gun-owner 'would as soon part with his lubra or child as his gun'.[25] This Act was disallowed by the British Government in 1841 on the grounds that Aboriginal people were theoretically equal before the law.[26] However, the settlers' fear of Aboriginal guns was somewhat misplaced. These smooth-bore, muzzle-loading weapons were inaccurate, slow to load and less of a threat than the accuracy and rapid fire of a handful of spears.[27] Besides, Aboriginal people rarely used guns aggressively against whites, and their own domestic violence and inter-group fighting were almost exclusively engagements with waddies and spears. William Thomas explained to an inquiry in 1858 that 'although scarcely an influential black but has a gun, yet they never use them in battle: they consider guns a cowardly means of defence'.[28] However, some squatters in the 1840s claimed warriors attacked them wielding both spear and gun.[29] And in 1838 Jack Weatherly of the Boonwurrung related a revenge story to a squatter, James Clow, to excuse his absence in the bush for weeks with Clow's guns, supposedly on a quick hunting trip after lyre-birds. Weatherly explained that before white settlement the Gunai/Kurnai killed 25 Boonwurrung at Western Port in a sneak attack, so he and other Boonwurrung ventured to Gippsland for revenge, killing seven warriors and some old men and children using Clow's guns.[30]

The Kulin rejected many European novelties, but embraced some enthusiastically. Dogs became great favourites, Aboriginal groups being trailed by packs of 'half-starved' dogs. These were European dogs, not native dogs (dingoes). Indigenous people kept them as pets, and embraced them as such, literally so at night for their warmth. William Thomas claimed that 'if a European's favourite dog but one night sleeps in a black encampment, it will do all it can to get back to them'.[31] Europeans kept dogs as work animals, rarely cuddling and fondling them as did Indigenous people. Aboriginal attitudes to dogs, while shared by many dog-owners today, were seen by colonists as spoiling, and even as unnatural and abhorrent.

Aboriginal people also embraced metal items once they appreciated their properties. They fingered the metal buttons on European jackets, collected scraps of iron hoop and marvelled at the blacksmith's forge. Reverend William Waterfield displayed his watch, compass and magnet in a Melbourne street to a Kulin man, who 'seemed quite astonished and in extasies [sic]'.[32] Blades appealed to their utilitarian sense. Peter Beveridge recalled being told about the intense Aboriginal interest in the first steel axe seen on the Murray, and similar scenes must have been enacted elsewhere. People travelled from afar to view the axe, and 'when it was produced to their astonished gaze, much ejaculation and clucking with the tongue ensued'.[33] It was duly passed around and tested on wood. Indigenous people in Melbourne started to shave with blades and glass fragments and, when invited to dinner with Europeans, mastered knife and fork.

These people were not 'savages', gaping in the face of magical innovations, but people willing to incorporate new artefacts, foods and technologies into their culture once they appreciated their advantages. The botanist Daniel Bunce described possum-skin cloaks being embossed with traditional designs—kangaroos, emus, human figures—

'Corroboree' from *Australia Terra Cognita* (1854) by William Blandowski.
(Courtesy of Mitchell Library, State Library of New South Wales, PXE864)

not with sharp stones or shells as before contact, but with fragments of glass or the sharpened edge of a metal spoon.[34] In his account of the metal axe, Beveridge noted that a debate emerged about who would have access to it, the decision being that those making canoes could use the metal axe. This indigenising of items of new technology—fitting them into the social structure—occurred with the gun as well. Aboriginal men, not women—and indeed only 'influential' men at that—predominantly possessed them.

All sorts of novelties and innovations were being adopted, and on both sides of the frontier, as items flowed across the cultural divide. Wild quail and crayfish were swapped for sugar and sheep's kidneys. For every bottle, blade and gun crossing over, spears, clubs, and baskets moved in the other direction. As Mrs P. Russell wrote to George Russell, a squatter, in 1839: 'When you ransack the Native Dens could you not secure for us some of their spears . . . they are rarities here.'[35] Traffic was heaviest in the indigenous direction, partly because they were more curious than self-possessed Europeans, but also because there were more visible European novelties than Aboriginal ones, whose culture possessed fewer material items. Besides, as they were less powerful in the colonial relationship, they experienced more pressure to change. Aboriginal people embraced flour, tea and sugar, but a few settlers cultivated *murnong* and other native foods in their kitchen gardens.

Words flowed across the cultural boundary as well. Europeans talked of *miams* (dwellings), of kangaroos, of corroborees (ritual dancing), of *quombaed* (sleeping). English words also travelled the other way. As Richard Howitt wrote of Aboriginal speech: '[A] vast deal of English and the native language we heard the first few days, chopped up together, and odd enough it sounded'.[36] Again, the flow was weighted in the indigenous direction. Aboriginal people, who routinely spoke several dialects, quickly mastered sufficient English to deal with the new realities, whereas few colonists learned Aboriginal tongues. Some Aboriginal English was structurally close to English, such as Billibellary's question to Thomas 'What for you go away?', while other remarks were less so, such as the man who complained about a lack of free bread when Governor Bourke visited: 'plenty gammon that one Governor no give it—plenty hungry blackfellows'.[37]

Once Aboriginal people mastered English words and mimicked English gestures, conversations were possible with settlers and knowledge and resources extracted. Richard Howitt saw Aboriginal people conversing with colonists in the street and shaking their hands. They requested or were given 'white money' (silver), food and tobacco. They discussed the making of glass and metal. They debated theology, being sceptical of Christian miracles such as the Resurrection, and showing preference for God the father. As one Kulin man exclaimed on being shown an engraving of baby Jesus: 'such a fellow was no good—he was weak and small, and could not protect them—no good little Jesus, very good the old man'.[38] With a great ear for languages, they spoke the new words in their own soft, musical tone, but with colonial accents. They enjoyed singing, expressing pleasure at Rev. Waterfield's choral service, and sang about town and bush. George Robinson met one group near Melbourne in 1840, who sang in a perfect brogue: 'Hura my boys, it's time for us to go bonny highland laddie', and Howitt heard a man singing: 'I'd be a butterfly'.[39]

Colonial dangers

Some novelties were dangerous, notably alcohol. At first Aboriginal people were loath to try it, but by 1839 Daniel Bunce claimed that

'Benbo is the only teetotaller I ever met with among the aborigines', implying all the rest drank alcohol.[40] There are no accounts of sensible use of alcohol by Indigenous people—perhaps it was not thought worthy of reporting—but plenty about alcohol abuse. Reverend Waterfield reported that 'many of the poor natives were made drunk by brutal whites', the idea often being to make them fight each other and thus gain amusement at their expense.[41] Aboriginal use of alcohol at best led to some time in the stocks, and at worst caused deadly harm among those with little experience of and tolerance to its perils. In March 1839 James Dredge, an assistant Protector, recorded that a woman died from drinking brandy, a litre being found in her stomach, and three days later one of Batman's Aboriginal servants from Sydney drowned after drinking 'a large quantity of rum'.[42] An amendment to the *Publican's Act 1838* made it an offence to sell or give Indigenous people liquor, and some convictions and hefty £5 fines followed.[43] But there were always whites willing to supply Aboriginal people with alcohol for some favour or other. William Thomas even suspected the publican of the now-prestigious Melbourne Club of doing so.

Derrimut was among the young men who experimented with hard drinking, perhaps as a way of managing their altered world, or just lashing out. William Thomas frequently witnessed drunkenness and uproar, which made people 'more like maniacs than rational beings'.[44] In November 1839, Derrimut and Joe (a Sydney Aboriginal man in Batman's employ), arrived at the Yarra camp wet and roaring drunk, as they had fallen into the Yarra. Derrimut yelled abuse at whites, who he claimed had stolen his hat and stick. He then threatened to spear his own mother, whom Thomas sheltered—'Derrimut is otherwise very fond of his mother', Thomas wrote. He also recorded in despair, having been up until 3 a.m., that 'drunkenness and swearing is all that these people seem to have learned, and firing off a gun'.[45] Settlers like Richard Howitt considered them 'firm as marble to retain their old freedom and habits, and soft as wax to take the impression of what there is degrading and demoralising amongst us. We have done them some good, and much harm'.[46]

However, Woiwurrung elders attempted to stop the trouble. Thomas recorded in mid-1841 that Billibellary and his cousin and fellow elder, Murrumbean, warned the young against drunkenness, the former beating a young man for repeated offences.[47] Their warnings seem to have moderated the abuse, as Thomas, in several of his 1844 quarterly reports, listed no or few cases of drunkenness. In April 1846 there were 160 Indigenous people in Melbourne but only three cases of 'gross drunkenness'. However, Thomas later pointed out that Billibellary's own son, Kulpendurra, drank while in the Native Police and died in a drunken fight with the Goulburn people.[48]

Disease stalked Aboriginal people in Melbourne as the town's European population reached 4,000 by 1840, increasing the germ pool immeasurably. In May 1839, Dr P. Cussens, the settlement's medical officer, attended the Yarra camp where he found people suffering from dysentery, typhus fever, catarrh (respiratory infections) and syphilis, which could 'if unchecked, render them extinct in a very few years'. Cussens pronounced their health the poorest since settlement, noting six recent deaths and that another six were imminent. The people lacked food and were without blankets in over-night May temperatures of 10°C. Cussens added that the people received medical care 'with avidity and gratitude'.[49]

Despite accepting European medicines, Aboriginal people remained deeply traditional in their medical beliefs. This is revealed by the illness of Billibellary, the most powerful Woiwurrung *ngurungaeta*, one of the signatories of the Batman Treaty, and close friend of William Thomas's. Billibellary had a 'slight cough' for about ten months and was given European medicines. When his case was pronounced as hopeless Billibellary consulted Aboriginal doctors. They advised that an up-country Aboriginal man had stolen some of his hair while he slept, and now his *marmbulla* (kidney fat) was wasting, draining away his life force. Thomas tried to convince him he was suffering from lung disease, but to no avail. Indeed, Billibellary soon recalled waking some months earlier to see a strange Aboriginal man near his fire, who must have stolen a lock of his hair. Billibellary died on 10 July 1846 to Thomas's great grief. He buried his friend in the European manner, but his attempt to erect a memorial tablet over the fenced grave was prevented by 'horrified' Woiwurrung. It was possibly the publicising of Billibellary's name, that of a now deceased person, to which they objected. A revenge party soon departed north-wards against the Daungwurrung people, as tradition demanded, for the deaths of mature people were always deemed to be the result of sorcery from afar. So powerful were traditional ideas of death, that the revenge party included a Christian mission youth whom Thomas believed 'has learnt to know better'.[50]

The European presence, along with their seductive foods and arte-facts, initially did not dent the strength of Aboriginal beliefs. Interested observers recorded, albeit uncomprehendingly, the practice of tradi-tional customs and rituals. In 1858, William Thomas recalled ten days of ceremonies in the early 1840s near present-day Birrarung

Park (Heidelberg), at which huge bark figures were carried. After the ceremony these were discarded and settlers used the bark sheets for roofing.[51] In 1843 one settler, Mr McCabe, reported seeing a 'closed' ceremony beside the Merri Creek, near Melbourne. McCabe saw 'a huge and rude temple of stringy bark, covered with various hieroglyphics in white chalk'. He returned the following dawn to souvenir the bark but found it dismantled and destroyed. McCabe perhaps described the same ceremony for readers of the *Port Phillip Gazette*. Men, some of them body-painted in ochre with white clay faces and all bearing branches and wearing cockatoo feathers in their headbands, danced with stamping feet and serpentine movements, uttering hisses as they

Winberry, sketched by William Thomas, Aboriginal Protector, 1840.
(R.B. Smyth Papers, Courtesy of La Trobe Australian Manuscripts Collection, State Library of Victoria)

whished their legs with the branches, all in time to the women's singing and clapping of sticks. The branches were wiped over, then thrown at a painted bark *miam*. He was told it was a *gageed* ceremony to send the current epidemic of sickness onto the Goulburn tribe.[52]

Many Melbourne settlers saw 'play' corroborees as well, which Europeans were allowed to attend, perhaps to bind them to Aboriginal country and culture and show them the power of ritual. These performances impressed McCabe, but not others, and often confirmed the 'savagery' the viewer believed Indigenous people possessed. Captain Wood thought the dancers 'cut throat looking fellows', while Richard Howitt saw things that 'will haunt the soul years after such exhibitions. You hear the wild songs, see the dusky moving figures'.[53] In 1839 William Thomas witnessed other ceremonies. In one, some Daungwurrung women stole locks of hair from Woiwurrung young men, allegedly paralysing them. To save the men from death, all their bodily hair was shaved with a piece of glass, their bodies oiled with ochre and fat and the hair buried, in a procedure lasting almost four hours. At the end their relieved kin 'wept or moaned for joy'.[54] Thomas also witnessed traditional healing in which the doctor vigorously rubbed the patient's body with dust, then carefully gathered the dust up and threw it away, presumably along with all the sickness.[55]

The Kulin's most spectacular ritual appeared to Europeans simply as fighting. Early colonial accounts invariably describe fights between Aboriginal people, as they were dramatic and confirmed the image of Aboriginal 'savagery' in an entertainment-starved town. Richard Howitt reported that a thousand Melbournians watched one such action in the mid 1840s. Humanitarians were continually trying to break-up these supposed 'savage' affairs, Rev. Waterfield and James Dredge among them, with Dredge reporting 'some bad wounds' in one fray.[56] On closer inspection, however, these were not fights, instances of warfare, or chaotic savagery, but trials in which honour was defended and restored. Howitt reported a fight over a Woiwurrung woman taken by a Daungwurrung man from the Goulburn River. After much shouting, the surging back and forth of both groups, and the throwing of boomerangs and spears, just *one* man was speared in the leg.[57] In most of these encounters, elders watched from the sidelines and it was the young warriors who cracked heads with clubs and threw spears at each other. Sometimes the women joined in with clubs, or held 'women's only' proceedings on another day. Not only was artful dodging taking place, often behind deftly held shields, but restraint was also shown in these ritualised conflicts. If not, elders intervened. Usually few people were wounded—speared in the side or limb—but sometimes deaths did occur. Once justice was seen to be done, a corroboree of reconciliation followed. This was age-old Aboriginal law at work, not 'savagery', war and chaos. In early 1844, 675 Aboriginal people from eight groups gathered to watch Wurruck and Poleorang, 'men of great importance', face trial for the murder of a Werralim youth from afar.[58]

It was just one of many such murders that took place as Aboriginal people, following colonisation, moved beyond their own country into that of others, sometimes as workers for Europeans or lured there by novelties such as tobacco, tea and sugar. Once they entered the territory of others they were seen as a threat. Peter, a Murrumbidgee youth who came to Melbourne with George Langehorne's cattle in 1839, was killed by three Boonwurrung, one of whom was Derrimut. While it was a dreadful murder, it was carried out in defence of the Boonwurrung and their land: Peter, as the stranger, could potentially work sorcery against them. He was killed as an enemy in a ritualistic manner, William Thomas reporting of the body that 'some of the flank and arm seem to be cut off and [an] incision [made] in the side'.[59] His kidney fat was taken as the source of his strength and it is possible the killers ritually consumed his kidneys. As one man told William Thomas when Thomas was investigating the killing, 'no good that black fellow, no his country this'. He added 'and no good you', raising his tomahawk as if to strike Thomas. He went on to accuse Thomas of reporting his findings to his superior, thus getting in the way of traditional Aboriginal justice. In twenty years it was the only reported occasion that Thomas was threatened, such was the importance of Aboriginal law concerning intruders. In the end nothing came of the murder investigation, as it was an inter-Aboriginal killing with no witnesses, and Aboriginal people—being non-Christians—were not permitted to give evidence in British courts.[60]

Despite making Melbourne their own, walking its streets and doing as they pleased, Kulin tradition became progressively more difficult to practise. Though groups maintained customary movements across their lands, they found that areas were now closed to them. It became harder to find places to hold ritual undisturbed, and Aboriginal judicial proceedings were broken up as outsiders saw lawful punishments as fighting. Disease and violent deaths swept away important bearers of oral tradition and ceremonial knowledge. By late 1839, the Woiwurrung had been reduced to 139 people and the Boonwurrung to 83 people. Thomas estimated perhaps 20 more people remained uncounted. Amongst the Woiwurrung, 34 of the population were under ten years of age, but only 12 were four years or younger; among the Boonwurrung only 4 of 19 children were under four years old, meaning fewer children had been born and survived since the whites arrived than in a similar period before their arrival.[61]

The European arrival had subtler impacts as well. Their very presence threw into question the continuation of the Aboriginal world. There were now known to be other ways of using the land, earning one's living, exchanging things, ordering one's affairs, relating to kin, and being religious. Aboriginal people resisted these influences at first, but European knowledge was always there challenging them. New imaginings emerged to compete with traditional ideas. In 1844, two Aboriginal men from Melbourne travelling in Gippsland with the Chief Protector, George Robinson, commented that the thick vines draping from the trees looked like ships' cables. Indigenous people were exposed to new ideas: writing and paper, guns and steel, farming and Christianity—there was much to fathom about the intruders.

A final indignity for the Kulin was the authorities' attempt to expel them from Melbourne. The Police Magistrate William Lonsdale had initially ignored their presence, admitting in February 1837, five months after his arrival, that he had not reported as yet on the Kulin.[62] But as more Kulin camped in Melbourne, concerns were raised. In December 1839 George Augustus Robinson, the Chief Protector, noted that large numbers of Kulin had gathered, including those from Melbourne, Western Port, the Goulburn and Geelong region, to conduct important 'business'.[63] Asked to report on the situation, William Thomas wrote in despair about the continued trouble in the Yarra camp. 'They are fighting almost every evening,' he wrote on a day in which three were severely wounded, 'and in the night indulging in the most awful scenes of debauchery, which create fresh frays for the coming day'. A young Goulburn woman was pack-raped, and Thomas commented that other Goulburn women, as well as the girl's sister, had abused her for 'making a noise and not quietly submitting to their brutality'. Thomas misunderstood much of what he saw, concluding that these things revealed 'the moral state of the people'—by which he meant their immorality.[64] This was only Thomas's eighth month in the job, however, and he did not realise both the fighting and the rape were legal punishments in Aboriginal society. We should not be too quick to judge those in the past, as people did things differently then. English people hanged and whipped people for serious offences and Aboriginal people speared and raped for gross transgressions. But Thomas, an English evangelical Christian, was appalled at what he thought was barbarous brawling and a sexual offence. Later he would realise such events were Aboriginal law in action.

When Superintendent Charles La Trobe heard of these things, he was similarly appalled that such 'disorder' and 'disgrace' existed in *his* town. He wrote to Chief Protector Robinson that 'the continued location of such a numerous body of natives in the immediate vicinity of the town cannot be endured much longer'.[65] La Trobe issued orders in September 1840 that 'no Aboriginal blacks of the District are to visit the township of Melbourne under any pretext whatever',[66] a directive that proved impossible to implement over the years. Thomas informed the Woiwurrung and Boonwurrung people that they must select a campsite beyond Melbourne 'to sit down'. They talked among themselves, night after night, first at their Kurruck camp and then at Bolin. They then met Robinson who produced a map of Port Phillip. The Kulin preferred to draw their own map on the ground, which they did, and pointed to a spot where they agreed to go and 'sit down': it was called Narre Narre Warren.[67]

Another stark example of arbitrary state power occurred in Melbourne in October 1840, and pays further witness to the government's growing impatience. In early 1840, frontier trouble—killings and loss of property in the Goulburn District—led to government action. One Major Lettsom was sent from Sydney to investigate and arrest Aboriginal wrongdoers; with authority to treat them as 'subjects of the Queen, and not as aliens'; and to act as a 'civil magistrate, and not in a military capacity'.[68] He pursued the Daungwurrung (Goulburn people) to Melbourne where the Kulin were gathering for a large initiation. Superintendent La Trobe described this gathering as 'a pretty numerous armed body'. Despairing of Aboriginal hostility and their 'resistance to the arm of the civil power', La Trobe permitted Lettsom to apprehend those he sought, but ordered that he avoid bloodshed unless in 'extreme and imperative necessity'.[69] Major Lettsom and eleven troopers rode into William Thomas's camp by the Yarra at dawn, seeking two Kulin. Thomas refused to cooperate, unhappy that charges had been laid against the two Aboriginal men. Lettsom crossed the Yarra, sending the Aboriginal camp of 200 Kulin into a panic. Thomas recorded: 'Many jumped into the River, others climbed the trees, the women and children running into huts or wherever they could shelter themselves'.[70] After riding hard all that week in search of the offenders, at daybreak on 11 October (as Protector James Dredge recorded in his diary), Major Lettsom and a military detachment surrounded the camp and arrested all but a few who escaped. One young Woiwurrung man, Winberry, resisted and was shot dead. The Kulin warriors' spears were burnt and a stand of arms confiscated. Over 200 people, including Woiwurrung, Boonwurrung and Daungwurrung, were taken at bayonet point to the barracks. It seemed much more like a 'military' than a 'civil' action. The Woiwurrung and Boonwurrung were later released and about thirty Daungwurrung men were detained. Overnight some escaped, but one man was shot dead while escaping. As no charges were as yet laid, Dredge, who recorded these events partly by hearsay, rightly believed the escape was justified and the killing of the escapee 'cold blooded murder'.

On 13 October, Dredge visited 35 men and youths in the jail, 'chained together two and two', who were 'overjoyed' to see him.[71] Eight months later, nine were convicted of robbery, and sentenced to ten years transportation for theft. La Trobe later admitted that they could not plead or testify in court, and were not defended. Ironically, all but one of the men escaped in January 1841 by diving into the Yarra during prison transfer and swimming to shore in leg irons. The leg irons were apparently filed off by their Woiwurrung kin. Dredge met six of them on the Goulburn two months later and, despite their fugitive status, fed them and sent them on their way.[72] The Woiwurrung and Boonwurrung, who were still loath to go to Narre Narre Warren reserve, were induced to go there according to William Thomas, due to fear arising from Lettsom's raid.[73]

The pressures on the Kulin were now intense as land was fenced, traditional resources lost, and ceremony disrupted. Death whittled away at families and tradition. In late 1843, William Thomas and his friend Billibellary, the most powerful *ngurungaeta* of the Woiwurrung, frankly discussed infanticide; in short, the group's future. Infanticide was traditionally practised when children were born too close together, as the younger could not be carried while the older was still unweaned and lacked mobility. Billibellary admitted that of eight women he named who had borne children since Thomas's arrival in 1839, only two of their children survived. The others died from 'strangulation or smothering'. Billibellary said that 'blackfellows all about say that no good have them Pickaninneys now, no country for blackfellows like long time ago'. Derrimut similarly declared to William Hull: 'all along here Derrimut's once, . . . you have all this place, no good have children, no good have lubra, me tumble down and die very soon now'.[74] These apparently deliberate deaths, and people's unwillingness to have children, are clear indications of the despair that colonisation had wrought among the Kulin. Without country, Aboriginal children had no birthright, and thus no reason for existence. However, Billibellary was

not a fatalist. He promised Thomas to dissuade women from killing their children. He added, like a statesman: 'if Yarra blackfellows had a country on the Yarra, . . . they would stop on it and cultivate the ground'.[75]

Billibellary himself 'tumbled down' in 1846, dying of respiratory disease in his mid-fifties. What was lost to early Melbourne when an elder such as Billibellary died? Thomas spent two long hand-written pages extolling the virtues of Billibellary, a man he knew well through travelling with him and sharing a campfire and long discussions. Thomas viewed him as a man of peace. Billibellary had signed Batman's Treaty, warned the early settlers of an attack from up-country Kulin, sent his own son to the first government mission and his two younger children to the Merri Creek School, joined the Native Police Corps (though he later resigned), tried to end revenge killings (although he fell to tradition in allowing his own imminent death to be revenged), and tried to prevent infanticide and drunkenness. This tall, athletic man was a visionary leader who tried to find a way forward without violence. As Thomas concluded: 'It may be said of this Chief and his tribe what can scarce be said of any tribe of located parts of the colony that they never shed white man's blood nor have white men shed their blood. I have lost in this man a valuable councillor in Aboriginal affairs'.[76]

Billibellary's reconciling nature was in no way a surrender of Aboriginal values. However, with his death a store of traditional knowledge and power was lost, and his passing made the Kulin's survival even more difficult. His son, Simon Wonga, succeeded him as *ngurungaeta*.

Wonga and his kin continued to struggle for the land by the Yarra desired by Billibellary. He and others later gained Coranderrk—a reserve at Healesville—which they cherished and, after much struggle, retain today.[77]

3

Countering Civilisers

The efforts to impose 'civilisation' on the indigenous peoples of Port Phillip is a British settler story. After the loss of the American colonies in the War of Independence (1775–83), Britain sought a second empire befitting an emerging world power. This imperial mission was softened by Enlightenment attitudes, at least in Australia's case. Arthur Phillip, who was to govern the new convict settlement of New South Wales, was enjoined in 1787 to treat indigenous people with 'amity and kindness' and to punish offenders against them. At the same time Phillip was also encouraged to discover how 'use' might be made of them.[1] The British seaborne empire was at that time underpinned by the inhumane transport of slaves and slavery in the West Indies, but there was already a movement afoot to end this stain on the Empire, with the transportation of slaves in British ships being banned in 1807. The enlightened element within the Empire was boosted when British Evangelicals and humanitarians captured the new Whig Liberal Government in 1830, ending slavery in British possessions in 1833. Led by Thomas Buxton, this reforming group turned its interest to the treatment of indigenous people within the Empire, securing an influential Select Committee on Indigenous peoples in the House of Commons in 1835.

The Buxton Committee's Report, tabled in June 1837 just as Port Phillip was becoming an official colony, criticised the government. It argued that colonisation had cast Aboriginal peoples into a 'deeper shade of wretchedness' by placing a convict colony in their midst and failing to protect them from violence and moral contamination. Because sovereignty was claimed over indigenous lands, the report recognised Indigenous peoples as British subjects equal under law. The report called for the governance of these new British subjects from Britain and not by local settlers; the provision of labour contracts to protect indigenous workers; and the provision of appropriate education and Christian instruction. As indigenous lands were taken without recompense, the report argued that indigenous people were owed a debt, and so the cost of their administration should be taken out of moneys raised from the sales of colonial (formerly indigenous) lands. However, the Buxton Committee Report, with its view of Aboriginal people as 'probably the least-instructed portion of the human race in all the arts of social life', was ethnocentric as well as enlightened, desiring that Aboriginal people become British and Christian: the 'apex' of human advancement. Such hierarchical views of human progress were common among enlightened and evangelical thinkers, whose world view sought social and moral advancement to Christian and respectable Western standards.[2]

The Port Phillip settlement was officially proclaimed on 14 September 1836 in this atmosphere of benign imperialism. The concerns of British reformers and Evangelicals were strongly echoed in the colony by the liberal NSW Governor, Sir Richard Bourke, which led to a series of Christianising and humanitarian efforts in the new colony. The first, a Government Mission, began in Melbourne in 1837, and the Wesleyan Buntingdale Mission opened at Birregurra just east of Colac in late 1838. Following the recommendation of Buxton's report, the British Government established an Aboriginal Protectorate in 1839, and, after three attempts, a Native Police Corps was established in Port Phillip in 1842. A Government School operated at Narre Narre Warren in 1841, and the Baptists initiated the Merri Creek School in 1845.[3]

These institutions had similar aims: to teach Aboriginal people the arts of British civilisation, transforming them from hunter-gatherers to a farming people; and to protect them from the worst effects of colonisation. Their common educative purpose was evident even in the Native Police Corps. Captain Alexander Maconochie conceived the idea of a corps in June 1837 after his concern that Aboriginal people faced 'severe suffering and eventual entire disappearance'. Maconochie, a penal reformer interested in rehabilitating convicts into respectable colonists, applied these ideas to Port Phillip. An indigenous military/policing force—such as the Roman Empire had possessed—would ensure frontier peace and also assimilation, by binding Aboriginal 'affections' to the government. Those who enlisted would develop pride from their duties, their uniforms, their equipment and their guns. The military code of neatness and cleanliness, and the work ethic, would have a 'humanizing effect' and increase their status in settlers' eyes. Life with their families in the barracks would civilise and settle them, making them models for other Indigenous people. Maconochie believed that 'a knowledge of and taste for European manners and civilization might be thus extensively yet silently implanted', for 'the Port Phillip natives, like all savages are great imitators'. All would benefit: the colony would be won, Aboriginal people would be saved and remade, and Maconochie—looking for employment—was 'very happy to be entrusted with the command of it'.[4]

These protective and civilising institutions had one thing in common: none endured. The Government Mission closed in 1839, the Government School in 1843, Buntingdale Mission in 1848, and the Aboriginal Protectorate, Merri Creek School and the Native Police Corps closed in

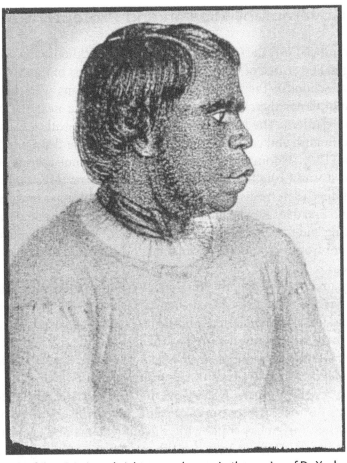

'Billy, Native of Port Fairy' aged eighteen—who was in the service of Dr Youl of Melbourne since a boy—by Ludwig Becker, from 'Select Committee of the Legislative Council of Victoria on the Aborigines', 1859.

1849, 1850 and 1852 respectively. Colonists, government and later historians summed them up as 'failures'. While considering the outcomes of Aboriginal policy, Superintendent La Trobe pointed out in 1848 that despite the outlay of £61,000 over thirteen years (equivalent to about $70 million today) all the plans, with the exception of the Native Police, have 'either completely failed, or show at this date, most undoubted signs of failure'.[5] In his 1941 book, *Australian Native Policy*, J. B. Foxcroft came to the same conclusion. But from an Aboriginal perspective these institutions were perhaps 'successes', as Aboriginal people turned them to their own advantage. It is this aspect of their story, rather than their administrative history, that is told here.

The Government Mission and Protectorate

In November 1837, the Quaker traveller James Backhouse saw fourteen Aboriginal boys, one of them named Barak and most of them Woiwurrung, at school in the Government Mission. Lessons were held in a mud and plaster thatched schoolhouse by the Yarra near the present Botanic Gardens. The boys were dressed in 'frocks' with a waistband, learned English and counting, and how to eat, wash and sleep in British fashion. They seldom left the mission house without asking permission, as it was a rule that they forfeited one of their three daily meals by so doing. Their meals consisted of bread, tea and sugar for breakfast, meat and bread for lunch, and bread, tea and sugar for dinner. The food was filling and free, but hardly a balanced diet. Another six older boys, who wore trousers, worked the mission's boat, ferrying supplies across the river.

Sixty adults camped by the mission. Two hours of fencing or digging in the garden each day earned them a ration of 450 grams each of meat and flour, and sometimes a little tea, sugar and soap.[6] None were forced to be there, but were lured by the promise of food and the sheer novelty. Interestingly, the site by a bend in the Yarra (later straightened by engineers) was also a traditional meeting place. The mission began in January 1837 after the NSW Governor, Sir Richard Bourke agreed to Justice Burton's call that missions and 'black villages' were needed to provide Aboriginal people with 'the enjoyments and security of a civilized life'.[7] George Langhorne, the missionary in charge, held the prejudices of his day, believing Aboriginal people to be 'degraded savages'—that is, people without God—as well as 'promiscuous, indolent wanderers', who must be weaned slowly to a settled life. His strategy of change and conversion was aimed at the 'rising generation' as being the more malleable.[8]

Upwards of twenty children, mostly boys, were accommodated at the school. Their parents moved about, using it like a childcare centre as their trust in Langhorne grew. However, most people scattered in April 1838 after two violent incidents. The first incident occurred when several Aboriginal men who were camped at the mission raided the potato patch of a neighbour, John Gardiner, who subsequently set his men to watch. During the next raid, Gardiner's man William Underwood accosted several Kulin men. They produced a gun and threatened Underwood, but at the same time they pleaded hunger. Given the abundance of food handouts at that time around Melbourne their plea was probably untrue, but in principle the potatoes were on their land and in their eyes Gardiner was a neighbour, and as a neighbour was considered almost kin. Underwood escaped and returned with weapons and men, and the Kulin were chased across the Yarra, shot at, and two were arrested: Tullamarine and Jin Jin. The two men were put in jail, but set fire to it, escaped, were recaptured, sent for trial in Sydney but never proceeded against, and finally returned to Melbourne. The second incident occurred the following month when Captain Lonsdale, the Police Magistrate, tried to apprehend several men, while they were camped at the mission, for alleged sheep theft up-country. There was a desperate scuffle with weapons, and shots were fired. Langhorne alleged the shots were fired *at* the Kulin; Lonsdale, however, claimed the shots were more of a danger to his own men. The two incidents ended any chance for the mission, as Langhorne and Lonsdale fell out, and the alarmed Woiwurrung dispersed, leaving only the old and sick.[9]

In reality, the Woiwurrung had had little interest in the mission's preaching, lessons and work regime. They preferred the town itself where they attached themselves to European individuals who were on Woiwurrung land, 'from whom they obtain money in part payment for their services'—'white money' (silver) no less, whereas Langhorne could only pay them 'in coarse flour with a little meat'.[10] Langhorne's regime of work and prayer was also less exciting than Melbourne with its gun shops, activity and street life. In December 1838 the Woiwurrung left Melbourne for the mountains, taking with them nearly all the boys from the mission, leaving only a Murrumbidgee boy. Important business was afoot, probably an initiation, as this would explain why some of the young Native Police trainees went as well and why the young boy from the north was excluded. As Langhorne lamented, 'no inducement . . . will operate to prevent a black from undergoing certain rites or assisting at certain ceremonies'.[11] By late 1838 he admitted failure, arguing that missions had to be isolated from towns, and their inmates drawn from distant places, so they depended on 'their white friends for protection, and [would be] render[ed] . . . more available to the missionary or instructors who should be placed among them'.[12] Langhorne acknowledged the power of Aboriginal kinship and tradition and also the lure of European goods. This same Aboriginal customary power sealed the failure of the Buntingdale Mission at Birregurra, placed uneasily on the boundary of three rival clans.[13]

The Port Phillip Aboriginal Protectorate commenced as the Government Mission closed. Its Chief Protector, George Augustus Robinson, had conducted the 'Friendly Mission' in Van Diemen's Land, which brought surviving Tasmanian Pallawah people to Flinders Island as well as a few to reside temporarily in Port Phillip.[14] Four Protectors assisted him. They were to itinerate with Aboriginal people, but the practicalities of being family men caused them to form central stations instead. By 1841, stations existed at Narre Narre Warren, the Goulburn River, Mount Rouse and Franklingford on the Loddon River. The stations issued rations, but these were always too few to keep Indigenous people there.

The Protectorate caused settler resentment as its policy was devised in London's armchairs, but paid for by the colonial land fund. Settlers were angry that each Protectorate station used five square miles of desirable land. They claimed the Protectors favoured Aboriginal people in disputes with settlers and were useless, being inept family men of unrealistic Christian and humanitarian ideas, ill-suited to the demands of 'taming a race of wild and lawless savages'.[15] Some slandered the Protectors as self-serving, and most believed the very existence of the Protectorate demonised the colony in the eyes of the world. Settlers claimed they did not need help to care for Aboriginal people. One settler called the Protectorate 'a curse to the land'.[16] Such criticisms, which stemmed from settler self-interest and rivalry with Aboriginal people for land, were endless and withering. They served to undermine the Protectorate even in the eyes of officials, who found its maintenance expensive by the time depression hit in 1844. Some colonists publicly defended the Protectorate, but behind *nom de plumes*: 'Humanitas' argued for more resources, while 'Memorabilia' claimed it protected the 'rightful owners of this splendid continent' from those 'rapacious and sometimes dissolute intruders' who forced Indigenous people from their land.[17]

Aboriginal people visited Protectorate stations, at times in significant numbers, but they remain largely faceless to us. The Loddon station, also known as Mount Franklin and Jim Crow, and which was formed in

Aboriginal Farmers at Parker's Protectorate Station, Mount Franklin.
(Courtesy of La Trobe Picture Collection, State Library of Victoria, H84.167/43)

early 1840 by ex-London printer and strong evangelical Christian, Edward Stone Parker, attracted most. In its first triennium the daily average attendance was almost 100 people, mostly DjaDjawurrung, although their attendance was halved over the next six years.[18] The stations lured people—as did Melbourne town—by food, the novelty of European things, and by being a refuge. Parker told a NSW Legislative Council Select Committee on Aborigines in 1845 that the Loddon River region was in the 'greatest confusion' and threatening to descend into 'a war of extermination on both sides' when he arrived in early 1840. He reported that two settlers, now magistrates, had told him on his arrival that blacks and whites in the same country were incompatible, and 'one-half of the Aboriginal population must be shot'. He added that after the Lettsom raid on the Kulin in Melbourne in October 1840, 'some of the most influential' Aboriginal men frequenting Melbourne proposed 'killing every white man they could find unprotected'.[19] To this region Parker brought peace.

There was a genuine affection between Protector Parker and the DjaDjawurrung, despite the cultural and religious gulf between them. Parker's evangelicalism moved him to deem them 'immoral', as they practised polygamy, allegedly infanticide, and other 'savageries' as well. They were also 'degraded' to his mind, as he believed they were descendants of the biblical Ham, Noah's son, who was expelled to the wilderness because he had looked upon his father Noah while Noah was naked and drunk in his tent.[20] However, Parker liked them, and his station was successful because of this and because he cut through 'red tapeism'.[21] The DjaDjawurrung thought him strange, a man different from other whites, as he was always praying from a book. But they liked him too, and from the outset carried his children on their shoulders into the bush and cooked them bush food. They called Parker *Marmingorak*, meaning 'father'. The DjaDjawurrung, Parker and his men set to work pioneering the Loddon station, quickly enclosing 15 hectares and planting several hectares of crops. As the people worked, felling trees, splitting timber, building huts and fences, and gardening with steel tools, they constantly asked the purpose of these labours. They expressed pleasure when Parker said their work was for their benefit. Indeed, as the DjaDjawurrung worked and spoke of their loss of land to settlers, Parker constantly told them that the station, its rations and clothing were for them—by way of compensation—as long as they were peaceful and left the settlers' stock alone.

Parker hoped to effect change through Christianity, and focussed his efforts on the young. However, he found it almost impossible to translate Christian ideas and morality into the DjaDjawurrung's language that he was attempting to master. His prayers were crudely evangelical, typically speaking of sin and evil, and may have offended. One prayer pleaded to God of the people: 'Take from them their bad spirit. Give them a good spirit. Be not angry with them. They are very stupid. They steal, they fight, they kill, they tell lies'. It was little wonder that Parker's efforts were not always appreciated. Two elders reproached him for interfering with their traditional education of the young: 'Why do you sit down with blackfellows? You were not born of a black woman! Why don't you go back to your own country—up to *woorerwoorer* [the sky] where you came from'.[22] Yet resentments were not permanent. When three Aboriginal children died shortly after overseer Bazely's own daughter died, the people wanted their children buried alongside Bazely's child. In 1848 the DjaDjawurrung people left for six months, claiming there was too much sickness and that they wished to hide from their enemies the Pyrenees people, who were venturing into the region. By the time they returned, to the delight of some of the young men (according to Parker), a school had been established at the Loddon station. However, a Legislative Council review then underway led to the Protectorate's closure in December 1849.

Parker lamented its demise as he sensed 'success seems to have dawned'. A young boy and also an Aboriginal man, 'one of the worst savages of the tribe', had both recently died, asking for Christian salvation. There were also 400 bushels of wheat in sacks from the last harvest and sheep numbers had soared from 500 to 3,000: a settled station was evolving. Yet there was little evidence that the DjaDjawurrung as a group were turning from their customary ways. Indeed, in his last report Parker admitted: 'The mass of the Aboriginal population of this District remains unchanged in their characteristic habits and inclinations, and in some instances I have witnessed more determined hostility to religion, and more inveterate attachment to their own sensuality and superstition than ever'.[23] Parker was appointed as visiting magistrate to the Loddon Aboriginal School. He leased the station's land, employing the Kulin as pastoral workers, and preached and ministered to their elderly.

The Native Police

The Native Police Corps, an instrument of change and control, also provided opportunities for Aboriginal people. Its commandant, Captain Henry Dana, claimed the routines they practised at their Narre Narre Warren barracks (near where present-day Stud Road crosses Dandenong Creek)[24] enabled young Aboriginal men to be 'kept under proper control, taught discipline, obedience, and respect, and made of some use to the country'.[25] The forty or fifty who were enlisted each year filled their days keeping themselves spick and span, doing an hour's drill, cleaning their equipment, building and maintaining their barracks, as well as cutting wood, gardening and playing ball games for fitness. These activities taught them the European work ethic within a lifestyle they found congenial. The artist William Strutt sketched them relaxing in their barracks like any British troopers. For some months of each year the Native Police Corps patrolled outside of Melbourne. Their work took them across the colony and into the white community and varied from searching for a shipwreck and an alleged gold mine in the Pyrenees, to tracking stock thieves and guarding Pentridge Stockade. They had authority over black and white. The troopers even paraded at official occasions, escorting Superintendent La Trobe. In September 1849 they were near the front of the procession celebrating the news of Victoria's imminent creation as a separate colony.[26]

About 140 Aboriginal troopers—mostly Woiwurrung and Boonwurrung—had enlisted by 1852, eagerly, voluntarily, and for their own reasons and desires. Each trooper used a variety of guns—carbines,

'Aboriginal Black Troopers, Melbourne: Police with English Corporal.' (By permission of the Parliamentary Library, Parliament of Victoria from William Strutt's *Victorian the Golden: Scenes, Sketches and Jottings from Nature 1850–1862*, plate 71)

muskets and pistols—a cutlass, and also a horse, which was a prestige item possessed only by gentlemen and masters in early Port Phillip. They also wore a uniform complete with cap, gold braid and polished leather belt and boots, and were provided with a pair of blankets and plentiful food. They were to be paid at three pence a day, a quarter of a shilling, equivalent to about a quarter of a shepherd's wage. However, as William Thomas testified in 1859: 'I have had many complaints made to me that they never did get their money; they would get 2s 6d or 3 s[hillings] at the end of a quarter'; that is, about two weeks pay instead of thirteen weeks. Where the rest went is unknown.[27]

The initial enlistments followed seven days of deliberations by Billibellary and his people in February 1842. Their induction occupied several hours, as Dana and William Thomas explained to the twenty-two recruits, resplendent in their uniforms, the duties of policing and the benefits they would receive. Each were sworn in and made their mark. Billibellary hesitated at this point, saying: 'I am king; I no ride on horseback; I no go out of my country; young men go as you say, not me.'[28] He eventually signed, although he only played a ceremonial role in the corps, parading in uniform for several hours daily, and soon quit. Within a year most recruits received good service reports, which noted their orderliness and obedience, their cleanliness, intelligence and improvement. Billibellary's record noted: 'general conduct good. A chief, he has a great deal of influence with his tribe; very useful in assisting to prevent quarrels'. Only six were deemed 'bad' characters, one 'a great savage, careless, disobedient, intractable and dangerous'. Three of these problem recruits were said to be 'improving'.[29]

Billibellary's presence in the Native Police Corps as the most prestigious elder of the Melbourne region was no accident. Marie Fels, who studied the corps in great depth, found that the first twenty-two enlistments 'were nearly all either clan heads or heirs to clan heads. In terms of traditional power and authority they constituted a formidable group of men'.[30] These men were not joining the colonial power structure, but enlarging their power by extending it into a new sphere. They were both troopers and Aboriginal men of significance. They received favourable service reports but also used their role for traditional ends. They moved the Narre Narre Warren camp to the Merri Creek at one stage, lured the young Aboriginal boys from school when it suited them, and arrested only whom they chose. As William Thomas recognised in 1844:

> an order from their own people they must obey . . . nor dare they do an act
> that may lead to any fearful results upon their Tribes or those [with] whom
> their Tribe may occasionally have intercourse. Let there be an outrage among
> the Barrabools, Mount Macedon, Goulburn, Yarra and Western Port Tribes
> and it will be seen what I have asserted is correct. This body dare not act,
> in tracking they will mislead, in acting evade or object, but they will readily
> pursue the far distant unfortunate Aboriginal tribes, or successfully act
> against the whites, this will ever render them inefficient and dubious.[31]

The mounted troopers even broke service regulations at times. In April 1847 they came on duty at the Melbourne races, but on foot, and the next day sent their uniforms back to Narre Narre Warren and stayed at the Merri Creek, seeming to want time out. In early 1849 about five 'bolted' despite knowing the consequences. Dana gave them some latitude, but Warringalpoop was one trooper who was court-martialled and flogged.[32]

Their tours of duty in the country were controversial too, predictably so, given Thomas's remarks above. Fels argues they did not practise inordinate violence against 'distant tribes'. However, evidence reveals the Native Police were violent to those whom they saw as *mainmet*, wild men, who were practitioners of dangerous sorcery. Other historians believe they played a significant role in subduing Aboriginal resistance in the Western District and Gippsland.[33] Contemporaries thought the same. If the Native Police were hard on other Indigenous people in the interior, it was as much or more for the traditional reasons of neutralising *mainmet*, as for the colonial reasons of clearing the land and protecting settlers.

The troopers were exhilarated by their military actions, an experience common to many truthful fighting men the world over. Rolf Boldrewood, who settled the Port Fairy area in the early 1840s, recalled the arrival of the Native Police, summoned there by fearful settlers. Corporal Buckup dismounted, saluted Boldrewood and said: 'We have been sent up by Mr Dana, sir, to stop at this station a bit. Believe the blacks been very bad about here'. Buckup added: 'They only want a good scouring, sir'.[34] Some weeks later the Gunditjmara were caught out in the open by the mounted Native troopers and received such a 'scouring' that resistance was broken in the region. Back in Melbourne William Thomas heard the results from the jubilant troopers: 'This black related to me how many had been killed, how many each shot—the gross number 17'. Thomas questioned why no prisoners were brought back. The trooper said: 'Captain say big one stupid catch them very good shoot them, you blackfellows, no shoot them me handcuff you and send you to jail'.[35] A Gippsland man told Mr Edgar, the teacher at the Merri Creek School, that 'Captain Dana come down with him black police; shoot him black fellar there, black lubra there, black picaninni there, shoot him pla-a-anty'. No doubt stories became embellished, but many were convinced of the violence of the Native Police in distant parts. One historian, Beverley Nance, estimated that the Native Police killed 125 Aboriginal people over a decade.[36]

The Native Police Corps ended in 1853 due to a combination of events. Resignations among the white officers occurred in the gold rush; Captain Dana died of pneumonia in November 1852; and the Aboriginal troopers dwindled in number due to disease and misadventure. William Thomas claimed in 1854 that they were all 'drunkards' and in 1859, that they were all dead.[37] However, one Native Policeman, William Barak, lived until 1903. Thomas's information on their lives after the abandonment of the force suggests they were driven by traditional relationships and that the force had not 'detribalised' them as the political scientist J.B. Foxcroft had suggested. Indeed, Marie Fels concluded that becoming a Native Policeman was a 'creative and adaptive Aboriginal strategy'.[38]

Aboriginal schools

Schooling was the final method of engineering change among Aboriginal people. A small bark schoolroom with forms and school requisites, run by Noble Keenan (and later E. Peacock), was built at Narre Narre Warren Protectorate station in August 1841. Keenan began with over thirty pupils, boys and girls, one of them Billibellary's son. He aimed to 'gradually bring them to civilized habits and let them have as little communication with their parents as possible'.[39] Within a fortnight the girls left with their parents and the boys soon followed. The people moved to the Merri Creek camp and into the bush as Keenan provided insufficient food. This was a pattern over the next two years, which led to daily attendances mostly of less than ten. Sometimes no children attended for days on end. Keenan tried numerous strategies, including following the children to the Merri Creek and into the bush with chalk and writing tablets, prevailing upon sixteen to sing lessons in the forest on one occasion. However, their lack of interest in lessons was such that in November 1842 the children told their teacher: 'no damper, no school'.[40] Captain Dennis of the Native Police urged the 'chief', probably Billibellary, to encourage the children to attend, which had a temporary effect. When attendances again dropped within a few days, Dennis told Billibellary that non-attendance would result in all Kulin being driven from the Police Paddock. Numbers instantly climbed to eighteen for a few weeks, and then fell away again. The school closed in early 1843.[41]

The Baptists of Melbourne began a more sustained educational effort at the Merri Creek in 1845. It began after Peacock, the former teacher at Narre Narre Warren, attracted five children to his Richmond Baptist Sunday School with bread and prayer. As the number of Aboriginal children increased to 26, the Baptists moved to a building on the Merri Creek immediately above Dight's Falls and just below the Aboriginal camp. With government help they opened a day school where the children could be educated 'and in a great measure domesticated, and led into habits of industry', as Rev. John Ham wrote.[42] Protector William Thomas was sceptical after the failures at Narre Narre Warren, fearing the Kulin's mobility and Peacock's lack of skill. However, in May 1846 Thomas was amazed at the progress of the 27 clean and neatly clad pupils, mostly Woiwurrung, who had only a few months before 'formed a portion of the great nuisance in Melbourne, begging, and often pilfering about'. The students were able to read words of one or two syllables, and one boy read a portion of 'our Lord's parables'. They received 'three good meals a day of the best food' and occasionally slept at the school, although the girls slept at camp. The school gained more land and commenced a garden. The *Port Phillip Gazette* reported good progress.[43]

For a year the pupils shone in Melbourne's estimation, and revealed their ability to learn new languages—spoken English, the written word and arithmetic—as well as ideas and skills. Three public performances of their learning took place, the first before 600 people in a packed Mechanics Institute meeting. Thirteen boys and seven girls were on show, the boys dressed in white duck trousers and regatta shirts and the girls in pink dresses, their hair shining and their skin scrubbed to a glorious bronze. Their singing drew applause. The youngest of eight children spelt three-letter words, and the older ones read Scripture. The Mayor of Melbourne presented the oldest boy, Wydelong, with a New Testament. He opened it and read from Matthew 13: the parable of the sower and the seeds sown on barren and good soil, raising hopes among the Christians present. Donations of £30 were raised, a sum equal to half a labourer's yearly wage, and doctors offered their services free to the school. In November a second presentation focussed on the students' written and craft work. More donations flowed, a Geelong squatter alone sending £30.[44] Reverend John Ham later claimed: 'I never saw cleaner copy-books from any white school. They could not as yet write a sentence or spell properly, but could write text and round hand'.[45] Melbourne's humanitarians sensed progress. Ham lamented two years later that the students' performance was marred only by their speaking too softly. This was to be expected, especially as Aboriginal youths were taught to be self-effacing.

These accomplishments probably amounted to little more than a thin veneer over Aboriginal customary ways, although we cannot discount their sincerity. Ham recalled: '[The Aboriginal students] first wanted shirts and trousers, then hats and shoes, and after they had got shoes, they were not content till they got jackets. Then they wanted frock coats, and had them as the fruits of their own labour out of their own garden'.[46] Their interest in material things made their Christian interest appear a compliant and manipulative strategy by a people becoming paupers in their own land, to gain food, shelter and access to tradable goods. Their efforts revealed fine imitative skills, but we cannot underestimate their interest in the novelty of schoolwork and the Christian message, which within a few years yielded Christian converts. Even their gardening, which five of the boys undertook with diligence, was done with tools and blades, whose novelty might have intrigued them.

However, resentments emerged and customary demands arose. In December 1846 the boys proved so unruly that William Thomas was summoned to draw up rules of behaviour to assist Peacock. Within a month some boys left and others refused to dress and clean themselves for Sunday church. The next year the girls misbehaved. Their home culture was blamed, a school report in 1848 stating: 'direct authority cannot be employed to the same extent as with European children' due to the 'indulgence native children have had at home'.[47] Certainly, school discipline—which included strapping—would have shocked children unused to such strictness. A few boys, including Billibellary's son, left in excitement to join the Native Police. Some absconded to taste bush life, telling Thomas 'they liked the bush better than the school'.[48] Others left to be initiated and maturing girls were claimed as brides. In early 1847, three families from Western Port arrived to take a nine-year-old away, no doubt to prepare for her education, initiation and eventual marriage, but on being refused, and 'after five days waiting in the rain to obtain her', they left. In September 1847 parents sought to recover other children, complaining that they were 'worked like long ago government men', meaning convicts. Despite only a handful of convicts being present in Melbourne working on government projects, Kulin people still had a vivid impression of their drudgery. Perhaps Batman's 'Sydney blacks' told the Kulin stories of convicts in their home country. In late 1847, the people abandoned the Merri Creek camp after two years residence and moved further up the Yarra taking their children with them.[49] The school was left without pupils, causing the *Argus* to chortle that the 'school for savages' had failed. However, Rev. Ramsey wrote: 'There is nothing wanting on the part of the native population either as respects quickness of mental apprehension, or the ordinary sensibilities of our nature to hinder them from rising in Society, and one day taking their place amongst the civilised and Christian portion of mankind'.[50]

The Merri Creek School lingered until 1848 with a new teacher, Mr Edgar, and family. His daughter Lucy Anna published an account of the experiment in 1865. The school's original pupils were five youths around the ages of twenty. Murrumwiller (renamed Charley) was from the Murray (or perhaps Gippsland); Jackey and Little Jemmy were from Gippsland; two more students were from Port Fairy—Jemmy and Figur (renamed Tommy)—and one was a Melbourne youth, Gurren Gurren-boop. William Thomas had brought them all to the school. A young woman Parley (renamed Kitty) and her two young sons, Wurrabool (renamed Harry) and Tommy, also came to the school.[51] They were the family of Bungaleen, a Gippsland man apprehended for allegedly holding as hostage in Gippsland a fabled 'wild white woman'. This woman—a fantasy constructed from images of white maidenhood held in savage hands—was first rumoured to exist in 1840. The 'wild white woman' supposedly held by Bungaleen was sought by three white search parties, which gallantly rode out in knightly quests in the mid 1840s, causing the deaths of numerous Gunai/Kurnai.[52]

The youths were at first disinclined to work or take lessons, but their existing appetite for tobacco was used by Edgar to gain their cooperation. The boys' lessons initially proceeded well. They attended the Collins Street Baptist Church each Sunday, in white trousers and jackets, discussing the sermon and the church rituals over dinner that evening. They particularly enjoyed the hymns, which they sang about the house and in bed before sleeping. Little Jemmy (James White) and Kitty were married around 1850 by Rev. Ramsey before the School Committee, William Thomas claiming it as the first Christian marriage among Aboriginal people. The School Committee tested the students regularly and rewarded their efforts with gifts, including 'white' money. Even Superintendent La Trobe heard them read and deemed their progress pleasing. Together with the Edgars the students refurbished the school's garden and built a bridge over the Merri, which earned them cash tips from grateful travellers before it was washed away in a devastating flood. The youths had pleasant, even amusing times with the Edgar family, there being a genuine mutual affection, if tinged with paternalism on the part of the Edgars who thought the youths amusing—'half-civilised', 'half-savage'. But a melancholy intermittently haunted the boys. They (and the Edgars) called it a 'beeg one sulky', which caused them to be uninterested in life and eating for several days on end, before regaining their hunger and cheerful disposition. The Edgars explained it as part of their 'savage' make-up. Perhaps it can be read as an alienation or depression, experienced by youths separated from their families, culture and their home country, and placed amidst an experiment in social change to form them into Christian rural labourers.

Charley from the Murray had aspirations to be more than a labourer and evolved a plan. He admired the gentlemen of the School Committee and others about Melbourne with their fine clothes and horses. If Charley was to join white society, he aimed to join its upper ranks, not the lower ranks as imagined by European humanitarians. Charley knew where power and status lay. He perfected his spoken English and observed the manner and deportment of a gentleman. Indeed, Charley expressed the desire to be white. The Edgars replied that a well-conducted dark man could be as respected as a white. He then declared: 'I like to be a gentleman. Black gentleman as good as white'. Indeed, Charley declared

'Portrait of Charles NEVER, Civilised Aboriginal.' (By permission of the Parliamentary Library, Parliament of Victoria from William Strutt's *Victorian the Golden: Scenes and Sketches and Jottings from Nature 1850–1862*, plate 72)

he desired a white wife and when the Edgars laughed, retorted: 'plenty white woman marry black man'. He even penned the first line of a love letter to a lady he admired, writing: 'My dear Mary, I love you sweet as honey'.[53] Charley realised that Europeans had two names and that gentlemen had formal ones, so he renamed himself Charles Never. (The other youths wanted two names as well and, with the help of the Edgars, became James White, Jacky Warren, Thomas Gurrenboop, and Kitty, Harry and Tommy Bungaleen). To make his way in the world, Charles Never apprenticed himself in April 1850 to Mr Foreman, a tailor in Elizabeth Street, in order to gain indoor employment and learn to sew, so he could make his gentleman's clothes.

Charles Never was soon parading around Melbourne like a dandy in black coat, trousers and waistcoat with a white starched stand-up collar, black boots, black kid gloves, a black satin stock (whip), and a tall black hat, apparently to the mirth of passers-by. Colonial and racial ideas were against Charles joining the powerful classes, as has been the case in all colonial regimes.[54] Aboriginal people were enjoined to become like whites, but derided when they sought to aim high, and do it in style. His fellow students also mocked his attempt—but we should not. Charles Never chose to assimilate but on his own terms. He also made a keen political point saying: 'I mean to write to the Queen and ask her to give me a piece of land . . . to build a house on; and I mean to ask her for 400 pounds . . . to build my house'. Mrs Edgar explained that the Queen would not entertain such a letter unless it went through the proper channels. Charles quickly replied:

> You say one time the Queen a good woman. And yet she send white man out here, take black fellar's land, and drive them away, and shoot them, and build planty house and garden on my land; and when I say, I ask her to give me back a piece of my land and money to build a house, you say she think I not know better. I know better. This land, my land *first* of all. 400 pounds not much to the Queen, and she take planty land from me.[55]

Mr Edgar said the School Committee might support his request for land if he worked better, but his master did not think that Charles worked hard or consistently enough. Charles disagreed. The letter it seems was never sent, but Charles's intention revealed his political stance.

Charles Never made a success of being a tailor. Lucy Edgar claimed Charles refused to call the tailor 'master' as an apprentice should, and referred to him simply as 'he'. In April 1851 William Thomas went in pursuit of Charles after hearing he had left his master, and found him at the Native Police Barracks. Charles Never claimed his master urged him to work when he was unwell. He returned to his master on Thomas's urging and finished his apprenticeship despite this rebelliousness. He then joined the Native Police as a tailor, probably gaining a smart uniform of his own. Charles Never told Thomas in May 1851 that he was very happy at Narre Narre Warren and 'that Capt Dana and all are very good to him'.[56] It was reported at a missionary meeting in July 1851 that he continued to study his Bible and attend Sunday school.[57] He apparently attempted to 'call on' some genteel families— unsuccessfully. Lucy Anna Edgar, who recalled Charles's words above (probably loosely) and told the story of the Merri Creek School, again from memory more than a decade later, also recalled Charles's fate from hearsay. Edgar wrote that some Aboriginal people eventually killed Charles Never while he was guiding missionaries to the Murray (no doubt the Anglicans to Yelta Mission in 1855), suggesting that he might have tired of breaking into white society and was perhaps heading for home.[58]

The other youths at the Merri Creek School did not share Charles Never's aspirations to go into the wider world, partly from fear of local Aboriginal people. Figur attempted to make his way home to Port Fairy on a bullock wagon in June 1848. He was waylaid and killed by a group led by the Goulburn man, Billy Hamilton, which contained four Woiwurrung students from the School, including Wydelong who had read Matthew 13 so impressively. Figur's killing was traditional business. He was a stranger, Billy Hamilton commented to Thomas: 'no good long way blackfella that'.[59] Figur's brother Jemmy returned home safely, but in sorrow. The two Gippslanders also headed home. After weeks of pressure from the Woiwurrung—'wild blacks', the Edgars called them—Kitty departed, leaving her two young sons with the Edgars. With only a few students left, the Merri Creek School closed in 1851. The two Bungaleen boys were to move with the Edgars to Tasmania, but for some reason this did not occur, much to their chagrin: yet another happy home was wrested from them. Instead, in January 1851 William Thomas gave them to the care of John Hinkins, who ran an Anglican school in Pentridge village (now Coburg). The boys became showpieces of assimilation as will be seen later.

4

Accommodating Sheep Herders

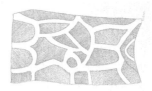

The speed of pastoral settlement in Port Phillip's interior was startling, making it one of the fastest land occupations in the history of empires, as sheep and their European keepers spread over the central third of Victoria in less than a decade to 1845. The movement stretched northwards from harbours along the coast from Portland to Port Albert, and south-west along Major Mitchell's 1836 line of march between present-day Howlong (west of Albury) and Portland, which was rutted and easily visible with his wagon tracks for decades. Mitchell prophesied this rapid colonisation of the grasslands prepared by millennia of Aboriginal fire-stick farming. Calling the region *Australia felix* (happy south land), Mitchell claimed that Providence had left it for Englishmen to settle and cultivate.[1]

Aboriginal traditional owners and European settlers interacted in complex and varied ways during this frenzied decade of settlement. The 5–10,000 Aboriginal people in the swathe of expansion consisted of thirty different cultural–language groups and hundreds of clans, each with their own elders, ideas, and strategies. Aboriginal people—elders and youths, men, women and children—all experienced the occupation differently. The 10,000 Europeans who occupied rural Port Phillip by 1846 were not a unified group either. The squatters (masters) and their overseers were from all parts of the United Kingdom, some young, some old, some educated, some not. Their servants were similarly diverse, comprised of convicts/ex-convicts (a third of rural adult males) and freemen as well. Less than fifty men were government officials: protectors, land commissioners, magistrates and police. Several were missionaries. Most European intruders were men, which made it a masculine and often violent frontier. On both sides of the frontier people and groups had their own desires and the stakes were high. Many squatters risked up to £2,000 in capital (over $1 million in today's terms) on sheep ventures on leased government land, which they knew in their hearts and acknowledged in their diaries was traditionally someone else's country. Their servants worked for their daily bread in a new land far from kith and kin. For Aboriginal people, their very ownership of land, which was not only their livelihood but the source of their culture, identity and spiritual essence, was at stake.

Forming frontier attachments

Ironically, Aboriginal people assisted the European possession of Port Phillip lands, unaware of what the long term would bring. Aboriginal guides, for novelty and adventure, often accompanied squatters seeking new country to lease. They ate European food en route. George Russell remarked of his journey near Western Port that 'we found we had given the two blackfellows too much of our provisions and had not sufficient for ourselves'.[2] Guides gained other goods such as tobacco, and perhaps had use of a gun to forage for food. They paved the way as they knew the country and had kin there, or, through common dialect and signs, they introduced the Europeans to land and people. George Robinson remarked of one squatter in 1840: 'it was the natives that showed him his run and I believe half of the runs have been shewn by the natives'.[3]

Without Aboriginal guides, Europeans were blind to what lay ahead, and vulnerable. Having Aboriginal guides saved many exploring parties, especially in rugged country like Gippsland. In 1840 Paul Strzelecki, a Polish scientist leading a party of six from the Alps through Gippsland, was saved from starvation by game caught by Charley Tarra. William Brodribb's party also depended on Charley Tarra for food and for good relations with Gunai/Kurnai people while exploring around Port Albert in 1842. When George Hawdon's party became lost near Wilson's Promontory in 1844 their two guides caught a 'native bear' (koala) and offered the seven Europeans only a hind leg between them. Hawdon thought it an unfair division, but accepted it in case 'the blacks might leave us in the lurch to find other food as we best might'.[4] These journeys had Aboriginal outcomes as well. Tarra was asked by one group to cicatrise one of their youths similar to his own scarred shoulders and back. He obliged, breaking a bottle and operating on the youth's back, who did not wince as the flesh was sliced open ready to be rubbed and filled with ashes.[5]

'Stockman Talking to Natives', by Samuel Thomas Gill. (Rex Nan Kivell Collection, courtesy of the National Library of Australia, AN2377106)

Most initial meetings on pastoral runs were wary but peaceful. Aboriginal people usually had forewarning from neighbouring groups about Europeans and their flocks, but the shock of meeting men on horses and seeing bullocks, wagons and sheep was still great. George Walker, accompanied by six Aboriginal guides on his route overland from Sydney in 1838, met a party of Kulin people at the Ovens River who had seen Europeans and even knew what guns were, but were still agog. He recorded that 'they examined and touched our clothes and skins, with wonder and admiration, and asked us to give them many articles they saw in our possession'. They followed the overlanders for a day and wondered at matches being struck, crackers being lit and other items they saw.[6] Other groups showed hostility from the start, especially if caught by surprise when parties came from seaward, as did Brodribb's group at Port Albert in 1842. A group of Gunai/Kurnai approached their encampment, surrounded them and proceeded to inspect the Europeans' goods. When a man attempted to steal Brodribb's pipe, Brodribb 'pushed him back and held my fist in his face'.[7] The Europeans then demonstrated the power of their guns on bottles and targets and even fired a small cannon out to sea. The people were unimpressed and the next day chased them in the bush, though Brodribb's party, being on horseback, escaped.

Many Aboriginal groups initially fostered peace as they pondered the newcomers and wondered how they might be controlled, even made useful. They sought the whites' origins and intentions. Naturally they understood Europeans in Aboriginal terms and thus did not initially conceive of them staying and settling, as Aboriginal people did not come onto another's land if it had no spiritual meaning for them. As their other cultural imperatives were kinship and reciprocity, they tried to establish an attachment with Europeans to control the rupture of the Aboriginal world and gain access to their resources in exchange for guest-status on Aboriginal land. Women were offered or offered themselves, which was a traditional form of peace-making between groups. Before long new names were bestowed on Indigenous people. This pleased Europeans, who were unable to master Aboriginal names and their tricky pronunciations, with soft 'ng' sounds and all syllables emphasised. The bestowal of names also suited Aboriginal people for it established an attachment and avoided the use of traditional names that were hedged with protocols and strictures. In terms of kinship, it was not uncommon for Indigenous people to think these first whites were former relatives returned from the dead. How else could their appearance be explained?

Trade was initiated on both sides with metal and wood, flour and fish, sugar and game changing hands. Europeans, who were outnumbered, initially cooperated and humoured their more numerous hosts. An accommodation emerged on both sides as Aboriginal people sought to incorporate the Europeans in their web of tradition and Europeans sought assistance in a strange country. Aboriginal men often helped to establish pastoral stations by ferrying sheep across creeks, cutting brush for the sheep folds and slabs and bark for huts. In return they were given flour and tobacco and a sheep was killed for food. As peaceful relations developed, intimacies grew between some groups of First Nations people and Europeans.

Good relations prevailed in the most unlikely places as fellow humans of vastly different cultural backgrounds sometimes found delight in each other's activities. David Fisher, who was manager of a Geelong run in 1837, was shaving himself in the open air much to the amusement of an Aboriginal audience. One asked to be shaved as well, and 'I undertook the task, which I accomplished amidst the yells, shouts, and laughter of some fifty savages with their lubras, who enjoyed the affair very much'.[8] In Gippsland in 1843, H. B. Morris was alarmed when the Tarra Creek mob visited a hut where he was staying. However, after these Gunai/Kurnai people entered, their Irish host danced 'in the most approved fashion last imported from Donnybrook fair'. As the 190-centimetre Irishman worked into a Gaelic frenzy, several Gunai/Kurnai imitated him, dancing right and left as he did, twisting as he pirouetted in mirror-like fashion in an extraordinary performance.[9]

People on both sides of the cultural frontier engaged in ordinary relations of human interest. Work and sometimes sex was exchanged in return for tobacco, tea and damper. The sense of attachment and loyalty on both sides could be strong. The Clow family, who settled the foothills of the Dandenongs, sent Jack Weatherly, an Aboriginal man at their station, on an errand to take four dozen home-cooked biscuits over twenty kilometres to their son, the payment being six for himself. En route Weatherly became involved in a kangaroo hunt, but organised another Aboriginal man to complete the task, the biscuits arriving safely.[10] Other everyday interactions reveal similar closeness.

In 1841, Edward Curr, an educated young man in his early twenties, tried squatting on behalf of his father, first near Heathcote, then on the banks of the Goulburn River in the Shepparton region. His party of eight were heavily armed and fearful of being 'killed by the Blacks'.[11] As they felled trees, three Aboriginal men appeared and a conversation in broken English ensued. Curr stressed the sanctity of his sheep and the power of his guns, but also offered each of them 'as much meat, tea and damper as would serve two ordinary whites for a meal'.[12] The two groups found common ground in admiring the beauty of Curr's kangaroo dogs. The Aboriginal men set to work for Curr. As the weeks unfolded, more Bangerang people arrived, and he encouraged them to work for food and tobacco. As was now customary, he named them, and some attached themselves to his station. An exchange relationship developed as they learned sheep work and Curr, bored with his own company, learned bushcraft from them. Curr recalled that 'yarning with the Bangerang, swimming, climbing trees in native fashion, throwing spears, and hunting' filled his leisure hours.[13] The Bangerang never felt inferior to Curr, being his superior in the bush and, only half joking, reminded him that 'I could make neither a gun, nor a tomahawk, nor sugar, nor flour, nor anything else', whereas they made all they used.[14] Although his leasehold expanded to 900 square kilometres, they never acknowledged the land as his. When he expanded his leasehold further he was confronted by an elder who abused Curr, asking 'why I came to the Moria? What I wanted? That I was a demon from the grave! That the water, the fish, and the ducks belonged to his tribe. That he spat at me and hated me'.[15]

In 1844 John Hinkins, a widower, became overseer at 'Gunbower' station on the Lower Murray west of Echuca. He was accompanied by his five-year-old daughter Jenny. About 300 Yorta Yorta visited the

Detail from Eugene von Guérard's 'The Barter', 1854, oil on canvas. (Courtesy of Geelong Gallery, gift of W. Max Bell and Norman Belcher, 1923. Reproduced in black and white with permission)

day after their arrival to see the golden-haired child. To foster good relations, Hinkins re-named Najara, the most formidable man among them, 'Cockie', and the rest quickly demanded names as well. Najara attached himself to Hinkins, coming each dawn to his hut to make the tea and engage in station work. Such trust developed between the two that Hinkins left Jenny in Najara's care for several days at a time, while on station work. Hinkins, who admired these people, always kept his word, ministered to their illnesses and cared for their elderly. They in turn were scrupulously honest with his property, the young men shepherding for him, and saving several of his workers from drowning. Jenny was taught to swim by the women and spent much time at the camp with Aboriginal playmates, becoming fluent in their language. Hinkins would often gravitate to the camp for a chat. He talked religion with Najara, who on occasion laughed so much at Hinkins's views that he had to stuff his mouth with his possum-skin cloak: 'he would run out of the hut, throw himself on the ground, and lie rolling about laughing'.[16]

These were relationships of respect, more equal than those between white masters and servants. Hinkins hunted with the people and organised field sports days in which he held handicap shooting events, his gun against their spear, with damper being the prize. Yet a complex relationship developed, for Hinkins's field days were in part meant to reveal his own superior prowess with a gun. He admitted that he occasionally cheated by placing a musket ball in a distant sapling, then pretending from far off to shoot it there. This earned a 'cluck' of admiration from Aboriginal bystanders. Such demonstrations, he said, aided his control over the people. Surprisingly, given Najara's care of his daughter, Hinkins never fully trusted Najara, always having his gun at hand, as he conceived him still 'a savage'. Najara in turn disapproved of Hinkins's discipline of Jenny, to the point of physically holding Hinkins back on occasion till Hinkins cooled his anger towards her. When Hinkins departed after two years, the people as a sign of respect 'assembled in great numbers and the wailing and howling of the lubras and piccaninnies, and the cutting and burning of the men [by way of mourning], was grievous to hear and see'.[17]

Aboriginal people often responded very positively to white children on the frontier. When Katherine Kirkland took her baby to a pastoral station, the Aboriginal women inspected the baby and its clothes with interest and hilarity, the Aboriginal children mimicking its cry.[18] George McCrae, who kept a diary when a thirteen-year-old boy on the Mornington Peninsula in the 1840s, wrote affectionately of his relationship with an Aboriginal man, Ben Benjie, the family's huntsman. Young George went hunting with Ben and learned to spear fish and use a boomerang. They went swimming in the surf and attended corroborees together. McCrae later set down some of the tribal songs he had learned from Ben Benjie.[19] Similarly, six-year-old Jenny Hinkins was loved by the Murray people, being invited to ceremonies, and was able to demand anything of them. Her father once carried out a punishment-threat to strip her naked and send her to the blacks. To his astonishment, Jenny gleefully ran towards the camp singing out 'merrijig [good] blackfellow, no good whitefellow', forcing Hinkins to chase after her and bring her home.[20] Eleven-year-old James Hamilton met an Aboriginal couple on his father's run in the Wimmera while bringing in horses. His fear of them dissipated when the man, Jacky, put his spears in the ground and came up to James with 'a broad smile on his face'. From then on they 'were much together'. In later years Jacky addressed him as 'Mr Hamilton when in town, but in the bush it was "halloa Jim"'.[21]

Europeans, however, often perceived Aboriginal children as property. Sometimes children were acquired in protective mode. In Melbourne in 1839 Protector Parker snatched an Aboriginal baby boy from an Aboriginal man who was allegedly about to kill it. Parker assumed control of the boy, named Kolain, apparently without consulting anyone, and raised, educated and Christianised him as one of his own until he was seventeen.[22] John McLeod, an early squatter in the Geelong area, for nine years looked after a boy who travelled everywhere with him, including to other colonies. McLeod claimed 'his father and mother gave him to me when about ten years of age, and he, as well as his parents, appeared to at once consider him my property'. This may have reflected Aboriginal ideas of kinship, education and the forming of attachments with newcomers on Aboriginal land. McLeod stated that when the boy grew into a fine man, 'his tribe forced him to leave me'.[23] (The boy remained nameless in this recollection, indicating his servant-like status.) Dr Jonathan Clerke, from the area west of Geelong, acquired a boy in 1837, telling a government investigation that his mother consented to his being given over and civilised. Foster Fyans reported that Clerke's intentions were noble and that the boy 'speaks English well and knows his letters, he appears to have great affection for Dr Clerke, and detests the sight of a native'.[24] However, Aboriginal consent may not, in fact, have been given to Clerk. John McLeod recalled that two men approached him about that time near Geelong asking for the black boy 'Billy Clarke', adding: 'as it was about three weeks after Dr Clarke has taken him, they wished to know if we had eaten him, and said his mother was very sorry and cried very much'.[25]

Others took children to exploit them. Squatters and bullockies took boys they claimed were orphans and fought over them in court.[26] George Faithfull, who settled the Ovens in 1838, fought Aboriginal groups a number of times. He recalled that after one fight 'I picked up a boy from under a log, took him home and tamed him, and he became very useful to me'.[27] Thomas Browne, who wrote novels under the name 'Rolf Boldrewood', acquired an Aboriginal child through a squatter in Mount Gambier, who had heard 'I anxiously desired to become possessed of a black boy'. Browne named him 'Charlie Gambier' and took him back to his Port Fairy run. While these 'possessions' will perhaps be given a grim sexual interpretation in today's world, which in some instances might have been the case, Faithfull and Browne were probably looking for cheap roustabouts at a time when labour was scarce and putting young children to work was acceptable. But imperial attitudes also played a role in these relationships, as squatters assimilated these boys with European clothes, work routines and language. Indeed, Browne tutored and Christianised Charlie Gambier, but claimed the youth deteriorated rapidly at the age of fifteen, 'learning to drink spirits and copy the undesirable whiteman with painful accuracy'.[28] Boldrewood showed no understanding of the bewilderment of a young Aboriginal man who had been denied knowledge of his own

'Going to Work' by Samuel Thomas Gill, 1850s.
(Courtesy of the National Library of Australia, AN2381127)

and his country's identity—perhaps a bewilderment he tried to dull
by alcohol.

Relations with Aboriginal adult workers were less exploitative, as adults
could and did leave at any time. Perhaps 200 to 400 Indigenous people
worked at any one time during the 1840s as sheep washers, general hands
and as shepherds—about three to five per cent of the pastoral workforce
of Port Phillip. Aboriginal women did domestic work around the station,
shepherded, and also provided sexual services on a voluntary as much as
a forced basis. A few Aboriginal men became the aristocrats of pastoral
workers: stockmen on horses. Edward Curr praised these men, arguing
that 'as scrub-riders and rough-riders the average Bangerang excelled the
average stockman. He had better nerve, quicker sight, and stuck closer
to his saddle'.[29] George McCrae recalled of the Boonwurrung that 'the
youths, always fearless riders and fond of horses, made good stockkeepers,
and took great pride in their long, heavy whips and spurs'. He added that
most were honest and intelligent workers and the young women 'washed
and ironed well'.[30]

Aboriginal workers were invariably paid in rations and clothing,
although a few were paid in cash, especially after the discovery of gold.
Most white employers thought them poor workers, but used them
nonetheless as cheap labour. In reality Aboriginal people saw little
point in regular daily work, as it was not how their traditional economy

operated; traditionally, they foraged when hungry and stopped when they had gathered enough for the next meal. Aboriginal workers also placed Aboriginal business before white needs, leaving when it suited them and not their bosses. Ceremonies and time in their own country came first. Hugh Jamieson, a Murray squatter, recalled that in summer 'nearly all, from the oldest to the youngest in the various tribes, have the greatest desire to abandon every employment, and indulge in the roving life of naked savages'.[31] Besides, Aboriginal workers were aware that they were paid less than white workers, which did little to increase their loyalty to white bosses. Few adopted the work ethic and some positively opposed it, one group of Goulburn (Daungwurrung) men saying in 1840, 'we gentlemen, we no work'.[32]

Imagining savages

The peaceful working relations that existed between Europeans and Aboriginal people on some pastoral runs were absent on others. Many squatters had a strong sense of their absolute possession of the land, at least for the term of their annual lease. They wanted no impediments to their pastoral venture, and feared and distrusted Aboriginal people, who they believed were 'simply savages'. This idea was universally held in Port Phillip, even amongst the friends and supporters of Indigenous people. Hugh Jamieson, who had good relations with Aboriginal people, termed them 'naked savages', and others, like John Hinkins, Edward Curr, the Aboriginal Protectors and missionaries, all thought the same. The word 'savage'—which had a long heritage in Europe, associated with wildness and being uncivilised—was invested with many meanings. By definition, savages were degraded and immoral, feckless and untrustworthy, treacherous and violent. They were claimed to be low on the scale of humankind. Two other vivid claims made and believed by friends and foes of Aboriginal people alike, and repeated endlessly in letters, diaries, reports, newspapers and books, were that Aboriginal people practised infanticide and cannibalism—the classic marks of the 'savage'. While these topics are often avoided in recent histories, they must be confronted, as they shaped European attitudes and actions towards Aboriginal people. They also added to the justification that they were 'primitive' people of no account, who did not deserve to own a continent.

Most Europeans in Port Phillip believed Aboriginal people practised infanticide. In 1845, when the NSW Legislative Council held a Select

Committee on Aborigines, question 17 asked: 'Is infanticide known among them'? Many respondents believed it was 'common'; some, that its incidence varied between groups; several did not know; while John Watton, the Mount Rouse surgeon, only interested in the facts, was unique when he replied: 'I have never known an instance of it'.[33] William Westgarth, a Melbourne merchant, wrote a series of books on Victoria praising its progress to a flourishing colony. *Australia Felix*, published in 1848, trumpeted Port Phillip's spectacular advance in just twelve years. Westgarth devoted four chapters to Aboriginal people and their customs based on John Eyre's observations and the 1845 Select Committee report. In his chapter on the Aboriginal family, Westgarth was puzzled by the obvious affection of Aboriginal people for their children and their supposed practise of infanticide—'the extreme of barbarism and cruelty'—which he believed was 'undoubted and extensive'. He claimed infant girls and mixed descent children were killed most often. Westgarth believed this barbarism was compounded by the 'horror and astonishment' of parents eating their children. Infanticide in short proved Aboriginal savagery.[34] Numerous other colonial references to infanticide exist.

However, two things need to be said about infanticide. The first is that none of these European claimants acknowledged that infanticide, to which we could add the related practice of abortion, was also practised—but not condoned—in European society. Indeed, at this very time there was alarm among the English middle class about a perceived plague of infanticide, especially among the London poor. Yet, although English mothers who practised infanticide were often portrayed as misguided victims, Aboriginal people were seen as barbarians.[35] This interpretation demonstrates how claims about them were based as much on politics as on fact, and were used to demonise them as 'savages'.

The second thing to note about infanticide is that the evidence does not clearly show that it was 'common' at all, as most Europeans believed. As in England, there was a degree of moral panic about the issue. Billibellary acknowledged to William Thomas that infanticide occurred among the Woiwurrung, indicating a fatalism about there being no land for children to inherit. However, most if not all of the evidence about infanticide is hearsay. Even Billibellary's statement falls into that category. Foster Fyans, the Colonial Lands Commissioner for the Portland Bay District whose evidence to the 1845 Select Committee was repeated by Westgarth, claimed to have seen a child dashed against a tree by a 'native man' and to have later seen brains and hair on the tree. He witnessed the incident from the other side of the Marrabool River (not

'Bushman's Hut' by Samuel Thomas Gill, in his *The Australian Sketchbook*, 1865.
(Courtesy of the National Library of Australia, AN7150080)

now listed in directories), and does not tell us the distance of his line of sight. Did Fyans in fact see a possum being despatched against a tree from which it was caught? Fyans knew the colonial talk about savages, and perhaps *imagined* rather than *saw* a child. Westgarth also refers to Edward Parker's report of a mother eating her killed child, but again what Parker says to the Select Committee is that 'a well ascertained instance was lately made known to me'. In other words, it is again hearsay.[36] Thus, while infanticide occurred in Aboriginal society as it did in European society, its incidence and meaning is obscure, and not an obvious marker of savagery.

Westgarth also highlighted in his 1848 book another universal colonial belief, evident in the first entries of William Fawkner's diary in 1835, namely, that Aboriginal people practised cannibalism. Westgarth wrote that they not only eat the flesh of 'enemies slain in battle', but 'prefer the flesh of their own friends and relations who have died in the course of nature'. He gave lurid instances of people eating flesh for gratification, using emotional words such as 'unnatural', 'disgusting' and 'monster in human shape' to relate these stories. They were mostly unsourced hearsay. Westgarth concluded that 'the circumstances attending these occasions of festivity are sometimes of so callous and brutal a character as to be hardly credible of any section of human beings'.[37] Cannibalism is both a worldwide phenomenon and a universal way of slandering other cultures.[38] Westgarth used cannibalism to cast in doubt the humanity of Aboriginal people. We must treat such claims cautiously.

Despite the widespread claims of cannibalism, most reports did not refer to eating human flesh for pleasure or need, but rather to ritual consumption of parts of fallen enemies—especially the kidney fat—out of triumph and revenge. Traveller George Haydon claimed that 'on several occasions I have seen human flesh in their possession, and have been told by them without much scruple that they always make a point of eating certain portions of their enemies killed in battle or by treachery, under a feeling of revenge'.[39] Haydon then luridly described inter-group fighting where the 'dead bodies are savagely lacerated and the kidney fat torn out, large slices of flesh are cut from the legs, and every conceivable indignity offered to bodies lately tabernacles of living souls'.[40]

Many other observers including William Buckley, who had lived with Aboriginal people for 33 years, referred to 'kidney fatting' and the ritual consumption of flesh in warfare. Buckley, in measured terms, told George Langehorne in 1837:

> They are cannibals. I have seen them eat small portions of the flesh of their enemies slain in battle. They appear to do this not from any particular liking for human flesh, but from the impression that by eating their adversaries' flesh they themselves would become better warriors. Many of them are however disgusted by the idea, and instead of eating the flesh merely rub their bodies with a small portion of the fat as a charm equally efficient.[41]

Buckley added that they sometimes ate the flesh of a dead favoured child. Whether Buckley related the truth is unknowable for he was a man in the middle of a difficult situation, a man returned from living with 'savages', trying to make his way and his living amidst new social realities. He was certainly aware that his audience saw cannibalism as a marker of savagery. The politics of consuming human flesh is packed with emotion and value judgements, yet his observation has a ring of moderation and sincerity.

In 1858 the Protector William Thomas told a Select Committee that Aboriginal people were not cannibals, but did rub the kidney fat of vanquished enemies over their bodies. Certainly in 1839 he reported seeing the exhumed body of Peter, an Aboriginal youth from the Murray, who was killed in Melbourne because he was a foreigner. Peter's body had flesh cut off the arms and flanks and an incision made in the side.[42]

A squatter, Hugh Murray, stated some Barrabools killed some of the Colac tribe when searching for Gellibrand and Hesse and 'brought with them, on the end of their spears, portions of the man and child they had killed, which *I saw them eat* with great exultation during the evening'.[43] And of course Aboriginal people also believed cannibalism happened to them surreptitiously through sorcery. William Westgarth recalled meeting an ill Aboriginal man in an encampment near Brunswick in 1843 who believed his kidney fat had been taken and eaten, leaving a now healed wound and him 'sadly weak and death-like', soon to leave this world.[44] William Thomas, who doubted a sorcerer could make a cut while a man slept and then seal it over perfectly, was firmly told by an Aboriginal man that it could happen. This man proceeded to borrow Thomas's sharp knife, cut bark on a branch with it, and pressed it together, so that Thomas could not detect the cut. The man said: 'like it that the spirit of a black on another'.[45]

George Robinson also collected compelling evidence of cannibalism in Melbourne in 1839, when he publicly asked for proof upon hearing Aboriginal stories. The next day a number brought pieces of flesh said to be human, and a child's foot and hand, and one gave a vivid description of the killing of a man, woman and child who were *mainmet*, meaning distant enemies.[46] Robinson showed these items to James Dredge a month later who recorded it in his diary.[47] However, we cannot

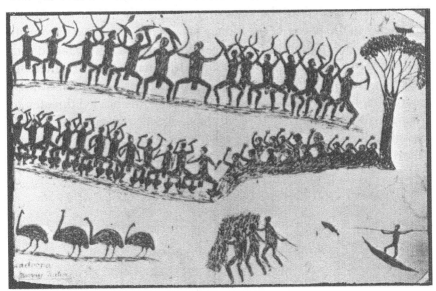

'Yackadoona, Murray Natives' by Tommy McCrae, R.E. John's Album, 1869.
(Reproduced courtesy Museum Victoria, XP2065)

discount the fact that individuals might have led Robinson on. Robinson was in the habit of giving gifts for ethnographic items and in this instance did so again. He recorded of their conversation:

> I was horror struck but compelled to suppress my feeling in order to elicit their customs. Some time after all the natives had assembled I entertained with boiled meat and soup, Mr Thomas who was to have given them blankets having not returned. I continued in conversation with them and in acquiring their language and customs. Distributed cigar, tobacco, pipes, beads. Gave a tommyhawk for a crooked club. Pm the natives all left. Mr Murry stopped behind.

Murry, an Aboriginal man, placed a child's hand on Robinson's desk and told a detailed story of the killing of these distant enemies, reiterating: 'the blacks very bad, killed were a long way off'.[48]

In an emotion-charged subject like cannibalism facts were never clear-cut, especially when meat, tobacco and tommyhawks were at stake. Individual Aboriginal people told William Mollison, a squatter for thirty years, further stories of cannibalism. Mollison commented in 1853: 'This does not prove it, because we know they will at any time admit or say anything which they think will please their interlocutor'.[49] The strip of flesh Robinson came to possess may not even have been human. And the child's body parts may have been pieces of a dead child, traditionally, and affectionately, carried in a bag by a mourning mother. However, Aboriginal belief in the power of the kidney fat and its removal was probably universal in Port Phillip. The bodies of some slain settlers were found with flesh sliced from them.[50] We cannot know what happened thereafter, but settlers steeped in the myths of savagery assumed the worst. John Fawkner recorded in his diary in December 1835: 'They [the blacks] threaten to attempt us to night, if they succeed they will Kill and eat us all'.[51] Such prevailing ideas shaped relations of violence on the frontier, as settlers believing in 'savagery' acted savagely to oppose it.

5

Dangerous Frontiers

An uneasy peace on new pastoral runs often gave way to mutual fear, mistrust, and then violence. Trouble erupted on runs in the Geelong region in 1836, on the Ovens and Goulburn Rivers in 1838, in the Western District from 1839, in Gippsland from 1840 and the Murray Valley and Wimmera–Mallee from around 1842. In most regions, violence lasted sporadically for several years, but in inaccessible places like Gippsland, intermittent violence continued for upwards of five years. There were literally hundreds of violent incidents of various magnitudes across all these frontiers. Each violent encounter was unique and not all people in a given area were involved in the violence, making generalisations difficult. Violence usually began as localised trouble—feuding and disputes over specific lands and particular events—and often remained that way. In places, however, it evolved into a kind of war, causing Aboriginal people and settlers to recognise a wider pattern.

The causes of conflict

Three main factors underpinned the violence: the nature and perceptions of the land and the contest over it; the pastoral economy's structure and the human relations this fostered; and the ideology dominant amongst Europeans.

The lands of Port Phillip, mostly beautiful pastoral and farming country today, looked similar in the 1830s, thanks to millennia of Aboriginal burning to foster feed for kangaroo and other game. This managed landscape was invisibly divided into dozens of discrete Aboriginal traditional countries, each with their own stories, sacred sites and clan owners to care for them. The land was locally owned, so specific clan owners met individual pastoralists to negotiate the challenges of intrusion. Clans initially acted alone, not as part of some wider Aboriginal response. Europeans were also initially vulnerable. Port Phillip to them was vast and uncharted, a fearful and alienating place. Government control and the rule of British law was minimal given the vast distances and scarcity of enforcement agencies. The frontier became a place of fear and of fragile relationships.

Both sides viewed land in absolute terms; that is, they believed they should hold it without restriction. Both sides had their *all* invested in the coming struggle over land. Aboriginal clans were owners by customary right and the acts of the great ancestors who had made the land and entrusted it to them. Land to them was much more than the source of their livelihood, and it certainly was not conceived of as property that could be traded, bought and sold. It was their mother, their spiritual essence, to which they were bound by their Great Tradition and by the totemic ties they shared with other living things on it. They traversed a landscape heavy with religious meaning, from which they could not be parted.

Europeans too came with a love for land, but their love was essentially different. Europeans could be sentimental over land and be prepared to die for it, but their ideas about it were bound up with personal power and wealth as well as affection. The shift in Britain from communal to capitalistic ideas about land in the eighteenth century caused land to be seen as a potent form of individualistic property to be held and enjoyed in an absolute way and thus capable of being bought and sold. Land could be left behind you too: were the Port Phillip sheep herders not all emigrants from England, Scotland and elsewhere? Pastoral land was held only on an annual crown lease between 1836 and 1849, yet pastoralists treated leased land as theirs. On taking up a run near Port Fairy Rolf Boldrewood exclaimed: 'Pride and successful ambition swelled my breast on that first morning as I looked round on my run. My run! My own station! How fine a sound it had'.[1] For European small holders near the towns—farmers—land fulfilled a dream of independence from wage slavery. Such a clash of absolute views about land found little compromise.[2]

The structure of pastoralism also underpinned frontier violence. Pastoralism—the newest child of nineteenth-century capitalism, linking the sheep walks of Port Phillip to the woollen mills of England—occupied vast tracks of land, and quickly displaced large numbers of Aboriginal clans. If farming had been the main pursuit, settlement would have been slower and marginal lands might have sustained Aboriginal numbers, perhaps even under some sort of mutual accommodation agreement. However, pastoral runs which spread rapidly tempted the original owners with large numbers of sheep, seen as property by Europeans but as easy targets and tasty feasts by Aboriginal people, especially as sheep displaced game and ate out traditional vegetable crops on Aboriginal land. The pastoral workforce was also sparse. Each run was worked by several men spread out from each other to tend flocks and separated from neighbours by perhaps ten or twenty kilometres. Fear thrived among Europeans in such vulnerable isolation; it also thrived among Aboriginal people, who saw a tide of sheep sweeping their land.

Aboriginal ambush of a shepherd, *Illustrated Sydney News*, 29 September 1869.

The pastoral workforce was mainly male, the ratio of men to women on the early pastoral frontier being over twenty to one. This led to much trouble over Aboriginal women. In 1842 the Protector Edward Parker reported the deaths of two Aboriginal men, shot by John Williams, an American Creole, because they 'would not give him their women'. Parker commented: 'It is my firm conviction, the result of nearly three years observation, that nine out of ten of the outrages committed by the blacks may be traced, directly or indirectly to such circumstances as these'.[3] Lands Commissioner Foster Fyans agreed, as he 'generally found the origin of theft and murder was from an over-intimacy on both sides'.[4] Sometimes amicable arrangements could be made between men, and even men and women, concerning women. But bad characters like Williams inflamed the delicate balance and caused violence. Settler James Clow sent a servant back to Melbourne to save him being killed after he gave 'great offence' to Aboriginal women.[5] Rutledge's servant was killed at his pastoral station on the Loddon in 1839 for interfering with an Aboriginal woman. This was a judicial killing, as his fat was cut out and Rutledge's other workers, though not interfered with, were informed of his crime.[6]

Ideology, especially the racial ideas held by many Europeans, along with preconceptions and rumour, also caused fear and violence. As most Europeans believed Aboriginal people were 'savages', barbarous, brutish people who killed and ate each other and killed their own children, they claimed 'the blacks' only understood firmness and force and could not be reasoned with. Thus the conception of Aboriginal 'savagery' led to savage treatment of traditional owners, as fearful and hard men battled for the land on which they had staked all their capital. A 'shoot first' mentality developed. Settlers built their huts like forts with slotted windows for firing, several mounting swivel guns and cannons. Most routinely carried guns, although their unreliability contributed to the atmosphere of fear. Edward Curr met one ex-convict shepherd at Wyuna Station who admitted shooting an Aboriginal man, Nosie, in the arm, despite Nosie approaching the hut unarmed. The shepherd declared: 'As many of them as comes here when I am alone, I'll shoot'.[7]

Besides land, economic structure and ideology, violence stemmed from a myriad of minor grievances which arose as the two groups interacted. These included conflict over the sharing of goods and food, personal disagreements and trouble over sacred transgressions of which Europeans were unaware. Intimacy existed because Aboriginal people initially saw white trespassers in customary terms, not as *mainmet*—traditional enemies to be quickly killed—but as relatives returned from the dead, or strange new people to be incorporated as kin. As kin, old or newly created by name-exchange and other methods, there could still be a falling out. Foster Fyans observed the frequent closeness of the two groups which could suddenly explode: 'In all my investigations I found where life was lost that blame was attributable to both sides—to the jealousy of the native and over-intimacy of the hut-keeper or shepherd, who was one day feeding the natives and the day following beating and driving them from the place'.[8]

Initially trouble on pastoral runs resembled feuding: local disputes over land, women or resources between specific and known people. But as the pastoralists and their sheep stayed to permanently occupy Aboriginal lands, as violence and reprisals increased, and as Aboriginal clans talked to each other about what was going on, a new generalised perception amongst at least some Aboriginal people emerged. Europeans had long conceived of conflict in terms of battles between anonymous, generalised groups over wealth and land, as in war, but this conception was alien to Aboriginal people. In traditional times Aboriginal disputes and feuding did not incorporate struggles over land because Aboriginal people did not covet the land of others to which they had no spiritual links. Fighting was with known enemy clans for customary reasons which did not include land. However, the Europeans' desire for land and claim over it, and the action of many in keeping Aboriginal people off their runs, led to a strange new concept for Aboriginal people: that of a war for the land. On some runs, Aboriginal people came to see all Europeans as enemies (as in war) rather than just seeing particular people as enemies (as in feuding). This was revealed by the not infrequent cry that they 'would attack all Europeans', calling them by the generic name: 'whites' or 'whitefellas'. At Willam Dallas Bernard and Dr Kilgour's run near Port Fairy in late 1841, a shepherd had his arms pinned by two Gunditjmara warriors, who before they unsuccessfully prepared to strike him a mortal blow patted him on the head and said: 'white fellows no good; must kill 'em'.[9]

As Aboriginal people shifted their perceptions, Europeans also developed a more sophisticated justification for what was happening on the frontier, based partly on religious principles and a pastoralist theory of value. Most colonists believed the Biblical account of God's covenant with Noah after the Flood (Genesis 9) that directed humankind to be fruitful and multiply and gave them control of the earth and all its resources. A settler, Charles Griffith, claimed 'these duties the savage has for centuries neglected, and thus, in my mind, abandoned his inheritance'.[10] It was believed that humankind had a right to property, but after the expulsion of Adam and Eve from the Garden of Eden (Genesis 3), this right was only realised through labour. As magistrate William Hull remarked in 1846, 'No nation or tribe can acquire or maintain a right to the soil, unless it profitably occupies or tills it'.[11] The pastoralists, 'squatters' as they were at first derisively known, also claimed that they were the true basis of colonial prosperity. This was the squatter theory of value, a claim with much truth, as wool was the colony's staple export. As Charles Griffith added, Europeans could make the land 'capable of maintaining millions of human beings'.[12]

The nature of warfare

Squatters invaded Kulin territory beyond Melbourne after 1835 and violence resulted. In February 1836 Joseph Gellibrand and his partner George Hesse disappeared while exploring pastoral country between

Werribee and Geelong. Three expeditions assisted by a group of Wathawurrung failed to find them and it was feared they fell victim to an Aboriginal attack probably by the Mount Macedon people.[13] In March 1836 two of David Fisher's shepherds disappeared. A year later an Aboriginal man, Woolmurgen, showed Fisher their bones and related how the armed men and their wagon were stopped by a party of Aboriginal warriors, separated by guile, and killed.[14] In March, shepherds employed by the banker and speculator Charles Swanston were attacked near Geelong. They retreated to Melbourne, Fawkner recording that, 'they are afraid to live in the Bush for fear of the Blacks'.[15] A squatter, Ferguson, found the bodies of two of his men who went missing in May, while in July squatter Charles Franks and one of his men were murdered near Werribee, beaten to death with tomahawks. Fawkner recorded in his diary that Franks had 'one deep & deadly cut on the Temple and one on the back part of his head', while 'the Brains were cut and beat entirely out of the man's head'.[16] Two days before these chilling details became common knowledge, the settlers resolved in a meeting to protect themselves, allowing Aboriginal people to 'deal with the Murderers as they think according to their Rules'.[17] Armed Europeans, assisted by Derrimut, Bait Banger, three 'Sydney blacks' and a few other Kulin men, made contact with a group who had the property of the murdered Europeans in their camp. Fawkner, who was not there, recorded that 'the Native Blacks took full satisfaction on the Murderers and they found several Huts and some of the Property in each Hut'.[18] Derrimut and the Kulin were acting for new kin, the white settlers, against Aboriginal people who were not close kin, or not kin at all.

Squatters tried to avoid violence, if only because they were at first outnumbered. But many had their entire capital tied up in sheep, which had to be protected. Some like Richard Howitt avoided confrontations altogether by farming in Heidelberg, fifteen kilometres from Melbourne and nearer to European power and control.[19] Others were prepared for action. Robert William Von Stieglitz told fellow squatter George Russell that 'on my way [to the Werribee] I met with a Mr Franks and got some lead from him to make what he called blue pills [rifle balls] for the natives, who were very fierce'.[20] Only a few colonists recognised the injustice of the land invasion. The Aboriginal Protector James Dredge observed that Aboriginal lands are 'taken from them at the mere will of the British Government, and sold or let to strangers without any reference' to the needs or wishes of Aboriginal people. Where else in Britain's dominions 'does there exist a people so helplessly situated, so degraded, so neglected, so oppressed'?[21]

As the violence moved beyond Melbourne's immediate hinterland, numerous Aboriginal attacks on whites were vividly reported. Many letters were written and depositions made, all of which are tempting to take at face value, but it must be remembered that these documents are white versions of the action. Aboriginal acts against persons, property or stock, which Europeans labelled as 'criminal', were to Aboriginal people the protection of home and kin. Similarly, European arrests or shootings of Aboriginal people were carried out in the name of defending property. It is a matter of perspective.

Often violence followed hours of wary interaction and standoff as both sides tested each other. Pastoralist John Mackay documented one such attack on his Ovens River station in May 1840. About twenty Daungwurrung warriors, men unaccompanied by women or children and thus bent on trouble, approached his hut. Mackay advanced to meet them, gun in hand. One called out to him 'what for you cooler [sulky]?' Mackay replied he was not sulky. The man named Merriman asked 'what for you mankin [carry] musket?' to which Mackay responded, why did the Aboriginal men carry spears? Merriman and one other discarded their weapons and came forward, asking in tolerably good English for food and for work. They desired to enter the hut but Mackay refused. The rest stayed in the bush nearby. Mackay gave them some food, warned them off, and watched their distant campfire all night. Tension mounted the next morning as a Daungwurrung man demanded a shirt, powder and shot, and others forced themselves into the hut and took food. Mackay chased them off, displaying his guns, but they returned, speared a horse to death and robbed several of the huts, burning one down. The third day there was a stand off as the warriors, dressed in the Europeans' clothing, fired guns at Mackay and his men, and tried to burn the remaining huts. Mackay's party returned fire and held them at bay. Eventually the warriors left, but only after having robbed an outstation of guns and sheep, burning the hut and killing a shepherd, mangling his body.[22]

In scores of accounts of Aboriginal attacks, a certain measured behaviour on the part of the warriors can often be detected. Many white depositions refer to attacks by large numbers in which only thefts occurred. Some described warriors disarming whites only to rob them of their sheep, but not harming them in their defencelessness. Indeed, on the Port Phillip frontier to 1850, in which whites were said to be in blood-curdling danger, only about 59 Europeans were killed.[23] Probably double that number were wounded, as in all wars, and many more were threatened. One squatter, William Dallas Bernard, reporting on trouble

'Mounted Police and Blacks', by Alfred Charles Mundy in Munday,
Our Antipodes, 1852.

near Port Fairy over several weeks in early 1842, listed significant stock losses, including valuable horses, much threatening behaviour, one death, and the injury of three men who survived multiple spear and waddy wounds.[24] Why expert Aboriginal hunters did not kill more isolated white shepherds, which clearly they were able to do, is unclear. In their own inter-tribal skirmishes Aboriginal people generally practised measured violence. While their relationship with whites remained in the feud phase this restraint would have continued. Perhaps Aboriginal warriors also sensed European power in the form of the Border and Native Police and the vengeful actions of settlers, and wisely exercised restraint accordingly.

If Aboriginal people refrained from causing personal injuries, they certainly attacked the settlers' stock on their lands. Superintendent La Trobe's desk was piled high with letters from settlers demanding protection for their flocks. Many squatters lost property and supplies, as well as scores, even hundreds, of head of stock and horses. The latter were scarce and expensive items in early colonial society. David Waugh, a squatter on the Devil's [Delatite] River near Mansfield who lost 638 sheep and property worth £1,100 (over $1 million today), even sought compensation from the British government. It was refused, as the risk of loss was deemed to be borne by the squatter. Two of his men were also killed.[25] The Port Phillip press had a field day with white stories of black 'theft' and violence from the frontier, listing stock and property losses and portraying

Aboriginal people as 'robbers' and 'murderers', which from a European perspective was indeed the case.

However, from an Aboriginal perspective these actions were not simply robbery, for possessions were nothing to them compared with protecting land. Yet how could they protect their land except by attacking Europeans through their property or person? What is most remarkable about these stock losses is that Aboriginal groups learnt how to harm squatters by waging what might be called 'economic warfare' on them. This was clearly so as scores, sometimes hundreds of sheep were taken at once, far in excess of the numbers that could be immediately eaten. Nor was it unusual for sheep to be maimed and left to die. The motivation was not robbery or food. Pastoralist John Robertson was with a party near Casterton that found over 600 stolen ewes worth over £2 each, more now as they were in lamb, 'all dead; some skinned; others skinned and quartered; some cut open and the fat taken out and piled in skins, but most of them just knocked on the head with a stick; meat, fat, and all mixed with the fine sand of the stringy-bark forest'.[26] The curious thing about this is that Robertson refers to the fat being removed and 'piled in skins'. This was possibly kidney fat, as was removed in human ritualistic killings, and its presence suggests an added meaning behind the killings. Historian Robert Kenny has recently argued that Aboriginal people were attacking not just the property of the Europeans, but their totemic animals. Certainly squatters revered their sheep as the road to wealth. To Aboriginal people, humans and animals existed in a deep relationship sanctioned by their dreaming stories. The settler and ethnographer William Howitt, who was closely informed by Aboriginal people about their culture, claimed they, 'in order to injure another person, would kill that person's totem'.[27]

Stock was also taken to aid survival in the face of falling traditional food stocks. Some warriors, like Billy Billy and his people of the Pyrenees region, evaded pursuit for several years and set up their own runs in the mountains. Billy Billy established his operation with pastoralist William Clarke's sheep, and 'they made a bushyard and shepherded the sheep during the day and yarded them in the usual way at night'.[28]

These events were repeated time and again, leading to large stock losses and Aboriginal deaths. John Cox of Mount Napier went in pursuit of his stolen flock—a third of his whole stock—and found them with their hind legs dislocated to immobilise them. Enraged by the loss of his property, and probably influenced by the fact that stock theft had been a capital offence in England until 1832, Cox and his party pursued the 'thieves'. Cox told Boldrewood that 'it was the first time I had ever levelled a gun at my fellowman . . . I did so without regret or hesitation in this instance . . . I distinctly remember knocking over *three* blacks, two men and a boy, with one discharge of my double barrel'. His Aboriginal servant Sou'wester, had a 'good innings that day', which he thoroughly enjoyed. He fired right and left, 'raging like a demoniac'. The party shot a 'few of the front-rankers', the rest escaping into a lake.[29]

The press published settler opinions, couched in the language of otherness in which Aboriginal people were 'ruthless savages', and their actions, 'native barbarity', 'aboriginal slaughters' and 'robbery'.[30] These epithets posed traditional owners as criminals not patriots fighting for country. Letters and editorials demanded more police and government protection and condemned the Protectorate as useless—or worse, a launch pad for Aboriginal attacks.[31] Deputations of squatters met with officials, those from Port Fairy telling La Trobe in early 1842 that 'life and property are in constant hazard' as Aboriginal 'numbers, their ferocity, and their cunning, render them peculiarly formidable'. Their statement listed 22 incidents over two months, including the deaths of four shepherds, the wounding of eight others, the robbing of four huts, and the loss of ten horses, 136 cattle and over 3,000 sheep.[32] These claims of sheep losses were hard to test but had the power of the written statement behind them. Several squatters claimed Aboriginal attacks had made them insolvent, forcing them to abandon their runs. George Faithfull, a squatter on the Ovens, never retreated, but reflected later that 'I would not undergo the same injuries, annoyances, and anxiety again for ten times the quantity of land I hold'.[33]

In the face of such resistance, settlers and their servants muttered murderous thoughts which were occasionally overheard, or recorded dark thoughts in private letters that have survived. In May 1839 Protector Dredge overheard a stockman stating that the 'government ought to issue an order to have every black shot—and declared he would like to have permission to shoot every one he met'. In July 1839 a stock agent in Melbourne told Dredge that thirteen Aboriginal people were shot at Captain Brown's run at Mount Macedon for stealing sheep.[34] Dr David Wilsone, who squatted near Ballan where he lost goods and valuable stock to Kulin raids, wrote to his family that the Protectors were 'fools'. Wilsone added of the traditional owners whose land he occupied that they were 'all ugly black pickinnies, and the most hideous ugly men and women I ever saw one link removed from the ourang outang'. He added: 'nothing will do I am afraid but to shoot a good many as example and you depend on it, it will be done one way or the other, they seem to be truly devilish, useless of human organisation whose extirpation would much improve the colony' as they were 'unworthy of life'. Wilsone and his family were clearly at breaking point, having 'gone beyond their tether' by borrowing half the £3,165 ($3 million today) needed to stock their run at ten per cent per annum interest.[35]

Aboriginal people had infinitely more to lose than Wilsone, as the land was not only their livelihood but their life and their spiritual essence. Yet it is harder for us to know this, as their culture, being oral, meant their frontier sufferings are obscured. There are no Daungwurrung newspapers of the 1840s, no piles of depositions in the archives—true or exaggerated—no letters and no diaries. The accounts that do exist are second-hand and fragmentary. They often lack the strength of a vivid narrative, like Mackay's deposition about his stand-off with the Daungwurrung at Ovens River, but they have a power nonetheless. Some Goulburn River people told Dredge of the killing of several Daungwurrung. They were out hunting possum when they met one Mr Mundy and party. He offered them flour, which they proceeded to make into damper. However, as they were eating, Mundy and party rode up and shot several dead, including women and children. Dredge later met Mundy who in conversation told him that he did not have trouble with 'blacks' as 'he had given them such a punishing as they would not readily forget'. Dredge added in his diary that 'no indeed, the poor creatures have not forgotten it, they continue to breathe revengeful threats at the remembrance of his name, nor would it be a matter of surprise if, at some favourable opportunity, retributive justice overtake the culprits'.[36]

The cost of war

Hundreds of violent clashes occurred across the grasslands during a decade of European invasion. The significance of this violence is still hotly debated, centring attention on black rather than white deaths and examining the moral issues of invasion and occupation. Some let the word 'genocide' slip easily from their lips. What can we know of the real death toll and what does it signify?

European deaths, more noted, tallied and investigated at the time, are much easier to reckon. In June 1844 Superintendent La Trobe tabled a document in the NSW Legislative Council which stated that between 1836 and June 1844, forty whites had been killed east and west of the Hopkins River near Warrnambool.[37] Historians such as Jan Critchett counted 35–38 in the Western District by 1847, Bain Attwood, six in Gippsland, while Beverley Nance counted 59 European deaths in Port Phillip at Aboriginal hands by 1850.[38] The overall figure could be closer to 70 or 80 as the deaths of some loners doubtless killed went unrecorded. Richard Howitt wrote in 1845 that 'more than thirty whites have been missed, besides what the blacks are known to have murdered'.[39] The number of wounded was perhaps twice this figure—maybe up to 150—as many Europeans survived spear and waddy wounds.

The Aboriginal death toll from white violence is harder to reckon due to a lack of records. White violence was covered up after the Myall Creek massacre in the New England area in 1838, when seven Europeans were hanged in Sydney for the murder of Aboriginal people in a controversial but isolated trial. Official inquiries into Aboriginal deaths were often met with settler silence and even collusion between settlers and police. When, in 1842, a missionary made an admittedly loose claim about white shooting-parties riding against Aboriginal people as a Sunday sport, Portland Police Magistrate J. Blair took fifteen statements, and each argued in curiously identical terms that any violent incidents happened two years ago; that the bad characters had left the district; that the settlers were respectable; and that Aboriginal people were 'cannibals' and troublemakers.[40] Yet within weeks renewed violence exploded in the Portland area. A year earlier, Blair had remarked to George Robinson that 'if he was Governor he would send down soldiers and if they did not deliver up the murderer he would shoot the whole tribe'. Blair added that Aboriginal people were without 'shame', being naked, and were 'hardly men'.[41]

Historians have made educated guesses of the Aboriginal death toll for Port Phillip ranging from 400 to over 2,000 Aboriginal deaths. However, more careful counts by Jan Critchett for the Western District south of the Grampians, and Ian Clark for most but not all of western Victoria, give counts of 350 and 430 respectively. Critchett stated in 2003 that her earlier estimate was too conservative. Bain Attwood estimated that between 250 and 350 deaths occurred in Gippsland, while Peter Gardiner has suggested a range for Gippsland from 430 through 610 to 820 Aboriginal deaths.[42] Realistically, total Aboriginal frontier deaths in Port Phillip from white violence range from about 800 to 1,000 deaths. The lower figure is the combination of Clark's tally and Attwood's higher estimate (430+350) and the higher figure is a combination of Clark's tally and Gardiner's mid-range estimate (430+610). Attwood's lower and Gardiner's highest tallies have been rejected. As tallies do not exist for the Northeast and Murray Valley, a total figure of a thousand black deaths at white hands in Victoria is likely.[43] This is approximately 10 per cent of the Aboriginal population at European settlement. The numbers of Aboriginal wounded who survived white shootings was likely to be only a few hundred, since 19-millimetre musket balls travelling at 300 metres per second left terrible wounds, shattering bone and smashing organs, often leading to death without medical attention.[44]

Given possibly 80 white deaths and 1,000 black deaths on the Victorian frontier, Aboriginal people died through inter-racial violence at a rate twelve times that of whites. Europeans also killed Aboriginal people with a greater intensity, for while most European deaths occurred in small-scale killings of one to three people, the majority of Aboriginal fatalities from white violence occurred in larger-scale incidents. Ian Clark's 1995 inventory of 107 fatal incidents in Western Victoria, which resulted in about 430 Aboriginal deaths, reveals that 55 incidents resulted in one to three deaths, amounting to 88 people; 19 incidents resulted in 5 to 10 deaths; while 13 incidents involved more than 11 deaths each. Thus, only 88 out of approximately 430 Aboriginal deaths from white violence in Western Victoria, or about twenty per cent, occurred in small-scale incidents.

Conversely, eighty per cent of Aboriginal deaths occurred in incidents of five or more. Such killings are often termed 'massacres'—the killing of defenceless or beaten people. However, the word is overused and portrays Aboriginal people as passive victims. Some incidents were not 'massacres', but battles in which one side suffered severe losses. The details of the action are too vague in many incidents to confidently label them 'massacres' rather than 'defeats'.

In 2010, historian Lyndall Ryan meticulously re-examined the Port Phillip frontier, arguing I had downplayed the extent of massacre by describing some as 'defeats'. Ryan used Jacques Semelin's ideas that massacres were often planned retaliations to a key incident; were a demonstration of power by perpetrators who felt vulnerable; and were marked by secrecy, making them difficult to investigate.[45] Ryan examined the pastoral regions of the Western and Murray districts and Gippsland, and killings of more than six defenceless people, which she termed 'massacres'. Ryan identified 68 massacres in these areas between 1836 and 1851 involving the deaths of 1,169 Aboriginal people. Forty massacres were in the Western District pastoral region, twelve in the Murray District and 24 in Gippsland. Ryan counted 169 more violent Aboriginal deaths than I estimated, and my estimate included killings of less than six people. Ryan concluded that massacre was responsible for more than half of all violent Aboriginal deaths at white hands. Twenty-three massacres were in response to the killing of a white person(s); 24 because of property losses, and about 20 were pre-emptive strikes motivated by settler fear.[46] Settler revenge parties perpetrated most massacres, however, thirteen were by official parties, eleven by the Native Police and two by the Mounted Police.[47]

Ryan concluded that massacre is not an over-used but rather an underused term to describe frontier violence. I now concur with her view. If more than half of Aboriginal violent deaths at white hands amounted to 1,169 deaths, then total deaths by white violence in Port Phillip to 1851 could be as many as 2,000. Ryan's research team has developed a digital massacre map of Australia to record the prevalence of massacre, why these events happened and how we know they happened.[48] The map reveals 400 Australia-wide massacres totalling 10,000 Aboriginal deaths, a truly horrific tally.[49]

Victoria features strongly in this massacre map for violent episodes, with over forty massacres of six people and twenty of over ten people in the 1830s and 1840s. In the Western District there were three clashes— massacres perhaps—in which more than thirty Aboriginal people died. These took place at the Convincing Ground near Portland in 1833–34 (about 60 killed); at Murdering Gully near Terang in 1839 (20–40); and at Fighting Hills near Coleraine in 1840 (30 to 50).[50] Incidents termed 'massacres' by locals also occurred in Gippsland, although details are extremely vague, which is why Gardiner's highest death tally is dismissed in the total count above. These included Warrigal Creek in 1843 (perhaps 60 killed); Brodribb River in 1850; and Slaughterhouse Creek in 1851 in which about 15–20 allegedly died.[51] There was only one incident of mass white deaths in Port Phillip—called the 'Faithfull massacre', when Daungwurrung warriors killed seven poorly armed shepherds near Benalla in 1838 after trouble over women. Further Aboriginal attacks followed, leading to a 45-minute battle at Yaldwyn's station that left seven or eight Aboriginal people dead.[52]

The violence stemmed from the efforts of hard men bent on taking and holding the land from a people they held in low esteem. One of Dr Mackay's men on the Ovens told Protector Dredge that Aboriginal people were not 'fellow creatures' but 'cannibals' and that 'the Blacks ought to have Bullets put through their heads'.[53] Too many acted on these desires. Neil Black who settled Glenormiston in the Western District in 1839 was told by Blackie, the former overseer of the property, that when it was leased by Frederick Taylor '35 to 40 natives had been dispatched on this establishment and that there is only two men left alive of the tribe'.[54] Oral history circulating in the 1870s claimed that an Aboriginal woman survived the attack at Murdering Gully by swimming across a lake with

'Villiers Fighting' sketched by William Thomas. (Courtesy of La Trobe Australian Manuscripts Collection, State Library of Victoria)

her child on her back. Neil Black wrote in September 1840 to William Gladstone (a future Prime Minister of England), 'the natives are daily robbing settlers . . . of hundreds even thousands [of sheep] . . . but I have no great apprehension of their ever troubling me much [as] they have had enough of this place. A few days since I found a grave into which about 20 must have been thrown. A settler taking up a new country is obliged to act towards them in this manner or abandon it'.[55] The authorities knew of this incident, most likely a massacre, but had no proof in law. Frederick Taylor left the district and turned up in Gippsland in 1844. Crown Lands Commissioner Charles Tyers failed to block Taylor's subsequent pastoral licence on the grounds of a 'bad reputation', and Taylor was soon driving the Gunai/Kurnai from his lease at Swan Reach.[56]

Many protested these murders. John Robertson, a pastoralist near Casterton from 1840–54, recalled in 1851 that the tally of Aboriginal deaths he had heard of from the Grampians to the sea was about 500. He had himself ridden out in four punitive parties, but recalled thankfully that he had not been called upon to fire at Aboriginal people, 'like many others' who were 'severe' on them.[57] Henry Meyrick, a Gippsland pastoralist, wrote in 1846 that 450 Gunai/Kurnai people had been killed and that 'no wild beast of the forest was ever hunted down with such unsparing perseverance as they are; men, women, and children are shot whenever they can be met with'. Yet he declared: 'For myself, if I caught a black actually killing my sheep, I would shoot him with as little remorse as I would a wild dog, but no consideration on earth would induce me to ride into a camp and fire on them indiscriminately, as is the custom whenever the smoke is seen'.[58]

The frontier years were wild times. Even decent men like Robertson and Meyrick put the life of a sheep above that of an Aboriginal sheep rustler, such was the prevailing worship of private property. They also believed they had rights to the land through lease and a manifest destiny to develop it. As Neil Black sighed about landholding: a settler 'is obliged to act towards them [the traditional owners] in this manner or abandon it' [the land]. Most learned to live with a background of low-level violence as 'severe' men took matters into their own hands. Meyrick wrote that he became 'so familiarized with scenes of horror—from having murder made a topic of everyday conversation', and Robertson believed 'no law could have protected these poor people from such men as we had to do with at that time'.[59]

Historian and polemicist Keith Windschuttle has disagreed, claiming that 'ever since they were founded in 1788, the British colonies in Australia were civilised societies governed by both morality and laws that forbade the killing of the innocent'.[60] This may have been true of the towns, but on the frontiers the law was often too distant to be effective. Even where the law reached, it favoured Europeans: through prejudice against the 'savage'; cross-cultural misunderstandings; the mysteries of court language and procedures; and the inadmissibility of Aboriginal evidence as non-Christians unable to take an oath. When the law tried to be even-handed, complex circumstances prevailed. Some Aboriginal murderers and thieves actually escaped sentencing because of problems of cross-cultural justice. However few Europeans were ever tried for violence to Aboriginal people. Only five Europeans were indicted for 68 murderous incidents in the Western District, one being found guilty—not of murder, but of grievous bodily harm, for which he received two months jail.[61] Squatter George Bolden who admitted he shot an Aboriginal man, Tatkiar, on his run near Lake Keilambete was acquitted in 1842 on legal technicalities. Despite the fact that Tatkiar was shot while Bolden and his men were driving three warriors from his run with whips, Judge John Walpole Willis deemed this act 'lawful', as they had no rights under the lease.[62]

The wild times, which ended around 1850, spelt tragedy for Aboriginal people. However, it was not a story of genocide, at least not according to the formal meaning of the word coined by polish jurist Raphael Lemkin in 1944—that is, of official, intentional, premeditated killing.[63] There was never an official policy of killing Aboriginal people, although police, both Aboriginal and European, were involved in 15 per cent of massacres counted by Ryan, on distant frontiers. These incidents appalled authorities, who tried vainly to end the violence. The British government attempted to be even-handed and, despite its failure, instituted the Aboriginal Protectorate for this reason. Most of the intentional killings and massacres were perpetrated by a small number of settlers. These were hard men prepared to kill to protect property and induce terror to subdue Aboriginal people and take their land.[64]

Inter-Aboriginal and disease deaths

During the wild times Aboriginal people also killed each other. These were termed *inter se* (among themselves) killings, and they had occurred for millennia, as murder exists within all societies. *Inter se* killings occurred because the Aboriginal world was divided into friends and dangerous strangers.

In the world of friends, each person belonged to a cultural dialect group, a 'tribe' in the old terminology. These tribes were related to neighbouring groups, forming culturally allied federations with a common language. People married into another group within the federation or nation, this law instinctively maintaining genetic diversity. While there was mostly harmony within these groups, there could be disagreements between families, clans or different cultural–dialect groups within the federation, mostly over marriage arrangements but also over ritual or site transgressions. These disputes took the form of controlled staged fights, in which bloodshed was necessary to reconcile differences. Deaths occasionally occurred. If a killing within the federation occurred that was not accidental it was seen as a murder, and death or serious injury was the punishment inflicted by the family.

Beyond the world of friends were strangers—*mainmet*, as the Kulin people called them—foreign language groups with whom you did not intermarry and who might wield dangerous sorcery against you. As William Thomas the Assistant Protector, who understood such matters, put it: 'All the tribes beyond the district of their friends are termed wild blackfellows, and when found within the district are immediately killed'. As one DjaDjawurrung man told Assistant Protector Parker at Mount William, when some people from the Pyrenees and Lake Boloke visited the station: '*mainmait talle, mainmait mirre-par-gar, mainmait nalderun: yurrong!* They are foreign in speech, they are foreign in countenance, they are foreign altogether—they are no good!'[65] Such people were liable to be killed as they were extremely dangerous, given that they could wield deadly sorcery. Aboriginal people believed all deaths of mature adults were due to sorcery from *mainmet* and must be avenged. The killer of a *mainmet* was honoured as protecting the group. Such killings were ritualised and often entailed disembowelling or the removal of the fat around the kidneys with a hooked stick. The life force, once taken, was rubbed over the avenger's body (and sometimes eaten) both in triumph and as a symbolic appropriation of power from the slain.

Europeans entered the Aboriginal world, creating wild times by challenging land holdings and thus the core of Aboriginal law and culture. Severe social disruption followed. Yet this colonial challenge enlarged the world for those Aboriginal people who survived. They discovered Europe, mentally speaking (although a few did journey there), met other peoples, saw new worlds of thought (writing, reading, arithmetic, Christianity and the market economy), and encountered metal, glass and gunpowder. Such expansions of the mind are difficult to document, but were present in the turn of metal screw on a gun barrel, the listening to a story of baby Jesus or the perception that vines looked like ship's cables.[66] This enlarging and rupturing effect rippled through to all aspects of Aboriginal life, including inter-group relations. People began to travel further than ever before to see and taste novelties, and thus interacted with *mainmet* as never before. The European presence caused this movement by creating towns, missions, schools, and Protectorate stations to which Aboriginal people were lured by food, tobacco and other exotic things.

This coming together of Aboriginal strangers caused fear and deaths. It is not known exactly how many deaths resulted, but Europeans all believed that *inter se* deaths were common. Reports of Aboriginal fighting and revenge parties were frequent in press reports, in settlers' diaries and reminiscences, and in official reports. There was no doubt some exaggeration in these reports, as whites projected their violence onto Aboriginal people and imagined this is what 'savages' did. Many mistook Aboriginal justice proceedings for indiscriminate warfare. However, all the evidence suggests inter-group violence was prevalent in the wild times, probably more so than in traditional times due to the opportunity created by a greater mixing of strangers. It is also likely, but impossible to prove, that white murders of Aboriginal people, at least for a time, could have induced Aboriginal revenge: not on whites but on blacks. This is because all deaths of mature people were related in Aboriginal belief to sorcery, about which Europeans were believed to know nothing. So whites could have been seen as the *means* rather than the *cause* of death—instruments of a black sorcerer from a distant *mainmet* group.[67]

No close counts have as yet been made of *inter se* deaths, but one historian has estimated that perhaps 200 Aboriginal people died at Aboriginal hands and perhaps 125 at the hands of the Native Police.[68] Because *inter se* deaths were by definition Aboriginal affairs, it is likely that Europeans did not hear of many such deaths or, if they did, that the information they had was inaccurate. However, George Robinson, the well-informed Chief Protector, commented in September 1839 that he knew of twenty to thirty Aboriginal *inter se* deaths in the previous fortnight.[69] He told a select committee in 1845 that perhaps it amounted to 'one in twenty [deaths] annually'—an alarming rate.[70] Peter Corris, in his careful study of the Western District frontier, thought 'the Aborigines perhaps suffered less from direct contact with the whites than from the intensification of hostilities amongst themselves' due to the presence of whites.[71]

Certainly *inter se* killings continued well into the 1860s after black–white frontier violence had ceased. Geoffrey Blainey has argued—by using William Buckley's reminiscences and post-contact evidence—it is possible that there were more Aboriginal *inter se* deaths across Australia in the century before the arrival of whites than occurred at the hands of whites in the century after their invasion.[72] However, this is based on the false premise that we can measure *inter se* death rates before whites arrived from post-contact sources—observations made in a changing Aboriginal world and framed by a notion of 'savagery'—or from Buckley's memories twenty years after re-entering European society. Instead, evidence and historical logic suggests *inter se* death rates were managed and contained in traditional times and rose due to the presence of whites—an indirect product of the mobility created by colonialism.

We can never know an exact *inter se* death figure due to lack of information and because the issue is bedevilled by politics. Some wish to 'prove' that Aboriginal 'savagery' killed more Aboriginal people than white savagery. It is not improbable that partly because of the European presence Aboriginal people killed 400–500 other Aboriginal people on the frontier to 1850—and several score more in the next two decades, judging by press reports—but we cannot know exactly. This was at least five times the number of Europeans killed by Aboriginal warriors, and constitutes evidence that Aboriginal people adhered to traditional ideas of death into the 1850s. Beverley Nance's study of violence in Port Phillip concluded: 'For Aborigines, murder represented a chain of relationships between killer and killed that was not present between races'.[73]

Although historians and their readers seem preoccupied with violence, disease killed far more Aboriginal people in the frontier period than any other cause. Again, details are sketchy due to a lack of information. Aboriginal people traditionally suffered few diseases due to their isolation from other populations over many millennia. Most modern human diseases emerged in the last 5,000 years, a product of disease mutations from domesticated animals and of larger populations living in villages and towns in the Middle East and Asia.[74] Aboriginal people suffered traditionally from the eye disease trachoma; a treponematosis skin disease; and the virus, hepatitis B. All were slow-developing diseases, only the latter being eventually fatal through liver failure.[75]

As we saw in an earlier chapter, the Macassans brought smallpox to northern Australia in the eighteenth century (and perhaps respiratory diseases), that survived the voyage of several weeks to the north coast. European-borne diseases after 1788 also impacted significantly on a disease-inexperienced Aboriginal population. These included respiratory diseases such as tuberculosis and influenza, common European childhood diseases such as measles and whooping cough, scarlet fever and typhus, water-borne diseases such as dysentery, and also the venereal diseases, gonorrhoea and syphilis.[76] In contacting new diseases, people can experience exaggerated symptoms and outcomes compared with those experienced by peoples with genetic immunities. Protector Parker wrote of one Aboriginal man's death from respiratory disease on the Loddon in June 1841: 'He was ill but a few days, but did not, till the previous morning, show any symptoms of internal inflammation. The progress of the disease was, however, so rapid, that in 24 hours his cause became hopeless'.[77]

The most prevalent disease in the frontier period was thought by many non-medical observers, such as Protectors, to be venereal disease. William Thomas stated that when he arrived in 1839 'old and young, even children at the breast were affected' around Melbourne, some infants being 'brought into the world literally rotten with this disease'. He and others blamed white men for its introduction despite its universality in just a few years.[78] In 1841, Protector Parker at the Loddon believed that syphilis or *wombi* was 'prevalent among the people', stating that near two pastoral stations 'nine-tenths of the women are affected by it, some of whom are scarcely able to crawl about'. Aboriginal people blamed the convicts for its introduction and the native doctors claimed no power to remove it.[79] However, when Dr Baylie began service at the Loddon station in 1841 he defined the malady as non-venereal in nature, remarking that it was an 'excrescence improperly called venereal by the whites'. Yet Dr Watton, Baylie's successor, told the 1845 Select Committee that syphilis was 'prevalent', and elsewhere he reported that 52 of the 182 cases he treated in 1845 had this diagnosis.[80]

It seems that significant numbers of Aboriginal people suffered from skin eruptions, but their nature is not entirely clear, as not all observers had a trained medical-eye. Besides, the French virologist Philippe Ricord only categorised venereal diseases in the late 1830s so medical men were still unskilled in their diagnoses. The question arises: did European doctors in fact observe syphilis and gonorrhoea, which could lead to infertility and sometimes death, amongst Aboriginal people or was it a prevalent indigenous treponematosis they saw? The latter was an ancient bacterial, non-sexually transmitted treponemal infection, which was often mistaken for sexual syphilis but was very different from it. Indeed, some evidence suggests the non-sexual treponematosis may have protected sufferers from syphilis.[81] The complaint was slow to develop and did not kill its host, but over decades it bowed the legs of sufferers and created eruptions and itchiness on the skin that drove sufferers mad at times. The medical men called it 'excrescence' but the Kulin called it *bubburum*. William Thomas told a select committee in 1858 that all adults were infected with it, and it even spread to their dogs, which lost their hair.[82] Henry Jones, the medical dispenser at Narre Narre Warren Aboriginal station, recognised treponematosis as a non-venereal itch, and wrote that it 'exists to a great extent', although Peter Beveridge suggested it cleared up in summertime.[83] Dr Baylie treated *bubburum* successfully with creams and lotions to which Aboriginal people willingly submitted. Even when he used 'the most powerful treatment'—*causticus*, or potash and caustic soda—'they evinced more readiness than would be anticipated placing great confidence in the means used for their good'.[84]

Those who definitely had venereal diseases were treated effectively with copper sulphate solution, but more radical treatments were also used. Dr Cussen told George Robinson and William Thomas in April 1839 that in the past year he 'had cut off the penis of five men the last he sent out quite bare, he had also amputated more arms and legs than he had ever done in town through excrescence'.[85] Whether people survived such treatments is unknown.

When Aboriginal people suffered from other complaints, such as dysentery, viral and bacterial respiratory problems, and European childhood diseases, for which Europeans had no real cures, they stuck to traditional medicine. There are many accounts of Aboriginal doctors and clever men rubbing the body of their patients, shaving them all over, secretly drawing or sucking the sickness in the form of a stone or object from the body, and even jumping on patients' bodies at times to 'cure' them.[86] Such treatments were less invasive and no more ineffective than bleeding, still in use then among Europeans.

The medical reports of the Port Phillip Protectorate and other sources reveal a constant trickle of deaths rather than a large number of fatalities through epidemics of respiratory or other diseases before 1850. Dr W. H. Baylie, at the Goulburn River station in January 1842, observed that 'a fever very painful in its symptoms made its appearance in the beginning of the summer increasing gradually as the season advanced, which required very active treatment and close attention'. However, it only caused one fatality.[87] Deaths through 'colonial fever'

Reproduction of the designs on the possum-skin rug found at Lake Condah Mission in 1872. (Courtesy of Museum Victoria, X16279)

(dysentery) and influenza were recorded as isolated and consistent occurrences, rather than as large outbreaks. Admittedly the medical records of the Protectorate are incomplete and under-researched, but they reveal mostly low-grade, slowly evolving health problems, rather than medical crises. In January 1843 Dr John Watton conducted 140 examinations at the Loddon Station, treating 102 patients for excrescence, 9 for opthalmia, 15 for constipation, 4 for psora (scabies), 3 for abscesses, 3 for fractures, 3 for gonorrhoea, 3 for 'ophalalgea', and 2 for catarrh. Patients were spread over most age groups up to forty years, except for one sixty-year-old woman who died from 'simple decay of nature'.[88] In January 1844, Dr Campbell at the Goulburn station treated 80 patients all of them for undefined ulcerations to the leg, fingers, penis and vagina.[89] Campbell did not identify whether these ulcerations were *bubburum* (treponema) or venereal. Again, none of the complaints were life-threatening, but perhaps seriously ill patients consulted only their own sorcerers, and chose to move away from the stations to die unrecorded.

Population decline

Multiple population shocks hit Aboriginal people over several generations from 1800. The Victorian Aboriginal population, which had survived for at least 50,000 years, was suddenly and dramatically reduced by colonisation. The question of what exactly occurred, why it occurred and what population impact it had is complex to answer.

The size of the Victorian Aboriginal population in 1788 is unknown. However, the impact of smallpox around 1790 and 1830—brought by the *Mindye* according to Aboriginal people, but, most likely to have been introduced by the Macassans in reality—was horrific. The 'guesstimate' of Noël Butlin, an economic historian, from assumptions about smallpox and economic modelling suggested a 1788 pre-smallpox population of about 250,000 for south-eastern Australia, which might translate to 60,000 in Victoria.[90] The historian Ian Clark supports this by close analysis of local clans, suggesting pre-smallpox numbers in Western Victoria alone might have been close to 30,000.[91] This population of 60,000 (conservatively speaking) was possibly halved and halved again to say 10–15,000 in two smallpox shocks before European settlers even trod Aboriginal lands.

The number of Aboriginal people at contact is not clearly known either. William Thomas estimated in 1858 that there were at least 6,000

Aboriginal people in Port Phillip at contact in 1834 (that is, after smallpox). Thomas calculated his '6,000 at the least' from a 'guesstimate' of a people per square mile ratio, using the ratios he observed as late as 1839 in the Melbourne area to make his calculations.[92] Edward Parker estimated in 1854 that there were about 7,500 Aboriginal people 'at the foundation of the colony'.[93] His calculation was also a 'guesstimate' of the unknowable 1834 contact figure based on what he knew in 1843. The estimates of both Protectors were too low, which Thomas sensed. Certainly they knew little of Aboriginal populations on the Murray itself or in the east and west of the colony. Archaeologists have argued that population/land ratios in the riverine areas of the Murray Valley and Western District were much higher than in other parts of Victoria.[94] On these grounds, it has been suggested that population at contact was likely to be 10,000 (conservatively speaking), and probably more.

Depopulation was massive and rapid during the frontier's wild times. The historian Beverley Blaskett (nee Nance) estimated that a contact population of about 10,000 fell to 1,907 in the two decades to 1853—a decline of 80 per cent in just under twenty years.[95] Regional statistics also reveal the population trauma. The Wathawurrung (Barrabools of Geelong) numbered 275 in 1837, 118 in 1842, but only 30 in 1852: a 90 per cent decline. The DjaDjawurrung (Loddon) numbered 282 in 1841, but only 142 in 1852: a 50 per cent decline. The Gunai/Kurnai of Gippsland were estimated to number 300 in 1844 and 32 in 1852: a decline of over 90 per cent. William Thomas carefully estimated the Woiwurrung and Boonwurrung people of Melbourne as collectively numbering 350 in 1836, 207 in 1839, and 59 in 1852: a fall of 83 per cent.[96]

Why did it happen? Why did a population of at least 10,000 at contact decline by approximately 8,000 or 80 per cent in two decades of white settlement? Probably about 2,000 Aboriginal people died violent deaths at white hands, half through massacre, and up to 500 more died from *inter se* killings; perhaps a further 1,000 died of natural causes over two decades; this leaves 4–5,000 who fell to diseases and debility due to disruption of food supplies and the trauma of cultural disruption. In 1858 William Thomas said that the young died two to one in proportion to adults. Edward Parker listed dysentery, liver disease, chest infections, and fevers as most prominent, while William Thomas emphasised pulmonary diseases—specifically 'endemic influenza', exacerbated by sleeping outside while intoxicated: 'cold comes on, and as soon as disease touches a black's chest you cannot save him'.[97] In an 1860 report on Aboriginal health, the common causes of death listed by 29 settlers were influenza and chest diseases, venereal disease and intemperance, often in combination.

Of the six Aboriginal patients in the Melbourne Hospital in 1860, five were admitted for chest diseases and one for burns.[98]

The related tragedy was that low birth rates prevented population recovery. William Thomas's journal from 1839 to 1859 recorded 135 deaths from all causes among the Woiwurrung and Boonwurrung, 29 occurring after 1850. During this period Thomas listed only 28 births, 20 before and 8 after 1850. Deaths outmatched births by almost five to one, leading to a population disaster. The low birth rate had many causes: poor nutrition, venereal disease, loss of land, and loss of faith in the future. Venereal disease, despite being confused at times with treponematosis (yaws), certainly existed and had a significant impact on the birth rate and infant survival rate as gonorrhoea created infertility and syphilis reduced live births.[99] Thomas believed his bluestone (copper sulphate) treatments had cured the Melbourne people of venereal disease by the mid-1850s. However, the damage had been done.

Birth labours were sometimes in vain. Thomas mournfully commented of his list that of the 28 live births, 'it is lamentable that most died before the first month, or [their mothers] removed from the encampment for a week or two and returned childless'.[100] Thomas implied some of these infant deaths were contrived—that is, were cases of infanticide, as Billibellary had admitted to him sometimes occurred—a view Thomas explicitly and consistently stated over two decades of writing. High deaths and low births: it was a common story across Victorian Aboriginal communities in frontier times, as diseases and violence took life, and malnutrition, trauma, venereal diseases and, to a lesser degree, infanticide, stalled Aboriginal population recovery.

Lyndall Ryan in her analysis of massacre also argued that violent deaths left Aboriginal survivors traumatised. We now know more about the impact of trauma on the psyche of individuals and whole groups. Trauma and post-traumatic stress disorder can impinge on wellbeing and increase vulnerability to disease. As Ryan concludes: 'If this is the case, then settler massacres, rather than disease by itself, emerges as a critical factor in accounting for the 80 per cent drop in the Aboriginal Victorian population in fifteen years' to 1850.[101]

Colonisation caused more than trauma from violent and disease deaths, as it changed Aboriginal societies, which lost control of land, food gathering, cultural practices and spirituality. Introduced animals and plants also disrupted the Aboriginal world, in a global process that environmental historian Alfred Crosby called 'ecological imperialism'. Along with the takeover from plants and animals came 'old world pathogens' that wiped out 'vast numbers of Aborigines'.[102] Tony Barta called these forces of human takeover and ecological displacement at the heart of colonisation 'relations of genocide'.[103] The colonisation of Port Phillip may not have had an official policy to effect genocidal outcomes, but a similar outcome was caused by the clash and structural incompatibility of two different societies determined to hold the land, and for some settlers by force if necessary.

Aboriginal numbers plummeted in the wild times with over eight of every ten Aboriginal people perishing. An indifference to their fate was common amongst early colonists, while those who did care felt they were witnessing a decline that was inevitable. The naturalist and evolutionist Charles Darwin learned the settler 'wisdom' of the frontier while at dinner with squatters during his visit to New South Wales in 1836. Darwin recorded in his diary: 'Wherever the European has trod, death seems to pursue the aboriginal . . . The varieties of man act on each other; in the same way as different species of animals—the stronger always extirpate the weaker'.[104] Some fatalists among Aboriginal people must have felt that too, given that so many of them had died. Others looked beyond the wild times, imagining their own survival, but perhaps not foreseeing their inevitable transformations.

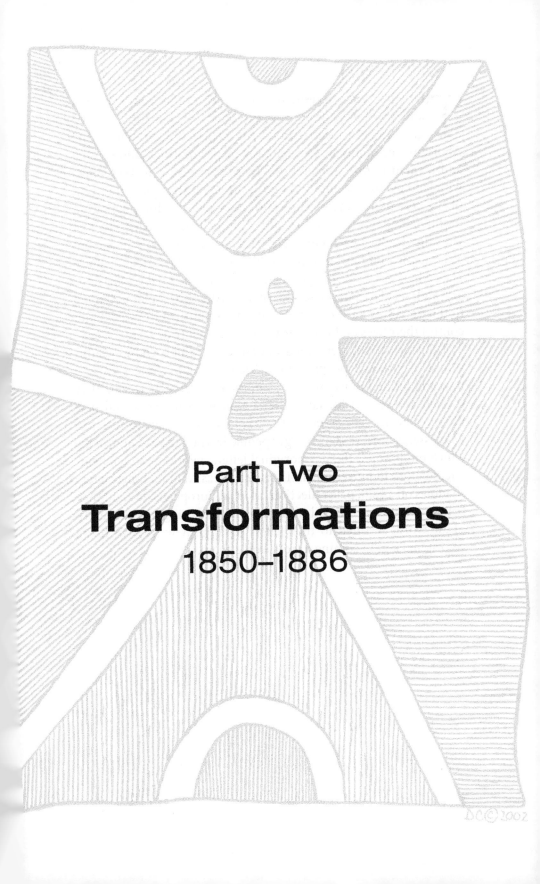

Part Two
Transformations
1850–1886

The wild times became quieter times as the frontier ended and white hegemony was extended over Victoria. Aboriginal and European cultures engaged, leading to change. The Aboriginal economy was swept away by pastoralism, gold mining and a small farming revolution. These disruptions to their links with land led to a decline and loss of the great Aboriginal tradition of the ceremonial cycle. The continuing catastrophic population decline compounded the loss of tradition, as knowledge was lost with the death of each elder. Diseases, especially tuberculosis but also measles, bit hard into the bodies of the people. Alcohol abuse played havoc as well. The population plummeted further. Missionary and secular enterprises to change Aboriginal people added to the pressures on them. A Board was established to protect and control their lives and transformations inevitably occurred.

Transformations were not always forced or imposed by circumstance. Aboriginal people across Victoria made choices from a new and limited range of options in the post-frontier world. They pushed and fought for land; they began to farm, work and play like Europeans; some adopted Christianity or began to listen to its message; most of the younger people learned to read and write, which empowered them. Aboriginal letters, petitions, and appearances before inquiries meant that their ideas were no longer mere shadows on a wall, pale reflections of what Europeans thought they believed, but were framed in their own words ringing out clearly. These words testified to their effort to forge new ways of being Aboriginal and becoming a free people again.

6

Negotiating Two Worlds

In the 1850s the Kulin sought to live as their great ancestors determined, but the pace of change quickened around them. The luck of geology deposited mineral wealth in Victoria which led to wondrous transformations once gold was discovered in 1851. As young men rushed from all parts of the globe to Victoria's golden gullies, Aboriginal people were shouldered aside in their own lands. The colony's non-indigenous population exploded ninefold in the decade to 540,000 people, while Aboriginal numbers fell by a further ten per cent to around 1,800 by 1860. Their percentage of the total population fell tenfold from 3.3 to 0.3 per cent over the decade.

Original owners were marginalised in their own lands, including in Melbourne where Aboriginal people were not now welcome. The land was progressively alienated by freehold sale from 1854, putting it legally beyond Aboriginal control. The newcomers controlled the land, government, the economy, and the infrastructure of education, religion, and the law. English was the official language. The newcomers also controlled the public discussion about Aboriginal people, which labelled them as 'inferior' and 'doomed to fade'. Across the colony Aboriginal people were obliged to negotiate with and adapt to aspects of this mega European world in the 1850s, while striving to stay enmeshed in their own cultural ways. It required great deftness and the skills of a diplomat.

Imagining Aboriginal people

As European colonisation swept across global frontiers, causing indigenous deaths through disease, dispossession and violence, a widely shared European notion arose: that indigenous people simply faded before the 'stronger' white civilisation.

This notion was a rationalisation for the usurpation of indigenes' lands. Colonisers invented 'laws' governing the contact of peoples and also 'flaws' in indigenous peoples to shift the blame for colonial destruction onto both the natural order of things and the victims themselves. This notion that the so-called 'weaker' races fell inevitably before the 'stronger' flourished in post-frontier Victoria and elsewhere, as Aboriginal numbers continued to decline. The naturalist William Blandowski, first head of the new Museum of Victoria, wrote in 1855 that it was a 'universal but mysterious law' that white settlement across the globe led to 'sweeping the backward races from the face of the earth.'[1] William Westgarth also commented in his *The Colony of Victoria* (1864): 'It could almost seem an immutable law of nature that such inferior dark races should disappear—people hardly see how—before the white colonist.'[2] This notion of an inevitable fading away led to a loss of respect for Aboriginal people, indicated by a decline in press attention and the frequent haughty comment made about them in documents.

Before the 1850s, Europeans in Australia believed they were technically and socially superior to Aboriginal people, due to environmental and cultural factors not biological ones. 'Race' was still a blurred category, interchangeable with 'people' or 'group', and it was not associated with immutable genetic inferiority. The keys to difference amongst peoples were environmental and historical forces, not biological facts, as

'Native Chasing Game', Eugene von Guérard, 1854. (Rex Nan Kivell Collection, courtesy of the National Library of Australia, AN2282444-1)

most people still believed that the world was one creation by God, and that all men were descended from the seed of Adam and Eve. Hence Aboriginal people were of one flesh with other men—albeit a flesh degraded over the five millennia since biblical creation. This sense of Aboriginal 'degradation' allowed settlers to believe that when 'civilisation', with its technology, was pitted against 'savagery', 'civilisation' always prevailed. Europeans were deemed 'progressive' and Aboriginal people 'primitive': a circular and self-fulfilling justification for Aboriginal decline. Colonists argued in essence that Aboriginal people were inferior simply because they were inferior. Phrenology, a popular pseudoscience that interpreted head shape as a key to intelligence, added *proof* of Aboriginal incapacity. 'Scientific' claims about Aboriginal decline were well publicised, which simply reinforced what many settlers believed already. Blandowski, head of the Museum, lectured on the Aboriginal fate at the Melbourne Mechanics Institute in 1856, which was featured in the daily press.[3]

By the 1850s, theorists overseas were increasingly convinced that biology or race, not environment, was the key to human difference. However, their ideas were slow to penetrate the Australian colonies.[4] Charles Darwin sharpened biological explanations for human difference when he outlined his theory of 'natural selection', but as his book *On the Origin of Species* was not published until 1859, his ideas did not have an impact until the 1860s. Indeed, educated and experienced opinion in the 1850s was still divided on the matter of Aboriginal humanness, equality and ability. The 1858 Select Committee on Aborigines collected divided opinion on Aboriginal intelligence. Missionary witnesses were optimistic about the future for Aboriginal people, but old colonists like William Thomas and William Hull were pessimistic. The missionaries, new to the colony, were embarking on a great spiritual adventure and were thus hopeful, whereas Thomas had seen far too many of his 'sable friends' die over a score of years to be sanguine. William Hull was more certain in his pessimism, claiming that the Aboriginal race would not survive as it was 'the design of Providence that the inferior races should pass away before the superior races'.[5] The Committee questioned how Aboriginal people 'could be saved from ultimate extinction', and blamed them for their own demise. It reported that they declined because of their alcohol abuse and because, unlike the 'strong' Maori, 'being weak and ignorant, even for savages, they have been treated with almost utter contempt'.[6]

By the 1850s colonists had invented an imaginary race against time. The *Argus* responded to Blandowski's 1856 lecture by arguing that cultural information and material should be collected before the Aboriginal people are 'wiped off the face of the earth'.[7] Similar calls were made over the years. In 1861, Governor Sir Henry Barkly, President of the Royal Society of Victoria, called for urgent research into Aboriginal 'dialects and traditions' as whole tribes 'are, under some mysterious dispensation, rapidly disappearing'.[8] Robert Brough Smyth, Secretary of the Central Board of the Aborigines, with the Board's approval embarked on the task of collecting 'every fact of importance connected with the blacks', assisted by information from honorary correspondents—the Board's unpaid local guardians.[9] The Mechanics Institute proposed a Museum in 1862 with an Aboriginal skull as the collection's nucleus, unearthed as settlers farmed the land. The National Museum began exhibiting Aboriginal materials.[10] However, in 1868 David Blair, a member of the Legislative Assembly, bemoaned a mere 'row of grinning skulls in the national museum' as the sole effort to collect Aboriginal cultural information from each group before extinction. Blair believed the gathering of ethnographic information was 'a debt, which we, the civilized and Christianized successors of these fast decaying savage races owe to science, to civilization, and to humanity'.[11]

Scraps of ethnographic information were gathered and disseminated. From the 1850s, public lectures of varying standards were given at the Royal Society, Mechanics Institute and elsewhere on Aboriginal culture by old colonists, including William Hull, Gideon Lang and Peter Beveridge, who were considered to be 'experts'. Aboriginal customs, beliefs, laws, government, ideas of birth, marriage and death, their weapons and warfare, and their languages were discussed, all according to white (mis)understandings. However, while Hull was pompous, Lang admired Aboriginal culture and openly discussed white brutality, calling for added protection for Aboriginal people. Beveridge, a former pastoralist, gave an affectionate and considered view of his former Murray River friends. These lectures were published in Melbourne and picked up by the regional press, the *Riverine Herald* publishing the lectures of Lang and Beveridge in their entirety, a fact that attests to some residual interest in Aboriginal people.[12] However, the reception of these publications was beyond the benign lecturer's control. A reviewer of Lang's humane lecture of 1865 doubted Lang's optimistic view of Aboriginal intellectual capacity and said Lang also failed to disprove the law of the 'inevitable degeneracy of the inferior animal'.[13]

Brough Smyth, Secretary of the Central Board, lectured learned societies on his research collection, demonstrating the use of Aboriginal tools. His views were encapsulated in a long awaited two-volumed work, *The Aborigines of Victoria* (1878). Although it remains of some interest and historical value to Aboriginal people today, the cultural information it contained was viewed predominately through white eyes, especially emerging racial (not environmentally-based) views of difference. For instance, in a section on 'mental character', Smyth claimed that while Aboriginal mental capacities varied as among whites, and that they learned quickly when young and had 'keen senses, quick perceptions, and a precocity that is surprising', an Aboriginal person had on maturity, he said, a limited capacity for improvement that prevented 'a complete change in the character of his mind'. Smyth and many of his European informants mistook Aboriginal cultural preferences and conservatism for an inherent inability to learn. The Victorian Parliament distributed the volumes of Smyth's book at no cost to Mechanics Institutes and libraries across the colony.[14] Readers who also consulted the *Encyclopaedia Britannica* of 1875 at these libraries would have read that Aboriginal people had 'little power of generalisation', lacked 'moral restraint', had 'no religion', and were a 'have not' people without cultivation, domestic animals, permanent buildings or much in the way of manufactures. The article claimed their 'want of ingenuity and contrivance' had 'undoubtedly been promoted by the natural poverty of the land in which the race settled'.[15]

The great European notion of the 'inevitable' Aboriginal decline was connected to another prevalent notion that developed from the 1860s: the notion of 'the last of the tribe'. This idea reflected white romanticism, guilt as well as emergent racism. The romanticism and guilt stemmed from a sense of loss, the idea that something unique in human history was passing, a form, perhaps, of their early selves. The racism was based on the growing belief that Aboriginality was defined immutably by physical attributes—especially the shape of the face, texture of the hair and skin colour—and not culture. Thus, only 'full bloods' in the terminology of the day were considered by whites to be 'real' Aboriginal people, and thus their passing heralded the 'end of their tribe'. Descendants from the union of 'full bloods' with Europeans were termed 'half castes', 'quadroons' (quarter caste) or 'octoroons' (one-eighth caste), to indicate the degree of Aboriginal descent or 'blood' remaining. They were not considered by whites as being 'authentic'; in fact, they were often considered superior to 'real' Aboriginal people as they had white 'blood' and thus possessed 'superior' attributes.

Europeans never considered labelling by degrees of 'blood' applied to themselves, yet the English and other European colonists were

'Native with Original Tomahawk and Shield, Fernyhurst, Australia Felix' photographed by Eugene Montagu Scott in 1853. (Courtesy of the Royal Historical Society of Victoria)

of mixed origin, despite their claims of purity. Most Aboriginal people did not and still do not distinguish between degrees of blood. Aboriginality was (and is) to them a cultural definition. Individual groups of dark-skinned people traditionally saw other groups of equally dark-skinned peoples as foreigners because they were not of the some dialect and cultural group. They identified with culture, not skin colour. Europeans did much the same thing among themselves—English and Germans often saw themselves as culturally different and racially the same—but increasingly after 1860 viewed Aboriginal people through the prism of biology and race.

Some of these 'last of' people were termed 'kings' and 'queens' by the European settlers who created these Aboriginal 'leaders' to enable better dealings or merely for their own amusement. The kings were presented with 'king plates', crescent-shaped brass plates with engraving. The 'king-plates' and titles were used for political and other advantage by Aboriginal people. At Geelong in 1866 King Jerry demanded 'restitution of all provinces of which he has been illegally deprived, after having held them by indefeasible title from time immemorial, together with all improvements thereon, and revenues accruing from all sources'. King Jerry, who had reputedly seen the Governor about the matter, was ejected from the Town Hall by Sergeant Morton to the amusement of the *Argus*, but not until he had made his point about original ownership.[16] Similarly, King Billy, 'the last of the Loddon tribe', described as a sober, peaceful man always 'tidily dressed', proposed in 1872 to erect a toll gate on the new bridge over the Loddon by 'the right which his progenitors enjoyed in the ages of antiquity'.[17] Aboriginal people not only appropriated these regal titles to gain power and status in the eyes of whites, but also to confirm their traditional power. Historian Edward Ryan has discovered that titles were passed on by

Aboriginal people, King Johnny being succeeded in the Donald area in 1883 by King Robert and in 1902 by King Anthony Anderson. As there were few remaining elders to confer his title, Anthony Anderson asked the local shire council to do it by presenting him with a 'king plate' inscribed: 'Anthony Anderson, King of Birchip, Morton Plains, Donald and surrounding country'.[18]

The colonial press recorded 'last of the tribe' deaths from the 1860s. Obituaries were given for King William of Tallock Bullock (1860); King Charley of the Goulburn (1868); King Jerry of the Dandan-noe (1870); and King Jack of the Wharparilla people (1880).[19] Virtually every district had a king or queen. Other elders, though not described as monarchs, were also farewelled as the 'last of' their people. The farewells of 'full bloods' were reported with pathos and regret and no doubt secret relief that the 'original owners' of the soil had passed on—settlers did not generally recognise the claims of 'half castes' to land. Sometimes local Europeans attended funerals—the residents of Ballan honoured King William in this manner in 1860. Occasionally other Europeans, such as residents of Murchison, raised (or proposed raising) a subscription to enclose the grave, as was done after the death of King Charley in 1868, who had requested to be buried in a coffin.

The reports of these 'last of' deaths were unusually respectful and sometimes laudatory, King Charley being described as a 'peacemaker', a man of 'great power' and 'very muscular'.[20] Henry Kendall's poem 'The Last of His Tribe', written in 1869, caught the pathos of this colonial notion, and became a popular poem for generations. Kendall's poem concluded:

> Will he go in his sleep from these desolate lands,
> Like a chief to the rest of his race,
> With the honey-voiced woman who beckons, and stands,
> And gleams like a Dream in his face—
> Like a marvellous Dream in his face?

Poems and sentiments like this helped colonists and their descendants to pass over the facts of usurpation and Aboriginal dispossession. Kendall's poem was read in schools at least a generation before it appeared in the *Eighth Book* of the *Victorian School Reader* (1928), which was used until the 1960s. Walter Robins of East Malvern studied it at school in Melbourne around 1900 and recited it to me in his nineties, eighty years later.[21]

The world of tradition

The Kulin around Melbourne in the early 1850s frequented traditional campsites, mostly along the many creeks and waterways encircling the town from the Maribyrnong River, through the Yarra, its wetlands and its tributaries, to the Mordialloc Creek. They refreshed themselves and caught fish, eels and fresh water mussels from grassy banks, as was customary. They continually moved about these campsites and back into the interior, following food, the movements of friends, ritual gatherings, because that was how life was to be lived. They occasionally entered Melbourne to sell things, particularly *bullen bullen*—lyre bird tail feathers—and clothes props, or to purchase supplies, including tobacco and, when they could obtain it illegally, alcohol.

There was less intimacy in the 1850s between Aboriginal people and settlers compared to the early Port Phillip days. (Goldrush society was bigger, faster and more self-possessed.) William Thomas, the Guardian of the Aborigines (after the Protectorate's closure), remained their daily advocate. He spoke their language fluently, believing it 'elegant' and a 'simple and harmonious' tongue. He compiled a grammar and extensive vocabulary of the Melbourne Kulin, and had translated into Kulin the Lord's Prayer, the Creed, parts of the Book of Genesis, and elements of the Anglican liturgy for church services.[22] But his old rapport with the Kulin was dented by the loss of his confidant Billibellary and other of his old friends, and a certain grumpiness overcame him in old age. Thomas's reports became more distant, rarely discussing Aboriginal individuals and personalities as before, describing people generally as 'the Yarra tribe', 'the blacks', and 'lubras'. The Kulin were not wanted in Melbourne—as had been made clear by Superintendent La Trobe a decade earlier—and their presence became a matter of constant negotiation. Thomas travelled on horseback most days and weeks in the early 1850s to check on the Kulin's whereabouts and to dissuade them from coming into Melbourne town, especially during festivals.

Each year during the 1840s the Kulin had visited the races at Flemington, no doubt to marvel at the commotion and join in the fun, as whites dressed up, wagered money on inconsistent horses and drank to excess. Thomas now sought to end their visits by vigorous action. In early March 1851 he scoured the outskirts of Melbourne for intending Kulin race-goers. On Tuesday 4 March he dissuaded seven Boonwurrung near Brighton from attending, warning them that there would be a great many constables at the races and 'any black found drunk would be immediately taken to the watch house'.[23] Grumbling, they retraced their steps, telling him that some Woiwurrung near the Plenty were also intending to go. On Wednesday 5 March Thomas warned off another party near Dandenong Creek, who with disappointment left for the bush. The next day he met eight Woiwurrung and three Daungwurrung people near the Darebin and 'had no difficulties in dissuading these from going to the Races, they had heard of my charge to the Western Port blacks [Boonwurrung]'. On the Friday Thomas met a South Sea Islander who had attended the race meeting and was amazed to find no Kulin there. Thomas replied that 'they could not go without getting drunk and they know it'.[24]

Traditional reasons usually drove the Kulin to Melbourne, groups coming weekly during some periods. Several Daungwurrung (Goulburn) people told Thomas at Heidelberg in June 1851 that 'they had arrived but yesterday and that they did not come to go to Melbourne but to talk with my blacks (the Woiwurrung)'.[25] Groups contacted by Thomas usually asked him the whereabouts of other Kulin. Clearly, inter-group relations among the Kulin were still vibrant in the 1850s. Day after day Thomas travelled Melbourne's outskirts checking the whereabouts of Aboriginal groups. The Kulin he met usually begged Thomas to allow them to stay and Thomas constantly begged them to leave. Although Thomas clearly badgered them, it was mostly a give and take relationship. However, with the inflow of overseas miners from 1852 the Kulin no doubt also came to observe and ponder the antics of a gold rush town. Thomas often expressed disappointment at the 'prodigal liberality of the gold diggers', who gave money and handouts to Aboriginal people in Melbourne.[26] Occasionally he appealed for police assistance, as he did in late April 1851, summoning them to break up a camp at South Yarra due to drunken behaviour, the group being shifted to Brighton.[27]

The desire for alcohol also attracted the Kulin to Melbourne. Thomas, whose Methodist religion opposed alcohol, deplored this and probably exaggerated its impact. The Kulin procured money to buy alcohol through the generosity of gold diggers or by working. Indeed, they acted like most white rural labourers of the time, who worked hard and drank hard. Thomas claimed of the Kulin: 'They work well for a few weeks, receive wages, and then a drunken bout they must have, notwithstanding they are eight or more miles from a country inn'.[28] Aboriginal drinkers often binged on rum and spirits to the point of oblivion, like many whites—for the colonial population as a whole drank spirits heavily, far more so than people in Britain.[29] Despite the law preventing sales of alcohol to Aboriginal people, they were still able to obtain it. Magistrate William Hull observed that they give money to a child to buy it for them or 'to some low man of the lower class of people, then they all drink it together'.[30]

Some Kulin asserted their right to drink, challenging William Thomas: 'white man get em drunk and why not blacks?'[31] And why not, we might ask? They were theoretically equal British subjects under the law. However, the consequences of drunkenness were dire for a people already dispossessed of land, facing severe cultural disruption and depopulation. Binge-drinking caused loss of authority, violence and sometimes death. The young seemed to be the most avid drinkers and Thomas claimed that respect for elders was being undermined. And alcohol-induced violence occasionally carried off key people, Thomas remarking after one drunken spearing that 'the Yarra blacks have lost by this death almost their last leading man'.[32] Alcohol abuse even affected ritual, Thomas lamenting in his description of a Kulin funeral that several Kulin were 'staggering round the scene in a state of intoxication, vociferating most awful curses'.[33] Several Kulin deaths occurred each year in the early 1850s from respiratory disease through lying drunk in the open.

The Kulin's constant visits to Melbourne created almost daily power struggles with Thomas. For instance, on Tuesday 6 May 1851, Thomas met a Kulin group north-east of the Merri Creek who begged him to let them stop there a few days. He visited them the next day and found more had arrived from the upper Yarra. He initially gave them until Saturday to leave. However, on the Thursday he came armed with a complaint about their dogs and 'pressed them to hasten again to the bush'. Thomas returned on Friday, begging them not to join the other encampments nearer town. On the Saturday the Kulin promised to leave that day, but were still in the Merri Creek camp that evening. Up before dawn, Thomas arrived on horseback at 8.30 a.m. on Sunday morning and to his relief found the people preparing to leave. He conducted a church service and with a handshake saw them on their way before noon. Thomas had finally prevailed but the Kulin had managed to stay an extra five days.[34]

Land sales and entreaties to 'move on' made it imperative for the Kulin to gain land that was acknowledged as their own. Indeed, Billibellary requested land in 1843 and the Kulin's demands soon became insistent too. In August 1850 Thomas reported that the Woiwurrung (the Yarra blacks) 'again point out the spot they would wish to locate upon. I again object, they reason the matter with some degree of art'.[35] Thomas did not identify the spot but in September he visited the Bulleen camp of the Woiwurrung, commenting that 'the blacks [are]

Young girl photographed about 1858 by Antoine Fauchery/Richard Daintree.
(Courtesy of La Trobe Picture Collection, State Library of Victoria, H84.167/47)

impatient for a station. I again state the impossibility of their having it in
their neighbourhood'. The suggestion was that they wanted it on the Yarra
at Bulleen, which was too close to white settlers for Thomas's liking.[36] In
1852 the Woiwurrung gained 782 hectares on both sides of the Yarra at
more distant Warrandyte. In August the Boonwurrung (Western Port
Tribe) 'selected the spot they would desire to have as a reserve', being
about 340 hectares on the Mordialloc Creek.[37] These two reserves were
both 25 kilometres from Melbourne, sufficient distance to isolate them
from the town.

These reserves remained low key. They were never staffed by whites
or permanently occupied by blacks. However, they acted as distribution depots. Thomas, encouraging a dependence on rations, convinced
Governor La Trobe that the only means to keep the Melbourne Kulin
from the town was to ration them from reserves: 'I would guarantee
to keep my own blacks out, and then I know the others would not
come'.[38] Rations of flour, tea, sugar and tobacco were soon provided,
an annual blanket distribution initiated, and tomahawks were, for a
time, handed out. During the first few years the Boonwurrung stayed
for some weeks at a time at Mordialloc, using the supplies there as well
as fishing in the Creek, but as Thomas said the 'Yarra tribe have not
[though passing through their depot] desired aught but a little tobacco'.[39]
The rations improved but remained little used as the Kulin were mostly
in work. By 1857 Thomas drew as usual for the year for both stations:
270 kilograms of flour, 70 kilograms of sugar, 7 kilograms of tea, 10
kilograms of tobacco and 8 kilograms of soap, and a pair of blankets
each, 'all of which last for a year or longer'. Home medicines were also

on hand, including salts, linament, castor oil, Dover's powders, sticking plaster, sulphur and bluestone.[40]

Other Aboriginal people besides the Kulin visited Melbourne. There was a constant movement of drays and stock from the interior and upcountry Aboriginal youths travelling with them. The youths who came from as far as the Murray stopped over in Melbourne, gaped at this gold rush boom town, and returned to the bush. Some individuals were extremely mobile. In June 1851 Thomas met two gold seekers, one black, one white, the Aboriginal man having travelled from the Sydney District with a consignment of horses for Geelong. His name was Thomas Walker, and Thomas recognised him as a celebrated 'converted black'. On hearing he had been in Port Phillip for five weeks Thomas feared for his soul in this godless society, but to his amazement Walker replied: the 'peace [of God] is all sufficient'. Thomas farewelled him saying, 'My dear brother, avoid temptation' and urged him to return promptly to his Christian friends. Walker replied: 'Christ will take care of me'.[41] Unfortunately, Thomas Walker, like many colonial men, soon fell to the demon drink.[42]

One incident in 1851 reveals the power of both tradition and change in Aboriginal society—and the fact that adult men outnumbered women in most Aboriginal groups by 1850.[43] In April a DjaDjawurrung woman from Avoca named Polly was brought to Melbourne by a settler, Mr Sanger, to wed a white shepherd with whom she had lived for two years. Polly was lodged at William Thomas's house which caused a commotion among some Gunai/Kurnai people visiting from Gippsland, some of whom were 'strangers' to him. About 50 camped on the Merri at Brunswick near his house. Thomas believed that the news had been passed from group to group: 'I cannot account in any other way for the appearance of so many strange blacks unless upon this errand'.[44] While Thomas was at church on Sunday 27 April, the visitors came to his house and insisted that Polly be turned over to them, one man saying she was his 'wife'. Thomas's daughter brought Polly into the house and bolted the doors. Thomas returned to news of the demands and went to the Merri camp and found that the group was searching for a Gippsland woman who had 'escaped' from them some months earlier. He resolved it thus: 'I then got two who were deputed (one who knew her) to accompany me and to see for himself, he at once said "big one bungallarly" (stupid) blackfellow, that not the lubra'.[45] Polly was 'awfully frightened at seeing them', as these were not her people, and she left within two days, there being difficulties 'in making the compact [marriage]'.[46] In January 1853, Thomas reported that the white shepherd 'has kept true to her and she to him, though on account of his occupation, he cannot be continually with her; when he can, he returns and brings her clothes and what she requires. She has been in my district from the time she left my roof, at Pentridge [now Coburg], and is a kind, faithful, and affectionate servant'.[47] However, in 1859 Thomas reported he saw Polly with an Aboriginal group, her 'white husband' having died.[48]

When the Gunai/Kurnai people of Gippsland visited Melbourne in the 1850s, extensive customary activities occurred. They were traditional enemies of the Kulin and in the past had engaged in bloody feuds with them, causing significant loss of life. But the pressures of colonialism had caused new alignments and in the late 1840s they had more friendly interactions. In April 1852 some Boonwurrung returned to Melbourne with about ten Gunai/Kurnai—'Warrigal [wild] blacks' Thomas called them. Thomas's efforts to remove them failed. Three camps formed as messengers brought more Gunai/Kurnai to Melbourne as well as Kulin from Geelong, Ballarat and the Goulburn. The people begged Thomas to allow them to stay for corroborees as they had not met in four years. He relented and collected them on the Yarra about twenty kilometres from Melbourne, probably near Templestowe. They held nightly corroborees for two weeks then moved camp regularly over the next few months, partying with the help of Melbourne's alcohol supplies. Thomas, disgusted at their 'debauchery' and riotous behaviour, broke up the camps with police help, but not before four murders and five deaths had occurred, some of which were alcohol induced. Thomas ordered the Aboriginal people home, 'assuring them that never more should there be an assemblage'.[49] (He later complained it took six months to remove them from Melbourne, such was the Kulin's desire to socialise.)[50]

Traditional meetings were at the core of Aboriginal *joie de vie*. Forty-three Gunai/Kurnai men returned to Melbourne in 1857, corroboreeing at Dandenong before camping at Brighton with the Kulin, who were 'highly delighted with their arrival'. They danced almost nightly, once for an audience of 300 Europeans. After ten days Thomas bribed them with rations and blankets to leave, but they pleaded to stay another day to see the races, to which he consented. He eventually got them on the road to Gippsland but not before messengers returned with more Kulin, delaying their departure, much to Thomas's grief. Some drunkenness continued, although Thomas remarked that 'a more quiet, orderly community would not exist when once beyond the pale of spiritous liquors'. Finally he rationed them and ushered them to Gippsland after a month in Melbourne. While en route

Thomas watched them playing cards, remarking: 'to my astonishment [they] played like white people, dealing out, proclaiming trumps, and following [suit] accurately'. They said a gentleman in Gippsland had taught them.[51]

Entering the European world

The Gunai/Kurnai's card skills were indicative of the increasingly enmeshed nature of cultural interactions between two very diverse cultures—one nomadic/semi-nomadic, one pastoral/farming. Apparently simple things like learning the rules of card games were being passed back and forth across the frontier. Such black–white transactions—economic, cultural, convivial and sexual—were myriad, as dramatic as negotiations over reserve land or as low key as a card game. Most encounters were not recorded and are lost to us or, if recorded, were not described in much detail so we don't get a sense of what such encounters meant to the participants. What did the Gunai/Kurnai take a card game to be: social interaction, a means of gambling, a ritual process? Certainly to play cards effectively they had to become numerate in the European way, make new associations in order to declare trumps, and perhaps adopt the rules of honourable play by always following suit and not reneging. But what did the kings, queens and jacks on the cards mean to them? For Europeans they conjured up ideas of dynasties of royal European houses, of heads chopped, castles defended and Divine Rights asserted. Even jokers held a special place in European culture as merry fellows able to tread a fine line between jest and social commentary in the face of the powerful. Perhaps Aboriginal people understood the joker only too well, having been forced to play his role too many times in the face of European power. We can never know such things, because these shifts in understanding were so subtle. It is certain that each culture was modified by these contacts, even if Europeans thought themselves more superior. Indigenous peoples were more vulnerable to change being the less powerful party in these transactions, and because the whites controlled the structures of the colonial world, but each side was influenced by the other nonetheless.

One repeated encounter on the frontier, often recorded but usually in a fragmentary way, were corroborees attended by whites. We can only guess at how these were understood on each side. What did whites make of them? Were their imaginings of Aboriginal people confirmed or modified by these performances? We know European artists drew corroborees as dramatic open-air, fire-lit events, exotic and archetypal representations of 'savagery'. Were Aboriginal people showing ritual about country to welcome, impress and claim ownership? Were they increasingly influenced by a new or additional profit motive, as moneys, rations and alcohol flowed their way at such events?

William Thomas recorded a new performance twist in January 1856, when six Yarra blacks engaged for six nights at the Queen's Theatre, dancing and demonstrating 'native habits', and entering the European world of theatrical performance. The *Argus* reported that attendances were good, the audiences being intrigued by the 'violent, muscular exertions' of the 'kangaroo' and other dances. Thomas attested to the Aboriginal performers' professionalism, saying 'to their credit they kept sober to the end of their engagement'.[52] Corroborees at Ballarat were also staged in a theatrical town awash with money and diggers to entertain. A group of Ararat Aboriginal people, 'advanced in civilization', frequented the town: 'The women have their hair neatly combed and oiled, and the men are dressed as Europeans. The King wears a white bell-topper, of which he seems as proud as if he wore the Crown of England'. At the suggestion of the impresario of Ballarat's Royal Theatre, a suggestion which the people 'accepted with avidity', the Ararat people took to the stage. After the first piece, one Aboriginal man stepped into the footlights and announced the program. The *Ballarat Star* commented that 'in his intelligence and manners he was a pattern to hundreds I have seen of Europeans attempting to address an assemblage'. One of the group left to round up 50 more of his kin for another performance, but the outcome was not reported.[53]

Work formed another frequent intercultural transaction. Europeans increasingly looked to Aboriginal workers in the gold-rush labour crisis and Aboriginal people sought work as their traditional bush-tucker economy faltered. They engaged as bullockies, stock handlers, wool washers, weeders, gardeners, harvesters, and on general farm maintenance, being paid in money and food like other workers. About forty Woiwurrung worked on farms and stations mostly in the Plenty River area, staying until the work was completed. Thomas reported in late 1852 that 'an experienced farmer gave me to understand that most of them were occupied on his and the surrounding farms; he had several reaping, two of whom each cut half an acre per day. All were not so ready, the middle-aged generally reaped sitting, working themselves forward as they go'.[54] Thomas noted that the Boonwurrung were less keen on steady work but assisted settlers along the coast and inland for some months 'in parties of three, four, and five'. Those on the Plenty in late 1852 worked below the current European wage rate at ten to fifteen shillings a week plus food. They went on strike for twenty-five, but Thomas persuaded them to return to work for fifteen shillings. By 1860 the Melbourne Kulin learned to work by contract and quotation. Billibellary's son, Simon Wonga, was observed by Thomas sizing up and quoting on supplying bark for a farmer's barn. Wonga stated: 'cut bark where we find good trees, *only cut it*, you cart it away, and white man put bark on, pay us blackfellows two pounds'.[55]

Throughout rural Victoria small groups of Aboriginal workers helped resolve the labour crisis of the 1850s. Most able-bodied DjaDjawurrung men washed sheep on the Loddon and Campaspe Rivers. Stations in the Wimmera employed Wergaia-speaking people as shepherds—their bush skills allowed squatters to let their sheep wander like cattle, to be tracked when needed. They had learnt the value of money and were paid wages, which magistrate Edward Bell claimed 'in ordinary times, would be considered high for emigrant labor [*sic*]'. He added that those acquiring 'a degree of European civilization in dress and habits of living' still left for 'their accustomed haunts', to engage in 'the sports and savage (though generally harmless) warfare of their respective tribes'. Similar continuities and change occurred at Portland Bay.[56]

At Alberton in Gippsland eleven Gunai/Kurnai males, three aged about 10, and eight under 20, as well as Henry, a Woiwurrung man aged 25, weeded and reaped 40 hectares over two months. Their wages of £2 were low, but their valuing of money was recent. Probably more important

Woiwurrung woman and child about 1858, photographed by Antoine Fauchery/ Richard Daintree. (Courtesy of La Trobe Picture Collection, State Library of Victoria)

to them were the added payments in kind: their share of a bottle of (diluted) rum, a fig of tobacco, a gun with some powder and shot, one blanket, three shirts, one pair of trousers, and a cap. Andrew McCrae, the Police Magistrate, reported 'they worked steadily, as many hours as the whites who were their fellow-labourers, and did the same amount of work'. Indeed, two Aboriginal workers and one white beat a team of three white workers in a reaping contest for nine litres of rum.[57] A year later they worked as sheep-washers, shepherds, stockmen, reapers, and house servants at various locations around Gippsland due to the labour scarcity, earning praise from settlers. W. O. Raymond reported that he 'could not have washed my sheep without the Dergo' people, whom he paid one shilling each per day. However, Charles Tyers, the Commissioner of Crown Lands, bemoaned that, despite this useful work, they are 'too idle to cultivate the soil and to lay up provision for to-morrow, they hold to their wandering propensities when unemployed by the white people'.[58]

Across the colony by the 1850s, Aboriginal people dressed like, worked like, ate like and, in some senses, acted like European rural workers, to the point of strike action at the Plenty River. Yet they were not the same, remaining staunchly Aboriginal in their identity and core culture. This was evident in Thomas's description of Woiwurrung labourers in January 1853, when he noted their refusal to become sedentary and to live in houses like Europeans:

> All efforts, however, to further improve their condition, have been tried without avail. I have pressed, and the farmers and others also have urged their becoming as we are, and not merely in work and diet; but to stop in houses and open convenient places at night, comfortably clad and stretched, is what they will not hear of; the hook, axe, or bridle down, and all further of civilisation for the day is over; off goes apparel, and they bask under the canopy of heaven as in their primitive wildness, evidently enjoying their freedom from incumbrance; nor do I conceive of any further advancement beyond what they have obtained practicable to those in the settled districts, nor have they any desire to be meddled with further. Such is their wandering propensity, that all the kindness, entreaty, or persuasion cannot secure them one day beyond their determination; and they have latterly been particularly cautious how they make bargains for labour on this account.[59]

Thomas was disappointed by this cultural tenacity, seeing them in biblical terms as 'voluntarily degraded', being like Ham, the son of Noah, and his descendants, 'fugitives upon the face of the earth', that is, itinerants.

Thomas despaired of their future in 1852, moved by both real concern and affection for the Melbourne Kulin whose numbers had plummeted to 39 Woiwurrung and 20 Boonwurrung, none of whom were under 14 years of age. Similar declines occurred elsewhere, but at least there were children inland and hopes for the future. Writing to Governor La Trobe in September 1852, Thomas prefigured aspects of later Aboriginal policy. He believed that the only hope 'to improve their condition and avert the extinction of their race', in fact to maintain 'a community of the race', was to create single-sex Aboriginal schools at inland locations. These pupils would graduate to Aboriginal schools in Melbourne, where they would be educated and taught a trade. Their centralising would stifle their ability to return to the wilderness and would 'amalgamate the tribes unconsciously, being young, they cannot have any prejudices'. Special Aboriginal legislation would facilitate 'marriages among themselves, also between them and the white population'. He was aware that removal of children was a radical step, which might earn him the title of 'misanthrope' (man-hater). However, he convinced himself that it was more humane to take them from their so-called 'miserable' parents, to 'rescue' them as he saw it, than not to do so. Thomas thus set aside the rights of parent and child to be with each other. His aim, unlike later policy makers, was not physical or racial absorption, but the opposite: to save the 'race'. Although he did not oppose marriage to Europeans, his plan was based on 'marriage with their own race'. Thomas clearly aimed at cultural assimilation, to 'materially improve the condition of the black population, and facilitate their permanent civilization'. They were to be settled rural workers sharing the gift of 'equal advancement'. But they were also to be 'a community of the race'.[60]

A few young DjaDjawurrung people, residents of the former Loddon Protectorate station, fulfilled Thomas's positive vision. An Aboriginal school begun by Edward Parker survived the Protectorate's closure and was attended in 1853 by 6 to 12 students. Eight young men who were employed by Parker on the former Protectorate land attended night school in winter, 'walking some miles in the dark wet evenings', returning late at night ready for work the next day. Three young women 'also received occasional instruction'. By 1858 there were ten pupils boarding at the school, seven with European names, and three males with traditional names: Morpoke, Warbourp and Weregoondet. Nine were aged 4 to 15 years and one, Mary Jane, was an adult. All of them could read and write, and some had knowledge of arithmetic.[61] A dozen other children had been through schooling for at least six months and had then left, a truancy mirrored by some white farmers' children. Parker also placed some Aboriginal children with white families to enable their Christian education. This followed his own experience of raising the young boy Kolain. However, one child educated by a Kyneton family was 'lured' away by a carrier to work and become, as Parker feared, 'the associate of drunken bullock drivers'.[62]

Two former young male residents of the Loddon Protectorate station at Franklinford, Yerrebullah and Beernbannin, were given four hectares each to farm. They fenced it themselves and, with some aid in ploughing, planted half of the land. Parker wrote in March 1853 that 'they are now fairly established as farmers, and their care and industry in cultivating their ground are combined with remarkable prudence in the disposal of their earnings'. They were expected to gain a handsome sum of £100. Parker reported in early 1859 that the two were still farming successfully, being no different 'from our ordinary peasants'. A few others sought to emulate them. Two other families took up land at the former Loddon station in the mid-1850s, but one family man died from pulmonary disease and the other from falling down a mine shaft. Parker sought to secure the land for their families.[63]

In all, six men and their families took up land at Franklinford. One of them, Tommy Farmer, told an 1877 Royal Commission that for six years he supported a wife and two children on the land which he ploughed and planted with potatoes and wheat, selling the latter in Castlemaine. He declared: 'Yes, I did keep myself; but a great number of my own people came and camped round me and eat me out'. Like other selectors, misfortune struck. He lost his bullocks: 'that broke me down, and I could not get on'. Then his family died and Tommy Farmer walked off the farm, moving to Coranderrk reserve in 1864. John Green, the Central Board's former inspector gave a slightly less admirable version. Green told the same inquiry that Edward Parker, the former assistant Protector, at times had to reap the wheat on Tommy Farmer's property, and the government received only a fifth of the property's value at the end. Joseph Parker, son of Edward, confirmed that all the Franklinford Aboriginal farmers, except Tommy Farmer, died from respiratory disease and misadventure and the land reverted to the Crown.[64]

Lost boys

The journey into the European world often left Aboriginal people disoriented and disappointed. The Bungaleen brothers, Harry and Tommy, cut adrift from Gunai/Kurnai society at the Merri Creek School as we saw in an earlier chapter, moved deeper into the European world as they grew. We left the two young boys, six and four, at the failing Merri Creek School in early 1851, eagerly expecting to go to Hobart Town with the school teacher Edgar and his family, to grow into 'white fellars'. But inexplicably the Edgars left without them, the two boys leaning against the playground fence staring after them, motionless, alone, without tears and without words, abandoned by those they thought loved them. William Thomas took the boys to John Hinkins, the schoolmaster of Pentridge (now Coburg) National School, who agreed to foster them for 5 shillings each per week and £5 for an outfit.[65] Hinkins was the settler who, with his young daughter Jenny, had lived amongst Yorta Yorta at Gunbower station some years before.

Harry, the older boy, acclimatised better than his brother Tommy who proved sulky and troublesome. Tommy bit Mrs Hinkins on the arm on one occasion before being flung to the ground, flogged and berated by Hinkins. Tommy also attacked Hinkins's son and initially displayed significant anger—as one might expect, having been left by both his mother, Kitty (Parley) and the Edgars. However, the boys reconciled themselves to the family, wishing to call the Hinkins 'father and mother' and kiss them good night like the Hinkins's own children. They became attentive and well behaved in church, particularly enjoying singing, and progressed well in their school lessons. They were baptised in great hope at Trinity Church Pentridge before a packed congregation on 1 January 1852. Harry, formerly Wurrabool, was renamed John after Hinkins (his third identity), and Tommy became Thomas after William Thomas.[66]

Hopes remained high. When Governor Hotham was welcomed to the colony in June 1854, Hinkins officially joined the parade from South Melbourne in his gig, sporting a white silk banner displaying a kangaroo and emu under the words 'Advance Australia'. The two boys, dressed in white, with blue kerchiefs and blue ribbon in their straw hats, stood on either side of Hinkins. Hotham shook hands with the boys and bowed after they sang 'God Save the Queen'. Hinkins recalled: 'Through the town the two boys were loudly cheered, and they, in return, shouted till they were hoarse'. The next day they regaled their playmates with descriptions of the grand events.

However, death stalked them. In the early 1850s Thomas was ill with colonial fever (dysentery) and both were very ill with measles. John, aged eleven, developed a fatal illness in early 1856. As he lay in the Government hospital repenting his sins before Rev. S. L. Chase, his last exclamation was in true believer style: 'I am so sorry'!

John's Moonee Ponds playmates accompanied his body to the Melbourne General Cemetery.

Thomas initially appeared unmoved by his brother's death: his third significant personal loss before the age of ten. However, he brooded, Hinkins noting that he 'was very careful of anything that had belonged to his late brother, especially his garden, which he kept with great care'.[67] Then he became rebellious. After becoming entranced by the theatre he regularly escaped to Melbourne in defiance of Hinkins, begging money for his admission and sleeping afterwards in a livery stable. Although School Inspector Geary declared in August 1857 that 'he stands first in his class and appears as intelligent and indus-

THOMAS BUNGEELENE.

Thomas Bungaleen in *Newsletter of Australia*, 1857. (Courtesy of State Library of Victoria LTF052.9N47)

trious as any other in the school', young Thomas played truant three times shortly afterwards. William Thomas pronounced him as 'very unruly'.[68]

After young Thomas attacked Hinkins with an iron bar in 1859, which suggests he was significantly angry and disturbed, the latter was forced to give him up. A place was sought for him at Scotch College and Melbourne Grammar, but both refused, so he was taught at Fitzroy, before becoming a messenger in the Department of Lands. Implicated with two white youths in an assault on a young girl, he was disciplined by being sent to the training ship SS *Victoria* in 1861 when aged fourteen.[69] Again he proved rebellious, until discipline and sea life controlled him. He saw service to the Gulf of Carpentaria during the search for Burke and Wills. When the *Victoria* was decommissioned, Thomas, then eighteen, became a map tracer in the Department of Mines, a report suggesting he 'writes very well . . . already he can plot from a simple field-book, and can draw plans tolerably well. He appears to like the work he has to do'.[70]

Ultimately Thomas Bungaleen became reconciled to his situation. Separated from his family through death and from his people by colonial circumstance, he embraced the white world as the best way to survive. Adrift in a white world, young Thomas denied his Aboriginality three times. Once when washing his hands vigorously with soap he asked Hinkins, 'I think they are getting a little whiter—are they not father?'; later he insisted to his fellow seamen that his parents were white; and later still, when it was suggested by a settler that a young Christian Aboriginal girl, Ellen Lassie from New South Wales, might be his wife, to 'propagate and continue your race', Thomas was livid, exclaiming: 'a black girl indeed! It's like their impudence to speak to me about a black girl as a partner for life'.[71]

So much did he embrace the white colonial world that when eighteen, Thomas asked John Hinkins to assist his admittance to membership of the Society of Oddfellows, a friendly society for men which advocated temperance, thrift, hard work, and respectability: core white colonial values. Before a room full of men wearing Oddfellows regalia in December 1864, the smartly dressed Thomas gave an acceptance speech, saying: 'Though I am the first of my race to receive this high honour, I sincerely hope I shall not be the last'. He then gave a twenty-minute recitation, as polished young men of his day did, to entertain his hosts. This was greeted by deafening applause and the high praise of Dr Greeves, a Past Grand Master of the Society.[72] Within a month Thomas was dead from gastric fever, his last words being to request a reading of the 23rd Psalm, the psalm of comfort for evangelical Christians of the day. As he was laid beside the body of his brother John, his Gunai/Kurnai people were being collected together at Ramahyuck, a mission on Lake Wellington, to continue in earnest their own adventures in the white colonial Christian world.

7

New Communities

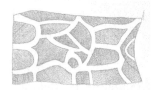

New Aboriginal communities emerged after the 1850s. Remnant clans, devastated by population decline and loss of land through colonial dispossession, looked to formerly hostile groups for wives, partners and, perhaps unconsciously, the critical mass required to form viable new Aboriginal communities. The Gunai/Kurnai and Kulin, often at enmity in the past, began novel marriage exchanges in 1847 and further social relations in the 1850s. The European presence also meant that Aboriginal groups met in non-traditional ways, which at first caused tensions and violence, but later enabled new alliances to be forged. Polly, the Aboriginal woman from Avoca, who partnered a white shepherd in the early 1850s and boarded in Coburg while he worked, upon his death took up with 'the first tribe of blacks she found' according to William Thomas.[1] If Thomas misrepresented how she came to be with a new group, she was with a new group nonetheless.

Europeans also played a part in forming new Aboriginal communities from 1860 by seeking to 'settle down' Aboriginal people and centralise them for European convenience, be it on a mission, school or government settlement. As Aboriginal groups formed or were encouraged into new groupings through missions, the power of tradition, marriage and Aboriginal kinship solidified these new communities. Traditional identities—clan, tribe and confederation names—were enlarged by new colonial identities. Thus, a person who was of the Wurundjeri-balluk clan of the Woiwurrung language group, which was part of the Kulin confederation, became also one of the Coranderrk mission people.

Policy making

With the demise of the Aboriginal Protectorate in 1849 there was virtually no Victorian Aboriginal policy. William Thomas was made the Guardian of Aborigines with, as well as his former duties, orders to manage two rations stations at Warrandyte and Mordialloc and 'to keep the blacks out of Melbourne'.[2] The Crown Lands Commissioners acted as local Aboriginal guardians but did little besides filing a few reports, as they did not distribute rations or even blankets to replace the declining production of possum-skin rugs. The one Aboriginal School, on a 46-hectare reserve at the Loddon, continued to be funded in the 1850s. Aboriginal people were prevented from drinking alcohol by legislation, but their free legal representation in Melbourne's courts ended due to budget cuts in 1854. No other official assistance was given to Aboriginal people in the 1850s, apart from the granting of 1,000 hectares and rations for several Christian missions at Lake Boga and Yelta and about ten hectares on the Loddon to six Aboriginal farmers. Thus, while about £70,000 was expended on Aboriginal people to fund the Protectorate, the Native Police and assistance to Buntingdale Mission between 1838 and 1850, only about £12,000 was expended between 1851 and 1858, a fourfold decline per annum. Admittedly, the Aboriginal population had also declined by a similar degree. In both periods, two-thirds of the money was devoted to white salaries.[3]

In this policy wasteland, some Christians expressed public concern for Aboriginal people, whom they acknowledged as being of the same creation as themselves. However, local Christians failed to turn their concern into any renewed effort after the demise of Buntingdale Mission in 1848. Indeed, the next move came from the Moravians, a distant German Protestant Church with a strong missionary commitment. Two missionaries, Revs Taeger and Spieseke, arrived in February 1851 and, after acclimatising on the Loddon with Edward Parker, formed a mission at Lake Boga, just south-east of Swan Hill. In July 1851 a packed meeting of Christians at the Melbourne Mechanics Institute (now the Athenaeum), chaired by Governor Charles La Trobe of Moravian heritage, resolved that the 'Christianization and Civilization' of Aboriginal people was of 'deep importance', and promised financial support. The Presbyterians in particular provided money.[4] Also, after meetings and discussions energised by Rev. Septimus Lloyd Chase, the Anglicans began a mission at Yelta at the Murray–Darling junction just west of Mildura in 1855, with the missionaries, Goodwin and John Bulmer. Christian hope abounded. Edward Parker argued in a published public lecture in Melbourne that Aboriginal people were 'just as capable of receiving instruction, just as capable of mental exercises, as any more favoured races'. He concluded with the ringing challenge: 'occupy the land,—till its broad wastes;—extract its riches,—develop its resources,—if you will;—but, in the name of God and Humanity, SAVE THE PEOPLE'.[5]

Aboriginal people proved wary of these Christian efforts at Lake Boga and Yelta. The Wotjobaluk waited two years before visiting Lake Boga and then came infrequently and in small numbers. The Moravians learned the Wotjobaluk's language and established gardens, but abandoned Lake Boga as the Wotjobaluk resisted its offerings and white settlers intruded on its boundaries. Defeated, they retired to Germany where they were severely criticised for their withdrawal. Reverends Spieseke and Hagenauer returned and initiated the Ebenezer Mission on the Wimmera River near Antwerp in January 1859.[6] Yelta fared little better. The Lower Murray people visited and, encouraged by an initial supply of government rations, helped to form huts, a school, fences and gardens, but the experience paled alongside working for wages on surrounding stations and the lure of grog at bush inns around Wentworth. In late 1866 Yelta was scaled down as only fourteen people attended on average. By 1865 Rev. Goodwin reported that only Fred Wowinda 'has remained very constantly with us, and I have good hope that the instruction he has received will bring forth fruit. I was much pleased when entering his hut some short time ago, to find him employed reading the Testament to a black from a neighbouring station'.[7] Few others responded as did Wowinda and Yelta closed in 1869.

Thomas McCombie, journalist, author, historian and politician, stirred a secular humanitarian conscience within the Victorian Legislative Council in the late 1850s.[8] In October 1858 he called successfully for a select committee to investigate the condition and needs of Aboriginal people. However, McCombie was also a colonist bent on the development of Victoria, its economy and government, having earlier been a champion of separation from New South Wales. McCombie expressed a fascinating mix of anger, sympathy and pessimism about the condition of Aboriginal people. They had been badly abused—he knew that from his recent researches into Victoria's history—and yet he firmly believed in the existence of 'inferior' and 'superior' races. He told Parliament: 'they had too frequently been treated savagely and inhumanly by the white population of this colony . . . they had in fact, been almost exterminated, and it was one of the darkest enigmas of the world that the progress of the civilised nations appeared always to eventuate in the extermination of the inferior race'. The 'higher race' had a 'right to take possession of this land', but also a duty to ensure the 'protection and support' of the 'inferior' race.[9]

The Select Committee that resulted from McCombie's calls interviewed the Moravians, William Thomas, Edward Parker and several other witnesses, and sought written replies from magistrates, crown lands commissioners and settlers to a questionnaire based on that of the Ethnographical Society of Paris. The Committee asked 388 questions of its witnesses and, with its written replies, collected 105 closely typed pages of information and opinion on the physical, family, cultural, social and political life of Aboriginal people and their present numbers and conditions. Its report claimed that the disastrous decline of the Aboriginal population should be 'attributed to the general occupation of the country', that is the colonial presence; 'hunger' from the 'scarcity of game since the settlement of the Colony'; and 'in some cases, to cruelty and ill-treatment'. Above all, it blamed the Aboriginal victims themselves, singling out the 'inveterate propensity of the race to excessive indulgence in spirits'.[10] Its witnesses were Christians and moral improvers, who disapproved of alcohol no matter who consumed it. McCombie had a protective reserve system in mind as a solution to the problem and his Committee questioned the witnesses on what was needed to help Aboriginal people and how it might work.

The report, tabled in February 1859 and influenced by William Thomas, called for 'reserves for the various tribes on their own hunting grounds' for agricultural and de-pasturing purposes, far from licensed taverns. More optimistic than when he started, McCombie's report (for McCombie was the Select Committee Chairman) stated that Aboriginal people who 'are possessed of mental power on a par with their brethren of the other races of man' should be 'civilized and christianized' by missionary managers. The report quoted Dr Pickering from his *Races of Men*, who stated Aboriginal people were 'the finest model of the human proportions I have ever met with in muscular development', were perceptive, apt learners, and had the heads of philosophers—alluding to the popular belief in phrenology, which assessed character from the shape of the head.[11] McCombie tabled the report on 1 February 1859 and the Legislative Council agreed to ask the Governor for land for reserves.[12] The conservative *Argus* approved of the report, declaring that the 'original owners of the soil' must be cared for and that the reserve system would be some atonement for past white cruelty and neglect.[13]

A reserve system emerged, as much due to Kulin pressure as to McCombie's Committee. The Kulin had continually reminded William

Thomas of their aspirations for land ever since Billibellary had articulated this in 1843. Thomas made their desires known to government. In late February 1859 Billibellary's two surviving sons, Simon Wonga, now a clan head aged 35, and Tommy Munnering aged 24, again visited Thomas—'marminarta' to them—at his home on the Merri Creek. They brought five Daungwurrung men with them: Bearinga, Murrum-Murrum, Pargnegean, Kooyan and Burrupin. They stayed the night as Thomas's guests. The next day Wonga, translating for the Daungwurrung, said they 'want a block of land in their country where they may sit down, plant corn, potatoes, etc.—and work like white men'. Thomas was pessimistic of success but spoke to the men for hours.[14] The two groups of Kulin, with Thomas acting as translator and mediator, waited on the Surveyor-General of Lands, who received them well. For their group of 32 individuals, they asked for a specific piece of land on the 'Nakkrom' (Acheron River) near Alexandra, where 'kangaroos and possums were abundant'. Regarding their use of the land, they stated: 'that blackfellows and lubras go look out food, but some always stop and turn up ground, and plant potatoes and food'. Thomas recommended that they be given 60 hectares each, in the form of about 2,000 hectares for the group, together with some initial provisions, implements and advice from a 'steady, sober agricultural family'.[15]

The Kulin lobbied Charles Duffy, the Minister of Lands, on 7 March 1859. The *Argus,* mightily impressed, reported that the seven, 'robust and well-made men, apparently equal in physical power to the average of Europeans', and all between 173 and 183 centimetres, wore 'coarse jumpers and trousers like sailors or labourers of an inferior class'. The paper continued: 'Their countenances were intelligent and animated. Their entrance into the boardroom was made in an unembarrassed and quiet manner', and upon being seated they listened with attentiveness and 'an air of grave courtesy'. Duffy was moved by these dignified land-seekers, perhaps as a result of his former involvement in land and tenancy protests in Ireland. He approved of the Acheron proposals and seemed startled to hear from Thomas that Kulin numbers had been reduced from 600 to 32 in just twenty years. This new immigrant of just three years residence in Victoria was learning some colonial facts! Duffy conferred *sotto voce* with his fellow members of the Lands and Survey Board. He then asked Thomas to accompany the Kulin home to see they were settled, and to report on their needs 'for we are anxious to make any reasonable experiment in this direction'. When told of Duffy's response, the Kulin made 'exclamations, apparently of approval', and withdrew with a slight bow in Duffy's direction.[16]

'Deputation of Victorian Aborigines at the Governor's Levée', *Illustrated Melbourne Post*, 18 June 1863. (Courtesy National Library of Australia)

The Kulin again displayed political savvy in 1863 before the Head of State, Queen Victoria and her vice-regal representative, the Governor, Sir Henry Barkly. The Kulin's pioneering of the Acheron land in 1860 was threatened by Hugh Glass, the most powerful squatter in Victoria, and he forced their removal to a colder site, Mohican Station. William Thomas was bitter that the government had broken its 'covenant', as he termed the promise over the Acheron land. Many Kulin refused to move. Ironically the new station proved unsuitable agricultural land and had to be abandoned. Finally in March 1863 the people selected a traditional camping site at Coranderrk (meaning white tea-tree) on Badgers Creek at Healesville and requested ownership. To expedite this, the Kulin applied to present gifts to the newly married Prince of Wales through Barkly at the Governor's levee in May 1863. They made a loyal address to the 'Great Mother Queen Victoria', promising to 'live like white men almost'. The qualifier 'almost' was significant. They presented weapons, rugs and baskets as presents for the soon-to-be-married Prince of Wales. They also spoke to Sir Henry Barkly about land. The DjaDjawurrung sent presents independently, including two letters and a crocheted collar for the Queen from thirteen-year-old Ellen, daughter of one of the Franklinford Aboriginal farmers, Dicky. The Kulin thereafter considered the gazettal of 931 hectares of reserve land at Coranderrk in June 1863 to be a gift from Queen Victoria, forming a powerful story of reciprocity: loyalty and fealty to a great kin in return for land of their own.[17]

The Kulin—mostly Daungwurrung, Woiwurrung and Boonwurrung at first, but later Wathawurrung and DjaDjawurrung—worked with a will on the Coranderrk land of their choosing. Their mentor John Green, a Scottish lay preacher who befriended the Woiwurrung in 1858, reported in July 1863 that they had erected sufficient huts to move from their traditional *willams* and had also 'made as many rugs, which has enabled them to buy boots, hats, coats, &c, &c, and some of them has even bought horses'.[18] In 1864 the Central Board reported: 'Wonga and Barak, who have made homes for themselves at Coranderrk, and who are now receiving instruction, are very intelligent men and in their behaviour would compare favourably with the better class of other races'.[19]

Parliament acted on the 1858–59 Select Committee, forming another in March 1860, which in June 1860 established the reserve and rationing system under a Central Board, local reserve managers and honorary correspondents.[20] Machinery was in place that—with tightening—managed Aboriginal people for the next one hundred years. The Central Board had seven members, self-improvers, but mostly radical and well-intentioned types, if ignorant of Aboriginal people. They initially relied on the ageing William Thomas, the Board's General Inspector of reserves, until he became ill and John Green replaced him. Thirty-nine honorary correspondents, who managed 23 depots, represented the Central Board in the countryside. The Board's General Secretary was Robert Brough Smyth, an intense workaholic of exacting standards and dictatorial temperament, whose public service career ended after an inquiry regarding his bullying of staff in another department.[21] The Board produced detailed annual reports, a mountain of correspondence, minutes and files, and prompted detailed inquiries in 1877 and 1881–82, which together asked 7,882 questions answered in 270 printed pages of minute type-face. This material created a massive body of information, albeit mostly from white perspectives.

Composed of liberal-minded men, the Board was initially very supportive as Aboriginal people lobbied for reserve lands on sites meaningful to them. The Board was advised by William Thomas who knew that 'hitherto, white-men have selected the spots. White-man's taste is widely different to the Aboriginal'. He warned about 'drawing them to a locality in which they took no interest, or felt no pleasure in encamping on'.[22] Thus the Gunai/Kurnai, like the Kulin of Coranderrk, determined the siting of two missions in Gippsland by steering missionaries to known and favoured camping sites at Lake Wellington and Lake Tyers.[23] A Warrnambool shipping company paid the fares of three Gunditjmara men to come by steamer to Melbourne to plead for land, which was soon reserved on the Hopkins River.

By 1863, seven reserves (also called stations and missions) and 23 handkerchief-size camping places and ration depots were in place, creating the most comprehensive reserve system in nineteenth-century Australia. Aboriginal people owned none of them as they were held in trust—such were the paternal views of the day. The reserves were small, being mostly under a thousand hectares, which made it difficult for Aboriginal residents to become self-supporting. They comprised about .03 per cent of the colony's land mass, an appalling outcome for the 'original owners of the soil', after 30 years of white colonisation. Five of the reserves were Christian missions, partially funded by the government, but salaried by the churches: the Anglican Yelta Mission west of Mildura (1855); the Moravian Ebenezer Mission at Lake Hindmarsh north of Dimboola (1859); the Anglican Framlingham Mission on the Hopkins River northwest of Warrnambool (1861); the Anglican Lake Tyers Mission, called Bung Yarnda by the Gunai/Kurnai, and separated by two kilometres of water from Lakes Entrance (1861); and the Presbyterian and Moravian Ramahyuck Mission on the Avon River at Lake Wellington outside Sale (1863). The two other reserves were government-controlled stations, namely: Coranderrk on Badgers Creek near Healesville (1863) and Lake Condah on the wetlands north of Portland (1867). Once Framlingham reverted to direct Board control in 1866 and Yelta closed in 1869, there were three missions and three government stations in Victoria, all under the oversight of the Central Board for the Aborigines. Most were 25 kilometres out of town—a convenient distance from temptation—which is why the Board revoked the two Kulin reserves at Warrandyte (Worri Yalloak) and at Mordialloc in 1862–63, considering them too close to Melbourne.

Understanding reserves

How can we evaluate Aboriginal lives on reserves? Each reserve had a unique history, whose details are beyond this study, and which has partly been told.[24] However, being under the one Board residents shared common experiences and outcomes, which have been explored by historians Michael Christie and Bain Attwood. Christie overviewed reserves until 1886 and observed that officials and missionaries aimed 'to eradicate Aboriginal culture and replace it with British forms', their work complementing 'the physically destructive work of the soldiers, police and pastoralists' on the frontier. He termed the reserves 'more like total institutions: they governed all aspects of the Aborigine's daily life'.[25] By 'total institutions' Christie meant institutions like convents, prisons and concentration camps, which sought to shape the lives and culture of their inmates in a 'total' way, as outlined in Erving Goffman's classic *Asylums*. While there is merit in this view, the reserves were never 'total', because finances, a lack of will, and the actions of Aboriginal people did not allow this. Christie, in discussing Aboriginal rebellions, implicitly acknowledges this.

Bain Atwood analysed the ways the missionaries, especially Rev. Friedrich Hagenauer at Ramahyuck, sought to replace Aboriginal ideas of place, time and the individual–community nexus with European notions, in order to remake Aboriginal people as civilised Christian farmers. Missionaries, he argued, won this battle through the power of food and the mission 'machinery', which reordered space and time, aided by the Central Board and its Aboriginal legislation. Attwood added that as Aboriginal people took up these new ideas, 'the seeds of oppression came to lie *within* Aborigines as well as *without*, making the task of liberating themselves even more herculean'.[26] His analysis is complex and incorporates discussion of the power of white paternalism and Aboriginal resistance.

However, Attwood underestimates the degree to which some Aboriginal people voluntarily embraced cultural enlargement and enrichment (not change). European ideas were often embraced in order to assist Aboriginal emancipation in the face of new realities, as Rene Maunier recognised decades ago in his *The Sociology of Colonies* (1949).[27] Aboriginal people did not just create oppressions 'within' by their actions, for their choices could liberate them. Schooling and Christianity, though shaped by European notions, produced literate Aboriginal people who petitioned Parliament for their rights and believed they were the equal of whites in the eyes of God and destined too for Heaven. Although Attwood sees Christianity as 'violent' and missions as 'oppressive', Aboriginal people became Christians by choice, something he only partially recognises. Their descendants have acknowledged this too, for instance as in Phillip Pepper's story of his Aboriginal forbears, *You Are What You Make Yourself to Be* (1980).[28] To see these people as lured or badgered into Christianity is condescending to those who chose to become 'settled down' Christians, and yet still desired to remain Aboriginal.

Coranderrk dwelling photographed by Frederich John Kruger. Dick and Ellen Richards are on the right. (BPA Album about 1870, courtesy of Museum Victoria, XP 1847)

Reserves are best understood in the light of prevailing attitudes of paternalism; a subtle two-way form of power, that had governed relations between people in the British world for centuries. Historian, David Roberts, argues that paternalism was a hierarchical relationship of ruling, guiding and helping from above with deference from below in return for protection. It was an intimate, face-to-face, two-way power relationship based on the view that all had an ordained place in the world: masters were to rule and underlings to serve, but with obligations on both sides.[29] The reserve managers, honorary correspondents and pastoralists who had the oversight of Aboriginal people, officially and unofficially, universally believed that they were 'inferior' and 'childlike', and thus needed ruling and helping. They constantly affirmed this to the 1877 Royal Commission on Aborigines, the words 'firmness and kindness' becoming a chant to describe how they must be managed. A number used the word 'patriarchal'. Reverend Hagenauer of Ramahyuck said 'the patriarchal system carried out hitherto is the only way to deal with them'. He acknowledged the importance of the personal relationship between missionary and an Aboriginal person: claiming rules and laws were secondary as 'the influence of the managers must be the thing which keeps discipline and order'.[30]

Many Aboriginal people acquiesced in this paternal relationship in the hard post-frontier colonial world, where protection and help was

needed, especially by children and the elderly. Such a reciprocal hierarchical relationship came naturally to people who traditionally had
elders to mentor, guide and protect them through the rigours of gaining
knowledge, becoming initiated, and living within a group surrounded
by *mainmet*—dangerous strangers. The people at Ramahyuck called Rev.
Friedrich Hagenauer and Louise, his wife, *moongan* and *yuccan*, meaning
'father' and 'mother'. They felt their power but also their parental affection
and respected them accordingly. William Thomas, Edward Parker, John
Green and their wives were also called 'father' and 'mother' in the local
dialect terms. Indigenous people and missionary were thus enmeshed
in a reciprocal relationship of two-way power and mutual dependence
that ebbed and flowed and varied from reserve to reserve. The reserves
were not 'concentration camps' as some have termed them, but places of
refashioned community and identity: places that became 'home', complete
with oppressions and opportunities like any home.

Within this paternalism, Aboriginal people developed a powerful
moral view of the world. It claimed they were a free people like other
British subjects and that Queen Victoria, her government and settlers
owed them a living because whites had occupied Aboriginal land and
because Aboriginal people had agreed to 'settle down' under the Queen
on reserves. James Dawson of Camperdown argued that the Framlingham
people were

> fully aware of the position the occupation of their country by the white
> man has placed them in, and of their strong claims on him for proper
> maintenance and protection. They are very sensitive on that point, and
> assert that they are entitled to be well housed, well clothed, and well fed, in
> consideration for the loss of their "hunting ground" and that they ought not
> to be called upon to work on the aboriginal farm without fair wages, any
> more than a hired white labourer.[31]

The 1877 Royal Commission was told repeatedly that Aboriginal people
existing on stations expected to be cared for. Hugh McLeod of Benyeo,
Apsley, declared that 'the Aborigines consider they have a right to be
kept by the squatters', and Joseph Watson of West Charlton observed of
the twelve Aboriginal people around his station that: 'most of them are
old and not fit for work; they have to be fed and clothed. Those who are
fit for work do so for a few months in the year, they expect to be fed and
clothed the remainder of the year'.[32]

Many who gave evidence to the Commission thought it fair to give
Aboriginal people sustenance, wracked as they were by the knowledge

and even guilt of possessing Aboriginal lands. They were inclined to be indulgent as they thought the problem was passing. A local correspondent, C. M. Officer of Mount Talbot, believed 'it is the inevitable fate of an inferior race to disappear before a superior; and in this belief I consider it to be the duty of the people causing this disappearance, not to look for the perpetuation of the race, but to endeavour to make the last remnants of it as happy and comfortable as is consistent with their position and habits of life'.[33] The Commissioners concurred, declaring: 'The care of the natives who have been dispossessed of their inheritance by colonization is a sacred obligation upon those who have entered upon the land'.[34] The danger of this view, which meshed with the Aboriginal moral idea of the government's duty and obligation to Aboriginal people, was a descent from self-sufficiency to dependency: a cancerous subjection that had the potential to sap Aboriginal initiative.

The reserve system aimed to order and control but these aims were only partially achieved. The Central Board issued instructions in 1864 for the regulation of reserves, ordering morning inspections of residents to determine 'that their persons are clean and their dresses clean and orderly', as well as daily inspections of huts, set school and work hours it enjoined the manager and matron to 'encourage all pursuits which are likely to preserve health, engender good feeling, and promote mirth and happiness amongst the Aborigines'. The regulations encouraged hunting, fishing and 'harmless amusement' one day a week. It is unclear how strictly rules were policed, but just as convicts found ways around regulations fifty years earlier, so did Aboriginal people, especially as managers of reserves varied in their desire to enforce them.[35]

The Central Board, experiencing difficulties 'with management of the blacks', especially their easy access to alcohol, soon sought greater powers.[36] After eight years of lobbying, Parliament finally obliged in 1869 with an Act for 'the Protection and Management of the Aboriginal Natives of Victoria'. The *Argus* argued: 'These children of nature, as they are poetically termed, are almost incapable of caring for or protecting themselves, and it is therefore necessary that the state with regards to them should assume a somewhat exceptional attitude'. It acknowledged that the Act contained 'very large powers'.[37] This 'management' Act, a sharp departure from earlier non-coercive policies, became a black mark in Aboriginal affairs and the history of human rights in Australia. It enabled regulations to prescribe where Aboriginal people should reside; what work contracts could be made with European employers on behalf of Aboriginal people who were 'able and willing to earn a living by their own exertions'; how their earnings might be apportioned and how the 'care, custody and education of their children' might be managed. It defined the term 'Aboriginal' culturally as well as racially, as: 'every Aboriginal native of Australia and every Aboriginal half-caste or child of a half-caste, such half-caste or child habitually associating and living with Aboriginals'. A magistrate could decide Aboriginality 'on his own view and judgement'.

Under the Act the Central Board became the Board for the Protection of the Aborigines with a revamped structure. The regulations issued in 1871 set out the six reserves (three missions and three stations) as prescribed places for Aboriginal people to live; set out the form of the work contracts and certificates for which they were eligible; modified the Board's meeting procedures; and gave the Board the power to remove 'any Aboriginal child neglected by its parents, or left unprotected' to a reserve, industrial school or reformatory. Reserve managers gained the power to compel those under fourteen to be in school, and to compel boys under fourteen and girls under eighteen 'to reside, and take their meals, and sleep, in any building set apart for such purposes.'[38]

The reserves grew gradually as Aboriginal people were drawn to them by their own people and Board staff. There must have been endless camp conversations about the benefits and problems of living permanently on missions but none have come down to us. Managers tried persuasion to boost reserve numbers, and were no doubt heavy-handed at times. Reverends Hagenauer and Bulmer and their Aboriginal emissaries made ventures into Gippsland camps in the late 1860s to convince people to come in.[39] The missionary Daniel Clarke attracted women and children to Framlingham by heavy persuasion, but this was resented by nine men who tried to reclaim them. In the scuffle a terrified 'half caste' girl reportedly thrust a gun into Clarke's hands and told him to use it against the Aboriginal men. The men were charged with assault, but Clarke was also reprimanded for keeping the women and children allegedly against their will, although this is unclear.[40]

As General Inspector for the Board, John Green was the most active in gaining new residents for the reserves. He claimed in 1877 to have brought in most of those at Coranderrk, although clearly a core of the Kulin desired to go there from the outset. However, he brought Aboriginal people from the Goulburn, Jim Crow (Mount Franklin), Sandhurst (Bendigo), the Terricks, the Murray and Echuca. He was adamant that all of them came voluntarily except for two women living 'immorally' at Mount Franklin on a pastoral run there. In all, Green brought sixty children to Coranderrk, many given up by their parents voluntarily as he convinced the parents 'that they were better off with

me than exposed to strong temptations'. Many parents followed later.[41]
People continually came in voluntarily over the years. In 1876 a group
of Bidwell people from the border region in far eastern Gippsland finally
came into Lake Tyers fifteen years after its creation. Reverend Bulmer
told the 1877 Royal Commission a measles epidemic drove them in:
'They got the idea that they were dying off, and they thought they
would be safer on the station, and also, that they wished to bring their
children to school. I had sent messages to them often in past years'.[42]

Life on reserves

The six Aboriginal reserves in Victoria experienced diverse development, making general statements about them difficult. The six
reserves comprised three governmental-controlled stations (Coranderrk, Framlingham and Lake Condah) and three Christian-controlled,
but government subsidised, missions (Ebenezer, Ramahyuck and
Lake Tyers). However, government policy and prevailing Christian
ideas made them similar, and their names, missions and stations,
even became interchangeable and are often termed 'reserves'. All
reserves started in a rudimentary way, the people living in traditional
miams until they were willing to leave them, or until bark and slab
huts could be built, followed by farm buildings, schools, boarding
houses and churches. At Lake Tyers as late as 1876, of the 94 people
resident, 57 were in traditional camps and only 20 resided in the six
huts. A boarding house, school, store, houses for the manager and
schoolmaster existed, but no church, which was not finished until
1878. Framlingham in 1875 had about thirteen small slab huts and
four *mia-mias* for the residents, but the store and the school shared
the one building. Nearby Lake Condah was much better off. A visitor
there in 1871 described the two dozen people's neat two-roomed slab
huts, some with verandahs: 'three or four have little fenced-in gardens,
gay with many old English flowers'. The huts were lined with engrav-
ings from English and other illustrated periodicals; some had 'white
window-blinds', cupboards displaying 'nice cups and saucers' and one
a bed 'covered with a bright patchwork quilt made on the station'. Lake
Condah had two cottages for the manager and schoolmaster and a
'substantial' stone school house.[43]

The reserves formed a hierarchy of excellence. In the Board's eyes
Ramahyuck was the most developed, with a physical layout designed for
surveillance. As Attwood has explained, the buildings were arranged on

three sides around a village green, all ordered by fences. The largest and most central building was the mission house, which overlooked the people's smaller cottages, the adjoining boarding house, school and church—the instruments of change and opportunity at Ramahyuck. The Aboriginal residents were only allowed to enter Hagenauer's study upon invitation, lined as it was with the registers and files that ordered their world.[44] Hagenauer helped John Bulmer, the missionary at Lake Tyers, to redesign it on the same plan in the mid 1870s, 'forming it in a square, and my house [said Bulmer] was to be at the top'.[45] The 1877 Royal Commissioners approved mightily of Hagenauer's ideas, commenting that 'the inculcation of tidiness forms part of civilization as well as of discipline'.[46] The well-ordered stone buildings and layout of Ebenezer mission met the Board's ideals as well. The Commissioners favoured missions as they were cheaper, being staffed and salaried by the churches, and more closely disciplined by dedicated and constant, religious staff. Reverends Spieseke, Hagenauer and John Bulmer were managers at the three Christian missions for over 110 years in total. The three Government-run stations fell short of these standards due to a lack of commitment as well as lack of funds and sufficient land to generate income for development. The Commissioners found that Coranderrk was unhealthy and untidy, Lake Condah needed 're-arrangement', and that Framlingham 'bears an unfavourable comparison with any of the others in the arrangement of the buildings, the management of the land, as well as the efforts to civilize the natives'. Order and regulation in 1877 were still more wishful thinking than reality on most reserves.[47]

However, Aboriginal people would probably have reversed the Board's ranking of the reserves, placing Coranderrk at the top during John Green's management (1863–1875), followed by Framlingham under William Goodall (1869–1882, 1885–1889) and Lake Tyers under John Bulmer's control (1861–1907). Green was a benign and consultative manager who treated the Coranderrk people as 'free and independent men and women', while 'remembering that they are but children in knowledge'.[48] Goodall was benign, gave the people freedom to move off the reserve for work and felt great affection for them, as did John Bulmer, who was kindly, tolerant and even interested in traditional Aboriginal culture. Even Ramahyuck's residents held Hagenauer in affection and publicly defended him, although he ruled like a patriarch. When asked about how he handled trouble on Ramahyuck he told the Royal Commission: 'I cannot speak about insubordination, because it never came before me'.[49] Hagenauer ruled by force of personality but also because he had perfected the 'machinery' of change at Ramahyuck and ruled the boarding house, the school and the church with an iron hand in a velvet glove. However, these instruments were not simply mechanisms of change, because young reserve residents also found them to be places of opportunity.

Coranderrk, the station near Healesville, began in 1863 with a boarding house for orphans. Within a year the Board was seeking children who were 'neglected', 'abandoned', orphaned or who might be 'surrendered' to Coranderrk by Aboriginal people. The Board found, unsurprisingly, that 'the blacks are reluctant to give up their children', and mooted legislation to force the issue.[50] The 1869 Act allowed for the removal of 'neglected' or 'unprotected' children to reserves. By 1872 Green was negotiating with Aboriginal groups on pastoral runs around Yackandandah and Wangaratta: 'I could not induce the old people to come with me, but they willingly gave me one girl (about twelve years of age), the other they would not give me, and I did not press them, as she was rather young (about four years)'. Another fifteen adults said they would come soon to Coranderrk, 'and as proof that they intended to keep their promise, they sent five children with me'. Several children remained 'who are on the list to be removed from the station'.[51] Green then moved wider afield to the Murray. By the following year the police were also involved in removing children from pastoral stations to reserves.

The removal policy existed in the name of protection. Until 1874 it was practised fairly benignly by John Green, as he usually respected the wishes of Aboriginal parents, whom he saw as 'free people'. Robert Wandin, a Woiwurrung man, told an 1881 inquiry that John Green 'took me when I was a baby, and looked after me as if I was one of his sons; and Mrs Green was very good too'. Of Green's gathering in of children Wandin stated that 'he never took them against their will. If they like to come down he fetches them down'.[52] The missionaries Bulmer and Carl Kramer (the latter replaced Spieseke at Ebenezer), also argued publicly that orphans did not exist in Aboriginal society, meaning that any children without natural parents would be cared for by kin. Kramer declared: 'the children are never abandoned; some other blacks take charge of them like the parents'.[53] Reverend Mackie, who visited Coranderrk regularly, agreed, adding that even illegitimate children of 'mixed descent' were cherished, and that their mothers 'would never dream of exposing or abandoning them'.[54] However, the Commissioners argued that 'no false sentimentality' should prevent the gathering in of children. 'It might be urged that they are happy where

Men of Coranderrk, around 1885. Robert Wandin is in the middle row, second from left (possible names of some others are in Museum Victoria's files).
(F. Shaw Collection, courtesy of Museum Victoria, XP2166)

they are, and that it were better to leave them alone; but it must not be forgotten that leaving them alone is, in fact, abandoning them to lower and lower stages of degradation.' White moral fears about Aboriginal camp life overwhelmed Aboriginal assurances of the protection provided children by kinship, and ushered in more hard-line practices.[55]

The Board sought to remake children through separation from their parents and through education. How far this power was used is unclear, but all reserves except Framlingham had a boarding house by 1870, those at Ramahyuck and Lake Tyers being run by Aboriginal couples, respectively the Camerons and O'Rourkes (then Thorpes). Boarding houses were formalised under regulations of February 1871, which gave managers the power to require all boys under 14 and girls under 18 to be placed there. Effectively, only those already on reserves were institutionalised. The boarding house was that part of a reserve that most nearly approached a 'total institution', although the less well-organised reserves found it difficult to restrict boarding house access. Ramahyuck had the most developed system to separate children from kin with its boarding house fenced off from the rest of the village. However, even at Ramahyuck there were opportunities for family to see each other as they were on the same site; overall, however, kin ties were weakened by the forced separation. The children were also separated from those of the opposite sex by partitions and separate beds in the dormitories and by separate playgrounds.[56] This was very different to the easy mixing of pre-pubescent children that occurred in the camps.

Coranderrk, where most 'orphans' were taken, had up to 40 children in its boarding house, all of whom were closely watched and kept under lock and key at night and during matron Halliday's absence. However, the matron's own teenage daughters were educated in the 1870s with the orphan girls and slept in their dormitory as well. James Deans, the schoolteacher, said Halliday's daughters 'make themselves very sociable with them'.[57] The same watchfulness was imposed on young women from both groups in a time of strict Victorian morality. The dormitory girls, mostly of 'mixed descent', were educated, reared and trained in European household management and were free of arranged marriage controls. The anthropologist Diane Barwick has argued: 'They could support themselves by working as assistant teachers or dormitory matrons at stations or in domestic service elsewhere, and could marry as they pleased. These completely emancipated girls became in turn exemplars as they and their husbands were given charge of the dormitories.'[58] Thus even the dormitory that separated families in a most terrible way had some opportune outcomes.

Schooling was another mechanism of change for Aboriginal reserve children, and it was compulsory, as for all Victorian children after 1872. Yet it was not without its opportunities as well. There is scattered evidence that Aboriginal families sought education for their children as a passport into the new world, like Billibellary had done in the 1840s. Some adults came onto reserves for the purpose of having their children taught. William Goodall, manager at Framlingham, in 1877 said the young men 'craved' for a schoolmaster as they had only him to teach them. He found them 'very quick ... much more intelligent than white'. Framlingham gained a teacher in 1878, fifteen years after most other reserves.[59] The 1877 Royal Commissioners continually asked about Aboriginal ability and the suitability of the curriculum, and were told by most witnesses that Aboriginal children were as able as white children and could manage the lessons. Miss Robertson, the teacher at Coranderrk in the mid 1870s, thought the children 'just as capable of receiving instruction as the whites'. Her successor, James Deans, agreed that 'they are quite as intelligent as the average class of white children, and I should be glad for the inspector to compare them with the white children at Healesville.'[60]

When Ramahyuck was brought into the national school system (as State School 1088) and compared to other schools, it shone. In 1873 it achieved a 100 per cent pass rate, the first school to do so since the passage of the free, secular and compulsory Education Act of 1872. Inspector Charles Topp wrote: 'The children showed not only accuracy in their work, but also exhibit much intelligence. Excellent progress is shown. The discipline is very good'. The perfect result was repeated in 1874 and dipped only to 95 per cent in 1875, while the average across the colony in those three years was 58, 63 and 70 per cent respectively.[61] However, Rev. Carl Kramer, the Ramahyuck teacher, spoke of the strain on both teacher and students of achieving these results. He dealt in the stereotypes of his day, adding that the Aboriginal children were no more apt than white children, perhaps not as quick, although the 'half-caste are a little smarter' than those of the white labouring class.[62] Reverend Hagenauer agreed that the 'half castes are superior on the whole in their mental capacities', and also agreed that the teaching of Aboriginal children at first was arduous.

But success flowed from the schooling. Hagenauer claimed that those who had finished school used the reserve library, reading religious tracts, works of history and geography and also 'yellow-back novels'—popular crime and romance reading of the day of which he disapproved—when they obtained them. Most were numerate, for all had money boxes, saving and paying small expenses from them; one had a bank account and another even held some mining shares. Reserve residents read newspapers, studied the advertisements and mail-ordered clothes from Melbourne, paying the accounts themselves. Reverend Bulmer wrote that mail-ordering happened at Lake Tyers as well.[63] Views of Aboriginal schooling varied however. In 1889 Ramahyuck's teacher and former missionary, Heinrich Hahn, claimed there was 'too much laziness which the teacher is powerless to correct'.[64] However, Hahn was embittered and made these remarks while seeking a transfer.

Ramahyuck's parents used their literacy skills to protest injustice and promote their moral view of the world. In March 1892 five mothers claimed two new teachers 'demoralised' their children, calling them 'horribly nasty creatures'. Again, in April 1901, Emily Stephen, Alice Login, Eliza Edwards, Florence Moffat, Helen Hood and Albert Darby protested in a neatly penned and argued letter against the school's closure. They recalled 'the promise from succeeding Ministers of the Government to us that our school should stand an Aboriginal School'. The alternate school at Perry Bridge was unsatisfactory as it was 'too far for the little ones' and they could not 'conscientiously send through the bush' the bigger girls. Hageneaur supported the parents in both protests, reiterating that 1088 was the first school ever to get a 100 per cent pass rate.[65]

Missionaries and those who were interested in and recognised the children's abilities gained the best out of the children, although school equipment, teaching skills and home support also shaped outcomes. At Lake Tyers John Bulmer taught school until 1872 when a German seaman, Lewis Hallier, took over for the six years to 1878. Both were sympathetic and committed teachers and thus were liked. Between 1879 and 1891 the teacher at Lake Tyers was David Morris, who dabbled in the distractions of a struggling farm near the reserve. Morris wanted the curriculum simplified. He rightly pointed to the fact that English was the Aboriginal children's second language, and was not practised at home—a place where homework was also impossible to complete because of the living conditions in camp and *miams*. But ignoring these disadvantages, and perhaps his own inadequacies, Morris then claimed his pupils were 'simply savages' with 'low' intellect, adding: 'what an English child of 6 or 7 could readily do would be an enigma to a black child of 13 or 14'.[66]

Ramahyuck residents in late nineteenth century, L–R: Tommy Scott, Alice Logan holding an unknown child, Adam Cooper and Bragen Scott. (A. & M. Jackomos Collection, courtesy of Museum Victoria, XP4257)

The children's educational outcomes looked similarly bleak under Thomas Starr, Morris's replacement, who believed that 'the children have not naturally the same degree of intelligence that European children have'. Starr, a compulsory transfer to the reserve, left after three years. The comments of these men also reveal that Aboriginal ways and language were still strong at Lake Tyers around 1890—Aboriginal people had not yet been successfully 'remade' there.[67]

While the boarding house and school aimed to 'civilise' the people, the church building and its rituals sought to Christianise them. Christianising occurred on all reserves, for even the

government stations were run by Christian men—such as Green and
Goodall—who believed in evangelising Aboriginal people to the knowledge of Christian salvation. Despite the claim by historian Michael
Christie that Aboriginal people found 'their fundamentalist version of the
gospel unpalatable',[68] many of the younger and a few of the older people
embraced this instrument of change, and at times, enthusiastically. Their
acceptance of Christianity was perhaps aided by the traditional emphasis
on religion in Aboriginal life, an emphasis weakened by still-recent
disruptions of the people's association with land, sacred sites and the
accompanying rituals. Christianity and its rituals thus fulfilled a cultural
vacuum and provided new ways of creating social interaction and a feeling
of community.

Sincere and deep conversions occurred amongst Aboriginal people in
the reserve period. Baptisms of the young had taken place in the 1840s but
an adult conversion, the true mark of comprehending Christianisation,
had eluded the churches in the earlier period of contact. However, one of
the earliest instances of voluntary adult Aboriginal conversion, uncovered
by historian Jan Critchett, did not even occur on a reserve. In 1853, Nora
Villiers was baptised in western Victoria at the age of seventeen. After
her marriage to Colin Hood, Rev. Hamilton pronounced her 'a sincere
and intelligent Christian' and baptised her children. The Pacific missionary, Rev. John Paton, visited her in 1863 and was so impressed with her
spirituality that he used letters from Nora in his Melbourne fundraising
campaign. In one letter she wrote: 'I am telling the blacks always about
God our Saviour and the salvation of their souls'. Nora appealed for more
missionaries.[69]

The most famous adult Aboriginal conversion in colonial Victoria
(though not the first as has been claimed) was that of Nathanael Pepper
at the Ebenezer Mission in 1860. His conversion has been written about
by his grandson, the late Phillip Pepper, who records that Pepper even
chose his own baptismal name. The historian Robert Kenny has written
incisively about Pepper's conversion. Kenny reveals Nathanael's careful
and heart-felt decision, a vision of hope for him amidst a destructive
frontier.[70] Nathanael and his brother Phillip, who also declared his
life for Jesus, like Nora Hood, went on to evangelise among their
own people.

By the 1870s conversions and baptisms were taking place willingly
on all the reserves, as many Aboriginal people embraced a new way to
give meaning to their existence. In 1877 Rev. Hagenauer told the Royal
Commissioners—although he had a vested interest in claiming
converts—that 'I could give you over a hundred instances of men,

consistent Christians to the end, really and truly from first to last.[71] Many
of the younger ones in the dormitories grew up in and professed Christian
beliefs, a phenomenon which Rev. Alex Mackie, visiting Coranderrk in
the 1870s, affirmed. Reverend Robert Hamilton, who visited Aboriginal
deathbeds on the same reserve, said many people 'were peaceful and
delighted in having hymns sung and in speaking about the way of salvation through Jesus Christ'.[72]

John Green, a lay Presbyterian who held twice daily prayers while
he was manager at Coranderrk and four services on Sundays, said the
residents came to his prayer-services 'almost to a man and woman'.[73]
However, what meaning did their attendance have? Not all reserve dwellers
were believers. Many, especially the older or more traditional people,
were what we might call 'rice Christians': that is, those who went along
with the flow for an advantage or a peaceful life. John Bulmer, like all
preachers, told biblical stories and added anecdotes in his services. He
wrote: the Lake Tyers people 'always listened', 'seemed interested', and
'understood what was said'.[74] Their interest is not surprising for a people
from an oral tradition—or in the process of transition from one. There
was wondrous talk by Bulmer and others of ancient times: of miracles,
of wrath and revenge, of journeys to a promised land, of blood spilt
and of a moving death on a Cross—and this suffered for others! These
parables, which parallel in some ways the stories of great Aboriginal
ancestors, also helped fill in their days in this new life on the reserve.
The people expressed great interest in singing too, and it is here on the
reserves that such hymns as 'Rock of Ages' and 'The Old Rugged Cross'
burned into the minds of many Aboriginal people, so that they are still
sung at funerals and wakes today. The rituals of church life—baptism,
communion, and marriage ceremonies—and even the sparse rituals of
evangelical Protestant churches such as the Moravian and Presbyterian,
struck a chord in a highly ritual people.

Christian marriage was the ceremony which most appealed to Aboriginal people for a diversity of reasons. First it combined their liking for
European dress—Revs Stahle and Bulmer both commented on how the
younger reserve residents loved fashionable attire and spent freely when
the hawkers came to the reserves with their wagons loaded with goods.[75]
Many of the young women sewed, some with newfangled machines, and
trimmed their dresses and hats with ribbons and lace from the hawkers.
Also, younger people wanted to experiment with European forms: the
wedding being a key symbolic moment in a life. The wedding dress,
ceremony and photographs also enabled them to assert their equality
with other Victorians.

There was also a keen interest among some Aboriginal people for what they call a 'likeness' or photograph. A delightful series of letters sent by some of the young people of Ramahyuck, including Bessy Cameron and Harry Flower, to Captain Charles Darby, ship's captain on the Melbourne–Gippsland Lakes route, constantly referred to their desire to exchange 'likenesses' with Darby.[76] This desire for 'likenesses' was apparently shared by many of those who married. In public and private collections there are many surviving wedding photographs of Aboriginal people dressed and posed like any other newly-married couples of the era.

The wedding bespoke change as well. Traditional forms of bestowal and elopement still happened on reserves in the early years, especially at Lake Tyers, and continued among the traditionalists off the reserves, but Christian, free-choice marriage became more common.[77] The anthropologist Diane Barwick observed that on many reserves Aboriginal people voluntarily banned traditional bestowals, and Bulmer wrote that by the end of the century the people 'consider a man not really (*maak*) married unless he has been wedded by a clergyman'.[78] Even traditionalists off the reserves saw the need for change, partly because the reserves, controlled by the missionaries, had so many young marriageable people as residents. As one elder from the Monaro country said when he and his daughter came into Lake Tyers: 'Marry her in your own way to a young man here, like the white people; I cannot because it is against my law. You marry them, and I will come back again'.[79]

The reserve system was also to teach time and labour discipline. When Aboriginal people felt they were free and properly consulted, as in Green's time as manager at Coranderrk, they worked with a will. He told them and the people of other reserves he inspected that the land would be theirs if they worked hard. Under more authoritarian management the people were disinclined to work and were threatened with withdrawal of rations. Work for rations became the Board's regime. However, this clashed with the ideas of Aboriginal people, who expected to be rationed in exchange for dispossession, and expected to be paid for their work just like free people. Within three years of Ramahyuck's establishment, Hagenauer was forced to pay wages to get the people to work. John Green thought it unwise to 'pay them for working on their own station, except [if] it was from the produce raised on the station by their own labor'.[80] However, Green was soon paying wages at Coranderrk due to the same pressure. Green also paid these workers as their efforts produced food to support many orphans and elderly people to whom the workers were 'in no way related but as

Lake Tyers residents with John Bulmer (front left) in 1886, photographed by Nicholas Caire. (Courtesy of Museum Victoria, XP2647)

countrymen'. A dozen men at Coranderrk—but, according to the idea of the day, no women—were paid between three and ten shillings weekly, according to their skill. Green soon believed they worked harder when paid and developed a more 'manly spirit'.[81]

Aboriginal residents forced wages at Ramahyuck, Lake Tyers and Ebenezer as well, although not at the rate of white workers or what they might receive outside. Bulmer, for instance, paid at half the white rate. However, the shearers at Ebenezer had to be paid at the same rate as white workers to keep them on the reserve. Due to lack of funds residents at Framlingham received only rations and the occasional gratuity for a fencing job or the like, which is why most left the reserve to undertake paid work.

The lack of pay on reserves was a significant reason why so many Aboriginal people either lived off the reserves or constantly moved between the reserves and the wider world. The Royal Commissioners in 1877 recognised this fact, which is why they urged that Aboriginal people should be paid for their labour—on a contract not a time basis—and that a cost-price reserve store be established, stocked with items 'suited to the tastes and wishes of' the people. The Commissioners aimed for stable reserves that would encourage 'industry and the saving of money received as wages'.[82] The missionaries welcomed these proposals for their fervent desire was to maintain permanent self-sustaining reserves isolated from the temptations of the wider world.

Aboriginal health

In the early years a health crisis threatened the viability of the reserves. While the Aboriginal population count was never exact, fairly accurate figures exist from the 1850s. In the 1850s when Aboriginal people were free to move unimpeded by governments, the population had declined by several hundred, from just over to just under 2,000, about one per cent decline per year. There were 1,907 Aboriginal people in Victoria in 1861 and 1,500 in 1874, a decline of about two per cent a year in this time. However, by 1877 there were just over a thousand, a further decline of almost 500 in four years—an average of about eight per cent decline per year for those four years.[83] Clearly the free life of the 1850s was far healthier than the sedentary life of reserve housing. It was little wonder that most witnesses to the Royal Commission of 1877 believed Aboriginal people were headed for extinction.

In the mid 1870s, all the reserves were struck by epidemics, exacerbated by poor diet and housing conditions. In early 1875 measles infected reserve dwellers, killing sixteen at Ebenezer, six at Framlingham, six at Coranderrk and four at Lake Condah, mostly from chest and other complications.[84] No figures are available for the other reserves or for those off the reserves, but they were certainly affected as well. Chest diseases were particularly rife. In 1875 there were 31 deaths at Coranderrk out of a population of 150, almost 20 per cent in one year!

Dr W. McCrae, the Chief Medical Officer of Victoria, reported in 1876 that the Aboriginal death rate was eleven times that of the general population. His critical survey of Coranderrk found that the houses there were poorly constructed, with cracks so large as to make them like 'bird cages', while their earthen floors were so poorly drained that the water rose to the surface when it rained. These 'wretched hovels' gave the inhabitants little resistance to diseases and he feared an outbreak of scarlatina might sweep them 'away altogether'. Toilets were constructions over mere holes in the ground, scattered about and 'insufficient in number for the wants and decency of the population'. The kitchen was 'wretched' and the children's dining room 'utterly inadequate'. Several families had built their own weatherproof houses and others had put in flooring to ward off 'the fatal effects of damp in the winter time'. McCrae recommended extensive redesign and rebuilding of the settlement, and the provision of toilets, better drainage, a new kitchen, dining room and school room, a hospital, higher meat rations and monthly visits by a local medical practitioner. Three years later he reported angrily that little had been done by the Board.

The Board rejected McCrae's views on the grounds that people on all the Aboriginal reserves had lung problems no matter what the nature of the climate or the buildings. The Vice-Chairman, Henry Jennings, believed the illness was 'a disease of the lungs peculiar to the natives'. He described it as a 'spitting of blood' that affected reserve residents between 12 and 25 years old.[85] What Jennings described was old-fashioned, murderous tuberculosis. Diane Barwick has meticulously analysed all 844 Aboriginal deaths (698 of them 'full bloods'), on and off the reserves, between 1876 and 1912. She found that 398 deaths were of children under fourteen years, and that forty per cent of the children died from respiratory diseases, with dysentery, gastroenteritis, associated high fevers and 'prematurity and weakness' at birth causing a further ten per cent of deaths respectively. Half of the 446 adult deaths, mostly occurring before the age of forty, were due to respiratory diseases, especially tuberculosis and pneumonia; fifteen per cent of deaths were from old age, with liver and heart disease being the other significant causes. Aboriginal people were victims not only of respiratory disease but also of contemporary medical knowledge, for the theory of germs and contagion was not yet accepted, so that tuberculosis and other chest diseases were not managed by isolation. Barwick also calculated that an horrendous fifty per cent of all Aboriginal children born in the second half of the nineteenth century died before they were one year old. Fortunately, high marriage and re-marriage rates and family sizes of about five children meant that the group survived.[86]

One of the frightening things about illnesses for the people at Coranderrk were their trips to Melbourne for treatment. The Board under Captain Page, its new Secretary, rarely bothered to meet people off the coach from Healesville and Aboriginal patients often faced a night without lodgings before meeting a strange doctor or hospital on their own. Friends like Rev. Robert Hamilton and Anne Bon, the latter from a Mansfield pastoral family which employed Aboriginal workers, often came to their rescue, but it was terrifying nonetheless. Hamilton said most Aboriginal patients felt 'isolated and lost' in these circumstances, especially the elderly and more traditional.[87] Matron Harriet Wylie of the Eye and Ear Hospital recalled a young girl who 'screamed dreadfully' and would not stay at the hospital.[88] No doubt young children generally were terrified by hospitals, but the Coranderrk children were less used to Melbourne and the medical world than other Victorian children. In 1881 William Barak, a Coranderrk elder who had just lost his wife through consumption, brought his son David to Melbourne for treatment for chest disease. David was so terrified that he fought to leave the hospital with his father, biting the arm of a staff member. William Barak was asked not to return because of the commotion, and David died alone in the Melbourne Hospital a few days later, leaving Barak childless.[89] The secretary of the Melbourne Hospital told an inquiry that Aboriginal people who died were not buried by the Board, but by the hospital in the 'same way as other people who have no friends'—alone and far from country, which is precisely what they dreaded about the trip to Melbourne to seek medical care.[90]

Reserves had become unhealthy places by the 1870s due to contagion spread by poor living conditions and medical ignorance. They were also places of momentous change, both imposed and embraced, as the people became agriculturalists and often Christian. Most had assumed a 'Christian' and a family name by this time, often given to them by missionaries or employers, and many could sign their names. Reserves became 'home' to a generation of people born on them. However, in the 1880s these people faced new difficulties as governments reconsidered the very existence of reserves. But first we must explore, as much as we are able, the lives of the other Aboriginal people: those living off the reserves.

8

Country 'Wanderers'

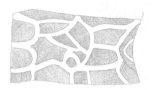

The reserve system created in 1861 was tightened in 1869 to give the Board for the Protection of Aborigines powers over Aboriginal employment, residence and the care of Aboriginal children. The aim was to locate Aboriginal people on reserves for their protection and control. As supposed 'savages' moving to a 'civilised' state, they were to become settled and taught the arts of civilisation: literacy, agriculture, work discipline, Christianity and European domestic life. Under the 1869 Act, the Board could prescribe places where Aboriginal people 'shall reside', namely the six reserves in existence at the time. However, despite these aims and powers, the Board lacked the resources and the will to gather all Aboriginal people onto these reserves. Besides, many Aboriginal people resisted the Board's efforts to centralise them.

The census of 1877 revealed that the Aboriginal population had dropped disastrously to just 1,067 people, comprising perhaps 100 family groups and scores of lone individuals. Of the 1,067 people counted, 774 people were described as 'Aboriginals', 293 as 'half castes', and of the total, 297 were children. For every six males there were four females. The census revealed (see table on following page) that just under a half lived on reserves. However, as many people came and went from the reserves, the majority had some experience of reserve life. As the table reveals, adult males of 'mixed descent' were over-represented off the reserves, and children, women and those of 'full descent' were over-represented on the reserves. The fact that two-thirds of children were on reserves is proof of the success of John Green and others in 'bringing-in' the children. The slight predominance of those of 'full descent' on the reserves was probably due to the movement of some of the elderly onto the reserves over time. Reverend Carl Kramer reported in 1881 that

Aboriginal People in Victoria On and Off the Reserves 1877 Census

Place	'Full Descent'				'Mixed Descent'				Total
	Adults		Children		Adults		Children		
	Male	Female	Male	Female	Male	Female	Male	Female	
Reserves									
Coranderrk	22	16	6	7	15	24	19	26	135
Lake Condah	23	13	6	9	4	7	8	11	81
Ebenezer	17	4	6	5	6	6	7	9	60
Framlingham	29	11	4	1	5	8	4	7	69
Lake Tyers	18	18	16	10	0	2	1	3	68
Ramahyuck	18	12	11	12	2	4	6	8	73
Total Reserves	127	74	49	44	32	51	45	64	486
Other Areas (off the reserves)									
North-West	216	94	14	5	15	9	16	8	377
South-West	44	19	2	3	12	6	5	5	96
North-East	15	12	3	1	1	1	0	1	34
South-East	23	11	8	9	4	2	8	7	72
Melbourne		1				1			2
Total Other Areas	298	137	27	18	32	19	29	21	581
Overall Total	425	211	76	62	64	70	74	85	1067

some of the Wimmera people had recently moved to Ebenezer: 'they are all old people, and several of them are blind'.[1]

The census of 1877 also revealed a thinly dispersed population, listing 61 places of residence for Aboriginal people besides the six reserves. These have been reduced to four compass segments of the colony in the table, plus a fifth for Melbourne, as two women were living in Melbourne: one in Cheltenham, and another in Fitzroy. Of the 581 people living off the reserves, two-thirds or 377 of them (mostly men), lived in the far north-west, primarily along the Murray. Moving west to east along the Murray, there were 24 at Ned's Corner, 15 at Kulkyne, 25 at Mildura, 114 at Swan Hill and 24 at nearby Cowana, 53 at Ulupna near Barmah, and 29 at Towanninie. About 80 lived to the south in the Wimmera. Another 96 lived in the south-west of the colony scattered in ones and twos, except for a few groups: 15 at Casterton, 12 at Cavendish and 12 also at Merino. In the south-east 72 people lived off the missions, including 40 at Bairnsdale, 16 at Livingstone and 11 at Bendoc. In the north-east only 34 people lived off the reserves, including 18 at

Wangaratta and 9 at Alexandra. Of the 61 non-reserve places where Aboriginal people were recorded as living in March 1877, 40 had five or less people living there: a family group perhaps. Eighteen places had just one Aboriginal person. The maintenance of tradition and the avoidance of loneliness in the aftermath of colonisation were increasingly real problems as the population declined—unless people travelled around.

Working off the reserves

Most of the able-bodied living off the reserves worked part of the year to sustain themselves and their young or elderly kin. Pastoralist Hugh Jamieson at Mildura reported in 1867 that 30 Aboriginal people were shearing for him and 'they spent nearly all the money they got on stores for themselves and others (about one hundred in all)'.[2] Other Murray River stations employed Aboriginal workers who supplemented their income with fishing and hunting or with supplies from the Board's scattered ration stations. Others moved off the reserves to work, returning on the completion of their contracts. Prevailing gender ideas, whether traditional or European is unclear, meant the men mostly did outdoor station work—sheep washing and shearing, fencing and droving—while the women generally did domestic work. The men earned 10 to 15 shillings a week, about half the rate of white workers, but double reserve wages. Indeed, some reserve workers received no pay, only their keep and housing.[3] Most workers moved around the stations like other contractors, but some worked permanently on the one property. Alexander Dennis of Tarndwarncoort station, Mount Gellibrand, wrote that Andrew Murray employed a Gulidjan woman Coinmaninin and her youngest 'half-caste' son Dickey [Richard Sharp], 'year after year, and I believe [she] is as well conducted as any servant'.[4]

Aboriginal workers were often admired, although their lack of constancy was criticised by some. Hugh Jamieson of Mildura stated he 'would rather have the Aborigines to be among his sheep than white men', while a John Jackson of Sandford who employed Jacky White and his wife, 'prefers him to a white man' and was going to build them a hut.[5] Reverend Hamilton employed a young 'half caste' woman as a domestic servant in Fitzroy under license from the Board for over five years. He deemed her completely 'faithful and honest', allowing her to handle the house-keeping money, and not needing 'to restrict her too much with regard to coming in at night, when she goes out to meetings'.[6] John Ralston at Casterton had a girl training as a housemaid at £10 a year, 'and she is doing better than several white girls we have had'. However, two married couples without families also living on Ralston's property—though good workers—were troublemakers, so he banished them from his station, being unable to control them any other way.[7] Mr Vectis in the Wimmera reported that he would not 'employ any of them another season, because they expend nearly all their earnings in drink. They will not take their payment in clothes'. He disliked not their work, but their independence, their desire for cash wages, and their spending preferences.[8]

Sometimes luck also produced cash for Aboriginal people, particularly for those who found gold as they journeyed. The Daisy Hill people from the Maryborough region, on a number of occasions in the mid 1860s, found surface gold nuggets in the Amherst–Talbot region worth £7 to £120, commenting after one find: 'white-fellow dig for gold and blackfellow pick it up'.[9] Three reports suggested they spent the money on clothing, dressing themselves in black suits, bell toppers and crinolines and 'swaggered about Amherst, cutting such airs as to greatly amuse everyone who chanced to see them'.[10] One group impressed the white community mightily by travelling to repay a debt to a white man. They had to run the gauntlet of tempting 'grog' shanties along the way, but only had ginger beer, one elder remarking to a shanty owner who tempted them: 'blackfellow could be a gentleman as well as white fellow'.[11]

Sport was also a money spinner. A local guardian, J. McLeod of Castlemaddie station, reported in 1877 that some Aboriginal men earned 'large sums by running and jumping at athletic sports'.[12] John Bulmer recorded the 'great love of sport' of Lake Tyers men who 'enter their names for every event in the district', then trained for them. Bulmer added that 'as they generally excel in most of the games which are in vogue, so they are sought by Europeans to compete'.[13] He bemoaned their subsequent loss of interest in steady 'manual labour', forgetting that he himself had taught them to play cricket in the mid-1860s.[14] The Wotjobaluk/Wergaia men in the north-west similarly engaged in country sports and regattas. Robert Kinnear, a Wergaia man who was born at Stawell in 1851 and mostly lived at Ebenezer, won the celebrated foot race, the Stawell Gift, in 1883.[15]

Some pastoralists made written contracts with their Aboriginal servants even before the 1869 Act introduced such agreements. In 1865 John and Mary Ann Jackson of Sandford, near Casterton, entered an apprenticeship contract with Sarah, whose surname Sandford was taken from the name of the place. She was of 'mixed descent' with her mother,

Looy, described as 'Aboriginal'. The contract stated that Sarah would be apprenticed for five years by 'her own free will' and the 'full consent' of Looy, who desired to have Sarah 'delivered from evil and vagrant ways'. Sarah would be taught the duties of a household servant and seamstress, and must 'conduct herself with honesty, sobriety, and good temper and respect' and not engage in lewd conversation, gambling or other immorality. She would be given work only appropriate for her 'years, strength, and sex', chastised only as a parent might correct their child, taught to read and write and to become a faithful member of the Church of England so as to become 'a good Christian and dutiful subject of Our Sovereign Lady the Queen'. She would be fed 'wholesome food in sufficient quantity', clothed in 'decent apparel', lodged, supplied with medicine in sickness, guarded from harm and paid £25 at the end of her term. The agreement, witnessed by two justices of the peace, was signed by the four parties, Sarah signing her name and Looy making an 'x' mark. John Jackson, who recommended agreements like this to the 1877 Royal Commissioners, said that Sarah 'is now married to a white man who has a selection, and she is now one of the most thrifty wives about, making her own and children's clothes, and most of her husband's. Having her apprenticed hindered the tribe taking her away, which they often tried'.[16]

Under its 1869 Act the Board introduced its own three-month work contracts and certificates in 1871 to manage work off the reserves. Employers applied to the Board's local Guardian for approval of their contracts. The Board could determine that the money be paid to the local Guardian and applied at his discretion for the welfare of the worker or his family. How many employers ever applied for approval of contracts is unknown. The anecdotal evidence from the 1877 Royal Commission is that such contracts were unusual for those living off the reserves and a free market operated instead. Thus, Aboriginal people off the reserves generally had control of their wages to the lament of those who disapproved of their spending decisions.

The Board certainly issued work certificates for reserve residents to accept outside work. The holder was identified by name and approximate age and height, 'having represented himself as able and willing to earn a living by his own exertions', and was entitled to enter into a binding contract of service with a European who was able to 'harbour him' without incurring a penalty. The employer was not 'to sell or give him any intoxicating liquor'. Work certificates, 89 of them, were issued between September 1871 and June 1874, all to men, except for one issued to Sophy, wife of Alec Campbell. The certificates revealed that the average age of the male workers was 31.2 years, the oldest being 50 and the youngest 18, and that the men on average were 169 centimetres tall and ranged in height from 150 to 188 centimetres. Sophy Campbell was 18 years old and a tiny 147 centimetres. These people were shorter than those described in the impressions of white observers at first contact, suggesting the effects of low or poor nutrition in the generation born after white contact. A dozen bore scars on the head, no doubt from fights—John Castella, 35, carrying 'a sabre cut on the side of one eye'— while one was deaf and two had lost an eye. Most had two names, with surnames largely bestowed by employers, names that still flourish in Aboriginal Victoria today—Moffatt, Mobourn, Mullett, Austin, Hood and Clark (with and without an 'e'). Five had a single name—Timothy, 28; Toby, 26; Edgar, 25; Luaky, 35; and Talgium, 23—while three, all from Lake Tyers, had descriptive names common on the frontier: King Charley, Big Charley and Billy the Bull.[17]

Some Aboriginal workers performed specialist work using traditional skills. At Linton, west of Ballarat, Aboriginal men in 1862 were employed at a house carving uprights for an alcove. The designs were to 'represent a serpentine coil, similar to that on the shields that the chiefs of the tribe use in times of warfare'.[18] Aboriginal people also played a part in rescues. Tally-ho rescued a woman and child from the Campaspe River near Echuca in 1867, while Aboriginal men, using their swimming skills, dragged a father and daughter from the Murray in 1868 after their boat had sunk, the latter surviving.[19] Hugh Clark and John Hennessy each received a Royal Humane Society bronze medal in 1886 for rescuing R. S. Sarlinens from a swollen creek at Avenel near Seymour.[20]

Trackers using traditionally-honed skills of observation and deduction helped find people lost in the bush, the most famous instance being the locating of the three Duff children in August 1864. The hero of this story, however, was Jane Duff, aged seven, whose resourcefulness helped her brothers survive nine days in the bush near Natimuk on the edge of the Little Desert. Her deeds were featured in the *Fourth Grade Victorian School Reader* for a generation after 1930. After the main search for the children was abandoned amidst rain and hopelessness, some Aboriginal men from Kaniva, including Dick-a-Dick (King Richard Jungunjinanuke), together with Jane's father, actually found the children.[21] The Aboriginal tracker's role became legendary in colonial society. The Victorian Police always had Aboriginal men on call for this duty.

Another group of Aboriginal men, mostly Jardjadwarli from western Victoria, used their traditionally honed hand–eye skills to play cricket and earn fame, though not fortune. Cricket was played by many Aboriginal people for leisure on reserves and stations. Reverend Hagenauer encouraged cricket in the early 1860s as a 'health-giving amusement' and, no doubt, because it was an English game. John Green and John Bulmer introduced cricket on their reserves as a recreation. By the early 1860s, Aboriginal people played cricket with the other workers on pastoral runs, and in matches against other teams. At Edenhope two young pastoralists, Tom Hamilton and William Hayman, coached Jardjadwarli and other men and formed them into a team in about 1864. District matches followed with varying success. On Boxing Day 1866 the team played before 10,000 people at the Melbourne Cricket Ground; spectators who came to view Indigenous people—by then a rare sight in Melbourne—playing sport. The Aboriginal cricketers lost, but they played again the next day and performed spear and boomerang throwing and other traditional sports on the third day, winning the applause of the crowd.

An inter-colonial and overseas tour was soon mooted and a tough contract drawn up by a promoter, Edward Gurnett, which exploited the players as cheap labour, promising £50 per player with food and clothing for the year, while Hayman, their coach, was to receive £1,000 as manager, and Gurnett the profits.[22] The team played matches in Sydney in February 1867, but three members died from ill-health, encouraged by alcohol abuse. The Central Board for the Aborigines opposed another tour, fearing the impact on players' health and their possible abandonment in England. However, before the 1869 Act was passed, the Board was powerless to prevent a tour. In August 1867 a Sydney cricket coach, Charles Lawrence, travelled to Edenhope, wooed pastoralists, coached the Jardjadwarli cricketers for two months and formed a team complete with a uniform of white trousers, red shirt and individually coloured sashes and peaked caps. The team of thirteen Aboriginal players, with Lawrence as their playing captain, secretly left for England in October 1867, stopping over in Sydney for several matches.

The tour itself is now famous, having been the subject of two books, discussed in many others and featured in a television and radio documentary. It was the first overseas tour by an Australian cricket team, and a great feat in its own right. The team faced the novelty and terrors of a sea voyage, then completed a gruelling tour, playing 47 matches in fifteen English counties over six months before good crowds, commencing at the Oval and ending at Lord's—winning and losing 14 and drawing 19 matches. Their rest days were spent travelling over rough roads in jostling coaches to the next venue. They were received

Aboriginal cricketers as portrayed by the English press, *Australian News (Melbourne)*, 20 December 1866.

with great interest, their race, blackness and physical features attracting press attention at a time when race was becoming the key concept in defining and explaining humanity. They were also seen positively as 'stalwart men' and, above all, were watched with 'curiosity and interest'.

Their cricket skills were applauded, especially those of Johnny Mullagh (Unaarrimin), Bullocky (Bullchanach) and Johnny Cuzens (Zellanach). However, most fascination was shown when they performed 'Aboriginal sports', throwing spears and boomerangs, and competed at the 'European sports' of running and jumping. They gained self-esteem from these events, Dick-a-Dick (Jungunjinanuke) and Cuzens usually winning the sprint, Dick-a-Dick excelling at sprinting backwards, and Mullagh often being the best high jumper. The latter two men generally won the cricket-ball throwing competition. Dick-a-Dick won applause—and money—when men failed to hit him with a cricket ball from ten metres, Dick-a-Dick warding them off in traditional fashion with shield and club. The team faced little overt discrimination. Indeed, they were generally fêted in luncheon tents at the game, moving amongst the guests, sampling the food and wine, no doubt being gazed upon as exotic.

In cricket terms the team made history and no doubt the tour boosted the personal confidence and self-esteem of the players. Unfortunately

King Cole (Brippokei) failed to make the trip home, dying of respiratory disease, Lawrence travelling back from a match to be at his death bed. He was buried at Bethnal Green, London. The twelve others returned and, having been poorly paid, returned to their former lives, living, despite some local reputation, mostly in obscurity. Their fame has only been revived in recent generations. Dick-a-Dick, the finder of the Duff children who also exhorted the other cricketers to avoid alcohol on the tour, lived at Ebenezer Mission until his Christian death in 1870. Bullocky played cricket for Lake Condah Mission before his death in 1890. Johnny Mullagh, an excellent all-round cricketer for his day, played a season with the Melbourne Cricket Club. He then retired to Harrow, surviving on station work, rabbiting, and as a Harrow Club cricketer until his death in 1891. He is now an Aboriginal and Harrow hero. (In 1995 an annual Johnny Mullagh Cup match was instituted between an Aboriginal team from the Warrnambool–Heywood area and a team from the Edenhope region.) The Aboriginal cricketers in England were considered exotic, according to the racial ideas of the day, but they knew in their hearts that they had played—and won—in England before any other Australian colonial team had.[23]

Twenty years later traditional skills were again called on for voyeuristic purposes. In 1885, James Thomson, Secretary to the Commissioners of the Colonial and Indian Exhibition in London at the Imperial Institute, requested that two Aboriginal boys be supplied for the Victorian Court at the Exhibition, to display the wonders of the British Empire. They were to throw boomerangs as part of the display 'as the most intense interest would be felt not only in the aboriginals themselves, but in everything appertaining to the fast dying race'. Judging by this comment, they were to reveal to white London viewers the 'primitiveness' of Aboriginal society and its passing, compared to the 'modernity' of British society. The two boys chosen were Gunai/Kurnai from Ramahyuck, William Clark and Willie King, but whether they received payment is doubtful. Thomson, who collected them from the Ramahyuck Mission, wrote en route to England that the boys were 'quite favourites with their fellow passengers'. One presented William Clark (Conebla) with an accordion which he mastered, giving 'promenade concerts to admiring audiences in the evenings'. The boys amused themselves playing drafts and attending church services on Sundays.[24] They appeared in London along with a diorama of an Aboriginal camp, complete with Aboriginal mannequins preparing food around a camp fire. It is not known how or what the boys actually performed. Their Ramahyuck school training no doubt surprised all London viewers who heard them speak, but mostly they were just gazed upon. An official report recorded that the diorama itself 'always [had] a crowd around' as it 'testif[ies] to a race now nearly extinct'.[25] The boys returned to Gippsland, surviving the gawking and the trip.

Less glamorous and more disturbing was the work done by the men who signed on with the Queensland Native Police in 1864 and 1865, a force with a violent and brutalising reputation. A Native Police force which had formed in northern New South Wales in 1848, and which was later transformed into a Queensland force, recruited some of its original members from the Murray region. In late August 1864, four surviving members who had joined fifteen years earlier and were now showing 'signs of age, one with sergeant's stripes', alighted gingerly from Cobb's coach at Echuca on home leave. They returned with a white officer, Murray, who reportedly sought 160 new recruits from the region. In mid-November about twenty Murray men 'dressed in a uniform of blue, with scarlet facings' ambled through Melbourne en route to the docks and a hard, perhaps exciting frontier life in Queensland, 'clearing' traditional owners from pastoral land with horse and carbine. In September

Aboriginal people at Caleguine Bay, Tooloo Arm, Lake Tyers, about 1890. Men with poles L–R: Big Joe, Ned Moffat and Larry Johnson. Three women on bank, (foreground) L–R: Alice Logan, Nellie Blair, Catherine Chase. (Hamilton Hendrie Collection, courtesy of Museum Victoria, XP2290)

1865 Lieutenant Walker, after four months recruiting in the region, gathered a further group of 22 men. They marched proudly in uniform through Echuca on their way to Queensland, trailed by 'two youthful gins'. Historians have not as yet uncovered their fate.[26]

Life off the reserves

Movement in the wider world wrought change. Work put money in Aboriginal pockets and they spent it as they saw fit. Clothes were a particular attraction and Aboriginal workers dressed like their white counterparts. One group of Aboriginal workers at Echuca in 1865 affected the dress of their class, the stock riders wearing 'cabbage-tree hat, shooting jacket, breeches, boots and spurs' and the shearers, 'twilled shirt and moleskin trousers'. Those without money wore cast-offs.[27]

The Gulidjan of Colac, like other Aboriginal people, transformed some of their rituals according to new influences. In September 1865 the Gulidjan gathered for the funeral of their elder, King Co-coc-Coine Snr. His body was conveyed in a cart—the property of the group and a gift from the government—followed by his son John Co-coc-Coine Jnr and other Gulidjan mourners. His widow was in another cart followed by 'a long line of horses and conveyances, with farmers, tradesmen and others with whom the deceased has long been a favourite. The body was interred in the cemetery'. What is fascinating is not only the adoption of European mourning ritual by Aboriginal people, but the esteem shown the deceased and his kin by the residents of Colac. Aboriginal workers and 'wanderers' enjoyed significant respect from those who knew them and valued their work skills. Indeed, as the funeral report added: 'The remnant of the tribe is well cared for in a brick house and their wants are well supplied'.[28]

Aboriginal Christian marriages had also become common by the 1860s. In August 1867, Jim Crow, a member of the Wannon people, married a woman of the Gulidjan (Camperdown) people at Colac. A Presbyterian and Wesleyan Methodist clergyman officiated and ladies of the district supplied the bride and bridesmaids with dresses. The bride, Donna Ives, was dressed in 'a wincey gown and cap', while the bridesmaids had 'their dark charms set off to advantage by dresses of a varied kind'. Many Aboriginal people, including John Co-coc-Coine Jnr, new King of the Gulidjan, other elders and local Europeans attended the ceremony. It was reported that Aboriginal people of the area had 'resolved to marry in future according to the Christian form'.[29] It was not the first Aboriginal wedding in a country town—Charles Gambier and Fanny Moorel, members of the local Anglican Church 'for years', married at Ararat in July 1861. The groom, from Mount Gambier, had lived among Europeans since childhood and Fanny Moorel was educated, had taught Sunday school, and had since childhood worked as a servant for a local pastoral family.[30]

The spending patterns of Aboriginal people off the reserves included purchasing alcohol, which could be harmful when drunk to excess. It was illegal to supply alcohol to Aboriginal people, but thirsty people and unscrupulous publicans found ways to circumvent the law. Some drank in defiance of the law and the expectations of colonisers. One group at Rosedale retorted to a complaint about their drunken behaviour that they were 'on the spree', which is what rural workers did after a bout of hard labour. Drinking heavily, and even to oblivion, was also a way of living for the moment, and of forgetting the frustrations created by European usurpation. Derrimut, the 'Chief or King of the Western Port tribe', drank to excess and often faced court and the police lock-up until his death in 1864 when he was buried in the General Cemetery under a headstone paying tribute to him as the man who warned Fawkner's party in 1835 of an impending Aboriginal attack.[31] For those with little tradition or incentive of saving, or who earned so little that saving was futile, drinking with friends was a logical pursuit.[32] The Board reported Aboriginal convictions annually, and drunkenness featured heavily. Indeed, the historian Jan Critchett, who analysed the annual reports for the 1860s, found that those locked-up for drunkenness and resisting arrest made up 76 per cent of all Aboriginal convictions.[33] Just over 60 people were locked up on average each year over the decade out of a population of around 2,000—a large though not massive number—but as many heavy drinkers no doubt avoided the lock up, these figures provide an insufficient picture of the problem.

The incidence of Aboriginal drinking was highlighted by the Board, missionaries, local Guardians and employers, who were all imbued with the values of self-improvement and temperance. The press also featured drunkenness in its news reports, fulfilling white expectations of Aboriginal riotous behaviour. Even the 'travelling correspondent' of the Catholic paper, the *Advocate*, commented on the drunken frenzy of a group who obtained grog at the Echuca race day and formed a 'disgusting spectacle'.[34] Witnesses to government inquiries such as the 1858 Select Committee and the 1877 Royal Commission were obsessed with Aboriginal drunkenness, reflecting general concern about colonial drinking patterns as well as concern about Aboriginal conduct.

Aboriginal people resented such attention. When one of the Board's concerned correspondents, S. H. Officer of Murray Downs Station, confiscated brandy from a camp, smashing the bottles, an Aboriginal couple responded with abuse and by burning their government blankets. Officer believed their action 'signified their contempt for my official position, their greater love for the spirit than for the blanket, and their present non-appreciation of my attempt to do them good'.[35]

Although a matter of choice, alcohol abuse was clearly destructive. Firstly, it exposed people to shame, humiliation and constant white criticism. In June 1864 'Spectator', in a letter to the Melbourne *Argus*, remarked that drunken Aboriginal people in Melbourne's streets were jeered by children who 'make sport of the sad sight'. 'Spectator' added paternalistically that 'though their skin may be dark, and their persons ugly and dirty, they have all been made by the same Power who created us'.[36] Secondly, the desire for alcohol exposed people to potentially violent situations. Fights often erupted amongst drunken men at inns and pubs, and deaths sometimes occurred. In 1865 Wathawurrung King Jerry was beaten up in a Geelong pub. The following year he and his kinsmen, Billy and Timbro, were in a fight with a European, Richard Haines, Timbro dying in the affray.[37] Aboriginal men gave as willingly as they received, one killing a German in 1867 during a drunken fight on the McKenzie goldfield.[38] Thirdly, drinking spirits—the drink easiest of access—induced rapid drunkenness and damaged health, exacerbating the continued high death rates of this period. Finally, drunkenness induced criminal behaviour. In 1863 two drunken Aboriginal men allegedly roughed up a seven-year-old boy at Bendigo, while Black Billy was sentenced to three months jail in Cranbourne Court in 1867 for theft of a watch while drunk.[39]

Drunkenness also caused domestic and kin violence which tore at the fabric of Aboriginal society. For instance, in 1861 Peter Gowrie, an Aboriginal man, murdered two Aboriginal women at Ettrick while drunk and was imprisoned for life; in 1866 Tally-ho was charged with beating 'his lubra' across the face with a tomahawk while drunk; in 1868 Thomas King of Warrnambool was charged with attempting to commit a capital offence on his fourteen-year-old daughter while drunk; and in 1869 at Ballarat East, Louisa and Caroline, mother and daughter, were arrested for a drunken fight in which the 'daughter was beating her mother unmercifully'.[40] The *Gippsland Times* claimed that on Sundays 'unfortunate creatures, half maddened with poisoned alcoholic and malt mixtures, may be found fighting and beating their gins'.[41] Most of these accounts come from the white press and tell us little beyond the

Campers at Aggie's Swamp on Edwards River, just north of Swan Hill.
L–R: Kathryn Janell, Jacky Logan and Agnes Edwards (Queen Aggie).
(A. & M. Jackomos Collection, courtesy of Museum Victoria, XP4822)

bald facts and the vivid representations of mayhem. However, in 1860 an Aboriginal woman named Lizzie related the events of a murder at Yambuck west of Port Fairy in court. She and three Aboriginal men, Billy Youlle, Governor and her man, Johnny, who were all drunk, were sitting in a *miam* when a fight broke out. Johnny punched Billy in the face before being felled by a *leangle*, a traditional club, and was then beaten to death, despite Lizzie's attempts to drive the men off.[42] Whether traditional enmities or drunken insanity lay behind the murder is unknown, but yet another Aboriginal life was lost to the grog. While a number of such drunken murders were reported in the 1850s and 1860s, leading to debates over the jurisdiction of the courts in *inter-se* killings, murderous drunkenness declined thereafter, once reserves reduced access to alcohol and provided other diversions.

Property and independence

Some Aboriginal people were teetotallers—non-drinkers—and others avoided excess, which allowed them to save and acquire property. In 1865 John Bulmer noted that Aboriginal stockmen around Lake Tyers owned a few head of stock, while Joseph Parker stated in 1877 that he knew of an Aboriginal woman on the Murray who owned two horses, which she hired out for 10 shillings a day. She shrewdly collected the money before hiring the horses and 'seemed to manage the money very well and clothed her children'.[43] Jim Crow, who married Donna Ives at Colac in 1867 and who was deemed by the local Guardian, Alexander Dennis, to be 'very steady and well conducted', owned a horse and cart for many years and occasionally drove his family to Geelong to attend a sports day.[44] Jim Crow was held to be a man of repute. Alexander Dennis told the Royal Commission that when Crow was leaving P. Manifold's employment he requested some old clothes. Upon finding three £1 notes in the pocket of the trousers, Crow returned the notes to Manifold, who promptly gave him one, saying: 'There are not many white men so honest as you are, Jim'.[45] Some self-reliant Aboriginal people owned or built houses. In 1864 John McIntosh was sued by a Chinese builder at Castlemaine for non-payment of a house he had built McIntosh, whose defence was that he had agreed to pay upon completion and the house was not yet finished.[46] In the mid 1860s a Wimmera family built a slab hut, and fenced and trenched a small garden, but left it in the traditional way when one of the family died. Neddy O'Rourke—a Gunai/Kurnai man—worked for six months and built a hut with the proceeds, employing a carpenter's help.[47]

A few people even gained access to land on an individual basis. In 1871 the local Guardian at Colac, Alexander Dennis, successfully applied on behalf of the people there 'to have a place of their own to reside on'.[48] Sixteen hectares were set aside as a temporary reserve at Elliminyt, near Colac, and the shire council spent £97 erecting fencing and a cottage. By 1872 Jim and Donna Crowe were on the land but had made few improvements. Dennis reported in 1877: 'I cannot get them to cultivate any part or stay there long together', as the few remaining members of the group, including Alice and Billy Murray, preferred to reside in town. Jim Crowe was widowed with three children when Donna, his wife, died from respiratory disease in 1879. In 1876 Richard Sharp, a 'half caste' son of Coinmaninin (Queen Kitty), who was married to a white woman and was a long-term steady worker in the district, rented half the land and controlled it all by default. However, in 1890 twenty-five-year old Joseph Crow, son of Jim, returned home, claiming his father's half of the land. The Colac Herald supported Sharp's claim, saying he had been in possession for many years and 'has laboured hard upon the land, and has respectably brought up a large family'. To divide the land would jeopardise Sharp's ability to keep his family. The Board returned Crowe's half to him while Sharp rented his half until his death in 1919. Joseph and Elizabeth Crowe (later spelt Crough) and their family occupied the land *gratis* and were occasionally rationed by the Board.[49]

A few men obtained individual holdings in more direct fashion. In 1863 the Board reported that some Aboriginal people had made applications for land—this being the time of the Selection Acts—many of whom 'were quiet industrious persons, who have for some time past maintained themselves by their own labour'. The Board supported them, as 'it is right that an opportunity should be afforded to every industrious Aboriginal to reclaim and cultivate the land'.[50] In 1860 Colin and Nora Hood applied for land as individuals and were granted a small allotment at Hexham, but little more is known about their use of it. Wirrimande Jackson Steward[t] and Hamilton Orr acquired land at Lake Tyrell, near Sea Lake, in 1863, although the Board later withdrew its support for their venture.[51]

Other Aboriginal people selected land under the Land Acts in the normal way, especially Grant's Land Act of 1869, which required them to improve the land and build a hut on it. Several selected the usual 320 acres (128 hectares), namely Jimey Uncles at Castlemaddie in the Wimmera. Jackson Steward, 'a most industrious man', and Hamilton Orr tried again, Steward selecting 320 acres at Fishpoint and Orr, 20 near Lake Boga. Steward was still there six years later and Orr paid off his land in 1894.[52] Others, like Charlie Hammond of Gippsland, applied but were refused. Hammond was forced to work for selectors until illness and a large family drove him back to Lake Tyers in 1883.[53] These efforts on the land were examples of Aboriginal people making choices about new ways of living, often within the confined alternatives created by colonial occupation. They did not sink into drunken hopelessness like some of their kinsmen or refuse to change like others.

All over the colony, Aboriginal people, especially younger people, were experimenting with new forms of living. Young women on the missions, several of whom became independent types and matrons of mission dormitories, as did Bessy Cameron (nee Flower) and Louisa Briggs, have had their lives meticulously recorded.[54] Young men like William Thorpe and George Thomas also experienced transformed lives. They lost their parents in the last Gunai/Kurnai *inter-se* battle at the Tambo River in 1855, before working for white pastoralists and then moving to Lake Tyers Mission. The youths stayed there, forming homes and gardens, learning to read and write, and becoming Christian. William Thorpe and his wife Lily ran the orphanage. Both men worked in the wider world as well, and were forced off Lake Tyers in 1889 by legislation. The missionary John Bulmer, their mentor, wrote of them around 1900:

> William Thorpe, who was one of the first boys we had, has now a nice little holding near the Lakes Entrance where he supports a wife and four children. He is often employed at day labour even before white men. As one employer said to me, Thorpe always will work whether you are there or not. In fact he is to all intents and purposes equal to any white man. There was another half caste, George Thomas, who supports by his own labour a wife and six children. He has for some years been employed by Mr D. R. Morris, our late teacher, who is farming at the Snowy River, and I believe Mr M. finds him just as useful as any white man, indeed he pays him the same wages.[55]

Thorpe, Thomas, Cameron and Briggs in no way ceased to see themselves as Aboriginal people. Indeed, they stayed in touch with kin, continually visiting and being visited by those on the reserves. Thorpe and Thomas appeared in photographs of community celebrations at Lake Tyers, and Briggs ended her days at Cummeragunja Mission on the Murray. In identifying as Aboriginal, these people who were earning their living in the European economy were at one with the conservative Aboriginal people who 'wandered' over their country and adhered to tradition.

The 1877 census analysed earlier revealed that two-thirds of the places where Aboriginal people resided off the reserves were inhabited by less than five people. Some resided permanently on stations, but most individuals or small groups moved between pastoral stations, the outskirts of towns and also between their own camps, eking out an existence from occasional Board rations, handouts, and by gathering bush foods: meats, vegetables, eels and fish, and possums out of which they still made rugs. A few who moved about in this way, Tarry Bobby and Wilmot Abraham, whose beat lay around Sale and Warrnambool respectively, have been written about at length.[56] Andrew Porteous, the local Guardian at Stockyard

Postcard image of Wilmot Abraham of Warrnambool. (Courtesy of Jan Critchett, Launceston)

Hill, remarked in 1873: 'The tribe is mostly composed of old feeble men and women, who are by nature restless, and, though they had every comfort, they would not stay long in one place'.[57] Most pastoralists were content to support these people out of a sense of paternal obligation and on the assumption that they were the last remnant of the original owners. Some lived in towns, two old men residing in the brewery at Camperdown, supported by the brewer, Mr Jackson, and a few friends. Even the Board, which had the power after 1869 to move the older people to reserves, did not have the heart, writing in its 1875 annual report: 'It is not practicable, nor perhaps humane, to compel the old natives against their inclinations to abandon the localities where they were born, and to which they are strongly attached'.[58]

These 'wanderers', and even those living on reserves, maintained many customary ways and ideas. Amateur ethnographers collected much information about what was recalled as 'traditional' life even by the 1880s. John Bulmer, stationed in the Wimmera in the 1850s and Lake Tyers from the early 1860s, observed fights, heard of judicial killings by 'kidney fatting', saw punishments meted out for wrong marriage, and experienced the strength of kinship. He was told about the power of sorcery to harm at a distance by singeing pieces of hair or tampering with the excreta of another person. Older people on reserves still buried their bodily refuse in the former way not for hygienic reasons but out of fear of sorcery. People believed clever men could fly, control the rain and wind, and were so powerful that they could catch bullets in their teeth. Bulmer witnessed mourning ceremonies, some of which he recorded in his *Recollections*. He was an accurate observer who cared for the people and was genuinely interested in their traditions. He remarked of one corroboree: 'It was wonderful to see how regularly they kept time to the women beating the rugs'.[59]

James Dawson and his daughter Isabella collected western Victorian language, traditions and customary information, which was published in his *Australian Aborigines* (1884).[60] Alfred Howitt's extensive ethnographic work created a mass of manuscripts (still extant) from which he produced many papers and several books, including *Kamilaroi and Kurnai* (1880) with Lorimer Fison, and his own *The Native Tribes of South East Australia* (1904).[61] Howitt even organised an initiation ceremony in Gippsland in 1884, finding enough Gunai/Kurnai men to conduct a shortened ceremony so he could record the proceedings.[62] However, a request by the Governor Sir Henry Loch in 1887 to see a corroborree was opposed by the Board. A similar request by the Australian Natives Association, a friendly society, was again refused by the Board, this time arguing that

Unidentified woman of the
Yarra tribe making a basket,
about 1870 (found in R.E. Johns
Album 1890, courtesy of Museum
Victoria, XP2120)

Aboriginal women had requested that their menfolk's bodies not be put
on display for white enjoyment.[63]

By this time tourists were continually visiting Aboriginal reserves to
gawk or buy 'traditional' items. This provided an income for the people,
but it meant they were being viewed as exotic, as a people moving to
extinction in the minds of onlookers. Several Aboriginal men produced
paintings in this period, partly for the tourist trade but also as an affirmation of Aboriginal culture. William Barak at Coranderrk expressed
his Kulin identity through a series of beautiful drawings of Aboriginal
ceremonial life, hunting and fight scenes in charcoal, ochre and pencil,
many of them available for viewing in public galleries in Victoria today.
They were executed from memory in the 1880s and 1890s, as these
actions and events were no longer practised, save for a little hunting
for recreation and the occasional taste of bush tucker. Tommy McCrae,
who lived off reserves at Lake Moodemere, a now defunct reserve near
Wahgunyah, drew similar subjects from the 1860s to the 1890s, as well as
post-invasion scenes of Europeans and Chinese interacting with Aboriginal people, including a series on William Buckley, the escaped convict.
McCrae became quite comfortable from the sale of his drawings, being
able to afford a horse and buggy.[64]

People off the reserves were more able to practise their customary ways and traditional values, free from the pressures of the reserve

agenda of cultural change. However, most of the children were moved to reserves, as we have seen, so the possibilities of cultural transmission were reduced to the occasional meetings between those on and off the reserves. However, traditional ideas of birth and death, of magical occurrences in the world, and of kinship and community—caring and sharing as people today term it—still flourished among Aboriginal people on reserves. So too did stories of bunyips, of messenger birds and kidney fatters, and also, Aboriginal moral ideas. An Aboriginal version of history grew up as well, including a story of invasion and of a people's resistance, as well as the story of working with the whitefellas. Increasingly these stories and this history were being related in English not the traditional language. On reserves and in most regions outside (but not along the Murray and with a few other exceptions), the elderly of the late nineteenth century and early twentieth century were the last of the full language speakers. John Bulmer testified in 1877 of the elderly at Lake Tyers that 'most of them understand broken English as a rule. I need not speak the native language to convey my meaning. To the very old ones I do sometimes, they like it best . . . they feel I belong to them'.[65] The last three words were heavy with meaning as to how Aboriginal people viewed their relationship with the missions—it was a reciprocal relationship, not an oppressive one. But it was also one corrosive of Aboriginal culture. While the elderly passed elements of language to the young, the impact of English on the reserves and in the wider culture whittled it away.

Aboriginal battlers and 'wanderers' within the wider white society fought in their own way to be free Aboriginal people: free to think, to move and to live as they wished. Reserve dwellers fought as well to be free people in permanent possession of reserve land. We must now examine their overt political struggles.

9

A 'Miserable Spadeful of Ground'

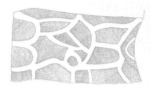

Following governmental neglect in the 1850s Aboriginal people welcomed the Central Board for the Aborigines' creation of reserves from 1861. The Board's human face was initially John Green, the brotherly General Inspector of Aborigines, who gathered children with parental consent (as we have seen) to Coranderrk, the reserve he managed. However, in the mid 1870s Green was removed, the Board lost its early caring zeal, and life on reserves under the 1869 Act became more restrictive. The Kulin at Coranderrk fought for freedom from the Board's increasing control of them and for the very survival of Coranderrk as an Aboriginal reserve—a 'miserable spadeful of ground', as one Kulin man put it. Other communities fought less public battles which cannot be detailed here. The Coranderrk struggle was eventually lost after a generation-long political fight.

A free and independent people challenge the Board

The Kulin forged a unique relationship over fifty years with John and Mary Green, Scottish emigrant lay-preachers. The Greens began evangelism in the Doncaster–Lilydale area soon after arriving in Melbourne in 1857. They made contact with the Woiwurrung camped at Yering, including William Barak: witness to Batman's treaty, a former Native Police trooper, Billibellary's nephew and Simon Wonga's cousin. Barak absorbed Green's message and converted to Christianity while still remaining firmly traditional as his later paintings reveal.[1] Others in the camp also responded to Green's evangelism. The Woiwurrung and the Greens collaborated over the building of an Aboriginal school at Yering in early 1861, just months before the Board appointed John Green as General Inspector of Aborigines. They pioneered the Acheron reserve together, and then Coranderrk. By 1863 Green performed two roles: General Inspector, gathering up children for Coranderrk and reporting on Aboriginal people across the colony, and manager of Coranderrk. He was never paid for the latter work.

The term 'manager' of Coranderrk was somewhat of a misnomer, as Green treated the people as 'free and independent men and women', and as Christian brethren. Green respected them and considered them truthful and honest. He once recalled he was able to keep the food store unlocked for nine years, up until some non-Kulin Aboriginal people arrived on the reserve. He did not distinguish between people of 'full' and 'mixed' descent, although he was aware that others did, and that they favoured those of 'mixed' descent. He enjoyed the residents' company and laboured with them on the reserve gardens and hop fields. During the picking season, once sufficient hops were picked each day for drying in the kiln, he reported that 'we were frequently playing at cricket and other things'.[2] Green knew the Kulin intimately and had brought many of them to Coranderrk. They seemed grateful for this and viewed it as a positive move to a homeland. One Aboriginal resident, Robert Wandin, remarked of Green in 1881 that 'he has taken the trouble to gather them [Kulin] from all parts of the country'.[3] Green and Mary, his wife, visited the people in their houses and tended the children in the orphanage. Tommy Michie declared that Mrs Green 'was like a mother to all the natives, and was good to the women when they were confined and she used to look after the sick'.[4] The Greens prayed with them and guided them through preaching.

Green, unlike most other reserve managers, worked *with* and not *over* Aboriginal people. He quickly became almost like a *ngurungaeta* (an elder) to the Kulin, certainly a mentor, an uncle. In turn, he conceived of their relationship, not as patriarchal but as a Christian brotherliness. By July 1863, within four months of the establishment of Coranderrk, but four years after first contacting the Kulin, Green outlined his approach to the Board's Secretary, Brough Smyth: 'My method of managing the blacks is to allow them to rule themselves as much as possible. When there is any strife among them this is always settled at a kind of court at which I preside'.[5] The Kulin worked with Green to manage alcohol use, farm work, movement off the reserve and community relations. In April 1865 they created their own reserve court which set punishments for drinking: a five shilling fine for the first

Men installing poles in Coranderrk's hop garden, about 1890. William Barak is standing third from the left. (Courtesy of La Trobe Picture Collection, State Library of Victoria, H141252)

offence, ten for the second and 20 shillings for the third, except for single men who forfeited their right to marry—the usual rule being that men could marry after two years residence at Coranderrk. Green assured the Royal Commissioners in 1877 that this fines system cured the intemperate from drinking. He added the people could not be ruled and could only be influenced by suggestions: it 'must be—come men, let us do this or that; or, I think it would be good to do this or that'.[6] Because they were 'very proud and sensitive', Green worked by appealing to their sense of pride, shame and duty. In this sense he empowered the people. As one Coranderrk resident remarked: 'Mr Green knows our inside—he speaks inside to us'.[7]

In 1874 the Board engineered Green's removal. He had been run ragged by inspecting the other five reserves quarterly and managing Coranderrk, as well as having to build his own house. He employed a European, Thomas Harris, out of his own modest salary to help as farm overseer during his absence, before the Board finally put Harris on the payroll. Despite being almost self-supporting, some minor farm matters at the reserve were let slide in his absence, leaving Green open to the Board's criticism. However, the real tension was that Green and the Board's Secretary, Robert Brough Smyth, who had formerly enjoyed a productive relationship, disagreed over Coranderrk's future and Green's advocacy for the Aboriginal people. In 1868 settlers coveted Coranderrk's lands, so Smyth proposed to sell the reserve and form another station with the proceeds—a policy Green vehemently opposed. Then in 1874 Smyth pressured Green with inordinate demands till Green declared in exasperation: 'I wish you would relieve me of Coranderrk, and put someone else here, I will do everything to help them'. Green meant it to be temporary relief, but the Board gleefully took it as his resignation as manager. Within fourteen months the Board had sacked Green from his position as General Inspector as well, as he still opposed the selling of Coranderrk and the Kulin's removal to a Murray River site. Green selected farm land near Coranderrk and maintained close relations with the Kulin, conducting church services there until forbidden by the Board in 1876. Thereafter, he visited the dying in their beds or, as he revealed in 1881, 'sick people come to me almost daily for medicine and advice, sometimes as many as ten and twelve'. He remained friend and confidante to the Kulin people until his death in 1908.[8]

The Kulin were alarmed by Green's removal, the threats to the reserve and the appointment of four uncaring managers over as many years. They protested about these injustices over a decade and formed them into a history of grievance. A number of historians have examined this episode, most notably Diane Barwick in her *Rebellion at Coranderrk* (1998), published posthumously.[9] The Kulin's protests are a classic example of the appropriation of the coloniser's political forms and tactics—the use of influential people and the press, the protest letter and petition, the protest march—to gain liberation from the coloniser. William Barak, *ngurungaeta* of the Kulin since Simon Wonga's death in 1874, led an impressive campaign, assisted by younger, educated men and women. His house was the place where many plans were hatched and petitions and letters composed that found their way into parliament and the press. Barak, whose status and traditional paintings gained him entry into the homes of local gentry, counted as his allies politicians and a Premier, Sir Graham Berry; David Syme, owner of the *Age*; some Healesville residents; and the tenacious Anne Bon. Bon, from an established pastoral family was perhaps the Kulin's most enduring supporter and she also employed some of them occasionally on her Wappan station near Mansfield. Several clergy were also vital, especially Reverends Mackie and Hamilton. Reverend Alexander Mackie advised the Kulin to lobby the Chief Secretary about their grievances. Mackie recalled that one Kulin man was almost in tears, saying: 'the white people have only left us a miserable spadeful of ground, and now they want to take that away from us'.[10]

The opening shot in the Kulin's political campaign of February 1876 was typical. Barak told the Melbourne *Leader* that his people would not leave Coranderrk, as 'the Yarra [is] my father's country', and, ignoring the Board, the Kulin walked 60 kilometres to appeal directly to the Premier in Spring Street. Frederick Godfrey, an MP and the Board's vice-chairman, was furious and attempted to block the deputation's path into Parliament House. The Chief Secretary, John MacPherson, received the Kulin and promised to visit Coranderrk.[11] The Kulin by this means gained Parliament and the Executive as allies in its battle with the Board.

Within a fortnight the Board was on the defensive over rumours of the break-up of Coranderrk. Godfrey, its spokesman in Parliament, argued that conditions at Coranderrk were not terrible as claimed and added that the Board did not intend to break up Coranderrk, merely wanting to create winter quarters on the Murray to counter the high pneumonia rates at the reserve. He bleated about visitors to the reserve being duped by the Kulin, for 'the blacks were very knowing—by no means the children of innocence they were sometimes thought to be—and pretty in discovering whether the persons who spoke to them possessed influence or not'.[12]

Following several Kulin deaths unattended by medical practitioners, Parliament again debated the state of the reserve in August 1876. Premier McCulloch requested a 'please explain' from the Board, with threats of a parliamentary inquiry. In October Chief Secretary John MacPherson commented that many of Coranderrk's children 'were half castes, and some of them nearly white'. An inquiry was needed to decide the children's future and Parliament's 'duty to those poor creatures'.[13] Godfrey, under siege, made a marathon speech in reply, claiming the Board acted in the Kulin's best interests, and arguing that the recent 30 per cent death rate at Coranderrk from respiratory disease made it imperative that its housing be improved or a new station formed. However, he still accepted Coranderrk's retention, for while the ill might be removed to a healthier climate for a season, and the 'young half castes' encouraged to seek work in the wider world, the reserve should remain for the old and infirm who 'looked upon it as their home'. Godfrey thought the Kulin well off and worried that they considered it was the 'duty of the State to support them'.[14]

Half a dozen Members of Parliament attacked the Board, one calling for a Member specifically to represent Aboriginal people. The radical Graham Berry called for abolition of the Board. However, parliamentary scrutiny had its downside. Gavin Duffy attacked the Board, which was in practice conducted by 'two or three members', but also chided the Kulin for not being self-supporting, and urged the boarding-out of 'octoroon and quadroon children . . . at a saving of expense to the State'.[15]

The McCulloch Ministry instituted a 'Royal Commission on the Aborigines' in January 1877 to inquire into their condition and the future of all reserves. The Commissioners interviewed reserve and Board staff, collected written responses from local Guardians, and questioned four younger Aboriginal men from Coranderrk. The latter were not community elders and were probably hand-picked by Rev. Stahle, the manager who replaced John Green. They were chosen in a twenty-minute meeting after no discussion—the antithesis of Aboriginal decision-making. Their testimony was certainly compliant. The evidence of other witnesses ranged over the reserves' agricultural, material, educational and spiritual practices. They discussed Aboriginal capabilities, their ability to survive in the wider world, and the impact of alcohol on their lives. Christian Ogilvie, former Board Secretary, considered that while the reserves had initially saved the lives of many people, it was time to move many residents into the world. However, most witnesses thought the people should remain on the reserves. Even Ogilvie thought the elderly and infirm needed sanctuaries.

The Commissioners recommended the retention and adequate funding of the reserves to make them self-sufficient. Residents should be paid for their work and provided with a store stocked with small luxuries to encourage industry and saving. The 'wanderers' should be collected on reserves, by regulation if necessary, although it was hoped they would need only 'gentle but steady and sustained suasion'. Any coercion was justified by the claim of needing to 'rescue' them, for to leave them off the reserves was to abandon them to 'lower and lower stages of degradation'. The Commission recommended that missionaries be employed as managers, that the Board be streamlined, and that the State continue to pay the comparatively small sum needed to fulfil its 'sacred duty' to those it injured by settlement.[16]

Little was resolved. The Board avoided making improvements to Coranderrk and continued to urge its closure. The Kulin's friends in parliament, led by John Dow, wrote reports and pushed their case, Epharaim Zox stating the Kulin were 'badly fed and clad and neglected in other ways'.[17] Twenty Kulin led by Barak headed for Melbourne in March 1881 to see Premier Graham Berry. They brought a petition written by Thomas Dunnolly and other of Barak's young scribes, asking for Green's reinstatement and the retention of Coranderrk. Most of the men wore their Sunday best clothes purchased from their own earnings, only two being in government-supplied work clothes. Several carried their shoes as they walked. John Norris, a fruitgrower at Boroondara, saw them on the road to Melbourne and, discovering they had not made an appointment with Berry, hurried to secure them one. Norris later recalled that he was sure they were not being manipulated by outsiders (an old anti-Kulin claim), as they had no appointment with Berry and arrived at Anne Bon's house in Kew unannounced.[18] Berry received them well, sympathising for the loss of Green, their poor treatment from the Board, and confirming Coranderrk's continuance. When his Ministry fell in July 1881, 46 Kulin petitioned the new O'Loghlen Ministry for the return of Green and the continuance of Coranderrk.[19] The O'Loghlen Ministry established a Select Committee into the condition and management specifically of Coranderrk. The following month the Coranderrk manager, Rev. Strickland, informed the Board that the Kulin 'men are in a state of revolt'.[20]

This inquiry in late 1881 interviewed Board and Coranderrk staff, medical men, missionaries, Healesville residents, police and businessmen, and John Green. It also questioned 22 Aboriginal residents, including four women, and received an Aboriginal petition and 7 written statements. Some of its 5,347 questions focussed on the Board and it transpired that most Board members rarely visited Coranderrk. Henry Jennings, a twenty-year member, admitted to several visits only, adding: 'I know very few of the Aboriginals personally'.[21] Yet he was very willing to order their lives. Many questions concerned Coranderrk's material state, its productive capacity, its day-to-day management, both of farm and people, the issue of its location and future, and the treatment of its residents.

Coranderrk's manager, Rev. Strickland, was grilled by the Committee. He was a decent man, even by John Green's account, but lacked Green's touch. The Kulin who valued Green's friendship and guidance thought Strickland too cold and too distant. They complained to the inquiry that Strickland did not mix with them, or visit them at their farm work or when they were ill. A visitor to Coranderrk, one of the many at this time, conveyed this perception to Strickland. Strickland replied: 'When I came here first I did so. I used to go into the huts and talk with them, and they took advantage of it. I found I was losing my position. I was losing my control due to undue familiarity'.[22] Strickland's authoritarian personality made him unyielding. For instance, he forbade the people from keeping their beloved dogs in their houses, causing older residents to refuse to leave their *mia mias*.

Thus, residents' stories and rumours about Strickland—moral weapons in their struggle with him—were rife on Coranderrk and

Louisa Briggs and family about 1874, photographed by Frederich John Kruger (BPA Album 1870, courtesy of Museum Victoria, XP1853)

these spilled over into the Inquiry. It was claimed by the Aboriginal witnesses that Strickland sold some wheels belonging to the settlement and kept the money; that he drank to the point of falling off his horse; and that he used youths and young women to chop his wood and clean his house without pay.[23] Some stories were true, but others were not what they seemed, causing Strickland to remark at the inquiry: 'if there is a hell upon earth it is Coranderrk'.[24] Strickland was grilled for allegedly withholding ten shillings from Robert Wandin, Coranderrk's stockman, which was a reward from a local settler for finding his cattle. Wandin threatened court action before Strickland handed it over. Strickland's version of this event was different, and we can never know the truth. The bottom line was that the people believed Wandin. Strickland was also in hot water for thrashing thirteen-year-old Phinnimore Jackson over a disciplinary matter. He beat him with horse reins, in the manner many boys of the nineteenth century were beaten by their fathers, but his head was gashed by a buckle. The Coranderrk men resented the thrashing and afterwards Alick Campbell and Alfred Davis took the boy away, causing Strickland to charge them in court for insubordination. As always for Strickland (and the Board) it was a question of control and authority.[25]

Most of the inquiry's questions revolved around rations of clothing and food. The Kulin received an annual government clothing supply of bedding and work clothes—a pair of blankets, two shirts, two trousers, one pair of boots, material for dressmaking and flannel cloth to make underwear—but no coats. While it is unclear whether they actually consistently received this supply, the clothing ration was not generous and had to be supplemented by their own efforts. Food rations were a more contentious matter. Each adult received a weekly ration on

Saturdays of 4.5 kilograms of flour, 0.9 kilograms of sugar, and 110 grams each of tea, rice and oatmeal, children under ten receiving a half ration.[26] Their friend, Thomas Harris the farm overseer who had married two Kulin women, measured out these rations—honestly it seems. The people believed the ration was too meagre. It represented for each adult: four cups daily of flour to make damper, which was probably sufficient, and 25 teaspoons daily of sugar, sufficient to sweeten the damper and tea, as well as one cup each of rice, oatmeal and tea to last the week. Milk was sometimes available. But if visitors came things were tight. Some witnesses claimed they often ran short by Friday and as Martin Simpson, a former Franklinford youth, said: 'We have to borrow bread off our neighbours'.[27] By 1881, the Kulin received few vegetables and little milk, unlike in Green's time when a kitchen garden and dairy operated. The official ration was boring, barely adequate, and devoid of vegetables and meat. The people were free to grow their own vegetables, but few did, partly because they believed these should be provided. Thomas Dunnolly among others grew cabbages and onions.

Most complaints concerned meat. After Green was dismissed the Board instituted wages for work performed, and stopped issuing meat, except to the sick and infirm. The rest had to purchase their own meat from their wages so as to learn self-reliance. However, wet weather and the constant need to cut their own firewood reduced the Kulin's weekly paid work time and thus wages, which were only paid every two months. Inadequate as they were, all the men's wages went to purchasing insufficient amounts of meat. All the witnesses complained of insufficient meat in their diet, Thomas Dunnolly testifying: 'I always feel faint when we are working'.[28] A Healesville butcher offered credit to allow them to purchase extra meat, and all stated they owed him money. Their indebtedness meant it was extremely difficult for people to save for the other items they were expected to provide for themselves, including candles and kerosene, towels and wash basins, clothes other than work clothes, coats, small luxuries and household items bought from the visiting hawkers, furniture, and even the costs of their marriage ceremonies.[29]

Rationing might have made it look as though Aboriginal people were on welfare, but all the able-bodied worked, and they received only a small part of their total needs as rations. It is difficult to know just how short of rations—how hungry and weak—the people actually were, because their resolute claims were countered by the Board's insistence that they were well rationed. What clouded the issue was that the ration was also political. It could be used as a weapon when withheld by management to enforce work, but it could also function as a weapon for the Kulin if it was claimed to be inadequate. Convicts in early colonial society also knew the power of protests over food—as these protests had to be taken seriously.[30] Complaints about inadequate food and insufficient warm flannels were sure to make the Board squirm and get attention from the humanitarians, press and parliament in Melbourne. Besides, the Kulin expected rations as part of the moral bargain following settlement: the usurpers on Aboriginal land had an obligation to share their bounty with the people. Food was thus a sign, a promise to be kept.

The real issue for the Kulin was as always: land and freedom. As William Barak testified: 'the Government leave us here, give us this ground and let us manage here and get all the money'.[31] Their petition to the 1881 inquiry signed by 46 Aboriginal people simply said: 'We want the Board and the Inspector, Captain Page, to be no longer over us. We want only one man here, and that is Mr John Green, and the station to be under the Chief Secretary; then we will show the country that the station could self-support itself'.[32] It was the 1843 dream of Billibellary reaffirmed yet again. Those on other reserves had similar desires and when they were attacked by the Board they responded in the same way.[33]

The 1881 Committee's report proved a fiasco when it was tabled in early 1882. Its nine members split into two partisan camps, leading to a main report and two rival sub-reports. The main report, supported by both factions, recommended the retention of Coranderrk, its material upgrading, a tightened management and the reintroduction of meat to the basic ration. Regarding its future, it recommended that the 'full bloods' be maintained in comfort and the 'half castes' be 'encouraged' to hire themselves out 'under proper supervision'. The sub-report written by the Kulin's friends called for an end to Board control of Coranderrk, attacked the Board secretary Captain Page for mismanagement and called for the abolition of his position. It recommended Coranderrk's permanent reservation, recognising the Kulin's attachment to it. It also urged training for those of 'mixed descent' bound for work outside, and that the reserve 'should still be considered their home', giving them a right of return. The sub-report written by the Board's supporters rejected the rival sub-report, arguing the Board could not be condemned on Coranderrk evidence alone. It recommended a committee of 'three gentlemen' to oversee Coranderrk. It claimed (yet again) that Coranderrk's residents were influenced by outsiders, a fact which, together with alleged climate problems, made the site near Melbourne unsuitable. The Board's supporters revealed the power politics behind the whole matter in their final recommendation: if 'discontents' existed after the improvements were made, Coranderrk should be broken up and the people removed to 'an isolated part of the colony, under missionary management'.[34]

New contexts, new policy

In 1881 Melbourne hosted a grand International Exhibition at the new Exhibition Building, complete with massive temporary annexes. The spectacle, ranging over many months, displayed the primary and secondary industry, technology, arts and cultural achievements of Europe and its colonies. It was a bid for Victoria to be recognised internationally as part of the vanguard of modern civilisation and progress and it was attended by most Melbournians and many Victorians who came to see exhibits from around the world.[35] Those in attendance included twenty Kulin protestors. The men, who appealed to Premier Berry on 29 March 1881, were taken after the interview with Berry by their friend John Norris to see the International Exhibition as a treat, before returning to Anne Bon's house in Kew to sleep that evening. It is unknown whether the Kulin realised that the wonders before them represented the forces against them. The exhibition was a metaphor for the competition of nations, and the progress and modernity of Western civilisation, while the prevailing discourse about Aboriginal people branded them as un-progressive and primitive. The exhibition embodied the arguments of Darwin's *On the Origin of Species* concerning natural selection (the survival of the fittest), but translated into social and national form. The Kulin's fate was shaped by these ideas on the competition between races and individuals. The general acceptance of these ideas by the 1880s explains the actions of white policy-makers.

After the 1850s ideas of 'race' and 'biology' increasingly appealed as key explanations of human difference. Theorists' claims about biological differences, especially of cranial capacity and racial ability, were reinforced by Charles Darwin's theory of natural selection, which provided an explanation for how biological difference developed as new and more favourable adaptations to a given environment created new types. This change in thinking can be seen in the press responses to Aboriginal reserves in Victoria. At first a positive and hopeful attitude prevailed, an *Age* editorial in May 1869 praising the moral, religious and educational progress at Coranderrk, which promised to make the settlement 'self-supporting'. Its weekly stable-mate, the *Leader*, suggested in August 1869 that the Aboriginal race might not die out as often thought, for 'as their moral and physical condition is improved, instead of diminishing, they increase and multiply just like other folk.' But tuberculosis and measles altered this optimism. By January 1881 the *Age*'s editor was convinced that Aboriginal people would 'simply vanish' as they were 'a bygone people', although he urged that they be helped to 'glide off the stage rather than pass away abruptly'. In 1888 an *Age* editorial, commenting on a Protection Board report, remarked that 'the aboriginal race is doomed', there was no weeping or calling for help this time because, as the editorial added in chilling fashion, their survival 'would have been a permanent drag upon our civilization and an incongruous element of the future Australian community'.[36]

In the face of evolutionism the old paternalism was fading in country areas as well by the 1880s, as new settlers arrived with less sense that the original owners were owed some recognition. Certainly, few settlers were willing to create permanent reminders of this past. James Dawson discovered this when he proposed a monument at the Camperdown cemetery to the Aboriginal people of the district and, in particular, to Camperdown George, the 'last of his tribe', whose tribal name was Wombeetch Puyuun. Camperdown George had died in 1883 while

School children at Coranderrk. (Frederich John Kruger Album, courtesy of La Trobe Picture Collection, State Library of Victoria, H141139)

Dawson was overseas and was buried outside the cemetery bounds in a bog. Dawson, who had just published his important *Australian Aborigines* (1884), was shocked at the burial site for Wombeetch Puyuum, and set about creating a tribute to local Aboriginal people. Dawson reburied Wombeetch's body in the cemetery and appealed for money to raise a monument, a project few supported. Despite having to fund it mostly himself, Dawson commissioned a magnificent seven-metre stone obelisk to Wombeetch Puyuun and his people that still inspires today.[37] When 'King Billy, the last of the Ballarat blacks', passed on in 1896, the *Age*'s only memorial was the comment that his death was further confirmation of 'Darwin's theory of the survival of the fittest that an inferior race has a tendency to wither away in the presence of a superior [race] . . . the aboriginals were of too low a stamp of intelligence and too few in number to be seriously considered'.[38]

By the 1880s an ethic of self-improvement as well as the theory of evolution prevailed. The gold rush immigrants, who were now the political and economic elite of Victoria, were, as Sidney Webb commented, the most individualistic members of an individualistic generation.[39] As immigrants in search of golden wealth, they believed more fervently than most in self-improving values. Their philosophy argued that individuals should educate themselves, work hard, learn to save and reject things like alcohol, gambling and the unchaste behaviours that degraded people. The power of this philosophy was evident in the self-help institutions that embedded themselves throughout Victoria: churches, friendly societies, lodges, temperance and debating societies, mechanics' institutes and libraries. These bodies helped individuals embrace self-help and make the right choices to self-improvement, values that were spread widely and deeply in colonial society. Victorians were haunted by the thought that old world poverty, symbolised by the Poor House, might infect the new world they were making. Central to this new world was a rejection of state assistance, which is why this was an era of no dole and no welfare payments. (The Old Age Pension, the first welfare measure, was not introduced until 1901.) Aboriginal reserves and rationing went against the grain of self-improvement and *laissez faire* economics (no state assistance) for many colonists. They were only tolerated because Europeans felt the guilt of the colonial usurper and were prepared to fund the 'full bloods' until they passed away. However, the fate of those of 'mixed descent' were another matter.

By the late 1870s a new Aboriginal policy was in the wind. In April 1877 the Board's General Inspector, Christian Ogilvie, who replaced John Green but was himself about to retire, wrote to the Board. Ogilvie

Kulin deputation to farewell Graham Berry from Melbourne, March 1886. William Barak is at centre (holding staff), with his speakers Robert Wandin on his right and Tommy Bamfield on his left. (Courtesy of La Trobe Collection, State Library of Victoria, H141267)

suggested that while 'centralization', moving Aboriginal people onto reserves, had protected Aboriginal people to date, 'this system, so analogous to that of a poor-house, does little to encourage self-dependence, provision for the future, and other qualities necessary to make people useful members of a community'. He suggested the policy be reversed 'gradually' and 'decentralization' embraced. Adult Aboriginal people 'should be encouraged' to leave the reserves in search of work and it 'should be compulsory' for the educated youths of both sexes to be apprenticed out to 'responsible masters and mistresses'. His aim was 'the absorption of the whole race into the general community eventually'. However, Ogilvie added that 'the stations should never being [*sic*] closed against any in periods of sickness or distress, nor to the young when wishing to visit their parents or friends during the holidays'. Ogilvie referred explicitly to notions of independence and the poor house, and did not distinguish between degrees of Aboriginality, only between adults and young, although degrees of descent entered the conversation when he faced the 1877 Royal Commissioners. At the

Commission Ogilvie emphasised the need for gradualism, with men working off and returning to their families on the reserves in the initial phase. Ogilvie also stressed that the people's attachment to their reserves should be respected.[40]

During the parliamentary inquiries of 1877 and 1881–82, and in the parliamentary debates over Coranderrk, racial and self-improving ideas, as well as paternal ideas regarding Aboriginal welfare, shaped the thinking of most white participants. Witnesses and parliamentarians mused over whether rationing off the reserves should be withdrawn or not; whether Aboriginal people should be on reserves or not; whether reserves should be and could be self-supporting permanent communities; and how long that might take to achieve. Ironically, Aboriginal people too desired self-supporting, permanent reserves, and wished for autonomy. As late as 1881 the Board still wanted to close only Coranderrk, Captain Page informing the government 'it is only on the Coranderrk station that discontent and insubordination exist'.[41] Indeed, the Board claimed in 1881 that 'half castes' were unfit to manage in the wider world, and predicted that if this experiment was tried the men 'would become loafers and vagabonds and the women prostitutes'.[42]

As the Board battled Aboriginal protestors, who were energised by educated young 'half castes', Ogilvie's decentralising ideas gradually appeared more attractive as a way of dispersing trouble makers. This was especially so after criticisms of the Board in the 1881–82 inquiry and in the face of the Board's increasing fears about the spread of Coranderrk's 'discontents'. By 1884 the Board was drafting possible amending legislation to implement Ogilvie's decentralisation policy. But this policy now was to be backed by compulsion, not encouragement, and had a racist edge, seeking to redefine Aboriginality by degrees of 'blood', rather than cultural ideas, beliefs and wishes of the people themselves.

In 1884, Graham Berry, one of the Kulin's staunchest allies, made Coranderrk a 'permanent' reserve, while all the others remained 'temporary'. This piece of justice was to assist the reserve's survival in name at least for another seventy years. As Berry was about to depart for London in February 1886 to become Agent General for Victoria, Kulin men travelled to Melbourne to farewell him. They presented him with weapons, a walking stick, baskets, a lyre bird's tail and a photograph album of their portraits. With these gifts they included an address of thanks from Barak and the group: 'You have done a great deal of work for the aborigines ... You do all that thing for the station when we were in trouble, when the board would not give us much food and clothes, and wanted to drive us off the land ... We had a trouble here in this country, but we can all meet up long "Our Father" '.[43] The Board's planned legislation was tabled in parliament nine months after Berry— their friend and defender—had reached London. It became the most draconian Aboriginal legislation of its time in Australia and was emulated by New South Wales in later years.

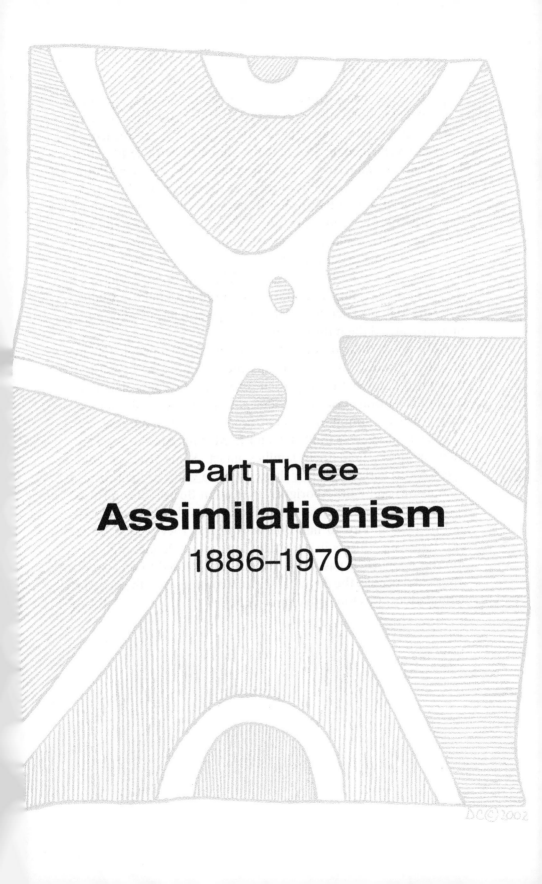

Part Three
Assimilationism
1886–1970

Times of transformation created pressures for Aboriginal people to assimilate, to relinquish their Aboriginality and become European. The assimilation policy enshrined in 1886 and reaffirmed in 1958 actually originated in the 1840s when Europeans first failed to accept Aboriginal people and their culture. From that time they sought to remake Aboriginal people in their own image. The first half of the twentieth century was the most dangerous of times culturally for Aboriginal people as the force of policy and the law sought to break up their families, remove them from their land and deny them their identity as Aboriginal people. It was also the time when the Aboriginal population fell almost to the point of no return due to diseases and high infant mortality. Only the high number of births and the persistence of Aboriginal mothers carried them through this crisis.

However, in these darkest of decades Aboriginal people fought for their families, their land and their identity with cultural tenacity, the stories they told each other and the political actions they took. During these years, Aboriginal people formed economically deprived communities on or near the remnants of reserves, by river banks across the State, and in Melbourne's slums where they sought to hold their families intact. Some lived at Lake Tyers. Most worked for their living in these years, as 'half castes' were disowned by the Aboriginal Protection Board. They formed sporting clubs and musical groups to express their camaraderie, and political groups to fight for their rights. They were assisted by white sympathisers in their fight for justice. Despite the pressures to forget their past the great majority refused to do so. For Aboriginal people, the denial of self and community—the price of assimilation—was too high a price to pay.

10

Under the Acts

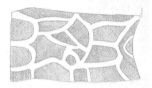

The two generations following the passage of the 1886 Act and its amendments were the most coercive time for Aboriginal people since white settlement. They lost significant civil rights as the Board dealt with families and moved people around as it pleased, all in the name of a grand design: the absorption and disappearance of Aboriginal people into the wider community. The Acts and their numerous regulations, while tediously detailed, make grimly rewarding reading for those exploring the Aboriginal experience under the Board's regime. Only by examining them closely can we understand why Aboriginal people, with wry humour, called the Aboriginal Protection Board the 'Aboriginal Destruction Board'. The Board never fully implemented its power to manage Aboriginal people, due mostly to a lack of will, resources and a modicum of compassion. The Board also believed its effort was somewhat superfluous, as time and the natural law of decline for 'inferior races' would simply take its course, and Aboriginal numbers would continue to fall.

The 1886 and 1890 Acts and their impact

The Amending Act of 1886, which followed the struggle for the reserves outlined in the previous chapter, was passed so swiftly through parliament on the eve of Christmas that one member termed it a 'disgrace'. Aboriginal people protested, but the Board now had the government and parliament on side. Its hasty passage meant several extremely coercive clauses were dropped to avoid delays, namely: a clause allowing removal from a station as punishment, and another allowing any 'half caste' found 'lodging, living, or wandering' in company with an 'Aboriginal' and unable to 'give a good account of himself' to be liable to a year's imprisonment.[1] In short, the Board had considered removal from home and removal from kin as possible punishments! The Government claimed the Act was aimed at reducing expenditure on Aboriginal people. However, as well as reflecting the self-improvers' fear of creating a permanent Aboriginal reserve pauper class, the Act also reflected racial thinking, for it only applied to 'Aboriginal' people so defined—those of 'full' and 'mixed descent' were treated differently.

The 1886 Act built on the 1869 Act, which controlled Aboriginal employment, place of residence and the management of children, but altered its definition of Aboriginality. Whereas in the 1869 Act a 'half caste' person or their child was also deemed to be an 'Aboriginal', the 1886 Act divided people into 'Aboriginals' and 'half castes'—the latter meaning those of any degree of 'mixed Aboriginal blood'. It sought to separate them along this racial category, but not strictly so, as 'half castes' under 14 or over 34, or those married to people of 'full descent' were treated like 'Aboriginals'; that is, age and gender as well as race shaped the definition. Thus, it was deemed that only 'Aboriginals', 'half castes' over 34, 'half caste' women married to 'Aboriginals', children of ' Aboriginals' unable to earn their own living, and licensed 'half castes' were able to reside on reserves. All unlicensed 'half castes' 14–34 years of age and 'half caste' women not married to 'Aboriginals' had to leave the reserves after 1 January 1887. The Board watched over those removed for seven years and, where it found 'necessitous circumstances', could ration them for three years, supply them with clothing for five years and with blankets for seven years after the gazetting of the Act. Concerning 'half castes', regulations or orders could be made under the Act regarding their assistance, the apprenticing of their children

Albert Darby and Alf Stephens rabbiting at Ramahyuck Mission, about 1900.
(A. & M. Jackomos Collection, courtesy of Museum Victoria, XP4256)

or the transfer of 'half caste' orphans to the Department of Neglected Children.[2]

In July 1890 an almost identical Act replaced the 1886 Act to consolidate legislation and clarify its possible regulations. This Act included one additional clause that authorised financial and administrative assistance to 'half castes' to 'select, acquire, hold, enjoy and be possessed of any such Crown lands'. Forty-six regulations were gazetted in September 1890, all designed to give the Board considerable power over Aboriginal lives.

'Aboriginals' were controlled by twenty regulations under the 1890 Act. These prescribed the places where 'Aboriginals' could live (at only five reserves now, as Framlingham officially closed in 1889); controlled their work off the reserves and their wages through certificates and contracts; and prescribed wages to those on reserves if any marketable goods were produced by their labour. The regulations ordered the removal of any 'neglected' child to a reserve, industrial or reformatory school; called for the instruction at school of those on reserves under 14 years of age, and set out that males under 14 and females under 18 on reserves may be required by the Board to reside in a dormitory.

'Half castes' were controlled by seven regulations, which offered some benefits. Two of these allowed the licensing of those ill or infirm to reside on reserves for three months with renewals, and prescribed their allowable rations, and authorised clothing and medical provisions. They were required to work like other reserve residents if able, on penalty of withdrawal of rations. Five clauses regulated the assistance available to 'half castes' off the reserves, including railway passes, but only in 'urgent and needful cases'; assistance to purchase land or other property but only to 'sober, honest and industrious' persons. The emphasis on assistance only to the 'deserving' was standard for the day.

A further thirteen clauses regulated apprenticeships of those over 14 years of age. Some clauses were clearly there for the protection of Aboriginal young people. These required employers to properly house, clothe and feed their charges, ensure 'female protection', allow them to attend church and provide them with moral training. They were to report the performance and illnesses of apprentices or any who absconded. They were to pay half their wages (of between four and ten shillings a week) to the Board for retention till the end of their service. Girls could not be apprenticed to single men, or hotel/boarding house keepers, and application forms had to detail the male members in the household and the sleeping accommodation. Those apprentices found unsatisfactory could be returned to the Board. An apprenticeship agreement, standard for the time, set out the mutual duties of master and apprentice. Orphans could be transferred to orphanages or the Department of Neglected Children. The Board could inspect these places at any time or the conditions of those in apprenticeship.[3] In short, reserve dwellers—considered as children—and children under 18 were under the Board's protection, but also, its strict control.

These revolutionary Acts and Regulations of 1886 and 1890 had at least four devastating effects over the next two generations. They limited the freedoms of Aboriginal people; they forced people from their homes and families on the reserve; they broke up families by the removal of children from their parents; and they undermined the reserves.

Land, family and tradition were attacked more coldly and ruthlessly than on any Australian frontier. Here was potential genocide, for the aim of the Acts was the 'absorption of the whole race into the general community', as Christian Ogilvie had succinctly put it in April 1877 when the policy was being developed. The word and thus the crime of 'genocide' did not exist until the United Nations Genocide Convention of 1948. However, the government's intention in 1886 of merging Aboriginal people into the community and increasingly denying access to land and children would inevitably extinguish Aboriginality: exactly what the 1948 definition outlawed.[4] Yet many at the time, including Ogilvie himself, drew back from the idea of genocide as later defined, stating it was wrong to use compulsion to achieve his stated aims. Even the Board did not explicitly discuss the need to end all Aboriginal tradition in the absorption process.

The first impact on Aboriginal people—the loss of freedom—is self-evident from the regulations detailed above, which were generally enforced to the letter. For instance, on 5 September 1894 the Board reported that a number of young men at several of the reserves had refused to work, preferring 'constant sports and [being] otherwise . . . insolent and disobedient'. The Board resolved to enforce 'the regulations' and direct them to work on penalty of exclusion from the reserve for a specified period. It was, of course, reasonable that they be asked to work. Barak and other elders would have wanted that, for work was the only way to be 'self-supporting'. But work on reserves under managers was not a free type of work. It was a directive, and the wages paid by the Board were infrequent and indeterminate, depending on produce sales. On 5 September 1894 it also regulated freedom in a more coercive way. It decided to prevent Aboriginal people wandering from place to place 'without good cause', for it 'upset all order and discipline', and was expensive for the Board by way of train fares. Managers were informed not to permit people to move about and to prevent visitors coming onto reserves 'without the express permission of the Board'. Managers also shifted people as a punishment. Thus, freedom of movement was restricted and connections with kin were at the behest of the Board.[5]

The Board also limited freedom by regulating marriages between 'full bloods' and 'half castes'. These unions were not prohibited by law, but the Board assumed the practice of issuing 'approvals' for marriages involving 'Aboriginals'. Those with 'half castes' were routinely refused. Couples who persisted in such relationships suffered financial hardship as rations were denied them. These things were done to uphold the wider policy. As the Board wrote in its 1888 report: 'the "Amended Act" was framed to merge the half-caste population into the general community: [but] by encouraging the intermarriage of blacks and half-castes that end would not be attained'.[6] It is clear that the Board was guided more by financial than racial reasons in its thinking. Historian Katherine Ellinghaus has noted that the Board was unconcerned by marriages between 'half castes' and other Victorians, or even between 'half caste' men and white women (there were two cases listed in the 1877 census), which were prohibited by law on racial grounds in many contemporary United States jurisdictions. Indeed, the Board welcomed such unions to advance its absorption policy. It permitted its own employee, Thomas Harris the Coranderrk farm overseer, to marry two Aboriginal women. Each such marriage was another family less under the Board's financial care and one more on the path to absorption.[7] In 1895 the Board boasted it had slashed its budget by half due to the 1886 Act.

The second impact—removal from one's home—did not occur overnight but over several years. The Board claimed it wanted to 'prevent individual cases of hardship' and 'interfere as little as possible with family life'.[8] But the gradualism of this policy was due as much to the reluctance of Aboriginal people to leave reserves, the need for them to find work and accommodation, and the compassion of managers like Goodall and Bulmer. The Board listed 233 'half castes' on the reserves in 1887, stating 60 had already left, a figure that rose to 80 departures by the following year. By 1892 there had been at least 120 removals, and managers reported there were few unlicensed 'half castes' remaining. Those removed from reserves worked as farm labourers, shearers, timber getters, and eked out a living as best they could. Some received wages equal to white workers, but it was up to employers to pay what they chose in industrially unregulated conditions. Family men found it difficult to manage and when illness hit, doubly so. Reverend Hagenauer, now the Board's Secretary as well as Ramahyuck's manager, fielded requests for assistance from Aboriginal people classified as 'half castes', and adjudicated whether they could receive rations or be licensed to return to a reserve. He generally licensed the ill to return until well. Settlers, and even managers, interceded. It was rumoured that Bulmer was illegally rationing 'half castes' off Lake Tyers, and Rev. Stahle at Lake Condah urged Hagenauer to give monetary aid to help them become successful, as otherwise they would return to the reserves.[9]

The onset of the 1890s Depression, just as the rationing period under the Act was due to expire, made survival off the reserves more difficult. People moved back onto reserves illegally in these tough conditions, also harbouring a desire to see home and family. Their kin secretly rationed them. Hagenauer reported of Framlingham in 1892 that a considerable number of unlicensed 'half castes' have returned and 'receive shelter and provisions from the blacks'.[10] In 1897 the Board threatened to cut rations to those who harboured kin. When Emily and George Edwards sheltered Mrs Alberts and her children at Framlingham, they refused to bend to the Board's threats, declaring that if it stopped their rations 'they could beg for their living and Mrs Alberts could stop with them'.[11] Others camped nearby and were secretly rationed by kin, their presence thwarting the Board's policy of mixing into the general community. Young men continued to associate with their families at Ebenezer during the 1890s, the manager reporting in 1899 that 'half caste boys are coming now and then to visit their parents, but they do not get any rations'.[12] At Framlingham a number of families camped in the forest adjoining the reserve.

The absorption policy also faltered because of the attitudes of whites. While some extended compassion to Aboriginal people, others lobbied the Board to move those near towns back onto the reserves. John Glasgow of the State School Board of Advice at Hopkins Falls reported that ten Framlingham children attended the school now that Framlingham and its school had closed. Subsequently most of the white children had been removed from the Hopkins Falls school. The white parents 'absolutely refuse to allow their children to attend the same school with the blacks. I may add that this [Hopkins Falls] Board did all that was possible to remove the prejudice, still the "strike" continues'.[13]

Some Aboriginal people returned to reserves after gaining permission to use reserve lands. In 1891 Frank Clarke applied for 16 hectares of Framlingham land for farming and the Board allowed him a 'temporary permissive occupancy'. Two years later it granted approximately 34 hectares each at Framlingham to John Wyselaskie, John Brown and William Good for similar purposes. Several were 'half castes', but were classed as 'Aboriginals' under the law, due to their being over 34 years of age.[14] Two 'half caste' families returned to Ebenezer in 1891 to occupy a portion of the reserve land 'to earn their living by growing wheat for their own support'.[15] The Board sought to encourage independent small landholding. However, in May 1894 P. Boglish, Ebenezer's manager, demanded Albert Coombs forfeit his block as he avoided church, served wine to his Aboriginal friends on Sunday afternoons and his wife allegedly failed to keep the house and children clean. The outcome is unrecorded.[16]

The third impact of the Act—dividing kin and removing children—was potentially the most damaging. The Act classified Aboriginal people according to their degree of 'blood' and sought not only to separate them physically, but to drive a wedge between 'Aboriginals' and 'half castes'. The policy encouraged ill-feeling as the former were on the homelands and rationed, the latter pushed off and generally denied assistance. Some 'full bloods'—300 in 1888—who insisted on living off the reserves were rationed by local Guardians, creating more potential for jealousy.[17] Not that all these 'wanderers' desired assistance. Tommy Smyth and his wife, living and working on a farm at Yea, refused rations as they wished to be treated 'like all British subjects'—that is, as an unrationed free people.[18] Occasionally tensions emerged between those of 'full' and 'mixed' descent. For example, the Board received letters from Framlingham 'Aboriginal' people complaining about the presence of 'half castes' on the reserve. A petition was sent to the Board in 1897

Aggie Edwards and R. Nichols boating near Swan Hill, 1910.
(Courtesy of State Library of Victoria, H2556/1–9)

requesting their removal.[19] Tensions still existed between those from different reserves as well. For instance, Colin Hood wrote to Rev. Stahle at Lake Condah in 1889 about Billy Wallaby, who had visited Framlingham. He complained that Wallaby induced residents to drink and wanted to fight him, 'calling me a bloody dog'.[20] However, most tensions were resolved by the residents.

The removal of children from their parents was the deepest outrage perpetrated by the Act, but the hardest to track in the records. Regulations under the 1869 Act had permitted the removal of any child to a reserve dormitory, or 'any Aboriginal child neglected by its parents, or left unprotected' to an institution. This was unnecessary in a protective sense, given the nature of Aboriginal kinship—orphans or neglected children rarely existed as there was generally family prepared to pitch in and care for children. The 1886 and 1890 Acts and regulations managed apprenticeships and orphans, and reaffirmed the 1869 provisions about dormitories and allegedly 'neglected' children. Those children boarded out with white families were collected after the Act and sent to institutions. Information on other early removals is scant. The children of artist Tommy McCrae were removed in the 1890s, although the reasons are obscure. Claims of 'neglect' were hard to sustain as McCrae was a teetotaller and earned sufficient from the sale of his drawings, fishing, poultry and possum-skin rugs to provide well for his children—even a horse and buggy.[21]

The Board seemed dissatisfied with the rate of removals in the 1890s. In November 1899 it issued a new draconian regulation that enabled it to transfer 'any child'—not just those 'neglected'—for its 'better care, custody and education' to an institution.[22] The Board announced in 1900 that it had adopted 'the practice of transferring these half-caste children on leaving the stations schools' to 'merge' them with the 'general population'.[23] These children were not neglected, merely of 'mixed descent' and now 14 years of age. The Board sent them to the Department of Neglected Children, which transferred them to Salvation Army institutions, the Bayswater Boys' Home where they learned farm skills, and the Albion Training School for Girls to learn domestic service. Initially ten children were taken, eight of them boys. Records of their experiences have been lost, destroyed or are available only to family.

The boys' new environment was difficult, as the 200-hectare Bayswater farm was for 'troubled' boys too young for the Reformatory. Bayswater's Superintendent James Bray admitted that some of the young residents 'are unfortunately very vicious, and others are intellec-

Billy and Julia Russell (nee Sutton), at right, outside their home at Coranderrk, 1916.
(F. Endacott Collection, courtesy of Museum Victoria, XP2231)

tually weak'.[24] However, D. McLeod, the Board's vice-chairman, claimed in 1900 that the Aboriginal boys were 'happy and contented', and added that they were undergoing training 'to make them upright and intelligent members of the community'.[25] Some Aboriginal parents visited their boys at Bayswater although their reactions are unknown. One boy from the Austin family, who developed tuberculosis, was sent home to die at Framlingham; another boy was returned to his parents as they had left the reserve; and the other eight were soon found positions.[26] Removals to institutions, and then onto white families or employers, continued until 1967.

The fourth and final major impact of the Act—the closure of reserves— happened over forty years as little by little these 'miserable spadefuls of ground' were whittled away. Aboriginal people on each reserve protested. Colin Hood of Framlingham told the Chief Secretary, Alfred Deakin, during a visit in 1889 that 'they only wanted enough land to be allowed to live quietly and comfortably'.[27] Framlingham was closed in 1889 and the land set aside for an agricultural college that was never built. Protests and the intervention of parliamentarian John Murray convinced parliament to retain one-eighth of it in 1892 as a temporary reserve. Framlingham survived as an unmanaged reserve in an administrative limbo.[28] By 1896 Coranderrk and Ramahyuck were reduced by 4,000 hectares and other losses were mooted.[29]

The dismantling of reserves

In 1901 the Victorian census recorded just 652 Aboriginal people, a 39 per cent drop from the 1877 total of 1,067, a one and a half per cent average drop per year. The census symbolised their inferior status, as Aboriginal people were still counted separately from other Victorians (as were Chinese-born people) and classified racially, with 271 deemed as 'pure' and 381, as 'half caste' people. In 1901, 36 Aboriginal people lived in Melbourne, most of them domestic servants, 151 in the western region (at or near Framlingham and Lake Condah); 101 in the north-western electorates (at or nearby Ebenezer and Swan Hill); and 175 in Gippsland (on or close to Ramahyuck and Lake Tyers). Central and north-eastern Victoria were almost devoid of Aboriginal people. In 1901, of the 52 country electoral districts, 39 had less than five Aboriginal people living in them and 28 of these had only one resident identified as Aboriginal.[30] Colonisation—in Victoria, the clearing of indigenous people from their land—was clearly an ongoing process.

The Victorian Aboriginal population declined further in the generation after 1900. A census by the Commonwealth Statistician in 1927 revealed there were 514 Aboriginal people in Victoria, a decline of 27 per cent since 1901. This was a slowing from the 39 per cent decline between 1877 and 1901, but still a disastrous situation. In 1927 there were only recorded 55 'full bloods' and 459 people of 'mixed descent' in Victoria—293 being in 'supervised camps' (reserves).[31] Their numbers equalled the size of several primary schools, the lowest point in terms of population in the 40,000-year history of Aboriginal people in south-east Australia.

Reserves struggled to remain viable under this population decline, a situation exacerbated by the 1886 and 1890 Acts. In 1901 the combined reserve population dipped below 300—ranging from 26 at Framlingham to 78 at Coranderrk—and fewer residents were suited to the demands of farm work, being either under 14 or over 40 years of age. The annual report on each reserve became a sad chronicle of departures under the Act, with little farm activity recorded. Reverend J. Stahle at Lake Condah candidly wrote in his report for 1900: 'As the blacks are dying out, and the Board removes the half-caste boys and girls by handing them over to the Industrial Schools Department, finality is greatly facilitated, and will, doubtless, be attained within a few years'.[32] Hagenauer's son Johannes, who now managed Ramahyuck, thought 'finality', that is the clearing of reserves, might be achieved in twenty years. In 1901 the Board again urged reserve closures for 'greater economy in management' and complained of government inaction on the matter.[33]

The Board drew back from an absolute hard-line policy on reserves. Rumours of closure flowed concerning Ebenezer and Ramahyuck and the Board suggested possible transfers to Lake Condah and Coranderrk. However, it hesitated to use its coercive powers to move people under an Order in Council, as 'the Aborigines are a free people, and not prisoners, who cannot summarily be deported against their will [and] some are so attached to their homes that it is almost impossible to move them'. Besides, the Board added, 'it is a much more difficult matter to deal with twenty educated blacks than four times that number of the original and totally uneducated people'.[34] The Board eased up on removals, reporting in 1905 that Coranderrk still has 'some half castes to be merged into the general population'.[35]

However, its attack on the reserves was relentless over the long term. Ebenezer was closed in 1904 and given over to selectors with the acquiescence of the Moravians. The cemetery was retained as a reserve, as it held the remains of 150 Aboriginal people and five missionaries. Rumours from 1902 about Ramahyuck's closure and the residents' transfer to Lake Tyers had also caused 'considerable anxiety and grief', especially among the older Ramahyuck residents, according to Hagenauer. John Bulmer at Lake Tyers told the Board that 'it is well known that there exists bad tribal feeling between the two stations, therefore it would be very undesirable to amalgamate them at present'.[36] However, Ramahyuck was closed in 1908: Hagenauer's pride, its school and orphanage were pulled down, and residents were transferred to Lake Tyers or sent into the wider world. William Edwards, Billy Clark and others applied for a grant of the mission land but they were refused and the land was opened for purchase.[37] A tiny reserve at Duneed and small reserves at Tallageira (near Edenhope) and Gayfield (Wahgunyah) were also revoked. By 1910, 3,706 hectares of reserve lands remained, about half of the former area, comprising Coranderrk, Lake Condah, Framlingham, Lake Tyers and tiny reserves at Elliminyt (Colac) and Lake Moodemere.

Those pushed off reserves did not move far from home territory and family, and generally sought work in the district. Reverend Stahle at Lake Condah reported in 1907 that 'there exists a regular network of relationship [sic] between the blacks here and the half castes who live as a little community by themselves about 2 miles from here'.[38] At Ebenezer the 'half castes' did not work, according to the manager. As professional sportsmen, he added, they 'still manage to live without work as they get supported by the football and cricket clubs at Jeparit and other town-ships, where they are much required for those sports'.[39] Others moved off voluntarily for variety and freedom as they always had. Some left Ebenezer in 1901 stating that 'as free British subjects they may go where they please'.[40] Most of these movements were short term. In 1909 Mrs Saunders and her son left Framlingham to live with her daughter in Colac, but she returned after a time. As Stahle said of Lake Condah residents in 1907: 'Although natives like to go away at times for a change, they invariably return after a while to their own home, and those who had once or twice to be sent away for correction and for the good of the little community, were never at rest until permission was given to them to return to their own home'.[41]

The Board assisted the family of Joseph and Elizabeth Crough (formerly spelt 'Crowe'), not generously, but consistently and adequately when they were in need, despite their 'half caste' status. Since 1890, the family had resided on a temporary Aboriginal reserve at Elliminyt near Colac, paying no rental for a house and fencing originally supplied by the local council. In 1891 Crough, a horse breaker, asked for rations and boots for his wife and two children. In 1904, with six children under 13, the Croughs asked the Board's Chairman and Chief Secretary, John Murray MLA, for rations due to the winter and a drought that left no grass for their horses. In July 1905 Joseph and Elizabeth Crough (nee Saunders) again appealed for help because the family was 'starving', their clothing and shoes worn out. They also owed food and funeral bills as they had recently lost a child. Elizabeth criticised the Board for not helping them with farm equipment in the first place and threatened to write to Murray if Hagenauer would not help. The Board minuted that both were 'half castes' and not eligible for assistance, adding the hearsay that 'it is reported that he drinks'. It left the decision to Hagenauer—who gave assistance.

In October 1905 Joseph Crough was admitted to Colac Hospital with respiratory trouble and Elizabeth again wrote for help. Joseph also asked that his family be taken into Coranderrk while he was convalescing at Echuca Hospital, 'as they have no friends hear'. He added: 'I am verry thankfull to you and the Bord for you kindness in supling my famly . . . the Bord I must thank for letting me stay on this land'. Joseph Shaw, Coranderrk's manager, opposed the family's stay, saying it was best to keep 'half castes' away 'as there is a great difficulty in getting the boys and girls away from the blacks once they get mixed up and become familiar with them'. He was in fact talking about extended families mixing between reserves, as Crough's sister lived at Coranderrk! Shaw

Coranderrk families at a Christmas camp on the Yarra River in the 1920s.
L–R: Jim Young, Elsie White, Julia Russell (seated), Bill Russell, Dan Russell, Michael Davis, Joe McDougall and ? White. (F. Endacott Collection, courtesy of Museum Victoria XP2214)

added: 'If it is intended to give help or assistance to the half-castes I think it would always be well to do so apart from the stations and the blacks so that we don't reverse the policy we have been trying to carry out for years past'.[42]

The Crough family, which grew to nine children, continued to receive clothing, rations and building materials for house extensions from the Board until about 1918 despite their 'half caste' status. The Board offered to transfer the family to Lake Tyers in 1918 but Joseph Crough declined, saying 'I am quite able to take care of myself. I am not like my poor colored friends. I am a man to try to get on in the world'. He thanked the Board for carrying him in his earlier sickness, but as he was now well, wrote 'let some poor frend [sic] get the ration that I have been getting'. Crough said he now survived by horse breaking, and by planting fifteen acres with his own horse and plough, together with the pay of his two sons—Joseph and Kenneth—both in the AIF for the last three years. He now had some savings and 'I have partly bought a little farm for my boy[s] if ever they come back. I am sorry to say I got one of them wounded now in England'. (Both men returned to Colac, but died in 1931 and 1925 respectively, being farewelled by the RSL (Returned & Services League) at the graveside.)

The family's regular rations stopped in 1918. Elizabeth Crough wrote in 1922, seeking clothing, blankets and three months rations, as Joseph was again ill. In 1932 the Board assisted with some plumbing repairs and household items: mattresses, chairs, and a kitchen meat safe. In 1933, during the Depression, Crough, now almost seventy, received payments from the Sustenance Board before being moved over entirely to the Board's care as he could no longer work in return for sustenance. The Board quibbled about Crough being below 'half caste standard', and suggested he was able to work, but they gave him some rations—certainly in 1939, anyway. Crough was too 'white' for the Sustenance Board's liking, and too 'black' for the Aboriginal Protection Board. Joseph Crough, 'a well know shearer and horse breaker', died in 1947, aged 85, while watching a buckjumping competition, and Elizabeth passed away a year later, aged 77. They lie in the Colac cemetery along with the rest of the community that accepted them and their family who grew to become soldiers, shearers, horse breakers and country wives.[43]

The Board reluctantly helped other 'needy half castes'. For instance, while the number of 'full bloods' receiving aid dropped by about 20 each year through natural attrition, the number of 'half castes' receiving aid rose from 80 to 116 between 1909 and 1911.[44] The government, led by John Murray, who had a long association with Aboriginal people, passed legislation in 1910 to formalise such aid. It allowed the Board to ration those 'half-castes [in need] if it thinks fit and subject to approval of the Minister'. 'Half castes' could also be licensed to reside on a reserve and be controlled like 'aboriginals' under the 1890 Act.

The Board's reluctant compassion is revealed in the case of Harriet King, who asked for help in 1916. Harriet King was the widow of Angus King, who was pushed off Lake Condah reserve in 1890 under the 1886 Act, but who was allowed back for two years in the late 1890s due to his ill health. He died during an operation and left his wife and two children with a lease on 20 hectares of poor and mostly uncleared land, as well as a few head of stock. In 1916 Harriet King had two teenage children, 16 and 19, her eldest bringing in wages from casual farm work. She also cared for four-year-old Nassen Young whose mother had died. She received rations from the Board for herself and Nassen until 1929. In 1916 Harriet appealed to the Board for assistance in fencing the land so she might run a few stock on it for her support. Despite her doubtful prospects on such poor land, and the fact that she was not Aboriginal, but of mixed African–American and European descent—a 'negress' as she described herself—and thus not strictly eligible for assistance in the Board's eyes, the Board fenced the land.[45]

However, the 1910 Act also contained some pedantic and harsh clauses aimed at controlling Aboriginal people. It stated that any clothing or bedding distributed to Aboriginal people was on loan and could not be sold by them. It deemed that anyone harbouring an Aboriginal person under the Board's control without permission, or enticing them to leave the State, or supplying them with alcohol, could be fined £10 or imprisoned for up to three months. Premier Murray, a friend of Aboriginal people, was a true paternalist (and anti-missionary), who believed Aboriginal people had 'little moral fibre' and needed to be made to 'work rather than pray'.[46] Murray shared the racial thinking of his day as he worried about 'half caste girls [who] were allowed to go astray because no authority could be exercised over them', and claimed the 'half caste is frequently a more helpless individual than the full-blooded black'. However, he publicly acknowledged the State's obligations to the 'original inhabitants of this country'.[47] Privately, however, Premier John Murray confessed the usurper's anxieties about ownership, writing that 'though the white man may have a legal right to the land, we must not forget that, after all, in a higher court, the blackfellow would be able to establish a much stronger moral right to the land than any of our white friends who own them today'.[48]

War service

It was right that the State assisted 'half castes' like the Crough family, for they responded well to the duty call in 1914. Indeed, Joseph and Kenneth Crough of Colac who went to the Great War were not unique, for other Aboriginal men joined the First AIF to save the Empire and Belgium from the Kaiser's designs. This response was extraordinary given the lack of freedom experienced by many Aboriginal people. AIF soldiers came from Lake Tyers, Coranderrk, Lake Condah, Framlingham and other parts of Victoria. Five of Hannah and James Lovett's boys—Alfred, Leonard, Edward, Frederick and Herbert—all from Lake Condah, enlisted. All those who enlisted from Victoria were of 'mixed descent', a situation shaped by racial laws. A regulation under the Defence Act of 1903 had deemed that only people 'substantially of European origin or descent' could enlist, and the Board implied the same when it stated in 1916 that 'it had no objection to half castes enlisting for military service if they be accepted by the authorities'.[49] Jim Rose recalled the day the recruiting sergeant visited Lake Condah. Rose enlisted but was soon discharged as being under-age at sixteen.[50]

Lanky Manton demonstrating fire-making for the Governor, Arthur Stanley, about 1918. This was part of the continuing long tourist interest in Coranderrk.
(F. Endacott Collection, courtesy of Museum Victoria, XP2236)

However, once enlisted, the men were well treated by the army, receiving equal pay and treatment because that was how the army dealt with its men. None became officers but this was perhaps a product of their lack of education and status as labourers as much as their Aboriginality. Few of their service records referred to the enlisted men as being of Aboriginal descent. Private Gilbert Stephen, born at 'Ramyuck', was described in his record as a 'half caste aboriginal'. Soldiers no doubt picked up on each others' backgrounds and there may have been trouble between them, but little evidence of this remains. One story survives about Chris Saunders of Framlingham/Lake Condah. Chris Saunders later became a noted Australian Rules footballer and father of Reg, the first Aboriginal serviceman, who became an officer in the Second AIF two decades later. Chris Saunders was informed on the troopship *S.S. Ascanius* that a fellow soldier objected to eating at the mess table with an 'abo'. Saunders promised to punch him on the nose: 'we'll get the gloves if you like. I'll show you I'm equally as good as you'. This brought an apology from the man. Saunders recalled 'next day he came looking for me, and we sat down to eat together. He turned out to be the best mate I had on the ship. We went through a fair bit of action together, and we stayed good friends after the war until he died'. [51]

The Aboriginal commitment to 'serve our Sovereign Lord the King in the Australian Imperial Force' was as high as that of the rest of the population. While the RSL estimated in 1931 that 30 Aboriginal men from Victoria served in the First AIF, research reveals that at least 42 enlisted (whose names are listed in this endnote).[52] The Defence Act and the Board discouraged the enlistment of 'full bloods' so the number of eligible Victorian Aboriginal men (all designated 'half castes') of military age was around 120, there being 113 'half caste' males between 15 and 45 in the 1911 census. Of those eligible the proportion of Aboriginal Victorians who served was one in three, the same as in the general Victorian population.[53]

However, the Aboriginal sacrifice was greater; eight of the 42 Aboriginal servicemen being killed in action, approximately one in five, while one in eight of all servicemen died in action or from wounds.[54] One of the eight Aboriginal men killed was Dan Cooper, son of William Cooper the Aboriginal activist from Cummeragunja (see chapter 14). His sister Sally learned of his death through nuns at the Catholic boarding school she was attending in Fitzroy.[55] Other Aboriginal servicemen were wounded. Private Henry Thomas of Lake Tyers lost an arm, Private George Terrick of Coranderrk who enlisted in the 14th Battalion in January 1916, aged 18, was gassed once and wounded twice in 1918. Private Percy Pepper of Lake Tyers who enlisted in the 21st Battalion in 1916 at the age of 38, and who was wounded in the head from a shell blast in 1917, was permitted to return home in May 1918 as his wife Lucy was ill and they had seven children.[56]

Two Aboriginal men served with distinction. Private William Rawlings, son of Billy and Bessie Rawlings of Purnim near Framlingham, and Corporal Harry (Henry) Thorpe, son of William and Lillian Thorpe of the Lake Tyers area, were both awarded the military medal after enlisting in the 7th Battalion in early 1916. While one in every 42 enlisted men in the AIF earned the military medal, two out of the 42 Aboriginal Victorians who enlisted did so.[57] Rawlings earned the military medal for storming and destroying a German machine gun pill-box and its defenders with grenades. Harry Thorpe suffered gunshot wounds at Pozières in 1916 and at Bullecourt in 1917. He became lance corporal in 1917. After showing initiative and displaying bravery in mopping up enemy dugouts and pill-boxes he was promoted to corporal and awarded the military medal in October 1917.

Both Rawlings and Thorpe were killed in action at Vauvillers on the Somme, and on the same day—8 August 1918—three months and three days short of the Armistice. Their bodies lie blended with French soil at Heath cemetery, Harbonnieres on the Somme.[58] Thorpe's widow, Julia (nee Scott and later Julia Edwards) was unable to receive a war widow's

Aboriginal members of the First AIF. Henry 'Banjo' Patterson (left) and George Terrick of Coranderrk. (Alick and Merle Jackomos collection, courtesy Merle Jackomos)

pension as she was living at Lake Tyers and deemed to be cared for.[59] The family suffered further insult in October 1923, when prejudiced people in Lakes Entrance tried to smear Harry Thorpe's name. The secretary of the Lakes Entrance RSL wrote to the Army to request Thorpe's records 'as some exceptionally slanderous statements have been made to the effect that this soldier saw no fighting and died of disease and the old people are very upset, appealing to the branch to contradict these and uphold the man's integrity'. The army rapidly confirmed his military medal of 1917 and his death in 1918 from wounds sustained the same day in fighting.[60]

Managed lives

While these men were away fighting for their king and country, new legislation was introduced which further confined their freedoms and determined who was, and who was not, 'Aboriginal'. The Aborigines Act of 1915 consolidated and repealed the Aborigines Act of 1890 and 1910.[61] Fifty-six regulations issued in 1916 under the 1915 Act not only maintained existing controls, but extended the Board's coercive powers over the lives of those Aboriginal people who came under the Act.

The 1916 regulations contained new hard-line controls concerning reserve management and relations between 'half castes' and reserve residents. Managers were required to keep a record of residents' age, gender and name, health and work details; inventories of rations; financial accounts; records of economic production; as well as manage buildings and the cultivation of the land. They were to ensure the residents' 'good order and conduct', ensure only licensed 'half castes' entered the reserves, 'restrain' defined 'Aboriginal' residents from leaving the stations, and ensure they did not visit public houses or squander their earnings. A 'reasonable amount of work' was demanded of residents, who were to be paid at a rate determined by the manager, on threat of removal of rations or removal from the reserve. A scale of rations for the management and Aboriginal residents gave each adult weekly: 4.5 kilograms of flour, 0.9 kilograms of sugar, and 110 grams each of tea, with children receiving half these rations, as in the 1870s. However, while staff were to receive 3.2 kilograms of meat, 3.2 kilograms of potatoes, 0.5 kilograms of soap and 0.5 kilograms of butter or 0.9 kilograms of jam as well, Aboriginal residents only received the meat, tobacco, rice, oatmeal, salt and soap 'as required'. There was no specific ration for clothing, which was to be issued 'as may be considered necessary'. The Board could prevent anyone other than a defined 'Aboriginal' under the Act from entering a reserve, and could remove residents for misconduct or if it was considered they 'should be earning a living away from the reserve'. Those harbouring expelled residents were guilty of an offence, punishable by a hefty £20 fine. All 'quadroon, octoroon and half-caste lads' had to leave the reserve at 18 years of age and could only visit 'at the discretion of the manager' and only for a maximum of ten days.[62] This would apply equally to returned servicemen wishing to see family after the War. A consolidating Aborigines Act of 1928 and its regulations of 1931 virtually mirrored these provisions.[63] The legislation was to govern Aboriginal people for another thirty years.

Thus, as Aboriginal servicemen fought for 'freedom from tyranny' at Gallipoli and then in France, the Board increasingly controlled the lives of their families back home. This can be glimpsed in a surviving Board letter book for 1915–1916. The Board's Secretary decided whether families could meet across the miles. In December 1915 Bertie Stephen and family at Lake Tyers unsuccessfully requested permission to move to Coranderrk, but were only allowed to visit for four weeks at Christmas if they paid their own travel expenses. In February 1916 Edward Foster was refused permission to return to his birthplace, Lake Tyers, and where his kin resided. In the same month William King, who

'Rafia Workers at Coranderrk, Healesville', photographed by E.S. Fysh.
(Courtesy of Museum Victoria, XP2590)

wanted to leave Lake Tyers for three months work was refused permission until he could state a 'more definite objective'. The same day Alex McCrae and family were forbidden to return home to Coranderrk from Lake Condah, where they had been staying, and had to go to Lake Tyers instead. Only Mrs McCrae's illness en route stayed the Board's hand and the family made it to Coranderrk. Lucy Pepper and her five children were given permission to move from Lake Tyers to Lake Condah in December 1915 as Percy, her husband, had taken work on rail construction at Heywood. Within five months, Percy enlisted, his son Phillip recalling: 'he didn't tell Mum he was thinkin' of joining up, he just went and did it'.[64]

The Board controlled the supply of rations and clothing to non-reserve residents, and distributed such household items as linoleum and fire fenders, but the recipients had to acknowledge their receipt in writing to the Board. A possible marriage at Lake Tyers between a man deemed an 'Aboriginal' under the Act and a woman not deemed 'Aboriginal' under the Act, which would be 'against the spirit and intention of the Act', was to be counselled against by the manager. Families continued to be broken up by Board decree. Minna Hood, aged sixteen, was sent from Lake Tyers to a reformatory in February 1916 for 'continued misbehaviour'. At the same time the Board refused to return Elsie Barrett to her family at Lake Tyers from the Salvation Army Girls' Home in Brunswick.[65]

The case of Elsie Barrett was a long and complex affair. In 1911 Elsie, aged fourteen, fell pregnant to Alfred Stephens, a 'half caste' man living near Lake Tyers. Stephens was sentenced to three months imprisonment in 1912 for carnal knowledge as Elsie was under the age of consent. The two continued to see each through 1913 and a marriage was mooted, Stephens allegedly sneaking onto the reserve, mostly at night, and Elsie allegedly crossing the lake by boat to his camp. Her family and the community did not object, but R. Howe, the manager of Lake Tyers, saw it as an issue of his authority and disapproved of Stephens. He suspected Stephens was aiming to live an easy life on the reserve after marriage—a marriage that was contrary to the Board's vision as Elsie was a 'full blood'.

Howe urged Elsie's removal and in June 1914 she was sent to the 'Harbour', a Salvation Army Home for Girls in Union Street, Brunswick. Elsie Barrett's mother Elizabeth and her stepfather Isaac Jennings, together with her grandparents, Andrew and C. Chase, began a valiant seven-year effort for the return of their 'Dollie'. The family wrote constantly to Elsie and to the Board, which did not pass all the letters to Elsie. They wrote letters and petitions to solicitors, three members of parliament, and the Governor, Sir Arthur Stanley, to have Elsie returned to them. Elizabeth told parliamentarian James Cameron in December 1915 that 'I am real disappointed about my daughter Elsie the only girl I got not home to have Xmas with me I would really like her to be home as same as a white mother would feel if they was in my place I am just worrying my head over her now because Xmas Day is near'.[66] The family tried to visit her, but only one visit was begrudgingly allowed by the Board, which claimed it was not in the 'girl's best interest' to return to Lake Tyers and her mother's control.

By 1921, Elsie, then 25 years old, was seeking an independent life, free of the 'Harbour', the Board and, ironically, her family. (It is unknown how the Board kept her in the Salvation Army Home given she was over eighteen.) Barrett wanted to leave the 'Harbour', absconding and refusing to eat. She desired to go into service rather than go home to Lake Tyers and pleaded until the Board let her do so. She worked for two mistresses but absconded from each after only a week. She found herself not skilled enough for the work—an indictment on her seven years at the 'Harbour'—and that it was not to her liking. Elsie then pleaded with the Board to send her home to Lake Tyers. She said she missed her mother, who was 'very cross with me for not going home to them she 'as never written to me since I told her that I was going to service and she said that she wanted me home to do the work for her seeing she is not very strong'. Elsie added that she 'would like to be earning for myself' rather than going home to Lake Tyers, but 'if anything did happen to her I shall never forgive myself because I never went home'.[67] Elsie made it home on 22 June 1921 but by early July was seeking a return to Melbourne to visit the Dental Hospital. It was a pretext, as she confessed to Parker, the Board's Secretary, in a letter mostly devoid of punctuation:

> I am very sorry I ever put my foot back on the Station I am very miserable here and discontented because I fell in love with a boy here and they won't allow me to have him but I am going to have him I am my own boss I am twenty five years of age now they wont allow me because he is an half-caste and I will have him they want to force me to have another man and I don't want them I want the man who I am after so I am full up with the place since I came back to it I am sorry I never stopped in Melbourne now I suppose it is no use of being sorry now if they don't allow me to get married to Carter I wont stop here.[68]

The 'they' who wanted to 'force' Elsie was more likely to be her family than the manager, especially as she was appealing to Parker for help. The outcome for this independent young woman who sought freedom from all authority is unclear, as her case file ended with this letter. Marriage and death records for Victoria do not reveal any further details of Elsie Barrett.[69]

By 1916 the Board's management was not only autocratic but unsupervised. Its affairs were run by its Secretary, as the Board's membership had dwindled to three, and it had not met for two years or issued an annual report to Parliament for four. In 1916 it was reconstituted by the Chief Secretary to comprise those members of Parliament in whose districts Aboriginal reserves and depots existed, although the ageing Anne Bon remained on the Board.[70] Board and Parliament became closely linked and this made the reserves more vulnerable to budgetary arguments. In 1917 the Board surveyed the remaining reserves, the Chief Secretary commenting that, 'a great waste of effort had been going on and that the best efforts could only be attained by concentration in one settlement'.[71] It resolved 'that Blacks be concentrated at Lake Tyers on account of climatic conditions, & isolated situation, lack of main roads & absence of hotels in District'.[72] Donald McLeod told Parliament in 1919 that an industrial training centre was mooted for Lake Tyers to provide the people with work skills, as they were a 'race of vagrants' who went shearing or fencing, then headed to town where they drank their cheque and caused trouble.[73]

James Menzies, a Board member (and father of Prime Minister R.G. Menzies), acknowledged Aboriginal sentiment for their land. However, he added that, as many of Cummeragunja's residents (a mission in New South Wales on the northern bank of the Murray River near Moama) were from across the border in Victoria, this was proof that Aboriginal people could 'settle down on a station far remote'. This was drawing a long bow as those Victorians settled at Cummeragunja were not from afar but only from across the Murray. Menzies also made a remarkable statement that appeared to turn the policy clock back to pre-1886 times, declaring that 'the half-castes are principally concentrated in the [ration] depots, and legally they have no claim upon us, but we considered that they, too, should be brought together with the aborigines, and the whole lot segregated at Lake Tyers, which is veritably a blackfellow's earthly paradise'.[74] Menzies' views were both coercive, ludicrous and in opposition to those of the Board, which strove to remove as many Aboriginal people as possible from government support.

Reserve closures

The decline of each reserve has its own history, but again Coranderrk's fate, being near Melbourne, was the most controversial. Around 1900, its population was over 80, including 13 children who still attended the Badger Creek School being somewhat 'shy' among the white children. The farm and hop gardens were productive, cows were milked to supplement rations, and bush tucker supplemented the meat ration. Visitors came to view Aboriginal people and the residents compensated for these gazes by selling boomerangs and crafts. Miss Valentine Leeper, interviewed in 1989, said she was cradled in Barak's arms as a one-year-old during a visit with her family around 1900.[75]

But age and the Act took its toll on Coranderrk. Barak died in 1904 aged about 85, and one of his 'speakers', Robert Wandin, died in 1908 from heart disease at 54. Wandin's son Joseph, a pupil teacher in 1902, was by 1908 a qualified teacher at Mordialloc State School—a potential leader lost to the reserve. By 1910 hop production declined as the plants needed renewal, but there was insufficient labour to replant.[76] However, the women were taught raffia weaving and were soon preparing baskets for sale to visitors. In 1910 the adults and children, all apart from two men, pledged themselves to total abstinence from alcohol and formed a branch of the Band of Hope Temperance Society, which met on Thursday evenings, 'the natives taking an active part in it reciting, singing etc'.[77] The residents formed a football team in 1911 and the manager, C. Robarts, reported in the same year that 'the school room is lit up nearly every evening for games, club swinging, ball punching, dancing, etc. This gives them pleasure during the long evenings, keeps them out of mischief and from seeking pleasure elsewhere'.[78] The people visited nearby Healesville, the women and children attending the picture theatre, but the men were still attracted to drink by the 'half castes' free of the Act.[79] In 1915, when the Chief Secretary suggested that Aboriginal people might be concentrated at Coranderrk, the Healesville Shire Council feared the town's tourist potential would be endangered by such a 'congregation of a degenerate race' and foreshadowed a public protest.[80]

The fate of most reserves was sealed in 1917 once Lake Tyers was designated as the point of concentration for all reserve dwellers. In 1917 Lake Condah was closed, its land leased and its residents scattered. Some, like Angelina McRae's family, went to live at Bunyip with a missionary, Sister Heatherington, before moving to Lake Tyers, while others went directly to Lake Tyers.[81] By 1921 there were only 331 Aboriginal people on the Board's books, 154 at Lake Tyers, 52 at Coranderrk,

Children outside Lake Condah school, about 1927. The church remained open to the people and a point of contact. Back row, L–R: Angus Alberts, Murray Lovett, Joyce Taylor (McKinnon). Front row, L–R: June Lovett and Rene King. (Connie Hart Collection, courtesy of Museum Victoria, XP2341)

66 at Framlingham, 19 at Lake Condah, 33 at ration depots such as Lake Moodemere, three in institutions and four in service.[82] The Board began transferring residents from all remaining reserves to Lake Tyers. In January 1922 government ministers, including the Minister for Soldier Settlement, inspected Coranderrk with a view to moving the fifty residents once sufficient houses had been built at Lake Tyers.[83] George Terrick, an Aboriginal ex-serviceman, wrote to Ann Bon in October 1922 for help 'to get a block of land at Coranderrk when it is broken up. I have been wounded at the war and unable to do any hard work and I would like to have some land to do a bit of farming'.[84] His request failed. Many of the residents were moved in 1923, the Mullett family, for instance, being forced to leave the reserve (and their aged parents) under police escort.[85] The twelve remaining residents protested by letter and after a further ministerial visit in January 1924, a compassionate Cabinet allowed them to remain at Coranderrk for the rest of their lives.[86] Similar agreements were made for elderly Lake Condah and Framlingham residents.

The Board's memorial and centenary tributes

The Aboriginal population fell by 27 per cent between 1901 and 1927 to number 514 by 1927. Victorians leafing through their newspapers read of the continued decline in Aboriginal numbers, especially those of 'full' descent, the only people popularly considered to be 'real' Aboriginal people. The headlines told the story bluntly. One headline in April 1923 read, 'Dwindling Aborigines. Only 84 of Full Blood Remain', while another in March 1927 stated, 'Aboriginal Population Numbers Declining. Only 55 in Victoria'.[87]

Articles listed the deaths of those people claimed to be the 'last of the tribe'. In 1911 Peter Maginnes, 65, 'last of the Lake Corrong' people, died, being farewelled by the press as 'an intelligent native' who was 'well liked'. In 1929 Benjamin Manton (called 'Lanky' as he was just five feet tall), died at Lake Tyers aged 86, the 'oldest full-blood' there. 'Lanky' and his wife had been removed from Coranderrk to Lake Tyers, allowed to return for a while, but then in 1927 returned to Lake Tyers to be near their children and many grandchildren. In 1937 Archie Pepper of Mystic Park died aged about 80, allegedly the 'last of the aborigines in Swan Hill'.[88] Then, in 1942, Mary Woorlong, daughter of Chief Woorlong and Minnie, 'last of the Mildura tribe', died aged 63, amidst much sadness as she was 'well-liked by all Mildura and popular with visitors'. Mary

Woorlong achieved fame when a London magazine published her story, and her photograph is still featured in the Mildura Historical Society's exhibition.[89]

These 'last of the tribe' claims emerged, as we have seen earlier, from racist views of Aboriginal people based on biological definitions of group membership, which only ascribed a true Aboriginal identity to those of 'full blood' and denied it to those of 'mixed descent'. Aboriginal people themselves emphasised a cultural and associational definition of Aboriginality, not a biological one. The passing of those of 'mixed descent' was, however, sometimes deemed newsworthy. Pelham Cameron of Dimboola was given an obituary in the Melbourne *Herald* when he died in 1932, aged 79. Cameron was 'highly respected in the district and was considered the greatest living authority on the history and legends of his mother's tribe'—not 'his tribe' as he was not considered truly Aboriginal. He was also remembered as being a great sportsman in rowing, cricket and football.[90]

Ignoring the claims of those of 'mixed descent' to Aboriginality, Victorians wrongly assumed they were witnessing the demise of Aboriginal people—judged only as 'full bloods'—and became nostalgic about it. This is particularly evident in the plans to erect a memorial over William Barak's grave. The Board proposed this after Barak's death in 1904, as he was a 'prominent and respected old blackfellow who lived and died a Christian', but the Chief Secretary would not release the £20 for this memorial (equal to ten weeks of a base salary).[91] In October 1931 the Healesville branch of the Australian Natives Association, a patriotic friendly and health society, successfully launched an appeal for £70 to erect a memorial stone over the grave of 'King Barak of the Yarra Tribe'.[92] Anne Bon had already donated an Italian marble slab worth over £300. Sir John Macfarland, Chancellor of Melbourne University, called for a national appeal in memory of the whole Aboriginal race, as well as in memory of Barak, for 'we have not only dispossessed this people, but by our vices and diseases we have largely hastened their extermination'.[93] The appeal led to an outpouring of sentiment, with Barak made more noble through nostalgia. Johannes Hagenauer wanted to recognise 'in this Australian Black the essentials of character and greatness'. Margaret Cameron, whose father was Rev. Robert Hamilton, recalled being at Barak's marriage ceremony performed by her father. Reverend Douglas Bruce, who conducted services at Coranderrk, said Barak attended church 'possessing a heart as white as the suit he wore'. Reverend Hugh Jones of Ormond, who had conducted Barak's funeral service, recalled that John Green had told him Barak was a 'man of great intelligence'. Frances Fraser remembered his 'unconscious royal bearing'. Other correspondents discussed the drawings of Barak's they had in their possession, Eva Hughes recalling the colours being made from 'leaves and berries then found in the Lilydale hills'. Other letter writers discussed two paintings made of him from life.[94]

The *Argus* published a long appreciation of Barak by his old friend Anne Bon who outlined his career from his presence at the signing of the Batman treaty, his training in Rev. Langhorne's school and the Native Police, and his Christian conversion, to his artistic and political work at Coranderrk.[95] The newspaper also published an edition of Barak's own 'My Words', dictated in 1882 and edited by Mrs Aeneas Gunn, author of *We of the Never Never*.[96] The *Argus* wrote a long and remarkable editorial, 'Barak's People', which was sparked by the memorial idea and permeated by the guilt and regret of the coloniser. It mused on the rise and fall of civilisations and nations, adding that it is a 'poor people which does not remember the past'. It stated that, besides the ethnological importance of Aboriginal people, it was 'time their importance in the story of the land was recognised. They make one of the last links with an Australia that is changing beneath our hands'. It concluded that they were worth remembering 'as some atonement for the undoubted wrongs which they suffered' and as 'Australia has little enough of tradition and story, little enough of the riches of the past to call upon for colour and wonderment in the present, is not the aboriginal race fit subject for speculation and romance as wild and startling as any the world has known?' It pondered their origins, their antiquity, and their relationship 'to the cradle of mankind'. The editorial added: 'The aborigines are going. It is good that monuments should be raised while there is yet time'.[97]

William Barak photographed by Charles Walter about 1866. (Charles Walter Album courtesy of John Green Parkinson, reproduced courtesy of Museum, Victoria, XP1952)

Months later, the site for Barak's memorial was debated and Healesville was decided upon, as Coranderrk was now under lease to a grazier. After the memorial's erection in the main street in mid 1934, controversy erupted due to its impact on property values, as some believed it looked too 'unsightly as it is too much like a grave stone'.[98] Others defended it as a reminder of 'a departing race and its departed king'.[99] The Council agreed to soften it with landscaping. Councillor Kay reportedly stated:

> Had the monument been altered into the shape of a column, with a bronze medallion by Mr Paul Montford, as originally intended, it would have been suitable and an acquisition to the town. But a tombstone in front of a ratepayer's property was really objectionable. If it could be obscured by trees and otherwise camouflaged it would have to serve the purpose for the time, and its removal could be left to future generations.[100]

The future dealt with the memorial—and quickly. W. J. Dawborn reported in 1946 that the memorial suffered a 'mishap' and it 'fell to pieces' and was lying uncared for at the Shire Council's depot.[101] In 1955 the Melbourne Bread and Cheese Club urged that the Coranderrk cemetery be cleaned up and Barak's memorial relocated there, where it remains today.[102]

In 1934 the centenary celebrations of Victoria's first European settlement at Portland further memorialised a 'passing race'. F. Wood Jones, Professor of Anatomy at Melbourne University, chaired the formation of the Victorian Anthropological Society in February 1934 with the words: 'it was up to us to do something for the remnant of the aboriginal race which was on the verge of extinction in Victoria'. He proposed a focus not only on their general anthropology, but on treating them as a 'living people' by appreciating their arts and crafts and other knowledge, and considering the 'humanitarian side' of their situation.[103] Within a month he and several colleagues, including anthropologist Donald Thomson, were hard at work photographing and taking total body measurements of thirty-three 'full bloods' at Lake Tyers.[104] Wood Jones, a liberal thinker, remarked that Aboriginal hair patterns on the back of their heads showed they had advanced one step further from the apes than had whites.[105] Thomson lamented the lack of research into their kinship and language, claiming only two speakers of any traditional language remained, due to the mixing of language groups on the reserves.[106] The Eltham artist Percy Learson was also at work painting portraits of the 'forty-six' listed 'full bloods' at Lake Tyers, Framlingham and elsewhere, which were exhibited at the Athenaeum Gallery in September 1934 under the title 'The Last of the Victorian Aborigines'. The Exhibition catalogue listed the biographical details of those thirty-one painted and the fifteen still to be painted. Learson discussed the gathering of these details and concluded there is 'little prospect that there will be another generation of full-bloods'.[107] Most of Learson's paintings are now held by the State Library of Victoria.

While these people were busy recording a 'passing race', historians were compiling their own version of Victoria's past. The official publication, *Victoria's First Century, a Historical Survey* (1934), devoted five pages to Aboriginal people. The book was framed by hierarchical thinking, claiming 'the lower race had absorbed the vices and evil habits of the superior one'. However, the authors admitted that about 400 Aboriginal people had been slain by whites, with blacks in turn killing about 50 whites, and added that 'probably in no other country has occupation been accompanied by less bloodshed'. The comparative claim was debatable, but the estimate of deaths was not wildly inaccurate and the use of the word 'occupation' rather than 'settlement' acknowledged forced entry onto Aboriginal lands. However, the foreword written by W. Russell Grimwade contradicted the text, showing he had not read it. He wrote: 'We are the gainers by the foresight, courage and hardihood of those who came to an empty land . . . uncoloured by the light of battle'.[108]

Writer Kathleen Ussher's *Hail Victoria* (1934) was at one point dishonest too: writing of Victoria's 'quiet pastoral' beginning, she claimed it was free of the 'clash of war', as the 'blackfellows for the most part were singularly uninterested in the white invaders'. Yet Ussher contradicted her own claim of peacefulness by using the word 'invaders' and writing of a 'certain resistance from the natives' in defence of their women and hunting grounds.[109] Ambrose Pratt's work, *The Centenary History of Victoria* (1934), was more critical. He argued the demise of Aboriginal people was due mostly to disease, and that the 'first settlers and Government sinned, if they sinned, in ignorance, and that they sincerely and assiduously endeavoured to preserve and improve the conditions of the people whose country they had invaded'. Pratt acknowledged Aboriginal land ownership and that this had led to clashes in its defence. He termed Justice Willis's acquittal of Bolden over the killing of an Aboriginal man, Tatkiar, in 1842 as 'revolting', as it allowed Aboriginal people to be cleared from legally licensed runs. This, he said, led to the 'total deprivation of their human rights and put their lives at the mercy of the white settlers'.[110] All three books discussed Aboriginal people in the dim past with no recognition of their current situation or status.

These histories, like Barak's memorial, promoted the old but still vibrant idea that Aboriginal people would not survive. Daisy Bates, the well-known philanthropic figure who ministered to Aboriginal groups at Ooldea on the Nullarbor in the interwar years, produced a widely publicised account of her life in 1938 under the title, *The Passing of the Aborigines.* In 1946, one in five Australian households purchased a children's swap-card encyclopaedia issued by Sanitarium breakfast foods, in which it was claimed Aboriginal people were a 'dying race'.[111] The old idea of their doom was popular and tenacious.

Advertising in the interwar period made much play on Aboriginal 'primitiveness', consigning Aboriginal people to a timeless past of spearholding hunters and gatherers. Others made smart play on words, advertising 'Lubra-Kate' lubricants. Much of this advertising made comment on blackness, as if their colour summed up Aboriginal people. The most blatant advertisement was for 'Nulla-Nulla Australia's White Hope the Best Household Soap'. It was claimed 'knocks dirt on the head'. This slogan was accompanied by a drawing of an unmistakable Aboriginal bust complete with brass kingplate around the neck, on which was inscribed the word 'dirt'. A wooden spoon was whacking the person on the head.[112] The unmistakable implication was that Aboriginal people were dirt. Advertising was a powerful purveyor of ideas for all people. In the interwar period an Aboriginal girl from Lake Tyers was found wandering the streets of Melbourne with a suitcase full of soap she had bought, which was advertised with the words 'leaves the skin soft and white'.[113]

The fate of reserve lands

During the interwar years, the Board urged governments to sell up all reserve lands, except for small living areas where it allowed a few older residents to live out their days. However, although legislation was constantly drafted by the Board, governments failed to act. For almost thirty years the Healesville Shire Council, the local Progress Association, the Returned Soldiers League and the local member William Everard, repeatedly tried through public meetings, petitions and parliament to excise Coranderrk for soldier settlement. However, Premier Graham Berry, who had made Coranderrk a 'permanent' reserve in 1884, made its break-up difficult. In 1941 the Board valued Coranderrk, Framlingham and Lake Condah at over £21,000, and the government again considered soldier settlement on the land.[114] During the Second World War local

The Marks and Harrison families, Dimboola–Antwerp region, about 1920.
(Alick and Merle Jackomos collection, courtesy Merle Jackomos)

graziers still leased the reserves except for small living areas which housed three people at Coranderrk, fourteen at Lake Condah, seven at Elliminyt, and a dozen at Framlingham.[115] Not all settlers coveted Aboriginal land. In 1942 the Portland Shire Council resisted moves to open the Lake Condah reserve for soldier settlement, arguing it should be retained for Aboriginal people.[116] Three residents still on Board's rations at Lake Condah by 1943 were Mrs Hannah Lovett, her brother Alf McDonald and Mrs H. Connolly, all of them in their mid-eighties. Five of Hannah's sons served in the Great War and four of them and a grandson were away in the Second World War.[117] Soldier settlement on remaining Aboriginal reserve land was mooted at the close of war.

In 1945 protests by Fitzroy's Aboriginal residents extracted a promise to reserve at least the Coranderrk cemetery.[118] In early 1948 Aboriginal activist Shadrach James argued for Aboriginal smallholders to settle on Coranderrk.[119] However, later that year Coranderrk's unique 'permanent' status was revoked by Act of Parliament, and the land, except for the cemetery, handed to the Soldier Settler Commission. In 1948 Elliminyt and Lake Condah were sold as well, except for the land around St Mary's, Condah's church. Aboriginal returned serviceman Herbert Lovett, who served in both wars, asked the Board for land at Lake Condah once it was converted to soldier settlement. There was deep anger when neither

Herbert nor any other Aboriginal serviceman received a block. This anger was still expressed to me by descendants over fifty years later, arising, as it did from their deep love for Lake Condah.

Affection for reserve lands burnt strong. Aboriginal people who lived near Lake Condah at Greenvale, Dunmore and the area known as 'the forest', maintained a strong community life through Lake Condah, visiting most Sundays for church services at St Mary's, and for dances and singing at the old school. Euphemia Day (nee Lovett) recalled of the immediate postwar years that: 'the Mission was still the central point for Aboriginal families in the area. We would walk from Greenvale, about 30 of us, to the Mission and have a great day playing tennis and cricket'. However, authorities claimed St Mary's bluestone walls developed a 'fatal' crack and instead of saving it, conveniently dynamited it in 1957. Euphemia Day added: 'Our whole being was in that old church. They just wanted to break any ties we had with the Mission'.[120]

In 1932 the Secretary of the Board, A. E. Parker, told the *Herald* that while the 'full bloods' continued to decline, 'half castes' were maintaining their numbers. In fact he should have admitted they were increasing in number. Parker added: 'There is evidence that they will continue to be a problem for the state'.[121] The reverse was also true—that the State was a problem for Aboriginal people of 'mixed descent', because the Board maintained the fiction until the 1950s that they were not Aboriginal. In the two generations after 1886, reserves were whittled away and closed, and Aboriginal people, mostly of 'mixed descent', were scattered across Victoria: some at Lake Tyers and Framlingham; some in camps new and old; and others in Melbourne.

In 2008 new demographic research using genealogies revealed two things about the survival of Victoria's Aboriginal people. First, the 'disappearance' of many Aboriginal people by 1900 was due to the Board's definitions of Aboriginality. After the 1886 Act and removal of those of 'mixed descent', they were not counted as Aboriginal people. Similarly, the research explained the rapid growth of the Aboriginal population after the Board's definition of Aboriginality changed in the 1950s. Second, the research revealed that the reserves did in fact protect those on them, despite the controlling nature of the Board. The researchers argued Aboriginal Victorians are: 'descended from the approximately 500 individuals collected on the Board's reserves in the 1870s. The other 500 to 1,000 people recorded by the Board and the colonial census as living outside the reserves appear to have left scarcely any descendants except a handful of families who, significantly, had some land of their own'.[122]

11

'Old Lake Tyers'

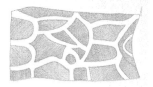

The Anglican Church formed Lake Tyers reserve in 1861 and the kindly and paternal John Bulmer (a Reverend after 1904) managed it until the Board took control in 1907. The reserve residents were fearful of the change and relieved when Bulmer was retained as their spiritual guide until his death in 1913. However, secular management backed by new legislation in 1915 created a tougher regime. Then, in 1917, the Board made Lake Tyers its central reserve to bring greater efficiency into its management of Aboriginal people under the Act. Strangers were brought to Tyers over the next decade as Lake Tyers grew and the other reserves declined. Despite some progressive staff, Lake Tyers became a place of control, offering little 'incentive and much despair. Paradoxically, it remained a cherished home—'old Lake Tyers'—for many people.

The Board takes control

Captain Howe, appointed assistant manager to John Bulmer in 1905, took control of the sixty residents at Lake Tyers from 1907 to 1917. The 1886 Act and that of 1915, which extended new powers over reserves, together with Howe's personality, brought a new harshness to this remote Gippsland reserve. Residents' movements, work, leisure, rations, family and kin contacts, and also relationships with children, were controlled by the Board and the manager. Howe sent people to Lake Condah for 'misbehaviour', refused the return of others, held back the wages of those who gambled in their spare time, destroyed the people's beloved dogs, and generally made their life under the Act difficult and sometimes miserable. It is thus ironic that eleven men from Lake Tyers

Wedding at Lake Tyers, 1905, photographed by H.D. Bulmer. Rev. John Bulmer is in clerical robes on the left. (Courtesy of La Trobe Picture Collection, State Library of Victoria, H18850)

enlisted to fight for freedom and the Empire, four being killed in action.[1]

The Board had a say in people's lives right down to the smallest detail, including how they lived in their houses and what clothes they wore. The women did not sew as they had on earlier missions, but had their clothing made at Pentridge Prison in Melbourne from waist and height measurements.[2] Some people resisted Howe's despotism. Emily Stephens, who moved from Ramahyuck to Lake Tyers in 1905, fought a prolonged campaign against Howe over conditions there and control over her children, related in Pepper and De Araugo's *The Kurnai of Gippsland* (1985).[3] Stephens was eventually removed to Lake Condah for making trouble.

Life at Lake Tyers was beyond close scrutiny by outsiders, although visitors might have gleaned information on the regime there if they had not been distracted by the colourful nature of reserve life. The Board worried that 'a number of the tourists sympathise with the inmates and lead them to believe they are not being well treated'.[4] Trips to Lake Tyers were so popular with tourists that the Board limited visits in 1914 to a few hours a day.[5] The residents welcomed visitors as they sold artefacts and performed for them, earning more than they did from paid reserve work. On Boxing Day 1925, 500 visitors witnessed minstrel performances with voice and piano, gumleaf band renditions of popular songs, boomerang throwing, traditional fire-lighting technique displays, and purchased baskets and artefacts. At each performance the hat was passed around. Aboriginal children posed before picturesque scenes, but averted their eyes until a penny was offered. Children also scrambled for coins thrown by tourists. A journalist, Marjorie Pryor, worried about the 'combined pleasures of a zoo and a circus' and a writer for the *Bairnsdale Advertiser* bemoaned the relationship of 'mendicant to a patron' that operated, marked by 'wholesale and offensive and demoralising "cadging"'.[6] The Board reduced visits to two afternoons a week in the 1920s, and in 1930 ordered that proceeds from artefact sales go to reserve income and not individuals.

Authority was contested daily at Lake Tyers as residents, the manager and Board manoeuvred over freedom of movement on and off the reserve. The Board initially allowed men to work off the reserve, so fulfilling promises they'd made to lure people there. However, in 1923 this ceased, with the Board reasoning that the men were 'competing unfairly with white workers for three months of the year and being supported by the Government for nine months'. In 1924 the Board tried to enlist police support to stop the men leaving for work, but the police refused to act, saying no law was being broken.[7] At the individual level battles raged. Jack Green moved between Orbost and Lake Tyers frequently between 1922 and 1925, being at various times licensed, placed on probation and expelled. He was reported for drinking and gambling at Orbost, no doubt like many other rural labourers, but this was unacceptable to the Board. His wife also complained 'he would not give her any money. That he gambled all he got'. Green was rebellious too, being involved in pilfering from the station food store in 1927.[8] However, when the police searched the reserve to expel him, they 'received a hostile reception from women'.

Resistance to the Board's control continued as the number of Aboriginal people living under the Act at Lake Tyers swelled to over 250 in 1925–26 due to transfers from Coranderrk, Framlingham, Lake Condah, and the Ebenezer area.[9] Trouble erupted publicly in 1927 after a new assistant manager, Thomas Hollingsworth, disagreed with the manager, George Baldwin, about the degree of familiarity Hollingsworth allowed the Aboriginal residents to display, including the use of his first name. Hollingsworth reported that while he 'hounded' the residents to work, he would not treat them 'like dogs'. The Board dismissed Hollingsworth after an inquiry in August 1927. Within days the residents, led by Braggin Scott and Jack Green, went on strike, demanding his reinstatement and an inquiry into conditions at Lake Tyers. The Board retaliated, expelling several men from the reserve.

Postcard of Lake Tyers 1910. L–R: Sarah Moffat (nee Scott), two children on the wheelbarrow unidentified, Lance McDougall (holding the barrow), Kassy McDougall (black dress), Ellen Hood. (Courtesy Museum Victoria, XP2765)

In October 1927 some unnamed Aboriginal residents visited W. Gordon Sprigg, secretary of the Collins Street Baptist Church, who alerted the Baptist Assembly to conditions on the reserve. Sprigg claimed that conditions were deplorable, rations for reserve workers were inadequate and there was a lack of milk for the children.[10] The government denied the allegations and invited Sprigg to tour Lake Tyers. Sprigg demanded 'unrestricted' access, but Baldwin, the manager, backed by the Board, refused him permission to interview the residents without Baldwin being present. Sprigg left the station in disgust, but agreed to these conditions six weeks later. Sprigg's report neglected his original claims, but called for repairs to the bath house water supply and replacement of fishing equipment, the institution of a regular vegetable ration, and better control of the young to prevent immorality. He denied outside influence had caused the recent strike, saying the residents told him they struck 'for more tucker and more freedom'.[11]

When Chief Secretary George Prendergast visited in April 1928 he complained that Lake Tyers was a mixture of 'trouble and expense'.[12] The Board lost faith in Baldwin and he resigned. The government also introduced a new Aborigines Act (1928) which mirrored the 1915 Act, but its regulations finally issued in May 1931 included several new clauses. One clause, 34(b), empowered the manager to fine those breaching 'good behaviour' or committing minor offences a maximum of £2 (equivalent to several weeks reserve wages). Another, (clause 37), allowed for those refusing to work to be expelled from the reserve.[13]

Newman's reforms

The Board selected a new manager, Captain J. A. Newman, formerly commander of the boys' reformatory training ship 'John Murray', head of the French Island reformatory, and a farmer with ten years experience.[14] Despite this disciplinary background, people on the reserve liked and respected Newman and his wife the matron, as they introduced new ideas to increase the residents' sense of responsibility and freedom. These included vocational training in carpentry, manual arts and cookery, Aboriginal participation in a rebuilding program, and the instilling of a capitalistic ethic. The latter was attempted by placing several families on small individual farming blocks on unused reserve lands with rations and equipment for the first year and the freedom to create and keep any surplus produce. The Wandin and Marks families were chosen to participate in the scheme because of their light skin colour and were the first to make a go of it.[15]

Newman also introduced improvements to the herd, introduced farming machinery, and suggested ways of creating a permanent water and electricity supply. The Board approved many of his recommendations. When Board members visited the reserve in October 1929 they were delighted by the transformation. They reported that 'discontent' among the residents had disappeared, the people were more 'industrious' and healthier, and that the facilities had been improved at little cost by Aboriginal labour. Houses were repainted and landscaped, the jetty remodelled, pasture improved, land cleared and more placed under cultivation. The Board summed it up: 'Newman is a wizard. He has added a couple of thousand pounds or more to the material value of the mission' and improved the morale. It added that 'grievances have evaporated, work has become popular and cooperation a factor'.[16]

Newman fostered self-discipline and self-reliance much as John Green had done at Coranderrk, although in a more paternal and less brotherly way. He instituted a police patrol of three ex-servicemen residents to maintain order and keep trespassers away. He introduced (with the sanction of the Crown Law Department) a native court that dealt with disciplinary issues, and punished offenders by extracting supervised unpaid labour on land clearing projects at an outstation, Spring Creek. It is unclear who ruled this court, but it was probably Newman. He fixed the bath houses and urged their use, and organised two youths to be apprenticed to a Melbourne landscape gardener. Newman also levied four shillings a month, about five per cent of the male reserve wage, for a sports fund. This guaranteed one film screening on the reserve per month, purchased sports equipment, and established a fund to pay half-wages to those sick or injured. The Board heard no complaints from Aboriginal people about all this. Newman even allowed sports teams to go to Bairnsdale on their 'honour' without 'white supervision'.[17]

The Lake Tyers School benefited from the new approach. The school files revealed that from 1900 a succession of teachers came through the school, many staying less than a year, some finding the experience 'distasteful'. A teacher, Dorothy Tonkin typically reported in 1915 that the 'reasoning power of the aboriginals was very low' and that they lacked 'animation'. She feared they dragged down the four white pupils who attended from neighbouring properties. Tonkin admitted that reserve life gave Aboriginal pupils a 'poor general background on which to build new knowledge, and then again, their home life is not conducive to learning'.[18] She suggested a shift to manual training, a shift which was indeed made in the 1920s and provided an educational focus that seemed more relevant to the community.

George Chapman, a teacher who came to Lake Tyers School in 1924 and liked the people there, consolidated this shift to vocational education, making 30 per cent of the timetable woodwork or sewing. He reported in April 1929 that the boys were 'keenly enthusiastic' in woodworking and their parents were 'very interested too and take a keen delight in examining the finished models of the boys'. Whereas Tonkin found their standard of work to be below that of white children in 1915, Chapman wrote in 1929 that it 'compares favourably with that of white children'. Useful items were made by the boys, and the girls sewed 1,219 garments in eighteen months for themselves, the young and the ill at Lake Tyers. All children worked in the experimental gardening plots which assisted the reserve's agricultural development.[19] The boys' products—knife boxes, nut dishes and crumb trays—were featured at a schools' display at Bairnsdale and sold to viewers.[20] Newman and Chapman also encouraged self-expression through a minstrel troupe and sport.

The residents were encouraged to take their minstrel performances— usually given on visitors' days—off the reserve, establishing important

Gum Leaf Band, Lake Tyers. (Courtesy of Amy and Robert Lowe, Warrnambool)

connections with the outside world. The minstrel group first performed at the Bairnsdale Mechanics Institute in November 1929 before a large and enthusiastic crowd, raising £22 to add to the £38 they had already raised for the Bairnsdale Hospital. The group performed forty items, most accompanied by Miss Moffat, playing the piano from memory. Many were popular American minstrel songs, 'Old Black Joe', 'Old Kentucky Home' and Home Sweet Home', which they sang at the reserve, but they performed 'Going Back to Lake Tyers' as well. The highlights of the program were Herb Murray's comic interpretation of the song 'All Along the Road', which brought down the house, and the gumleaf choir and gumleaf solos also proved popular. The Lake Tyers minstrels also raised money for unemployment relief.[21] More concerts in Bairnsdale, Sale and Lakes Entrance followed. Within eight months the group, whose members had so little themselves, had raised £160 for charities, an amount equal to an average male worker's annual salary. In 1934 Lake Tyers people appeared on ABC radio 3LO. Lake Tyers' then oldest resident, Gwennie O'Rourke, aged 80, talked of the old days, 'Chook' Mullett and Laurie Moffat sang solos, a chorus of 60 children performed and the gumleaf band played.[22]

While there are no details of other appearances by the band, music played a large part in the people's lives, their identity and their attachment to land. Mary Pepper, when in Melbourne recovering from an illness, asked for the song 'Neath the Mia-Mia's Leafy Shadow' to be sung to her, which she said Captain Newman wrote.

Its chorus went:

> Rolling home, rolling home
> Rolling home fair land to see,
> Rolling home to old Lake Tyers,
> Rolling home fair land to thee

Pepper told Anna Vroland, with whom she was staying:

> That little bit of land at Lake Tyers is ours. I was born there. Lakes and trees
> and hills. Some day the dark people must get it back. We really own the soil.
> They can't always separate us from it. Some day we'll come and go from
> our homes just like white people do; just as we want to. And we'll invite our
> friends. I'd like you to visit me in my home, without having to ask anyone for
> a permit. I want my little ones to have a better life than I have had.[23]

The Lake Tyers residents were sports fanatics and Newman again
encouraged their participation in the wider world of competitive sport to
increase self-discipline and self-esteem. In April 1929 he sought admittance
to the East Gippsland Australian Rules Football seniors' competition for
a Lake Tyers team. Newman asked a meeting of the Association's club
delegates why the Lake Tyers Club had ceased playing earlier in the
junior competition. Was it for financial reasons, misbehaviour or was the
'colour line' drawn, he asked. Several delegates said the club just 'dropped
out', while another alluded to some trouble at several matches. Newman
guaranteed the Lake Tyers Club's financial obligations to the League and
assured them that he or another member of staff would accompany the
team to matches. The delegates were divided. Some were inclined to
support the admittance of the Lake Tyers team as they were 'a fine body of
young athletes' and they and Newman needed support. However, others
pointed to problems for the draw from an uneven number of teams if
they were admitted. Some argued that 'every club has players who object
to play with aborigines'.[24] The application was refused on the grounds
that the Lake Tyers team was not strong enough. Newman, who believed
prejudice was involved, told delegates it was 'an extremely parochial view
to take when you consider that these people are native Australians and
under proper discipline'.[25]

During a bye in the competition, Bairnsdale agreed to play Lake Tyers
as a fund raiser, and beat Lake Tyers by 17 points in a dashing match
before a large crowd. Herb Murray, the Lake Tyers club secretary, said
they were beaten but not disgraced. The Bairnsdale Club agreed and

presented them with the ball, autographed and mounted.[26] A juniors match followed to raise funds for the hospital, Bairnsdale winning by one point. The following season (1930) Lake Tyers was admitted to the East Gippsland Association competition without a fuss, losing all seven of the matches recorded in the local press. Many Lake Tyers families were involved: the Mulletts, Moffatts, Mobournes, Hoods, Edwards, O'Rourkes, Harrisons and others. The team soon improved and were runners-up in 1933, 1935 and 1936 and premiers in 1934, 1938 and 1939.[27]

The Lake Tyers men excelled at other sports as well, in which they found they were as good, and sometimes better, than outsiders. In 1930 a Lake Tyers team played in the East Gippsland cricket competition, performing well with team members drawn from families such as the Wandins, Thorpes, Mobournes, Mulletts, Moffatts and Edwards. The cricketers won the Challenge Cup three years in a row, 1933–1935 and were runners-up in 1936, the year the Board visited and reported that the young men's hero of the season was Eddie Gilbert, the Aboriginal fast bowler who played Sheffield Shield for Queensland.[28]

Lake Tyers' runners often entered local handicap athletic events. In February 1930 the Lake Tyers Athletic Club staged its own sports meeting, which drew a large attendance at the Lakes Entrance Sports Ground, the programme 'running smoothly and up to time'. The reserve residents did well, E. Andy winning the 75- and 440-yard handicaps; R. Thorpe, the hurdle race; and Con Edwards, the 130- and 220-yard handicaps.[29] Edwards later won the Sale Gift in 1933 and Bert Hayes, the Bairnsdale and Bruthen Gifts in 1934. In 1936 boxers from Lake Tyers also won 7 of the 12 matches in the Bairnsdale and Orbost Open Tournament.[30] As Mrs V. Glen, wife of the current Lake Tyers manager in 1936, wrote: 'They are playing football today. I can hear the cheering from the house. They dearly love all kinds of sport, and Mr Glen encourages them in every way, as he thinks it gives them a much healthier outlook and gives them interests which counteract their moral shortcomings'.[31] For Aboriginal people, sporting competition and victories made them feel the equal of other Victorians.

Minstrel performances, woodworking displays and sporting competition were important means of interaction with other Gippslanders for the otherwise isolated community. However, it was perhaps vain to hope these meetings countered what ancient folklore, rumour and imagination said about those on the reserve. This is evident from a glimpse at the court reports of the *Bairnsdale Advertiser*. When a 'full blood' man was before the bench on a drunkenness charge, having been

Sonny Johnson of Lake Tyers skinning a kangaroo for a young audience.
Photograph by Alan West. (Courtesy of Museum Victoria, XP2757)

supplied with alcohol by 'half caste' friends at the Lakes Entrance Sports
Day in February 1929, Magistrate Brown repeated age-old scuttlebutt. He
commented that Aboriginal people were like children, 'their brain development ceases at 12 years of age, and they acquire undesirable habits by
memory and association'. Whites up on drinking charges did not face the
same stereotyping. Still, the slander worked in the man's favour, for this
prejudiced claim, along with Newman's testimony of his good character,
earned him a suspended sentence.[32]

The hothouse nature of the reserves—several hundred people
confined on 2,000 hectares day-in and day-out—caused flare ups. In
January 1930 police were called to Lake Tyers and suspended sentences
given out to some young people after a fracas caused by 'jealousy'.[33]
Some high-spiritedness spilled over to Lakes Entrance, causing one
correspondent to the *Bairnsdale Advertiser* to complain about the
reserve residents' use of alcohol, which had turned their creditable
behaviour to the 'unseemly'.[34] War memories rather than 'reserve-itis'
perhaps underpinned one reserve ex-service patrolmen's drinking
charges in 1930. Others clearly earned their sentences, particularly
an Aboriginal man at Stratford who assaulted a woman with a paling,
leaving her hospitalised with severe head injuries. One reserve resident,
having assaulted his wife for the fourth time, causing her finally to press

charges, was given a month in the Sale jail. He seemed unrepentant, heading for prison 'with a broad smile on his black face and a conspicuous yellow feather in his hat', wrote the *Bairnsdale Advertiser*.[35]

Aboriginal attachment to home and family was violated by the Board, which kept some people on the reserve and others off. People had to ask permission to come and go on family visits and not all reasonable requests were granted. Other people were ejected from the reserve for various reasons. Reginald Thorpe was thrown off in the late 1920s. He tried to return three times before being given a month's suspended prison sentence in May 1930. While relations with his wife were not always harmonious, he pleaded to the parliamentarian Albert Lind in July 1930 to be allowed to go to the 'edge of the Lake at Lake Tyers to see my wife & children also my mother. As Captain Newman won't allow me to go out even to this side of the Lake as I will be arrested'. Thorpe added hopefully that 'my father [Harry Thorpe] done his bit over there & through him being killed I am treated like this'. He concluded: 'it is a hard thing to be treated like this'.[36]

The Board pushed 'light coloured' families off Lake Tyers to make good in a 'white environment'.[37] John and Alice Connolly and their daughter Alice, as well as Leslie and Dora Green and their two children, were removed with the promise of child welfare assistance just as the Great Depression hit. They moved to Pinnock Street, Bairnsdale, where the police described the men as 'good working and respectable citizens', who managed to secure only scattered days of work in the tight labour market. The families lived together and pooled their resources but the child welfare assistance of 10/- per week each proved insufficient. In September 1930 Dora Green appealed to the Board for rations for Leslie and herself, saying he was looking for work, did not drink, and that they both were 'in need of clothing very bad & foot wear', also flour, tea, baking powder, soap and jam.[38] This was given as well as oatmeal, treacle and rice.

Alice Connolly wrote to Albert Lind, their local member of state parliament, claiming that whites received job preference, forcing her to be shamed by going twice to the benevolent fund. She pondered asking for a tent to save rent, but worried lest it encourage Welfare to take her child. She added: 'our colour is a curse to us we are too white for the station & when you ask for help here they say why ain't you on the station'. As other families were not put off Lake Tyers 'its not fair play at all'.[39] A year later the families still struggled, each surviving on 10/- child welfare and 10/- Sustenance payments. Alice Connolly wrote to the Chief Secretary: 'we hardly see a bit of meat and to tell you the truth

Mr Tunnecliffe we are nearly bootless & for clothes I haven't seen a new thing since we left the station'. The Board's policy created resentments. Alice Connolly complained that while her family struggled, those at Lake Tyers 'get everything they need on the station as well as their wages'.[40] By 1940 the Connellys moved to Fitzroy to continue their independent life, disappearing from the Board's records—and our view.

The removal of children by the Board continued. Albert Mullett had three brothers taken around 1934. He saw one ten years later, but two others died in the Western District, and he only found their graves in the 1990s. The Mulletts and other families moved off Lake Tyers to avoid the Board and sent their children, including Albert, to the safety of relatives in Bateman's Bay. Diane Barwick reported that banishments became more frequent during the 1930s, being 'frequently ordered at the manager's sole discretion and were automatically confirmed, without reservation, by the Board at its infrequent meetings'. She added that many families found refuge in Orbost, but amidst appalling living conditions, which were ignored by the Board, and which 'disclaimed any responsibility for those who had left Lake Tyers'.[41] Albert Mullett believed about 200 children from Lake Tyers were placed into white foster care or institutions over a generation. However, in retrospect he mused that being removed and 'growing up in the wider community made us stronger to be activists for the rights of our people'.[42]

Mounting criticism

Outside criticism of conditions at Lake Tyers continued in the 1930s. The regime became more severe under Major Glen, a former soldier, Alfred Hospital administrator and businessman, who replaced Newman in 1931.

The first criticisms were benign, coming from the Victorian Aboriginal Group, formed of philanthropic genteel women of independent means, led by Valentine Leeper and Amy Brown. The Group asked questions from 1933 about health, morality, educational and medical facilities, and suggested the appointment of an expert advisory board.[43] The Group's members were easily manipulated by Glen who fed them the official line. Amy Brown and M.A. Browne visited Lake Tyers in 1935 with Glen's approval, making rough notes as they toured with him. They described 'the school & church all buildings clean and beautifully kept', the 'cottages 3 & 4 rooms some with verandah & room at back fenced gardens in front, some cultivated others laid out nothing in them. Walls painted or calsomined flowers, table cloths, pictures & everyone tidy bright fire burning on the cold wet day'. As these houses were inspected twice weekly by Glen, they were no doubt primed for the visit. There was no evidence the two women talked with the people, who they described through Glen's eyes as being like 'natural boys of 12 childish irresponsible', as revealed by their use of building materials for firewood. The women added that the residents, although good sports, had 'no team work among themselves', lacked application and that 'girls sport quarrels, jealousies'.[44] They may just have caught the tensions produced by tight management in a closed, segregated environment.

The Group's educational sub-committee visited in 1936, praising the staff as 'strong, efficient and self-sacrificing', but criticising the residents' lack of 'moral standards and strength of character' and lack of 'a purpose in life and urge towards industry'. The sub-committee recommended vocational education, and education for 'health, for leisure and for culture, including sport, music, gardening, hobbies'. However, it saw Lake Tyers as a 'temporary expedient', and believed 'the ultimate aim should be to make this colony unnecessary'.[45] The Group clearly had no understanding of the people's attachment to 'old Lake Tyers'.

Issues of authority arose in late 1935 and W. Gordon Sprigg lashed out again. He told the Baptist Union that the Council of Churches' recent report on Lake Tyers' administration as 'satisfactory' was wrong, as banishments were frequent, immorality was 'far too common', and two youths had been flogged with a whip, causing bruising and bleeding and weeks of soreness. The Baptist Union included Sprigg on an investigating committee.[46] The Board reported that Major Glen claimed the boys were caned not whipped, and it had been done 'on the recommendation of a committee of Aborigines' in the presence of the president and secretary of this committee and a police officer. The youths had soon returned to work. The police, not unexpectedly, affirmed this account.[47] In January and February 1936 a crossfire of claims were made in the press about the Baptist report, by Sprigg, the committee members, and the government, concerning the truth of Sprigg's accusations.[48] The Baptist committee found that unauthorised punishments and banishments were made by the manager himself, not by the Board 'sitting judicially' and the 'committee of Aborigines' did not rate a mention. Its report pointed out that while the boys were not caned excessively, no regulation authorised such punishment. It also upheld Sprigg's claim of prevalent immorality 'amongst a primitive people, especially when congregated in one settlement'.[49]

Reactions to these injustices varied. The Chief Secretary claimed

Maria Harrison and children outside a Lake Tyers house, about 1960.
(A. & M. Jackomos Collection, courtesy of Museum Victoria, XP3402)

there was nothing in the allegations or the report to undermine the public's confidence in the Board and Major Glen.[50] Later that year L. Chapman, Secretary to the Board, using colonial language, declared of those at Lake Tyers: 'these natives were really better off than natives in other states ... and than most of the natives outside the station'.[51] One of the two youths caned made a written statement—out of truth, bravado or duress is unclear—and claimed they had been cheeky and their punishment had not made them cry out or bleed. He told the chaplain at Lake Tyers that 'I was not a mass of blood and bruises. It did not hurt very much'. The other youth, then in prison, was unable to make a statement about his injuries.[52] William Cooper, Secretary of the Australian Aborigines League, privately thanked Sprigg for his efforts, writing: 'For far too long there has been ruthlessness in dealing with our race and it is from friends as you that we feel an improvement will come. We know the truth of what you said'.[53]

Stewart Hood of Lake Tyers made a statement on oath not published at the time. He stated: 'There is a distinct feeling prevailing on the station that the native residents are at the mercy of the manager who summarily banishes them without first consulting the Board'. He accused Mrs Glen of inattention to residents' health needs. She inspected their houses twice a week, but did not visit when there were 'cases of known sickness'. Hood stated that one of the boys who was flogged had come to his house bleeding. He affirmed that 'immorality' was 'far too common' on the reserve and that Glen failed to check it. Glen showed too little concern for residents' 'spiritual, moral and general interest and welfare'. Hood added: 'The station is our recognised home and that of our children. It should be made a safe and attractive settlement where peace and happiness are enjoyed by all the residents'.[54]

In 1938 Alick Jackomos a Greek–Australian from Carlton, then fourteen, stayed at Lake Tyers as an illegal guest. He recalled: 'Lake Tyers had a population of 250–300 people. Most cottages were around the football ground, but the larger houses which had a bathroom and amenities were for the manager and white staff. Lake Tyers had a sewing room, maternity hospital, butcher shop, dairy, a hall for dances and concerts and a billiard room at the end of the hall. There was a primary school and a community bathroom near the swamp about 600 yards from the cottages'. The bathroom was located there, as it was the site of the original houses and had never been moved despite the inconvenience. The men grew beans for the Melbourne market for wages of three pence an hour. However, 'the local farmers complained that they were competing against cheap Aboriginal labour . . . and the project collapsed'.[55]

Pressure continued to mount from new Aboriginal support groups. In June 1941 a joint party of the Aborigines Uplift Society and the Victorian Aboriginal Group visited Lake Tyers. The party praised Lake Tyers management, but criticised the Board's policy, 'which admits of no future for the people'. Their report also condemned: 'The deplorably lazy and unambitious character of the men, and the low moral tone of the community, [which] are unavoidably perpetuated under the present system'. They recommended better training and education: a nursery school, kindergarten, handcraft and rural sciences training, followed by apprenticeships. Women should be given mothercraft and infant welfare training in sanitation and nutrition. There should be school, hall and recreation committees, the introduction of scouts, guides, a young farmers club, and of cooperative bodies such as a credit union and cooperative store. Residents should be paid for all work in order to pay for food and clothing and rent—in return for larger and more decent housing. The party's report called for reform of the Board along the lines of reforms just instituted in adjoining States, and urged a policy 'to facilitate the ultimate absorption of the native population into the economic and social life of the white community'. Their destiny was still conceived of as a white one, but the emphasis on dignity and self-reliance was important.

The Second World War provided opportunities for independence, which Glen and the Board encouraged to aid the manpower shortage in Victoria. Almost forty men volunteered for the 2nd AIF in 1940 and over twenty were accepted. By 1942 fourteen men were granted permission to leave the reserve to work: seven began labouring in Melbourne, five worked in glass manufacturing and two worked in munitions. Most resided in Fitzroy. Another seven worked on farms near Orbost.[56]

Milliken succeeded Glen as manager in 1945 and immediately caused trouble with some of the 300 residents. In January 1946 he halved the sugar ration due to low stocks, but did not consult the people. Strike action was threatened by a deputation of three men, Tom Foster, Eugene Mobourne and Bert Hayes, unless the ration was restored. Milliken ordered them to work and told Mobourne to leave the station immediately. During ration distribution at lunchtime, the men, according to Milliken, became 'noisy and used insulting language' to Mrs Milliken.[57] On Milliken's request the Board expelled Foster for six months, Hayes and Mobourne for three months (but not their families), and fellow troublemakers Carter and McDougall were expelled 'for many years, if not life'. Milliken expelled eight Aboriginal people during his two years as manager, causing great resentment as well as challenges from at least one man to fight. Milliken was bitter, saying Bert Hayes, who won £41 at Bruthen and Lake Entrance Sports meetings, feels 'almost independent of the station and work of any kind is beneath him'. This was understandable as Lake Tyers' wages were below the minimal award wage.

Milliken also claimed Tom Foster, aged 52, was 'lazy' and 'indolent' and a 'menace to the morale of the station'.[58] However, Rev. Gillespie Douglas, President of the Aborigines Uplift Society, claimed Foster, whom he described as 'one of the only four or five full-blooded Aborigines in the State and the last of the Yarra Yarra tribe', has 'an excellent character, does not smoke, drink or gamble and is endeavouring to lead a decent Christian life'.[59] J. Hawden of the Melbourne Fish Market, where Foster worked after his expulsion, wrote that he was 'very trustworthy, conscientious, sober and industrious'.[60] Management thought the worst of the people rather than the best—and probably brought out the worst in them as well.

Aboriginal frustration continued to build due to the tight control exercised at Lake Tyers. By 1950 many had moved off to find work and freedom, causing the reserve's population to fall to 150, half that of a decade earlier. Some stayed away longer than their permits allowed and thus lost their right of return and access to their houses. By 1951 half of the houses were vacant. Murray Bull recalled a happy childhood at Lake Tyers in the early 1950s, playing bush games with mates and diving for tourist coins as they had a generation earlier. He also remembered the compulsory teacher-supervised wash in the communal bath house at the end of each school day before home time: 'there was no choice'.[61] However, adults saw things differently. The people were rationed like children, and required to do work, for which they were paid in a month what they could earn in a day outside. Few worked, or worked well, as rationing and low wages induced a feeling of hopelessness. A committee of the Women's International League for Peace and Freedom which visited in 1951 wanted to increase the people's self-reliance by bringing rationing and communal bathhouses to an end, and providing postschool vocational and horticultural training. Its report noted that family members could not visit the reserve without a permit, which was 'an unnatural way of living'.[62]

Removal of children continued. One of those taken from Lake Tyers was Ronald Bull, who was removed at infancy, returned and removed again at the age of ten in 1953 to the Tally Ho Boys' home. Ronald became inspired by landscape painting, viewed the Old Masters' at the

Tommy and Herb Bull jamming at Lake Tyers in the 1950s. (A. & M. Jackomos Collection, courtesy of Museum Victoria, XP4297)

National Art Gallery and was mentored by well-known Australian landscapists Hans Heysen and Ernest Buckmaster. He spent some time in Pentridge for petty crime, painting a notable mural of an Aboriginal camp while there in 1962. Dubbed the 'new Namatjira', he exhibited European-style landscapes with leading Australian artists. Bull married in 1964, lived in the Dandenongs and exhibited frequently before poor health caused his early death in 1979.[63]

Despair and frustration grew at Lake Tyers and fighting became common. Cora Gilsenan, from a Metung pastoral family which employed, defended and sheltered Gunai/Kurnai people over the years, despaired as well. In 1953 she wrote to a fellow member of the Women's International League for Peace and Freedom, Anna Vroland, saying: if the 'dole control system is not ended' it will be useless to try and help even the reserve's children. 'For the young boys all life seems to hold is to get drunk and gamble, and for the girls all they can think of is having babies along with gambling drinking and brawls'.[64] In another letter Gilsenan wrote that the residents were receiving more help than ever but that it had 'come too late . . . the damage that was done in the Chapman reign [the Board's secretary from 1931–55], went far too deep to rectify. Turning to the drink in despair and frustration has signed their own death warrant'. She commented that 'Freddie and all the other good types of a few years ago, are today in the no hoper group. The Sale gaol is kept going by the number of dark prisoners within its walls. They are released Monday mornings and always return the following weekend'. Gilsenan added: 'My own thoughts on these regular outbreaks of violence, [is that they] may be a fore-runner to revolts. Quite often during these outbreaks all the white residents on the station are threatened and told to leave'.[65] The possibility of revolt against the system and the growth of self-control were the few bright hopes for 'old Lake Tyers' by the 1950s.

12

Fighting for Framlingham

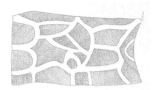

When the government set aside Framlingham's 1,640 hectares for an agricultural college in 1889, ex-reserve residents and their friends managed to claw back 225 hectares in 1892 for Aboriginal use, some of it in individual 32-hectare blocks. By 1910 Gunditjmara people John Wyselaskie, Frank Clarke and the Egan family still worked these blocks

Framlingham gathering about 1910. Back row, L-R: Unknown, William Good, Frank Clarke, Ted Mullett, Reg Rawlings, Lena Austin, Ada Austin, unknown. Centre row, L–R: Bearded man unknown, Chris Saunders (child holding hat), Herb Murray, Bill Egan, Norman Clarke, Ted Egan, unknown, unknown. Front row, L–R: Unknown, Lucy Egan, Hilda Egan, Jessie Clarke, Isabel Rawlings, Dina Rawlings, child side-on unknown, Helen Good holding Maude Fairy. (A. & M. Jackomos Collection, courtesy of Museum Victoria, XP4208)

but struggled on such small areas. The college failed to materialise on the adjoining land, which was used by 'poor men' and Gunditjmara as a living space. It reverted to weeds and bush and became rabbit-infested, to the annoyance of local farmers, but it was not alienated beyond the grasp of Framlingham people.[1] With the help of some white friends and the people's determination not to forsake it, the land was still within reach by the 1960s.

In April 1918 the Board visited Framlingham to explain the new policy of concentrating those under the Board's care at Lake Tyers. Board members claimed some Framlingham residents warmed to the idea. However, 111 people from the Warrnambool district, including 34 Aboriginal people—mostly Austins, Clarkes, Alberts, Blairs and Wyselaskies, but also Edwards, Rawlings and Couzens—petitioned parliament at the same time, requesting a new church at Framlingham to replace the one recently burnt, and stating that 'the Aborigines are very desirous to remain at Framlingham & altogether opposed to removing to Lake Tyers'.[2] Eighteen of the Aboriginal signatories resided on the reserve—'Fram' as they fondly called it—in Protection Board housing. A further sixteen lived on the adjoining agricultural college or forest land. Edna Brown, born in 1916, recalled: 'We all lived in bark humpies; our fathers cut wood or split posts for a living and that was only in the winter. There was no dole or endowment then; they also caught rabbits for their skins, the women used to make baskets and sell them in Warrnambool, we also gathered mushrooms to sell'.[3] Saturday was devoted to catching and eating bush tucker, Sunday to going to the reserve's church.

In the 1920s John Egan lived in a Board house that other 'Fram' residents called 'the Highland'. He ran some milk cows and a few horses on his block, helped by his sister Mrs Rose, who owned some stock and worked in domestic service. The other blocks were no longer worked. In 1926 Egan heard that the Board intended to lease most of the remaining reserve land and wrote anxiously to Henry Bailey the local member of state parliament for help. Egan admitted that gates were left open at times (but not by him), fences needed repairing, and that the reserve was 'growing nothing but "capeweed", "thistles" and rabbits, and harbouring and feeding stock off the roads', but not on his block. Egan, who received rations, stated: 'I would rather do without the "rations" "clothes" etc. (which the Board has always so generously allowed me) rather than be deprived of my little holding'. He added: 'It is only a matter of a few more years Sir, and the Board won't be troubled with me, I am not a young man, hospital life has left its mark on me'.[4] The

Board decided to lease all but 20 acres, twelve acres of which would be used as a living area and eight acres for cultivation—the eight acres being set aside, presumably, for Egan, provided he did actually cultivate it.[5] In 1928 the Board advertised 200 hectares of reserve land for lease, which was poorly fenced and degraded with weeds. An Aboriginal man, John Couzens, tendered, but his offer was rejected, despite being the only one submitted.[6]

'Forgotten Colony'

On 27 December 1933, the newly born Melbourne *Star*, an evening tabloid, described living conditions at Framlingham under the headline 'Forgotten Colony'. The *Star* catalogued a place with no water supply, sanitation, made roads or paths, where people lived in earthen-floored humpies, one-roomed structures divided internally by a bagging screen. These contained little except beds and a few boxes, and were dimly lit owing to a lack of windows. Some humpies contained families of up to eight people. The *Star* wrote evocatively: 'Outside the shacks dogs sleep in the sun, while inside, in gloomy darkness, innumerable kittens steal into corners or huddle before the sickly fire which burns in a ramshackle chimney of old tins'. Four photographs accompanied the story, two depicting humpies made of timber slabs, bark sheeting, flattened corrugated iron, and canvas. Nine unnamed residents were pictured, six of them children, some of 'the many who are living in the squalor of the Framlingham settlement'. One of those children, Ivan Couzens, recalled these conditions, but added: 'I didn't know any better, I thought it was all right!' Besides, he was happy with his family.[7] Another who lived there as a boy, Bill Edwards, recently constructed a replica of a hut for the First Australians Gallery at the new National Museum of Australia.

Seventy people lived on Framlingham in 1933, only eight legally, in Board houses and on Board rations. Some received Sustenance (the Government's Depression work-for-the-dole payment). The remainder survived by scrounging, catching rabbits, occasional work, wood-cutting, and through help from local farmers and storekeepers.

The *Star's* article noted miscegenation as well as poverty. Its second headline, 'Tragedy of the Half-Caste', argued that 'while most of those at the reserve appear little different from full-blooded blacks, some of them closely resemble pure-blooded whites. One woman's clear white skin is betrayed only by the shape of her face and her flattened nostrils'.

While some of the residents misbehaved in town, most were 'well-mannered and well-spoken' and 'thoroughly trustworthy in the work they have been given'. However, the *Star* claimed they experienced prejudice, and 'are mostly distrusted and unwanted in farm or household service'.[8]

The *Star's* revelation led to calls for action, highlighting the problem of race as much as the problem of poverty. Reverend M. Jones of the Australian Board of Missions urged action to 'absorb' these 'half castes', as experts theorised that absorption into the white community could occur without danger of 'throwing back'. By this he meant that intermarriage would lighten the skin of offspring without the fear that some children would be as black as their Aboriginal forebears. He also inferred that, through this 'absorption' Aboriginal ideas would also be lost. Jones advocated that land be made available to the people for agriculture or grazing, but paternally suggested leases rather than grants.[9] The more progressive Presbyterian *Messenger* called for an inquiry and condemned the government's absorptionist policy as 'a tragic failure and a shameful cruelty'. The Victorian Branch of the Australian Labor Party focused on equity issues, proposing material help, land and education 'to enable [them] to be self-supporting and to enjoy the full opportunities of our social system'.[10]

Dr John Henderson, who knew Framlingham through his medical practice, urged the appointment of a special committee and state help not only for the 'full-blooded blacks', but for others, as 'those whose veins carry "white" blood constitute a problem, for they are increasing in numbers each year'.[11] The Premier, Sir Stanley Argyle, defined Framlingham as a 'problem', but declined to make further comment until the Chief Secretary and Chairman of the Board, Ian Macfarlan, considered the matter. The *Star* published a sympathetic cartoon, with the caption 'ATLAS: ABO BRAND', showing a naked Aboriginal man with boomerang and camp in the background struggling under a huge spherical burden, marked 'OFFICIAL LETHARGY'.[12]

The story of the appalling conditions at Framlingham broke just as the Board attempted to lease the Aboriginal reserve to outsiders.[13] Someone alerted the *Star* that Framlingham was a scandal, ripe for a story. Perhaps it was John Egan himself. In a letter to the *Star*, Egan, the block holder at Framlingham rationed by the Board, congratulated it on its coverage, claiming: 'no one thinks of us'. Now sixty years old and with one leg,[14] Egan wrote in defence of his people, who were 'hard livers' but also 'hard toilers'. He said they found life in the Depression tough, as even wood-cutting jobs were scarce. He chided those who did not have

Framlingham people. L–R: Clive Hood, Henry Alberts, Jimmy Hammond, Mrs Brown. (Courtesy Amy and Robert Lowe, Warrnambool)

time for the 'darkey'; those who spread rumours about Framlingham; and those church people who 'tut-tutted' about immorality, when the 'half castes' had arisen from whites preying on 'coloured girls'. Egan declared: 'We are British subjects and by the laws of our country we should be treated as such. But we are not'.[15]

Deep concern was expressed in Warrnambool where the local paper, the *Warrnambool Standard*, reprinted the *Star's* exposé. J. A. Rollo, the Shire President, stated the people were 'half-starved now and they are increasing in numbers. Unless something is done the problem will become acute. They may be forced to steal'. Rollo expressed greatest concern for the children, who received little schooling, and faced prejudice as 'their colour is against them, because even if they have only a little aboriginal blood in them, they are patently "black". Only a few are "white". The colour bar is very real'.[16] The local state member of parliament Keith McGarvie believed 'the blacks are not a menace, and if their half-caste and quarter-caste children were handled properly and educated they would develop into decent citizens'.[17] The local branch meeting of the Australian Natives Association sparked discussion, which was led by Fletcher Jones, the humanitarian Victorian clothing manufacturer who operated from a Warrnambool factory. He claimed but two in a hundred locals knew what conditions were like at Framlingham. Only eight people now received rations under the Aborigines Act (1928); the other 84 residents were not recognised as 'Aboriginal' by the

Board and so were not entitled to assistance, nor to be resident on the reserve. However, as three-quarters of them were born at Framlingham, they did not wish to move. Jones said a further 41 people had left to live in the slums of Melbourne in 1933 due to the poor conditions at Framlingham. He identified five problems: a lack of education for the mostly illiterate youth; poor and unhygienic housing; unemployment, as farmers reduced their labour costs in the Depression; threats to the morality of the children; and threats to young girls from white men who visited the settlement. The Australian Natives Association called for a public meeting and the Shire Council agreed to act and also urged State Government action.[18]

The prospects of government help looked slim given the prevailing Aborigines Act. The Chief Secretary and Board Chairman, Ian Macfarlan, and the Board's Secretary, E. A. Parker, agreed to visit Framlingham. However, a government statement before the trip declared that the settlers adjacent to Framlingham Aboriginal reserve 'who have more white blood than black blood in their veins' could not be given free land or sustenance, and the taxpayer could not support 'every person who has a dash of native blood in his veins'.[19] Local civic leaders accompanied Macfarlan and Parker to the reserve. They spoke to some residents there, who indicated their willingness to work and improve themselves, if given a small-holding with some security of tenure.[20] The official party—though not the Framlingham people—reconvened that evening to consider measures for 'those unfortunate coloured people who did not come under the scope of the Board for the Protection of the Aborigines'; that is, those living and working in the forest. McGarvie proposed that some of the forest area under the control of the Agricultural Colleges Council be leased for 30 years and split into four-hectare blocks to be held by individual Aboriginal families as long as they worked it. The families would build their own houses, being supplied with rations during construction. Schooling was required for the children. He suggested the formation of a local committee to manage the scheme.

Macfarlan indicated the Government might approve the scheme if these people were likely 'to work and prove worthy'. He agreed they were more disadvantaged than the 'ordinary unemployed' as they 'lack education and they have colour, which in the minds of a large proportion of the population, is sufficient to debar them from employment'. Macfarlan, like most, was fixated on 'colour'. He stated the people's 'colour' should be taken into account by the Sustenance Department (which normally demanded work for rations), as he claimed 'these folk are like people with one arm or one leg only, and consequently I think they should be treated along different lines from those [rules] adopted in the case of persons who are 100% employable'. Macfarlan also supported the creation of a school, and firmly rejected any notion that Aboriginal children should be separated from their parents, because of 'the great bonds between coloured parents and their children'. Macfarlan concluded to applause:

> This is a particularly thorny problem. No doubt we owe a debt to these people. We are trying to fulfill it to the full bloods and half-castes, through the Board, but there the law stops and doesn't recognise the quadroons and octoroons. Apparently down here the people had come to regard the reserve as their home, and anything that could be done without undue strain on the finances should be done.

Parker agreed that a local management committee of farmers was preferable to a form of central control and praised those willing to serve. The meeting concluded with mutual congratulations.[21] Aboriginal opinion on the outcome was not recorded. However, they may have been pleased, as there was a prospect that the forest land lost to them in 1889, and on which they had camped 'illegally' ever since, was being set aside for their use—but not ownership.

A meeting with an officer of the Sustenance Department, Farquharson, to discuss the possibility of immediate relief for the forest settlers, revealed the town's humanitarian streak, and its prejudice, Fletcher Jones observing Warrnambool's 'colour bar is very real'. Constable McNamara, the local Guardian of Aborigines, claimed that 'in the majority of cases, the blacks were no worse off than the white unemployed'. He knew of three Aboriginal families at Framlingham who owned 38 cows between them, had rent-free grass, no rates, free firewood, although admittedly no security of tenure. But he agreed that 'in outside employment, the color bar was their disadvantage'. R. Crothers commented that the colour bar 'even went so far as to affect those who employed black labour'. Some suggested a segregated school for Aboriginal people's own good, but Farquharson rejected this, declaring that he had 'seen those black kiddies, and they were fine kiddies. If any mothers objected to such children mixing in the schools with their own, they should be permitted to object as long as they liked, and have no notice taken'. He added that 'they must be taught that they are not inferior'.[22]

Investigations followed. T. Isles, the Wangoom storekeeper who knew the Framlingham people well, submitted a list of 32 groups of names

Framlingham residents in the late 1930s. Back row, L–R: Henry McCrae, Billy Austin, Jim Rose, Nicholas Couzens, William Cooper (of Australian Aborigines League, and a visitor). Front row, L–R: Mary Lancaster, Esther Rose, Lucy McDonald. (A. & M. Jackomos Collection, courtesy of Museum Victoria, XP4212)

(households), mostly families, living in the forest and not eligible for assistance under the Aborigines Act. His list comprised 54 adults and 48 children, 102 people in all. Eight of the families were Clarkes and seven, Austins. Of these 32 listings, six groups were receiving Sustenance Department assistance, namely 11 adults and 14 children. Isles rated them as 'good' or 'bad', based on their work ethic. He rated only 3 of the 32 listed groups and a few other individuals as 'bad'. Four of the men were listed as working for nearby landholders.[23] The Board returned its own list to Isles, containing 20 household groups of 67 people, complete with comments. Only two were deemed by the Board as being bad workers, due to being 'cunning', 'lazy and indolent'.[24]

Farquharson's report supported the call for four-hectare blocks, adding that security of tenure should be given to allow the people to build permanent houses at no cost to the government. Sustenance should be granted but only until the block holders had cleared their land and built their homes. The children should be made to attend school, either locally or at a new school on the reserve, as one boy aged nine could not add '6 + 6'. However, he sided with Constable McNamara rather than Macfarlan, arguing that these people are 'no worse' off than those in Melbourne's slums, as they paid no rates or rent, enjoyed free open air and firewood, and had the opportunity to grow vegetables. He also disagreed with both, adding that they were 'no different than the average casual worker receiving sustenance', as 'work is no harder to obtain for either. Color [sic] does not debar—this from the employers themselves'.[25]

The Star's campaign gained immediate results for Framlingham's people. The Sustenance Branch of the Department of Labour granted sustenance in the form of food and grocery orders at the lowest (that is the non-working) level to those eligible and also to those classed as 'unemployable', which covered everyone not supported by the Board.[26] A school also commenced on the reserve, managed by representatives from Rotary, Toc H, Apex and the Country Women's Association, assisted by local churches, the Girl Guides, the Australian Council for Educational Research and the Victorian Council of Mental Hygiene. The service groups and the Department of Education equipped the school, while the other two bodies provided specialist services. In late 1936 there were 28 children in the school. Unfortunately their experience was shaped by the fact that A. W. Meadows, the head teacher, like many white teachers before and after him, gave them aptitude tests which labelled them as being of 'low' intelligence. He described the parents as having an 'excellent' attitude, as they provided him with a horse and participated in 'working bees', but claimed that 'drunkenness and immorality [was] very prevalent, very few being thoroughly reliable'. Meadows recommended that future teachers at the school be 'enthusiastic and interested in the problems of sub-normality'. Like many teachers of his day he equated Aboriginality with abnormality. If there was any truth to his IQ grades of 50 to 105, it was due to the students' poor nutrition, or the cultural inappropriateness of the test.[27]

Urged on by Warrnambool's civic leaders and Melbourne's Aboriginal support groups, Chief Secretary Macfarlan asked the Council of Agricultural Education to release eighty hectares of the unused forest land to enable him to lease four-hectare blocks to twenty families for thirty years.[28] The Agricultural Council curtly refused.[29] Pressure was applied to the Board from all quarters to allow settlement of those from the forest on the Board's 220-hectare reserve instead. The Board opposed this idea in July 1934, as it would reverse the policy of concentrating Aboriginal Victorians at Lake Tyers, and create pressures to re-open other reserves. It argued that the present distress was temporary due to the Depression and that those living in the forest would in the future be self-sufficient through wood-cutting. However, they deserved help and the Board advised that the government should excise land from the Council of Agricultural Education and lease it to them in small blocks.[30]

Many Framlingham people took matters into their own hands, moving from the forest and squatting on the reserve proper, claiming the protection of McGarvie, the local state member, and that they had 'a perfect right to the Reserve'.[31] In early 1935 there were twelve Framlingham people legally on the reserve receiving Board rations but living in dilapidated housing; 34 people in six families living there 'illegally' in bark huts receiving unemployed Sustenance; 3 living near the reserve on their own block; and 59 people still living in huts in the forest, who worked or received Sustenance.[32] The Board panicked, claiming this move to the reserve might eventuate 'in every coloured person in the western district congregating on the land under unhealthy and unsanitary conditions'. It showed no appreciation of the fact that Aboriginal people had little interest in permanent moves to places to which they had no historical connection. The Board urged Cabinet to ensure that the forest people be 'mixed with the white people of the community as individuals . . . rather than that they should congregate and breed with their own poor types'. These 'quadroons and persons of lighter blood' should be charged with trespass for squatting on the reserve despite the likely 'local criticism'.[33] The Cabinet chose to ignore the Board's plea and did nothing for four years.

The help of 'earnest and progressive men'

In May 1938 Chief Secretary Bailey announced that humanitarian pressure, particularly from Warrnambool community groups, had persuaded the Board to allow those camped illegally on the reserve and those still in the adjoining forest to be assisted with housing and support. The Board allowed the reserve to be divided into twelve four-hectare blocks, as long as the funding for housing and the people's upkeep was provided by the Board of Land and Works and the Sustenance Department. Also, a local committee was to manage the farm scheme. The Board remained financially uncommitted, apart from the value of the land loaned for the scheme, stating that under the Aborigines Act (1928) it could not expend money on 'quadroons and octoroons'. Its aim was simply to 'provide a home and a small patch on which vegetables could be grown and a cow kept as an assistance to living' through outside work.[34] Continued tenancy was dependent on the payment of a small rental and good behaviour, and no outsiders were to be permitted to settle. Fletcher Jones thought it could be a model for Australia, and 'make the people self-supporting and fit them for citizenship', but some doubted four hectares would prove viable.

Civic leaders, the heads of local service organisations and teachers formed the Framlingham Reserve Board of Management (hereafter called the Framlingham Management Board) to expend the money, mentor the 'farms', and manage their production. Service organisations would assist: Rotary would teach business and employment skills; the Rechabites would ensure the residents' sobriety; Manchester Unity and IOOF, their thrift, home improvements and gardens; Toc H would foster their education; Apex would run a sporting program; and the Australian Natives Association would instill a love of Australia and 'teach the tradition of the race'—no doubt the Anglo-Australian race. Local farmers would provide farming expertise, and the local Guardian, Sergeant West, would collect the rent.[35] Local Christians and self-improvers with a social conscience, 'earnest and progressive men' as their first Chairman, G. H. Newnham, termed them, formed the Framlingham Management Board.[36] They were paternalistic but, in terms of Victorians of their day, they were prepared as few others were, to push for equality for Aboriginal people.

It was a remarkable and idealistic plan of individual citizenship and hope, but there was not one Aboriginal person involved in the forming of this white vision of cultural assimilation. The Framlingham Management Board merely informed the reserve community of the housing plan. The residents would construct their own houses (under supervision) while on Sustenance. This and their farm work would uplift them and train the rising generation for work. The Framlingham Management Board would visit weekly, inspect the houses and report to the Board monthly. Rental was set at 3/- weekly. The *Warrnambool Standard* reported that 'several local residents spoke, expressing determination to leave behind the mistakes of the past and to make the most of the new era about to begin'. The *Standard* hoped the settlement could be 'something of which the district might be proud', revealing the Eurocentric nature of the whole enterprise, infused as it was by the self-improving values of white respectability.[37] Arthur Burdeu of the Aborigines Uplift Society in Melbourne claimed the Framlingham settlement 'can make history for the race, and that success will reverberate through Australia, while failure will put back Aboriginal progress for years'.[38]

The first house built under the 'New Deal' scheme was dedicated at a gala occasion in November 1938. The Mayor of Warrnambool,

Councillor Christian, spoke of a 'new era', especially for Aboriginal children. 'There must be no idea of inferiority complex. They had ability and brains just as the white children did, and there was no limit to the positions to which they might rise'. An exchange of gifts followed. The settlement's children presented the Lady Mayoress with bouquets, the Australian Natives Association gave the community a cricket kit and the Victorian Aboriginal Group presented the school with a film projector. R. Glasgow, a white farmer who had visited the reserve since boyhood and had been friends with the community for fifty years, launched an appeal for £200 for farm equipment and £30 was raised on the day. Nicholas Couzens, his wife Georgina (nee Winters) and their then six children were chosen as tenants of the first timber house of four rooms, three of which were bedrooms. (The family had won the Rotary Home Improvement competition the year before.) Nicolas Couzens took the key, unlocked the door and entered his 'new era'. Tea was served and Apex ran an athletics program for the Framlingham residents.[39] It was a golden moment, but one in which Victorians of European descent watched Aboriginal Victorians intently—waiting for results.

Ivan Couzens was six years old when he moved into this first house. He said everyone thought it was wonderful because the houses were far

Nicholas Couzens, whose family inhabited the first 'New Deal' house in 1938, photographed with his parents Harriet Couzens and John 'Jack' Wyselaskie about 1912. (Courtesy of Noel Couzens, Geelong)

superior to the huts in which they had lived. They had a kitchen and living area, a laundry and toilet outside and water tanks so that water did not have to be carried in kerosene tins from the river. The houses were built one by one, scattered about and backed onto the Hopkins River, where each family had an eel-trap. He recalled the church and the school house which was dragged up from the lower paddock. The men were given work repairing these buildings and making roads in the settlement. The families also survived on the sale of the men's woodcutting and the women's basket-making. There was sufficient food, including wild foods—eels, ducks and rabbits—and the occasional sheep and bag of spuds, which the men had 'found'. Ivan Couzens recalled plenty of 'caring and sharing'. The people would gather on Uncle Jim McKinnon's verandah, who had the only radio, 'and he'd have it sittin' on the window sill and everybody'd be sitting around outside listening to "Dad and Dave" and those sorts of things'.[40]

Idealism soon faltered. Within six months, the Framlingham Management Board claimed neither the local white settlers nor the Framlingham people understood its aims. Within a year, some residents had stopped paying rent out of hardship, or out of the sense that the land was theirs and need not be paid for. George Clarke told his fellow residents that if they all refused to pay, the Board could do nothing about it.[41] The Framlingham Management Board and the Board discussed the need for evictions. In February 1940 the Framlingham Management Board and the local Guardian, Constable Witham, met with the Chief Secretary to discuss rent arrears, and a lack of fencing and agricultural effort. Witham suggested that any people who were evicted would simply move to 'humpies' on the adjoining College forest lands, beyond any control. The Chief Secretary suggested threatening to remove their children instead, to make them conform to white expectations. However, Sustenance was given to some struggling families instead, though several evictions and removals did occur.[42] In April 1940, Nicholas Couzens wrote to the *Warrnambool Standard* complaining that the four-roomed houses were too small for large families; the women were sick of claims by the Framlingham Management Board that they kept 'dirty houses'; and the promised water supply for agriculture had not eventuated, so how could gardens be started? He concluded that there was too much interference. 'Let us do our own planning, we have taken enough advice . . . We might be told to do a few things, but we won't be driven by anybody.'[43]

In May 1940 the Framlingham Management Board, together with Witham and the Board's Secretary, inspected the reserve and that evening lectured the people in the school building on the aims of the farm scheme and its current progress. Each householder was then questioned on their house-keeping, fencing and outside improvements, their rental status and conduct. Close control had rapidly emerged, just when autonomy was needed—and desired—by the people.[44] The Framlingham Management Board urged the Board to allow the appointment of a missionary couple to guide the people. The Board feared this might indicate a commitment to those not under the Board's control, or that Framlingham might revert to an old-style mission, with the missionaries as advocates for the people.[45] However, in September 1941 Peter and Adele Mathieson from the United Aborigines Mission took up residence in one of the houses, supported by local donations.

Children were removed from some Framlingham families at this time, although the contemporary records of how and why are scanty and are only now accessible by family. However, in the 1980s people began to testify publicly about their removal. Francis Hutchins was removed from Framlingham around 1940 and only met up with her siblings forty years later, remarking that 'the sad part is what we missed growing up together as a family'. The same thing occurred to Albert Jackson, who went to a succession of six orphanages and boys' homes in Geelong, Frankston, Royal Park and Phillip Island. He too met up later with his family, after wishing many a time as a boy that 'they were by my side'. Lloyd Clarke and his six siblings were taken from nearby Lake Condah in 1945. He went to St Cuthbert's Boys' Home in Colac, while his siblings went in pairs elsewhere. Lloyd recalled in 1986: 'Sometimes I would dream I was back home, but woke up and no one was there'.[46] He once asked about his parents and was told they were dead.

Some parents were no doubt neglectful of their children, but in most cases Board officers and police mistook poverty for neglect. Others were young unmarried mothers and fathers. However, authorities rarely considered that there were always other Aboriginal families willing to take children in, for what missionaries observed in the nineteenth century still held true: with its strong extended family ethic, there were no orphans in Aboriginal society. However, Aboriginal relatives were rarely asked to care for children, as the Board wished to blend children into the general population.

The Board, the Child Welfare Department and the orphanages themselves were never consistent in their decisions to break up families. After four years, Lloyd Clarke was joined in Colac by his younger brother, whose arrival was announced to him. They were then sent to the Ballarat Orphanage in 1953 to 'be with our sisters'. Nor could the Board ever hope to end Aboriginal kinship feelings. So dense were Aboriginal kinship networks, now growing strongly through large families from a base of perhaps fifty surviving units in the 1920s, that it was impossible not to meet up with other kin in institutions. Lloyd Clarke recalled how at Ballarat 'we met up with our first cousins Betty and Nancy King then in 1954 the Foster kids came there, Gloria, Ronnie and Eunice'. Gloria McHenry (nee Foster) hated the experience of institutions but later said she and her sister 'were one of the lucky ones because we knew our people'. As Lloyd Clarke remembered: 'at the Ballarat Orphanage all us Koori kids had a strong bond together, whether we were related or not'. Clarke also found out from kin at Ballarat that his mother was still alive. Years later he inevitably found her and the rest of his kin in the still small Aboriginal communities of Victoria. He discovered his father too, and two sisters to whom he did not know he was related. In 1986 Clarke exclaimed: 'I was satisfied I had found my true identity and my family at last'.[47]

The war economy impacted on Framlingham too. People left to take up work in the district, several share-farming successfully, including Nicholas Couzens and his family, who had occupied the first 'New Deal' house in 1938. Others sought work in Melbourne's munitions industry. The reserve's population of 123 in 1941 fell to 45 the following year. This created a problem of vacant houses on Framlingham and led to tensions between the Framlingham Management Board, which wanted to rent them to other tenants, and the Board, which feared an enlarged and ongoing reserve population. The Board upheld its grand vision of 1886, telling the Framlingham Management Board that 'to permit new settlers, can only result in the Government ultimately accepting responsibility for the maintenance of people who should be well able to maintain themselves, and a further difficulty is that were such a policy adopted at Framlingham, it would also have to be applied to Dimboola, Condah, Orbost, and other parts of the State where there are numbers of people with an admixture of aboriginal blood residing'.[48] Framlingham threatened to open the floodgates.

The two Boards were at odds between 1942 and 1944. The Framlingham Management Board accused the Board of being 'unworthy, unsympathetic and psychologically unsound', while the Board claimed the Framlingham Management Board was shirking its promise to manage the housing.[49] The Board decided to evict those owing rent, and to sell the houses of those who left, but it allowed John Couzens and John Brice, who were interested in cattle grazing, to rent extra reserve land. Faced by the postwar housing shortage, the Board relented in 1945

Framlingham youths, 1944. Back row, L–R: Walter Austin, Sid Austin, Henry Alberts. Front row, L–R: Roy Rose (father of Lionel), Chris Austin. (Courtesy Amy and Robert Lowe, Warrnambool)

and allowed the Framlingham Management Board to let houses to those 'of Aboriginal blood'.[50] In 1946, the housing crisis drove people back to Framlingham, forcing 102 people to crowd into the twelve small houses and others to rebuild huts in the forest. In this year the Framlingham Reserve Board of Management became the Framlingham Reserve Welfare Committee, apparently in order to focus on assistance rather than on control. Warrnambool's 'earnest and progressive men' on the former Framlingham Management Board, despite their paternalistic and assimilationist vision, had successfully stalled the Board's efforts to sell Framlingham in the 1930s and 1940s.

The Framlingham community battles evictions

By 1950, 86 people resided in 14 houses at Framlingham, 38 of them children, most taught by John Sharp at the reserve school. Noel Couzens and his brothers, sons of Nicholas Couzens, now share-farming at Panmure, rode their bikes ten kilometres each way to attend the Framlingham School. The school was a vital link that Aboriginal people off the reserve maintained with the 'Fram' community. Community was also sustained by the Mathiesons who conducted religious services there until 1954. The reserve's families were sustained by the men's contract wood-cutting for the Forestry Commission, basket-making by the women, and pension and child endowment payments. Several white female activists who visited in 1950 thought 'the women at Framlingham seemed abler than the men'.[51]

A new crisis arose at 'Fram' in late 1949. Doris Austin and her three children, moved into a vacant reserve house from a hut in the forest, but were ordered off by Constable Rowe. Austin's brother and aunt wrote to the Board asking: 'Are they to camp in hollow logs and carry their swags about with their children behind them?'[52] A similar thing happened in August 1950. Peter and Phyllis Dunnolly and family, who had left to work in another district, returned after six months and paid £9 rental owing. Dunnolly then requested that his sister-in-law, Ella Austin, and her five children be allowed to live in their house. This was denied. Phyllis wrote to her aunt Mary Clarke and asked her to seek help from Doris Blackburn, President of the Women's International League for Peace and Freedom, to stop them 'robbing us poor black people, they took our pines [trees] away and one house and now they want to take another'. In a second letter Phyllis claimed Constable Rowe had refused a further rent payment, saying the house was to be sold, and again appealed for her aunt to seek help.[53]

A Women's International League for Peace and Freedom deputation assisted by Helen Baillie, a white activist, gathered facts at Framlingham and lobbied the government. The Board and Chief Secretary denied there would be any evictions, but stated the Framlingham houses were built for emergency accommodation in the Depression and were never to be transferred. They were to be sold when the original occupiers left or fell behind in their rent.[54] The Dunnolly house was sold and Ella Austin and family faced eviction. A public outcry forced a Board back-down in December 1950. A public meeting was sponsored by the League in February 1951 at the Australian Church in Melbourne, at which white women activists for Aboriginal people spoke, notably Helen Baillie, Cora Gilsenan and Anna Vroland.

Mary Clarke of Framlingham, a granddaughter of Louisa Briggs and thus a descendant of Tasmanian Aboriginal people (but not Truganini's great-grand-daughter as she claimed), also spoke.[55] This was a supreme effort for her, as she remarked ten months later on the theme of Aboriginal 'shyness':

> The truth is our people dodge white people because we feel we are not wanted. I know this is not always true. I have met a lot of very sympathetic white people and a few very helpful ones. Even so, it takes all the courage I have to shake off the old fear of the white community and mix with white people, even when they are kindly. When I want to help my people I feel I have to nerve myself for a struggle, but now and again, with the help of a few good friends, I have a victory, and it is all worth while'.[56]

At the meeting Mary Clarke claimed that the Board was attempting to evict the people of Framlingham and sell up the houses and the reserve.

In a ringing appeal she said: 'Leave us this tiny corner where our homes are . . . Why should we pay rent for it at all? We regard that little bit of land as ours still.'[57] A journalist, Frank Stephens, who travelled to Framlingham and wrote about it for the *Argus*, echoed her plea: 'Couldn't we afford to give them, as Mrs Clarke so earnestly appeals to us to do, "this tiny corner"'.[58] The house sale was cancelled in response to the pressure.

However, the Board was as tenacious as the 'Fram' people. In 1954 it sold two houses and placed pressure on several families to move. The house of Amy Lowe was apparently sold and was to be transported elsewhere. It was alleged by activist Helen Baillie that the purchaser had threatened Robert Lowe with a gun.[59] Robert Lowe junior recalled that his mother, Amy, confronted a man measuring up her house for removal in the 1950s. She fended him off with a broomstick and her husband, Robert Lowe, ploughed around the house to prevent trucks entering.[60] Even the Framlingham Reserve Welfare Committee wanted the houses removed to Warrnambool and the reserve turned over to two of the remaining people who wanted to farm: Percy and Henry 'Banjo' Clarke, amongst others. By 1956 there were still 64 people in residence at Framlingham ready to fight future battles.

The tenacity of the Framlingham community in the face of these constant struggles was founded on an attachment to community and land. John Egan, Walter Brice and John Couzens had chosen to use the reserve's land for grazing stock. Percy Clarke continued this tradition by running a small dairy herd for over forty years, wheeling his cream on a bike to the Framlingham Butter Company twice daily. He recalled: 'We didn't have a permit to milk. There were illegal dairies in the bush but the Government did nothing about it. You weren't allowed to have your stock in the forest. We had to farm illegally to make a living. We used to graze them on the side of the road or in the bush and bring them back at night to a fenced paddock'. He made ends meet by cutting wood and selling rabbit and fox skins as well. He worked hard all his life and recalled he 'never had time to get married'.[61]

To others Framlingham was a place of their own where they had a reasonable house in which to live. Robert Lowe remembers visiting his grandfather's house (Norman Clarke) in the early 1950s. His 'garden was beautiful, the hollyhocks were huge, and there were all types of different flowers. They were unreal when they came out. And rose bushes, they were beautiful, cut like a hedge they were. And on one side there were plum trees, fig trees, beautiful fruit trees. Cherry bushes, quinces—you name it he had it growing there'.[62] Much of the reserve beyond the houses and the few grazed areas had returned to scrub, which made a wonderful adventure area for the children. Beyond that was the forest, the reserve lands taken in 1889 but still used for bush tucker by the community, who caught rabbits with snares or by stunning them with *nulla nullas*, and collected grasses for basket-weaving. The nearby Hopkins River provided holes for spearing eels and trout, and places to catch swans or their eggs. The forest was the place for spiritual connection with the old ones and where *murrups* (ghosts) were said to roam. These things, which held echoes of traditional life, are recalled in Robert Lowe's book, *The Mish* (2002).

There was also a strong attachment to family at Framlingham, intensified by the feeling that beyond the reserve lay an alien world. The thirteen houses built by the Framlingham Management Board in 1939 were spread along a curved road, shown as 'Newnham Avenue' on early sketch maps.[63] Several of the older reserve houses stood nearby, as well as a school, church and cemetery. In 1944 the houses were occupied by six extended families—the Clarkes, Couzens, Alberts, Roses, Austins, and McKinnons—as well as Walter Brice. They were not always united. Brice and Nicholas Couzens argued over a fence in 1940, and George Clarke complained to the Board about the drinking and vandalism of some Austin and Rose teenage 'hooligans'.[64] However, the people generally socialised and pulled together, all the children attending the reserve school and Sunday schools while they were in operation, and later catching the same school bus into town.

The Framlingham adults spent much of their leisure time together and helped each other in adversity, even raising others' children at

Ella Austin and her children (L–R) Laurence, Wayne and David outside their Framlingham home in 1966. (Courtesy Herald and Weekly Times Ltd)

times. Brendan Edwards, Nicholas Couzens' grandson, recalled that in the 1960s 'it was a community, people used to go to people's places. And if anybody didn't have anything they'd come up home, and they would get stuff off us because Mum and Dad worked . . . they'd get bread and milk and eggs'.[65] Tim Chatfield, a Clarke descendant, remembered it as 'a safe place' in the 1970s: 'You felt secure, you knew everybody, everybody knew what was goin' on, and you met pretty regular because of the social plonk'.[66] Christmas time was the best for gatherings—Brendan Edwards recalled good times, 'just sitting around the table, mucking around and carryin' on, playing footy, goin' fishing, going down to the swimmin' hole down at the bridge and rippin' around in cars in the paddock, they were the good times'.[67] At these gatherings stories were told about work, family and the past. An Aboriginal history of massacres, dispossession, discrimination and life on the missions was passed down, all solidifying what it was to be Aboriginal.

Sport, a dominant cultural marker of the wider society, also fostered a sense of Aboriginal identity and esteem at Framlingham and elsewhere. Professional boxing in particular was popular among the Framlingham people as it required little equipment, only basic skills and courage, and promised financial rewards equal to a week's wages in the space of under half an hour. And, despite a reputation for passivity, Aboriginal people enjoyed a good fight. Bouts were held monthly in the Warrnambool Town Hall or Palace Stadium for several years in the mid-1940s, the majority of fights boasting an Aboriginal fighter: the Austin, Clarke, McKinnon, Alberts, Rose, Couzens and Roach families providing fodder for these events. The boxers won as many fights as they lost, despite a lack of coaching and the fact that their training at 'Fram' took place around a sugar bag hanging from a tree using bandaged hands instead of gloves. These wins built fighters' self-esteem, as they performed in front of crowds, often being touted as capable glove men before the bout. Fights became a fund for heroic fireside stories back at 'Fram'—I was told some such stories in the 1970s. These contests with townspeople sometimes built local respect and also enabled people to mix as never before. A local boxer, Billy Primmer, recalled that families of the boxers, black and white, often shared a pie at the pie cart outside venues in Warrnambool after bouts. They certainly fought and cheered alongside one another.[68] Boxing contests also helped counter negative images of the Framlingham people, which arose when some of them invariably appeared before the Warrnambool Court on drunk and disorderly charges.

However, boxing and other sports fed on racism as well, and even inflamed it. When travelling boxing tents visited the annual agricultural

Harry Johns' boxing troupe, Bombala Show 1950. From L–R: Harry Johns, Monty Faye (tent boss), Danny Marks (Western Victoria), Alick Jackomos and three unidentified boxers. (Courtesy Alick Jackomos collection)

shows in the Warrnambool District, Aboriginal boxers were much in evidence, 'Banjo' Clarke recalling that 'Aborigines were a big drawcard in the boxing tents. A lot of people would come to see the Aboriginals fight . . . they thought that Aborigines were better fighters and they were wild looking blokes up there on the boardwalk'.[69] Opposites were usually matched to increase the drama and because, as Warrnambool sports commentator Eddie Gibbon claimed, 'you never get a good game out of two niggers'.[70] This drama led to name calling—'Kill the black bastard!'— often being heard. Noel Couzens, one of Nicholas Couzens' sons, met similar racism on the football field in the 1950s—especially recalling abuse from the Mortlake team and supporters: 'They hated Aborigines, they hated black people'.[71]

Yet these fights gave Aboriginal boxers the chance to show they were as good as their white opponents, or better. 'Banjo' Clarke recalled one incident in triumph a generation later. Having overheard his opponent say before the fight, 'The nigger's already beat', an enraged 'Banjo' hopped into the ring barefoot, too impatient to borrow a friend's boots, and went to work. He recalled jubilantly:

> I went straight over and went bang with a straight left, hit him straight in
> the jaw, and he swung back at me, and I got underneath him and gave him a
> left rip and doubled him up and I hit him with a left hook and I hit him with

a right and I felt him go at the knees and I went in again just before he hit the canvass, and I gave him another left hook right in the chin . . . all the blood came out of his mouth, nose and ears . . . It was the first time I was wild in the ring.[72]

This story flowed out when Banjo told it to me in 1978, revealing he'd told it many times before, and had no doubt somewhat embellished it over the years. It revealed the pent up rage of a history of discrimination. However, Aboriginal boxers like 'Banjo' Clarke could be posed as everyone's hero when matched against strange boxers who came to town.

While most confined their boxing to the District, some like 'Banjo' and his nephew 'Muscles' Clarke travelled with boxing tents throughout Victoria and interstate. They were paid equal wages, gained the status of tough men—tent boxers—and socialised with many people, black and white. They experienced a wider world. As 'Muscles' Clarke recalled, they would meet people on the showgrounds and 'after we'd finish our session . . . we'd drink in their houses and drink in pubs or go to one of the houses and a girl would say "would you like to dance" and we would go to the dance hall. So we had a pretty good social life'.[73] These experiences formed heroic stories for the retelling and are discussed in a book by Richard Broome and Alick Jackomos, *Sideshow Alley* (1998)[74].

The Framlingham men participated in other sports as well. 'Banjo' Clarke won the Port Fairy Gift in 1948—and £70—while Stan Couzens won district cycle races in the late 1940s.[75] Many played country football. Noel Couzens became a local champion for Bushfield and other clubs in the Warrnambool District, kicking 97 goals in one season and 15 goals in a final.[76] These sporting trips also gave some Aboriginal men experience in dealing with *gubbahs* (whites) to fit them for leadership, as in the case of 'Banjo' Clarke, who later became a Gunditjmara elder. At the school level, sport gave Aboriginal children victories over their better-off country rivals. The Framlingham School, for instance, won the Grasmere and District School Sports Association's athletic carnival two years running (1948–49). Dawn Austin was thrilled to accept the shield second time around. The publication of each event's winners in the *Warrnambool Standard* broadcasted the children's achievements.[77]

Land, family, daily struggles and achievements: all underpinned a sense of being Aboriginal and being part of the Framlingham community. There were disagreements, arguments and old-fashioned 'blues' with fists—even appeals to the Board at times over personal disputes—but, once settled, the people buried their differences. As Tim Chatfield recalled: 'when there was a meeting called, everyone went there and put their concerns across and talked and rallied and supported, that's where it was really strong . . . people had their say and everyone had a right to speak'.[78] That sense of belonging kept the fight for 'Fram' alive into the 1960s and beyond, culminating in a series of land handbacks in 1970 and 1987.

Stan Lowe on the steps of his Uncle Frank Clarke's Brisbane house after winning the Queensland amateur lightweight title in 1956. (Courtesy Amy and Robert Lowe, Warrnambool)

13

Country Campers

In the first third of the twentieth century almost half of the Victorian Aboriginal population of about 500 lived at places controlled by the Board: Lake Tyers and the remnants of other reserves. The remainder—a little more than half—lived in camps either close to these reserves or at traditional camping places, including Dimboola, Antwerp, Swan Hill, Echuca, Nathalia, and Jackson's Track near Drouin. Most camp sites adjoined river banks, where clean water and fishing was available. Many Aboriginal Victorians resided by the Murray, that traditional place of high population density. After it became a white colonial boundary, it was a convenient place to move from the control of one administration to another. Some of these campers, or 'fringe dwellers' as they were called at the time, were pushed off the reserves by the Act and others fled the reserves to escape control. They lived in freedom—and poverty—in these camps until the Board took notice of them in the 1950s.

Campers lived in poor material conditions, sustained by cash from casual rural work, and rabbits and other bush food gathered in the hinterland behind the river. Most of them lived on the edge of white society, interacting with particular landowners for work and dealing with known storekeepers or publicans. They attended race days and country shows to watch their men run races or fight in boxing tents. They frequented the hotel or beer tent—if allowed. Some places refused service to those of 'mixed descent' even though the Licensing Act (1928) forbade supply to 'any Aboriginal native'—usually only interpreted as 'full blood'. If refused, campers found a friendly white who supplied their illicit drinking parties, sometimes joining them, sometimes interacting sexually with Aboriginal women. Aboriginal campers were served last in shops, were not permitted to try on clothing before purchase, and, when they had the price of admission, were restricted to the front seats in some theatres, for instance at Dimboola. Many Aboriginal children did not go to school because they were excluded by unwelcome looks, and because their frequent moves with parents to see relatives or chase seasonal work made attendance difficult. Some children did not attend because their parents did not value white schooling. Most campers were decent people but, like all groups, they contained a dissolute minority who lived life rough. Pastor Schultz of Jeparit stated of the campers at Antwerp around 1940 that 'there are some good people amongst them, honest, upright, and firm believers in Christ, their Saviour. Others have inherited and copied the lowest principles from their white fathers or their contact with the whites'.[1]

There are numerous personal stories that reveal the campers' desire for freedom and independence, and the constant threats they experienced on this head. Around 1940, Robert and Christina Pinkie of Bordertown, their daughter and son-in-law, Emily and Alan Karpany, and two children, Lettie and Betty, crossed by wagon into Victoria to avoid the removal of the children by the Board. They travelled for a month on back roads to dodge the authorities and eventually settled in what became 'Wamba' (Murray Downs), a newly formed 'fringe camp' in New South Wales across the river from Swan Hill. But the NSW authorities stalked them, and Betty Karpany and her cousins once had to swim the Murray back to Victoria to avoid being taken.[2] Betty Clements, her parents Clarence and Evelyn Atkinson, and her two siblings left Cummeragunja to avoid removal of the children and shifted to Swan Hill in 1935. Betty Clements also recalled children being removed from 'Wamba'. One single mother who worked to keep the cupboards full in the hut and her children fed, and who left her children in the care of their sixteen-year-old sister during the day, arrived home one day to find the little ones taken by the welfare. Parents like this woman, said Clements, were 'happy people until the children were taken away, their light was gone, that's when they started drinking. A few of them died from the alcohol, a few of them got drowned in the river because they were too drunk'.[3]

The Pinkies, Karpanys, Atkinsons and others survived in the area during the 1940s through hard work fruit picking, shearing, rural labouring and knitting (undertaken by the women for a Swan Hill baby shop). They supplemented their earnings with traditional bush tucker. Betty Tournier (nee Karpany) said they ate many bush vegetables and meats: rabbits, possum, kangaroo and emu, except koala as they 'cried like babies'. Her grandparents still spoke in the traditional language

Betty Tournier (nee Karpany) with son David in 1958, while working at 'Clithro Park' South Australia. (Courtesy of Betty Tournier, Geelong)

and they taught Betty words and the use of bush medicines as remedies for colds and even as contraceptives. Betty Clements (nee Atkinson) recalled learning how to find swan eggs on the Murray by observing the parent birds: the way the male swam furiously away from the nest as a diversion, and the female swam to guard it. They were taught to take only a third of the eggs from any one nest. Her parents did not speak Yorta Yorta, having grown up at Cummeragunja reserve, but her father Clarence Atkinson was strong on family values and the traditional custom of never marrying your cousins.

Some families moved more in the mainstream than on the fringes. Kenneth and Dulcie Stewart married after the Second World War and moved to Lake Boga. Kenneth had worked in local wineries in the 1930s, being a grandson of Rob Roy Stewart, the Aboriginal postman who settled there with his brother Jackson Stewart. Kenneth and Dulcie Stewart gained a soldier-settler block at Robinvale after the War, which they worked successfully until retirement. Daniel and June Atkinson moved off Cummeragunja reserve in the 1930s to avoid the risk of their children being removed. They became share farmers at Deniliquin, then Daniel worked as a vine dresser at Swan Hill and as a storeman for the Country Roads Board at Horsham. Both the Stewart and Atkinson families were hard-working country battlers, aware of the value of education and eventually able to give their children a high school education in the 1960s. They also adhered to their Aboriginal heritage by keeping in touch with family—and their children and grandchildren still identify strongly—but life in the mainstream made it difficult to maintain Aboriginal traditions.[4]

Many of these families, whether on the fringe or part of the mainstream, led respectable lives. Betty Tournier recalled that her parents, Emily and Alan Karpany, and her elders taught her 'honesty, caring, looking out for each other ... and you didn't tell lies'. They were also taught to keep the camp tidy even though they lived in a tent:

'everything had its place ... And we were always taught our manners'. Their punishment was the shame of silence. Hard work was another lesson. Betty Karpany was working in the paddocks at seven and in a Swan Hill bakehouse at thirteen before she went off to school each day. She then worked as a kitchen hand and shearers' cook. Betty Clements (nee Atkinson) was taught these things as well and started scrubbing floors beside her mother Evelyn at twelve, before graduating to fruit picking and waitress work—eventually trying the wider world of café work in Melbourne.

These young people were also taught to be proud and to defend themselves against racial abuse from other kids. Betty Clements was told to bemuse taunters by saying: 'I can't help it if God made me in the night time and you in the day time'. She was also told to 'be proud of what you are, be proud that you are a Koori. Don't ever deny it, be proud of it and don't ever hide behind a wall of shame'.[5] Myra Grinter (nee Atkinson) was told by her father Daniel that she could be anything in life, adding: 'You have two things against you—one you're a woman, two you're black—but it makes you twice as good'.[6] Albert Mullett was fortified by the elders with: 'Aye, you're better than the white-fella, remember that. You have something they will never have: your values, your connection with the land. It goes back to your ancestors, through your bloodline'.[7] These are the memories and experiences of many Aboriginal people. But the remainder of this chapter will examine closely just two camp communities: one at Mooroopna-Shepparton—which had its antecedents in the Cummeragunja reserve on the New South Wales side of the Murray—and the other at Orbost.

From 'Cummera' to the 'Flat'

The origins of Mooroopna-Shepparton's Aboriginal community at the 'Flat' by the Goulburn River lay sixty kilometres north-east, on the Murray's northern bank in the Barmah area. In 1874 Daniel and Janet Matthews, inspired by the work of John Green at Coranderrk, formed the Maloga Mission to 'rescue' Aboriginal people and make them Christian. The work was slow as funds were short, but within a decade eighty people, mostly now Christian, lived there in decent housing amidst gardens and farm buildings. A detailed history of the mission is to be found in Nancy Cato's *Mister Maloga* (1976). In 1881, when Matthews took the residents fund-raising in Melbourne, they met Thomas Shadrach James, a young Indian from Mauritius. James had reputedly just dropped out of Melbourne University's Medical School due to a career-ending bout of typhoid, which left him with shaking hands and unable to perform surgery. James agreed to become Maloga's teacher and in 1885 married into the community, taking Ada Cooper as his bride.

The Maloga men were inspired by stories of Coranderrk to have land of their own. In 1881, 42 Maloga men petitioned the NSW Government for land. They argued that 'we have been under training for some years' and 'we are earnestly desirous of settling down to more orderly habits of industry, that we may form homes for our families'.[8] The petition was rejected, but two years later New South Wales formed its own Aboriginal Protection Board along Victorian lines and created some reserves, one of them just upstream from Maloga.

The people yearned for individual blocks as well. In 1887 several men, including William Cooper, Thomas James's brother-in-law, unsuccessfully applied for land. Cooper requested 'a grant of land that I can call my own as long as I and my family live and yet without the power of being able to do away with the land'. Cooper sought forty hectares near to Maloga, which was but a 'small portion of a vast territory which is ours by Divine right'.[9] Matthews' paternalism began to grate by the mid 1880s and one of the petitioners, John Atkinson, left to farm land nearby, with others joining him for a time. In 1888, due to discontent with Matthews and policy changes by the mission's backers, most of the people left Maloga and settled at the nearby government reserve. They called it 'Cummeragunja', meaning 'my country', or affectionately, 'Cummera'.[10]

By 1900 Cummeragunja was a thriving Aboriginal community of over 300 residents, mostly Yorta Yorta and some Bangerang people. It had almost fifty houses, several gravel streets, a store, school, church and other out-buildings. Farming thrived and production matched that of the rest of the district. Families were given the use of individual blocks in 1896, although these were removed in a change of government policy in 1907, for reasons relating to the Board's finances. Thomas James was a key personality as the school teacher and the spiritual leader of the reserve. He built on the people's desire for independence by his fostering of Christian and self-improving values, and helped forge an Aboriginal political leadership. The reserve's population peaked at 394 in 1908.

In 1909, New South Wales adopted legislation similar to Victoria's 1886 Act, and people of lighter skin were removed and apprenticed out. Cummeragunja declined as a result, just as the Victorian reserves had done under similar legislation. The NSW Board also attacked the reserve in the 1920s by pulling down the houses of those who had moved temporarily to seek work, removing farm equipment, and leasing some of the land to white farmers. Clarence Atkinson and others became woodcutters in the Barmah forest. Other men sought work off the reserve on farms, shearing about the district and labouring with the Victorian Water Commission. Bevan Nicholls recalled the meagre and short rations they received, but Merle Jackomos remembered well-kept houses and gardens, a frequently used dance hall, concert bands, music, sports days and regattas. While rations were basic, they were supplemented by rabbits and by the Murray, 'full of fish, turtle, yabbies, swan, ducks and fresh water mussels'.[11] By 1937 there were 172 persons living in 25 cottages on the reserve.[12]

The fierce independence of Cummeragunja's residents caused many to leave in the face of the NSW Board's hardline policies after 1909. Thomas James retired around 1922 and moved over the river to live with some Aboriginal people at Barmah. He later became a herbalist in Fitzroy, before moving to Mooroopna in the late 1920s, where a few Aboriginal people lived on the riverbank. He shared their shanty living conditions, and joined the Methodist Church, where he was 'very much respected as a Christian gentleman'.[13] His son Shadrach was not kept on as a trainee teacher once Thomas James was dismissed, and so he left. Independent types William Cooper, Bill and Eric Onus left in the early 1930s. Cooper went to Melbourne where he formed an early Aboriginal political organisation—the Australian Aborigines' League—before spending his last days in the Mooroopna Hospital. Others headed to a camp across the river at Barmah to stay close to family on 'Cummera', there being 113 at Barmah in 1937.

Amended NSW legislation in 1915 gave the Board more power to remove children, with neither parental nor a magistrate's approval being needed, or 'neglect' having to be demonstrated. If the Board desired, children were removed. Boys were apprenticed out, while girls, like Margaret Tucker and her sisters, were sent to the Cootamundra Girls Home for domestic training before being put out to service. Trouble brewed on most NSW reserves over child removals, and Aboriginal political activity challenged the Board. In Cummeragunja's case, the people were extremely dissatisfied with the manager, Arthur McQuiggan, and they petitioned against him in October 1938. The NSW Board provocatively showed McQuiggan the petition, and he proceeded to insult and persecute the people responsible for it. Helen Baillie, a white supporter in Melbourne, reported that

McQuiggan was frequently drunk and threatened a resident with a revolver.[14]

President of the Aborigines Progressive Association, Jack Patten, who had been visiting NSW reserves to make people aware of their condition, arrived at Cummeragunja in early 1939.[15] On 4 February 1939, about 200 residents left the reserve in protest over inadequate rations, repressive management, the loss of reserve lands and fears for their children.[16] Patten was arrested, convicted of enticement and placed on a bond.[17] He spoke to the Melbourne University Labor Club, the Railways Union and other groups, demanding an inquiry.[18] Back at Cummeragunja, Bevan Nicholls recalled leaving the reserve in a boat 'full of the belongings we could carry but the valuables handed down from my grandparents to my parents are lost because we were afraid to go back over there'.[19] More left in April, and very few had moved back. Fortunately some stayed to maintain their claim on the reserve land. Many people remained at Barmah, while others moved to the Shepparton area, where Thomas James was living, and where they had previously picked fruit. The Victorian Aboriginal Protection Board refused to ration Aboriginal people from across the border, but the Sustenance Department distributed rations to some at Barmah. Shortages of food urged Helen Baillie, a nurse, to form a support group, which ferried car loads of supplies northwards.

Many Yorta Yorta remained permanently at Mooroopna after 1939. It was not exactly a haven as they met prejudice there. Ten years earlier in about 1929, an Aboriginal girl had taken a job at the fruit cannery, the first Aboriginal person to do so. Other workers walked off the job, some yelling: 'We don't have to work with black trash'. The union and the Melbourne press fought the case and the woman was reinstated.[20] During the 1930s Depression the Shire Council expressed concern about people in economic difficulties who camped by the Goulburn River. These anxieties increased after Aboriginal people camped on government land adjoining Daish's paddock, which became known as the 'Flat'. The 'Flat' was outside the town council's jurisdiction. It also adjoined the tip where people could extract building materials and spoilt but edible fruit. In May 1941, W. Edgar, member of the Legislative Council, criticised their living conditions, forcing Doug Nicholls, President of the Australian Aborigines' League, to defend them. Chief Secretary Bailey, Chair of the Board, criticised Edgar's remarks by denying their identity: the campers were 'not Aborigines' as 'they were quadroons, octoroons and of like colour, and were ordinary citizens entitled to the benefits and privileges of citizens, also their responsibilities'.[21]

The 'Flat' was well named, as it was partly below flood level. Betty Lovett remembers regular removals to higher ground and one flood in which water lapped her bed in the night.[22] In a police report of September 1946, Sergeant McGuffie listed 130 people aged from 8 days to 80 years, a third of them under 15 years, camped at the 'Flat'. They were members of the Cooper, Muir, McGee, Nelson, Smith, Peters, Edwards, Jackson, Atkinson, Charles, Briggs, Morgan, Murray, Patten, Dunolly, Burns, Aulton and Smith clans, living in 29 dwellings, 22 being tin or bag huts, and the rest tents. Wayne Atkinson, who grew up on the 'Flat' recalled, 'the floors were just hard dirt but it was a clean tidy place' which Hugh Hamill of the Aborigines Uplift Society confirmed, as did photographs.[23] Others have told me the earthen floors were polished hard so they almost shone. The men McGuffie listed were labourers, cannery workers, railway workers and wood-cutters, and several of the women were waitresses. McGuffie believed they had a 'desire to improve their standard of living'. The foreman at a local cannery said that Aboriginal girls were among his best workers. Others worked in the local tobacco factory. Selwyn Briggs ran his own wood yard in Shepparton.[24] McGuffie claimed in his report that they were philosophical about their hardships and had 'hopes of being rewarded in the hereafter for the sufferings imposed upon them by mankind', which included living in tents or huts 'made from pieces of iron rescued from rubbish tips or flattened out kerosene tins'. He added that they had hopes of land 'on which they could establish a home free from the fears of flooding in the winter, and be able to grow food stuffs for their requirements, especially vegetables'.[25]

The poor housing conditions on the 'Flat' left Aboriginal children vulnerable to

John and Carmelia Satchel and friends outside their substantial iron-clad hut at the 'Flat', Mooroopna, before its demolition in 1958. (A. & M. Jackomos Collection, courtesy of Museum Victoria, XP2917)

being removed. However, unlike on reserves where the Board removed children to assimilate them, end Aboriginality and phase out the reserves, children deemed by the Board not to be 'Aborigines' were more likely to be removed where neglect was evident. In 1944 two children were removed from a couple who had a history of convictions for drunkenness and domestic violence. The crunch came when they were both drunk in public and police observed the father throw the children down the river bank. The children were crying and allegedly in danger of falling in. Their hut was said to be 'dirty' and there was only flour, jam and powdered milk on hand. A police constable said in court: 'I have known the accused about three years. I have frequently seen them on the streets of Shepparton in a drunken condition with their children. There have been convictions against both of them. In my opinion they are not fit and proper persons to have control of children. The children have no boots and few clothes'. They were convicted of causing neglect, jailed, and their children were removed.[26] In 1948 three more children were removed from a family at the 'Flat' as their shanty was 'filthy' and the children 'covered in vermin'. However, Sergeant McGuffie said there 'are camps down there, which are a picture of cleanliness and where the children are well looked after by devoted parents but the surroundings cannot be any help in making them good citizens of the future'.[27]

The authorities' error was to place these children in institutions and not with other Aboriginal families, a policy that revealed a deep suspicion of Aboriginal family structures and the belief that good citizens could not be bred in material deprivation. So these children ended up, amongst other places, in the Ballarat orphanage. Anna Vroland, a white activist, visited and wrote to Aboriginal children in institutions. She remarked in February 1950 that 'all of them tell that they are kindly treated, but most of them are pining unutterably to be with people of their own colour'.[28] In 1956, the police introduced a more aggressive policy, removing 34 Aboriginal children from Mooroopna families. It is unlikely that all were 'neglected'. Local white supporters and the Aborigines Uplift Society of Melbourne took court action against the police and stopped the wave of removals.[29]

In June 1946 the Aboriginal community at the 'Flat' led by Shadrach James, son of Thomas James and Secretary of the local Aborigines' Progressive Association, lobbied Cabinet for land for housing and independent living. He argued that missions made paupers of his people. The Aboriginal community entertained several Cabinet ministers including Chief Secretary Slater, and civic leaders, at a banquet at St Mary's Hall in August in a consummate piece of political lobbying to push their plan.[30] In November the Cain Labor Government approved the purchase of 60 hectares of land at Daish's paddock.[31] However, it lost the election a fortnight later, putting the deal under threat again.

In autumn 1947 alarm spread as many other Aboriginal people arrived for the picking season and the 'Flat' population doubled. The police and the Mayor of Shepparton expressed concern. Doug Nicholls, by then a leader of the Fitzroy Aboriginal community, and Bill Onus, President of the Australian Aborigines' League, visited from Melbourne in March 1947 and expressed dismay at the conditions they found. When told by the police that those on the 'Flat' 'were a menace to the good conduct of the town', Nicholls accused the town of discrimination as Aboriginal people were not welcomed, and the police of 'victimisation'. Nicholls wanted Aboriginal housing scattered throughout the town and an Aboriginal community centre built. The Goulburn Shire was dismayed when the Board again denied any responsibility for these people, saying in the racial categories of government policy they were 'legally white', that is, there were not 'half caste' or 'full blood' people.[32] Concern deepened from town authorities in 1948 when a child at the 'Flat' contracted typhoid, due to lack of sanitary facilities. Health authorities from the Council demolished several Aboriginal huts in 1948 and 1949.[33] The 'Flat' burnt into the Shepparton community's imagination, some thinking it 'a blot . . . a menace to the town', while Rev. N. Fairchney mused: 'that blot over the river is a rain on my conscience'.[34]

Shadrach James lobbied for assistance between 1946 and 1950 despite government lethargy. In ten letters to government over these five years, he sought the land promised by the government, 'vested in our own rights where we could settle permanently and have homes of our own'. He argued that 'after all the Aborigines really are homeless and landless proletarians in a country with millions of acres that once belonged to them'.[35] As the 'Flat' was too flood-prone, James suggested 80 hectares of well-watered land owned by a local landowner, Agnew, which could be used for an experimental vegetable farm to prove to Australia that Aboriginal Victorians 'could take their place in any community and work equally as hard and as well'. However, this land was sold, so James submitted a list of three other suitable blocks in April 1947, including some set aside for an agricultural college. As so often happened with Aboriginal land proposals, a neighbour and current leaser of the college site opposed the idea. James and members of the local Aborigines' Progressive Association agreed in October 1948 to accept the Daish's paddock land and engineer away the flooding, but acting Premier McDonald opposed the idea. Shadrach James wrote in frustration in March 1950, calling for immediate assistance after record floods and for the promise of land to be honoured. He wrote in vain.

Sporting and community life

Sport was a vital part of community life at Cummeragunja and this tradition was carried on at Mooroopna-Shepparton. Their skills were honed originally on 'Cummera's' sports ground, which they had cleared and levelled themselves. Cummeragunja men played football in scratch matches as early as 1888 and formed a football club in 1894. Their team were premiers of the Nathalia and District Football Association in 1898 and 1899 and played in that league until the First World War. They played in the Western and Moira Riding Football Association from 1921 to 1931, being premiers five times (1926–1929, and 1931). Their deeds made them feel the equal of others, which they voiced in their team song:

> We are from Cummera, we are the team
> We can't be beaten, that's easily seen
> At the end of the season, you know the reason
> We are the premier team.[36]

They also inspired the next generation of Aboriginal athletes. Paul Briggs, a footballer and athlete of note at Shepparton in the 1970s, recalled: 'My greatest motivation to play came from the stories of the old Cummeragunja football teams. All my Dad's brothers played in the 1926–27 Premierships and Dad was constantly talking about them. They were folk heroes. Their exploits were extraordinary and I was inspired to emulate them.'[37]

Some of the Cummera men played for district teams and in Melbourne. In 1925 brothers 'Dowie' (Howard) and Doug Nicholls and Billie Muir joined the Tongala Football Club while working for the Water Commission. At first they took some racial abuse, mostly from the crowd but sometimes from players as well, but won respect through their football skills. Doug Nicholls decided to try Melbourne football in 1927 and, after failing to make the Carlton League team, was accepted by Northcote Association team despite nervousness about his Aboriginality. His first game was sensational and he was soon given a labouring job with the Northcote Council. His brother 'Dowie' joined him for a season but Doug Nicholls stayed for five, being named 'best and fairest' twice and being an active part of a premiership team. Known as the 'flying Abo', he also became one of the best known players in the game for his speed on the wing, spring and agility, his weaving and his courage in playing the ball—skills concentrated in a very short but well-muscled body. He brought pride to those at Cummera who would 'gather by someone's radio on Saturday night, and listen eagerly to Northcote's score, and an account of Doug's play'. He was head-hunted by Carlton and Collingwood, but ended up playing with Fitzroy alongside the great Haydn Bunton from 1932 to 1937, winning further awards and playing interstate games as well. While playing football, he made an adult Christian conversion to the Church of Christ. He won respect for this, as he did for his Aboriginality, by force of his conviction. He played a final season with Northcote in 1939.[38]

Doug Nicholls after winning the Warracknabeal Gift, 1929. (Courtesy Herald and Weekly Times Ltd)

Cummeragunja's sportsmen often competed in athletics sports, professional running being very lucrative. There were several carnivals a week in country centres, especially in the Depression, and runners could earn £10 for a heat win and up to £30 for a final—ten times the basic weekly wage. Big races offered prize money of £100 or more. Additional income could be made from appearance money and betting, which led to sharp practices in professional running. *Millers Guide* to sports claimed that no town in Australia produced more gift winners than Cummera, it having provided fourteen, including Bobby MacDonald, Peter Dunnolly, Larry Marsh, Stan Charles, Alf Morgan, Bill and Eric Onus, 'Dowie' and Wally Nicholls, and Selwyn and Eddy Briggs. The first runner listed used the crouch start in the 1880s before it was officially sanctioned, and the last one listed was runner-up in the Stawell Gift in 1930. Doug Nicholls won the Nyah and Warracknabeal Gifts, winning £100 in each. He won many modest heat and place prizes, and possibly received appearance money as well.

Lynchy Cooper, son of William Cooper, was one of the best of them. He ran professionally for over twenty years from the mid 1920s and, besides casual work, supported himself from his earnings. Cooper won the Warracknabeal Gift (1926), the £250 Stawell Gift (1928) complete with gold cup and sash, and many minor events and heats. Runner and coach Merv Feenan estimated his career earnings as possibly £3,000. In 1929 Cooper failed in the Melbourne Thousand, Eddy Briggs running third, but the same day won the gruelling World Sprint Championship from Englishman Tom Mills, run over four races: 75, 100, 130 and 220 yards. He retired in 1946, aged forty, to become a painting contractor in Shepparton and President of the local Aborigines' Progressive Association. He made an unsuccessful comeback in 1948 to contest the Bendigo Aboriginal Gift over 130 yards for £60. The race was won by 41-year-old ex-serviceman Frank Stewart from Swan Hill, the son of rodeo rider Galloway Stewart. Stewart ran professionally in the l940s, boxed in the travelling tent shows, and later became a minister in Swan Hill.[39]

The Cummera sporting tradition was carried on by many at Shepparton. Harry James (Jimmy) Murray was a fine professional runner in the 1940s. His trainer, Clive Wiltshire, believed he was unfairly handicapped in the Shepparton Gift in 1945 at a crucial time in his career, preventing him from becoming 'one of Australia's really great runners'. Lynchy Cooper agreed, remarking that in his prime, Murray 'could have downed the best Australian runners'. He was still running well in 1950, achieving five firsts and a second in one week. The *Shepparton News* praised his abilities in several sports and referred to him as a 'fine ambassador to his race' and 'an acquisition to any community'.[40] Sport thus had the power to transform, for this praise was given to Murray at the same time as the Aboriginal campers were being called a 'menace' to the Shepparton community.

Jimmy Murray was also a leading footballer for Shepparton East and later the Lemnos club from the mid 1940s to late 1950s. He also played in the Aboriginal 'All Blacks' team. Murray was also a good middleweight boxer as well, and was wooed by promoters. He also fought in the travelling boxing tent shows when they visited Shepparton, being recruited beforehand as the 'good' local hero to take on the 'evil' out-of-towners. He recently recalled a visit around 1950 from Jimmy Sharman, 'Mr Tent Boxing', who pleaded with him to fight as the 'local champion'. Murray finally agreed to do so, but only for a large sum.[41] Aboriginal people gained power and prestige from sport to counter the hurts of being Aboriginal in a town that disparaged them. In 1958 Hurtle Atkinson won the Victorian junior bantamweight title, Jeff Cooper won the Morrison

Medal for the 'best and fairest' footballer in the Goulburn Valley competition, and Rosalind Atkinson was 'best and fairest' in Mooroopna School's A Grade 1959 Premiership Basketball team.[42]

The 'Flat' had a strong community life despite outward material privation. Wayne Atkinson recalled that 'there were four children plus my parents, plus my grandparents—eight people—living in our place. And sometimes you have your cousins coming and going, so it could be anything from eight to twelve people living in a "humpie" the size of a lounge room in a modern house'. Family was the rock of their survival. Atkinson continued: 'There was a sense of freedom there. You could wander around, you could visit your relations, then you could go into the bush and get a bit of bush tucker. Some of the old people taught us to find bush tucker'. Betty Lovett agreed, saying: 'Everyone cared for each other and helped each other'.[43] The people were bound in networks of family and kin into a supportive community. If there was a flood they all pitched in. If someone was short of food they all helped. If there was trouble from the police they sympathised. Someone could always give assistance, as many earned reasonable money in the fruit season, picking or working in the canneries.

There were times when crime disrupted the community, especially alcohol-induced violence. This is evident in court reports found in the *Shepparton News*, although the incidence was not large. People were mostly in court on drunk and disorderly charges, and for vagrancy and indecent language. There were some cases of domestic violence and assault, and several cases of sexual assault and theft, all over a period of fifteen years. Some incidents no doubt escaped detection, while other charges were trumped up or resulted from 'victimisation' as Doug Nicholls called it. Aboriginal drinking was usually more public than that of whites in town and thus easier to target. Many Aboriginal people abhorred drunken behaviour. When his brother Thomas Carey James was on a drunk and disorderly charge, Shadrach James told the court that 'it was very hard for him to help Aboriginals who were in the habit of drinking. But he felt that spending the week-end in jail might be a lesson to his brother'.[44] Mostly the people were law-abiding, reflecting their strong religious and moral upbringing under Thomas James.

The Mooroopna-Shepparton Aboriginal community continued the strong religious life of Cummera. When Thomas James retired in 1922, Eddy Atkinson took over the spiritual leadership of the reserve, in between earning a living from rural work and playing football. Atkinson also ministered to those in Mooroopna. Sergeant McGuffie reported in 1946 that the Aboriginal campers were a 'god fearing' people who held their own church services in the Mooroopna Court House. About fifty attended and the 'Preacher, Choir and Organist are all aboriginals'.[45] In 1946 the Church of Christ Aborigines Mission Committee appointed Atkinson and his wife to work in Mooroopna and a church building was promised. By 1950 no church had been built. Atkinson wrote to Amy Brown of the Victorian Aboriginal Group: 'The flood has scattered quite a lot of our people and they have gone from the flat to different places, probably until the summer comes again. There is still a number of people here. And I go around to their homes and have meetings. It is a big job because I have to travel some 6 miles out and back . . . I manage to have the Sunday school when I can in the homes of the people'.[46] Eddy Atkinson died in 1953 and Pastor Doug Nicholls stepped in, causing Shadrach James to form a breakaway group for a time. The Aboriginal community raised sufficient funds to buy a block of land in 1956 and the Church of Christ purchased a prefabricated building from the Eildon Weir project to be used as a church and further bind the community.[47]

Orbost and Newmerella Hill

Aboriginal people settled in the Orbost area of Gippsland by the Snowy River during the 1930s, and by the mid 1940s, there were five to ten families—including the Solomons, Hoods, Harrisons, Mulletts and Mongtas—living there semi-permanently in bark or hessian-bag huts and tents. They had been pushed off Lake Tyers reserve for being 'too white', were expelled for defying authority, or chose to leave for freedom's sake. Cora Gilsenan of Metung (an old friend of the Gunai/Kurnai people and granddaughter of Richard who was a school teacher at Lake Tyers), wrote of Lake Tyers in 1948: 'food, clothing, housing and firewood do not make up for lack of freedom . . . a dole and control system robs them of incentive and self-expression'.[48] George Slaney of the Melbourne City Mission, who worked with Aboriginal people in Orbost, was also told by ex-residents of Lake Tyers that 'they disliked the restrictions; that they are treated like children; because they have to ask permission even to go to Lakes Entrance to do some shopping'. Slaney's informants added that food rations were meagre at Lake Tyers and there was no minister there.[49]

The numbers of Gunai/Kurnai people at Orbost swelled to two hundred during the bean picking season—December to March. Albert Mullett recalled generally good relations between workers and farmers, who supplied their pickers with farm vegetables, milk and eggs; there were also always plenty of rabbits and meat and sometimes a bullock was killed.[50] However, few farmers provided adequate accommodation and there was none in town, so the people camped along the Snowy River and on Newmerella Hill. Conditions were rough, with mostly bags and coats as blankets. Eric Onus complained about this on the Gunai/Kurnai's behalf in December 1942, and about their inability to buy alcohol if they wanted it, as other people did after a hard-working week. He pointed out that the kinsmen of some of these people were fighting for freedom overseas at that time with the 2nd AIF.[51] Most of the people probably preferred the bush in summer, away from whites and amongst their own, but some would certainly have found the drinking situation unjust.

Aboriginal bean-pickers were vital to the industry in Orbost, as well as other places like the Mitchell River near Bairnsdale, as they formed a large proportion of the seasonal workers. They were proud of their work skills. They would start at dawn, break in the heat of the day and resume in the late afternoon, picking till dark, a ten- to twelve-hour day. The work was done with lots of chat, with children beside the adults, and babies in boxes under umbrellas. Nights were spent eating and socialising around the fire. Friday was a day off in town, washing, shopping, playing cards and drinking a bit of illegal alcohol. During picking, the 'gun' pickers ('loners') would not stop for dinner or a smoke, but ate and smoked as they worked. Albert Mullett recalled his times as a 'loner', picking 22 bags a day. He prepared his own bags, stretching them to hold more, and had them at hand ready for a fast start. 'The pressure was on you when you are a gun picker because someone always wants to beat your tally. So each morning I was keyed up'. He learned to work steadily all day and his fingers became nimble.

> Good pickers don't pick the little beans, they just pick all the big beans. They
> lay the bush back and get them off the bottom, both sides, and they leave
> the young beans so that there is a good crop for the next pick. You have
> to run your fingers in and out the bush until your hands are full of beans.
> Sometimes you get a few leaves or a bit of stalk in your hand but you learn
> how to get rid of those . . . I can get a job picking anywhere—a fast picker but
> a clean picker.[52]

However, the mechanisation of bean-picking in the 1970s curbed the market for these skills.

Some whites sought to help the Gunai/Kurnai people in Orbost. George Slaney of the Melbourne City Mission spent two years from 1945

Emma and Bill Murray, bean pickers, photographed by Derek Fowell in 1988.
(Courtesy of Museum Victoria, XP3849)

working amongst the people. He ministered to their spiritual needs, helped them petition the Board, and met the Board at Lake Tyers on their behalf, surveying their opinions beforehand. Slaney asked if they desired houses and '13 of the dark people (almost each one representing a family) signed this questionnaire stating they wanted mainly 3 roomed cottages and were prepared to pay from £2 to £10 deposit and pay them off by rent'. The Board was hostile and ignored the subject of housing. Within weeks, Slaney claimed the Chief Secretary requested the Orbost Shire Council to remove the people from the area, and force them back to Lake Tyers. Slaney, a tent dweller himself when in Orbost, unsuccessfully scoured the district for houses for himself and the Gunai/Kurnai during the post-war housing crisis.[53]

Slaney also gave practical help with a dash of religion. Each morning in early 1947 seven children came to his tent to have a wash, their hair combed, and shoes cleaned. Whether this was necessary is unknown, for most mothers were scrupulously clean, despite the difficulties of life on earthen floors without tap water. However, some children were excluded from school in 1944 for being dirty. Reverend M. Green of Orbost claimed in 1947 that some white families withdrew their children because some 'half caste' children 'were so dirty and unhealthy'.[54] Slaney was perhaps making sure they would pass the test; he also gave them a piece of fruit. In return for sixpence in the middle of the day he gave them an 'Oslo' lunch—a wholemeal salad sandwich, milk and fruit lunch popular in wartime. They returned after school to do their homework and several stayed for tea and bible lessons.[55]

In 1947 an Orbost Aborigines Welfare Committee was formed by local clergy and the school teacher. Its aims were to preach the gospel and encourage assimilation. Slaney did not join but worked with it. The Committee chided the farmers for not providing accommodation for seasonal workers, and lobbied the Shire Council for land for the people to reside upon and for better housing, but to no avail. The Shire Council provided an Aboriginal Infant Welfare Centre for a six month trial, but only one Aboriginal mother attended, which was probably due to the Centre's non-community nature. The Committee also wanted the children's education to be addressed, as many did not attend the school when their parents were in the area. It stated that there were a 'number of respected families of dark people who have lived here all their lives, and are an asset to the community', but said 'THE problem' was 'the indolent type'.[56]

George Slaney diagnosed things differently. In June 1947 he wrote: 'studying the situation here now for two years, I am convinced fully, that the fault of the Aboriginal problem is mainly the so-called white people of Orbost and the Aborigines Destruction [crossed out] Protection Board'.[57] Slaney said farmers objected to people camping on the river bank near their property and claimed Aboriginal people left gates open, which the 'permanent' campers denied. He wrote that neither he nor the Gunai/Kurnai people were 'wanted by the majority, and yet the farmers want them to do the maize picking'.[58] The white children of the town felt the same. When Slaney took some Aboriginal children to Sunday school he found after the second week that 'the white children interfered with them in class and were positively rude'. As he walked three girls home, they were met with cat calls from the white children: 'Get out you black niggers, we don't want you'. He wrote: 'It gave me such a shock that I did not know what to do; nor do I yet know what to do'. The children probably coped better, as they had heard it all before. The school teacher, Mr Hassell, told Slaney: 'This is the attitude of many children in Orbost'.[59]

In early 1951 Cora Gilsenan of Metung spoke on radio about the plight of Gunai/Kurnai people in East Gippsland fringe camps, particularly their high rate of child mortality, and attacked the Board for refusing to take responsibility for 'the dark people who have left Lake Tyers to seek freedom and independence'. She wrote to Anna Vroland, the Secretary of the Women's League for International Peace and Freedom, applauding their stance on Framlingham housing and suggesting the group pursue the Gunai/Kurnai's cause.[60] The Women's International League sent a retired doctor, Hilda Greenshields, and Sister L. Miller, a former matron with experience in Aboriginal child welfare, with Gilsenan to investigate.

The three were 'shocked' by what they saw, especially in seasonal workers' temporary camps. Gilsenan reported that most lived in wooden structures covered in hessian bags. Three families sheltered under a bridge, one under a buggy, one in a disused maize crib and another on a cement-floored disused dairy. Others were in somewhat better accommodation on farmers' properties. Dr Greenshields stated that there were 200 Aboriginal children in the region, 'living under such appalling conditions that their very lives were threatened, the rate of mortality in some families being as high as 50%'. At this time the overall rate in Aboriginal Victoria was a 20–25 per cent loss of life by the age of fifteen, whereas for the total Victorian population in the 1940s, 2–3 per cent of infants died before the age of one year.[61] Greenshields added that 'camps of this kind provide no real shelter or warmth, and no cooking or bathing facilities'. Many people contracted pneumonia and, given their inadequate diet and insufficient warm clothing, blankets and beds, 'the miracle is any escape'. Sister Miller remarked on the love of the parents for their children and the large families, few women having less than six children and some up to twelve. She noted most babies she saw were bottle-fed and that most deaths occurred in the second year. Indeed 'we met very few families who had not lost one or more babies at that age'. She called for infant welfare training in feeding and hygiene. Miller also noted that most adults 'we met had lost most if not all of their teeth'.[62]

The Women's International League Committee sent the report to Chief Secretary Keith Dodgshun, as it was his Department's duty 'to promote the well-being of these people'. Dodgshun gave the standard Board answer that these people were not officially considered to be Aboriginal people, adding that no 'man should be denied the right to endeavour to establish his own independence and to earn his own living, but once he does so, he accepts the responsibility of providing for the proper maintenance of his family'. If conditions were hard, the people could seek help from local health and education authorities like any other citizen, but not from the Board. Voluntary organisations could help them if they chose. He said he intended to initiate a police investigation and have any neglected children removed. In a second letter, Dodgshun blamed the people for their own predicament, saying they had proper parental training while at Lake Tyers, that there was plenty of work

Farm labourers from Lake Tyers and elsewhere in Gippsland in the 1930s.
L–R: Alf Harrison, Fred Johnson, Albert 'Choppy' Hayes, Rupert Harrison, Jimmy
O'Rourke, Jack Lynix, Ted Foster, Charlie Brown, Tom Foster. (A. & M. Jackomos
Collection, courtesy of Museum Victoria, XP3468)

available at award rates as well as social benefits if they needed them.[63] His
letters sounded reasonable, but Dodgshun failed to acknowledge several
factors: the discrimination the Gunai/Kurnai faced in Gippsland towns;
the fact that seasonal workers were classed as contractors and not under
awards; that, being untrained, they were trapped in low paid and seasonal
rural work; they lacked capital to get a start with housing; and they had
an (understandable) fear of officialdom and were thus unwilling to utilise
welfare benefits. Dodgshun also overestimated the effectiveness of any
training at Lake Tyers, where dependence and a lack of responsibility
were nurtured, not the reverse.

The members of the Women's International League for Peace and
Freedom lobbied politicians, unions, and the Council of Churches. The
Minister for Lands and local member, Albert Lind, who was sympathetic,
met with the League and promised some crown land, saying that 'any
dark family who shows us that they are prepared to go on a piece of
Crown Land would receive sympathetic consideration from me'. He
also promised building materials, and a mobile health unit staffed by
someone who 'understands the needs and purpose of the dark people'.[64]
In 1952 the League followed the matter up with Lind and the Shires of

Orbost and Tambo, and suggested empty Lake Tyers houses be transported to Orbost. As a stop-gap, Cora Gilsenan and her father donated
a few hectares and negotiated with the transport company, Mayne
Nickless, to supply eight car cases for temporary accommodation.
However, political instability led to three different non-Labor governments in 1952 and Lind left office without making any headway on
the land issue.

In September 1953 the League told the incoming Lands Minister,
Robert Holt, of Lind's broken promises, commenting that 'nothing
came of the matter except disappointment and additional bitterness
among those it was hoped to benefit'.[65] Holt replied that the file showed
no Indigenous people had applied for land, but offered to help any who
did. His answer was surprising as Gilsenan had referred in January 1953
to a couple 'Dick and Mary' still awaiting a reply to their letter from the
Lands Department.[66] Richard Harrison, a former Lake Tyers resident
and ex-serviceman, with his wife Mary—the 'Dick and Mary' to whom
Gilsenan referred—and their seven children again requested land at
Metung in September 1953, 'to get security for my children and give
them the opportunity I never had'. He had almost ten years experience
working with a grazier, did weekend contract work and had offers of help
to clear the land and build a house. Holt promised to investigate despite
most land being occupied, but he resigned two months later.[67] Gilsenan
lamented that Harrison had been: 'as keen as mustard. He said "I would
work night and day in an effort to get some security for my children"'.
He met with more disappointment.[68]

Campers' culture and their benefactors

Campers were not considered by the Board to be Aboriginal and were
thought by anthropologists of the day to be a people 'in-between' and
without a culture. A leading anthropologist, A.P. Elkin, who influenced
governments, believed that those of 'mixed descent' were 'cultureless'
and on the road to becoming white. That was their destiny.[69]

However, Aboriginal campers were not the same as 'poor whites',
some of whom camped out in 'humpy'-style accommodation in the
1930s Depression and even lived off the land. They lived their lives
in a distinctively Aboriginal way, as we have seen. For instance, at the
'Flat'—a complex camp—they had their own pastor and church, their
own political organisation, and their own sports teams; thus they forged
their own traditions. They also had a distinctive history based around a

sense of injustice about land, and about heavy-handed treatment by the Board, which had extended to the abhorrent removal of their children. They affirmed their sense of injustice as they yarned around camp-fires, and it was reinforced when they suffered discrimination in employment—or 'special' treatment from police.

Campers had their own ideas about family, kinship and sharing. Connie Barling of Save the Children Fund, who worked with the Dimboola camp community in the 1950s, recalled: 'The families were very close, and any relatives passing through were always welcomed with a bed or tucker. Money, also, was lightly handed around or loaned and when I suggested that this may not be the best idea, I was merely told: "He is my brother", and there is no answer to that'. The campers had their own space, separated from whites by way of choice, as well as due to unofficial caste barriers. They experienced cold stares when they ventured into the white world. Barling also recalled: 'The families lived quite near the main street but were out of sight in their dwellings. When walking along the street the children would hang their heads'.[70]

These people shared an Aboriginal culture that was not exactly the same as that which their grandparents shared—as is the way of all cultures. They now spoke English, but did not speak an Aboriginal language as well. They were still a spiritual people believing in things

Unidentified camper on the track in the Mallee, 1944. (Courtesy of Herald and Weekly Times Ltd)

they could not see, but these things now included God and Jesus as well as *mindye* and *bugeens*. They enjoyed music as they socialised, but did not sing in the language of their grandparents, except for a few surviving songs. Margaret Tucker set down several of these around 1950 with her friend Anna Vroland.[71] One was called 'Rough Road' and it was sung to her by her uncle in the Yorta Yorta language when she was a child. It went:

> Gul cul je-mah chee, gul cul je-mah, Chu-ju-mah pull pull je mah
> Long is the journey, rough is the track, till we come to the end of the road

Another was called 'Nowwa Bora Pharoh' and was about Moses leading the Israelites from the Pharaoh's tyranny. It was adapted by Thomas James and translated into Yorta Yorta by Margaret Tucker's grandmother. Other songs were Westernised but still expressed distinctive Aboriginal ideas. The song 'Jacky Jacky' is set in the Depression and describes how Jacky the consummate hunter is now on rations:

> White Boy he now pays all taxes
> Keeps Jacky Jacky in clothes and food
> He don't care what becomes of the country
> White boy's tucker him pretty good.

> *Chorus:*
> Clicketa Boobilah wildy maah
> Billying etcha gingerry wah

> Now the country's short of money
> Jacky just sits and laughs all day
> White boy wants to give it back to Jacky
> No fear, Jacky won't have it that way.

Anna Vroland heard this sung by Aboriginal people at a support meeting in Melbourne in 1935. It was attributed to Captain Newman, manager of Lake Tyers. However, a typescript copy in the archives of the Victorian Aboriginal Group claims it was written and composed by Leslie Mullett, a Sydney man staying at Lake Tyers, noted down and recorded when an Indigenous man sang it while travelling to Framlingham in 1938. However, an earlier claim is that it was a song by Jimmy Scott sung to Chief Secretary Macfarlan at Lake Tyers in 1932, making him laugh.[72] Whatever its true origins, it captured the essence of Aboriginal humour.

Daryl Tonkin pioneered forest land near Drouin with his brother in the late 1930s and allowed Aboriginal workers to live there, on an area called Jackson's Track, in the 1940s. He married one of the community, Euphemie Mullett, and together they raised twelve children. In his life story, *Jackson's Track* (1999), evocatively told by Carolyn Landon, Tonkin describes the Gunai/Kurnai culture of the campers. They maintained a unique family and work culture based on shame and respect, used bush tucker and the forest in their own way, practised traditional crafts of carving and basket-making, maintained a belief in *bugeens* and other spirit beings, and entertained themselves with distinctive stories and music. The residents sent their children to school and allowed them to participate in sport, producing many Victorian Badminton champions from the Mullett family and a world bantamweight boxing champion in Lionel Rose (1968–69). However, development in the area, attention from local authorities and 'do-gooders' caught up with Jackson's Track. The people were forced or cajoled into moving into town. Some refused and headed for other places, but those enticed by religion or cowed by authority gave it a go. Their Jackson's Track bark huts were quickly bulldozed and burnt by the authorities. But the promised houses in town were slow to materialise and initially the Gunai/Kurnai lived in tents. Men and women who rarely or never drank, soon felt isolated and bored in town, and some of them despaired and took to drink. In his book Tonkin is scathing about the do-gooders and religious types who played a part in the end of the Track.[73]

Few whites had any experience of this world, save open-minded types like Tonkin, and some rough men with a bottle in their hands looking for a good time in the camps. However, a few people who felt 'a rain on their conscience', mostly locals, tried to help with food, clothing, and religion, or by lobbying the government as did Cora Gilsenan. But were they meddling 'do-gooders' as Tonkin portrays them?

There are many examples of local individuals who offered assistance. In Antwerp Pastor Schulz helped campers in the 1930s, and in Hamilton in 1941 Rev. I. L. Graham spoke with the Chief Secretary about a family which was in difficulty. In the north-west in 1940 Arthur Burdeu of the Aborigines Uplift Society of Melbourne planned improvements to Aboriginal self-made 'humpies' after touring Bordertown, Antwerp and Dimboola. Burdeu stated that 'the type of house should be as at present but with all objectionable features removed and obvious needs added'. His plan was that 'humpies' would still be made of second-hand materials and in the same way, but would have three not two rooms, a galvanised roof (not bark) with gutters and water tank, glass windows

Children at Jackson's Track, photographed by Richard Seeger. L–R: Russell Mullett, Lynette Rose, Cheryl Mullett, Dorothy Mullett, Raymond Rose, Phillip Mullett, Lionel Rose. (Courtesy of Museum Victoria, XP1679)

not bagging, washable tar floors not earth, and a fenced area for a kitchen garden.[74] It could be done for just £30 per hut, about six weeks basic wage. It is unknown if any such modifications were made. In 1955, residents of Robinvale, a new soldier-settler orchard town, arranged black versus white basketball and football matches to encourage interaction. Elderly Aboriginal man Thomas Pearce said of the whites: 'people are all right round here. Not high minded like they are in some other places'. However, a local garage man when asked about 'Aborigines' in 1957 by activists visiting the town, replied: 'We just call them niggers'.[75] Sergeant Arthur Feldtmann, an energetic Swan Hill policeman, raised funds and donations of labour to build a children's centre for two extended families adjoining their parents' huts. The centre was just three metres away from the parents' accommodation, and provided a boys' and girls' bedroom, sleeping three each room, a recreation room, and a bathroom. The children attended the state school.[76]

By 1955 the Save the Children Fund supported four field officers in Victoria, two in Shepparton, and one each in Orbost and Dimboola. The Fund assisted the children's education and performance at school. Connie Barling, the Fund's welfare officer at Dimboola between 1954 and 1966, who ministered to seven families, was shocked by their housing which was even devoid of rainwater tanks. The children stayed at school until fourteen but never moved beyond grade four: 'Absenteeism was rife; any excuse served and no one cared.' They 'had to fight as they were called "niggers", which they hated'. Barling was amazed at 'how they all loved one another' and shared what they had. Many of the townspeople were hostile to her as she was helping the 'niggers' and one police officer told her 'the aborigines should all be sterilized and allowed to "die out"'. Barling encouraged school attendance, combing and washing hair in readiness, assisting with books and uniforms and providing lunch for a shilling. She took the children each year to the Lord Mayor's Camp at Portsea—to their delight. Barling also established a centre for recreation, sewing classes for the women, a teenage club and accompanied Aboriginal people when they faced court. She let a homeless couple share her flat.

Barling left Dimboola in 1966 when the families moved into public housing in town and the children had grown up, several reaching high school, which was a coup. She reminisced:

> Looking back over those thirteen years I remember many times when I almost gave up, especially when the hostility of some of the townspeople made things difficult. It was as though there were two communities there, and I was in the middle. But I had developed a very strong attachment to the aborigines, and was never in any doubt as to where my loyalties lay . . . whatever I was able to do for them, they gave me a great deal in return.[77]

It is not known exactly what these efforts achieved or what Aboriginal people thought of them. Cora Gilsenan, who showed Florence Grylls of the Save the Children Fund around Orbost on a fact-finding tour in August 1953, gives us some insight:

> The dark people were as usual reluctant to talk to strangers, and to make the situation more strange Miss Grylls did not wish to make her name or her organisation known to them. I think they were non-plussed by the abruptness of the visit to each group of people throughout Orbost. It went much like this. 'Good morning? How many children here? Would you like a scrap book for the children? Would you like a tin of dripping? You would? Here you are. Well we must be going: Good Bye'. The lack of explanation as to the purpose of the visit puzzled them. I felt pretty uncomfortable at times. The dark people looked at me for some kind of explanation but it was not my place to give it. So hence I don't think much could be gained from the visit.[78]

However, Cora Gilsenan had an intimate and longstanding relation-ship with the people, who visited and worked on 'Noonahcullah', her father's Metung property. The Gilsenans provided food and shelter for Aboriginal people during flooding in East Gippsland. Alick Jackomos recalled that they hosted 'up to two hundred Aboriginal people on their property at Metung and they stayed there some months'.[79] Slaney at Orbost and Barling at Dimboola also developed a complex relationship with Aboriginal people over time. No doubt reactions to these three whites were mixed but were generally favourable. At an Aboriginal Congress meeting in Melbourne, Mrs Harrison of Kaniva stated 'Miss Barling is a great help'.[80]

Certainly, welfare workers upgraded the material conditions of Aboriginal families and increased the children's access to school. They created models of discipline and self-reliance, qualities Aboriginal people possessed before white colonialism managed and infantilised them. The danger was that these well-meaning helpers might take too long to stand back and let Aboriginal people look after themselves, thus undermining Aboriginal self-sufficiency. Gilsenan was certainly

Broadcasting hymn singing, Jackson's Track in the 1950s, photographed by Richard Seeger. L-R: Lilian Nicholls, Anna Cooper holding young Daisy Cooper, Gladys Nicholls, Irene Moffat, Roy Rose with guitar, Norman Coombs (?), Doug Nicholls conducting. (Courtesy of Museum Victoria, XP1640)

aware of the problems of paternalism. Probably the example of welfare workers was most important in convincing whites that Aboriginal people were worth the effort. Barling and Feldtmann were often asked by service clubs and church groups to speak of their work. As Barling recalled: 'My work was becoming known in other country towns and I was asked to give talks, sometimes travelling up to fifty miles, which resulted in a lot of extra help'. In this way they highlighted the qualities and achievements of Aboriginal people.

By the early 1950s the Aboriginal population of Victoria was about 1300, 1000 of whom were campers, free from control but in poor material circumstances. Arthur Feldtmann, the Swan Hill police officer, compiled a brief survey of Aboriginal people in Victoria in 1955, which gives us a frozen demographic moment in the ever-moving Aboriginal population of campers. He compiled it from 'information received', excluding the 150 Aboriginal people who resided at Lake Tyers. Of the 796 people listed, 188 were male, 165 were female and 443 were children, 231 of whom attended school.[81] The 142 listed as being employed were mostly men, as the work listed was mostly men's paid work of the day (with the exception of picking), namely: wood-cutting, shearing, and railway work. The survey suggested most of the 188 men were at least in part-time work. Feldtmann noted the housing of 754 of these people: 507 being in huts or 'humpies' and 247 in houses. He listed ten districts of residence (clockwise around the State): Dennington (60); Dimboola (58); Mildura (4); Robinvale (80); Swan Hill (39); Lake Boga (11); Echuca (62); Nathalia (100); Shepparton (201); and Orbost (162). Feldtmann believed there were people in other centres as well 'but I would say they would be very few indeed'. In fact he missed over 500 across the State, as he did not list Framlingham, Jackson's Track, and Aboriginal people living in Melbourne, to whom we now turn.

14

Melbourne and Aboriginal Activism

In early 1951 William Bull, an elderly Gunai/Kurnai man, was arrested for begging on Princes Bridge while playing the gumleaf. He was sentenced to six months jail. This added to Bull's decades-long list of sentences for offences that regularly snared Aboriginal people—drunkenness, vagrancy and offensive behaviour. After seven weeks in Pentridge Prison, Bill Bull successfully conducted his own appeal as Justice Streeton acquitted him. A letter to the press from 'Australian' of Murrumbeena claimed Bill Bull 'was arrested a few minutes after I gave him 3d. He did not ask me for it, nor did I see him ask others'.[1] He was in effect 'busking' in today's terms, not begging. Bull was assisted in court two years later by prominent barrister Frank Galbally over the same offence, causing Bill Bull to weep: it was the first legal aid offered him in 30 years before the courts. Bill Bull died in 1954 in the Fitzroy lock-up. Sergeant Joyce described him as a 'real gentleman', adding 'he was just a wanderer. Many times we brought him in just for his own sake'.[2] He was given an Aboriginal funeral with a gumleaf requiem funded by white supporters.

Bill Bull's presence on the streets of Melbourne challenged the century-old policy of keeping Aboriginal people out of the metropolis. Indeed, from the late 1920s Aboriginal people reclaimed their right to live in Melbourne. As a denser Aboriginal population emerged, fuelled by the Depression and the Second World War, an Aboriginal community life emerged, which included fledgling Aboriginal political organisations, encouraged by white support groups.

Aboriginal Fitzroy

In the 1920s Aboriginal people began to move to Melbourne's working class suburbs for a diversity of reasons. Thomas James came to North Fitzroy after he retired as Cummeragunja's school teacher in 1922. Grace Brux left Cummeragunja to run a boarding house in North Melbourne in the late 1920s. She hosted a number of young Aboriginal women, including Margaret Tucker, who, having turned 18, was freed in the mid 1920s from a forced apprenticeship in domestic service under the NSW Aborigines Act. William Cooper left Cummeragunja in 1932 when almost seventy and settled in Footscray. Others came to try life in the big city or search for a job. Many gravitated to Fitzroy, perhaps because Grandpa James had been there, and because the rents were lowest, for Fitzroy was then classed as Melbourne's worst slum. Slum crusader F. Barnett argued in 1931 that slums were morally, not just materially bankrupt, and described Fitzroy as 'a hotbed of drunkenness, dissoluteness, slovenliness, and crime'. The *Herald* agreed, claiming areas like Fitzroy were 'breeding grounds for stunted, rickety bodies, crime, immorality and pauperism'.[3] About a hundred Aboriginal people lived in Fitzroy in the 1930s and this trebled by the early fifties. An equal number lived in other parts of Melbourne, mostly inner suburbs; Doug

Keith Nelson, Clorrie Nelson, Les Hudson and Clarry Harradine at Collingwood, about 1960. (A. & M. Jackomos Collection, courtesy of Museum Victoria, XP3407)

Nicholls lived in Northcote, and the Hunters and Pattersons from Coranderrk in South Melbourne. Some Aboriginal people never or rarely visited Fitzroy because of its rough reputation.

Aboriginal people from three main regions shifted into the south Fitzroy area bounded by Victoria Parade and Brunswick, Johnston and Hoddle streets, but were mostly located around Gertrude Street. The initial migration from the Barmah-Cummeragunja area, stemming from the reserve's overbearing management, increased after the 1939 walk off. Others came from Framlingham in search of work and better housing in the early 1930s when the Depression bit hard. From 1940 there was a flow from Gippsland, as some of the independent-minded escaped Lake Tyers, or took the opportunity to leave with permission to do war work in Melbourne's factories. But few came from the north-west of the State.[4] The interaction of these groups in Melbourne was not new. Movements to and between reserves had occurred from the 1860s onwards, as kin kept in touch, people moved for work and others were shifted as punishment. The concentration policy of 1917 sent people to Lake Tyers from reserves across the State. The continual movement led to some intermarriage between Wotjobaluk and Gunai/Kurnai, Gunditjmara and Yorta Yorta, Woiwurrung and Gunai/Kurnai, which increased the density of the kinship networks. The streets of Fitzroy continued this process.

However, distinct regional identities remained and most people still married those from their own region. Diane Barwick, a Canadian anthropologist who researched Melbourne's Aboriginal population in 1960–62, found that four out of every five Aboriginal men and five out of every six Aboriginal women, who married Aboriginal partners in the generation before 1960, had married partners from their own region. Elders were careful about maintaining older marriage patterns (which defended genetic diversity) by opposing first and even second cousin marriage, despite being legal in the general community. These regional in-marriage rates were based on parochial feelings that reduced inter-mixing. Barwick overheard Aboriginal people making such comments as: 'Those people don't know how to behave down in Gippsland. Real shy of white people they are, seem to have inferior complexes. Of course they've never mixed with white people and learned how to deal with them the way we have.'[5] Gunai/Kurnai people reciprocated with similar prejudices towards other Aboriginal Victorians.

Social interaction had not forged a strong pan-Aboriginal identity, as people remained loyal to family and regional groups. But by 1960, some used a traditional NSW word for 'man'—'Kuri', 'Koorie', 'Koori'—to describe themselves as Aboriginal Victorians. The last two spellings dominated over time. It was an 'in' word some used, while others did not, a situation that continues to this day.[6] Most disliked intensely being called 'blacks' or 'blackfellas' by whites. Even when Archbishop Mowll suggested the inclusive term 'black Australians' in 1952, Doug Nicholls replied: 'I do not think it would help us much. We prefer "aborigine" or "native".'[7] Anna Vroland who knew the Aboriginal community well, said in 1948 that they claimed they were brown not black, and thought the term 'black' was derogatory. One young woman said to her 'how would you like to be called a "Gub-eye" (pig-eye) at a public meeting'— this, or the word 'loon', being the Aboriginal term for white people. Vroland added that they liked to be called the 'dark people'.[8] However, Melbourne Aboriginal footballers played, ironically, as the 'All Blacks', perhaps inspired by cross-Tasman rugby.

Many Kooris used Fitzroy as a stopover. Some were searching for work. As 'Banjo' Clarke from Framlingham recalled: 'Herb and I went on taking jobs we could get in the city: builders' labourer, pick-and-shovel work, digging trenches, or delivering briquettes around town from the Fitzroy railway yard'.[9] When work was offered in the country they were off. Others came and went to visit kin. One old Gunai/Kurnai man, who came from Gippsland to visit kin, camped in the backyard of a Gertrude Street house. He fashioned boomerangs from wooden blanks brought from Gippsland's forests and sold them around Fitzroy and the Victoria Market before moving on. Diane Barwick observed in 1960 that there was a rapid turnover of population as people moved back and forth from the country to the city. She added: 'Many householders are exceedingly gregarious and are prepared to accommodate numerous casual visitors, if only to hear the latest news and gossip from the country'.[10]

The people forged a vibrant social life in Fitzroy. Young men played sport and their heroes were Aboriginal footballers Laurie Atkinson and Ron Edwards who played for Fitzroy Football Club around 1950, and Jim Wandin and Ted Jackson who played for St Kilda and Melbourne respectively. The young men trained for football and boxing at the Exhibition Youth Club, part of the Exhibition Building complex. They also socialised at the Builders Arms Hotel on the corner of Gertrude and Gore Street. Some young women, like the six who boarded with Mrs Clark in Kerr Street, tasted the freedom of night life in the city. In 1949 Margaret Tucker and the community's friend, Cora Gilsenan, organised an Aboriginal Debutante Ball in the Church of England Hall in Fitzroy Street. They rehearsed about forty young people for weeks before the smart suit-and-gown affair. On a daily basis, family men and women gathered in houses to yarn and discuss the problems of city life. The adults also entertained themselves at cards, often gathering at the Moyles and Edna Brown's house. Diane Barwick remarked: 'Kinship duties, scandals, quarrels and the organisation of community activities were normal topics of conversation'.[11] As a Canadian outsider, Barwick had to be placed into the kinship system in order to mix, and was introduced around the Aboriginal community as a 'cousin'.

Aboriginal children attended Fitzroy's George Street Primary School. Albert Mullett remembers there were about 100 Aboriginal children there in the early 1940s. It was his first schooling, even though he was eight, but he did not last long with stories of Captain Cook and the daily singing of 'Gawd Save the King'. He soon decided that he 'didn't want to be part of that system', preferring life as a hunter and gatherer on Melbourne's streets, picking up wood and pine cones for the fireplace at home, travelling to the markets with billy carts and returning with spoilt fruit and vegetables for the family table.[12]

Some of the Aboriginal residents of Fitzroy were strong Christians, and formed their own religious communities. Pastor Eddy Atkinson, who ministered to the Barmah and Mooroopna communities, had links to Fitzroy. He influenced Doug Nicholls whose interest in Christianity was renewed while a Fitzroy footballer. Church services were also held at a rented terrace house in Gertrude Street near Little Smith Street in the early 1940s. 'Dowie' (Howard) Nicholls, Doug Nicholls' brother, conducted services and the congregation often spilled onto the footpath. The people petitioned to get Doug Nicholls out of the army to lead the community after 'Dowie's' death from a car accident. Doug Nicholls took over the spiritual leadership, married 'Dowie's' widow, Gladys, in 1942 and helped raise her three children.

Doug and Gladys Nicholls formed an Aboriginal chapel at 258 Gore Street in 1943, which was donated by the Church of Christ, and became affiliated with the Church of Christ in 1944. Before long Nicholls' Sunday congregation had risen to eighty, who enjoyed his quietly persuasive preaching and the inspiring gospel singing. Not all of the community attended, some going to the Fitzroy Anglican Church, the Bethesda Mission, or not attending any church. Others went to Gore Street for the social life, as Albert Mullett recalled: 'There was always a good feed and time to catch up with "rellos" and listen to a vision for the future by our elders'.[13] Gore Street probably influenced more than half the community in some way. It became an alternate symbol of Aboriginality for whites in Melbourne counteracting the image of Aboriginal people as dissolute vagabonds. It also provided role models for Aboriginal people, as Nicholls invited visiting Black American entertainers to his church, including Harry Belafonte and Winifred Atwell. The church lasted for 27 years, moving to Fitzroy Street in its latter years.[14] Some Aboriginal people distrusted or were jealous of Nicholls, thinking him a 'jumped-up' man from Cummera who was too thick with whites. Certainly Nicholls had a rapport and influence with whites through football. He also led the Cummera faction in Fitzroy, which held the political influence—such as it was—of the day.

Many of the Aboriginal community were hard-working decent people who were independent and self-supporting. The wartime economy provided work for all who wanted it and the chance of independent living. A number came from Lake Tyers and they now had control over their own movements and associations, even their diet. Some saved enough to purchase a piano. Those who were not in work, due to injury or poor life choices, were helped by their kin. The paid workers had a 'kitty' to help out those in need. They also raised money for others, an Aboriginal concert in the Fitzroy Town Hall in 1944 netting £200 for the Salvation Army.

The notion of 'respectability' or worthiness was defined a little differently in the Aboriginal community than in the white middle class, being less connected to morals and self-help individualism, and more to ideas of kinship. The Aboriginal community, as Diane Barwick noted, had definite views of 'good' men and women based on how well they protected their families. Men were thought to be 'good' if they were good providers and did not threaten the strength of the family. They were not expected to be always faithful, sober, or in work. Indeed, discrimination against Aboriginal workers and the seasonal nature of much of their labouring work, meant that under or unemployment was often their lot. Women's 'goodness' was defined not so much in terms of being a good wife or worker and staying with just one man, although that was important, but in being a good mother. The 'good mother' kept the family together, battled for and protected her children, kept them clean and well fed and away from the hands of the welfare system. Women were also expected to maintain kinship networks. While men were not condemned if they deserted their wives or families, and family break-ups were not uncommon, a woman who deserted her children was universally condemned.[15]

Some Aboriginal families were mixed, those in the city being twice as likely as country families to contain non-Aboriginal partners. Barwick found that in Melbourne Aboriginal women were twice as likely as Aboriginal men to have a white partner: 28 per cent of married

Aboriginal men and 47 per cent of married Aboriginal women had non-Aboriginal partners. Such mixed marriages were clustered in particular Aboriginal families, which suggests that certain families were more open to cultural change and diversity. There was considerable misgiving about such marriages in the Aboriginal community because of prevailing racial views and the frequency of failed relationships. Margaret Tucker married a white man and suffered shame from the prejudice of his family until they finally came to love her and her daughter. The marriage did not survive and years later she wrote with some anguish: 'Why didn't I marry one of my own people'.[16]

Most children of such mixed marriages identified themselves as Aboriginal and so there were few losses to the Aboriginal community. This identification occurred because the non-Aboriginal community was less tolerant of mixed marriages. Also, as Aboriginal people reasoned, why would children identify as white, when whites rarely did anything but harm to Aboriginal people? As Daphne Lowe (nee Proctor), whose father was white, recalled: 'We never grew up on the white side, we never knew anybody on Dad's side, we just grew up on Mum's side'.[17] Barwick found that few families tried to 'pass' into the white community in Victoria. This suggests that Aboriginal people married non-Aboriginal partners for love and affection, rather than

Mattiwilda Dobbs, African-American coloratura soprano sensation, visits the Gore Street congregation around 1950. (A. & M. Jackomos Collection, courtesy of Museum Victoria, XP3433)

ideas of prestige or advantage, as none was forthcoming.[18] Mixed marriages and cross-racial friendships were small in number in the sea of indifference, intolerance and distrust that existed between the white and dark communities in the interwar period and immediately after.

Out of the mutual distrust incidents arose between the Fitzroy police and Aboriginal people. 'Banjo' Clarke claimed: 'The police were locking people up just to keep them off the street . . . Police would pull you backward, then pull you all over the street, making out that you were drunk and staggering'.[19] In February 1941, the *Truth* newspaper, which delighted in sensations, published an encounter between Norman Clarke ('Banjo's' brother) and Constable De Vere in Gertrude Street. Elderly Aboriginal Ebenezer Lovett said he was walking home one evening when a man tried to fight him. He roused Norman Clarke from his Young Street house but the would-be attacker had disappeared. As Clarke was standing there, Constable De Vere approached and accused him of being in a brawl that had happened in Victoria Parade. What followed was a matter of opinion, but the court, perhaps not surprisingly, believed De Vere rather than Clarke. Clarke claimed that De Vere began to haul him down to the station and started to use the baton on him. When he arrived at the station De Vere challenged him to fight and broke his jaw. However, De Vere claimed that Clarke resisted arrest and as a tent-boxer was so strong that he had to be batoned into submission. While at the station he claimed Clarke became violent, slipped and fell, striking his face on the counter and breaking his jaw. He joined a long line of Aboriginal people who had 'fallen' in police stations. Norman Clarke received a £6 fine or 33 days in jail. Norman's brother Henry ('Banjo') told Sergeant Williams: 'We don't like De Vere. He always has a shot at us for nothing'. Norman's mother, Mary Clarke, was also on a charge, with De Vere claiming she attacked him with a shoe and yelled: 'All into the—and kick him to death'. Her case was adjourned for six months.[20]

Alick Jackomos, who mixed with the Fitzroy Aboriginal community as a teenager in the late 1930s, recalled a significant fight that erupted in the Builders Arms Hotel. 'Banjo' Clarke was chased into Little George Street by a group of white youths. Then 'they closed the street off . . . The whites were at both ends of the street . . . Aborigines were locked in there. This was for the full weekend'.[21] Such incidents attracted the attention of the Fitzroy Council, which had taken little notice of Aboriginal people up till then. Councillor Foley expressed anxiety about brawling in Gertrude Street.[22] In early September 1941 Aboriginal men fought in Gertrude Street with soldiers and civilians—possibly the same event recalled by Alick Jackomos above. The Council ordered a health and police report on the Aboriginal community. Councillor Foley declared: 'During the last six months small streets leading into Gertrude Street have been invaded by an Aboriginal colony. Street fights are frequent, and women are afraid to walk along the street'.[23] In late 1941 the Health and Public Works Committee referred to complaints 'of the objectionable conduct of Aborigines or half-castes in the streets'. Councillor Baker urged drastic action 'to stamp out the objectionable conduct of certain coloured people who are now making women and even young schoolgirls objects of their attention'.[24] Aboriginal men were being made scapegoats for street violence.

Aboriginal residents were indignant at such claims. One young woman told a *Herald* reporter that 'all the aborigines are being persecuted for the behaviour of a lot of hooligans and two or three badly behaved blacks'. The reporter questioned the Fitzroy police who unexpectedly supported this view: 'These aborigines give us little trouble. Although there are about 100 of them in the district we rarely have to arrest any of them. Of course, they are not all good, and we may have to lock one up now and then—probably one in six months'.[25] Margaret Tucker, vice president of the Australian Aborigines' League defended the people as 'generally quiet and decent' and said they had become fearful because of persecution.[26] Doug Nicholls, now a private in the Second AIF, praised those fellow Aboriginal Victorians who sought an independent life away from the reserves and said that 'Aborigines were fighting beside white Australians overseas and serving beside them in Australia and they deserved the right to live quietly without persecution'.[27]

The Fitzroy Council became anxious about the housing of Fitzroy's Aboriginal residents, a situation exacerbated by a high rent crisis. The *Truth* claimed in early 1941 that 'the unprecedented house famine in the metropolis, which has given blood-sucking landlords the chance to get tenants by the throat, is a direct product of war conditions'.[28] The Council wanted some terraces in Little George Street demolished due to their shocking state, but the Housing Commission delayed several demolitions as Aboriginal families were in desperate need of housing. Councillor Baker condemned the overcrowding and the exploitation of Aboriginal people by sub-letting.[29] Alick Jackomos remembered that families lived in a single room, with three or four families occupying a house. Others lived in shop fronts.[30] Some Aboriginal residents of Little George Street told the *Herald*: 'We know these houses are shocking but we can't get anything better. We are lucky to be able to get houses at all'. The reporter observed that most of the male residents in this street were munitions workers. One stated that Aboriginal men were fighting abroad in the AIF and 'since these men had gone, [white] hooligans pestered their women'.[31]

In 1949 the Victorian Council of Social Services commissioned a study, 'The Dark People of Melbourne', by Melbourne University's Social Studies Department, to evaluate their need for a social worker. The researchers focused on Fitzroy but did not speak to any Aboriginal people living there. Police and welfare workers reported that 'on the whole, the dark people are, if anything, more law-abiding than the whites' and showed a higher church and Sunday school attendance. They were handicapped by poor education and 'intolerable' housing, discrimination in employment, and being confined to 'unskilled and irregular work', and were trapped by their 'dark clannishness'. The researchers surveyed fifty non-Aboriginal people finding that 18 were unprejudiced; 23, prejudiced; and 9 had no opinion on Indigenous people. None of those who knew Aboriginal people were 'prejudiced', while none of those who were unhappy living in Fitzroy were 'unprejudiced'.[32] Social unease, poverty and unfamiliarity with Aboriginal people underpinned prejudice.

The Fitzroy Aboriginal community, about 300-strong by the late 1940s, was by then the largest in Victoria. The Fitzroy Council and support groups asked the Protection Board to assist, but it once again refused to recognise those of mixed descent living off Lake Tyers as Aboriginal people for whom it had any responsibility.[33] Some individuals gave self-sacrificing help. Sister Maude Ellis, a deaconess in the Methodist Church, formed the Bethesda Aboriginal Mission at 406 Fitzroy Street in 1938, which later moved to the Independent Hall on the corner of Fitzroy Street and Brunswick Place. She held church services, distributed food and clothing to the needy, and ran a kindergarten for about twenty children, most of whom were Aboriginal. She visited hospitals and prisons as well. Ellis survived on donations, including free milk daily from the Milk Board. Her efforts are remembered fondly by elderly Aboriginal people. Sister Ellis ran the Mission into the 1950s and continued hospital visiting and monthly visits to Framlingham till at least 1964.[34]

Helen Baillie, a spinster and nurse with some independent means, was another staunch advocate for Aboriginal people. She was descended from the Baillie brothers who were Port Phillip pioneers. She lived in England during the 1920s, becoming interested in the issue of slum clearance. She returned to Australia in 1931 and by chance read works by white activist Mary Bennett, including *The Aboriginal as a Human*

Being, and embraced the cause.[35] Baillie travelled to other States seeking information on Aboriginal matters and joined the Victorian Aboriginal Group and formed the Aboriginal Fellowship Group to bind Christians interested in Aboriginal welfare. She was described by ASIO in contradictory terms as a 'Christian Communist'.[36] Valentine Leeper, secretary of the Victorian Aboriginal Group, recalled that Baillie was 'driven by a feeling of guilt that her ancestors had taken the land'.[37] Baillie assisted rural communities as well, including Yorta Yorta people who walked off Cummeragunja in 1939. She joined many other groups working for Aboriginal rights, including, after 1951, the Women's International League for Peace and Freedom and the Council for Aboriginal Rights. In 1944 she offered to leave to the Board the enormous sum of £1,000 for a scholarship to train a social worker to work with Aboriginal people, but finding no response, offered it to the Victorian Aboriginal Group to administer.[38]

Baillie gave constant practical help. Mrs J. J. Clark of Little Gertrude Street thanked Baillie for fitting her daughter Muriel with a tunic to attend the Bell Street Fitzroy School in 1939.[39] Baillie often had her hand in her pocket. When Baillie's mother died, she turned her mother's Punt Road home into a hostel for Aboriginal people. In 1956 Baillie wrote to fellow white activist, Shirley Andrews, apologising for giving only a little for one particular cause:

> I am very hard up as I have had so many Aboriginal folk staying in my home. They came up from Framlingham looking for work and I have been keeping them and paying fares while they were looking for work. They have *very* big appetites and I have a huge food bill . . . I have one boy who is doing well. He is in regular work as a builder's labourer and always pays his board regularly but many of the others are a problem. The boy who is doing well is Jimmie Berg, aged 18 from Nyora S. Gippsland . . . and he is a cousin of the lads from Framlingham.[40]

'Banjo' Clarke stated that some 'drunks' took advantage of Baillie. In 1958 a *Herald* reporter visited her home, described as a hovel, inhabited by a dozen Aboriginal people—men and women—in the grip of alcoholism. The reporter described Baillie as unwell. She said she used to help people find their feet in Melbourne, 'but it's no good now. There's too much drinking. Most of the aboriginals are out of work, and they're not paying rent. I'm old and sick. The aboriginals won't help me keep the place clean'.[41] Helen Baillie was still making small donations to Aboriginal causes from her bed in the Harcourt Private Hospital,

Victorian Aboriginal Football team, 1948. (Courtesy of Alick Jackomos Collection)

Hawthorn in 1968. But when she died in 1970 there seemed little of her money left, certainly nothing to fund a social worker.[42]

Most Aboriginal people did not abuse those who helped them, and many did not even seek such help, being independent types, or people who battled to be independent. Indeed, the 1949 study 'The Dark People of Melbourne', which reaffirmed this desire for independence, found that 'the severest judges of the dark people are dark people themselves. They complain bitterly when a small minority brings discredit on the whole group. They have a continual fight against the whites' "stock picture" of the aborigines'.[43]

Aboriginal people challenged stereotypes in many ways. One was by performing on the sports field or musically. Margaret Tucker was part of an Aboriginal music group which performed from the 1930s and in wartime for charities and the war effort. Tucker often sang as 'Princess Lilardia'.[44] Aboriginal people also performed in pageants which functioned as political statements. The first, in 1948, was sponsored by the Australian Aborigines' League with a political intent to 'advertise the Aborigines' claims for citizen rights'. The pageant was held over a week to big crowds at Wirth's Olympia. Produced by the League's President, Bill Onus, it featured corroborees, boomerang-throwing by Onus himself, fire-lighting, a gumleaf band and choir conducted by Ted Mullett, whip-cracking by Billy Bargo, as well as standard vaudeville items, such as comedy by Eric Onus and James Scott. Queenslanders performed as well, including George Hill, the blind guitarist, and celebrated baritone Harold Blair.[45]

In early 1951 Victoria was preparing to celebrate its Centenary of Separation from New South Wales. The Australian Aborigines' League discovered that Aboriginal people were to play no part in the proceedings. They held a protest meeting in Fitzroy to consider their involvement, and an embarrassed Celebrations Committee invited Doug Nicholls to organise Aboriginal participation. The Onus brothers, Eric and Bill, developed a concept that, with the help of theatre producer Irene Mitchell and script writer Jean Campbell, became 'Out of the Dark, an Aboriginal Moomba', featuring Victorian and Queensland Aboriginal people. The exercise appeared tokenistic and a likely failure, but it was a hit with audiences—especially the Aboriginal items. Critics urged that it tour overseas.[46]

The show did not tour. However, Bill Onus sought to join the United States theatre circuit the following year to perform boomerang-throwing, as he was considered the Australian champion. Onus, a clerk on the Melbourne docks, was also a member of the ALP, a State Councillor of the Federated Clerks Union, and was on the Australian Peace Council. The last body ensured that he was excluded from touring under the United States Exclusion Act, but in 1946 he was also reported by ASIO as saying the Australian Aborigines' League had affiliated with the Communist Party of Australia because it was the only party trying to assist Aboriginal people. ASIO passed on a 'derogatory' report to their US counterparts, then so paranoid about Communism. Onus told the US consulate when applying for a visa that he had spoken from the Communist platform, but added: 'I have also spoken from Liberal and Country Party platforms and at trade union and church meetings. My only subject has been the plight of my people. I have tried in every way to get the Aborigines' message to the public'.[47] Actors Equity protested on his behalf and tried to at least retrieve his finger print file from US authorities, but to no avail. He lost payment of $750 and fares for an eleven-day US engagement.[48]

The 'Out of the Dark' show reverberated with Aboriginal people as well. Doug Nicholls mused: 'We began to realise that we should be proud of our Aboriginal culture—that we should remember we were a great people'. He added: 'We've been missing out because we've lost the interests of our own hearts—we've disgraced ourselves by not holding on to it. Instead of teaching ourselves about ourselves, we've been studying whites . . . I'd like to see our children taught—fairly and conscientiously—about their ancestors. It would give them self-respect. Self-respect would breed mutual respect between us and the whites'.[49]

The Fitzroy community continued strongly into the 1950s.[50] However, it splintered physically from the late 1950s as some families drifted away to other parts of Melbourne or were rehoused in Housing Commission homes in Preston, Reservoir and Broadmeadows. This was a natural move in search of better housing and jobs, but it was also due to regional differences as the Fitzroy leader Doug Nicholls specifically represented the Yorta Yorta or 'Cummera' power base. Others distrusted his affiliations with a white church—the Church of Christ—and with whites generally, which they believed undermined Aboriginal independence. However, Doug Nicholls preferred a strategy of dialogue with other Victorians, as did others from Cummeragunja, who were known for their openness and tolerance. As he told a Fitzroy Australian Natives Association Smoke Night in 1937: 'Although we have not been given a fair deal we hold no grudge against the white people who govern us ... Give us a chance to take our place in the life of the Australian community in cooperation with you'.[51] This basic cooperative strategy was revealed in an earlier Yorta Yorta creation, the Australian Aborigines' League.

Political life

The power of education is evident in the influence of Thomas Shadrach James, the Indian man who became the Cummeragunja school teacher and married into the community there. For almost forty years he gave the children of 'Cummera' the skills to defend themselves and articulate their view of the world. James retired in 1922 with hopes that his son Shadrach, his teaching assistant, would replace him. However, Shadrach James was not appointed by the NSW Board, which resented the family's independence. Shadrach worked off the reserve. He became a law student (it was later claimed, though he seems not to have completed his degree),[52] then gravitated in the 1930s to Shepparton where he worked in the canneries and became a union representative.

In 1929 Shadrach James began to make speeches to missionary and other associations and to write to the press about Australia-wide and local issues concerning 'my people'—by which he meant all Aboriginal people. He conveyed his view of Aboriginal history, and proposed solutions, learnt in years of political discussions over meals and campfires at Cummera. These were not his ideas so much as the combined political wisdom of many Yorta Yorta and Bangerang men and women. In 1930 in a letter entitled 'Help My People', he set out ideas that represented an

Aboriginal charter of reform. James wrote that 'no sooner had the white man invaded our land that the extermination of our people began, and it has gone on, and is still going on, under various guises'. He here alluded to police actions still occurring in the North and continued poetically: 'The whole attitude of the white man towards the aborigine has all along been to dis-pirit and humiliate him, to extinguish his self-respect, to suppress his ambition, in short, to kill his hope'. James added that 'the aborigines of today are different from those of yesterday. They are more industrious, more ambitious, more intellectual, more provident and less vicious', yet they are 'landless and homeless wanderers [for] we are the descendants of the people you have unjustly disinherited of their land, and of their privileges'. He called for land, homes and education to be given us 'by public law and not by regulation of the Aboriginal Protection Board'. He yearned for equal citizenship, to be achieved by federal control of Aboriginal affairs, a 'native representative' in federal parliament, and a 'native protector' heading an advisory board of whites and Aboriginal people in each State.[53]

William Cooper, Shadrach's uncle by marriage, had unsuccessfully petitioned for land in the 1880s. He mostly lived and worked off Cummeragunja, earning a living by shearing and rural labouring, but settled there in his retirement after the Great War in which he lost a son. He moved to Melbourne in 1932, aged seventy-one. Being eligible for the pension as he was now living off the reserve, he rented in Ballarat Road in 1932, then 27 Federal Street, Footscray in 1936. Cooper began a remarkable political career in Melbourne, reiterating and expanding the ideas of Shadrach James and other Yorta Yorta political thinkers. Fuller details of Cooper's campaigns have been given by others, most meticulously and recently in Bain Attwood's *William Cooper: An Aboriginal Life Story* (2021) and Bain Attwood and Andrew Markus's *Thinking Black: William Cooper and the Australian Aborigines' League* (2004).[54]

Cooper believed the ill-treatment of Aboriginal people to be a white moral problem. He invoked his strategy of the 1880s, which was to use a petition to effect change. This new petition was to be presented to the King himself, as the Yorta Yorta—like the Kulin of Coranderrk—had long believed the monarch to be bound to them in kinship, to have bestowed reserve land on them, and to be their protector. Cooper's petition argued that by 'moral duty' and by the 'commission' that had ordered settlement, governments were to care for the 'original inhabitants and their heirs and successors'. However, Aboriginal lands had been 'expropriated' and their legal status denied. The petition called for royal protection to 'prevent the extinction of the aboriginal race and give better conditions for all, and to ensure an Aboriginal representative in parliament'.[55] By December 1934 Cooper, writing as honorary secretary of the Australian Aborigines' League (AAL), a political body he founded, claimed 3,000 Aboriginal people had signed and 'signatures are still coming freely from all states'.[56]

Cooper was first and foremost a proud Yorta Yorta man. He based his petition on a history of injustice, and on his position as an 'heir' to the 'original inhabitants'. He claimed civil rights as an Australian, but also as a descendant of the 'original Australians'. His Cummera heritage was fiercely Aboriginal and he always rejected the Board's classification of people into 'full' and 'half caste'. At public gatherings, Yorta Yorta songs

William Cooper in the 1930s. (A. & M. Jackomos Collection, courtesy of Museum Victoria, XP3659)

from the mission days were sung and AAL vice presidents gave 'Aboriginal performances': Margaret Tucker sang songs of Moonahcullah Mission in New South Wales and other missions, and Doug Nicholls played a gum leaf solo.

In January 1935 Cooper, representing 'the aboriginal population of Australia', led a deputation to the federal Minister for the Interior, Thomas Paterson. It included Shadrach James, Doug Nicholls, Anna Morgan, and white supporters, Helen Baillie and Rev. William Morley. Affirming his faith in God and the British Empire, Cooper called for a duty of care from the government for a people 'faced with extinction', many of whom were not citizens and did not have citizens' rights. Calling for federal representation—the substance of his still-unpresented petition—Cooper reminded Paterson that the Maori had enjoyed such representation since 1867. Shadrach James spoke of the need for land and education, and Anna Morgan the need for the education of women. Helen Baillie supported Cooper's call, saying Aboriginal people received little education and training, and were often refused the old age pension for being 'too dark'. She outlined how the New Zealand system of representation worked and called for a federal Department of Native Affairs and an expert advisory committee. In his reply Paterson was sympathetic but pointed out that all the requests posed constitutional difficulties as the Commonwealth only had jurisdiction over Aboriginal people in the Northern Territory. He referred to the two large reserves recently created there. This sparked the interest of Cooper who wrote back asking for the 'exact locality' of these reserves and the 'most convenient route to take to get to these areas'. Whether the elderly Cooper seriously contemplated this extremely difficult trip over bush tracks is unknown. He also requested remuneration for his efforts on behalf of 'the Aboriginal cause' over the past three years to cover postage and travel expenses, but was, predictably, refused.[57]

In his AAL annual report for 1936 Cooper addressed his 'fellow members of the Dark Race' and expressed mixed feelings: disappointment at the slowness of progress, but belief that 'the Star of our Hope is in the ascendant'. He reported that the petition was imminent.[58] However, Cooper held it back on the promise of government action, including federal control, to emerge at the August 1936 Premiers meeting. However, as little occurred at the meeting to give him hope, he finally presented his petition in October 1937 with 1,814 Aboriginal signatures. The London *Times*, believing that Aboriginal people were facing 'racial decay' in the face of white colonisation, sympathetically called the petition 'pathetic'.[59] The comment reflected the AAL's small voice in the white Imperial and Australian political context.

William Cooper, the honorary secretary of the AAL, like all honorary secretaries did the real work of the organisation, writing, thinking and planning. In the AAL's 1936 annual report Cooper referred to 'heavy' correspondence to all States and to England on many issues. He was assisted in his struggle by Shadrach James, Margaret Tucker, Doug Nicholls and other Yorta Yorta people. Arthur Burdeu of Essendon was the presidential figurehead of the AAL and its only non-Aboriginal member. Burdeu, an operations officer and union representative with the Victorian Railways for forty years, appears not to have dominated or influenced the key ideas of the AAL. Burdeu, who once remarked that he was considered by other AAL members to be a 'dinkum abo', praised Cooper, the organiser of the petition, as a 'self-educated and born leader'.[60]

Arthur Burdeu was very active in his own group, the Aborigines Uplift Society, formed in 1937 and which outlasted him to 1954. It was a Christian-based organisation, which provided social services and complemented the political work of the AAL. Uplift offered practical help with clothing, food, housing materials, furniture, books and

Christmas presents for those at Lake Tyers and elsewhere. The group found accommodation for people visiting city doctors and ran a small hostel for young Aboriginal working girls in Melbourne. Burdeu lobbied hard for social welfare payments—the aged and invalid pension and maternity allowance—to be paid to Aboriginal people, often considered too light-skinned for the Board's help and too dark-skinned for social welfare. He argued that those who paid taxes should be supported. The Uplift Society's motto was 'self help' and it sought a farm scheme at Lake Condah, put forward better designs for 'humpy' housing, and assisted Aboriginal girls to find work in Melbourne.[61] Its eighteen points affirmed Aboriginal ability and equality; their right to education and training, social welfare and employment; their right to inalienable reserve land and the mineral wealth thereon; and the need for Aboriginal women's views to be represented. Their objectives also included parliamentary representation, as demanded by the AAL.[62] Burdeu sought to develop a white 'conscience' through lectures, radio broadcasts, his magazine *Uplift* (1938–41), a ladies' auxiliary and an Uplift branch at Hamilton. Membership never topped 400 but *Uplift* sold 2,000 copies. And the message Burdeu espoused in *Uplift* could be strong: 'The story of blood and misery which is the record of the manner in which the country was taken is your responsibility equally with those whose hands dripped with aboriginal blood'.[63]

Cooper and Burdeu's message of Aboriginal equality was radical for a society still gripped by the great notion that Aboriginal people were unfit for the modern world and doomed to extinction. However, the 1930s ushered in new thinking about race and indigenous peoples, which challenged older ideas. Race began to be seen as something made up in the human imagination, rather than as an immutable and determining fact. Older bodies like the British Anti-Slavery Society and the Association for the Protection of Native Races continued their work, but new groups—often dominated by educated white women—emerged in Aboriginal affairs, raising the community's conscience.[64] These groups held meetings; raised and donated moneys; wrote letters to press, politicians, governments, and the Board; visited Aboriginal reserves to gather facts; and worked *with* Aboriginal people.

The Victorian Aboriginal Group began in 1929 as a study group of the Citizens' Education Fellowship, led by the historian A. S. Kenyon and naturalist R. H. Croll. Valentine Leeper recalled that some Fitzroy Aboriginal people were invited along, but they did not continue to attend. The Group was formalised in 1933 and lasted for almost forty years under the same leadership. Amy Brown, the spinster sister of

Professor E. Brown, and involved in both the Seamen's Mission and the YWCA, was its energetic long-serving honorary secretary to the end. Valentine Leeper, spinster and daughter of Dr Alexander Leeper, Warden of Trinity College for 42 years, was its only honorary treasurer.[65] The Group gathered facts, discussed them rationally, and then lobbied over Lake Tyers, Framlingham and other Victorian, as well as national, issues. The members were liberal rather than radical, remained always at arm's length to Aboriginal people, and during the 1930s shifted from protectionism to assimilationism, which was radical enough for their time. The Victorian Aboriginal Group remained small and was past its prime and becoming outdated by 1950. It was wound up by Amy Brown, Valentine Leeper and two others in 1971, having amalgamated with the National Association for the Advancement of the Native Race in 1959, a struggling umbrella organisation it spawned in 1952. The latter group, headed by A.O. Neville, the former Chief Aboriginal Protector of Western Australia, then living in Melbourne, remained steadfastly assimilationist.[66]

These groups were part of a Christian, liberal network of women's associations. Amy Brown, for instance, was also honorary secretary of the Citizens' Education Fellowship which began in 1932 to promote active citizenship and progress through education. It was an off-shoot of the New Education Fellowship of London. Anne Bon, in her nineties, still a member of the Board, and living permanently in the Hotel Windsor in Spring Street, continued to write letters to the press about Aboriginal Victorians 'to whom we are so much indebted and for whom we have done so little in return'.[67] Bon was a matriarch of the white female movement promoting the Aboriginal cause. She wrote to Amy Brown in 1934, two years before her death aged 99, apologising for not attending the Victorian Aboriginal Group meeting, wishing it well 'in arousing the public to a sense of duty, although it is very late in the day', and requesting that 'Miss Baillie' call on her.[68] Baillie led the Aboriginal Fellowship Group. While Amy Brown and Valentine Leeper did heart-felt lobbying; Burdeu, Baillie, Bon, like other activists, Cora Gilsenan and Anna Vroland all worked *with* and not *on* Aboriginal people.[69]

While the AAL awaited news of its petition—probably with no great hope, given decades of failed petitions (admittedly to lesser beings than the King)—it convened a joint meeting in November 1937 with William Ferguson and his NSW-based organisation, the Aborigines' Progressive Association. The two bodies jointly organised a 'Day of Mourning', to be held on 26 January 1938 in Sydney at the Australian Hall, while the rest of Australia was celebrating the 150th anniversary of Australia's white

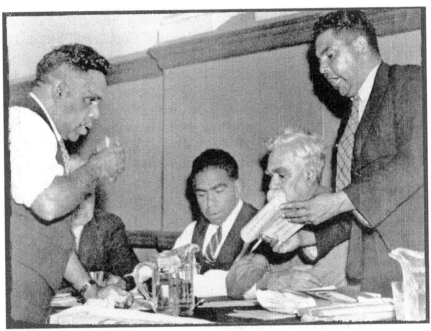

Jack Patten reads from the agenda of the Day of Mourning Conference in Sydney on 26 January 1938, as Committee members listen. L–R: Tom Foster, Jack Kinchela (obscured), Doug Nicholls and William Cooper. *Man* magazine, March 1938. (Courtesy of Mitchell Library, State Library of New South Wales, A4290036)

settlement.[70] It was a brilliant political strategy. Cooper and Doug Nicholls travelled to Sydney where Cooper told the meeting 'we must continue our struggle until we win our objectives'. A resolution was passed calling for a 'new policy which will raise our people to full citizen status and equality within the community'.[71] William Ferguson and Jack Patten published a manifesto—'Aborigines Claim Citizen's Rights'— supporting this resolution with facts about Australia's poor treatment of Aboriginal people, the tyranny of the Protection Boards, the pervasiveness of racial ideas and the need for a 'New Deal for Aborigines' based not on charity but justice. A deputation presented ten objectives to Prime Minister Joe Lyons, including federal control over and equal rights for Aboriginal people as enjoyed by all other Australians, and the retention of reserves for the aged and those made incompetent by past policies of segregation.[72] The events of January were recorded in a new Aboriginal publication, *The Australian ABO CALL*, edited by Jack Patten of the Aborigines' Progressive Association, 'representing 80,000 Australian Aborigines'.

Historian Bain Attwood persuasively argues that the idea for a 'Day of Mourning' was probably Cooper's. Early in 1937 Cooper had attended a service in Melbourne for Victorian pioneers at which he heard a spokesman for the Australian Natives Association, a patriotic and health-benefit society, appropriate the term 'native', claiming it for white Australians. Cooper was livid and wrote to the organiser, Isaac Selby, that 'what is a memorial of the coming of the Whites is a memorial of death to us'.[73] It was the germ of a brilliant idea. The events of January 1938 were the most effective moment in Aboriginal politics to that date, but the moment was dented somewhat by the news in March 1938 that the federal government would not act on Cooper's petition, as it had no jurisdiction in Aboriginal affairs under the Constitution. The petition was never sent to the King. Cooper retired as Honorary Secretary of the AAL in November 1940 and went to live at Barmah with his third wife Sarah Nelson (nee McCrae) until his death in 1941.[74]

War and postwar reform

As the world moved to war in January 1939, William Cooper wrote to Prime Minister McEwen urging all Aboriginal people be given citizenship, for 'to put us in the trenches, until we have something to fight for is not right'.[75] When war began in September 1939 the Second AIF was formed and Aboriginal men answered the call to war yet again. Their reasons varied as with other Australian soldiers: adventure, a job, an escape, a sense of duty. One Lake Tyers man told Helen Baillie in 1940: 'We heard the Motherland was in danger'.[76] In January 1940 twenty men from Lake Tyers volunteered. In all, of 43 men at Lake Tyers eligible to serve, 37 volunteered and 26 passed the medical examination.[77] This was an impressively high proportion, as 86 per cent of those eligible volunteered. Army regimentation was preferable to that of life on Lake Tyers. The men provided gumleaf accompaniment on training marches and later played at recruiting drives in Melbourne. However, during 1940 and 1941 the Services and the Government debated whether Aboriginal people should be allowed to enlist, as sections 61 and 138 of the Defence Act exempted those 'not substantially of European descent' from serving. Confusion reigned as Aboriginal men had enlisted and been accepted, especially by Southern Command which recruited in Victoria.[78] In March 1941, eighteen Lake Tyers men were discharged after some months of training, because of the confusion. However, the growing Japanese threat in the Pacific caused a reversal of policy and Aboriginal enlistments were accepted from late 1941 onwards.[79]

Gunditjmara men joined up as in the Great War. Reg Saunders from Lake Condah (son of Chris who fought in WWI) served in the Middle East, then New Guinea and made history in 1944 by being the first Aboriginal soldier to become a commissioned officer—a Lieutenant in Australia's armed forces. Reg told the press that 'if the barriers are removed in civil and social life the first Australians can lift themselves to the level of our white brothers'.[80] Reg's brother Harry, who also served, was wounded in Syria in 1941 and killed in heavy fighting in late 1942 on New Guinea's north coast. When these Aboriginal servicemen returned home they never received access to Lake Condah and Coranderrk when they were broken up for soldier settlement. Saunders was also denied a position in the Occupation force in Japan due to a blanket ban on Aboriginal soldiers being sent there. He worked on Melbourne's trams instead, before enlisting for Korea where he was promoted to Captain.[81] Over 150 Aboriginal men from Victoria enlisted in World War Two and some of their experiences are recorded in Alick Jackomos and Derek Fowell's *Forgotten Heroes: Aborigines at War from the Somme to Vietnam* (1993).[82]

Enlistments boosted the cause for Aboriginal civil rights. In June 1940 Arthur Burdeu wrote to Prime Minister Menzies pointing out that Aboriginal soldiers in the Great War who were under Aboriginal Acts did not enjoy the rights of others, despite the fact that 'the blood of the aboriginal was blended with white men who gave their all too when the soil of Flanders and Palestine was sanctified with the blood of Australia's best'.[83] Burdeu requested that once this new war ended, enlisted Aboriginal people classed as 'Aboriginal' under Aboriginal Acts, should be granted full citizenship, including the right to military, old age and invalid pensions; the federal franchise; and the maternity bonus for their wives. Federal Cabinet agreed to Burdeu's proposal and a Bill was drafted. However, it was deemed unnecessary until the expiration of the Commonwealth Electoral (War-time) Act 1940, which gave all soldiers the vote until six months after the war ended. Burdeu pushed this issue for Aboriginal people up north as Aboriginal Victorians (as well as those in New South Wales and South Australia) already had the right to vote, since their State Electoral Acts did not mention 'Aborigines' or 'half castes'. This State-based right also allowed Aboriginal people to vote in federal elections. Many Aboriginal people did not vote in Victoria due to indifference, lack of mobility, and a sense of futility, but they were never chased up under the compulsory voting provisions.

Helen McDonald, Aboriginal servicewoman. (Dawn Lee Collection, courtesy of Museum Victoria, XP4067)

In 1947 the Caulfield branch of the RSL renewed the push for the vote for all Aboriginal servicemen. Gillespie Douglas, the President of the Aborigines Uplift Society, also declared in 1948 that taxing Aboriginal workers without giving them the vote was against the British principle of 'no taxation without representation'. The Chifley Government amended the Commonwealth Electoral Act in 1949 to give all Aboriginal ex-servicemen the vote. Other Aboriginal people throughout Australia without the vote were finally enfranchised progressively after 1962.[84]

Others continued Cooper's work. In 1949 Shadrach James and Doug Nicholls revived the key aspect of the petition—an Aboriginal member for federal parliament—setting out proposals as to how it might work. Shadrach James wrote to Prime Minster Chifley as honorary secretary of the Aborigines Progressive Association of Victoria complaining that the Minister for the Interior, Herbert Johnson, refused to meet an Aboriginal delegation on this matter. 'Perhaps he thinks we may speak in broken English or may remind him of painful things that happened long ago'. His words must have stung, as a deputation of ten Victorians—all Yorta Yorta people—was received by Johnson, which included four women, Shadrach's sister and niece, Mrs Muir and Mrs Charles and the daughters of Thomas James's brightest pupil Theresa Clements: Margaret Tucker and Geraldine Briggs.[85] The Chief Electoral Officer advised Johnson that their proposal was impossible under the Constitution. Nicholls then requested that Chifley initiate the necessary Constitution amendment to bring Australia in line with the 'spirit and principles of the Charter of the United Nations'.[86] (In fact a referendum in 1944 had included a question on federal powers in Aboriginal affairs but it was rejected by a usually suspicious electorate along with other questions on federal powers.) An Aboriginal federal representative, elected purely by Aboriginal people, never eventuated as it did in New Zealand. Instead, Aboriginal rights activism shifted from an emphasis on indigenous rights special to Aboriginal people, to civil rights the same as those enjoyed by other Australians.

The fervour for postwar reconstruction brought a new era of social reformism, which emphasised welfare and equal citizenship, not protection. This placed pressure on the Board, now a miserable body that had not reported formally to parliament since 1925. Scandals and inquiries in New South Wales had caused the Protection Board there to be replaced by a Welfare Board in 1940 with a policy of proactive assimilation. From 1943 two Aboriginal representatives were appointed to this new NSW Welfare Board.

Pressure for similar reforms mounted in Victoria from Aboriginal, Christian and women's groups. In May 1947 the Cain Labor Government appointed Shadrach James to the Board, the first Aboriginal voice on the Board in 86 years. He was chosen due to his prominence, but also because of his relative moderation. He was to serve on the Board until his death in 1957. Shadrach James had formed the Aborigines Progressive Association (Victorian branch) in 1946 to improve Aboriginal living standards and educational opportunities and create an Aboriginal Christian community. His program was different to the AAL's, being more overtly Christian and more practical than political. Once on the State-based Board, James changed his views to oppose federal control of Aboriginal affairs. However, he was not an assimilationist, as he identified with Aboriginal people across Australia, struggled to gain land for Aboriginal people and supported Aboriginal aspirations, including an all-Aboriginal football team in the Shepparton League. James made strong statements as well, arguing in February 1946 that Aboriginal people had been 'herded into compounds like animals which left them a disgraced, withered people, trampled, branded with a soul devoured by despairing bitterness and broken hearts'. Yet he believed human difference would largely disappear if all were fed, clothed and educated alike.[87] His appointment in May angered Bill Onus, President of the AAL, who was overlooked as the more radical candidate.[88]

In September 1947 the AAL called for more reforms, including an inquiry into Lake Tyers and its administration, and action from the Board on housing, education and health issues.[89] This necessitated a reform of the Board itself. Various groups supported the AAL's call for the Board's reform and a 'New Deal' as Doug Nicholls put it. In November 1948 the New Education Fellowship, a body devoted to the realisation by all peoples of their full potential, called for a new

Aborigines Act for Victoria based on democratic and constructive lines not the 'dole and control' approach of the Board. Shadrach James and Cora Gilsenan spoke in support. The New Education Fellowship was led by an educationalist, Anton Vroland, who headed a sub-committee that drafted ideas for a new Act. The Fellowship's interest was driven by Anna Vroland, a teacher and Anton's recent and much younger left-leaning wife, who was developing an intense interest in Aboriginal issues and closeness with Aboriginal people.[90] It ran a national conference in Melbourne on 'native rights' in May 1949, which discussed national Aboriginal policy, a charter of rights for Aboriginal people, surveys of health and Aboriginal administration, and issues of cultural survival and citizenship.[91] Anna Vroland became a tireless lobbyist for Aboriginal causes in Victoria and encouraged the Women's International League for Peace and Freedom to support Aboriginal equality.

The Council for Aboriginal Rights formed in 1951 also pursued Aboriginal affairs aggressively. Some of its members had Communist affiliations which caused ASIO to place its activities and members under surveillance, including some Aboriginal people connected with it.[92] During the early years of the Cold War, the security organisation kept files on Helen Baillie, Anna Vroland, Barry Christophers and Shirley Andrews (the last two were members of the Council for Aboriginal Rights), as well as such Aboriginal leaders Doug Nicholls, Harold Blair and Bill Onus. The files today are as uncontroversial as shopping lists, but during the tensions of the early 1950s, they collected seemingly important information.[93]

In April 1949 the Hollway Liberal Ministry announced that the State Government would consider 'bringing all castes of aborigines in Victoria under jurisdiction of the state [sic] Aborigines' Protection Board': a radical change to the policy of 1886 onwards, and in line with Aboriginal thinking.[94] However, the incoming Macdonald Country Party Ministry failed to send a delegation to the national Native Welfare conference in 1950 and 1951, as it believed it did not have a 'native problem' as only nine Victorian 'full bloods' survived. The federal Minister for Territories, Paul Hasluck, who championed the new assimilation policy nationally, in 1952 termed Victoria the most 'backward and most self-righteous' of all the States.[95]

The activists kept pegging away at the Board and conservative governments but, as Anna Vroland wrote to a Queensland unionist in 1950, 'because there are so few dark people in this state [sic], the white people tend to think the question a remote one'.[96] Politically, Victoria was also in too great a period of instability to give much time to the affairs of only a thousand people—Victoria had ten governments between 1943 and 1955, and six governments between June 1950 and June 1955. However, Henry Bolte's government brought what proved to be long-term stability to the State's political life after June 1955. Between September and December 1955, Arthur Rylah, Bolte's Chief Secretary, instituted a reform process concerning the Board's administration and the conditions and affairs of Aboriginal people in Victoria: a 'New Deal' for Victorian Aboriginal people was imminent.[97]

15

Assimilation and its Challengers

Colonisers try to conquer minds as well as lands and attempt to remake their subjects, for all peoples believe their ways are best. The British sought to refashion Aboriginal people in missions, farm schemes and schools from early colonial times. This enterprise intensified after the 1886 Act which moved 'half castes' off reserves, their children into apprenticeships once they turned fourteen, and removed other children if deemed 'neglected'. Yet the assimilation policy was pursued in a half-hearted and rarely proactive way by an under-resourced Protection Board after the First World War. The Board pushed people off reserves and left social forces to do its work of assimilation. It let some back on reserves and supported them under certain conditions. However, the Board in general refused to recognise those of 'mixed descent'—whom it deemed as being less than 'half caste'—as being Aboriginals. They were left to their own resources, often in appalling material conditions. The Board practised daily tyrannies, mostly at Lake Tyers, and by the removal of children. From the 1930s some Victorians criticised the Board, both for what it did at Lake Tyers and what it did not do for Aboriginal campers. Pressure finally forced an inquiry into the Board and led to reforms that increased the intensity of assimilation—an intensity soon felt by all Aboriginal Victorians. However, by the 1960s Aboriginal people and their supporters fought for greater rights—not civil rights, which they now had—but indigenous rights that recognised difference.

The McLean Report and the Aborigines Welfare Board

In 1937 the so-called Native Welfare Conference of all States and Territories adopted the radical policy of assimilation. The onset of war had shelved its implementation, but in the early 1950s it was revived as national policy, led by Paul Hasluck. Hasluck, a journalist-historian turned conservative politician, observed while a back-bencher in 1950 that Australia's defence of human rights in the international sphere was 'mocked by the thousands of degraded and depressed [Aboriginal] people who crouch on rubbish heaps throughout the whole of this continent'.[1] When he became Minister for Territories in the Menzies Government in 1951 he pursued a proactive policy to encourage all States to turn to assimilation.

The power of the photograph—a blend of horror and concern—impacted on Aboriginal affairs in the 1950s. Photojournalism found drama at Daish's Paddock adjoining the Mooroopna tip—home to about eighty permanent Aboriginal campers. A similar number lived on the 'Flat' by the river. In 1954 journalist Graham Perkin (later editor of the *Age*) described in lurid terms the 'housing horror' of makeshift 'humpies' that could not resist heat, cold, wet or flood, into which people were closely packed. The campers lived a little above Shepparton's water supply, and Perkin claimed there 'remains a lurking fear that it could become polluted'. People's nutrition was poor, as most ate cheap meat and bread with few vegetables and had little fruit and milk, and the children's schooling was infrequent. It all amounted, he wrote, to a 'social cancer' that must be eradicated. Four campers' children died in early 1954, partly though malnutrition, and a young girl had been hospitalised eighteen times between the age of two and five for diarrhoea, ear infections, chest infections, tonsillitis and burns: typical medical incidences for campers.[2]

The Save the Children Fund supported Sister Melba Turner from 1952 to ameliorate the children's conditions with a kindergarten, which supplied lunches, and a girls' club. A New Deal Committee of concerned Mooroopna-Shepparton residents erected a pre-school building for Turner's work in late 1956. Turner claimed the campers ranged from decent families, ten of whom had recently made it into housing commission homes in town, to those caught in a cycle of fighting and drinking, fuelled by job discrimination and poor opportunities.[3] The New Deal Committee sought affordable housing on crown land for the campers.[4] The local community feared the campers, one person referring to their 'filthy, unhygienic, disgraceful, communist-breeding' conditions.[5]

As concern mounted, individuals mobilised. Within weeks of Henry Bolte's Liberals assuming office in May 1955, Irene Newton John, wife of the Master of Ormond College (and mother of the singer, Olivia),

Aboriginal Sunday school in postwar Central Victoria, probably Mooroopna.
(Val Heap Collection, courtesy of Museum Victoria, XP2502)

invited Aboriginal support groups to quiz several public servants about Lake Tyers and the Aborigines Act. Notes kept by Valentine Leeper reveal that the new permanent Under-secretary of the Board, A. James, admitted that 'some regulations may go beyond the power of the act [sic]'.[6] The heat was clearly on. In September James's boss, Arthur Rylah, the Chief Secretary, suggested that the Victorian Council of Social Services review Lake Tyers and the Act. The Council formed an impressive committee of activists: Irene Newton John, Anna Vroland, Cora Gilsenan, Shirley Andrews, Doug Nicholls, and Richard Seeger, a photographer who often visited Jackson's Track.

On Christmas Eve 1955 the Bolte Government announced an inquiry by Charles McLean, a retired Chief Stipendiary Magistrate with a strong middle-class work ethic and a court reputation for being hard on vagrants.[7] McLean was to evaluate the current Aborigines Act (1928) and its operation, and inquire into the number, distribution and living conditions of permanent Victorian residents who are 'believed to be of not less than one-fourth part aboriginal blood'. In particular he was to assess their employability, their capacity to maintain themselves and families according to the 'general standards of the Victorian community', and assess what factors militated against their absorption into the community. McLean was to examine the future of Lake Tyers and how those of 'aboriginal blood' should be administered. These were old questions asked anew. Not surprisingly, the Board's Secretary, N. Garnet, became McLean's secretary. McLean took some months to peruse the Board's annual reports and minutes—no doubt with Garnet's help—from which he wrote an approving 'potted history' of its activities. He visited Aboriginal communities, interviewed some Aboriginal people including Doug Nicholls and Shadrach James, as well as Board staff, police, welfare workers, local councillors and teachers. He reported in January 1957.

McLean counted 1,346 Aboriginal Victorians, about 150 each at Lake Tyers, Melbourne, Nathalia, Orbost, and Mooroopna, with between 50 and 70 each at Robinvale, Dimboola-Antwerp, Echuca, Heywood and Framlingham. This count underestimated the population by at least 500, according to Diane Barwick's figures in 1962.[8] McLean described the living conditions of Aboriginal campers at Mooroopna and elsewhere as 'squalid', often 'immoral', and claimed that 'many of the children are dirty, undernourished and neglected'. McLean noted that the police removed 24 children following his visit, ignoring family ties and affection, and assuming family neglect was the norm rather than the exception. He disapproved of campers, a view honed no doubt while dealing out sentences to vagrants from the Bench. McLean rejected the idea of Aboriginal mental inferiority, ascribing their position to cultural factors that made them improvident, itinerate and casual workers, who lacked education and were clannish. Older racial ideas surfaced in the language and thrust of his report as historian Corinne Manning has so ably argued.[9] McLean admitted that whites have a 'racial and colour prejudice', and some employers exploited or discriminated against Aboriginal Victorians. He wanted Lake Tyers reduced twenty-fold and its residents encouraged to leave, the diminished reserve being for those who are 'aged, sick, infirm, or otherwise necessitous'. An Aboriginal administration under a Superintendent was needed to maintain a 'positive endeavour' in the 'direction of assimilation'. He favoured the NSW model, including its name, the 'Aborigines Welfare Board'.

The McLean Report highlighted housing and education as keys to Aboriginal 'absorption into the community'. He advocated the NSW housing model of placing Aboriginal families in a few houses in towns providing employment. Education and youth training would speed absorption, but he urged the closure of 'all-aboriginal' schools at Lake Tyers and Framlingham, as he believed they would retard assimilation. The Superintendent of the Welfare Board should practise 'close personal contact' with Aboriginal people, but needed wide powers under the Child Welfare Act, as 'sympathetic treatment must be allied with firmness'.

Coached by the Board's man Garnet, McLean became a committed assimilationist, acting in the shadow of the 1886 Act and of Paul

Hasluck's influence at the federal level. Thus it was perhaps surprising and against the Government's brief of investigating those of 'one-fourth Aboriginal blood', that McLean wanted 'Aborigine' in the new Act defined as 'any person having an admixture of Australian aboriginal blood'. This was a broad definition that the Board had long resisted and Aboriginal people had long promoted.[10] However, McLean was not influenced by Aboriginal ideas of identity. Rather, he included those with one non-Aboriginal grandparent and parent as 'Aboriginal', because he believed campers had not been assimilated and needed the active surveillance of the state to do so. As he reiterated privately to Valentine Leeper, 'the only real progress [to assimilation] will lie in subsequent vigorous and sympathetic administration'.[11]

The response to McLean's Report from the press and parliament was generally enthusiastic, revealing the overwhelming community desire for an assimilation policy. Within a day, the Bolte Government announced that a new Aborigines Act would be drafted following McLean's suggestions.[12] Several Aboriginal people spoke approvingly of the report, including Harold Blair and Doug Nicholls.[13] Aboriginal support groups gave varied responses, the Victorian Aboriginal Group approving the report's emphasis on assimilation. However, Anna Vroland and the Council for Aboriginal Rights, while welcoming certain aspects, criticised others. They were unhappy with McLean's white judgements of how Aboriginal people should behave; his unwillingness to speak to residents at Lake Tyers; his recommendation for Lake Tyers' reduction and eventual closure; his desire to close Aboriginal schools; and his view that there should be only one Aboriginal Board member. They also opposed his use of the old term 'blood' in his definition of Aboriginality, as inferring a genetic difference, and his support for the term 'welfare' which had bad memories for Aboriginal people. Finally, they urged him to use a capital 'A' for Aborigine/al.[14]

The new Act's parliamentary debate focused on Lake Tyers and the number of Aboriginal people sitting on the Board. Sir Albert Lind for the government saw 'no necessity' for more than one Aboriginal representative, while Valentine Doube, member for Oakleigh, quipped that 'the Opposition realizes that this is the old deal under a new guise'.[15] The Aborigines Act (1957) created an Aborigines Welfare Board with ten members, two of whom were to be Aboriginal people—assimilationist advocate Harold Blair and the popularly acceptable Doug Nicholls were appointed. The Act was significant in that it followed McLean in defining 'Aborigine' widely as 'any person of Aboriginal descent'. However, the new Board, like the old, was to manage money, food and

Visitors outside the home of Tom and Rose Dunnolley, Barmah Lakes 1967.
L–R: Esmai Jackomos, Merle Jackomos (nee Morgan), Rose Dunnolley, Viney Morgan,
Denise Morgan, Andrew Jackomos, with Greta Morgan at the rear.
(A. & M. Jackomos Collection, courtesy of Museum Victoria, XP5294)

clothing according to Aboriginal need and assist Aboriginal people 'to become assimilated into the general life of the community'; that is, it aimed at the erasure of Aboriginality over time.[16]

Regulations under the Act gave the Board and manager of Lake Tyers power to issue permits to allow people to move on or off the reserve; demanded residents' obedience to the manager on penalty of a fine of £50; and required them to do a 'reasonable amount of work' at a rate arranged by the manager. Residents were not permitted to fight, be riotous, use indecent or abusive language, gamble, become drunk or be indecently clothed. Residents could form an advisory committee but it was given no power or definition. Those off reserves were treated with the old paternalism as well. Employers of Aboriginal labour—the legislators had seasonal pickers in mind here, not city workers, although they kept definitions vague—had to provide accommodation, sanitary facilities and sufficient food and water, and no Aboriginal male under eighteen or Aboriginal female of any age could be employed without the Board's consent. The latter provisions were unworkable and revealed the truth of the new Welfare Board being an 'old deal under a new guise'.[17]

The Welfare Board at least spoke the language of citizenship, freedom and equality. Following changes to the licensing and consorting laws in 1956, it claimed in its first annual report that Aboriginal people enjoyed the 'normal rights and obligations of citizenship which are shared by other Victorians'. The Board boasted they had given Aboriginal Victorians the right to vote, to own property, enjoy freedom of movement, to sue or be sued, and to be protected by normal social and industrial legislation. It aimed to assist Aboriginal people to become 'fully accepted member[s] of the general community'. The Board argued that assimilation meant people of 'Aboriginal descent will be merged into the general community and live in the same way as white Australians'. This was a definition lifted from the national Aboriginal Welfare Conference, which Victoria had earlier refused to attend. It stressed that assimilation did not have to occur through inter-marriage or 'the extinction of the racial identity of the aborigines'. Like Paul Hasluck's federal government assimilation policy it sounded reasonable, but in practice it was still aimed at making Aboriginal people white.[18]

For the Board, housing policy was the key, as it could dramatically improve the material conditions of Aboriginal people and place them physically alongside whites. Health and education and even employment prospects would improve with better housing. Public attitudes could also play a role. While the Board argued that Victorians were generally 'free from serious expressions of racial prejudice', it acknowledged there were 'some people who are prejudiced or hostile towards the aborigines' and that 'citizens of country towns do not realize the conditions under which aborigines live on the outskirts of their towns'. The Board urged Victorians 'to recognize their aboriginal fellow-citizens as beings of the same human clay, with much the same abilities and imperfections' as themselves and to accept them as neighbours.[19] These fine words— perhaps written by Philip Felton, the new Superintendent and former social worker with the NSW Board—gave a humane and rational face to the assimilation policy and aligned it with national policy. Yet how were these ideas practised in the real world of housing policy and child welfare?

Assimilation in practice: housing and children

The new Welfare Board acknowledged in 1958 that 150 housing units were needed across the State for Aboriginal people. It focused initially on Mooroopna where local housing solutions were already being discussed by an anxious Rodney Shire Council and the local New Deal Committee. The Save the Children Fund also stood ready to help. Concerns were raised in 1956 about Daish's Paddock and 'the Flat' due to the former being beside the shire tip and the latter beside the Goulburn River, which flooded twice that winter. Some new houses were proposed.[20] Concerns increased when McLean's report described both camps in early 1957 as 'squalid'. In mid 1957 Senior Constable H. G. Haag wrote to the Council as its prosecuting officer and recommended that eight unoccupied 'humpies' at Daish's Paddock be bulldozed before they were again occupied by the inflow of summer fruit pickers. He wrote a vivid account of the 'appalling conditions' there, the smelly and unhealthy nearby tip that hospitalised children, the parental 'neglect' that led Mooroopna police to remove 34 children to institutions in 1956 alone, and the decent families hoping for something better.[21]

The Council resolved to demolish any vacant huts, but within two days Charles Huggard, a Council foreman, bulldozed the lot. The bewildered and angry campers were given an hour to collect their possessions before being moved by police to the 'Flat'. Witnesses claimed they were forced to move in with relatives or into tents. Gwen Evans of the New Deal Committee called the demolitions premature, 'ruthless' and inhumane. The demolitions brought to fifty the number of huts removed that year.[22] Mrs Magee, one of those residents moved, said: 'We were promised a house two years ago. When I heard that there was a chance now of getting a house, I came down [from Cobram] and went back to the tip. And when the huts at the tip were demolished I was given a tent to live in'.[23] The last hut was flattened in late 1960.[24]

Ten new houses were built in 1958 on 'Blue Moon Estate' behind the Ardmona cannery, a kilometre from town. The settlement, called 'Rumbalara' (meaning 'rainbow'), was opened by Chief Secretary Rylah as a 'New Deal' for the people 'after years of blackness and being put aside'.[25] The houses were made of prefabricated concrete and were built at half the cost of other Housing Commission homes. They were in imperial measure: 26' × 17' or four squares in size and contained a living area (19' × 10'), three tiny bedrooms (9' × 7' or 10' × 7') and a laundry-bathroom (7' × 6'). They had running water, a fuel copper for hot water, electricity operated by a coin slot-machine, but no back or internal doors. They were an improvement on 'humpies', but smaller and cheaper than the usual Housing Commission home and inadequate for the size of most Aboriginal families. Design faults soon became evident—doors too narrow to admit standard furniture—and building defects were discovered. They were also ill-suited to extremes of temperature. The carefully selected initial residents paid an admittedly subsidised rental of 16 shillings per week, the other 13 shillings required by the Housing Commission being paid by the Board.

The houses were designed to be 'transitional', which was the way slum-dwellers in England, as well as Aboriginal people across Australia, were managed into living in modern homes. They were a stage between the

Residents of Rumbalara contemplate the mud, 1961.
(Courtesy of Herald and Weekly Times Ltd)

huts on the river and the Housing Commission houses in town sprinkled amidst white neighbours. Alan and Betty Charles were the first Mooroopna couple to move to the latter in June 1959, and Violet Harrison moved to a Drouin house in 1960.[26] Despite the initial euphoria about Rumbalara, complaints from all quarters—Aboriginal people, welfare workers, even the Board itself—meant that twelve houses built in 1960 at Manatunga, a second estate just outside Robinvale, were better built, 20 per cent bigger, a third more expensive and more suitably designed, being fitted out with internal doors.[27]

The residents initially believed these transitional houses did offer a 'New Deal'. Their huts at the 'Flat', Daish's Paddock and at Robinvale on the Murray were home to them, but they offered harsh and insecure living conditions, few amenities and the slavery of carrying each drop of water used. The new houses seemed like 'palaces' or, at least, a 'step up'.[28] However, most residents seemed unaware that they were the subjects of an experiment. These houses were in reality training facilities where they would practise thrift and sobriety in order to pay the rent, undertake gardening and home-making like suburbanites, and live as nuclear rather than extended families—all to copy the ideal white, middle-class family home of the post-war years. Rules existed to order their behaviour, and a manager was appointed for each settlement—Charles Huggard, who had so happily bulldozed Daish's Paddock, was made Rumbalara's manager, and Ray Hicks, the manager at Manatunga. The

Board supervised rent payments, home-making and visitors. Evictions occurred for those not shaping up. Those who responded earned the chance of a house in town, depending on availability. The Save the Children Fund ran facilities and activities for women and children at both housing settlements, gave Christmas parties and even made cash payments to those with good school attendance. The Fund acted as an unofficial trainer as well as a welfare agency. Florence Grylls, its founder, reported its aims in 1957 as helping 'these people to achieve better standards of living and better education, so that they may become fully assimilated to the general population of Victoria'.[29]

An inevitable power struggle emerged between the management and the Aboriginal residents. As Violet Harrison recalled: 'We didn't have the same freedom . . . There was no longer the same spirit of sharing and supporting each other that we had on the river bank . . . There were too many rules'.[30] The Housing Commission also had rules, but these concerned rents and property. Only the Board's houses had the extra rules about visitors and moral behaviour. The claims of the Welfare Board about equal treatment of Aboriginal people were clearly untrue. Socialising, as had occurred at the 'Flat' was still allowed, but visitors and 'blow-ins' were not allowed to stay overnight. The managers collected the rent and reported to the Board and the police almost every visitor, every lapse, every indiscretion, and each inebriation. One resident recalled of Huggard: 'If someone came up to visit their people, the police would be right behind him and he [Huggard] would be right behind the police'; another remembered: 'He was a mongrel . . . He used to come down here a lot, just snooping around'. The scheme attacked Aboriginal kinship, and Aboriginal people resisted it. One resident recalled that when Huggard found out that her own daughter from Melbourne was staying in her house, he asked her to leave. She chased Huggard off with a frying pan.[31] The residents had their internal disputes, and drunken fights erupted in some households—as they did in white houses in town. Townspeople sometimes drove by just to stare and 'confirm' what they had heard.

Rumbalara and Manatunga bred criticism from the outset: the Board slandered the residents and the residents attacked a well-meaning, but misguided Board. Alf Bamblett, aged twenty, said the houses were 'not fit for pigs'.[32] Thirteen-year-old Esme Bamblett claimed she lost a school friend after her friend visited her Rumbalara house: without internal doors, with wood stacked in the bathroom to keep it dry— there were no sheds provided—and a sink for washing both clothes and dishes.[33] A West Indian cricketer of the 1930s, who became a West

Indian parliamentarian in the 1950s, Learie Constantine, when shown Rumbalara in 1959, commented that it was better than the fringe camp, but 'the person who designed them has a poor opinion of aborigines as humans'.[34] The Australian Aborigines' League also attacked the houses, Doug Nicholls believing they 'segregated' Aboriginal people who 'are being treated as second class citizens'.[35] In June 1966 thirty Aboriginal people called for Rumbalara's closure as it had served its purpose and they wanted housing equal to the general standard. Doug Nicholls led a deputation to government.[36]

The Board undertook several major renovations in the 1960s but the transitional housing experiment was doomed. Manatunga and Rumbalara closed in 1968 and 1969, leaving the residents to be housed in a town at higher rental. Alice Cooper was relieved, commenting: 'We want to go and live in Mooroopna among the white folk. Give our kids a chance'. Jean Atkinson added: 'I wish they'd bomb it'. A Shepparton resident agreed: 'It is a rotten place. In the summer the stink from the swamp is unbearable and you could suffocate in the houses'.[37] Some elders today look back on the experience as 'the good old days', a 'stepping stone' to being able to deal with whites in town. Historian Corinne Manning has argued that they form an important community focus of history and identity to this day.[38]

The Harrisons on show in 1966. L–R: Peter Gordon, Irene Gordon (nee Harrison), Dick Harrison, Mary Harrison, Veronica Harrison, Mervyn Harrison.
(Courtesy of Herald and Weekly Times Ltd)

The Board went backwards in its effort to match Aboriginal housing needs in the face of a rising population. The housing shortage of 150 dwellings in 1957 had blown out to 220 houses by 1967.[39] The Board's three- or four-bedroom, asbestos-clad houses had combined kitchen-living area and separate bathroom and laundry with hot water, blinds, linoleum flooring and sewerage connection where available. From 1966 two-thirds of families benefited from subsidised rental of $2 to $5 depending on income and family size. The Board favoured 'scattering' the new houses to speed assimilation, itself being helped by such service organisations as the Country Women's Association, Apex, local New Deal committees and church groups. The 106 new houses built by 1967 were located in 36 country towns, six towns having between 5 and 8 houses—Dimboola, Robinvale, Mooroopna, Morwell, Nowa Nowa and Orbost—and 30 having one to four houses (of these, 18 towns had just one Board house).[40] The Housing Commission provided other housing which the Board subsidised. Many people wanted to be in town to avoid the conditions of riverbank and transitional housing and to be closer to services. Some, including Doug Nicholls and Bruce McGuinness from the Victorian Aborigines Advancement League, even advocated 'scattering' in 1962, although they were not advocating an end to Aboriginality. This approach soon fell out of Aboriginal favour through hard experience.[41]

Those who moved into these houses experienced the pressures of being role models for assimilation. Between 1958 and 1960, Violet Harrison moved from riverbank to Rumbalara, to a house in Drouin provided by the Board and fitted out by the Country Women's Association on land bought by the Victorian Aborigines Advancement League. She paid a subsidised rent of £1 ($2) per week. Harrison told a reporter she felt 'like a little queen in a palace', and wanted her grandson to 'grow up like a white child'. She indicated a television her children had bought for her.

Dick and Mary Harrison and their six children became celebrities at Lakes Entrance when they saved and built a home in 1961 with the help of white neighbours, who proudly erected a sign in the street: 'to Harrison's house'. The Harrisons—good workers and decent people who lived in a 'humpy'—were given two hectares outright by Joe Rickman in 1959. An appeal raised £400, to which the Harrisons supposedly added a huge £1500 they had saved over 14 months, to complete a house furnished with carpets and cut-glass cabinets. Cora Gilsenan said the Harrisons had to 'contend with the resentment of some residents and the jealousy of some of their own people'. Indeed, Mary Harrison told the *Herald* that 'it hurts. You have no idea how it hurts. A lot of aboriginal friends visit me and I am happy to entertain them.

But never once will I allow any of them to spend the night here. If I weaken once, this home we built could easily be ruined and I can't do that to my children. Not after coming so far'.[42] Three years later, and despite much local unemployment, the two oldest Harrison boys had maintained their jobs as a mechanic and a salesman.[43] However, the Harrisons remained in contact with their Aboriginality. Alick Jackomos who was in charge of Lake Tyers in 1967 commented: 'They would attend the dances and participate in all the functions at Lake Tyers'.[44]

The experiment of scattering was only partially successful despite the hopes of Aboriginal people and the good intentions of many townspeople. On the one hand Aboriginal Victorians were bound in webs of extended family and kinship that succoured them and shaped their identity. And as one observer wrote: 'When Aboriginal people go into new houses many take their problems with them: failure results'.[45] On the other hand non-Aboriginal Victorians held stereotypical views of Aboriginal people's work skills, drinking, health and intelligence, based on generations of myths and were thus mostly unwelcoming.[46]

Despite such an atmosphere, the Board was especially keen to rehouse those from Lake Tyers so as to close the reserve. It shifted 39 families into the La Trobe Valley and as far as Stawell, Horsham and Ararat. Alick Jackomos, who was a field officer for the Victorian Aborigines Advancement League in 1965, recalled:

> Families that were housed were harassed by [Welfare Board] officers for having relatives (unauthorised tenants) staying in their houses yet the authorities made no provision for pensioners, childless couples, single persons many who had lost their spouses . . . I witnessed officers threatening families with police action if the extra members of the family did not leave the house. Where could the children go, they had no home and the only alternative was to live in a humpy. Of course there was always the threat of your children being taken away and placed in an institution.[47]

Some were evicted for rent arrears, some left in disgust at the rules about visiting and orderliness, others because they felt alienated from a town without relatives or affirmations of Aboriginality.[48] When Claude and Ivy Mobourne and their five children moved from Lake Tyers to the only Board house in Horsham in early 1963, their new neighbours cleaned the house, provided cut flowers and chopped wood ready for their arrival. The Mobournes claimed to have no misgivings about leaving Lake Tyers, although some new neighbours were nervous that 'if Mr Mobourne's place becomes a happy hunting ground for aboriginals from all over the place, it will ruin the whole area'. The Mobournes left within a year and in 1966 were living in a Housing Commission home in Wonthaggi, closer to their Gunai/Kurnai roots.[49] Less than half of those shifted off Lake Tyers were still in their Housing Commission or Board houses by 1966, the rest were camping in huts, living with relatives, or trying to return to the reserve.[50]

The Board tried to clear Lake Tyers completely by proposing to build a 'transit village' on industrial land two kilometres from Morwell in 1965. The village was to house the remaining reserve families, young or elderly couples, and a small number of single men, providing trade and domestic training, and access to town employment. Families would 'shape up' under the manager's guidance, and then move into town. The Board admitted that 'Aboriginal resettlement places strains on the white community as well as the dark people' and argued such a centre would allow the residents to 'rub shoulders with [the] general community' and avoid 'the feeling of loneliness that attends the isolated resettlement case'.[51] The Shire Secretary, R. Lord, welcomed the proposal, saying that 'an aboriginal is a creature of God, and entitled to live beside anybody and share the privileges and responsibilities of citizenship'.[52] However, others disagreed. Local landowners opposed the idea, claiming 'we do not have a colour bar, we simply say the site is unsuitable'. The Council voted against rezoning the land as residential, effectively ending the idea. Aboriginal people also vigorously opposed the proposal, partly because Rumbalara and Manatunga were failing by then, but more because the 'transit village' was a dagger at the heart of Lake Tyers.[53]

The Board's housing policy caused community tension. In September 1958 the Victorian Aborigines Advancement League built a house for Sid and Margaret Austin and their seven children at Neerim South. They had been influenced by church people to move into town according to Daryl Tonkin, a white Victorian who married into

Mr Veldon, left, a Nowa Nowa grocer, selling wares at Lake Tyers, 1965. Gladys Edwards is at centre. (Courtesy of Museum Victoria, XP2593)

the Gippsland Gunai/Kurnai community.[54] The Austins welcomed the move as their hut at Jackson's Track was freezing in winter and school was a six-kilometre walk away. However, some local residents protested to the press. An ex-serviceman, W. Millnes, said: 'Most of us paid big money for our land and houses, and they would not be worth a cracker if aboriginals moved into the street', while George England stated: 'Had we known the Austins were coming to live next door, we would not have bought the house'. Geert Joustie, a Dutch immigrant, agreed, saying: 'I've got no hard feelings against aboriginals, but I would not like to see them next door'.[55] Other Victorians were outraged by the Neerim South residents' objections. This caused the objectors to retract their statements, claiming they had misunderstood the proposal, and a single house with one family would be acceptable.[56]

The same fear gripped the small Gippsland town of Nowa Nowa in March 1960 as the Board prepared to move families into three adjoining houses brought from Lake Tyers. Mrs P. Kingston warned: 'We intend to move if we possibly can. The whole thing is shocking. I don't look forward to living next to them. I have two little boys and my husband is away all the week'. Mrs A. E. Toner, a widow with an invalid daughter, stated: 'We'll just have to get out and let the aborigines take over ... I couldn't keep my daughter here if they are living up the hill'.[57] Again there was dissent from such views. However, Bill Tregonning, a member of one of the town's four existing Aboriginal families—which were all in work and well respected—agreed that the three houses should not be sited together and that a police presence in the town would avert any trouble.[58] Police at Lakes Entrance confirmed that two-thirds of the previous year's criminal charges were against Aboriginal people: not the steady locals in work, but the 'blow-ins'.

In January 1966 protests emerged at Traralgon against the overcrowding, property damage and partying of Gunai/Kurnai living or staying at four Board houses. Mrs Jean Stephens said they moved in 'two years, seven months and three days ago'. She had tried hard to welcome them, she said, and they had tried hard to settle. It was the Board's fault: 'It dragged these people here from Lake Tyers, which they did not want to leave and dumped them in Traralgon. It was too big a break'.[59] Doug Nicholls said this was the problem of the assimilation policy: it threw people into society without help. 'They are out of work and in crowded houses'.[60] Lindsay Mobourne and his wife wanted to return to Warragul where they had been happy. They needed a bigger house for their children and grandchildren. A Gunai/Kurnai woman, Norma Harrison, also attacked assimilation. 'When I first came here, I used to keep my people out. We love one another . . . we are very sentimental people. It hurt me to tell my own flesh and blood to go away from the gate. I made a lot of bad friends with my own people—and most of the white neighbours still did not have much to do with me'.[61] The Minister of Aboriginal Affairs, Lindsay Thompson, inspected the houses and found some mess and disorder, but said that, statistically, less than ten per cent of 3,000 Aboriginal Victorians gained the attention of police. The Board promised repairs and a social worker. At a public meeting in February, Laurie Moffat, 67, spoke his mind courageously, saying: 'We were kicked out of Lake Tyers. We just aren't ready to face living in a white man's town. I want to go back to the place where I was born and be among my own people. Most of us feel this is best'.[62] Similar tensions flared at Robinvale in 1968 when there was an influx of 'out-of-towners', and at Warrnambool when Daphne Lowe recalled a petition was raised to prevent people from Framlingham being placed in town.[63]

The Welfare Board put most of its effort into housing policy and still failed to make any significant inroads into the Aboriginal housing 'waiting list' over ten years. Historian Mark Harris argued the Welfare Board was more notable for its 'inactivity than reform' and consistently ignored the advice of its own Superintendent, Philip Felton.[64] It should be noted that it faced a massive 214 per cent growth in the Aboriginal population in the decade after 1958—from 1,400 to 4,500 people. However, the population was small enough to be housed—despite being underestimated by perhaps a thousand—if the will was really there.[65]

The Board left health, employment and education issues to other agencies, which was appropriate given its lack of resources. It recognised the value of education for assimilation, as most Aboriginal children left school at fourteen with an inadequate primary standard of education due to poverty, ill-health, truancy, insufficient encouragement at home, and the problem of mobility. However, it made few efforts of its own to boost education. Indeed, community groups helped Aboriginal children as much as the Board did. From 1958 a dozen Aboriginal children were sponsored yearly to the Lord Mayor's holiday camp at Portsea and several other groups ran holiday camps. Clothing and toy appeals were directed to Aboriginal children. The Save the Children Fund made payments from the 1950s for regular school attendance and provided several school bursaries.[66] The Country Women's Association offered bursaries in 1958. In 1959 Carey Grammar School began an Aboriginal scholarship and a few other schools followed suit. Apex, the Master Plumbers Association, the Victorian Printers Union, as well as other bodies, created bursary schemes.

Secondary school attendance soared from 35 in 1961 to 243 by 1967, mostly at the lower levels, with only two students in their final Year Twelve in 1967. Despite the fact that two-thirds of students received some financial assistance—government and non-government—only about ten per cent reached Year Nine in the 1960s.[67] The Melbourne Conservatorium of Music offered a scholarship after 1958 which was held by Isabel Kuhl and later, Vic Lovett. A scholarships scheme initiated by tertiary students to fund Aboriginal students to university (ABSCHOL), begun in 1952, awarded scholarships at Melbourne University to Aboriginal students from interstate from 1958. Monash University offered its own scholarships in 1963, but there was still no Victorian student qualified to accept one in the 1960s. However, ABSCHOL began a tutor scheme in 1969 that promised future results. Ten-year-old Carl Atkinson of North-cote, who was failing all his school subjects, gained a 70 per cent average after tutorial assistance. He was one of almost 200 Aboriginal students in Melbourne receiving voluntary help from university students by 1971.[68] The tutoring scheme was phased out in 1972 once ABSCHOL was convinced governments and parents had become adequately involved.

The assimilation policy also involved the removal of children, a policy dating back to the 1870s. While housing policy was debated fiercely and publicly, evidence about child removal is scant, secretive, and locked away in the archives of private charities and in the hearts and minds of damaged people. In 1962 Diane Barwick reported that in 1956 about 150 Aboriginal children, more than ten per cent of the State's total, were in institutions. Most had been seized by police on the grounds of 'being in need of care and protection'. Their parents did not know they had the right to refuse entry to their homes and the right to reclaim their children when their circumstances improved.[69] Barwick's estimates seem sound. Cora Gilsenan ran a Christmas party for a total of 28 Aboriginal children in the Ballarat Orphanage in December 1955, and Senior Constable Haag reported that the police had removed 34 Aboriginal children from Mooroopna in 1956.[70] Barwick claimed the Welfare Board, which commenced in late 1957, reduced the number of committals and helped families reclaim their children. However, Alick Jackomos, who worked for the Victorian Aborigines Advancement League in the early 1960s, commented around 1990 that the 'AWB was an adoption agency. They don't admit it but they were'.[71]

Glenda Austin (nee Proctor) and three siblings were removed from their parents in 1964 when Glenda was nine. Her Aboriginal mother had left Framlingham where the family lived and her non-Aboriginal father was away on weekdays working for the Country Roads Board.

Playmates in Pye Street, Swan Hill, 1965. (Courtesy of Herald and Weekly Times Ltd)

The children were in the care of their teenage sister, Daphne Lowe (nee Proctor), and partner Robert Lowe, who had a child of their own. Glenda and three siblings were rounded up by the welfare on a charge of 'neglect' and driven to Melbourne by a male and female police officer. She, Daphne and Robert are still angry and bitter today, for they have now read their own welfare file with its claims of 'neglect' and 'exposure' to moral danger. They deny this, Daphne adding: 'I might have been young but I knew how to clean the house! You never had the house in a filthy condition when you had the Welfare poppin' out every month. They went in the bedrooms and pulled back the blankets to see if we had clean sheets, and in our cupboards and our fridge to see if we had food and what we had to eat'.[72] The children's father, Harry Proctor, brought food home every weekend. However, as Glenda remarked of the Welfare, 'they could write anything up, I suppose, just to, you know, take the kids away'. The irony is that Glenda claims the two police officers had sex beside the car on the way back to Melbourne in front of the children. And then there were the dangers of institutions. After some months in Allambie and then the Ballarat Orphanage, which 'wasn't bad but wasn't home', Glenda's grandparents Evelyn and George Alberts were permitted to care for the children. Unsettled, Glenda left home at thirteen, stayed with relatives, became a too-young single mother at fourteen and had her baby removed just after birth: 'They gave me a nurse of her and they just took her off me. They said I was too young'.

She found her daughter in another city 25 years later and experienced an emotional reunion with her.[73]

Sometimes family tragedies caused removals. Charlotte Jackson, who was born and grew up at 'The Flat' in Deniliquin, southern NSW, was removed because of an accident she suffered on the night her mother, Isabel Whyman, died in the Deniliquin Hospital. Charlotte, then thirteen, was returning from the hospital when she sat on a smouldering log by the river to warm and comfort herself. Her nylon dress caught alight, flared and melted, burning her face and hands terribly. She jumped into the river then ran back to the hospital. She was admitted, then sent to the Royal Children's Hospital in Sydney. Her long hospitalisation and reconstructive surgery caused the authorities to remove her from her father, Cyril Jackson of Cummeragunja, to the Cootamundra Girls' Home: was there no other solution? She came home scarred inside and out by the experience and the loss of years with her family.[74]

Occasionally news of the removal and fostering of Aboriginal children surfaced in the press. In 1964 it was publicised as 'a good deed' that the Slea family of Geelong had adopted four Aboriginal children and the Stallion family of Doveton had three adopted Aboriginal girls. In 1965 the Smiths adopted a girl after having her as part of a holiday program run by Harold Blair, the celebrated Aboriginal tenor.[75] Blair started the Harold Blair Aboriginal Children's Project in 1961 to bring children to Melbourne, mostly from interstate, for a six-week holiday with a white family to show them the advantages of an education. Over 300 had come by the late 1960s and some never went home. In December 1967 Stan Davey of the Aborigines Advancement League called for research into the general issue of adoptions of children from northern Australia.[76]

Challenging assimilation

The Victorian Aborigines Advancement League (the League or Advancement League) emerged in May 1957 (see Richard Broome's *Fighting Hard*, 2015). It was stimulated by the forced removal of people from Maralinga to the Warburton Ranges in Western Australia to allow for rocket and atomic testing under a 1946 British–Australian agreement. Bill Grayden and Doug Nicholls filmed the Maralinga people's third-world conditions, shocking Australians. Subsequently, Nicholls, federal parliamentarian Gordon Bryant, women's and peace activist Doris Blackburn, and Church of Christ Pastor Stan Davey formed the League. It became a dynamic group, with many local branches, most of whose members were white. It played a role in the formation of the Federal Council for Aboriginal Advancement (later FCAATSI) that pushed for Aboriginal rights across Australia and was behind the 1967 Referendum on federal control of Aboriginal affairs. The League became a powerhouse of ideas and critiqued the assimilation policy. In 1959 it defined its role: 'to work towards the complete integration of people of Aboriginal descent with the Australian community with full recognition of the contribution they are able to make'. It defined 'integration' as the ability of a minority to retain its identity. Aboriginal self-reliance and self-respect were other key aims.[77]

The League created a unique infrastructure. It employed Doug Nicholls as a full-time field officer, who sought practical help for Aboriginal people—emergency assistance, employment, legal advice—and spoke to countless public and club meetings.[78] Stan Davey was the full-time secretary, who operated out of 46 Russell Street and then 336 Victoria Parade, East Melbourne. He was assisted by an elderly woman, Vera Dyer, who came in daily for years to do office work on a voluntary basis. The offices provided a focus for all those visiting the city. The League established an opportunity shop and women's auxiliary run by Gladys Nicholls and other Aboriginal women. It formed 28 branches in Melbourne and country Victoria, all of which were busy fund-raising for clothing, bursaries, holiday programs and building projects.[79] In 1965 it had 2,000 members and a survey identified that 88 per cent were professionals or white collar workers—Protestant Christians and Jewish people were also over-represented.[80] It published its own magazine called *Smoke Signals* in 1957 which ran till the 1970s.[81]

Before the Advancement League's creation, Doug and Gladys Nicholls dreamt of a hostel for Aboriginal girls coming to Melbourne. An Aboriginal Girls Hostel Committee was formed in 1956 and it was given the use of an old Church of England manse at 56 Cunningham Street, Northcote, which, under the Nicholls' supervision, accommodated nine girls who worked in Melbourne factories and retail outlets. Myra Grinter (nee Atkinson) lived there for four years and said many of the girls 'went onto better things' because of the influence of the Nicholls: 'They gave us kids a vision'. Doug and Gladys Nicholls guided the girls to church each Sunday and encouraged them to attend [Advancement League] meetings as well as Aboriginal socials'.[82] In 1957 the Hostel amalgamated with the Advancement League. The League built its third office next door at number 58. A Boys Hostel began nearby in 1963, as well as one at Nathalia set up to accommodate ten Aboriginal children attending the local high school. A holiday house, 'Tanderra', opened at Queenscliffe in

1963, following a private gift of land and donations of money, material and time to convert a building moved to the site.[83] The League built its own hall in 1966 at 58 Cunningham Street, Northcote, named the 'Doug Nicholls Centre', raising eighty per cent of the capital itself. It became a focus for Aboriginal community and political life. Bill Onus donated a boomerang-shaped plaque which read: 'This centre is erected to honour humble Australians and to provide a meeting place for those who believe that all human beings are born free and equal in dignity and rights and should act towards one another in a spirit of brotherhood'.[84]

The Australian Aborigines' League (AAL) was reformed in the early 1960s and had close links with the Victorian Aborigines Advancement League, being referred to as the Aboriginal branch of the Advancement League. Alick Jackomos, a Greek Australian who had married into the Aboriginal community in 1951 and who did much voluntary work with Doug Nicholls in the 1950s and 1960s, was president. The rest of the membership was Aboriginal. Jackomos edited fourteen issues of *Aboriginal News* between 1963 and 1966 in order to strengthen a sense of community and history. It was a roneo'd, typed newssheet, which contained news, job information, a 'Does Anyone Remember?' column, and birth, death and marriage information. AAL ran socials and dances at the Doug Nicholls centre—often to piano and gumleaf accompaniment—a Christmas tree gift-giving for children, a 'Most Popular Girl' competition and an annual Aboriginal Ball at the Northcote Town Hall. The League and AAL combined to fight battles over transitional housing schemes, supported the revitalisation of Cummeragunja with a farm scheme, and regularly criticised the Welfare Board—although it conceded it was doing a better job than its predecessor, the Protection Board.

Other all-Aboriginal groups emerged. In 1957 the Aboriginal Elders Council of Australia held an 'all-Aboriginal' conference at 'Moomba', its clubrooms in Gertrude Street, Fitzroy. Delegates representing 90 per cent of Victorian Aboriginal people called for an end to child removal, the retention of Lake Tyers and better housing and employment. Chris Saunders, a World War I Aboriginal veteran, stated: 'Only one man can help the black man, and that is the black man himself'.[85] The next Elders Council conference at Newmerella, Gippsland concluded with a concert of Aboriginal performers.[86] In June 1964 the AAL held an Aboriginal Congress in Fitzroy, followed by two more over the next two years, each ending with a dinner dance and entertainment by Aboriginal performers. They were addressed by white activists and officers of the Welfare Board, but held Aboriginal-only sessions, chaired by Alick Jackomos.

Jackomos was not only the AAL President, but was seen by the vast majority of the community, from young radicals like Bruce McGuinness to older, more conservative people, as a 'gubboriginal', that is a *gubbah* (non-Aboriginal person) totally attuned to and accepted by the Aboriginal community.

Doug Nicholls photographed in 1966 by Albert Brown. (Courtesy of Museum Victoria, XP2726)

Pan-Victorian links were being built with each meeting. The first Congress in 1964 called for the rehousing of Aboriginal people within three years and the appointment of more social workers, with which Philip Felton—the Board's Superintendent—agreed. The second in 1965 called for the retention of all reserves, and the election of five Aboriginal members to the Welfare Board. It howled down Felton for a lack of consultation when he outlined the Board's Morwell 'transit village' proposal.[87] Alick Jackomos hoped to initiate half-yearly regional meetings, but wrote privately: 'It is so hard, the committee is so weak, it looks big on paper, but after being elected at Congress, you don't hear from them again, although I write to so many'.[88] In 1967 a United Council of Aboriginal Women was formed. Its President, Margaret Tucker, declared the Council aimed to fight for 'higher moral standards which would mean higher living standards in our homes' and would 'give unity amongst all my people to close the gaps of division'.[89] Unity was a problem as in any community. An Aboriginal man in 1964 told a white activist that he wanted to do something for his people, but 'Bill Onus is a "commo" and Doug Nicholls is a red'.[90] It was the Cold War era after all.

The biggest fight of the 1960s between Aboriginal people and the Board was, as we have seen, the struggle to retain Lake Tyers. The Welfare Board announced in February 1963 that it would close Lake Tyers and move its remaining residents into country towns. The reserve's population had declined from 198 to 84 between 1958 and 1963, as the Board rehoused people in towns, demolished the vacant houses and refused to allow people to return when unhappy.[91] Doug Nicholls resigned from the Board in protest and a campaign was mounted, which has been covered in detail in *Victims or Victors?* (1985) and Bain Attwood's *Rights for Aborigines* (2003). Nicholls led forty Lake Tyers residents in a march through Melbourne to Parliament House in May 1963. They presented a petition with nine points, which called for Lake Tyers' retention, adequate finance to develop it, the end of all restrictive rules, and moves towards its full control by the people within five years.[92] It was significant that Nicholls and the Advancement League also petitioned the United Nations, writing in a cable: 'Australian Government ignoring minority rights of Aborigines. Two million acres of reserves alienated since 1859, further half million threatened. Residents moved without consent or compensation. United Nations inquiry requested'.[93] In the face of such Aboriginal opposition, significant public support, lobbying by the Council for Aboriginal Rights and several years of intense press attention, the Board backed down and in May 1965 declared Lake Tyers a 'permanent' reserve.

The mid 1960s witnessed the emergence of a new phase in Aboriginal affairs, as Aboriginal groups pushed for both equality and also specific Aboriginal rights. Aboriginal militancy forced minor amendments to the Aborigines Act in 1965. The League petitioned parliament, opposing a possible move of Aboriginal affairs into the Social Welfare Department, and fearful of being lost in the mainstream. It called for a department of Aboriginal affairs—asserting Aboriginal difference on

The Lady Gladys Nicholls Hostel for Girls in Cunningham Street, Thornbury, 1958. Standing from L–R: Beverley Carter, Elvie Carter, Valmai Atkinson. Seated from L–R: Beverley Briggs, Lois Peeler (nee Briggs), Gloria Hood, Lena Gaston. (A. & M. Jackomos Collection, courtesy of Museum Victoria, XP2909)

the grounds of history and identity—to be assisted by an advisory council with elected Aboriginal representatives.[94]

However, the government retained the Welfare Board and moved it to the Ministry of Housing, which reflected the Board's preoccupations since 1958. There was no advisory body, but the League was invited to offer three names for Board membership, one of which was to be selected by the government. It chose Colin Tatz from the League's list. Tatz was a white South African, a new politics lecturer at Monash University and Monash's first Director of its Centre for Aboriginal Research. He joined anthropologist Donald Thomson, an existing Board member, and together with the Aboriginal appointees, Margaret Tucker and Con Edwards, they challenged the Board from the inside. Groups like the League and the Council for Aboriginal Rights (with its union and Christian affiliates), along with publications like Ian Spalding's *On Aboriginal Affairs*, attacked the Board from the outside. Opponents on the Board—J. H. Davey, the Chairman and Ministry of Housing bureaucrat; Don Howe, a Mooroopna employer of Aboriginal people; and Arthur Holden, a Morwell accountant involved in Apex—formed a powerful coterie, which, according to historian Mark Harris, dominated the Board, its agenda and its staff.[95]

In 1966 the ginger group gained a sub-committee assisted by Super-intendent Felton to examine policy. It issued a lengthy and revolutionary report which was accepted by the Board, bringing an end to eighty years of hard-line assimilationism. The report sought to end the tyrannical rule of the coterie, arguing that Board members, staff and Aboriginal clients must work together. It redefined 'assimilation' quite radically, accepting the looser definition of the 1965 national Aboriginal Welfare Conference. This changed the 1951 Conference's definition of assimilation that Aboriginal people in their daily lives 'will attain the same manner of living' than other Australians, to read: Aboriginal people 'will choose to attain a similar manner of living to that of other Australians'. The report explicitly rejected 'European insistence on Aborigines conforming to what Europeans deem is in their best interest' and gave full recognition to 'Aboriginal customs, cultural values, beliefs, manner and place of living'. It recommended minimum rights and standards for Aboriginal people and included policy statements on education, health, employment and training, and housing. Lake Tyers was to be retained and developed, and Framlingham made a permanent reserve.[96]

Criticism intensified in 1967. In March, the League called for the dumping of the Board's chairman, J. H. Davey. Colin Tatz threatened to quit in support. A frustrated Donald Thomson actually did so, accusing

Davey of 'blustering bullying tactics' and of not only treating Aboriginal people as 'children', but as 'stupid children'. The government promised changes and consulted with the League.[97] Colin Tatz maintained the heat, saying relations between the Board and its staff was 'at bedrock'. He added—later claiming to have been misquoted—that too many in Aboriginal affairs were 'dead-beat no-hopers' who 'did not make the grade in the white community', whereas work in Aboriginal affairs demanded considerable skill due to the 'extreme complexity of the problems'.[98] In November the government passed the Aboriginal Affairs Act (1967), which abolished the Welfare Board and created a Ministry of Aboriginal Affairs.

The sea change in Aboriginal affairs continued, with the League itself experiencing radical change. In March 1967 Bill Onus was elected the first Aboriginal President of the League, declaring: 'Now Aboriginals will really have a feeling that they are running the show'.[99] In August 1969 Roosevelt Brown, a Bermudan MP and representative of the Latin American Black Power movement, visited Melbourne on the invitation of some officers of the League and offered assistance in Aboriginal land rights battles. Brown's visit was met by strong condemnation from the Melbourne press because of the radical nature of the Black Power movement in the United States. His visit also sparked a power struggle within the League between those who wanted or did not want white members in the League, a battle outlined in the *Victims or Victors?* (1985). Doug Nicholls briefly resigned in protest at the militancy of Black Power, which he described as a 'bitter word'.[100] He soon returned as patron and a statement was issued rejecting violence and black supremacy. It read: 'Black Power was the empowerment of black people to make their own decisions'.[101]

A deputation of three Aboriginal members—Bob Maza, Harry Penrith (later known as Burnam Burnam), and Geraldine Briggs—speaking for AAL, the Aboriginal branch of the League, and the Victorian Tribal Council, asked the League's white paid workers and committee members to step down. Stan Davey, the secretary, had already left to work with Aboriginal people in the Kimberley, but others who remained went after a brief struggle. It was a bitter pill for those who had given so much of their time and energy to uplift Aboriginal people. But if they thought about it, this coup represented what they had been working for—Aboriginal people showing initiative and doing things for themselves. Bob Maza took over as director assisted by Bruce McGuinness. Myra Atkinson (now Grinter), who was nineteen, became a secretary. She recalled of the change: 'There was sadness at that happening, but it was

Eugene Mobourne and Laurie Moffat (L–R) at the 'Save Lake Tyers Campaign' meeting, Scott's Hall, Melbourne, March 1963. (A. & M. Jackomos Collection, courtesy of Museum Victoria, XP4395)

also self-determination for us to start handling our own affairs and helping our people to make changes. I got the feeling that they understood and that they were very, very supportive of us . . . they were people who were really dedicated to seeing big changes, for our part we felt sad because they were like family to us'. McGuinness sent Myra Atkinson to a secretarial and deportment course to give her the necessary skills for her new job. He also gave her two months to read every book concerning Aboriginal affairs in the office so her knowledge would be accurate, justifying it by saying: 'When people ring in I don't want you giving bullshit to them'. She graduated to be a liaison officer and 'saw the biggest changes that ever happened in the Aboriginal movement'.[102]

In January 1969 Lin Onus, son of the late Bill Onus, announced the creation of an 'Aborigines only' Koorie Club at 41 Gertrude Street, Fitzroy. The club carried the name 'Koorie', a Wiradjuri word from north of the Murray River that McGuinness, who was from that region, began to use around Melbourne. He did so because the word was distinctive, and was an Aboriginal word for themselves.[103] Others, but by no means all, began to adopt it. The Koorie Club was managed by Bruce McGuinness and contained an Aboriginal souvenir shop. McGuinness edited its newsletter, the *Koorier*, which sold for five cents per issue.[104] The club had a short life, but symbolised the Aboriginal rejection of assimilation, and the beginning of an Aboriginal cultural renaissance that is still unfolding.

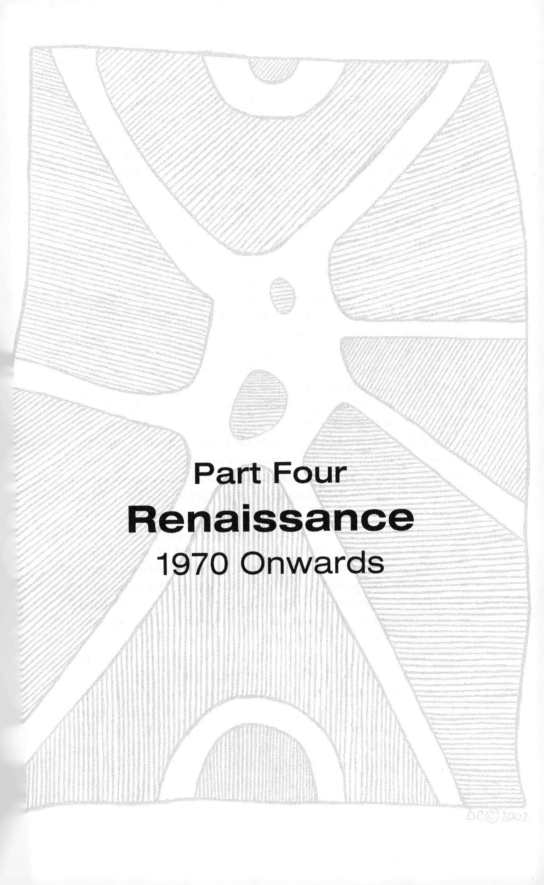

Part Four
Renaissance
1970 Onwards

The long years under the Aboriginal Protection Board and its successor, the Aboriginal Welfare Board—each termed the 'Destruction' Board by Aboriginal people—ended after 108 years. A Ministry of Aboriginal Affairs followed for a further seven years, and then Aboriginal people became freer to manage themselves. Governments still existed and still held the purse strings and thus ultimate power, but Aboriginal people were more able to manage their destiny than at any time since the 1840s. In this period the Aboriginal population was restored to levels that had existed when the Europeans arrived—this provided the critical mass for a political and cultural renaissance.

A burst of organisational activity from the 1970s onwards saw Aboriginal people forming their own organisations in city and country areas to provide a range of essential services and employment, which were inadequately provided for them by the mainstream. A newly emerged Aboriginal leadership drove these organisations and grew up further skilled young people. Cultural awareness was raised by such welfare groups as well as by specific cultural organisations. An Aboriginal renaissance occurred as cultural forms were revived, reinvented and adapted to the late twentieth century. Poor life chances—a product of racism, colonialism and the removal of children from families, but also due to ill-discipline within the Aboriginal community itself—led to challenges from poverty, health problems and substance abuse.

Colonialism had reshaped Aboriginal people, physically, culturally and economically—in fact, in every way. Yet people still had an indelible sense of being Aboriginal and could articulate how that was acted out in respect for land, ancestors and family, culture and traditions. Aboriginal culture, like yet another layer of paint on an ancient rock art drawing, is vibrant today: being continually altered and refreshed by new hands.

As the twenty-first century unfolded Aboriginal people in Victoria, now often referring to themselves as Kooris or First Nations peoples, began to work with governments, particularly with the Andrews Labor government from 2014, to seek new structures. The inspiration for this came from the United Nations Declaration on the Rights of Indigenous Peoples (2007) and the Uluru Statement from the Heart (2017). Aboriginal people and government together forged a First Peoples' Assembly, which is pushing for a voice, truth-telling and a treaty.

16

Seeking Autonomy

The Aborigines Act (1967) ended 108 years of being under a 'Board', which had begun as a protective device only to become one of control. The word 'Protection', which had been turned to 'Destruction' in grim Aboriginal humour, and the word 'Welfare', which had connotations of surveillance and the removal of children, were also gone. The 1967 Act promised more Aboriginal autonomy through consultative mechanisms, and the end of official assimilation, but was it an illusion? And if it was of substance, what responsibilities and opportunities might autonomy hold for the 6,000 Aboriginal people living in Victoria in 1970?

Battling the last Victorian Aboriginal administration

The Ministry of Aboriginal Affairs replaced the Welfare Board in January 1968. Its history does not concern us, save for how it interacted with Aboriginal people. The Victorian Government chose Reginald Worthy, a social worker, as Director of the Ministry. Worthy had long experience in youth work and four years in Aboriginal administration in the Northern Territory, where a proactive policy of change then operated. Under Worthy and the Minister-in-charge, Ray Meagher, significant resources were devoted to Aboriginal Affairs, some coming from the Commonwealth after the 1967 Referendum gave it a role in State Aboriginal affairs. The Ministry grew to about 80 staff, of whom 30 were Aboriginal people. Of the latter, about half were employed as farm hands at Lake Tyers, but those employed elsewhere included a visiting nurse, stenographer, liaison officer, housekeeping adviser and rent collector. Some were clearly to teach and police the Ministry's objectives.

Worthy was assisted by an Aboriginal Affairs Advisory Council of twelve nominated members, at least three being Aboriginal people. This minor representation was initially criticised by Stewart Murray, a member of the Advancement League and Doug Nicholls's son-in-law. Murray demanded that the Advisory Council be elected and claimed the currently appointed Aboriginal members did not have the support of most Aboriginal people.[1] The Ministry responded. An Act of November 1968 allowed for six members of the Aboriginal Affairs Advisory Council to be elected by Aboriginal people, with the government appointing a further two, giving Aboriginal people a majority. However, shortly after the first election, Stewart Murray resigned, saying *all* members should be Aboriginal and the Council should have executive powers and be free of ministerial influence. Eric Onus, Chairman of the Tribal Council of Victoria, which sponsored Murray, and Council appointee Margaret Tucker criticised Murray's decision, but activist Bruce McGuinness admired his guts and style. Murray, a Wemba Wemba man and ex-serviceman, also criticised the Ministry for a lack of consultation and claimed (correctly) that the differential payments of its home grants policy was aimed at moving people off Lake Tyers.[2]

The Ministry, energised by Worthy, wished to make Aboriginal people independent, responsible citizens, a goal no doubt shared by Aboriginal elders. Its first annual report stated: 'The Ministry had rejected policies of paternalism and expediency and espouses a programme which will lead ultimately to self-determination by Aborigines'. The welfare handouts given since 1834 had to stop, as they 'have taken away their initiative, responsibility, and even the desire for anything better'.[3] Under this approach people had to pay their own rent, medical bills, fulfil their own hire purchase agreements and (perhaps unfairly) those with prior convictions were denied government legal aid. Aboriginal rent subsidies were phased out, those in need coming under general Housing Commission subsidy schemes. Those moving into new homes no longer received furniture selected and paid for by the government, but chose and paid for their own, the government acting as guarantor.

Assistance was given to those seeking independence. The Ministry introduced a scholarship scheme to support all levels of schooling, which was vital as 54 per cent of the Aboriginal population in 1971 were under twenty. Scholarships were paid to over 1,500 children by 1973. Over twenty Aboriginal students were in tertiary education by this time. The Ministry provided funds for local government to employ some men in rural areas. Its rental stock rose to 186 houses by 1973 and in that year it wrote off rental arrear debts accumulated over fifteen years. Regular payers were rewarded with a $500 bonus towards rent reduction or a housing deposit. Deposits of $1,500 were offered to all and $9,000 to those leaving Lake Tyers. Worthy ended communal bathhouses at Lake Tyers and introduced award wages for workers there.[4]

In 1968 Worthy dropped a bombshell while addressing the Aboriginal branch of the Victorian Aborigines Advancement League. He stated: 'We do not believe in taking children from so-called "substandard" conditions and putting them in with a middle class white family. This will stop dead. No home is better than the one provided by your own mother'.[5] A fortnight later he told the Victorian Council of Social Services that there were 300 Aboriginal children (not all born in Victoria) in foster homes in Victoria, mostly with white foster parents. Worthy said most white foster parents were excellent but some were not. Some made private arrangements to take children and sometimes farmed them out to others. In one case twins were passed on and separated by the decision of a second set of foster parents. Another foster parent had 15 Aboriginal children and six of her own. Some people thought they were doing good, but others, he declared, used fostering as a status symbol and treated their Aboriginal foster children as pets. One woman was found to have bleached the skin of a child in her care.[6] The Minister for Aboriginal Affairs, Ray Meagher, was shocked at the number of children being exploited by the fostering system and promised discussions with colleagues interstate, and legislation if necessary, to prevent it but at present fostering was only illegal if money changed hands. He added: 'It has come to my attention that some people are getting aboriginal children through holiday schemes and not sending them back'.[7] Stan Davey of the League welcomed the attention given to unofficial adoptions: 'Families are split up and the child feels violated, different and lost'.[8]

Worthy also believed that 'unless they [Aboriginal people] are able to stand on their own feet they will never be independent'.[9] However, his strongly directive efforts were criticised by Aboriginal leaders, who thought he moved too fast and consulted too little. In 1969 Bob Maza, Queensland Aboriginal entertainer, activist, actor and the first Aboriginal director of the League, cautioned against 'forcing them to take immediate responsibilities in matters which have so far overwhelmed them'. Aboriginal people should not be pushed too quickly into 'the ruck of our aggressive competitive society', for to force them from one extreme to another causes 'despair'.[10] David Anderson, a member of the Advisory Council, accused Worthy in 1972 of being 'arrogant, perhaps racist' when he said that if Aboriginal Victorians wanted to be treated equally they had to measure up to equal responsibility. Anderson said: 'We are still reeling under the blow of white man's invasion, so it's absurd for Mr Worthy to talk about taking off the kid gloves and giving the Aborigine equality'. He also accused Worthy of paternalism for chairing the Advisory Council when an Aboriginal person could do it.[11]

The Advancement League was the focus of Aboriginal assertiveness in Victoria in the early 1970s, once it became an all-Aboriginal organisation after a power struggle in 1969. Its leadership developed a new message partly inspired by the American Black Power movement, but firmly rooted in Victoria's own colonial past, and mentored to a degree by Doug Nicholls, though more directly by Bill and Eric Onus. The League's Aboriginal president/director after the takeover, Bob Maza, quickly set the tone with an article in *Smoke Signals* on the importance of pride in Aboriginality, which was widely quoted in the metropolitan press. Maza slammed those 'integrates' who denied their own past, and criticised the majority of Aboriginal people who 'would not bother to find out the tribal name of even one of their ancestors'. He attacked white colonialism which 'successfully has beaten the black man into submission, taken away his culture and land, made him wear clothes, turned him into a beggar and forced him into becoming a black parasite, continually living on handouts, even to the present day'. His vision was that Aboriginal people would relearn their culture and 'having learned, we could then teach the whites how to live, simply by adopting the ethics and principles of our people which are almost completely lost'. Aboriginal culture was given a premier position, as he claimed it provided 'the key to making Australia a better place'.[12]

Bruce McGuinness was also important in setting new directions for the League and, over the longer term, Aboriginal Victorians. McGuinness was born in southern NSW at Cootamundra in 1940 but shifted to Fitzroy at the age of two. He attended several schools in the area and met racism in all of them, being called 'boong' and 'coon'. He moved in with his grandmother after his parents separated, but at age twelve joined his mother at Daish's Paddock in Shepparton. McGuinness met further racial abuse in Shepparton's schools. He left school at thirteen, entering a succession of thirty jobs over five years, including circus work and fighting in a boxing tent. Of these years he recalled: 'I resented being an aboriginal. If I had been granted one wish in life it would have been that I could turn white'.

In 1958 when McGuinness was eighteen, Bill Onus persuaded him to come to work for him in his Belgrave boomerang factory, and while there he mentored McGuinness in Aboriginal politics and activism.

He also nurtured his pride in his Aboriginality. McGuinness recalled in 1972 that Bill Onus 'was the most intelligent man I ever met. We would sit talking for hours about religion, about justice, and he awoke a sense of human dignity that had been buried in me'.[13] McGuinness claimed he only courted white girls and soon married one. His marriage broke down after three years on cultural grounds, as 'it was terribly embarrassing for me to get up on a platform with a white wife and advocate that aboriginals preserve their identity by marrying other aboriginals'. By 1970 he declared: 'I am proud to be an aboriginal. By the white man's reckoning I am quarter-caste, but as far as I am concerned I am an aboriginal in every sense of the word. My left leg is not aboriginal and my right leg white. I can't consider myself anything but aboriginal'.[14]

McGuinness became the League's liaison officer in 1969, and initially enjoyed good relations with the Ministry. He worked hard on welfare work, educating the public and fostering black pride through a rudimentary black studies program at the League. He became co-director in 1971 and in April he argued unsuccessfully for a change in the League's name. McGuinness wanted 'Koorie' instead of 'Aboriginal' to be used, as he claimed the latter was 'derogatory'; he also claimed the word 'Advancement' was inappropriate as 'we are not seeking to advance in the white man's world, but to find the self-identity of our people'.[15] McGuinness was aware of international developments, particularly the Black Power movement, but eschewed violence, unlike certain elements in Sydney and Brisbane, which modelled themselves on the Black Panther movement in the United States. There was little such militant activity in Melbourne, although Michael Anderson had visited Lake Tyers and spoken about Black Power with little response.[16] Indeed, the League was daubed with metre-high Black Power slogans in December 1971, which McGuinness found disappointing, as the League was not an 'Uncle Tom' type organisation.[17]

However, McGuinness and others became militant over land. This issue came to the fore across Australia after the Gurindji walk-off from Wave Hill station in the Northern Territory in 1966. The climate for land rights was unsympathetic in Victoria, as Reg Worthy stated in an off-the-cuff remark in June 1968 that it would be of little value to give Aboriginal people land as they were not farming people, and 'within a year, 80 per cent of the land would be in white hands at a cost far less than the real value of the land'.[18] In early 1969 David Anderson, an Aboriginal mature-aged matriculation student from Mildura, called for compensation for land taken and minerals removed, based on land values at the time of settlement. The money could be placed in a trust fund for Aboriginal health, education and housing needs. The following year he called for the handing back of the Little Desert for a tourist area run by the Wimmera people.[19] In 1969 Doug Nicholls attended yet another John Batman commemoration—for Aboriginal people admired Batman as the one person who had dealt with them over land—but this time Nicholls wanted to give the treaty back. He pointed out that the promised ongoing payments had not been made. Bruce McGuinness said there were some descendants of Jaga Jaga, (a signatory of the treaty) living around Healesville who could be paid the back rent. Nicholls repeated this in subsequent years, asking for half a million dollars for a trust fund in 1972. Ray Meagher was less light-hearted about it this time and replied that as the treaty had been declared void by the British Government, nothing was owed.[20]

The Victorian Government seized some kudos when it announced in April 1970 that 1,600 hectares at Lake Tyers and 240 hectares at Framlingham would be 'permanently reserved' and held under 'perpetual licence' by two Aboriginal trusts, making them the second hand-back in Australia behind the Pitjanjatjara in South Australia. A large crowd of locals and dignitaries witnessed the Lake Tyers hand-back, the deeds being presented to Aboriginal elder Charlie Carter by the Governor Sir Rohan Delacombe. Carter declared: 'This is our land and we are proud of it. After all, you white fellows weren't the first to discover Australia—we were here first'. Doug Nicholls added: 'This is the biggest thing in the history of the Aboriginal people of Australia . . . We have fought for this with bitter experience but the winds of change are blowing'.[21]

However, the Aboriginal Lands Act (1970) proved divisive. The reserves were given to those registered as being resident there between January 1968 and October 1970 and the children of mothers so resident. The Minister could exclude any member of a family which had already received a grant for a house off the reserve. Adult members were allotted 1,000 shares and children 500 shares. Shares could only be transferred to the trust, another trust member, an immediate family member or back to the government at a price fixed by the auditor. The land was held under communal title, which prevented its sale if any one shareholder objected. Those not registered were excluded, causing 213 people to petition over rights to Lake Tyers they claimed were denied them as they had left before 1968. Many who protested were Gunai/Kurnai. They were aggrieved that they had no rights as traditional owners or as being born at Lake Tyers, whereas others from Ebenezer or NSW families who were living at Lake Tyers in the registration period, received shares. At

Framlingham a similar complex split developed between those with and without rights to the land, a spilt which exists to the present day.[22]

In 1970 Bruce McGuinness and others appealed to international opinion on the land issue. In July he wrote to the United Nations on behalf of the National Tribal Council, charging the federal government with trying to defraud Aboriginal people of land. He attended the Congress of African Peoples in Atlanta in September that year, which he described as 'more than useless to Australian aboriginals', but he met American land rights lawyers and claimed to have instructed them to sue a number of mining companies. By October 1970 there were

Charlie Carter receives Lake Tyers freehold title deed from Victoria's Governor, Sir Rowan Delacombe, July 1971. (A. & M. Jackomos Collection, courtesy of Museum Victoria, XP3666)

two Aboriginal petitions circulating at the United Nations, accusing the Australian government of genocide and demanding $5.3 billion in compensation and the return of all vacant crown land. Its five Aboriginal signatories across Australia included McGuinness and Stewart Murray.[23]

Action followed in February 1971 when twenty-two-year old Yorta Yorta man Lin Onus and ten others occupied sixteen hectares of the Sherbrooke Forest, a Dandenongs tourist spot. They demanded land rights and action over health and the preservation of Aboriginal culture. The League quickly endorsed the protest. John Newfong, its publicity officer, claimed the government tried to bribe it with much-needed funds to oppose the forest occupation, a view the government denied. Onus declared: 'We are determined this will not be just a rabble living idly in the forest. We will start a small aboriginal settlement with a view to becoming self-sufficient'. A painter himself, Onus suggested an artists' colony like that at Montsalvat might arise.[24] The Forest Commission threatened him and his co-camper Donald Bux with court action if they created a permanent occupation by erecting other than a tent. Locals showed support with food, and Aboriginal people visited at the weekend. A week later Framlingham people occupied the forest adjoining their newly won reserve and sent observers to Sherbrooke—they eventually regained Framlingham forest in 1987 but at the cost of a further split in the community.[25] Within a month Onus claimed that over 3,000 people had visited the Sherbrooke occupation. He built a round hut-like structure and Ray Meagher, the Minister, threatened action.[26]

In mid April a resolution over Sherbrooke seemed likely as Onus and Meagher had met and issued a joint statement that the campers had acted responsibly and with integrity. The 'roundhouse' was to remain for public use and a plaque placed in it, inscribed: 'Erected by a small group of Victorian aboriginals as a gesture of protest. Its message to all Australians is simple—aboriginals as citizens of this country are entitled to the opportunity to own the land on which they reside, thus enjoying the dignity of equality under the law'. Misunderstandings arose. Onus refused to budge without a written assurance from the government on land rights, while Meagher claimed Onus broke his word to move on.[27] In the early hours of 18 April 1971 the 'roundhouse' was destroyed by fire, Lin Onus and his friends barely escaping before the tar and paper structure was engulfed in flame. Onus claimed he heard two bangs and believed it was set alight deliberately. Police reportedly found pieces of three milk bottles stuffed with rags, as in a petrol-filled 'Molotov cocktail'.[28]

The Sherbrooke occupation was a seminal moment. The *Age* called the protest 'half-cocked' and without clear objectives, but admitted its success as a public relations exercise. It added—in words that would have pleased Onus—that the protest was 'a reminder that the problem of putting two civilisations into one continent has not been solved and cannot be ignored'.[29] A few days later McGuinness, as the National Chairman of the National Tribal Council, issued a claim for title to all reserves throughout Australia to be given to Aboriginal people, mining royalties to be directed to them and each to receive $15,000 compensation for white colonisation, managed by a trust and paid over twenty years. The policy, honed by Barrie Pittock, the Council's white adviser, was to cost $6 billion, two hundred times the annual Aboriginal Affairs budget.[30] All these demands of April 1971 preceded those presented at the now-famous Aboriginal Tent Embassy in Canberra on 26 January 1972.

While these events were unfolding, the League slipped into a financial crisis that killed any remaining cordial relations with the Ministry of Aboriginal Affairs. Funds became so short by February 1971 that the League could not pay wages for a time or meet other debts. Appeals went out to Aboriginal affairs at State and federal level for help but this was refused until an audit took place. McGuinness was trying to do everything: acting as director, manager, cultural officer, rabble-rouser and book-keeper and his skills at the latter were inadequate. McGuinness stated in December 1971 that when he was not being paid earlier in the year, due to the League's financial crisis, the League made his private car repayments. He admitted: 'I realise now that, for the purposes of book-keeping and accounting this was wrong. A few of my private accounts were met in this way and have since been repaid. We can account for all the money'.[31] Meagher refused to give any more grants until an audit was done. He also stopped the League from running a funding campaign in State schools in early 1972, which caused Bob Maza to call Meagher 'incompetent'.[32] The League's new treasurer, and only non-Aboriginal employee, Eric Weeks, said the League's financial problems were due to 'inexperience' and that the banning of the school fund-raiser was part of a campaign to denigrate it. It was 'Mr Worthy's way of hitting back at people who dare argue with him. His attitude is that the League should conform to his ideas of what is good for aboriginals'.[33] McGuinness stepped down to attend Monash University and Doug Nicholls came out of retirement to be interim director until Stewart Murray took over.

The Ministry and the Victorian Aboriginal political leadership were at odds from 1971. Worthy argued in his 1971 and 1974 annual reports that he and the Ministry sought to 'influence rather than control', but he had a vision of 'social engineering', which suggested a more direc-tive process on his part.[34] In 1974 he believed this 'engineering' was succeeding: the public were more aware of Aboriginal issues; Aboriginal self-esteem was higher; Aboriginal people were making a 'contribution to their own and to the general community['s advancement]'; and they were escaping 'welfare paternalism'. Worthy suggested the advances were due to his department, not to Aboriginal people. He hoped that Victoria would be the first State to 'be in a position to abolish any Governmental service set aside for Aboriginal people' and predicted it would be less than twenty years away. However, in his 1973 annual report he referred to tensions in Aboriginal affairs, of being 'damned if we do and damned if we don't'. Worthy gave a long list of scenarios, including: 'If we employ Aborigines they are accused of being "stooges"; if we don't employ them we are accused of denying them employment opportunities. Even on invitation, if we attend Aboriginal meetings, we are often abused and told to get out; if we don't attend we are accused of being disinterested in Aboriginal affairs'.[35]

In February 1974 Reg Worthy actually experienced this. He attended a meeting at the League to discuss a federal takeover of Aboriginal affairs. Stewart Murray pointed to Worthy and said: 'I did not invite that person here. If it was up to me I would toss him right out the door. He is a racist pig'. Bruce McGuinness also pointed and added: 'That man had done nothing to help Aboriginal people'. Both were unfair remarks, but understandable. They unsuccessfully urged the meeting to 'blacklist' Aboriginal people dealing with the Ministry. Worthy took the criticism and abuse for two hours, for which McGuinness expressed admiration. Reportedly Aboriginal people at times even 'rose to their feet and applauded Mr Worthy'.[36]

The Ministry of Aboriginal Affairs was far more consultative and benign than the Welfare Board or the Protection Board before it. Under Worthy it had taken definite action on child removal in 1968 and he had tried to foster independence and responsibility in people. However, it faced the winds of Aboriginal assertiveness and anger against a long

Dr John Beaumont tends to Jaymaya Atkinson at the Aboriginal Health Service, Fitzroy, 1981. (Courtesy of Fairfax Photos)

colonial rule. It was probably with relief that the Ministry transferred its functions to the Commonwealth Department of Aboriginal Affairs in December 1974.[37] After the 1967 Referendum and the election of a centralist Whitlam Labor Government in December 1972, the federal government was looking to administer the whole of Aboriginal Affairs in the country. However, while this federal department administered Aboriginal affairs from 1975, mainstream State departments actually operated health, housing, education, and other services for Aboriginal people—often with former staff and the same old attitudes. In 1982 the Victorian Premier's Department created an all-Aboriginal unit to liaise between the Victorian Government and Aboriginal Victorians. This still exists as Aboriginal Affairs Victoria but with a mixed staff, and has recently assumed important heritage functions. In the 1980s Victoria's Ministries of Housing, Health and Education also established Aboriginal advisory units.

Stepping out to Aboriginal autonomy

The struggles in Victoria against white authority strengthened the Aboriginal leadership and led to the birth of new Aboriginal organisations and a new confidence. As one young Victorian woman, Jill Johnson, wrote in the national Aboriginal magazine *Identity* in 1972:

> Before the whiteman came to this country our wise men were greater
> than the world's best scientists, our tribesmen survived in the most harsh
> conditions . . . but times have changed. We have to show the Europeans that
> we are as good as they are, even better. I am in a Black Studies Group which
> studies Aboriginal culture and reveals many astonishing facts about our
> people . . . Watch out whiteman, these Aborigines are stepping out.

The Black Studies Group she referred to was probably at Monash University's Aboriginal Research Centre headed by Colin Tatz. Johnson and other Aboriginal people were soon active in a growing network of Aboriginal service and community organisations.

Aboriginal organisations emerged in Melbourne from 1973 (following Sydney's lead), to provide services not otherwise offered, or only available in the mainstream where many Aboriginal people felt unwelcome. An Aboriginal Legal Service, Aboriginal Health Service, an Aboriginal Education Consultative Group and Aboriginal (Housing) Cooperative were formed in Melbourne by Aboriginal people, with the assistance of professionals—lawyers, doctors, dentists—some of whom provided their services free. Initially these organisations operated out of shopfronts in Gertrude Street Fitzroy, beginning on a shoestring with a small staff and struggling in their early years. They all performed multiple functions, providing welfare and emergency assistance beyond their legal, health or housing briefs. The Legal Service found places to care for alcoholics or endangered children, ran a hostel in Melbourne, and operated a funeral fund, assisting with the transport of deceased people for burial in country areas. Stewart Murray later created a funeral transport service through the League. These organisations were social and information centres as well, where people of all ages sat and yarned with fellow Kooris.[38]

Funding was a perpetual problem, making Aboriginal organisations dependent on the agreement of white bureaucrats. Jim Berg revealed how in the mid 1970s these organisations borrowed frantically from each other to pay the bills on a weekly basis and stay afloat until the next grant was approved. They also competed with mainstream services which received the lion's share of federal funding. By the early 1980s, governments agreed to channel most of the Aboriginal affairs budget through these bodies and not mainstream services, but this commitment has wavered over the years. In 1981 the Legal Service closed its doors due to a lack of funding, the federal government having threatened to direct its funding elsewhere, unless 'better' use of money was made. A director of the Legal Service, Mollie Dyer, returned her Order of Australia in disgust. Her story of the establishment and early years of the Legal Service is detailed in her *Room for One More—The Life of Mollie Dyer* (2003). This was by no means the last crisis. In 1995 the fraud squad investigated the Legal Service after a federal government report into many Aboriginal organisations across the country suggested irregularities, most of which proved to be inefficient rather than dishonest practice, although there were elements of the latter. Allegations arose against a so-called 'Koori Inc', whereby certain Victorian families dominated various organisations and favoured their own. This is not an uncommon story in community organisations, but does not necessarily suggest a corrupt nepotism. Members of the Aboriginal community certainly believed there was substance to these claims revealing the survival of family-based politics in Aboriginal Victoria.[39]

The history of these organisations is yet to be written but the work of the Health Service in the late 1970s was evaluated by Pam Nathan in her *A Home Away From Home: A Study of the Aboriginal Health Service in Fitzroy* (1980). Within a generation the Victorian Aboriginal Health

Service, now based in Nicholson Street Fitzroy, employed over eighty staff, including seven sessional doctors, who saw over 300 patients per week. The Health Service by then offered clinical and specialist consultations, dental, physiotherapy, optometry, mental health and drug and alcohol services, as well as a women's clinic, birthing program, children's, aged, home care and education services. It also conducted research. However, its CEO Tony McCartney in 2000 referred to 'cramped working conditions', up to five months waiting lists for dental work and stretched resources to provide over 35,000 consultations each year. The old issue of competition with the mainstream remained. McCartney stated: 'Taking account of government efforts to mainstream Aboriginal health services, it has become increasingly difficult to maintain service delivery amid growing demand and limited funds'. McCartney might have added that staff are paid less and often work harder than in mainstream bodies. The Health Service's old social function persisted, for he added that 'it is also a focal point for many community members to catch up with family and friends, and in this way fulfils a very important social purpose. As a community gathering place it plays a vital role in extending networks and strengthening community and culture'.[40]

These community and service organisations expanded across Melbourne in the 1970s and developed in the regions in the 1980s. Besides health, legal, education and housing services they also offered language and cultural programs and sport and recreation services. They grew in number from a few bodies in the early 1970s to about 150 Victorian Aboriginal organisations in the 1990s. Their number exceeds that today.

A typical regional organisation emerged in Sale in 1992 from the vision of a few families, including the Yarrams, Noongar immigrants from Western Australia. Bessie Yarram was related through marriage to the Flower family, Bessy Flower being one of the young brides brought to Ramahyuck Mission over a century earlier. Noel Yarram, a professional soldier, had once liaised with Sale Council, the local hospital and other bodies on Koori matters as there was no Aboriginal organisation in the town. After his death in 1989, his wife Bessie and daughter Daphne decided there was a need for an Aboriginal voice in Sale. They convened a meeting of local families and the group formed an organisation. The group met in Daphne's lounge room, then, as Bessie Yarram recalled, 'when she had two babies it went to my lounge room, then to my dining room'. After some years of scrounging furniture and with the help of ATSIC and the State Government, they gained a renovated building in Sale (upgraded and extended in 2003) and later acquired a warehouse for art and crafts and a small farm. The organisation is a blend of Gunai/Kurnai and Noongar talent, symbolised by the adoption (with Gunai/Kurnai permission) of the old mission's name—Ramahyuck—with a Noongar motto on its logo: *boon-ya-bur werna*, meaning 'to join us', set beneath two swans, one black, one white.[41]

Its founders did not want Ramahyuck to be a welfare organisation offering food vouchers and other hand-outs, preferring to refer people elsewhere. Instead, it focused on education and training, by running Community Development and Education Programs (CDEP), through which Aboriginal people worked for the dole, paid direct to the community, and often enhanced with other matching government moneys. In 2002 Ramahyuck's Board, representing 300 Aboriginal people in the area, and with the help of Dr Ali Khan, its non-Aboriginal CEO who had a management and development postgraduate degree, developed a corporate plan. Their vision was to make Ramahyuck a professional community organisation to provide health, employment and other services by establishing viable business enterprises. The plan's managerial tone referred to budget planning, quality assurance, information technology, human resources, customer service, public relations and other corporate 'buzz words', precisely the approach needed in many Aboriginal organisations if they are to succeed and obtain grants. It laid down plans for health, maternal and children's services, drug and alcohol education, home and community care, cultural heritage and business possibilities, including: joinery, screen printing, lead lighting, car detailing, lawn mowing, catering and diversifying produce from its farm.[42]

These organisations performed many functions, not least a social and cultural one. Charlotte Jackson who suffered terrible burns and scarring at Deniliquin when thirteen, had a difficult life, being removed from her family, and after hospitalisation, placed in the Cootamundra Girls Home. She later experienced unhappy, violent relationships with men and a broken marriage. She now attends the Wathaurong Aboriginal Cooperative in Geelong where she enjoys activities and friendships: 'I enjoy myself with the people, and I've got nice friends . . . I feel safe'. Charlotte Jackson is also finding her cultural roots. She remembered little about Aboriginal culture from her parents—Cyril Jackson of Cummeragunja and Isabel Whyman of Moonahcullah—before the death of her mother and her removal when aged thirteen. Charlotte Jackson was pleased when told recently that she is Yorta Yorta. She also keeps some Aboriginal artefacts on display in her home. After a difficult life, the Cooperative has made her 'happy and proud just to find out who I am. I walk around with my head up in the air now'.[43]

Nindeebiya Aboriginal self-help kitchen, Fitzroy, 1979.
(Courtesy Herald and Weekly Times Ltd)

Around the countryside regional communities are creating employment as well, aided by CDEP moneys. The Worn Gundidj Aboriginal Cooperative in Warrnambool, formed in the early 1990s, generated employment in several ways: by developing landscaping, lawn mowing, rubbish removal and a mechanics business. However, a member of the Cooperative, Robert Lowe, said these had little to do with Aboriginality, for 'we never, ever had a culture component in the business, so our heart and soul wasn't in it. We were survivin' but we wasn't surviving in a way where we could say: "Well we need to go out the back, dig a hole, and make a damper", because that component wasn't in the business, because the business was set up to be a business.'

In the late 1990s some rethinking occurred. Lowe stated that the community agreed to inject 'a compulsory, cultural component into the business and it has blossomed. We were reborn'. The move has boosted pride and identity. The floor of their conference room is now painted in Aboriginal designs representing message sticks and the symbols of men and women. Outside in the front court yard there is a large brick-paved turtle—Worn Gundidj. Robert Lowe explained:

> When you see the turtle's image, we always say, "You don't look at the turtle, what you're looking at is Worn Gundidj, and its satellites". Cos that's what

the turtle represents. The shell represents Worn Gundidj, and the feet and the head represents the satellites [Budja Budja, Winda Mara (Heywood), Tower Hill, Ballarat and Framlingham Trust]. And the symbols inside the shell, represents men and women, and they all work in the organisation'. The Cooperative currently produces a range of silk scarves, purses, bags, and other items silk-screened with local designs. It manages the Natural History Centre at the Tower Hill State Game Reserve. It also runs Worn Gundidj Environmental Services, which combines caring for country with employment, by revegetating and controlling weeds at mining sites, coastal zones and Framlingham's land. The Cooperative grows seedlings for these purposes and employs 120 people, mostly Aboriginal people, in all centres with CDEP help.[44]

Budja Budja Aboriginal Cooperative at Halls Gap is forging efforts at reconciliation as well. Its combined Health Service and Aboriginal Cooperative in 2004 offered services to all of Halls Gap's residents including visits by specialist health and welfare professionals from Stawell. These services were offered through partnership with main-stream health services in Stawell and funded by the Commonwealth government. Tim Chatfield, the Chair of ATSIC's Tumbukka region, is located there as well, which facilitates these partnerships. Budja Budja has just built a small gymnasium, the only one in town, to promote healthy living. In Budja Budja's new premises, non-Aboriginal people using these services rub shoulders in the waiting room with Aboriginal community members. Community relations have been strengthened by such simple human contacts. Local police have expressed interest in using Budja Budja's gymnasium and, instead of sideways looks, now acknowledge Cooperative members in the street.[45]

Many people who staff these Aboriginal organisations undertake enormous workloads. Bessie Yarram, mother of six children, also fostered 45 mostly non-Aboriginal children, over 35 years. Her husband Noel said: 'There is always room for one more'. She now receives calls from all over Australia, from young people who call her 'Mum'. ('Who am I speaking to'? she has to ask. One caller, a man now of 39, replies: 'It is your little black duck'.) Besides parenting so many and chairing Ramahyuck for eight years, in 2002 Bessie Yarram was a full-time regional development officer of Home and Community Care (HACC); Chair of the National Indigenous HACC Reference Group; on a State Advisory body for Senior Victorians; Chairperson of the Community Justice Panel and coordinated 'camps' for senior citizens and elders (that is, all elderly Victorians) to discuss health issues, the last attracting

An Aboriginal apprentice. (Courtesy of Herald and Weekly Times Ltd)

200 people. Bessie Yarram recalled: 'My Dad was a worker. We were taught that if you wanted something done you had to get up and do it'.[46]

The workload often leads to considerable stress. Sandra Neilson, who was a HACC and CDEP employee, now works at Ramahyuck as a drug and alcohol educator, and is studying for a tertiary qualification part time. She also serves on the local Community Justice Panel, negotiating with police over charges laid against Aboriginal people. Some of her workload occurs after hours. As Neilson commented: 'Someone might ring your home at 10 o'clock at night in a dilemma, so you sit there and talk to them for an hour or so'. She added: 'We have found the burn-out of Aboriginal people working in organisations is very high'.[47] Sociologists have recently coined new terms for this total commitment to work in one's community, calling it 'emotional labour' and 'obligatory community labour'.[48]

Brendan Edwards knows about 'emotional labour' all too well. He managed a drug and alcohol resource centre at Wathaurong Cooperative in Geelong and faced the gamut of problems experienced by some Aboriginal families: substance abuse, domestic and family violence, poverty and incapacity to make rent payments. Edwards threw himself into the job and 'it started to get to me'. There was no counselling to help him to avoid taking his work personally. Because of what he experienced each day Edwards shut himself off from his own family. It was a half-time job that he made full time. It became so stressful he had to give it up after two years. He now manages a CDEP outdoor work gang at Budja Budja Aboriginal Cooperative, Hall's Gap and is a cultural heritage officer for the south-west Wimmera. This story of exhaustion is repeated in many organisations.[49] Myra Grinter, who currently works in drug and alcohol education and in the courts for the Mildura Aboriginal Cooperative, said: 'We're expected to work 7 days a week, 24 hours a day. When it gets too overwhelming and I get too tired and emotionally drained, I take a break and go back into mainstream services'.[50]

These Aboriginal organisations are also vital sources of employment. A survey in 1994 revealed that community organisations provided a quarter of all Aboriginal employment, while another quarter was employed in government, perhaps mostly Aboriginal Affairs positions. Noel Couzens, whose family occupied the first 'New Deal' house at Framlingham near Warrnambool in 1938, is one who now works within the community after forty years of mainstream work in the farming, building, transport and cleaning industries. Seven years ago Couzens was severely injured in a road accident and was unable to work as before. However, he was offered part-time work as a cleaner under a CDEP scheme for Wathaurong Aboriginal Cooperative and Wathaurong Glass, Geelong, which assisted his rehabilitation. He now works hard and cooks hamburgers weekly as a fund-raiser for the Cooperative at a Geelong play group. Asked about work he said: 'I love it! It motivates you, you get up earlier. I've always been an early riser'.[51]

Since the creation and growth of CDEP work-for-the-dole, community-based employment, the numbers involved have climbed. An indigenous employment consultant recently estimated that, including the CDEP run by Aboriginal organisations, perhaps 80 per cent of all Aboriginal employment is provided by or through Aboriginal organisations, a figure paralleled by other anecdotal evidence. With the current Aboriginal unemployment rate at least three times the rate of other Victorians, this is a welcome contribution.[52] Besides, as Jamie Thomas, a drug and alcohol worker at Gunditjmara Cooperative in Warrnambool, remarked: Aboriginal people would 'rather work within their own community 'because it feels so safe, it's warm and friendly, you're with friends and your family is living up the road'.[53]

However, Aboriginal Victorians made impressive individual gains in a range of diverse mainstream fields from the 1960s. These individuals were held up initially as models of assimilation by the press and Aboriginal affairs, but most strived because they wanted to enter the wider world, not escape Aboriginality. In the 1970s young Aboriginal women, such as Muriel Harrison and Doreen Wise, successfully completed secretarial courses under bursaries, while Avis Egan of Robinvale completed a nursing qualification assisted by a Save the Children Fund scholarship. Robert Austin became a motor mechanic. Glen James, a trade teacher, was later a Vietnam Vet, AFL umpire and Victorian of the Year. Lois Briggs and Beverly Briggs became fashion models, the former working in television. Annabelle Charles and Marjorie Thorpe entered the Miss Australia Quest. When the latter had trouble with sponsors, 75 men of the 7th AIF Battalion came to her rescue with $131 in donations, as her grandfather had been one of the 'most honoured men in their battalion'. Mollie Dyer, daughter of Margaret Tucker, was appointed to the Victorian Equal Opportunity Advisory Council. Others became actors, including Monica Hoffman and Jack Charles. The latter, among his many roles, played Bennelong in Alex Buzo's *Macquarie* at the Melbourne Theatre Company in 1972. Charles also pioneered the Aboriginal drama group, Nindethana. Eric Onus, an old stager, appeared in episodes of 'Homocide'. In sports, as always, Aboriginal people excelled, Lionel Rose from Jackson's Track winning the world bantamweight boxing title in 1968 and being named Australian of the Year in 1969. The Mullett children from the same settlement—Cheryl, Linda, Sandra, Phillip and Russell—were top Victorian Badminton players by 1970. Australian Rules football increasingly experienced the magic of Aboriginal players, both Victorian and from South and Western Australia.

Doug Nicholls, Margaret Tucker and Reg Saunders were honoured with MBEs by the Queen in the late 1960s, Doug Nicholls being raised to a knighthood for which he and Gladys Nicholls travelled to London in 1972. In 1973 he was named 'King of Moomba'. The name of this festival was suggested by Bill and Eric Onus in 1953. Lin, Bill's son, revealed in 1969 that their suggestion was a joke, as *Moomba* was not an Aboriginal word for 'let's get together and have fun' as the Onus brothers had claimed, but came from the Aboriginal word *moom* meaning 'backside', with the 'ba' added for effect.[54] In 1976 Nicholls was appointed, at the age of 69, as Governor of South Australia by Don Dunstan's Labor Government. As always, however, it was hard for Aboriginal people to break through and be seen to do so on their own terms, rather than as 'fine representatives of their race', as the well-worn phrase went. Even Nicholls said, after he was sworn in in December 1976, 'It is a great honour not only for Lady Nicholls and me, but for the Aboriginal people throughout Australia'.[55] Gladys Nicholls calmly faced the prospect of being a governor's wife and Nicholls was excited, but the gloss was dulled when a television journalist asked how he would fit in with Adelaide's garden party set. Nicholls was naturally upset at the implication that he would not, and Aboriginal protests were vented at Channel 9. Unfortunately, Nicholls was forced to retire due to ill health after four months in the job.

Talented people continued to emerge in the 1980s and beyond. Eleanor Bourke became director of Aboriginal and Torres Strait Islander Services in the Commonwealth Department of Social Security in 1985. In 1983 Sandra Bailey was accepted as Victoria's first Aboriginal woman solicitor and barrister. In 1989 Ian Anderson became Victoria's first Aboriginal medical practitioner after completing a Bachelor of Medicine/Surgery. There is also a growing tradition of Aboriginal people in small business. As early as 1953 Bill Onus opened a boomerang-making factory and souvenir shop at Belgrave, running it successfully until Japanese-made boomerangs undermined the business in the late 1960s. His brother Eric and his wife Wynnie operated an Aboriginal art shop at Narbethong. Harold Blair ran another such shop at the Southern Cross Hotel, Melbourne, and Harry Williams ran one in Gardenvale for a time. In 2003 there were 26 small businesses run by Aboriginal people in the north-west of the State alone, mostly in tourism and arts and crafts, although one business person is a locksmith and another is in trucking.[56] Throughout Victoria there are currently about 250 sustainable Aboriginal small businesses assisted by the Koori Business Network, mostly operating in arts and culture, community services, consulting and, more recently, in agriculture and horticulture.[57]

Many Aboriginal people are also entering higher education. Graham Atkinson, a fitter and turner, entered tertiary studies after national service. He was one of only three Aboriginal people at Melbourne University in 1973 where he studied social work. Atkinson worked in Aboriginal administration before opening his own consulting business in the early 1990s. His brother Wayne Atkinson was one of the hundreds of Aboriginal Victorians undertaking tertiary studies in the 1990s. Wayne Atkinson proceeded to postgraduate studies and graduated as a PhD in 2002 with a study of the land claims of his people, the Yorta Yorta.

Workers at Bill Onus' boomerang factory, Belgrave, 1955. L-R: Eric, Wynn and Teddy Austin. (Courtesy of Herald and Weekly Times Ltd)

Troubles of family life

Such achievements were against the odds in the face of significant welfare and socio-economic problems, discrimination and family welfare issues. The latter remained a key issue despite Reg Worthy's declaration in 1968 that the removal of children would end. Worthy's policy did not affect those placed in care before 1968, those in crisis, or those who had made private arrangements about children.

Crises, when they arose, arose suddenly. Ray Marks recalled his mother Daphne's death around 1970, leaving his father Norman, a railway worker, to raise six children, the oldest daughter becoming the 'mother' at about fifteen. Instead of counselling Norman Marks and finding an Aboriginal solution to the crisis, the Welfare decided to swoop unannounced. When the children were at school they were called to the principal's office and promised a trip to the pictures. They left school in high excitement but were taken to 'Warrawee', a Ballarat children's home, instead. Norman Marks, on his return from work, found the children were missing. Marks eventually got them back through court action, to the eternal gratitude of his son Ray, who says his father will 'always remain in my heart' because of his efforts. Thereafter, the children stayed with their father, but were able to do so only with the help of Doris and Dick Kennedy, to whom Ray Marks is still deeply grateful. The Kennedys agreed to care for the children while Norman Marks worked, despite having nine of their own, revealing the Aboriginal commitment to children. Ray recalls seeing other Aboriginal children when in the Victoria Street Ballarat Orphanage: 'Clarks, Austins, Atkinsons—there was a big population of Aboriginal people there in the children's homes . . . we were related to some of these children'.[58]

Some Aboriginal families fought for their children in the courts, especially over private arrangements. A case involving young Donna Charles was particularly complex, and caused sensational reporting in the press. In September 1970 Fay Charles, aged 18, one of fourteen children of Noreen Charles of Kyabram, privately gave Donna, her 22–month-old daughter, into the care of Blanche and Kenneth Bausch who had six children of their own. It is unclear from press reports if the father, her de facto husband Anthony Bono, approved of this arrangement or not. In June 1971 Fay Charles had a second daughter, Liza, with Anthony Bono. A battle erupted in the Supreme Court in October 1971 when Charles wanted Donna back. Competing accusations and expert opinions were given. Doctors claimed Donna was malnourished before coming into the Bausch's care, while it was revealed that several of the Bausch's own children had convictions and two were placed in a reformatory. Reg Worthy gave evidence that 80 per cent of informal adoptions did not work. The court also heard from a social worker about the impact of removal on young children and that Donna seemed happy in the Bausch's care. Justice Stephen asked to see Donna and to hear evidence on whether she had 'distinctive Aboriginal features' to determine if this would have a bearing on the choice to be made. Worthy claimed she had 'Aboriginal' features and skin colour but, under cross-examination, agreed with the Bausch's lawyer that she could be said to take after her father, Anthony Bono, who was of Italian heritage. The press made great play of pictures of all the participants, including a beautiful, big-eyed Donna. To the Bausch's sorrow, Justice Stephen found in favour of the mother. A happy Fay Charles said that she and Bono, with whom she had lived for five years, would marry as soon as he got out of Pentridge.[59] In March 1973 a new battle erupted after Anthony Bono took the children from Fay Charles. This time, for reasons that are unclear, Fay Charles supported the Bauschs in their quest for custody of Donna and her sister Liza. The action was contested by Bono and some of the Charles clan.[60]

It is difficult to gauge what proportion of Aboriginal children were in white care at any one time. Possibly 200 to 250 of the 300 Worthy said were in white Victorian foster homes in 1968 were Victorian Aboriginal children, the rest coming from interstate. And Worthy made no mention of those in institutions. Perhaps a total of 350 Aboriginal Victorians were in white care in the late 1960s but we will never know until agencies and churches open their records. In 1967 the Welfare Board believed there were 750 Aboriginal children of school age (5 to 14) in Victoria, which would equate to a total of about 1,100 under 14.[61] However, Diane Barwick has shown that the Board always underestimated population figures and stated there were 3,000 permanent Aboriginal residents in Victoria in 1962, 50 per cent of them under 14.[62] By 1968 the number of children would have been close to 1,800. Therefore, if 350 Victorian Aboriginal children were not in the care of their families, this represents a removal rate at this time of close to one in five. This figure is corroborated by an Australian Bureau of Statistics survey in 1994, in which 15 per cent of 840 Aboriginal Victorians aged 25 and over reported being taken away from their natural family.[63] Given average Aboriginal life expectancy of about 55 years old, most would have been removed between 1950 and 1980. Sometimes all siblings in a family were removed: certainly all families were touched in some way through their extended networks.

The rate of Aboriginal child removal has varied since the 1869 Act. Levels were low before 1899, although children were still separated from reserve-dwelling parents by being placed in nearby dormitories. An 1899 regulation allowed removal of children of any age, and without them being deemed 'neglected', leading to the removal of between five and ten children yearly for several decades, or over 5 per cent of children.

Removals declined in the interwar period when the Board ignored Aboriginal people, denying that those of 'mixed descent' were Aboriginal. Most interwar removals centred on Lake Tyers. Removals increased from the 1940s, numbers being taken from families at Framlingham and Mooroopna, 24 being removed from the latter in 1956 alone. In 1958 the new Welfare Board listed 70 Aboriginal children in institutions, a removal rate of over 5 per cent, while those in private arrangements, which were then common, perhaps doubled the number. The Welfare Board's proactive assimilation policy after 1958 increased removals to over 15 per cent. Alick Jackomos, a field officer for the Advancement League, who was seconded to the Board in 1967, claimed in the early 1990s that the Welfare Board was 'an adoption agency'.[64]

The level of removal is almost impossible to fathom, something the Victorian Government admitted to the National Inquiry into the separation of children in 1996. Board records have been lost or destroyed, while other records (if they exist) are in the hands of private agencies and church homes which oversaw most removed children. An overall rate is difficult to estimate; rates were below 5 per cent before 1900, above it from 1900 to the 1940s, and closer to 20 per cent in the 1950s and 1960s, after which they declined to below 5 per cent once more. There were still between 250 and 350 children in foster care each year in the mid 1990s, accounting for about 3 per cent of Aboriginal children in the state, and the current fear is that the number is rising. In the twentieth century, with rates between 5 and 10 per cent for most decades and closer to 20 per cent in the 1960s, an average close to 10 per cent is likely; this is at the lower end of the National Inquiry's estimate of 10 to 30 per cent, but enough to touch every Victorian Aboriginal family.

The critics of the 'stolen generation[s]' have argued that many removals were in fact rescues. This was certainly true in some cases. However, before the 1970s, the authorities never considered that children should be placed with extended kin or other Aboriginal families. Their aim was two-fold: to take children from an Aboriginal family structure, seen to be in 'depravity', rather than just in poverty; and to take children permanently from families to end Aboriginality. The fall-out of the removal of about one in ten Aboriginal children from their natural parents over several generations since 1900 is incalculable. In 1974 Diane Barwick wrote that 'the majority of Aboriginal adults heading today's problem families—those most likely to lose their children—were themselves reared in institutions and have never known the secure affection of family life or experienced the socialisation processes of their own community'.[65]

In 1976 the Aboriginal Legal Service formed the Victorian Aboriginal Child Care Agency (VACCA) with Mollie Dyer as director. VACCA was to be an Aboriginal voice in the child welfare system and part of its story has been set down in Mollie Dyer's life story, *Room for One More* (2003). VACCA claimed that white fostering did not work and that 90 per cent of those fostered returned or were returned to institutions. It aimed to minimise the removal of children. Where placements were unavoidable, VACCA urged they be with the extended or other Aboriginal families and with white Victorians only as a last resort. In 1976 Hilary Islam, an Aboriginal woman, and her husband Frank were permitted to foster two children despite their temporary and cramped housing.[66] This indicated a changed attitude among child welfare authorities. In 1978 the Department of Social Welfare accepted VACCA as the official voice of the Aboriginal community on child welfare matters, and the 1984 Victorian

Adoption Act incorporated its placement principles.[67] VACCA, under Dyer's leadership, also supported non-Aboriginal families who cared for Aboriginal foster children and needed help on cultural issues or with counselling. VACCA also ran a 'link-up' service to reunite fractured Aboriginal families.

The public was made keenly aware of the personal devastation caused by child removals in cases examined by the Royal Commission into Aboriginal Deaths in Custody in 1988–89 which became daily news. The heartache was also vividly portrayed in the case of Russell Moore (James Savage), who was removed from his mother, Beverley Whyman (nee Moore) then aged fifteen, just after his birth on 31 January 1963. Beverley Moore and a family member consented to the adoption on 13 February under pressure from Welfare Board officers. She revoked the consent within the statutory thirty days, but was told that such revocation would not necessarily lead to the return of her baby and police action might follow her return home to Deniliquin for her sexual relationship with the baby's father. Under this pressure she signed another consent form. Russell Moore was adopted by a white family, the Savages, who moved to the United States in 1969 but returned in 1983, leaving their adopted son Russell in prison in the United States for car theft. Alienated and removed from his roots and his home country in Victoria, Russell Moore knew he was Aboriginal, but this had little meaning for him away from family, community and country. He was a group of one. Moore drifted into drug abuse and crime, eventually raping and murdering a woman during a drug-induced robbery in 1988. Presented with information about child removal the Florida Court commuted his 1988 death sentence to life in prison in 1992.[68] In 1990 Beverley Whyman and James Savage threatened to sue the State Government over the legality of the adoption, alleging coercion, but dropped the case.[69]

Singing couple Archie Roach and Ruby Hunter were both removed from their parents before the age of three. Their story has been told many times in the media, particularly Roach's personal pain, anger and alcohol abuse while searching for his identity.[70] Roach's moving song 'Took the Children Away'; theatre work like Jane Harrison's *Stolen*; and the institution of an annual national 'Sorry Day' have revealed the issue dramatically to other Victorians. The Victorian Government, unlike its federal counterpart, formally apologised on 5 April 2000 for past removals of Aboriginal children and expressed 'deep regret at the hurt and distress this caused'.[71] VACCA continues to focus on 'the physical, emotional, spiritual and cultural well being of Aboriginal children and their families', with special emphasis on children's rights to 'their cultural identity'.[72]

Fractured family life, and institutional upbringing or fostering provided poor modelling for parenthood for some Aboriginal people. Others must take personal blame for behaviour—violence and substance abuse—that affects family life. Some Aboriginal families remain vulnerable. The incidence of abuse and violence is under-reported and has existed within some families for a long time, as part of a syndrome of poverty, despair and alcohol abuse. A report in 1996, completed by the Monash University Koori Research Centre, found that Aboriginal women in Victoria suffered rape at four times the rate of other Victorian women and assaults at six times the rate.[73] Children are vulnerable to physical and emotional violence and, to a lesser degree, sexual abuse. In 1999, 2,010 Victorian Aboriginal children were reported as abused, mostly involving violence and substance abuse. Aboriginal children were ten times more likely to be abused than other Victorian children. In 2001 a Department of Human Services leaked report stated that while child abuse report rates had jumped 16 per cent in the general community in the previous four years, it had jumped 72 per cent within the Aboriginal community. VACCA reported that the numbers were so great that there were insufficient Aboriginal foster families to handle the case-load, so children were again being placed with white families, despite previous laws and agreements.

The problem of child abuse occurs across all social groups and is growing—in 2003 in Victoria there were 37,630 notifications.[74] In 2001 Sally Jo Sherger, a family services coordinator at the Mildura Aboriginal Cooperative, admitted that 'sexual abuse is rife and there is a type of collusion within the Koori community that is hard to break down. I'd be hard pressed to find a Koori girl in this community that hasn't been sexually abused. The issue is just too hard for us. Aboriginal people are so used to being branded as drunks and welfare cheats that it's impossible for our community to confront a serious problem'.[75] Sherger was correct, as little public discussion followed her comments, although local communities began to educate themselves, issue pamphlets about substance abuse, and create women's and men's support groups and family refuges.

Some Aboriginal youths and children are unruly and cause trouble. No doubt the colonial condition is partly to blame for this, but poor parenting and self-indulgence has also failed to instil them with goals, self-discipline and self-esteem. Drug and alcohol abuse is rife among some, who take little responsibility or show little regard for what they

'Sorry Day' March, Melbourne, 1997. (Courtesy Giuseppe Stramandinoli, ATSIC)

put in their bodies. However, efforts are being made to counter such destructive behaviour. In 2002 Albert Mullett, a Gunai/Kurnai elder, ran a week-long gathering at Windarra Camp at Buchan for forty boys and their fathers and elders. There was no television, 'pop' music, substances to abuse, or 'normal' youth culture, but bush and Aboriginal cultural activities and 'men's business'. The theme was learning and instilling respect for elders, law and all people. For the total cost of $4,500, which was difficult to raise from government, some youths had life-shaping ideas placed before them.[76]

The issue of violence against women was dramatically reignited by a series of accusations against Geoff Clark, the Framlingham-born head of ATSIC (1999–2004). Criminal charges against Clark for the rape of a cousin in 1971 were dismissed in the Warrnambool Court in 2000 due to a lack of evidence.[77] However, the *Age* in 2001 aired these rape allegations as well as those against another woman, producing an Australia-wide controversy and calls for him to resign, which split the Aboriginal community. Clark claimed it was 'trial by media' and an 'anti-Aboriginal attack' on him as a high profile leader, but he did not attempt to sue the *Age*.[78] A police investigation declined to lay charges, but court action in June 2003 and January 2004 enabled the women to undertake civil action against Clark despite the time lapse, a decision Clark is currently appealing.[79]

Clark's claims of victimisation have strong resonance within the Aboriginal community, for Aboriginal people have been victims of a smear campaign lasting 170 years, ever since early European settlers made false claims about so-called Aboriginal 'savagery'. The smear campaign grew into claims of general Aboriginal 'laziness', 'drunkenness' and 'intellectual inferiority' over the decades, claims which have been shown in earlier chapters to be unfounded. In recent times it expanded into 'welfare rorter', which again is erroneous, as Aboriginal people for a long time were considered too white for Board assistance and too black for social welfare. When welfare assistance was finally available to them many failed to receive it, being reticent about filling in forms and wary of authorities.

Clark was also found guilty in March 2003 of obstructing police in a fracas in a Warrnambool hotel. The hotel licensee in the case declared he would not serve Clark in future, a ban which could spread to 21 other hotels under a local licensing accord. Clark again cried victimisation, but the licensee, John Palmer, stated that of the six people currently banned from all Warrnambool hotels under the agreement, none were Aboriginal people.[80] Clark was suspended in August as ATSIC's chair by the federal government pending his appeal. In December 2003 his sentence was reduced on appeal to a $750 fine. Clark requested his reinstatement as ATSIC's chair in the Federal Court, which ruled in August 2004 that the Federal Government had acted unfaithfully and in a racially discriminatory way by suspending him. However, the intention of both major political parties to disband ATSIC (currently under challenge in the High Court) threatened to leave Clark without a job.[81]

Police and community attitudes

The history of colonialism in Victoria had been marked by police victimisation of Aboriginal people. In the nineteenth century police were local Aboriginal Protectors and in the twentieth century were often their controllers. Elizabeth Eggleston's 1965 study of Aboriginal people and the law revealed difficult relations with police. Alick Jackomos, who did voluntary work for the League, witnessed police victimisation. At Rumbalara 'it was common practice for the police just to walk into places there and a police patrol, the panel van, just drove around to arrest people'. Jackomos was harassed at Rumbalara until his identity was known.[82] Poor police–Aboriginal relations were corroborated by a study in 1980 by Greg Lyons.[83] In 1983 there were renewed stories of police harassment of Aboriginal youths, especially in Fitzroy. The drinkers at the Builders Arms received frequent visits and were called 'coons' by some police. Stewart Murray of the League called for more understanding of Aboriginal culture by police as there were only two Aboriginal members in the force at the time.[84] The State Government quickly formed a police–Aboriginal Liaison Committee. Len Clarke was appointed Aboriginal liaison officer in 1985 to establish more local committees, work with Aboriginal communities on crime prevention and lecture to new recruits—not always successfully—about Aboriginal–police relations. In 1988 the State Government formed community justice panels to minimise the detention of Aboriginal people for minor offences. They were staffed by Aboriginal volunteers who attempted to find alternatives to incarceration. Len Clarke left in 1989 after tensions over police and community support for his position as Aboriginal liaison officer. He was replaced in 1990 by Ken Saunders, who left three years later, claiming inherent racism in the police force.[85]

Evidence given to the Royal Commission on Aboriginal Deaths in Custody in the late 1980s, and the 1991 Human Rights and Equal Opportunity Commission National Inquiry on Racial Violence by Irene Moss and Ron Castan both found significant police violence and prejudice against Aboriginal people and over-policing of them in some areas. Their report called for sweeping changes in police procedures.[86] A 1992 Victorian study found Aboriginal people were apprehended by police at six times the rate of other Victorians, predominantly for public order and drunkenness offences (19 per cent of Aboriginal apprehensions), which almost outweighed the combined Aboriginal apprehensions for burglary, theft and car theft (22 per cent). There was considerable regional variation, with half the offences of Mildura's Aboriginal people being for drunkenness, while in Fitzroy drunkenness accounted for 34 per cent of offences; in Swan Hill, 31 per cent; and in Shepparton, 30 per cent. In Bairnsdale only 13 per cent of offences were for drunkenness, and in Warrnambool, just 4 per cent.[87] The regional differences were probably due to victimisation stemming from racism in some areas. Discussion with people in Mildura revealed claims of police victimisation, while police attitudes in Warrnambool were much better due to the approach of a particular officer who set a tone of consultation. While the RCADIC investigated only three Victorian deaths, they were all in police custody, and were found to be due to 'the archaic and ludicrous laws relating to drunkenness that still apply in this state'.[88]

These findings highlight the continuing importance of Community Justice Panels. A report in 1996 by the Monash University Koori Research Centre expressed concern that Aboriginal youths had detention rates six times that of other Victorian youths for 'minor summary offences', particularly indecent language and offensive behaviour.[89] It is hoped that the creation of a Koori Court in 2002 at Shepparton and later at Broadmeadows will have an impact on detention rates for public disorder and minor offences. The Koori Court was devised to be informal and culturally sensitive, with an elder sitting at an ordinary table beside the magistrate (not a court bench), offering cultural advice.[90]

Police mostly reflect community standards. Racism against Aboriginal people festered from the 1970s in the playgrounds, workplaces and lounge rooms of Victoria. Children were jeered as 'chocolate ice-cream' or 'burnt toast' by their peers. Schoolyards were, and still are, brutal places at times, but all of this is learned behaviour. Aboriginal children went home angry or bemused about name-calling and harassment when they first experienced it. Lynette Bishop, a Gunai/Kurnai woman who believes her life has been remarkably free of racism, still recalled a teacher at Bairnsdale who in 1975 used to tell anti-Aboriginal jokes and then turn around and say to the class in a sly and bullying manner: 'Oh, I hope we haven't got any blacks here'. Bishop said: 'I'd just shrink in my seat'. She also remembered that one of her children played happily with another kindergarten child until the family's Aboriginality was discovered. The next invitation to play extended by the Bishop family received a written reply: 'He won't be allowed to your house any more and don't bother contacting us any more'. The adult world's intolerance has poisoned many a

Postcard to register interest in becoming an Aboriginal Bail Justice, Department of Justice, Victoria.

young mind, yet in this case 'that young boy still sneaks around to see my son today', Bishop says.[91] However, the federal Racial Discrimination Act (1976) and the Victorian Equal Opportunity Commissioner have both influenced behaviour. The Human Rights and Equal Opportunity Commission in 1993 awarded $20,700 in damages to Murray Bull against Sale caravan park owners, the Kuchs. They would not rent Bull a van because he was an Aboriginal man. In court Mrs Kuchs gave evidence that Aboriginal people were 'non-Australian people'.[92]

Community racism was also evident in the now-famous incident involving the St Kilda footballer Nicky Winmar during an AFL football match against Collingwood in 1993. Winmar, suffering the usual football racial abuse that Aboriginal players receive from a partisan crowd, suddenly faced his abusers, lifted his shirt, pointed to his skin and yelled 'I'm black and I'm proud to be black'.[93] A period of soul-searching followed within Australian Rules Football circles, which led to a sea change in football on-field behaviour, backed by AFL Rule 30 introduced in 1995 to combat racial and religious vilification. It was upgraded in 1997 to included mandatory conciliation, education and fines.[94]

There are, of course, other problems within the Aboriginal community, which are in large part their own responsibility. A number of middle-aged people and elders I interviewed admitted to the presence of reverse racism—an Aboriginal prejudice against non-Aboriginal people. Aboriginal school children now give as good as they get, and often take the lead in abuse and name-calling. Some Aboriginal adults think the worst of other Victorians, rather than the best, and quickly stereotype them. To them, all *gubbahs* are materialistic, uncaring about family, greedy and hard-hearted. Most, however, deplore such attitudes as contrary to racial harmony. Many spoke about the problems of the current generation involving drugs, alcohol and crime, boredom, lack of discipline, aimlessness, and the influence of American television culture. There was also concern at the loss of respect for elders. Many thought the blame lay with some Aboriginal parents who allowed their kids to roam at night and could not be bothered disciplining them. Some thought police and teachers were too soft on wayward Aboriginal children for fears of cries of racism and victimisation, and thus the ill-disciplined became bolder.

Aboriginal responsibility

But there are positive signs. The Victorian Aboriginal Education Association Inc (VAEAI) in partnership with government, introduced in 1995

Koori Open Door Education (KODE) schools, of which there are now four in Victoria at Glenroy, Morwell, Mildura and Swan Hill. These are Aboriginal driven, community-based schools, offering education up to Year 10. They are controversial, concerns being expressed by both the Aboriginal and wider community about their standards and isolation from the rest of the community. The KODE School at Swan Hill was the initiative of VAEAI rather than the local Aboriginal community and currently has minimal local support. KODE schools do not suit all children but are important alternatives for certain families with significant domestic and unemployment issues and for Aboriginal children in foster families. These schools, attended mostly by Aboriginal children, provide positive environments and peer support, and openly acknowledge the children's home problems, seeking to deal with them to enable education to proceed. Sandra Stewart, one of those behind the formation of the Mildura KODE School in 1998, is adamant: 'It is a choice, it is not a dumping ground'. Stewart pointed out that the School was now giving cultural and dance performances at other schools. The Mildura KODE school had 70 enrolled by 2002 from fourteen families, mostly branches of several extended families.[95]

In August 2002 Marie Stopes International, a philanthropic organisation concerned with reproductive health, ran a 'Photovoice' program with Mildura KODE on the theme of minimising substance abuse and maximising responsible sexual practice—pertinent issues for all teenage children. In one week, thirteen KODE junior secondary students devised, photographed, processed, captioned and mounted a black and white photographic exhibition of over forty items, which was shown in the Mildura Council's Gallery. It was the 'most focused' the students had ever been on a project and twelve of the fourteen families attended a preparatory meeting. The photo panels were lively, funny, honest and hard-hitting. They contained mature messages and modelled responsible behaviour. Justin Williams captioned his photograph of a backyard party as follows: 'You need to get an education and settle down to a healthy life. Because people who do drugs and drink alcohol, they are not only hurting themselves, they are hurting other people around them'. Scott Hills captioned his photograph of water reflections: 'What it means to me is the reflections of the water could be like a reflection of your life. The smooth is when things are going calm. The ripple could represent all things that could happen. Like having a child at 15 and not knowing what to do and to miss out on your teenage years because you did not think of what the results could be from your actions'.[96]

The Victorian Aboriginal population has grown strongly in the last generation. In 1971 there were 6,371 Aboriginal and Torres Strait Islander people living in Victoria; there were 16, 570 in 1991 and 25,900 in 2001: an increase of 306 per cent over thirty years. This is due to a continued high birth rate, a lowered infant mortality rate, a preference for large families, better health, and a greater willingness for some people to identify as Aboriginal. Of these 25,900, about 20,000 people identified specifically as Aboriginal, most of them from Victorian families, the remainder being of Islander heritage. Around 1990 the Aboriginal population finally equalled that when the Europeans arrived 160 years earlier. The 2001 census revealed the indigenous population in Victoria was young, having an average age of 20 as opposed to the 35 years average of other Victorians. Half lived in Melbourne, scattered over most suburbs, but still with concentrations in Fitzroy, Northcote and Preston. Regional communities also existed mostly in traditional areas, the largest being at Morwell, Sale, Bairnsdale, Lakes Entrance, Lake Tyers and Orbost in the east; Geelong, Warrnambool, Portland, Ballarat and Horsham in the west; Echuca, Swan Hill, Robinvale and Mildura along the Murray; Bendigo and Mooroopna-Shepparton to the north of Melbourne and Healesville to the east.

Aboriginal life chances are now the best they have been since the European arrival, but are still not equal to those of other Victorians. Indigenous health is poorer, especially from heart and lung disease and diabetes, and their life expectancy is twenty years lower than that of others in the community. Domestic violence and substance abuse threaten family life. A survey in 1994 revealed that over half of those over thirteen smoked, and at least half were overweight or obese, far higher rates than in the general community. Their schooling rates to Year Twelve and tertiary education participation is less than half that of other Victorians. Aboriginal household incomes and home ownership rates are lower, unemployment levels three times higher and imprisonment rates over ten times as high. After 170 years of white settlement, Aboriginal people are still poorer, less educated, less healthy and more at risk from violence and death than other Victorians. This is a product of the colonial legacy, but is also somewhat of their own making. By looking to the future as well as to the past, and by taking responsibility, like the KODE children's exhibition suggested, Aboriginal people can create positive lives. Aboriginality can be a prison or a liberation, depending on how it is lived.

It is extremely difficult in such a diverse community to portray a typical Victorian Aboriginal family, as it would be to paint a typical non-Aboriginal Victorian family. The majority of Aboriginal people now live in suburban dwellings, indistinguishable on the outside from those of other Victorians of modest incomes. There are cars out the front—new ones for those with executive jobs in community organisations—and lawn mowers at work out the back on weekends. More Aboriginal houses are rented and they contain a higher percentage of low income and unemployed people than the Victorian average. While many older Aboriginal people live alone, most Aboriginal households contain extended families. About two-thirds of households have a non-Aboriginal member, but the children of mixed relationships mostly identify as Aboriginal—'Koori', as many now say. The furnishings inside are modest, purchased from the usual places, and most homes contain symbols of Aboriginality on the walls and mantelpieces—ornamental boomerangs, Aboriginal paintings, posters and indigenous artefacts. A few backyards have hearths for open fires to yarn beside. Families have crises and problems too, on average more than other Victorians as we have noted above. However, there is a different feel to the human interactions within the Victorian Aboriginal household—there are more young people, perhaps more noise and joking, and easiness about the passage of time, fondly called 'Koori time'. Friends and relations are often present, and there is a warm bond between people who call each other 'sis', 'cuz', 'uncle' and 'auntie'. What then underpins being Aboriginal in Victoria today?

17

Being Aboriginal

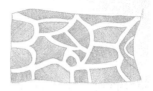

After six generations of European settlement, the colonial onslaught had done its work in Victoria. Indeed, well before the 1990s Aboriginal people were significantly remade in the colonisers' image, culturally, economically, and physically—a process to which they themselves contributed. The Aboriginal economy was quickly fractured by settler capitalism. Much Aboriginal cultural and ceremonial life had been undermined before 1900 by the attacks of colonialism, missionary activity and government control. Language was all but lost by the 1920s due to direct prohibition and the indirect power of English as the colonisers' tongue. Many traditions disappeared with the deaths of key elders. Aboriginal social structure was reshaped by inter-marriage between regional groups and, more recently, inter-marriage with non-Aboriginal people. A survey in 1994 revealed that two-thirds of indigenous families had non-indigenous members.[1] Intermarriage has diluted Aboriginal skin tones, leading some Victorians to doubt people's Aboriginality. However, as Sandra Neilson, a Gunai/Kurnai woman, stated: 'You don't stop being Aboriginal if your skin is lighter, as long as it's in your heart and you believe you are. It's basically an insult to Aboriginal people to ask them if they are half caste'.[2]

The Aboriginal world has been greatly altered since 1834, but not totally so. Aboriginal attachment to country, to cultural group and kin, to family and to Aboriginal core values remains indelible. Gestures, a sense of humour and an attitude to time and space that is peculiarly Aboriginal also survive. The experience of a shared history of injustice and life as victims of colonialism—the things that happened 'in them days'—also shape their sense of self. Above all, a belief in being Aboriginal—or Koori as many now say—remains fixed. Things that have been lost are being rediscovered and tradition is being reinvented, in the same way that humans have always used ideas of the past to shape their present. Despite the fluidity of identity, a deep sense of being Aboriginal remains. Sandra Neilson stated: 'You can tell another Aboriginal person straight away, even though they might not be really dark. It might be the way they are standing, the way they're looking, or even the way they speak, you just sort of pick it up'.[3] Many Aboriginal men greet each other with a special double hand shake—a clasp of thumbs, then hand.

Respect for ancestors

Like all people, Aboriginal people had a deep respect for the dead. In traditional times bodies of the deceased were treated in particularly reverential ways, either by reburial after a period, or even by the carrying around of a desiccated part of a child's remains (which fuelled colonial misconceptions about cannibalism). The spirit of the dead was helped on its way by purifying the last resting place with smoke.

In colonial times Aboriginal people's respect for the dead was violated by the zest of some whites for collecting relics and placing them in private or public museums. The viewing of such collections helped shape the colonists' sense of self, for they defined themselves as 'civilised', by knowing the 'savage'. Aboriginal respect for the dead and for relics of the past carried through the colonial period to become a highly contentious matter in the present as people battled with museums and academics over the ownership of cultural artefacts.

By the 1970s relics both in the ground and in museums became topical. Aboriginal people themselves expressed public concern over the loss of relics, but the initial push for action was by archaeologists with an academic concern for both Aboriginal and European relics. The Victorian Government passed the Archaeological and Aboriginal Relics Preservation Act (1972) which was orientated to the interests of archaeologists, but did include one nominated Aboriginal representative on its advisory committee. It allowed for the control and management of any land declared to be of Aboriginal importance, though instructing that private land could only be 'declared' with the consent of the owner. In 1975 an Archaeological and Aboriginal Relics office, which became the Victorian Aboriginal Survey, was established to survey sites throughout the State and it listed about 8,000 within a decade.[4] An amendment of 1980 made the National Museum of Victoria (later Museum Victoria) the usual place for safe-keeping of Aboriginal relics owned by the Crown.

Aboriginal people busy fighting battles on many fronts broadened their concerns to include relics in 1973 when the Advancement League protested that Alan Thorne and other researchers from the Australian National University and the National Museum of Victoria, had been working each summer on human remains found at Kow Swamp in 1969. The League demanded this 'desecration of our burial grounds' cease immediately and threatened an appeal to the Privy Council in London, then Australia's highest court. In 1974 the League also requested the return of skeletal and ceremonial material in the Museum to Aboriginal communities—but to no avail.[5]

The issue was revived in 1983 and 1984 when Jim Berg, Director of the Aboriginal Legal Service and a warden under the 1972 Act, took the initiative on the matter of Aboriginal relics. Berg, supported by the Act, seized a hundred Aboriginal artefacts listed for auction by Leonard Joel, sending collectors and auctioneers into a spin.[6] A prosecution failed and the Act was clarified in March 1984 to make it illegal to buy, sell or display (but not to privately own) Aboriginal relics without the minister's permission. The government also spent money buying sensitive items and encouraged Aboriginal groups to establish keeping places to store artefacts.[7] Berg promptly impounded 500 relics at the Museum as he claimed it had improperly arranged to loan artefacts to American museums, including the irreplaceable and very old Keilor skull and Kow Swamp material. It had also made loans to other institutions, including 400 to primary schools, without the consent of the minister in charge. Some of the loaned material had been lost or damaged. In court the Museum claimed authority to make loans under the Museum Act, but Justice Nicholson found it had acted wrongly, although in good faith, and ordered the return of all relics on loan within 48 hours.[8]

In May 1984 Jim Berg again served impounding writs, this time on another powerful institution—Melbourne University—for possessing a collection of Murray Valley skeletal material without ministerial approval. The University's collection was donated by a Gippsland grazier in the 1940s, Murray Black, who dug up and boxed the remains of 800 individuals between 300 and 14,000 years old. More remains were later found housed in Canberra. Melbourne University was ordered by the Supreme Court to remove the collection to the Museum by August where a committee would decide its fate.[9] When Jim Berg indicated that the Aboriginal community wanted the remains reburied, the archaeological community panicked that valuable material for scientific study would be lost. A debate developed over whether the bones belonged to Aboriginal people or humanity in general. Both sides wanted protection, but

Gary Murray, carrying baby Jaara's remains, leads other DjaDjawurrung elders at a hand back ceremony, Bunjalaka Gallery, Museum Victoria, September 2003. (Craig Sillitoe/Fairfax Photos)

while Aboriginal people wanted to protect the spirit of the remains, archaeologists wanted to protect them for science.

Sacred sites also caused concern. In November 1980 Aboriginal protestors in Portland unsuccessfully tried to stop bulldozers levelling land for an aluminium smelter. After a protracted court battle against Alcoa launched by Sandra Onus and Christina Frankland, the Supreme Court ruled in February 1982 that Alcoa had to protect five sacred sites near its smelter.[10] In 1984 the relics issue spilled over to sacred sites when the government contemplated accepting a committee's recommendation—with a majority of Aboriginal members—that the government assume ownership of all Aboriginal relics and remains, both in private possession and on private land. It was claimed that some farmers were hiding or destroying sites out of fear of a loss of control over their land.[11] Federal legislation in 1984, the Aboriginal and Torres Strait Islander Heritage Protection Act (and a 1987 amendment), was applied to Victoria, giving Aboriginal communities control over access to sites, excepting those on private land. In 1985 a Wurundjeri Tribe Land and Compensation Cultural Heritage Council was formed to help manage sites remaining in the Melbourne region.[12]

Finding a resolution over relics and remains took some years of heated debate and soul-searching. By 1989 it was agreed that 1,240 items from the Murray Black collection, including 127 remains from Coobool Creek indicating head-binding 14,000 years ago, were to be returned to six communities for reburial. Some archaeologists still found it hard to accept, arguing the significant Coobool Creek remains were 400 generations removed from present people. Aboriginal people were unmoved, despite always being ready to accept the benefits of scientific analysis, which proved the great antiquity of the remains. A year later the remains of a hundred individuals found at Kow Swamp were handed back for reburial. In early 1992 Mungo woman, a 27,000 year-old individual (a recent dating claims an age of 40,000), was also handed back for reburial just north of the Murray.[13]

Aboriginal attention has turned recently to overseas museums and universities that hold remains, an estimated 6,000 items being held in Britain alone. Some spectacular returns have occurred, mostly involving other States: Yagan's head, Truganini's hair and skin samples and beads. In 2003 a British working group recommended changing British law to allow the repatriation of culturally sensitive remains. The process of hand-back continues as Museum Victoria is still repatriating material. In September 2003 the body of a girl taken from a hollow tree at Charlton in 1904, who had died fifty years earlier, was named and reburied in a tree in home country by elders of the DjaDjaWurrung. The following November, members of the Kirrae Whurrung clan gathered at Framlingham to bury the remains of 174 people, returned after a ten-year campaign directed at museums in Australia and overseas.[14]

Respect for land

A respect for land as the source of our sustenance, livelihood and wealth is inherent in all cultures. The space that is called 'home' or 'country' is also the source of our cultural and often spiritual inspiration, and this applies for all people. However, Aboriginal people traditionally had a peculiarly intense and symbiotic relationship with particular country of which they were spiritually a part, to which they were bound by totems and by their responsibility as custodians. Land, people and the great ancestors were fused together, as recorded in stories, paintings and ritual. This traditional relationship continued into the colonial period and, although totemic ideas and ceremonies about land faded over time, a special and spiritual relationship to country continued, often focused on a reserve. When people were moved to or from reserves, they maintained attachments to land, sometimes forming additional ones due to

Wayne Thorpe leads a welcome dance for the thirty-year anniversary celebrations of the Lake Tyers hand back, July 2001. (Courtesy ATSIC)

marriage or their new place of residence. With the loss of reserves or removal from them, people have often broadened their land affiliations back to the wider country of their forebears. Land lost in the colonial period also assumed the importance of a great injustice and people fought to regain it.

Efforts to regain land intensified from the 1970s. The Sherbrooke Forest protest of 1971 discussed earlier was followed by claims over Crown and local government land at Collingwood in 1973. The Liberal Government was unresponsive, but the following Cain Labor Government proposed a land tribunal in 1982. A South Eastern Land Council was formed in that year, which claimed a traditional camping site at Clifton Hill, and groups around the State claimed another thirty sites.[15] The government gave 1.1 hectare of land in Watt Street Northcote to the League for a community centre, and planned to hand over the Framlingham forest and other land once a Land Claims Bill became law. But many Aboriginal people believed the Bill did not go far enough. The Liberal Party opposed it as well, claiming outside influence on Aboriginal people and fears that forty per cent of the State could be claimed. As the Bill only applied to State Government land and protected current leaseholders, these were ignorant claims, but strong enough to end the Bill's life.[16]

Since then there have been further hand-backs of small parcels of land. In 1985 forty hectares of land at Lake Condah were returned and the Winda Mara Cooperative there is currently working towards world heritage listing for its ancient eel traps through the Lake Condah Sustainable Development Project. The vision is one day to rebuild St Mary's Church, dynamited in the 1950s.[17] In 1987, 1,130 hectares of the Framlingham Forest was returned with the help of legislation passed by the Federal Government, adding to the land handed back in 1970. In 1992 Manatunga land was given to the Aboriginal Cooperative in Robinvale. In the 1990s, negotiations with a local landowner finally produced access for the Gunai/Kurnai for repairs and visits to the Ramahyuck cemetery. However, from the early 1980s a conservative backlash over Aboriginal land claims descended over Australia, making such progress hard. It was exacerbated by the High Court decisions in the Mabo (1992) and Wik (1996) cases, leading to anxiety and hard fought legislative responses.

In the Mabo case over a Torres Strait island claim, the High Court ruled in June 1992 that 'the Meriam people are entitled as against the whole world, to possession, occupation, use and enjoyment of the lands of the Murray Islands'. In doing so, it upheld that native title had not been extinguished by the act of possession and settlement in 1788 and that *terra nullius*, the belief that Aboriginal people were 'too low in the scale of social organisation to be acknowledged as possessing rights and interests in land', was not part of the common law.[18] Eighteen months of hysteria and misinformation followed, before federal native title legislation was passed in late 1993, creating mechanisms for native title claims.

In July 1993 the Yorta Yorta people filed a claim with the High Court for a massive 4,000-square-kilometre area of Crown land, State forests and waterways straddling the Murray River from Cohuna to Tocumwal. The thousand Yorta Yorta, 200 of who still lived at Cummeragunja on the Murray's north bank near Barmah, believed they had a very strong claim. Their spokesman, Bill Belling, stated: 'People have maintained their connection with the land'.[19] But native title demanded a 'continuous' link with the land. Would that be found to be the case? About 300 parties—farmers, graziers, timber cutters, fishermen, local councils and two governments—registered as interested parties in the case. A year later, in compulsory mediation, the Yorta Yorta appealed for an out-of-court settlement, but by then the local community was deeply divided. The Yorta Yorta's claim was large and provocative, claiming ownership of minerals, natural resources and the right to exclude others or any actions that might damage land over a wide area of public land

and parts of the Murray River. The Yorta Yorta claimed the right to
control and hold a veto over a proposed board of management. The
mediation over this ambitious claim inevitability failed and the road led
to the courts. The conservative State Government decided to oppose the
claim and became the main respondent in the case.[20]

Aboriginal infighting created complications for this and other claims.
The Bangerang, based in Shepparton, were unhappy with the Yorta Yorta
claim. Spokesperson Richard Atkinson thought it was inflammatory to
whites and was angry that it also made claim to Bangerang land in the
Goulburn Valley.[21] Another Bangerang spokesperson, Eddie Kneebone,
added: 'We are not asking for control, we are asking for official recognition as the descendants of the original occupiers of the Goulburn
Valley region'.[22] Four other native title claims in Victoria were initiated
by groups over the next few years: by the Gunai/Kurnai, the Gunditjmara, the Wotjobaluk and by groups based at Robinvale. Most of these
claims over local areas created long running controversy, tension and
bitterness between local Aboriginal groups. In December 2003 there was
still a row over boundaries between the Daungwurrung, Boonwurrung,
DjaDjaWurrung and the Wurundjeri (Woiwurrung). Most Aboriginal
informants I interviewed in 2002 believed that native title was utterly
divisive. Mark Matthews wisely commented that the three communities
in his area that were fighting over land should put in a joint claim and, if
successful, fight over the bits and pieces, 'because they are fightin' over
something they haven't got yet'. Ivan Couzens, an ATSIC representative
simply said: 'Native title, it stinks'.[23]

Five years and five months after the Yorta Yorta case was first registered,
Justice Howard Olney handed down a decision in the Federal Court in
December 1998, after hearing 201 witnesses on 114 sitting days, who
gave 11,664 pages of transcribed evidence. Justice Olney rejected the
large Yorta Yorta claim in a 75-page judgement. He discussed at length
three tests for the existence of native title, being: that the current group
are proven descendants of the indigenous group who occupied the land
prior to the assertion of Crown sovereignty; that the traditional laws and
customs of this original group in relation to their traditional land can be
established; and that the traditional practices and connection to the land
have been substantially maintained.

Olney found that of the eighteen named people in the case from
whom the current Yorta Yorta are descended, only two could be confidently traced to the indigenous group of the area in the 1840s (for all
intents and purposes, at the moment sovereignty was asserted: that is, at
1788). And while Olney established the laws and traditions that existed

in the 1840s through the writings of a squatter, Edward Curr, and the Chief Protector of Aborigines in Port Phillip, George Augustus Robinson, he argued these laws had ceased to be practised by 1881. Indeed, Olney argued directly from the 1881 petition for land of the Maloga people (discussed in chapter 13) which was used as evidence by the applicants. He found that this petition revealed that the Aboriginal petitioners believed they had been dispossessed, and it showed they no longer practised laws and customs based on tradition in relation to land, and indeed sought to be farmers like Europeans. He stated: 'The tide of history has indeed washed away any real acknowledgement of their traditional laws and any real observance of their traditional customs. The foundation of the claim to native title in relation to land previously occupied by those ancestors having disappeared, the native title rights and interest previously enjoyed are not capable of revival'.[24]

The judgement revealed the problems of the legal doctrine of 'native title' for Aboriginal people living in long-settled Australia: the fact that people moved or had been moved around; the fact that pastoralism and settlement had undermined their economy; and the fact the people embraced or had been forced into a different economic mode, such as agriculture. This definition of native title created in the Native Title Act has been termed 'repressive authenticity', that is, only so-called 'real' (traditional) Aboriginal people can win claims. It also revealed that other aspects of Aboriginal culture besides those connected to land practices—and changing cultural practices within the framework of Aboriginal identity—are of no account in law in determining native title. So while the Yorta Yorta people still have a strong sense of kinship, of adherence to Aboriginal core values, of identification as Aboriginal— being recognised (and discriminated against) as such by those around them—this could not be taken into account when judging 'continuity' under existing native title definitions.

The Yorta Yorta appealed, but in February 2001 the full bench of the Federal Court upheld Justice Olney's decision. However, the Victorian Bracks Labor Government offered to negotiate.[25] The people welcomed this gesture but decided to appeal to the High Court. However, in December 2002, almost a decade after the claim was first filed, the High Court upheld the Federal Court's decision in a five-to-two decision. The majority argued that the 'forbears of the claimants had ceased to occupy their lands in accordance with traditional laws and customs'. The dissenters, Justices Michael Kirby and Mary Gaudron, argued that traditional connection did not have to be continuous; the important thing was that they continued to identify as members of a community.[26]

The Yorta Yorta were bitter and shocked by the legal decision. Local landowners were relieved, but were not inclined to rejoice in public, sensing the depth of Yorta Yorta grieving. One compensatory factor was that the Indigenous Land Corporation purchased 259 hectares of Murray River farmland for the Yorta Yorta in late 2000 to transform into bushland. The Bracks Government also proved willing to negotiate as promised, which culminated in an agreement in May 2004, which was signed off the following month. The Yorta Yorta and the Bracks Government reached a management agreement, whereby the community will have a majority on a Board to advise the Environment Minister on the management and protection of public lands in a designated area. Their status as the original owners will also be recognised.[27] However, the Bangerang people, who favoured negotiation over land in the first place, and whose lands were part of the claim, were left out of the deal by a Government Minister listening only to the most vocal.

Meanwhile, at least one family chose to avoid the native title process and gained a small piece of land through purchase by the Indigenous Land Corporation. The Chatfield clan of Gunditjmara and Djap Wurrong descent gained 800 hectares as freehold at Mount William Creek between Lake Fyans and Stawell. The land, which they named 'Martang'

Yorta Yorta claimants Monica Morgan (speaking) and Wayne Atkinson (on her right) outside the Federal Court in February 2001, photographed by Giuseppe Stramandinoli. (Courtesy ATSIC)

meaning 'white clay', contained 27 Aboriginal sites. It was able to carry up to 5,000 sheep, but Tim Chatfield said: 'It's not there to make a profit or make us a million dollars, it's there to break even so we've got a place to go and have time out among ourselves as family . . . and for training especially the younger members of our family in shearing or whatever'.[28]

While the Yorta Yorta risked court, the Wotjobaluk followed more modest claims through negotiation under the Native Title Act (1993). In 2002, this group and the Victorian Labor Government agreed to a grant of non-exclusive native title rights to hunt, fish and camp along the Wimmera River (much like the rights enjoyed by the public); an advisory role in managing national parks and Crown lands in certain areas; and freehold title to 45 hectares. The Wotjobaluk would be recognised as traditional owners. The agreement would also declare that exclusive native title rights did *not* exist over 98 per cent of the land claimed, to bring certainty to land use in the region. The agreement needed ratification by the Federal Court. A Federal Government lawyer intimated in October 2003 that the Federal Government may oppose the deal, following the Yorta Yorta case's reasoning, that the evidence for native title was not 'strong'. However, in November 2003 the Federal Government backed the deal and other parties fell into line, making the Wotjobaluk the first acknowledged native title holders in Victoria, a decade after the passage of native title legislation. Spokesperson for the group, Jennifer Beer, said it would be the first stage in rehabilitating Wotjobaluk law, customs and language.[29] Ten other native title claims in Victoria are still in process.

Respect for tradition

Tradition is what cements families, groups and societies. It was and is especially important in a society that has lasted for over 40,000 years and at least 1,500 generations. This does not mean Aboriginal society was unchanging in the past, for all the evidence of the archaeological record shows that it was dynamic and went through enormous changes in technology, from a stone to a wood and bone tradition, and from low to more intensified food-gathering strategies. Changes in technology and climate also meant developments in culture. However, these developments respected the continuities of culture. Due to colonisation much tradition has been lost or abandoned. Conversely, important core values have remained and culture is being revitalised and even reinvented. The later process is ongoing in all cultures. Indeed, the historian

Hugh Trevor-Roper has revealed that even the revered Scottish clan tartan designs were largely invented by woollen manufacturers in the nineteenth century, yet are now highly valued as 'traditional' symbols.[30] The symbolic nature of culture underpins its continual reinvention. Anthropologist Jocelyn Linnekin has written that a shift in thinking now rejects 'the objectivist concept of culture as a thing-like bundle of traits amenable to scientific description, and [shows] an increasing tendency to view culture as symbolically produced or "constructed" in the present'.[31] Tradition is valued highly in a society with a four millennia heritage, and Aboriginal organisations across the State have emerged in the last twenty years to protect and further this great tradition.

Jim Berg's cultural awareness was heightened by the battles over Aboriginal skeletal remains as outlined above. In 1985, Berg, together with lawyers Ron Merkel and Ron Castan—his non-Aboriginal friends from the Legal Service—established the Koorie Heritage Trust. Its purpose was initially to store returned skeletal material, but the Trust was soon part of an exhibition space at Museum Victoria, where an exhibition, 'Koorie', celebrated the survival of Aboriginal culture in Victoria. 'Koorie' (which also became a book of the same name in 1991) was moved to the Trust's own building in Flinders Lane in 1999 and elements of it reappeared in its new multimillion-dollar exhibition space in King Street in 2003. Over the years the Trust established a remarkable collection of 600 pieces of contemporary Koori art, 10,000 artefacts, a research library of books, documents and 50,000 photographs, and an education service, all serviced by over a dozen staff. Ongoing funding has not always been abundant, but the new cultural centre was built with money from ATSIC, the Community Support Fund, and from the Gandel, Pratt and Castan families.

The Trust's 'rival' is 'Bunjalaka', the Aboriginal gallery within the new $290 million Museum Victoria, opened in October 2000. 'Bunjalaka', the first gallery in the Museum's history dedicated to indigenous exhibitions, was developed with the input and cooperation of the Aboriginal community, channelled through a community-based advisory committee. Indigenous staff members devised the exhibitions. The gallery was meant to be thought-provoking and received significant criticism from conservative commentators when it opened.[32] Its exhibitions feature the voices and stories of Aboriginal people and their ideas about identity, law and the land in a series of present-centred, not past-focused, presentations. A wax anthropologist sitting at a desk was placed in a glass case for viewers to observe, to indicate his observations are another form of knowledge-making, but do not necessarily represent

Thelma Carter making a basket at Lake Tyers, 1975, photographed by Alan West. (Courtesy of Museum Victoria, XP2625)

truth. 'Bunjalaka' also provides internal and external spaces for Aboriginal people to meet, bringing the past and the present together in a dialogue. As research student Tiffany Shellam has recently written, 'museums have become places of authority for indigenous people'.[33]

Aboriginal communities are also empowered by the creation of their own regional keeping places and exhibition spaces. The Krowathunkoolong Keeping Place and Museum at Bairnsdale was opened in 1994 through the efforts of the Gippsland and East Gippsland Aboriginal Cooperative. The centre houses artefacts and Gunai/Kurnai contemporary art and craft, fosters pride in Aboriginal culture, and presents it to the wider community. Keeping places and cultural centres exist in many regions, including: the Dharnya Cultural Centre of the Yorta Yorta at Barmah, and Brambuk Cultural Centre adjoining the Gariwerd/Grampians National Park of the DjaDjaWurrung and Djap Wurrung. Like Dharnya and Krowathunkoolong, Brambuk offers exhibitions and culture tours, has a video display, boomerang-throwing and craft classes, and a restaurant offering bush tucker. It also runs rock art tours. All these places foster Aboriginal identity and employment. Ray Marks and his two sons, Sonny and John Secombe, worked at Brambuk in 2002. He showed them songs and dance and they taught themselves didgeridoo. The didgeridoo is not a traditional Victorian instrument, but one embraced by the people here in recent times through interaction with Aboriginal people from up North.[34]

Aboriginal creativity has blossomed along with this reassertion of culture. Life stories are increasingly being told. Alick Jackomos and Derek Fowell produced *Living Aboriginal History in Victoria—Stories in the Oral Tradition* (1992) and Bruce Pascoe edited Wathaurong *Too Bloody Strong* (1997). Recent individual accounts include: Iris Lovett-Gardiner, *Lady of the Lake* (1997), Robert Lowe, *The Mish* (2002), Banjo Clarke, *Wisdom Man* (2003), and Mollie Dyer, *Room for One More* (2003), all of which were assisted by co-writers. Others explored their Aboriginality in plays, which were stimulated by the creation of Ilbijerri in 1990, an indigenous-controlled theatre company. Ilbijerri commissioned *Stolen* (1998), a powerful play about the removal of children. In 2002 Ilbijerri and the Playbox presented 'Blak Inside', a series of six exciting, challenging and deeply moving productions, written, acted and directed by indigenous people born or living in Victoria. One of the six by playwright Richard Frankland, entitled 'Conversations with the Dead', revealed the trauma of the Royal Commission into Aboriginal Deaths in Custody. Frankland has also produced thirteen short films, some winning awards.

Aboriginal music has blossomed as a new cultural creation drawing on diverse styles and Koori ideas. Richard Frankland has written songs and performed with 'Djaambi' (brother) in the late 1980s. This group inspired Koori women to form 'Tiddas' (sister), which performed in the 1990s and recorded five CDs.[35] There are other Koori bands in Victoria. Songlines Aboriginal Music Corporation, formed in the mid 1990s, promotes such Aboriginal music and protects its rights.

Aboriginal music is widely appreciated in pubs and on mainstream radio, but is played most solidly on radio 3CR, which hosts 'Koori Survival', 'Rap Attack' and 'Koori Youth'. The program 'Koori Survival' was begun in 1976 by Gilla McGuiness and others, and he and his son John, who writes Koori music, still host it. The two put a Koori voice on the airwaves, broadcasting positive community news and views, often in opposition to the Aboriginal establishment of ATSIC. Their message reinforces Aboriginal culture. Gilla McGuiness recently commented:

> We need to make things happen so pathways are available for all youth: to get out of poverty, get out of drugs and alcohol and unemployment. If you're going to teach young people, you've got to show them the way. I had good elders, good direction. That's what it is all about. Put it this way: I grew up in Fitzroy. Johnny grew up in Fitzroy. We're blackfellas. I'm 44, he's 23 and neither of us has a criminal record. To come up in a down-and-out place

with your people and not have a criminal record, that means you're doing something right. We need to show the way.[36]

The Koorie Heritage Trust encourages the production of contemporary Koori art from south-eastern Australia, and collects the works of many artists, including the late Lin Onus. His work, presented in a 2000–01 retrospective entitled *Urban Dingo*, epitomised the essentially political nature of the Aboriginal renaissance and its cross-cultural resonance. Onus, son of Bill, a Yorta Yorta man, and Mary, a Scottish woman, brilliantly reconciles Aboriginal and Western themes and imagery in his art, producing a seamless new creation with both political and humorous intent.[37]

This cultural renaissance has extended to education and language. In 1983 Worawa College, an Aboriginal boarding school, was opened by Sir Doug Nicholls in temporary premises at Frankston before moving to a permanent site at Healesville. The opening celebration ended with singing led by an ageing Nicholls and elders and sisters Margaret Tucker and Geraldine Briggs. Worawa (meaning eagle) was the inspiration of Hyllus Maris, an Aboriginal educationalist. Maris was also co-writer-producer of the groundbreaking four-part video series, 'Women of the Sun', winner of the United Nations Media Peace Prize (1983). The College began with about thirty students and continues to thrive, offering mainstream subjects combined with Aboriginal culture—songs, dances, art, history and language. The Yorta Yorta language is taught there and a 200-word dictionary has been researched and compiled by the students. Hyllus Maris's mother, Geraldine Briggs, provided the cultural teaching for the first decade and her place was taken by her granddaughter, Aretha Briggs.

In 2004 Wowara will offer a new VCE subject, 'Indigenous Languages'. Students will research and study one of five languages. Students at other schools can take the subject with Aboriginal community approval, as community involvement is essential.[38] This subject builds on renewed interest in Aboriginal languages. The Victorian Aboriginal Corporation for Languages was formed in 1994 to manage a national indigenous language initiative, especially aimed at language retrieval and promotion. There are currently four language programs across Victoria and much research is being done. The aspiration is for future generations to speak a Victorian language. A number of languages can potentially be revived from material in the archives, preserved and documented by missionaries, Protectors and other interested nineteenth-century Europeans. Woiwurrung grammar, vocabulary and phrases were

Margaret Tucker tells young members of the community what it was like 'in them days'.
(Alick and Merle Jackomos Collection, courtesy of Merle Jackomos)

meticulously recorded in the 1840s by William Thomas, the Protector, and located in the report of the 1859 Parliamentary Select Committee on Aborigines. Isabella Dawson, daughter of James Dawson, collected the Dhauwurd Wurrung language from the people of the Warrnambool region in the 1870s and recorded it for posterity. Ian D. Clark and Toby Heydon recently produced, on behalf of the Victorian Aboriginal Corporation for Languages, a *Dictionary of Aboriginal Placenames of Victoria* (2002).

The Aboriginal cultural renaissance has fuelled jobs, as well as much pride and cultural production. Wathaurong Glass in North Geelong emerged in 1998 as a CDEP project after negotiations between ATSIC, the Wathawurrung community and Royal Melbourne Institute of Technology, which advised on glassmaking. It manufactures fine glass individually designed and crafted for the domestic, commercial and architectural markets, including glass plates and large panels. Its brochure boasts: 'Our artisans are highly skilled in procuring a wide range of architectural glass products that reflect the true Australian culture and heritage . . . whether it be Aboriginal designs or contemporary designs'. Wathaurong Glass, managed by Mark Edwards and staffed by several others from the Edwards clan, as well as other Aboriginal people, began with the demanding aim of teaching ten trainees glass work from scratch and yet still being economically viable in two years. The business was performing satisfactorily after four years but still needed CDEP funding to be viable, as the CDEP paid a third of the wages of two-thirds of the workforce of nine. With this assistance—perhaps $70,000 per annum—nine Aboriginal people are in work and produce architecturally beautiful and culturally appropriate glass products.[39]

Respect for family

A culture is a web of evolving ideas and understandings that bind a group of people together. Cultures are dynamic, as ideas progress and change with the environment in which they operate. The relatively recent emergence in the Western world of human rights, and the rights of women and children is a case in point. Aboriginal society in Victoria has also changed over the years of European occupation. Religious and ceremonial rites, initiations, sorcery and many other aspects of traditional life are no longer practised. Yet, as we have seen, much remains in terms of respect for ancestors, country and tradition. The same goes for family and associated core values.

Allegiance to family is an essential element in Aboriginal thinking. Conversations between Aboriginal people who are strangers to each other always start by placing the other person in a family context and locating their attachment to a piece of country. If Aboriginal people are asked what is most important to them, 'family' will invariably be their first response. As Lynette Bishop, a Gunai/Kurnai welfare worker and descendent of the fighting Mobournes, said of her early life in east Gippsland: 'Everything stemmed from family, everything came back to family. If your family needed you, you were there'. Today she lives in Stratford near her father and near the families of her sister and brother. Lynette Bishop, like many other Aboriginal people, spends much of her leisure time with family. She adds: 'I do have friends outside my family, but I've got a big enough family that I don't *need* to visit friends'.[40] Her sister Sandra Neilson commented of growing up: 'If someone turned up to our doorstep—visitors—there were beds, you could find a bed easily. And you didn't need permission to visit someone, you just went'.[41] Aboriginal families were perhaps on average closer and warmer than other families, or that is what Aboriginal people believe. All resort to the catch phrase 'caring and sharing' when Aboriginal family values are discussed, although obviously this is not the reality with dysfunctional Aboriginal families. However, Aboriginal people feel a sense of responsibility to people in families to which they are not related. Lynette Bishop revealed that Aboriginal families in Gippsland today take in children from other families in crisis 'to keep police, welfare, teachers, anyone at bay, that's one good thing about Koori families'.[42]

Respect is another basic element of Aboriginal thinking. It is what underpins the deference given to elders. Tim Chatfield stated that as a young man he learned 'total respect. I always have respected whoever's older than me'.[43] Many others I interviewed used the word *respect* as well. The corollary to respect is shame. Respect is practised in many ways: there are those whom you meet and should avoid direct eye contact with; there are those who are elders and should be addressed with the terms 'auntie' and 'uncle'; there are those who are the traditional land owners of a piece of country; and there are those who have knowledge and wisdom. Respect is also shown to the dead and to their families. Name avoidance and the smoking and abandonment of houses is now rarely practised, but funerals remain key events in contemporary Aboriginal society—events not to be missed. People travel long distances at great expense to be present. Sandra Neilson commented: 'People will go out of their way to get to a funeral, even interstate, to show a sign of respect to that person and their families'.[44] Funerals are often held up to two weeks after the death as the family waits for all to arrive. The coffin is often open for a farewell viewing, particular hymns are usually sung, very occasionally there is traditional wailing, and generally a long wake celebrating the departed occurs. Thus special employment leave is appropriate, though rarely given—another reason why Aboriginal people like to work within their own community organisations. An Aboriginal-run funeral service and several Aboriginal pastors exist to cater for these distinctive needs.

Cultural revival

Across Victoria, Aboriginal people are working among kin in Aboriginal organisations and searching actively for their cultural roots. Many middle-aged people I interviewed told me that not much Aboriginal culture was passed on to them in the 1950s and 1960s, although when pressed, it is clear a lot was absorbed unconsciously and incidentally.

The search for family history is most evident among people like Sandra Stewart and Myra Grinter (nee Atkinson) who were brought up in the mainstream community. They were both daughters of independent-minded Aboriginal farming families. Sandra Stewart's father, Kenneth Stewart, was the grandson of Rob Roy Stewart, who pioneered the Lake Boga area. Myra Grinter's parents, Daniel Atkinson (Yorta Yorta) and June Murray (Wiradjuri) left Cummeragunja and went 'mainstream' to avoid their children being removed. Both farming families identified as Aboriginal—and proudly so—but the opportunities to 'live it' were narrowed. Myra Grinter's mother told her traditional stories, but the family only saw their relatives at Christmas. However, both women now work for indigenous organisations. Sandra Stewart helped form a KODE Aboriginal-driven school in Mildura and currently works in the Indigenous Business Unit. Myra Grinter, who worked for VAAL in the stormy late 1960s, lived in its hostel under Doug and Gladys Nicholls's care, and now works hard for the Mildura Aboriginal Cooperative. Neither speak 'Aboriginal English'—that is, they do not drop their aitches and 'ings', being well schooled in the mainstream (a sore point at first with some Aboriginal people, whom Myra recalled considered her 'uppity').[45]

The atmosphere is now ripe for this cultural search to flourish as the pressures for assimilation have faded and there is a new interest and tolerance for Aboriginality in the Victorian community. Murray Bull, a Gunai/Kurnai man, along with others, has also stressed the need for a cultural revival in order to reassert discipline, pride and respect within Aboriginal families and the Aboriginal community. Bull urged: 'You've got to get tradition and culture back, and education, to end abusive language, fighting and drug abuse within families'.[46] However, an active cultural search is not desired by or possible for all Aboriginal people. A survey in 1994 of Aboriginal people over thirteen years of age in the two ATSIC administrative regions, Binjirru in the east of the State and Tumbukka in the west, revealed that while 70 per cent in the west attended Aboriginal cultural activities, only 50 per cent in the east did so. The remainder did not attend for reasons of work, transport, cost or lack of interest. In each region almost 50 per cent of Aboriginal people identified with a clan or language group, while 70 per cent recognised an area as their home country, mostly because they or their ancestors came from that area. Almost 80 per cent said the role of elders was important in their lives.[47] However, since 1994 when this survey was taken, many individuals have begun searching for their cultural roots and reinventing their identities, spurred on by native title business.

Mark Matthews was born in Melbourne in 1968. His father, Ronald Matthews, is non-Aboriginal and his mother, Rhonda Clarke, was a Gunditjmara woman, whose own parents were from Framlingham and Lake Condah. Mark Matthews grew up associating with Aboriginal families in Melbourne with the blessing of his father, who associated with them as well. As a youth Mark mixed with a gang of Aboriginal youths who called themselves the 'Vic Tribe'. They battled or mostly postured with other Melbourne gangs in the mid 1980s, including the 'Lebo Tigers'. They tangled with police who were quick to sheet blame to this group for any trouble going on. They were wild and bored, rather than criminal young men, but the elders eventually broke up the 'Vic Tribe' to avert bad publicity.

Mark Matthews was an apprentice carpenter and joiner in the 1980s, an apprenticeship he finished. Despite being Aboriginal he knew little of his culture. He recalled: 'I knew there was Aboriginal culture there somewhere, but not knowing much about it, it was just something inside of me missing'. He eventually moved to Hall's Gap in the mid 1990s where he got a job cleaning at Brambuk Cultural Centre. There he overheard the culture talks, learning by listening and watching. He became a cultural officer five years ago and continues to teach Aboriginal culture throughout Victoria: the use of boomerangs, string-making, rock paintings, stories and bush medicine. Matthews not only found the work of dispelling ignorance about Victorian Aboriginal people immensely satisfying, but has been changed by the experience. As he stated: 'I have come a long way from my city life to learning my culture and then coming to be respected by elders'. He is now teaching his parents and uncles cultural knowledge, much to their delight. He plays didgeridoo for cultural presentations at public functions in Melbourne as well as in Halls Gap. Matthews also explains to overseas visitors why Aboriginal people in Victoria do not have dark skin, but are still Aboriginal. As he says himself: 'My skin might be different but I'm still here [and Aboriginal] in heart and spirit'.[48]

Each person has their own journey to make, but individuals can assist and inspire each other. Jamie Thomas is a case in point. Thomas, now thirty-two years old, is the son of Arthur Thomas, a Gunai/Kurnai man with Gunditjmara forbears—the Austins—and a non-Aboriginal mother, Jennifer Commons. He grew up with his mother, knowing his father was Aboriginal, and identifying himself as such as he grew, having occasional contacts with Gunai/Kurnai people, some of whom turned out to be family. He became a boxer like his father and rose to be a dual Australian amateur champion in his mid to late teens, fighting as 'Jamie Commons'. Boxing showed him the right direction, bringing focus and discipline into his life, which otherwise might have been given over to substance abuse and aimlessness. His mother once showed him where he was conceived in east Gippsland and eventually he met his father, who had never lived with them, and more of his kin. However, being Aboriginal to him involved something more. As he recalled in 2002: 'It's about culture, it's not just about my family that I'm Aboriginal, it's about my way of life and my beliefs, and my connectedness to country and to land, and my role as a custodian to look after things'.

Thomas travelled to Alice Springs to connect to traditional culture and worked in the Aranda community for two years. He found much support in his quest but met others who said: 'You southerners, you've got no culture'. He met an Aboriginal man in Katherine who asked:

> 'Oh, where're you from?' And I said: 'Oh, I'm from Alice Springs', and he goes: 'No, where're you from, where's your country?' And I said: 'Oh, from down south there, in the salt-water country', and he goes: 'Oh, yes, what are you doin' up here? Why aren't you home with your family, what are you hiding?' And I said: 'No, no, no! I've come here looking for Aboriginal culture and the northern language', and straight away he said: 'Oh, you want initiation?'

Thomas baulked at that thought, thinking of circumcision and months of trials in the bush. The man then asked him the 'Aboriginal question':

Albert Mullett teaching Aboriginal culture at Bairnsdale Primary School, 1983. One in ten pupils was Aboriginal. (Reproduced courtesy Fairfax Photos)

who was his family? And because the man had himself worked in boxing tents in the south he knew of the Thomas and Austin families. Thomas vividly recalled the conversation:

> Then he started saying stuff like: 'You should go home and you should get your own culture back. Go home and find yourself'. And I said: 'Oh, but it's all lost and gone', and he said: (kindly) 'Aye! Stop feelin' sorry for yourself! Get that chip off your shoulder. You go home and you start asking questions to your elders and to your community and to your family and talk about things. You get your own things happenin''. And he said: 'Have you've been up to the top-end there and seen the paintings up there on the rocks?' I said: 'Yes'. He said: 'There's a painting on a painting on a painting on a painting on a painting. Do you think our culture's been the same for 40,000 years?' 'No!' he said: 'That's too boring. It changes, it's evolved, even before white fella come in it kept changing, language changed, dance changed, songs changed, dreamings changed. Because that's our dreaming, you know, how we see it, and it is the way we do it. You go home, and get your initiations started up again, you get your stories and your language and your dance. You start it up. And if the white fella tells you it's wrong, who are they to tell you? And if a black fella tells you it's wrong, you ask him—"Please show me the right way", and if he can't show you, you keep doin' what feels good for you, and you get the support of your family and community, and you keep doin' it'. And, so I moved to Warrnambool . . . That's the beauty about having an identity, it's not just being Aboriginal, it's about being Gunai or being Mara, and I'm proud of that.

Back in Warrnambool, the country of his Gunditjmara roots, Thomas became a drug and alcohol worker, consulted with elders Robert Lowe, Ivan Couzens and 'Banjo' Clarke about traditions and country and, inspired by what he had seen at Echuca, formed an Aboriginal dance group. At first, the youths involved in the dance group were embarrassed, but soon warmed to the idea. Thomas developed dances which emerged from his experience with the land, a whale dance from watching the leviathans cruising off Logans Beach at Warrnambool, and a Brolga dance after seeing these birds dancing and floating in a paddock. Thomas remarked that it was not 'just about dancing, it's about language, it's about making the artefacts, it's about traditional values'. His greatest moment was taking 41 dancers from Warrnambool to the Yeperenye Festival at Alice Springs in 2001. He presented the Aranda people with a gift of ti-tree boomerangs made in Warrnambool. Aranda elder Max Stuart praised his group for their dancing, but also for correct protocol, as they and one other were the only groups out of dozens to bear gifts for the traditional owners of the host country.[49]

With the cultural revival furthered by Thomas and others like him across Victoria, and presented at places like 'Bunjalaka' and the Koorie Heritage Trust, a new respect forms among other Victorians. This is reconciliation grass-roots style. Aboriginal people are reclaiming aspects of their culture 200 years after first encountering the British. They are adding new layers of paint to a cultural canvas now over 40,000 years old—paint upon paint upon paint—the culture of Aboriginal Victorians is still in the making.

Indigenous dancers and musicians, Reconciliation Walk in Melbourne, 2000. (Courtesy of Peter Smith/ATSIC)

18

New Day Dawning?

As this book has revealed, European voyagers first made landfall in Victoria in about 1800, more than 220 years ago. The invasion began at Portland in 1834 and in Melbourne a year later. Colonial control was exerted rapidly over the land and by government instrumentalities. The Aboriginal population crashed fifteen years later through the impact of colonisation—disease, violence, and loss of land and culture—leaving only 10 per cent of the first contact population. It was a terrible and traumatic outcome to a colonisation that was without treaty or agreement, and in which Aboriginal people had no say.

Some legislative controls were imposed through the Aboriginal Protectorate (1839–49), and wider-ranging controls in the Acts of 1860 and 1869, which set up a Central Board for the Aborigines and a reserve/mission system. A more coercive Act in 1886 pushed those of 'mixed descent' off reserves to assimilate them, splitting families. Those on reserves would, it was believed, fade away, and, along with the assimilation of those off the reserves, this would end Aboriginality through a cultural form of genocide. For many First Nations Victorians, legislative control and official discriminations existed until the 1970s. Yet through it all, Aboriginal people survived, maintained their culture and, in recent times, have rebuilt their population and cultural strength.

Change coming

By the 2020s it was evident that a new relationship was forming between governments and First Nations peoples across Australia. In many respects, Victoria was leading the way. At the beginning of this book (see Reflections), the uniqueness of Victoria's colonisation compared to other Australian colonies was found to be due to the context of time and place. Victoria's continued distinctiveness in Aboriginal affairs is shaped by four main factors: continuing Aboriginal activism; government responses to the dramatic failure of native title; progressive government in Victoria; and governments that pay heed to the United Nations Declaration on the Rights of Indigenous Peoples (UNDRIP), which was ratified by its General Assembly on 13 September 2007.

Aboriginal activism in Victoria began in 1843, when Billibellary asked for the return of traditional land. His request was pursued by fellow Kulin and other groups, who gained reserve lands by 1860, then fought to retain them after 1886. Individuals, especially women, fought against the 1886 Act that split families apart.[1] Activism never stopped. It was ramped up to an organisational level by William Cooper and his Australian Aborigines' League (1934), and Sir Doug Nicholls and the Victorian Aborigines Advancement League (1957). From the 1970s, other community-controlled organisations emerged, concerning health, legal issues, housing, child care and other services.[2] There are scores operating today across the spectrum of conservative, progressive and radical groups, the latter represented by the Warriors of the Aboriginal Resistance (2014). All continually advocate and pressure governments for change.

Many Aboriginal corporations are defined by their traditional owner status, with Country being the centre of Aboriginal identity. This was why the failure of native title legislation in the Yorta Yorta case sent shock waves through Aboriginal groups. The Yorta Yorta lost their claim in 1998 and their appeal in the High Court in 2001, because Justice Olney of the Federal Court found that the 'tide of history' had washed away their rights (see Chapter 17). The Kennett Liberal government had vehemently opposed the Yorta Yorta's claim. The incoming Bracks Labor government, urged on by traditional owners, pursued a less litigious approach to native title, making symbolic hand-back gestures and land management agreements with the Yorta Yorta (2002). Agreements with Wimmera groups (2005) and Gunditjmara peoples (2007) followed.

Since 1999, the progressive Labor administrations of Steve Bracks (1999–2007), John Brumby (2007–10) and Daniel Andrews (2014–) mostly held power. Andrews came to power in 2014, was returned in a landslide in 2018 and again in 2022 despite some unpopularity because of Melbourne's world-record 262 days of Covid lockdowns over six cycles during 2020–22. Andrews, a progressive force, remained supreme. When he clocked up 3000 days in office in 2023, political scientist Professor Paul Strangio dubbed him 'the most significant reformist premier since

[John] Cain [jnr]'.[3] Some of that reform push was directed to Indigenous affairs.

Victoria led Australia's quest for justice for Aboriginal people and in fulfilment of much of the United Nations Declaration on the Rights of Indigenous Peoples (UNDRIP). Article 1 of the Declaration declared:

> Indigenous peoples have the right to the full enjoyment, as a collective or as individuals, of all human rights and fundamental freedoms as recognized in the Charter of the United Nations, the Universal Declaration of Human Rights and international human rights law.

The remaining 45 articles established minimum standards for the survival, dignity and wellbeing of the world's Indigenous peoples, and enjoined governments to ensure these standards were attained (see Appendix).

The aspiration of recent Victorian governments to meet these principles was vital to the impulse for change. The Victorian Indigenous population numbered 65,646 in the 2021 census (up from 37,991 in 2011); that is, 1 per cent (up from 0.7 per cent) of the Victorian population.[4] Aboriginal people continued to seek change by their own efforts, but because they made up just 1 per cent of the population, they depended on the willingness of non-Indigenous people, the law and governments to achieve that change.

However, Indigenous populations have grown faster in recent decades than the general population due to four factors. These are: declining (although still too high) mortality rates; high fertility rates; an increase in the decision to identity as Indigenous; and births by non-Indigenous mothers. Analysis of the 2011 census revealed Indigenous Australians had high rates of exogamy, that is, marriage outside the group, at 57 per cent for males and 59 per cent for females. This led to mixed partnership rates for Indigenous people of 79 per cent in major cities and 77 per cent in major regional cities, where Indigenous people were more likely to make contact and thus partner with non-Indigenous Australians. In Melbourne the mixed partnership rate for Indigenous people in 2011 was 85 per cent and in Geelong 87 per cent. And as Nicholas Biddle a demographer from the ANU argued, 'most children from mixed partnership will end up being identified [initially by their parents] as Indigenous (no matter which parent is Indigenous)'.[5] Janet McCalman and others have similarly argued that the population recovery began in the middle of the twentieth century with the high fertility of some families, the increasing decision to identify as Aboriginal as the pressures of assimilation receded, and significant recent out-marriage.[6]

Gadubanud Welcome to Country Ceremony, Lorne Biennale, March 2022.
(Richard Broome, with permission from Richard Collopy and family)

This chapter offers a snapshot of four key issues to assess how Victoria is faring in its efforts to create a new day in Indigenous affairs. First, it discusses First Nations peoples' wellbeing with a focus on their disastrous rates of incarceration. Second, it examines the state of community relations using racism in Australian Rules Football (AFL) as the most pertinent public window into these interactions. Third, it explores the existing levels of respect for Indigenous cultures and how this is shifting over time. Fourth, it outlines the growing search for truth, treaty and voice. It is a mixed story, one marked both by progress and inconsistency, but in the end it is more hopeful than not and reveals progress through ongoing Indigenous activism and non-Indigenous change as well.

First Nations wellbeing

One of the deepest traumas from colonisation was the removal of children from their families, spectacularly revealed by the Human Rights and Equal Opportunity Commission's (HREOC's) *Bringing Them Home* report (1997). In 1997 the Victorian premier Jeff Kennett, despite then opposing land rights, issued an apology to the Stolen Generations. It was an early and magnificent gesture that Kennett's conservative counterparts at the federal level, in the Howard government, could not

contemplate. Once in power in mid-2007, the federal Labor government of Kevin Rudd gave a landmark Apology in 2008. Compensation
remained elusive, however, and was sought by individuals in court. Bruce
Trevorrow, who was forcibly taken in 1957, received $750,000 in the
South Australian Supreme Court in 2007, although he died a year later.[7]

In 2011 Neville Austin, a Gunditjmara man, sought reparations in
Victoria's courts. In 1966 his mother Eileen Austin voluntarily placed him
as a toddler in St Gabriel's Baby's Home, Balwyn. When Eileen Austin fell
£8 behind in her payments, young Neville was fostered out, despite his
mother's continued efforts to get him back. Austin won an undisclosed
sum in an out-of-court settlement, creating a precedent.[8] Eventually, and
after consultation with Koori communities, the Victorian government
introduced a redress scheme of $10 million in 2020 to provide counselling,
monetary compensation and family funeral payments. Gavin Jennings,
Special Minister of State, stated that parliament 70 years ago 'made decisions to kill communities, to remove people forcibly . . . It was an act of
genocide . . . It was a conscious decision made in that parliament to rip
families apart.'[9] Ian Hamm, Chair of the Reparations Steering Committee,
thought $10 million may be insufficient because a sixth of Aboriginal
Victorians 'were descended from or part of the stolen generations'.[10]

Prime Minister Rudd's Apology also committed to Close the Gap
between Indigenous under-privilege and the socio-economic condition
of other Australians. Public servants set top-down targets for Indigenous
life expectancy, health and wellbeing, education outcomes, and incarceration rates. A report was presented to federal parliament each year on the
progress being made, but it soon became clear that few of the targets were
being met. In a sense, it was unrealistic to think that the disadvantage of
generations could make significant headway from year to year, especially
with little input from First Nations peoples.

Closing the Gap was also a failure in Victoria. A 2012 report revealed
that, compared to all Victorians, the life expectancy of First Nations
Victorians was ten years less, their unemployment rate three times more,
and their rate of imprisonment nine times more. Young Kooris were three
times more likely than non-Indigenous youths to be processed by police
on the street, rather than warned and sent on their way. Bundjalung man
and Australian Labor Party president Warren Mundine commented that
Indigenous people in southern Australia had unique and perhaps bigger
problems than those of Indigenous peoples in the north: 'the forgotten
people are the people in Victoria . . . they have huge problems in closing
those gaps'.[11] As state governments tried to implement targets set federally,
there were few improvements.

The 2018 federal *Closing the Gap* report conceded that future targets needed to be 'designed, developed and implemented in partnership with Aboriginal and Torres Strait Islander people'.[12] In March 2019, a Closing the Gap Partnership Agreement was forged between a coalition of peak Aboriginal and Torres Strait Islander community–controlled organisations (Coalition of Peaks) and the federal government. The coalition established four pillars to transform how governments worked with First Nations peoples: collaborative decision-making; a stronger community-controlled sector; a rethink at all levels of government; and a sharing of outcomes data. Twelve standard socio-economic targets were set, as well as five concerning wellbeing, land and waters, culture, language, and connectivity. The Productivity Commission had to collect, track and share the data on a live online dashboard. Pat Turner, Convenor of the Coalition of Peaks, called the agreement a 'historic achievement'.[13] The partnership's first report in November 2022 found that only a quarter of targets were met. Prime Minister Anthony Albanese lamented that, despite the best intentions of governments, 'for some of the targets, what we so gently call a gap has remained a chasm'. Like those before him, he promised a 'new chapter' ahead.[14]

Victoria had initiated targets before the federal government did. The Bracks administration created a framework to end Indigenous disadvantage in 2006, two years before their federal counterparts.[15] The Andrews government also preceded the Commonwealth's 2019 shift to partnerships. In June 2018 it established the Victorian Aboriginal Affairs Framework 2018–2023, which outlined how to plan, enact, measure and evaluate progress. Premier Andrews' preface stated the Framework represented 'A new approach to Aboriginal affairs, with the voices of Aboriginal people at its heart', and added, 'we only achieve better outcomes for Aboriginal people when that all-important work is led by Aboriginal people'. The Framework declared: 'Aboriginal self-determination is a human right as enshrined in the United Nations Declaration on the Rights of Indigenous Peoples, and we commit to working towards a future of equality, justice and strength'. A community informant from Morwell declared: 'We need more Aboriginal people's voices in decision-making . . . it's not just good practice, it's good business.'[16]

First Nations people now have a real say in their wellbeing, but disadvantage remains entrenched for a large majority of them. Their socio-economic profile will take many years to reach parity with the rest of the population, especially in a post-Covid world. And the evaluation of statistical outcomes from these partnerships will involve complex analysis too detailed to consider here. A word must be said about the incarceration of

Indigenous suspects and offenders, however, since altered justice provisions can bring speedy change much faster than shifts in socio-economic outcomes. And the issue of Aboriginal deaths in custody is open to the most rapid change, if the will is there.

Justice and incarceration

In 1991 the report of the Royal Commission into Aboriginal Deaths in Custody (RCADIC) investigated the causes of death of 91 individuals, three of whom were Victorians. It made 339 recommendations about custodial health and safety, especially how to make custody a means of last resort by Aboriginal involvement in the justice process and decriminalising public drunkenness.[17] A review in 1994 found little progress, however, and another in 1996 by Commissioner Mick Dodson of the Human Rights and Equal Opportunity Commission found, to his despair, that incarceration rates remained stubbornly high despite an expenditure of $400 million.[18] A ten-year review of the RCADIC found that, at 115, deaths in custody were higher in the 1990s than in the 1980s, at 110.[19]

The National Deaths in Custody Program, set up in 1992 by the Australian Institute of Criminology, has recorded 527 Indigenous deaths in Australia since the royal commission in 1991 until 2022. Between 2017 and late 2022, there were 94 Indigenous deaths across the country, or 23 per cent of total deaths in custody, while Aboriginal people form 3 per cent of the Australian population.[20] In Victoria, there has been a spike in Indigenous custodial deaths since 2017, from less than one per year from 1991 to 2016, to more than two deaths per year.[21] In March 2023, Pat Dodson, a Labor senator (and brother of Mick Dodson), termed deaths in custody 'a national disgrace'; called for the full implementation of the RCADIC recommendations; and said governments had a duty of care, not 'a licence to kill people'.[22]

The RCADIC found that First Nations peoples had higher rates of deaths in custody because they had far higher rates of imprisonment: a problem that has continued. Between 2011 and 2021, the Aboriginal imprisonment rate in Victoria doubled from 965.2 per 100,000 Aboriginal Victorian adults to 1903.5, while the rate for all prisoners increased by a fifth from 110.2 to 138.7.[23] The Indigenous rate in 2021 was 13.7 times that of the non-Indigenous rate. Prisoner numbers have climbed over the past decade, but more so the proportion on remand, especially after bail laws were tightened in 2018. This followed public outrage over the slaughter of six people and the injuring of 30 more by James Gargasoulos in 2017 while on bail. He mowed them down with his car on the footpath of Bourke Street, Melbourne. New bail laws meant that a higher percentage of those accused of an indictable offence committed while on bail, even if for an alleged non-violent crime such as shoplifting or public drunkenness, were incarcerated. Between 2010 and 2020, the percentage of Aboriginal people incarcerated while awaiting trial jumped from 20 to 44 per cent.[24]

This figure applied especially to Indigenous women. Between 2009 and 2020, their imprisonment rate jumped by an astounding 321 per cent, while those awaiting trial and sentencing jumped by even more at 440 per cent.[25] By 2020, Indigenous women in Victoria were being jailed at twenty times the rate of non-Indigenous women, which was higher than Indigenous males at 13.7 times the rate of non-Indigenous men.[26] Therefore, Aboriginal women were much more vulnerable to harm and even death, as revealed in the cases of Tanya Day and Veronica Nelson. Day, a 55-year-old Yorta Yorta woman, was arrested for public drunkenness on 17 December 2017 while asleep on a country train. She was sent to the Castlemaine watchhouse where she fell and died from a massive brain injury. The coroner's report found that the actions of police were not 'causative' of her death, but referred her death to the Office of Public Prosecutions in case an offence had occurred. The Public Prosecutor in August 2020 declined to press criminal charges.[27] New rules were introduced the following month, making a coroner's investigation mandatory in each Indigenous death-in-custody case.

Veronica Nelson, a 37-year-old Gunditjmara, Djadjawurrung, Wiradjuri and Yorta Yorta woman, was arrested in Melbourne in late December 2019 on suspicion of shoplifting. She represented herself in court and was refused bail. She died in agony in the Dame Phyllis Frost Centre on 2 January 2020 from drug withdrawal symptoms and complications from Wilkie's syndrome, a gastrointestinal condition. That night, Nelson appealed for help 49 times over the prison's intercom, but received indifferent and insufficient care and was not transferred to hospital, a move that would probably have saved her life. Nelson called out to her deceased father to save her; such was her torment. Her mother Donna Nelson and family grieved for her and wanted action.[28]

The Victorian Coroner Simon McGregor, amid tears, described Nelson's treatment as 'cruel and degrading', and slammed the justice, health and corrections system for failings over a 'preventable' death. He also criticised successive Victorian governments for failing to implement fully the RCADIC's recommendations. McGregor added that changes to the

Bail Act in 2018 were a 'complete and unmitigated disaster' and were against the Charter of Human Rights. The family threatened legal action and the case was reviewed by the Director of Public Prosecutions. Premier Andrews apologised to the family and announced changes to the bail laws to correct this 'dreadful tragedy'.[29]

Further changes followed as the law against public drunkenness was scrapped beginning in November 2023 and the age of criminal responsibility was raised from ten to twelve years. However, the tragic and avoidable deaths of Day and Nelson reveal the racism embedded in state and public authorities, which add to Indigenous disadvantage. We must ask: would a white woman or man have been arrested, refused bail and received inadequate care in the same circumstances?

To reduce the disadvantages of First Nations peoples before the law, a Victorian Aboriginal Justice Agreement was formed in 2002 between the Victorian government and Victorian Aboriginal communities. It was inspired by the RCADIC and in practical terms by the Nunga Court of South Australia established in 1999. The first Koori Court was created at Shepparton in 2002, which aimed to use therapeutic justice to help the wellbeing of offenders and be more collaborative rather than adversarial in style. Koori Courts give Aboriginal people a greater say in the justice system. They are now found at fifteen locations, four in Melbourne and eleven in country Victoria: from Bairnsdale to Portland, and north to the Murray River. Since 2006, eleven Koori Children's Courts have opened progressively and from 2009, Koori County Courts operated at the Latrobe Valley, Melbourne, Mildura and Shepparton to hear more serious cases.

Defendants must agree to plead guilty for their case to come before the Koori Court, so a positive outcome is already in process before the case begins. Koori Courts ensure defendants feel culturally safe with the presence of Indigenous artworks, native timber furnishings and the Aboriginal flag. Importantly, Indigenous Elders are present in all the proceedings, which are given in plain English, not legalese. Their role is to give cultural advice to the magistrate about appropriate sentencing, which remains the magistrate's prerogative. Elders converse with the defendant, admonish them for their misdeeds at times, making clear their offending is a 'shame job' for their family. The latter is a powerful statement in a culture that stresses the avoidance of shaming family publicly. Aunty Rochelle Patten, a court Elder at Shepparton, said, 'They don't like coming back to face the Elders'.[30]

These courts are not soft options and have been successful. In early research on the Shepparton and Broadmeadows Koori Magistrate courts, reoffending was halved to 15 per cent.[31] All who participate in the courts, including victims, find the experience worthwhile. The Aboriginal community has driven the Koori Court's expansion, which they realise empowers them by creating a real voice in the justice system.[32] In 2018 Judge Paul Grant stated, 'In 2002 there were very few—if any—Aboriginal people working in Victorian courts and now more than 100 Elders and Respected Persons are participating in Koori Courts throughout Victoria.'[33] At the twentieth anniversary of the Koori Court in 2022, Magistrate Rose Falla—a Wotjobaluk and Wemba Wemba woman, and the first Indigenous magistrate in Victoria—said the Koori Court had heard 3200 cases since 2002, adding, 'the evaluation when it took place did highlight that the number of the failures to appear, the number of warrants being issued by courts decreased'. For Falla, the court was 'an example of self-determination in action.'[34]

The criminal justice system is changing in incremental ways, but there is much to do. The death of Veronica Nelson revealed that the duty of care shown to Aboriginal people in custody was probably less than would have been extended to other Victorians. This was also the general finding

Bendigo Law Courts by John Wardle Architects, which opened in 2023, displaying a welcome image of Bunjil overseeing his people's conduct in the Koori Court. Djadjawurrung, Barapa Barapa and Boonwurrung artist Racquel Kerr formed Bunjil in hammered copper. (Richard Broome)

of the RCADIC: that deaths in custody reflected a general lack of care and attention. As Nerita Waight, CEO of the Victorian Aboriginal Legal Service, stated: 'There have been many reports that have highlighted systemic racism in Victoria Police and a lack of accountability for their behaviour.'[35] In 2022, 22 per cent of Indigenous Australians surveyed thought they had poor relations with police as opposed to 6 per cent of other Australians. It is likely that other government agencies have a similar level of Indigenous disapproval.[36]

Racism in sport

Since 2014, Reconciliation Australia has issued an annual 'Reconciliation Barometer'. In 2022 the Barometer found that, while 42 per cent of non-Indigenous Australians surveyed agreed 'Australia was a racist country', 57 per cent of First Nations people agreed with the same proposition. Of the latter, 60 per cent said they had experienced one form of racial discrimination in the last six months.[37] Racism is still at too high a level across society, and is not helped by the rise of populist politics in recent years; anxiety about migration movements across the world, due to war and global warming; and the stresses and strains of the Covid pandemic since 2020.[38]

The problem of racism manifests itself most publicly and powerfully in Victoria within the AFL. Racism has always found expression in sport, especially in football, boxing and other sports. Colin Tatz argued in 1995: 'Sport illustrates both the worst and the best in black–white relations.'[39] Due to the centrality of the AFL in Victorian life, along with the strong Indigenous contingent and their success in football, racism in the AFL is the touchstone of race in Victorian society. Sir Doug Nicholls experienced it when playing for Fitzroy (1932–37), Syd Jackson for Carlton (1969–76), Robert Muir for St Kilda (1974–80, 1984) and many others.[40] It seized widespread public consciousness in April 1993, however, when St Kilda's Nicky Winmar responded to taunts from Collingwood supporters by lifting his jersey, pointing to his skin and indicating he was proud to be black.

To create greater respect, the AFL created the Marn Grook game at the SCG (2002), the Dreamtime game at the MCG (2005), and the Indigenous Round named after Sir Doug Nicholls (2016), all to shift opinion about Indigenous players. Clubs also created Indigenous programs and listed more Indigenous players, following the lead of Essendon Bombers' coach Kevin Sheedy. The Bombers created the *Ngaalang Miya* Academy to foster Indigenous players, which was mirrored by most other clubs. In the 2022 season, 10 per cent of AFL and 4 per cent of AFLW players identified as Aboriginal or Torres Strait Islanders. The Indigenous percentage in the general population is 3 per cent, and in Victoria just 1 per cent.[41] St Kilda Football Club, which declared it is on a *yawa*, a journey, had the most Indigenous players in 2022, with eight on its list of 38 players, or 21 per cent.[42] Indigenous players are now over-represented in the AFL due to their love of the game and their willingness to work hard to get ahead through football. This attitude creates a high level of game skills, which draws the attention of fans as well as those uneasy with their prominence.

Adam Goodes, an Adnyamathanha man from the Yorke Peninsula in South Australia who played for the Sydney Swans, attracted scrutiny after he reacted to a racial slur from an opposing Collingwood fan during the Indigenous Round at the MCG in 2013. Collingwood president and radio host Eddie McGuire later compounded the matter with an on-air racist joke.[43] Match after match, the booing continued against Goodes, even into the 2014 season after he was named Australian of the Year. It erupted again in 2015 when Goodes did a war dance to the crowd following a brilliant goal.[44] Goodes was hounded out of the game in September 2015. He retired as an AFL great: playing 372 games over sixteen years with the Sydney Swans, winning two Brownlow medals (2003 and 2006) and three best-and-fairest medals during his career. Two films, *The Final Quarter* and *The Australian Dream*, exposed the racism and mental harm that traumatised Goodes. The films stimulated the AFL to issue an apology to Goodes. His fellow AFL players also admitted they had been unsupportive by not publicly condemning the racist behaviour.

Brazilian-born Héritier Lumumba (Harry O'Brien), who has Congolese heritage, played for Collingwood from 2005 to 2014 including in a premiership team. When he condemned the treatment of Adam Goodes, he was ostracised and traded out of the club. In late 2020, Lumumba claimed in a Supreme Court writ that he had been racially vilified while playing at Collingwood. While the writ was never served on the club, or the AFL, it caused Collingwood to commission an inquiry. The *Do Better* report of February 2021 upheld his claim. Collingwood's president Eddie McGuire silkily declared the report was 'a historic and proud day for the club', adding: 'we are not a mean-spirited club. We are not a racist club.'[45] McGuire declined to stand down as president, wishing to lead change from within the club, but soon resigned in the face of widespread criticism of his attempt to gloss the situation. Lumumba, now a lawyer and Director of the Kenyan School of Law in Nairobi, made fresh claims in May 2022.[46]

Eddie Betts endured racial abuse, notably from 2016.[47] Originally from Kalgoorlie, Betts played 350 games from 2005 to 2021 for Carlton,

410 Renaissance: 1970 Onwards

Adelaide and Carlton again, kicking 640 goals and 342 behinds in a brilliant career as a small forward. The AFL Players Indigenous Advisory Board issued a strong statement in April 2017 that slammed racial vilification for its profound impact on players and their families.[48] The AFL Players Association Summit in February 2019 demanded a united player front against racist trolls on social media.[49] The Melbourne Football Club responded by symbolically ripping up a banner of hateful words as they began Round 2 of the 2019 season.[50]

In August 2020, the shameful story of Robert Muir's racist treatment during his career in the Victorian Football League (now AFL) and South Australian League became known to the public. Muir, a Yorta Yorta man like Doug Nicholls, was one of the best players of his day, signing with St Kilda when he was twenty. Yet, he was continually abused while playing. Russell Jackson, who broke the story, wrote that Muir 'endured nothing but hounding and harassment—a decade-long chronicle of racial abuse and mistreatment, including incidents in which he was spat at, urinated on, pelted with bottles and set upon by mobs of racist fans'. A particularly ugly incident occurred at Victoria Park in May 1980, when Collingwood fans vented relentless racial abuse. His teammates did not do enough to defend him. Legendary AFL coach John Northey said Muir was 'more maligned than any player who's ever played the game'. The legacy of this treatment was alcoholism, homelessness and mental illness—and being ignored by St Kilda in his retirement. But with the help of his partner Donna Pickett, he gradually healed himself in recent years.[51]

The tide is turning. Overt racial vilification is slowly being eroded from the AFL and its fan base, easing the trauma of players. Despite the deep hurt, Adam Goodes reflected in September 2021 that the racist slurs he experienced were transformational for the nation and in the end for him too: 'there is a true and real empathy for Indigenous people at the moment'.[52] In August 2022, St Kilda Football Club welcomed Robert Muir and his family home to the club. Muir was deeply impressed with how Indigenous players were now embraced and valued by the club and made culturally safe with their own *Yawa* room to honour Indigenous contributions at St Kilda.[53] In 2022 Eddie Betts and his wife Anna Skullie wrote two children's books, which have been taken up by Netflix for children's programming. Betts reflected: 'if I didn't get drafted, I had nothing. The only thing I could do is work in the mines. Footy kind of saved me.'[54] Football can be a hotbed of racism, but also a place of hope and respect.

Growing respect for Indigenous cultural knowledge

More Victorians increasingly embrace Indigenous culture. In 2022 the Reconciliation Barometer indicated that 58 per cent of those surveyed felt proud of Australia's Indigenous cultures; 84 per cent believed it was important to know First Nations history and 85 per cent to know about First Nations cultures.[55] This positive attitude is also evident in the growing respect given to Indigenous knowledge, including by students, teachers and academics at all levels of educational institutions. The University of Melbourne created the First Nations Knowledge Institute in 2019. Governments are reflecting this new-found interest as well. Elders of the Wurundjeri Woi Wurrung Cultural Heritage Aboriginal Corporation have undertaken cultural mapping of the Yarra River and Jacksons Creek in the Melbourne region, and advised on strategic plans for their environmental management and revitalisation.[56]

Traditional fire knowledge has become more valued following the Black Saturday fires of 2009. The Andrews government funded the Victorian Traditional Owner Cultural Fire Knowledge Group, which asserts in Indigenous terms in its 2019 report: 'cultural burns are used for cultural purposes—they are not simply about asset protection'. The report establishes the vital principles of cultural burning: the right fire, at the right time and in the right way. Fires are also a cultural responsibility, living knowledge, a healing of country and culture; and they need to be properly monitored, evaluated and researched to grow the practice.[57] After the devastating Black Summer (2019–20) fires, authorities and landowners paid even more notice to cultural burning practices.

Respectful attitudes underpin the growing use of Indigenous names.[58] The year 2022 marked the beginning of the United Nations' International Decade of Indigenous Languages to restore and maintain Indigenous languages worldwide.[59] The then Department of Environment, Land, Water and Planning (DELWP)—now DECCA—agreed to partner with traditional owners to encourage the adoption of Indigenous placenames, led by DELWP's Geographic Names Victoria.[60] The Australian Broadcasting Corporation programming introduced dual placenames in its reporting around the country, often placing the Indigenous name first to stimulate learning. Australia Post includes a space for Indigenous placenames on its packaging. Acknowledgement of country and traditional owners has become widespread at public meetings of government, educational institutions, private industry and community organisations. Language recovery and revival, led locally by the Victorian Aboriginal Corporation for Languages, has made this possible.

Ultimately, the move to change names reveals respect for traditional owners' care of Country and their First Nations status. In 2017 after extensive consultation by Parks Victoria, Canadian Regional Park in Ballarat was renamed Woowookarung Regional Park, meaning 'place of plenty', to show respect to the traditional owners. In 2007, 133,000 hectares, including Mount Eccles National Park, was returned to the Gunditjmara people under a non-exclusive native title determination. In an agreement with the Victorian government, the park was renamed Budj Bim National Park and the Gunditj Mirring Traditional Owner Aboriginal Corporation formed to manage it. For a decade, the corporation pushed for World Heritage status, which was granted by United Nations Educational, Scientific and Cultural Organization (UNESCO) in 2019. It was given this special accolade because it is the site of extensive aquaculture works used by traditional owners for eel farming, deemed more than 6000 years old.[61]

Name changes are especially important where the existing name shows disrespect. In 2021 Moreland City Council confronted the history of its own name. 'Moreland', the 1840s name of the estate of Dr Farquhar McCrae (straddling Moreland Road west of Sydney Road), was named after his grandfather's slave plantation in Jamaica. 'Moreland' had only been the council's name since 1994, when the cities of Brunswick and Coburg were forced to amalgamate as a cost-cutting exercise. It was therefore not deeply cherished, and in December 2021 the Council voted six to three to change its name. The Wurundjeri Woi Wurrung Cultural Heritage Aboriginal Corporation agreed to make suggestions.[62] A postal ballot considered three names—Merri-bek, meaning 'rocky country', was the clear winner. More than 13,000 households voted and only 2200 people signed a petition protesting the process, objecting to the cost, the limited choices and, perhaps for some, the Indigenous name.[63] The name 'Moreland' still exists for a road and the local railway station, and street and other signage will take time to replace. Still, Merri-bek joined eleven other councils in the Melbourne area with Indigenous names.

Respect for Indigenous rights and culture was embedded in significant legislation passed by the Labor governments of Steve Bracks and John Brumby. In 2004 the Bracks government changed the Victorian Constitution to recognise Aboriginal people as the 'original custodians of the land' that is now the state of Victoria. In 2006 it passed the *Charter of Human Rights and Responsibilities Act*, which in its preamble proclaims that 'human rights belong to all people without discrimination, and the diversity of the people of Victoria enhances our community'. It adds: 'human rights have a special importance for the Aboriginal people of Victoria, as descendants of Australia's first people, with their diverse

Smoking Ceremony by Bill Nicholson (left) and Tony Garvey (right) of the
Wurundjeri Woi Wurrung Cultural Heritage Aboriginal Corporation to mark the
Council meeting at Glenroy Community Hub, 3 July 2022, at which Moreland
City Council officially changed its name to Merri-bek. (Richard Broome, with
permission from Bill Nicholson and Tony Garvey)

spiritual, social, cultural and economic relationship with their traditional
lands and waters'. It guarantees their distinct cultural rights to identity
and culture, language and kinship ties, and to maintain 'their distinctive
spiritual, material and economic relationship with land and waters . . .
under traditional laws and customs'.[64]

The Bracks government also passed the *Aboriginal Heritage Act 2006*
to extend heritage protection and established the Aboriginal Heritage
Council (2007). The Council's logo comprises four coloured shields
that protect Victoria, and that support, respect and celebrate Country,
Culture and Life. Their colours represent dry country (ochre); waters,
rivers and lakes (blue); forest country (green); and volcanic country and
the Metropolitan region (purple).[65] The Council manages the knowledge
of Aboriginal cultural material, its location and protection.

The Council also approves and oversees Registered Aboriginal Parties
(RAPs), which by July 2021 numbered eleven and covered 75 per cent
of the state (see the map on p. 415). Currently, only some Country in
the eastern Mallee, some near Wilsons Promontory and some in the
north-east of Victoria remain unallocated. RAP boundaries became

highly contentious given that traditional owner groups are the 'primary guardians, keepers and knowledge holders of Aboriginal cultural heritage' and therefore able to determine and negotiate on cultural heritage within their boundaries.[66] The RAP appointment process inadvertently led to suboptimal outcomes for some Indigenous people. Local traditional owners can be excluded from large Aboriginal corporations that receive RAP status from the government over an area by claiming to represent all of them, when they in fact do not. This appears to be the case in parts of south-west Victoria and elsewhere.

Seeking to avoid further costly and protracted native title litigation, the Brumby government followed Bracks's lead on agreements over land. It created a Steering Committee in 2008 headed by the respected Mick Dodson with representatives from government departments, Native Title Services Victoria and the peak body, the Victorian Traditional Owners Land Justice Group. Together, they forged a new cooperative pathway, the *Traditional Owner Settlement Act 2010*. Gavin Jennings, the minister for Environment and Climate Change, when presenting the Bill on 12 August 2010, told the Upper House that it recognised traditional owners' rights and was compatible with the *Charter of Human Rights and Responsibilities Act 2006*. It provided 'an alternative mechanism for the resolution of native title claims in Victoria through the making of agreements with traditional owners which offer a range of benefits, including rights equivalent to native title, in return for withdrawal of native title'.[67] In 2023 the Eastern Maar gained native title to access, use and protect public lands and to be consulted on their use by such agreement with the state government after four years of negotiation. The agreement was ratified by the Federal Court.[68]

The return of traditional land occurred in diverse ways. Small plots have been returned by churches and individuals. In 2022 the philanthropic body Trust for Nature agreed to transfer ownership of 30,000 hectares of land at Neds Corner in the far north-west of Victoria to the Millewa-Mallee Aboriginal Corporation. For twenty years, the Trust had restored the former grazing lands to a complex ecosystem. The state government gave $2 million to support the work of Indigenous rangers to care for and culturally manage this land.[69] Native title claims continue to be registered. In December 2022, the native title tribunal held hearings in Melbourne for the Boonwurrung claim over lands stretching around Port Phillip Bay from Werribee to the tip of the Mornington Peninsula. N'arweet (Elder) Caroline Briggs gave evidence about an ancient redgum in St Kilda near Junction Oval, which had ceremonial importance and 'significant cultural heritage value'. However, this claim is being contested not by

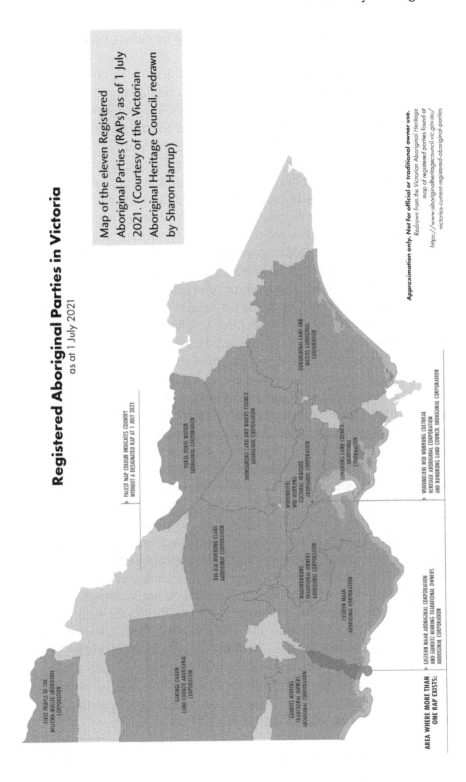

Registered Aboriginal Parties in Victoria
as at 1 July 2021

Map of the eleven Registered Aboriginal Parties (RAPs) as of 1 July 2021. (Courtesy of the Victorian Aboriginal Heritage Council, redrawn by Sharon Harrup)

PALEST MAP COLOUR INDICATES COUNTRY WITHOUT A DESIGNATED RAP AT 1 JULY 2021

FIRST PEOPLE OF THE MILLEWA-MALLEE ABORIGINAL CORPORATION

BARENGI GADJIN LAND COUNCIL ABORIGINAL CORPORATION

GUNDITJ MIRRING TRADITIONAL OWNERS ABORIGINAL CORPORATION

DJA DJA WURRUNG CLANS ABORIGINAL CORPORATION

YORTA YORTA NATION ABORIGINAL CORPORATION

TAUNGURUNG LAND AND WATERS COUNCIL ABORIGINAL CORPORATION

WURUNDJERI WOI WURRUNG CULTURAL HERITAGE ABORIGINAL CORPORATION

GUNAIKURNAI LAND AND WATERS ABORIGINAL CORPORATION

BUNURONG LAND COUNCIL ABORIGINAL CORPORATION

WADAWURRUNG TRADITIONAL OWNERS ABORIGINAL CORPORATION

EASTERN MAAR ABORIGINAL CORPORATION

AREA WHERE MORE THAN ONE RAP EXISTS:

EASTERN MAAR ABORIGINAL CORPORATION AND GUNDITJ MIRRING TRADITIONAL OWNERS ABORIGINAL CORPORATION

WURUNDJERI WOI WURRUNG CULTURAL HERITAGE ABORIGINAL CORPORATION AND BUNURONG LAND COUNCIL ABORIGINAL CORPORATION

Approximation only. Not for official or traditional owner use.
Redrawn from the Victorian Aboriginal Heritage map of registered parties found at https://www.aboriginalheritagecouncil.vic.gov.au/victorias-current-registered-aboriginal-parties

non-Indigenous counterclaims, but by the Wurundjeri Woiwurrung, Gunai/Kurnai and Bunurong.[70]

Trees were at the centre of another land dispute in 2018, during VicRoads' planned duplication of a dangerous single-lane section of the Western Highway between Ararat and Buangor. The Registered Aboriginal Party for the area (the Eastern Maar), the federal government and the Victorian Ombudsman all agreed to VicRoads' favoured route. Local Djab Wurrung representatives, however, formed an embassy on the site to protect sacred 'grandfather trees' and a magnificent eucalypt called the 'Directions Tree'. VicRoads had already shifted the route to save several 'birthing trees', but 3000 old-growth trees were still destined for destruction. More than 200 activists flocked to support the protest in August 2019.

A compromise was forged to save more trees and works recommenced. A year later in October 2020, however, anger erupted with further protests at the site, over the loss of more trees including the 'Directions Tree'. Victorian Senator and radical Gunai/Kurnai woman Lidia Thorpe called the tree-felling 'cultural genocide and colonial violence'.[71] Upon action from the Djab Wurrung, the Victorian Supreme Court extended its injunction on further works until February 2021 under the *Aboriginal Heritage Act 2006*. The Djab Wurrung also had a case before the Federal Court. In June 2022, Marjorie Thorpe, who was pursuing the Supreme Court case, agreed to drop it when the Andrews government promised to create a new Cultural Heritage Management Plan before the roadworks recommenced.[72]

Appeals to traditional culture, as on the Western Highway, had powerful resonance with a public more attuned to respecting traditional owners. Legislative instruments also give support to cultural protection. Indeed, a High Court decision in March 2019 to award damages for spiritual and cultural loss in the Timber Creek (Northern Territory) case opened the way for different sorts of cultural compensation claims into the future.[73]

The growing respect given to Indigenous people is revealed by the way they are being honoured in public spaces. Pastor Sir Doug Nicholls (1906–88) was honoured in his own time with a knighthood and many other accolades. In December 2007, he was honoured alongside his wife, Lady Gladys Nicholls, with statues in Treasury Place.[74] Lionel Rose (1948–2011) was the World Boxing Council (WBC), World Boxing Association (WBA) and *The Ring Magazine* world boxing bantamweight champion in 1968–69. Rose captured the hearts of the public with his winning smile and country songs, and in 2010 was honoured by a bronze statue in Mus Park, Warragul.[75] His death in May 2011 brought extensive press coverage.[76]

In Sarah Pinto's recent book, *Places of Reconciliation: Commemorating Indigenous History in the Heart of Melbourne* (2021), she describes the history of artworks and commemorations of Indigenous culture that challenges the settler dominance of public spaces in Melbourne. These include Birrarung Marr, the Barak and Tanderrum bridges, and Eel Trap alongside the Yarra River. A digitally displayed Aboriginal Honour Roll was also created in 2011, which grows by a dozen members each year—135 in all by 2022—to challenge lists of settler heroes.[77] The erection of Indigenous statues continues, including that of Archie Roach and Ruby Hunter in Fitzroy. Wurundjeri Elder Colin Hunter said of their figures in the landscape: 'Mob from all over Australia came to Fitzroy in search of family and community. Uncle Archie and Aunty Ruby will forever be memorialised here in Fitzroy, watching over their community from the cradle of Aboriginal activism and the birthplace of the Aboriginal rights movement.'[78]

Indigenous cultural icons engender widespread appeal. In late 2022, Victoria lost two of its most significant cultural icons and Indigenous Elders, who were widely respected. Singer/songwriter and Gunditjmara-Bundjalung man Uncle Archie Roach AC (1956–2022) died in July of that year, aged 66. Along with his wife and music partner Ruby Hunter (d. 2010), Roach transfixed audiences at music festivals and concerts for a generation. His song 'Took the Children Away' (1990) defined a historical phase as much as the term 'Stolen Generations'. It was one of many moving songs in a repertoire that gave all Victorians an insight into the world of those in *Charcoal Lane* in Fitzroy, the title of his first album. Over time his demeanour grew into one of calmness and forgiveness, not rancour,

Statues of Sir Doug Nicholls and Lady Gladys Nicholls in Treasury Place, Melbourne, by sculptor Louis Laumen, the first statues of Indigenous people in a public place in Melbourne. (Courtesy of Margaret Donnan)

the lines of his face reflecting both hardship and wisdom. Musician and composer Paul Grabowsky praised his layered voice and exquisite songs: 'he was as great an artist as any of them, our own, a true original'.[79]

The government honoured Roach in December 2022 with a state memorial service at the Sidney Myer Music Bowl. On behalf of the Victorian government, Premier Andrews apologised to Roach's sister at that event 'for the forced removal from your family, from your country, community, culture and language, and for depriving you of your birthright by actions perpetrated on you'.[80] Already honoured with the Australian award of AM, Archie Roach was posthumously elevated two levels in January 2023 to AC—Companion of the Order of Australia—the highest award that can be given.

Boonwurrung, Djadjawurrung, Woiwurrung and Yorta Yorta man Uncle Jack Charles (1943–2022) passed away, aged 79. He was a noted actor and mentor with a rich baritone voice. He too had been removed from his family when he was just four months old, and grew up at the Salvation Army's Bayswater Boys' Home. His removal led to an early troubled life. He entered acting in 1970 and in 1971 became a co-founder with Bob Maza of the first black theatre in Australia, Nindethana, at the Pram Factory in Melbourne. His illustrious career spanned films and stage plays, many of which tackled Indigenous injustice, including *Coranderrk: We Will Show the Country* (2013). Jack Charles was given a state funeral in Hamer Hall. Premier Andrews remarked: 'He leaves behind a legacy— one of profound honesty, survival and reconciliation—and one that every single Victorian can be proud of'.[81]

Jack Charles was an activist who was outspoken about his experience as one of the Stolen Generations. He was the first to give evidence to the Victorian Yoorrook Justice Commission in April 2022: stating: 'I wasn't even told I was Aboriginal. I had to discover that for myself. I knew nothing, was told nothing, and had to assimilate . . . I was whitewashed by the system'.[82]

Truth, treaty and voice

Seeking a new day for Indigenous people in Victoria involves listening to Indigenous voices and empowering them to shape many aspects of their own lives. The process was inspired internationally by UNDRIP and locally in Australia by constitutional recognition discussions at the federal level. These began in 2010 but, due to a change in government, spluttered to a stop under the Abbott government three years later.

In 2014 Noel Pearson in frustration called for a Voice to Parliament. Constitutional discussions begin again in 2015, culminating in a large and representative meeting in Central Australia in late May 2017, which issued the *Uluru Statement from the Heart*. That historic statement called for a Voice to Parliament to be enshrined in the Australian Constitution, a *makarrata* or treaty, and a truth-telling process—a trinity to create greater self-determination. The Andrews government responded to this trinity of voice, truth and treaty in the *Uluru Statement* and intimated in UNDRIP Articles 18, 19, 37 and 46 (see Appendix).

From early 2016, the Victorian government held forums with Aboriginal people across the state over recognition and treaty.[83] In 2017 Jill Gallagher AO, a proud Gunditjmara woman and former CEO of Victorian Aboriginal Community Controlled Health Organisation (VACCHO) was appointed as the Victorian Treaty Advancement Commissioner until the First Peoples' Assembly was created. Under the *Advancing the Treaty Process with Aboriginal Victorians Act 2018*, Gallagher, in consultation with Victorian Aboriginal communities, devised the First Peoples' Assembly of Victoria. It was essentially Victoria's own Voice to Parliament but created for the specific purpose of treaty negotiation. Aboriginal Victorians elected 22 general members across five voting regions, and another eleven seats were reserved for members of formally recognised traditional owner or RAP groups. The Assembly held its first meeting in December 2019. In consultation with the government, the members forged a Treaty Authority and a negotiating Framework.

The Assembly operated from Cambridge Street, Collingwood, and created an active and educational website, plus LinkedIn and Facebook pages. Its website invited those of our 'mob' and allies to join 'team treaty'. It provided educational articles and news of events, including Elders Voice gatherings, Treaty forums and barbecues.[84] The Melbourne City Council and the Assembly agreed to create a First Nations' precinct in the heart of the Melbourne central business district to be a permanent home for the Assembly, a keeping place for repatriated artefacts and a place of reconciliation. It would be 'Indigenous led, owned and operated and provide a platform for lifting the Indigenous community'.[85] To help drive the process, the government renamed the Ministry of Aboriginal Affairs as the Ministry of Treaty and First Peoples.

The Victorian Parliament passed the *Treaty Authority Act* in 2022. Marcus Stewart, Taungurung man and co-chair of the Assembly, welcomed this Act, as it placed 'First Peoples' lore, law and cultural authority at the heart of the journey to treaty'. Assembly co-chair and Bangerang and Wiradjuri Elder Geraldine Atkinson agreed, stating: 'now there is a real sense of hope growing. Hope that this country is ready to reckon with the past and make amends so we can create a better future together.'[86]

In 2022 the First Peoples' Assembly and government devised a Treaty Negotiating Framework to guide treaty-making in Victoria, based on Indigenous knowledge. Marcus Stewart and Geraldine Atkinson declared the framework recognised Indigenous 'lore, law and cultural authority' and established standards and criteria to guide traditional owner negotiations for treaties that reflected local needs and aspirations.

The First Peoples' Assembly wooed Victorians to its cause, celebrating Valentine's Day 2023 on Facebook and LinkedIn with a poem to fellow Victorians.

Roses are red, and violets are blue
We're leading the nation,
How bout you mob come too . . .
So let us embrace this Treaty with pride,
And walk together, with love by our side.
For a better Victoria, where all can thrive,
Treaty for Victoria, the time has arrived.[87]

A new Assembly of 22 people was elected in June 2023, by 4200 Aboriginal Victorians from an Indigenous electoral roll of 7000 people, to represent five regions. Its role was to negotiate a state-wide Treaty, through a process funded independently of government, 'that will deliver bold structural change, improving the lives of our people and ensuring we always have a strong voice and decision-making power'.[88] It would not be an easy process as one of the elected representatives, Gary Murray, asserted 'there are 38 [Aboriginal] nations in this state and they left out 28 of them'.[89]

The truth-telling process also began in earnest. The First Peoples' Assembly established the Yoorrook Justice Commission as the nation's first truth-telling commission, led by Professor Eleanor Bourke AM. Yoorrook held its first hearings in early 2022 and in June issued an interim report, *Yoorrook with Purpose*, heralded by strong speeches from Jill Gallagher and Eleanor Bourke. The report outlined Yoorrook's purposes, legal framework, values, challenges and emerging themes from the first yarning circles of 199 people at 29 different locations across the state. It developed a website, which enabled visitors to view the Commission's hearings.[90]

The journey to realise more fully the UNDRIP is ongoing. A new dawn through treaty-making, truth-telling and voice is slowly breaking through the darkness of injustice and indifference. Over time, this new light will be embedded into many spheres of Victorian life, ushering in a more united and reconciled future. Aunty Charmaine Clarke enthused: 'In Victoria we're already making good progress. We have a VOICE already in the First Peoples' Assembly. We have TRUTH-telling with Yoorrook, and we have TREATY within reach.'[91]

Appendix

United Nations Declaration on the Rights of Indigenous Peoples Adopted by the General Assembly 13 September 2007

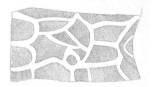

Most of the following articles of the Declaration have been abbreviated and the long prologue omitted. The full text is found at: www.un.org/development/desa/indigenouspeoples/wp-content/uploads/sites/19/2018/11/UNDRIP_E_web.pdf

Article 1 Indigenous peoples have the right to the full enjoyment, as a collective or as individuals, of all human rights and fundamental freedoms as recognized in the Charter of the United Nations, the Universal Declaration of Human Rights and international human rights law.

Article 2 Indigenous peoples and individuals are free and equal to all other peoples and individuals.

Article 3 Indigenous peoples have the right to self-determination.

Article 4 Indigenous peoples, in exercising their right to self-determination, have the right to autonomy or self-government in matters relating to their internal and local affairs.

Article 5 Indigenous peoples have the right to maintain and strengthen their distinct political, legal, economic, social and cultural institutions, while retaining their right to participate fully, if they so choose, in the political, economic, social and cultural life of the State.

Article 6 Every indigenous individual has the right to a nationality.

Article 7 Indigenous individuals have the rights to life, physical and mental integrity, liberty and security of person. Indigenous peoples have the collective right to live in freedom, peace and security as distinct peoples and shall not be subjected to any act of genocide or any other act of violence, including forcibly removing children of the group to another group.

Article 8 Indigenous peoples and individuals have the right not to be subjected to forced assimilation or destruction of their culture.

Article 9 Indigenous peoples and individuals have the right to belong to an indigenous community or nation.

Article 10 Indigenous peoples shall not be forcibly removed from their lands or territories.

Article 11 Indigenous peoples have the right to practise and revitalize their cultural traditions and customs.

Article 12 Indigenous peoples have the right to manifest, practise, develop and teach their spiritual and religious traditions, customs and ceremonies; the right to maintain, protect, and have access in privacy to their religious and cultural sites; the right to the use and control of their ceremonial objects; and the right to the repatriation of their human remains.

Article 13 Indigenous peoples have the right to revitalize, use, develop and transmit to future generations their histories, languages, oral traditions, philosophies, writing systems and literatures, and to designate and retain their own names for communities, places and persons.

Article 14 Indigenous peoples have the right to establish and control their educational systems and institutions providing education in their own languages, in a manner appropriate to their cultural methods of teaching and learning. Indigenous individuals, particularly children, have the right to all levels and forms of education of the State without discrimination.

Article 15 Indigenous peoples have the right to the dignity and diversity of their cultures, traditions, histories and aspirations which shall be appropriately reflected in education and public information.

Article 16 Indigenous peoples have the right to establish their own media in their own languages and to have access to all forms of non-indigenous media without discrimination.

Article 17 Indigenous individuals and peoples have the right to enjoy fully all rights established under applicable international and domestic labour law.

Article 18 Indigenous peoples have the right to participate in decision-making in matters which would affect their rights, through representatives chosen by themselves in accordance with their own procedures, as well as to maintain and develop their own indigenous decision-making institutions.

Article 19 States shall consult and cooperate in good faith with the indigenous peoples concerned through their own representative institutions in order to obtain their free, prior and informed consent before adopting and implementing legislative or administrative measures that may affect them.

Article 20 Indigenous peoples have the right to maintain and develop their political, economic and social systems or institutions.

Article 21 Indigenous peoples have the right, without discrimination, to the improvement of their economic and social conditions.

Article 22 Particular attention shall be paid to the rights and special needs of indigenous elders, women, youth, children and persons with disabilities in the implementation of this Declaration.

Article 23 Indigenous peoples have the right to determine and develop priorities and strategies for exercising their right to development . . . and, as far as possible, to administer such programmes through their own institutions.

Article 24 Indigenous peoples have the right to their traditional medicines and to maintain their health practices . . . and have an equal right to the enjoyment of the highest attainable standard of physical and mental health.

Article 25 Indigenous peoples have the right to maintain and strengthen their distinctive spiritual relationship with their traditionally owned or otherwise occupied and used lands, territories, waters and coastal seas and other resources and to uphold their responsibilities to future generations in this regard.

Article 26 Indigenous peoples have the right to own, use, develop and control the lands, territories and resources that they possess by reason of traditional ownership or other traditional occupation or use, as well as those which they have otherwise acquired.

Article 27 States shall establish and implement, in conjunction with indigenous peoples concerned, a fair, independent, impartial, open and transparent process . . . to recognize and adjudicate the rights of indigenous peoples pertaining to their lands.

Article 28 Indigenous peoples have the right to redress, by means that can include restitution or, when this is not possible, just, fair and equitable compensation, for the lands, territories and resources which they have traditionally owned or otherwise occupied or used, and which have been confiscated, taken, occupied, used or damaged without their free, prior and informed consent.

Article 29 Indigenous peoples have the right to the conservation and protection of the environment and the productive capacity of their lands or territories and resources.

Article 30 Military activities shall not take place in the lands or territories of indigenous peoples, unless justified by a relevant public interest or otherwise freely agreed with or requested by the indigenous peoples concerned.

Article 31 Indigenous peoples have the right to maintain, control, protect and develop their cultural heritage, traditional knowledge and traditional cultural expressions, as well as the manifestations of their sciences, technologies and cultures.

Article 32 Indigenous peoples have the right to determine and develop priorities and strategies for the development or use of their lands or territories and other resources.

Article 33 Indigenous peoples have the right to determine their own identity or membership in accordance with their customs and traditions.

Article 34 Indigenous peoples have the right to promote, develop and maintain their institutional structures and their distinctive customs, spirituality, traditions, procedures, practices.

Article 35 Indigenous peoples have the right to determine the responsibilities of individuals to their communities.

Article 36 Indigenous peoples, in particular those divided by international borders, have the right to maintain and develop contacts, relations and cooperation, including activities for spiritual, cultural, political, economic and social purposes, with their own members as well as other peoples across borders.

Article 37 Indigenous peoples have the right to the recognition, observance and enforcement of treaties, agreements and other constructive arrangements concluded with States or their successors and to have States honour and respect such treaties.

Article 38 States in consultation and cooperation with indigenous peoples, shall take the appropriate measures, including legislative measures, to achieve the ends of this Declaration.

Article 39 Indigenous peoples have the right to have access to financial and technical assistance from States and through international cooperation, for the enjoyment of the rights contained in this Declaration.

Article 40 Indigenous peoples have the right to access to and prompt decision through just and fair procedures for the resolution of conflicts and disputes with States or other parties.

Article 41 The organs and specialized agencies of the United Nations system and other intergovernmental organizations shall contribute to the full realization of the provisions of this Declaration.

Article 42 The United Nations, its bodies, including the Permanent Forum on Indigenous Issues, and specialized agencies, including at the country level, and States shall promote respect for and full application of the provisions of this Declaration and follow up the effectiveness of this Declaration.

Article 43 The rights recognized herein constitute the minimum standards for the survival, dignity and well-being of the indigenous peoples of the world.

Article 44 All the rights and freedoms recognized herein are equally guaranteed to male and female indigenous individuals.

Article 45 Nothing in this Declaration may be construed as diminishing or extinguishing the rights indigenous peoples have now or may acquire in the future.

Article 46 The provisions set forth in this Declaration shall be interpreted in accordance with the principles of justice, democracy, respect for human rights, equality, non-discrimination, good governance and good faith.

Recommended Reading

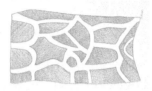

Note: The endnotes of each chapter reveal the extensive archival, official, press, manuscript, secondary and interview material on which this book is based. Below is suggested reading for those who wish to read further, but do not wish to engage in research from primary documents.

Anon., *Koorie*, Koorie Cultural Heritage Trust, Melbourne, no date.

Anon., *Victims or Victors? The Story of the Victorian Aborigines Advancement League*, Hyland House, Melbourne, 1985.

Attwood, Bain, *The Good Country: The Djadja Wurrung, the Settlers and the Protectors*, Monash University Press, Melbourne, 2017.

——, *The Making of the Aborigines*, Allen & Unwin, Sydney, 1989.

——, *Rights for Aborigines*, Allen & Unwin, Sydney, 2003.

——, *William Cooper: An Aboriginal Life Story*, Miegunyah Press, Melbourne, 2021.

Attwood, Bain and Foster, S.G. (eds), *Frontier Conflict: The Australian Experience*, National Museum of Australia, Canberra, 2003.

Attwood, Bain and Markus, Andrew (eds), *The Struggle for Aboriginal Rights*, Allen & Unwin, Sydney, 1999.

Attwood, Bain and Markus, Andrew, *Thinking Black: William Cooper and the Australian Aborigines' League*, Aboriginal Studies Press, Canberra, 2004.

Banivanua Mar, Tracey, 'Imperial Literacy and Indigenous Rights: Tracing Transoceanic Circuits of a Modern Discourse', *Aboriginal History*, vol. 37, 2013, pp. 1–28.

Barwick, Diane, 'The Aboriginal Family in South-eastern Australia', in J. Krupinski and A. Stoller (eds), *The Family in Australia*, Pergamon Press, Sydney, 1978.

——, 'And The Lubras are Ladies Now', in F. Gale (ed.), *Woman's Role in Aboriginal Society*, Australian Institute of Aboriginal Studies, Canberra, 1974.

——, 'Mapping the Past: An Atlas of Victorian Clans 1835–1904', *Aboriginal History*, vol. 8, no. 2, 1984, pp. 100–131.

——, *Rebellion at Coranderrk*, L.E. Barwick and R.E. Barwick (eds), Aboriginal History Monograph 5, Canberra, 1998.

——, 'This Most Resolute Lady: A Biographical Puzzle', in D.E. Barwick, J. Beckett and M. Reay (eds), *Metaphors of Interpretation: Essays in Honour of W. E. H. Stanner*, Australian National University Press, Canberra, 1985.

Boucher, Leigh and Russell, Lynette (eds), *Settler Colonial Governance in Nineteenth-Century Victoria*, ANU Press, Canberra, 2015.

Broome, Richard, 'Aboriginal Workers on South-eastern Frontiers', *Australian Historical Studies*, vol. 26, no. 103, October 1994, pp. 202–220.

——, 'Aboriginal Victims and Voyagers, Confronting Frontier Myths', *Journal of Australian Studies*, vol. 18, no. 42, 1994, pp. 70–77.

——, *Fighting Hard: The Victorian Aborigines Advancement League*, Aboriginal Studies Press, Canberra, 2015.

——, 'The Struggle for Australia: Aboriginal-European Warfare, 1770–1930', in M. McKernan and M. Browne (eds), *Australia: Two Centuries of War & Peace*, Australian War Memorial/Allen & Unwin, Canberra, 1988.

——, '"There Were Vegetables Every Year Mr Green Was Here": Right Behaviour and the Struggle for Autonomy at Coranderrk Aboriginal Reserve', *History Australia*, vol. 3, no. 2, 2006, pp. 43.1–43.16.

Broome, Richard; Fahey, Charles; Gaynor, Andrea; and Holmes, Katie, *Mallee Country: Land, People, History*, Monash University Press, Melbourne, 2021.

Broome, Richard and Jackomos, Alick, *Sideshow Alley*, Allen & Unwin, Sydney, 1998.

Campbell, A. and Vanderwal, R. (eds), 'Victorian Aborigines: John Bulmer's Recollections 1855–1908', *Occasional Papers Museum of Victoria (Anthropology & History)*, no. 1, Museum of Victoria, Melbourne, 1994.

Cannon, M. and Macfarlane, I. (eds), *Historical Records of Victoria, Foundation Series*, vols 2A and 2B, Government Printer, Melbourne, 1982 and 1983.

Christie, M.F., *Aborigines in Colonial Victoria 1835–86*, Sydney University Press, Sydney, 1979.

Clark, Ian, *Aboriginal Languages and Clans: An Historical Atlas of Western and Central Victoria, 1800–1900,* Monash Publications in Geography, no. 37, Melbourne, 1990.

——, *The Journals of George Augustus Robinson, Chief Protector, Port Phillip Aboriginal Protectorate, vols 1–6,* Heritage Matters, Melbourne, 1998.

——, *Scars in the Landscape: A Register of Massacre Sites in Western Victoria, 1803–1859,* Aboriginal Studies Press, Canberra, 1995.

Clarke, Banjo as told to Camilla Chance, *Wisdom Man: The Compassionate Life and Beliefs of a Remarkable Aboriginal Elder,* Penguin/Viking, Melbourne, 2003.

Corris, Peter, *Aborigines and Europeans in Western Victoria,* Australian Institute of Aboriginal Studies, Canberra, 1968.

Critchett, Jan, *A Distant Field of Murder: Western District Frontiers 1834–1848,* Melbourne University Press, Melbourne, 1990.

——, *Our Land Till We Die: A History of the Framlingham Aborigines,* by the author, Warrnambool, 1980.

——, *Untold Stories: Memories and Lives of Victorian Kooris,* Melbourne University Press, Melbourne, 1998.

Davis, Fiona, *Australian Settler Colonialism and the Cummeragunja Aboriginal Station: Redrawing Boundaries,* Sussex Academic Press, Brighton, 2014.

Dyer, Mollie, *Room for One More: The Life of Mollie Dyer,* Aboriginal Affairs Victoria, Melbourne, 2003.

Edmonds, Penelope, *Urbanizing Frontiers: Indigenous Peoples and Settlers in 19th-Century Pacific Rim Cities,* UBC Press, Vancouver, 2010.

Ellender, Isabel and Christiansen, Peter, *People of the Merri Merri: The Wurundjeri in Colonial Days,* Merri Creek Management Committee, Melbourne, 2001.

Ellinghaus, Katherine, 'Regulating Koori Marriages: The 1886 Victorian *Aborigines Protection Act',* *Journal of Australian Studies,* vol. 25, no. 67, 2001, pp. 22–29.

Evans, Julie, 'Living Together Justly in Settler Societies: Legacies of the Coranderrk Aboriginal Reserve and the 1881 Inquiry into Its Management', *Journal of Social History,* vol. 50, no. 3, 2017, pp. 555–71.

Fels, Marie Hansen, *Good Men and True: The Aboriginal Police of the Port Phillip District 1837–1853,* Melbourne University Press, Melbourne, 1988.

Furphy, Samuel, *Edward M. Curr and the Tide of History,* ANU ePress, Canberra, 2013.

Healy, Sianan, 'Aboriginal Mobility and the Search for a Home and a Job in Postwar Victoria', *Australian Historical Studies*, vol. 51, no. 1, 2020, pp. 38–53.

Horton, Jessica, 'Rewriting Political History: Letters from Aboriginal People in Victoria, 1886–1919', *History Australia*, vol. 9, no. 2, 2012, pp. 157–81.

Jackomos, Alick and Fowell, Derek (eds), *Forgotten Heroes: Aborigines at War from the Somme to Vietnam*, Victoria Press, Melbourne, 1993.

——, *Living Aboriginal History of Victoria: Stories in the Oral Tradition*, Cambridge University Press, Melbourne, 1991.

Jensz, Felicity, *German Moravian Missionaries in the British Colony of Victoria, Australia, 1848–1908*, BRILL, Leiden, Netherlands, 2010.

Lovett-Gardiner, Iris, *Lady of the Lake*, Koorie Heritage Trust, Melbourne, 1997.

Lowe, Robert, *The Mish*, University of Queensland Press, Brisbane, 2002.

Lydon, Jane, 'The Experimental 1860s: Charles Walter's Images of Coranderrk Aboriginal Station, Victoria', *Aboriginal History*, vol. 26, 2002, pp. 78–130.

——, *Eye Contact: Photographing Indigenous Australians*, Duke University Press, Durham, N.C., 2005.

Manning, Corinne, 'The McLean Report: Legitimising Victoria's New Assimilationism', *Aboriginal History*, vol. 26, 2002, pp. 159–76.

Mulvaney, John and Harcourt, Rex, *Cricket Walkabout: The Australian Aboriginal Cricketers on Tour 1867–8*, 2nd ed., Melbourne University Press, Melbourne, 1988.

Nance, Beverley, 'The Level of Violence: Europeans and Aborigines in Port Phillip, 1835–1850', *Historical Studies*, vol. 19, no. 77, October 1981, pp. 532–52.

Nanni, Giordano and James, Andrea, *Coranderrk: We Will Show the Country*, Aboriginal Studies Press, Canberra, 2013.

Pascoe, Bruce (ed.), *Wathaurong Too Bloody Strong*, by the author, Geelong, 1997.

Pepper, Phillip, *You Are What You Make Yourself To Be: The Story of a Victorian Aboriginal Family 1842–1980*, Hyland House, Melbourne, 1980.

Pepper, Phillip and de Araugo, Tess, *The Kurnai of Gippsland*, Hyland House, Melbourne, 1985.

Russell, Lynette, *Roving Mariners: Australian Aboriginal Whalers and Sealers in the Southern Oceans, 1790–1870*, State University of New York Press, Ithaca, N.Y., 2012.

Standfield, Rachel (ed.), *Indigenous Mobilities: Across and Beyond the Antipodes*, ANU Press, Canberra, 2018.

Tonkin, Daryl and Landon, Carolyn, *Jackson's Track: Memoir of a Dreamtime Place*, Viking, Melbourne, 1999.

van Toorn, Penny, *Writing Never Arrives Naked: Early Aboriginal Cultures of Writing in Australia*, AIATSIS, Canberra, 2006.

Endnotes

Reflections

1. See creation stories collected by Alfred Howitt including that collected by his uncle Richard, in the *Native Tribes of South-East Australia*, Macmillan, London, 1904, pp. 484–92. See also William Thomas, in Thomas Francis Bride (ed.), *Letters from Victorian Pioneers*, Heinemann, Melbourne, 1969, first published 1898, pp. 419–25.
2. John Mulvaney and Johan Kamminga, *The Prehistory of Australia*, Allen & Unwin, Sydney, 1999, chaps 9–10. See also Josephine Flood, *Archaeology of the Dreamtime*, Collins, Sydney, 1999; Josephine Flood, *The Riches of Ancient Australia*, University of Queensland Press, Brisbane, 1990.
3. Mulvaney and Kamminga, *Prehistory of Australia*, chap. 7.
4. Caroline Bird and David Frankel, 'Aboriginal Sites in the Grampians-Gariwerd Region', La Trobe University, Melbourne, 1998.
5. Mulvaney and Kamminga, *Prehistory of Australia*, chaps 13–14.
6. Harry Lourandos, 'Change of Stability? Hydraulics, Hunter-Gatherers and Population in Temperate Australia', *World Archaeology*, vol. 11, no. 3, February 1980, pp. 245–64.
7. Jared Diamond, *Guns, Germs and Steel: A Short History of Everybody for the Last 13,000 Years*, Vintage, London, 1998, chaps 4 and 8.
8. Harry Lourandos, *Continent of Hunter Gatherers. New Perspectives in Australian Prehistory*, Cambridge University Press, New York, 1997.
9. James Dawson, *Australian Aborigines. The Languages and Customs of Several Tribes of Aborigines in the Western District of Victoria, Australia*, George Robertson, Melbourne, 1881, pp. iii, 5.
10. N. W. G. McIntosh, K. N. Smith and A. B. Bailey, 'Lake Nitchie Skelton—Unique Aboriginal Burial', *Archaeology and Physical Anthropology in Oceania*, vol. 5, pt 2, pp. 85–101.

11. William Thomas, 'Brief Account of the Aborigines of Australia Felix', in Bride (ed.), *Letters from Victorian Pioneers*, p. 398. See also Diane Barwick, 'Mapping the Past. An Atlas of Victorian Clans, 1835–1904', *Aboriginal History*, vol. 8, part 2, 1984, pp. 100-31 and Gary Presland, *Aboriginal Melbourne. The Lost Land of the Kulin People*, Penguin, Melbourne, 1998.

12. On axes and trade see Isabel McBryde, 'Wil-im-ee Moor-ring: Or, Where do Axes Come From?', *Mankind*, vol. 11, 1978, pp. 354–82; Isabel McBryde, 'Exchange in South-Eastern Australia: an Ethnohistorical Perspective', *Aboriginal History*, vol. 8, pt 2, pp. 132–53; D. J. Mulvaney, '"The Chain of Connection": The Material Evidence', in N. Petersen (ed.), *Tribes and Boundaries*, Australian Institute of Aboriginal Studies, Canberra, 1976, pp. 72–94.

1. Meeting strangers

1. A. Campbell and R. Vanderwal (eds), 'Victorian Aborigines. John Bulmer's Recollections 1855–1908', *Occasional Papers Museum of Victoria (Anthropology & History)*, no. 1, 1994, Museum of Victoria, Melbourne.

2. For first contacts see R. D. Boys, *First Years at Port Phillip*, Robertson and Mullins, Melbourne, 1935, pp. 4–28; for Lady Nelson visit see F. Labilliere, *Early History of the Colony of Victoria From Its Discovery to Its Establishment as a Self-Governing Province of the British Empire*, Sampson Low, Marston, Searle and Rivington, London, 1878, pp. 89–92; for Milius see E. Scott, 'The Early History of Western Port, Part One', *Victorian Historical Magazine*, vol. 6, no.1, September, 1917, pp. 15–17.

3. For the Sorrento settlement see Rev. Robert Knopwood's Journal in C. E. Sayers (ed.), J. T. Shillinglaw, *Historical Records of Port Phillip*, Heinemann, Melbourne, 1972, (first published 1879), pp. 136–61; and J. H. Tuckey, *Account of a Voyage to Establish a Colony at Port Phillip*, London, 1805, pp. 167–81; David Collins quoted in Shillinglaw, p. 83.

4. E. Sayers (ed.), John Morgan, *The Life and Adventures of William Buckley*, Heinemann, London, 1967, pp. 20–3; M. J. Tipping, 'William Buckley', Douglas Pike (ed.), *Australian Dictionary of Biography*, Melbourne University Press, Melbourne, 1966, vol. 1, pp. 174–5.

5. See Diane Barwick exhaustive study of Louisa Briggs, 'This Most Resolute Lady: A Biographical Puzzle', in D.E. Barwick, J. Beckett and M. Reay (eds), *Metaphors of Interpretation. Essays in Honour of W. E. H. Stanner*, Australian National University Press, Canberra, 1985, pp. 209–11 and footnote 20.

6. For European exploration of Victoria, see Susan Priestley, *The Victorians: Making Their Mark*, Fairfax, Syme and Weldon, Sydney, 1984, chap. 2.

7. For the presence of smallpox in Australia see Judy Campbell, *Invisible Invaders. Smallpox and Other Diseases in Aboriginal Australia 1780-1880*, Melbourne University Press, Melbourne, 2002; Noel Butlin, *Our Original Aggression*, Allen & Unwin, London, 1983; A. S. Benenson (ed.), *Control of Communicable Diseases in Man*, Washington DC, 1980, pp. 315–21.

8. Journal of James Flemming in Shillinglaw, *Historical Records of Port Phillip*, p. 32.

9. Sayers, *Adventures of William Buckley*, p. 68.

10. Quoted in E. M. Curr *The Australian Race: Its Origin, Languages, Customs...*, Victorian Government Printer, Melbourne, 1886, p. 216.

11. Campbell, *Invisible Invaders*, pp. 152–6 discusses the widespread evidence.

12. Peter Beveridge, *The Aborigines of Victoria and Riverina*, Hutchinson, Melbourne, 1889, p. 180.

13. Campbell and Vanderwal (eds), 'John Bulmer's Recollections', p. 69.

14. William Thomas in C. E. Sayers (ed.), T. F. Bride compiled, *Letters From Victorian Pioneers*, Heinemann, Melbourne, 1969, first published 1898, p. 426.

15. *Port Phillip Gazette*, 11 February 1843.

16. Butlin, *Our Original Aggression*, p. 146.

17. E. Kolig, 'Bi:n and Gadeja. An Australian Aboriginal Model of the European Society as a Guide in Social Change', *Oceania*, vol. 43, no.1 September 1972, pp. 1–18.

18. Quoted in James Bonwick, *Port Phillip Settlement*, Sampson Low, Marston, Searle and Rivington, London, 1883, p. 185.

19. The quotations are from John Batman's Journal, 4 June, 6 June 1835, in James Bonwick, *Port Phillip Settlement*, pp. 181–8. The Batman treaty is contentious to this day and the literature is large. For the view of it as a trick see A. H. Campbell, *John Batman and the Aborigines*, Kibble Books, Melbourne, 1983 and for a reading of it from an Aboriginal perspective see D. Barwick, 'Mapping the Past. An Atlas of Victorian Clans 1835–1904', *Aboriginal History*, vol, 8, pt 2, 1984, pp. 106–7.

20. P. L. Brown (ed.), *The Todd Journal*, Geelong Historical Society, Geelong, 1989, especially 6 July 1835.

21. John H. Wedge,' Narrative of an Excursion Amongst the Natives of Port Phillip', *Tasmanian Parliamentary Papers*, 1885, vol. 5, no. 44, pp. 18–20.

22. Joseph Tice Gellibrand, 'Memorandum of a Trip to Port Phillip', in Bride, *Letters*, p. 20.

23. ibid., p. 31.

24. Fawkner's diary, 28 October 1835, in C. P. Billot (ed.), *Melbourne's Missing Chronicle*, Melbourne, 1982.

25. Fawkner's diary, 9 December 1835 in Billot (ed.), *Melbourne's Missing Chronicle*.

26. See Fawkner's diary from October 1835 to August 1836 in Billot (ed.), *Melbourne's Missing Chronicle*; Fawkner's reminiscences in SLV ms 8528; A.W. Greig, 'Some New Documentary Evidence Concerning the Foundation of Melbourne', *Victorian Historical Magazine*, vol. 12, no. 4, 1928, pp. 109–17.

27. M. F. Christie, *Aborigines in Colonial Victoria, 1835–86*, Sydney University Press, Sydney, 1979, p. 5; For Derrimut's status, see Barwick, 'Mapping the Past', p. 119.

28. William Thomas, Quarterly Report June–August 1846, VPRS 4410, unit 3 (hereafter without location numbers); and Daniel Bunce, 'Australasiatic Reminiscences', in his *Travels with Dr Leichhardt*, first published 1859, Oxford University Press, Melbourne, 1979, pp. 64–79.

29. Jan Penney, 'The Death of Queen Aggie; Culture Contact in the Mid-Murray Region', La Trobe University BA Hons, 1979, p. 48.

30. Billot (ed.), *Melbourne's Missing Chronicle*, p. 95.
31. G. H. Haydon, *Five Years Experience in Australia Felix*, Hamilton Adams, London, 1846, pp. 116–17.
32. Emphasis in the original, Gellibrand in Bride, *Letters*, p. 32.
33. The resolution is reprinted in H. G. Turner, *A History of the Colony of Victoria . . .*, Heritage Publications, Melbourne, 1973, first published in 1904, p. 151.

2 Melbourne, an Aboriginal domain

1. E. M. Curr, *Recollections of Squatting in Victoria*, Melbourne University Press, Melbourne, first pub. 1883, abridged 1965, p. 11.
2. G.G. McCrae, 'Some Recollections of Melbourne in the Forties', *Victorian Historical Magazine*, vol. 2, no.3, 1912, pp. 121–2.
3. Richard Howitt, *Impressions of Australia Felix During Four Years Residence in that Colony*, Longman, Brown, Green and Longmans, London, 1845, p. 185; Curr, *Recollections*, p. 11.
4. A. Russell, *A Tour through the Australian Colonies in* 1839, David Robertson—Duncan Campbell, Glasgow, 1840, p. 177.
5. Reprinted in J. Bonwick, *Port Phillip Settlement*, Sampson Low, Marston Searle and Rivington, London, 1883, p. 505.
6. John Cotton letters August 1843, in R. V. Billis and A. S. Kenyon, *Pastures New: An Account of the Pastoral Occupation of Port Phillip*, Macmillan and Co., Melbourne, 1930, pp. 228–9.
7. Howitt, *Impressions*, pp. 196, 197, 284, 196, 503, and 173–4.
8. See A. Hamilton, 'Blacks and Whites. The Relationships of Change', *Arena*, no. 30, 1972, pp. 41–3.
9. Fawkner's Diary, 9 March 1836, Billot, *Melbourne's Missing Chronicle*.
10. Russell, *Tour*, p. 177.
11. See William Thomas' Journal 5 April 1839, and James Dredge's Journal 28 March 1839, in HRV, vol, 2B, pp. 442, 451.
12. George Robinson to Colonial Secretary 13 May 1839, HRV, vol. 2B, p. 463.
13. William Thomas to Chief Protector George Robinson, 1 January 1840, VPRS 11.
14. Thomas Quarterly Report, December 1843–March 1844, June–August 1844; William Thomas to La Trobe, 1 October 1844, VPRS 10, unit 6 1844/1761.
15. *Victorian Year Book, Centenary Edition*, 1973, Commonwealth Bureau of Census and Statistics, Victorian Office, Melbourne, 1973, p. 1090.
16. Thomas Quarterly Report, June–August 1844.
17. Quoted in D. Frankel, 'An Account of Aboriginal Use of the Yam-Daisy', *Artefact*, vol. 7, no. 1–2, 1982, p. 44.
18. Quoted in William Thomas Notebook, p. 97 in R. B. Smyth Papers, box 1176/6 (b), La Trobe Library ms 8781.
19. Thomas Quarterly Report, March–May 1841.
20. Thomas Journal, 11 August 1844 in H. Sullivan, *An Archaeological Survey of the Mornington Peninsula, Victoria*, Victorian Archaeological Survey, Occasional Reports Series, no. 6, 1981, p. 17.

21. G. Blainey, *A Land Half Won*, Macmillan, Melbourne, 1980, p. 85.
22. William Thomas' Journal in *HRV*, vol. 2B, p. 538.
23. George Robinson to La Trobe, 19 September 1840, VPRS 10 unit 2, 1840/867.
24. Thomas Quarterly Report, February–August 1840.
25. Thomas Quarterly Report, August 1839–February 1840.
26. R. H.W. Reece, *Aborigines and Colonists. Aborigines and Colonial Society in New South Wales in the 1830s and 1840s*, Sydney University Press, Sydney, 1974, p. 188.
27. For a discussion of guns and spears see R. Broome, 'The Struggle for Australia: Aboriginal–European Warfare, 1770–1930', in M. McKernan & M. Browne, *Australia. Two Centuries of War & Peace*, Australian War Memorial/Allen & Unwin, Canberra, 1988, pp. 97–100, 104–5.
28. William Thomas evidence, 'Report of the Select Committee of the Legislative Committee on the Aborigines . . . ', *VPP VLC*, 1858–59, p. 69 (hereafter Select Committee 1859).
29. George Mackay in Bride (ed.), *Letters*, p. 212.
30. James Clow in Bride (ed.), *Letters*, p. 359.
31. Thomas, Select Committee 1859, p. 63.
32. J. H. Waterfield, 'Extracts from the Diary of the Rev. William Waterfield, First Congregational Minister at Port Phillip, 1838–1843', *Victorian Historical Magazine*, vol. 3, no. 3, March 1914, p. 109.
33. Beveridge, *Aborigines of Victoria*, p. 70.
34. Daniel Bunce, *Travels with Dr Leichhardt*, first pub. 1859, Oxford University Press, Melbourne, 1979, pp. 75–6.
35. Quoted in P. L. Brown (ed.), *Clyde Company Papers 1821–1850*, Oxford University Press, London, 1941, vol. 2, p. 239.
36. Howitt, *Impressions*, p.185.
37. Thomas Notebook in Smyth Papers, p. 99.
38. Quoted in Haydon, *Five Years' Experience*, p. 100.
39. G. Presland (ed.), *Journals of George Augustus Robinson, January–March 1840*, Records of the Victorian Archaeological Survey, no. 5, 1977, p. 12; Howitt, *Impressions*, p. 103.
40. Bunce, *Travels with Dr Leichhardt*, pp. 64–79.
41. Waterfield, 'Waterfield Diary', June 1838, p. 110.
42. Dredge Diary, 15 & 18 March 1839, La Trobe Library, ms 421957.
43. Reece, *Aborigines and Colonists*, p. 188; *Port Phillip Gazette*, 29 April 1840.
44. Thomas' Journal, 9 November 1839, *HRV*, vol. 2B, p. 558.
45. ibid., p. 559.
46. Howitt, *Impressions*, p. 196.
47. Thomas Quarterly Reports, June–August 1841 and June–August 1846.
48. Thomas Quarterly Reports, March–May, September–November, March–May 1846; Thomas in Bride, *Letters* (ed.), p. 406.
49. P. E. Cussens to G. A Robinson, 6 May 1839, *HRV*, vol. 2B, p. 461.
50. Thomas Quarterly Report, June-August 1846. On sorcery see B. Nance, 'The Level of Violence. Europeans and Aborigines in Port Phillip, 1835–1850', *Historical Studies*, vol. 19, no. 77, October 1981, pp. 532–49.

51. William Thomas evidence, 'Select Committee 1859, p. 62.
52. McCabe referred to in Hull, *Remarks*, p. 13. See McCabe in *Port Phillip Gazette*, 11 February 1843.
53. Wood quoted in P. L. Brown (ed.), *The Narrative of George Russell of Golf Hill with Russellania and Selected Papers*, Oxford University Press, London, 1935, p. 132; Howitt, *Impressions*, p. 189.
54. Thomas' Journal, *HRV*, vol. 2B, p. 564.
55. ibid., p. 549.
56. Waterfield, 'Diary of the Rev. William Waterfield', November 1838; Dredge Diary, 23 March 1839.
57. Howitt, *Impressions*, p. 187.
58. Thomas Quarterly Report, January–March 1844.
59. Thomas' Journal, *HRV*, vol. 2B, p. 543.
60. See the events in *HRV*, vol. 2B index entry 'Peter, servant of G. M. Langhorne'.
61. Thomas' census in *HRV*, vol. 2B, pp. 603–7.
62. Willliam Lonsdale to Sir Richard Bourke, 1 February 1837, in *HRV*, vol. 1, p. 87.
63. George Robinson to La Trobe, 6 December 1839, *HRV*, vol. 2B, p. 609.
64. William Thomas to George Robinson 17 December 1839, *HRV*, vol. 2B, pp. 609–10.
65. La Trobe to George Robinson, 18 December 1839, *HRV*, vol. 2B, p. 611.
66. George Robinson to William Thomas, 12 September 1840, VPRS 10, unit 2, 1840/39.
67. Thomas Quarterly Report, February–August 1840.
68. Colonial Secretary to Major Lettsom, 28 August 1840, in 'Papers Relative to the Aborigines, Australian Colonies', *BPP*, 1844, Irish University Press, Shannon, 1969, p. 92.
69. La Trobe to Major Lettsom, 10 October 1840, *BPP*, 1844, p. 5.
70. Thomas Quarterly Report, December 1840–February 1841.
71. Dredge Diary, 10–16 October 1840.
72. Dredge Diary, 15 January, 18 March 1841; see Christie, *Aborigines in Colonial Victoria*, pp. 110–12 for a full account of the case.
73. Thomas Quarterly Report, September 1840–February 1841.
74. William Hull evidence to Select Committee 1859, p. 12.
75. Thomas Quarterly Report, September–December 1843.
76. Thomas Quarterly Report, September–December 1846. For more on Thomas and Billibellary see I. Ellender and P. Christiansen, *People of the Merri Merri. The Wurundjeri in Colonial Days*, Merri Creek Management Committee, Melbourne, 2001.
77. Diane Barwick, 'Mapping the Past: An Atlas of Victorian Clans', *Aboriginal History*, vol. 8, part 2, 1984, p. 124.

3 Countering civilisers

1. *Historical Records of Australia*, series I, vol. I, pp. 13–14.
2. Extracts of the House of Commons Select Committee Report, in *HRV*, vol. 2A, pp. 62–9.

3. For an overview see J.B. Foxcroft, *Australian Native Policy. Its History Especially in Victoria*, Melbourne University Press, Melbourne, 1941; also *HRV*, vols 2A and 2B.

4. Alexander Maconochie to Lord Glenelg, 23 June 1837, *HRV*, vol. 2A, p. 240.

5. Memo to the Colonial Secretary, 18 November 1848, reprinted in *Argus*, 11 November 1849.

6. For this description see especially James Backhouse, *A Narrative of a Visit to the Australian Colonies*, Hamilton Adams and Co., London, 1843, p. 502; G.M. Langhorne to Col. Sec. 14 August 1837, *HRV*, vol. 2A, p. 12; and Mission Report November 1837, *HRV*, vol. 2A, p. 207; and other documents on pp. 191–236.

7. Justice Burton to Sir Richard Bourke, 22 November 1835, *HRV*, vol. 2A, p. 154.

8. Langhorne to Bourke, 26 November 1836, HRV, vol. 2A, p. 158.

9. For these two incidents see *HRV*, vol. 2A, pp. 213–26.

10. Mission Report November 1838, *HRV*, vol. 2A, p. 233.

11. Mission Report December 1838, *HRV*, vol. 2A, p. 234.

12. Langhorne to La Trobe, 15 October 1839, *HRV*, vol. 2B, p. 508.

13. For Buntingdale see C. Irving Benson, *A Century of Victorian Methodism*, Spectator Publishing, Melbourne, 1935; documents in *HRV*, vol. 2A, chap. 4.

14. See *HRV*, vol. 2B, chap. 15.

15. Aliquis' letter to the editor, *Port Philip Gazette*, 17 August 1839.

16. *Port Philip Gazette*, 4 March 1840.

17. 'Humanitas' and 'Memorabilia' in *Port Phillip Gazette*, 4 and 15 May 1839, respectively.

18. Return of Average Daily Attendance 1841–1849, Edward Parker Half Yearly Report to December 1849, VPRS 4410, unit 2, item 65, reprinted in E. Morrison, *Early Days in the Loddon Valley. Memoirs of Edward Stone Parker*, Daylesford, 1966, p. 82.

19. Parker evidence to 'Report from the Select Committee on the Condition of the Aborigines', NSWLC, 1845, p. 54.

20. Parker Report 1848, Morrison, *Early Days*, pp. 76–8.

21. Parker, Select Committee 1859, p. 23.

22. Parker's prayer and elders' reply in Parker Report, May 1842, Morrison, *Early Days*, p. 63.

23. Parker Report June to December 1849, VPRS 4410, unit 2 (where all his reports are to be found), item 65, reprinted in Morrison, *Early Days*, pp. 80–5.

24. See Marie Fels, The Dandenong Police Paddocks, Department of Conservation, Forests and Lands, Melbourne, 1986, for a description of the site.

25. Written evidence of H. E. Putney Dana to the 'Select Committee on the Aborigines and Protectorate', *NSWLC V&P*, 1849, vol. 2.

26. See Native Police Day Book 1847–1849, VPRS 90; H.E.P. Dana, Native Police Report June–December 1848, *NSWLC V&P*, 1849, no. 55a; E. Finn ('Garryowen'), *The Chronicles of Early Melbourne*, Fergusson and Mitchell, Melbourne, 1888, pp. 914–15.

27. Thomas, Select Committee 1859, p. 5.

28. Quoted by William Thomas, 'Brief Account of the Aborigines of Australia Felix', in Bride (ed.), *Letters*, p. 400.

29. Superintendent's Report 1 February 1843, reprinted in Michael Jones, *Prolific in God's Gifts. A Social History of Knox and the Dandenongs*, Allen & Unwin, Sydney, 1983, pp. 287–90.

30. Marie Fels, *Good Men and True. The Aboriginal Police of Port Phillip District 1837–1853*, Melbourne University Press, Melbourne, 1988, p. 55.

31. William Thomas Quarterly Report December 1843–February 1844, VPRS 4410, unit 3.

32. George Robinson to C. J. La Trobe, 13 April 1847, VPRS 10, unit 8, 1847/561 and Native Police Day Book, 9 January–1 February 1849, VPRS 90.

33. Peter Corris, *Aborigines and Europeans in Western Victoria*, Australian Institute of Aboriginal Studies, Canberra, 1968, pp. 114–16; Michael Christie, *Aborigines in Colonial Victoria 1835–86*, Sydney University Press, Sydney, 1979, pp. 71–7.

34. C. E. Sayers (ed.), Rolf Boldrewood, *Old Melbourne Memories*, William Heinemann, Melbourne, 1969, (first published 1884), p. 68.

35. William Thomas Quarterly Report September–December 1843.

36. Beverley Nance, 'The Level of Violence: Europeans and Aborigines in Port Phillip, 1835–1850', *Historical Studies*, vol. 19, no. 77, October, 1981, p. 540.

37. Thomas in Bride (ed.), *Letters*, pp. 404–13; Thomas, Select Committee 1859, pp. 4–5.

38. Fels, *Good Men and True*, p. 227. See also Foxcroft, *Australian Native Policy*, p. 90.

39. Noble Keenan's journal, Department of Aborigines Account Book, Schools Board August 1841–January 1843, VPRS 26, p. 6

40. Keenan's Journal, p. 151.

41. Keenan's Journal, pp. 143–52.

42. John Ham et al to C. La Trobe, 6 November 1845, reprinted in Edward Sweetman, 'History of the Merri Creek Aboriginal School, 1845–50', ANZAAS Report, no. 22, p. 177.

43. William Thomas to C. La Trobe, 5 May 1846 and *Port Phillip Gazette*, 18 March 1846, quoted in Sweetman, 'Merri Creek Aboriginal School', pp. 178–9.

44. See *Port Phillip Patriot* and *Port Phillip Gazette* reprinted in Sweetman, 'Merri Creek Aboriginal School', pp. 180–1.

45. Evidence of Rev. John Ham to 'Select Committee on the Aborigines and the Protectorate'. *NSWLC V&P*, vol. 2, 1849.

46. Evidence of John Ham and Merri Creek School report in 'Select Committee on the Aborigines and the Protectorate'.

47. Quoted in Sweetman, 'Merri Creek Aboriginal School', p. 182. See also Thomas Quarterly Report, December 1846–February 1847, VPRS 4410, unit 4.

48. Thomas Quarterly Report, March–May 1847.

49. Thomas Quarterly Report, December 1846–February 1847, September–November 1847.

50. *Argus*, 4 January 1848; Ramsey to C. La Trobe 4 February 1848, VPRS 10, Unit 9, 1848/296.
51. Lucy Anna Edgar, *Among the Black Boys: being the history of an attempt at civilising some young Aborigines of Australia*, Emily Faithfull, London, 1865, p. 35. Whereas Edgar says Charley was from Gippsland, Fels, *Good Men and True*, p. 90 locates Charley as a Murray youth named Murrumwiller.
52. For a recent account of this story, see Julie Carr, *The Captive White Woman of Gippsland: In Pursuit of the Legend*, Melbourne University Press, Melbourne, 2001.
53. Edgar, *Among the Black Boys*, pp. 28–9, p. 95.
54. The Albert Memi, *The Colonizer and the Colonized*, translated by Howard Greenfeld, Orion Press, New York, 1965, pp. 119–26.
55. Edgar, *Among the Black Boys*, pp. 93–4.
56. William Thomas Weekly Report, 12–18 May 1851, VPRS 2893, unit 1, 1851/27. See also 1851/20, 1851/21 and 1851/24.
57. *Argus*, 2 July 1851.
58. Edgar, *Among the Black Boys*, p. 110.
59. Quoted in Fels, *Good Men and True*, p. 103.

4 Accommodating sheep herders

1. Thomas Mitchell, *Three Expeditions into the Interior of Eastern Australia, with Descriptions of the Recently Explored Region of Australia Felix and of the Present Colony of New South Wales*, second edition, T. and W. Boone, London, 1839, vol. 2 pp. 159, 333.
2. P. L. Brown (ed.), *The Narrative of George Russell of Golf Hill*, Oxford University Press, London, 1935, p. 89.
3. Ian D. Clark, *The Journals of George Augustus Robinson, Chief Protector, Port Phillip Protectorate, Volume One, 1 January 1839–30 September 1840*, Heritage Matters, Melbourne, 1998, p. 125.
4. George Mackaness (ed.), *George Augustus Robinson's Journey into South-Eastern Australia, 1844, with George Henry Haydon's Narrative of Part of the Same Journey*, Mackaness, Sydney, 1941, pp. 57–8.
5. Geoffrey Rawson, *The Count. A Life of Sir Paul Edmund Strzelecki KCMG, Explorer and Scientist*, William Heinemann, Melbourne, 1953, p. 95; W. A. Brodribb, 'Exploration of Gippsland', in *Proceedings of the Australian Geographical Conference*, AIATSIS Library, P7718 pp. 197–8, 205.
6. Thomas Walker, *A Month in the Bush of Australia*, J. Cross, London, 1838, p. 26.
7. Brodribb, 'Exploration of Gippsland', pp. 197–8.
8. David Fisher in Bride (ed.), *Letters*, p. 42.
9. *Port Phillip Herald*, 19 May 1843.
10. James Clow in Bride (ed.), *Letters*, pp. 108–9.
11. E. M. Curr, *Recollections of Squatting in Victoria*, Melbourne University Press, Melbourne, 1965, abridged 2nd edition, p. 42.
12. ibid., p. 49.
13. ibid., p. 164.

14. ibid., p. 124.
15. ibid., p.81.
16. Hinkins, John T., *Life Amongst the Native Race: with Extracts from a Diary*, Haase, McQueen and Co., Melbourne, 1884, p. 46.
17. ibid., p. 45.
18. Mrs Thomson (K. Kirkland), *Life in the Bush, by a Lady*, Chambers Miscellany, London, 1845, pp. 13–14.
19. H. McCrae (ed.), 'Fragment of a Diary Kept by George Gordon McCrae, Thirteen Years of Age', in *Georgiana's Journal: Melbourne a Hundred Years Ago*, Angus and Robertson, Sydney, 1934, pp. 201–13.
20. Hinkins, *Life Amongst the Native Race*, p. 25.
21. J. C. Hamilton, *Pioneering Days in Western Victoria: A Narrative of Early Station Life*, Macmillan, Melbourne, 1923, p. 94.
22. Morrison, *Early Days*, pp. 10, 61.
23. John McLeod in Bride (ed.), *Letters*, p. 149.
24. Foster Fyans to Colonial Secretary, 13 July 1838, *HRV*, vol. 2B, p. 742.
25. John McLeod in Bride (ed.), *Letters*, p. 148.
26. *HRV*, vol. 2B, p. 739.
27. George Faithfull in Bride (ed.), *Letters*, p. 221.
28. Boldrewood, *Old Melbourne Memories*, p. 151.
29. Curr, *Recollections of Squatting*, p. 137.
30. G. G. McCrae, 'The Early Settlement of the Eastern Shores of Port Phillip Bay: With a Note on the Aborigines of the Coast', *Victorian Historical Magazine*, vol. 1, no. 1, January 1911, p. 24.
31. Hugh Jamieson in Bride (ed.), *Letters*, p. 380.
32. Quoted in Clark (ed.), *The Journals of George Augustus Robinson*, vol. 1, p. 287. See also Richard Broome, 'Aboriginal Workers on South-eastern Frontiers', *Australian Historical Studies*, no. 103, October 1994, pp. 202–20.
33. John Watton, to 'Select Committee on the Condition of the Aborigines', 1845, p. 58.
34. William Westgarth, *Australian Felix, or a Historical and Descriptive Account of the Settlement of Port Phillip, New South Wales*, Oliver and Boyd, Edinburgh, 1848, pp. 56–7.
35. See Anne R. Higginbotham, ' "Sin of the Age". Infanticide and Illegitimacy in Victorian London', in K. O. Garrigan (ed.), *Victorian Scandals: Representations of Gender and Class*, Ohio University Press, Athens Ohio, 1992, pp. 257–88.
36. Foster Fyans evidence to 'Select Committee on Aborigines', 1845, p. 54.
37. Westgarth, *Australia Felix*, p. 74.
38. On cannibalism see Gananath Obeysekere, 'Cannibal Feasts in Nineteenth Century Fiji; Seamen's Yarns and the Ethnographic Imagination', F. Barker, P. Hulme and M. Iversen, *Cannibalism in the Colonial World*, Cambridge University Press, New York, 1998, chap. 3.
39. Haydon, *Five Years' Experience in Australia Felix*, p. 105.
40. ibid., p. 107.
41. George Langhorne's Reminiscences, *HRV*, vol. 2A, p. 183.

42. William Thomas to Select Committee 1859, p. 4; William Thomas Journal, *HRV*, vol. 2B, p. 543.
43. Hugh Murray in Bride (ed.), *Letters*, p. 103.
44. William Westgarth, *Personal Recollections of Early Melbourne and Victoria*, George Robinson and Co., Melbourne, 1988, p. 15.
45. Aboriginal man quoted in Beverley Nance, 'The Level of Violence', p. 536.
46. Clark (ed.), *The Journals of George Augustus Robinson*, vol. 1, pp. 80–1.
47. Dredge Diary, 22 November 1839.
48. Clark (ed.), *The Journals of George Augustus Robinson*, vol. 1, pp. 80–1.
49. William Mollison in Bride (ed.), *Letters*, p. 258.
50. Stephen Henty statement, 12 January 1842, in *Papers Relating to Australian Colonies 1844, British Parliamentary Papers*, reprinted by Irish University Press, Shannon, 1969, p. 189 (hereafter *BPP, 1844*); Clark (ed.), *The Journals of George Augustus Robinson*, vol. 1, p. 280, 301.
51. John Fawkner Diary, 13 December 1835 in Billot (ed.), *Melbourne's Missing Chronicle*.

5 Dangerous frontiers

1. Boldrewood, *Old Melbourne Memories*, p. 35.
2. On competing ideas of land see H. Reynolds, *Frontier*, Allen & Unwin, Sydney, 1987, pp. 182–96; and H. Goodall, *Invasion to Embassy. Land in Aboriginal Politics in New South Wales, 1770–1972*, Sydney, Allen & Unwin/Black Books, 1996, pp. 1–19.
3. Morrison, *Early Days* p. 58.
4. Foster Fyans in Bride (ed.), *Letters*, p. 181.
5. James Clow in Bride (ed.), *Letters*, p. 109.
6. Clark (ed.), *The Journals of George Augustus Robinson*, vol. 1, p. 301.
7. Curr, *Recollections of Squatting*, p. 53.
8. Foster Fyans in Bride (ed.), *Letters*, p. 181.
9. William Bernard to Foster Fyans 16 February 1842, Australian Colonies 1844, *BPP*, p. 206.
10. C. Griffith, *The Present State and Prospects of Port Phillip District of New South Wales*, Dublin, 1845, p. 170.
11. W. Hull, *Remarks on the Probable Origin Antiquity of the Aboriginal Natives of New South Wales*, Melbourne, 1846, p. 21.
12. Griffith, *The Present State and Prospects of Port Phillip*, p. 169; William Hull, *Remarks*, p. 21.
13. See M. Cannon (ed.), *Historical Records of Victoria*, Victorian Government printing Office, Melbourne, 1982, vol. 2A, chap. 10.
14. David Fisher in Bride (ed.), *Letters*, p. 39.
15. Fawkner's Diary, 28 March 1836, Billot (ed.), *Melbourne's Missing Chronicle*; also A.G.L. Shaw, *A History of the Port Phillip Frontier. Victoria before Separation*, Melbourne University Press, Melbourne, 1996, p. 115.
16. Fawkner's Diary, 12 July 1836, Billot (ed.), *Melbourne's Missing Chronicle*.
17. ibid., 10 July 1836.
18. ibid., 16 July 1836.

446 Aboriginal Victorians

19. Richard Howitt, *Impressions of Australia Felix during Four Years Residence in that Colony*, Longman, Brown, Green and Longmans, London, 1845, p. 235.
20. Editor's note in Bride (ed.), *Letters*, p. 88.
21. James Dredge, *Brief Notes of the Aborigines of New South Wales, Including Port Phillip*, James Harrison, Geelong, 1845, pp. 29–30.
22. John S. A. Mackay statement 14 February 1841 of events on 26 May 1840, *BPP*, 1844, pp. 111–13.
23. Beverley Nance, 'The Level of Violence: Europeans and Aborigines in Port Phillip 1835–1850', *Historical Studies*, vol. 19, no. 77, 1981, p. 539.
24. William Bernard to Foster Fyans, 16 February 1842, 'Australian Colonies 1844', *BPP*, pp. 205–7.
25. See correspondence in 'Australian Colonies 1844', *BPP*, pp. 113–17.
26. John Robertson in Bride (ed.), *Letters*, p. 163.
27. Quoted in Robert Kenny, 'The Conversion of Nathanael Pepper. Human Unity and the Lamb of God in Nineteenth-Century Victoria', PhD Thesis, La Trobe University, 2003, p. 175.
28. William T. Clarke in Bride (ed.), *Letters*, p. 279.
29. Boldrewood, *Old Melbourne Memories*, pp. 58–9.
30. See for instance *Port Phillip Gazette*, 6 June 1840.
31. *Port Phillip Gazette*, 29 July, 8 and 22 August 1840.
32. Petition reprinted in 'Australian Colonies 1844', *BPP*, pp. 213–14.
33. George Faithfull in Bride (ed.), *Letters*, p. 221.
34. Dredge Diary, 28 May, 21 July 1839.
35. David Wilsone letters, 6 April 1839, 26 June 1840, 12 March 1839. La Trobe Library ms 9825.
36. Dredge Diary, 8 December 1839.
37. 'Return to Address by Superintendent Charles La Trobe being a Return of the Number of Whites and Blacks killed in Port Phillip since its Occupation, 1836–June 1844', *NSWLC*, 1844, vol. 1.
38. Jan Critchett, *A 'Distant Field of Murder'. Western District Frontiers 1834–1848*, Melbourne University Press, Melbourne, 1990, Appendix 2; Jan Critchett, 'Encounters in the Western District', in Bain Attwood and S.G. Foster (eds), *Frontier Conflict. The Australian Experience*, National Museum of Australia, Canberra, 2003, p. 55; Bain Atwood, 'Blacks and Lohans: Aboriginal–European Contact in Gippsland in the Nineteenth Century', PhD Thesis, La Trobe University, 1984, p. 63; Nance, 'The Level of Violence', p. 533.
39. Howitt, *Impressions of Australia Felix*, p. 221.
40. Depositions in 'Australian Colonies 1844' *BPP*, 1844, pp. 183–203.
41. Entry 20 May 1841 in Gary, Presland (ed.), *Extracts from the Journals of G.A. Robinson, May to August 1841*, Ministry of Conservation, Melbourne, 1980, pp. 15–16.
42. For the debate of Port Phillip violence and the various estimates, see, Nance, 'The Level of Violence', pp. 532–52; M.F. Christie, *Aborigines in Colonial Victoria 1835–86*, Sydney University Press, Sydney, 1979, chaps 2–3, espec. pp. 78–9; Anon., *Koorie*, Koorie Cultural Heritage Trust, Melbourne, 1991,

pp. 17–20; Critchett, *A 'Distant Field of Murder'*, chaps 6–7, espec. pp. 130–2, and appendices 2–3; Jan Critchett, 'Encounters in the Western District', in Attwood and Foster (eds), *Frontier Conflict*, pp. 52–62; Ian Clark, *Scars in the Landscape. A Register of Massacre Sites in Western Victoria, 1803–1859*, Aboriginal Studies Press, Canberra, 1995, passim; my count of Clark's register in Broome, 'The Statistics of Frontier Conflict', in Attwood and Foster (eds), *Frontier Conflict*, p. 94; Attwood, 'Blacks and Lohans', pp. 60–4; P.D. Gardiner, *Gippsland Massacres*, passim; Richard Broome, 'The Struggle for Australia', in McKernan and Browne (eds), *Australia. Two Centuries of War and Peace*, pp. 92–120; and Gardiner's recent overall tally of Aboriginal deaths for Gippsland ranging from 430 through 610 to 820, in personal communication to me 3 March 2002. See also Broome, 'The Statistics of Frontier Conflict', in Attwood and Foster (eds), *Frontier Conflict*, pp. 94–5. For the debate on frontier violence generally see Stuart Macintyre, *The History Wars*, Melbourne University Press, Melbourne, 2003, chap. 8.

43. I have suggested the figure of 1000 several times over the years. See also Broome, 'The Statistics of Frontier Conflict', in Attwood and Foster (eds), *Frontier Conflict*, p. 95.
44. Broome, 'The Struggle for Australia', pp. 97–100.
45. Lyndall Ryan, 'Settler Massacres on the Port Phillip Frontier, 1836–1851', *Journal of Australian Studies*, vol. 34, no. 3, September 2010, pp. 257–73. See also Philip G. Dwyer and Lyndall Ryan, 'The Massacre and History', introduction to *Theatres of Violence. Massacres, Mass Killing and Atrocity Throughout History*, Berghahn Books, New York, 2012, pp. xii–xxxv.
46. Ryan, 'Settler Massacres on the Port Phillip Frontier, 1836–1851', pp. 263–66.
47. Ryan, 'Settler Massacres on the Port Phillip Frontier, 1836–1851', pp. 266–67.
48. 'Colonial Frontier Massacres in Australia, 1788–1930', Centre For 21st Century Humanities, The University of Newcastle, https://c21ch.newcastle.edu.au/colonialmassacres/
49. Lyndall Ryan, 'The Australian Wars: New insights from a digital map', Australian Academy of the Humanities, March 2023, https://humanities.org.au/power-of-the-humanities/the-australian-wars-new-insights-from-a-digital-map/
50. Critchett, 'Encounters in the Western District', p. 57.
51. Gardner, *Gippsland Massacres*, passim.
52. See *HRV*, vol. 2A, pp. 312–42; Judith Bassett, 'The Faithful Massacre at the Broken River, 1838', *Journal of Australian Studies*, no. 24, 1989, pp. 18–34.
53. Dredge Diary, 28 Sept 1839.
54. 21 February 1839, Neil Black Journal 1839–1840, LT ms 8996.
55. Black to Gladstone, 9 September 1840, Neil Black papers, LT ms 8996.
56. For the oral history see Critchett, *Untold Stories*, p. 42; and Taylor's Gippsland career, see Pepper and De Araugo, *The Kurnai of Gippsland*, pp. 37–9, 46.
57. John Robertson in Bride (ed.), *Letters*, p. 167.
58. F. J. Meyrick, *Life in the Bush (1840–1847). A Memoir of Henry Howard Meyrick*, Thomas Nelson and Sons Ltd, London, 1839, p. 136.
59. Meyrick *Life in the Bush*, p. 137; John Robertson in Bride (ed.), *Letters*, p. 167.

60. Keith Windschuttle, 'The Myths of Frontier Massacres in Australian History. Part II. The Fabrication of the Aboriginal Death Toll', *Quadrant*, vol. 44, no. 11, November 2000, p. 23.

61. Critchett, *A 'Distant Field of Murder'*, p. 132. For a study of the law in Port Phillip, see Susanne Davies, 'Aborigines, Murder and the Criminal Law in Early Port Phillip, 1841–1851', *Historical Studies*, vol. 22, no. 88, 1987, pp. 312–36; see also Reece, *Aborigines and Colonists*, pp. 179–82.

62. Critchett, *Untold Stories*, pp. 120–2.

63. On genocide, see Henry Reynolds, *An Indelible Stain? The Question of Genocide in Australia's History*, Penguin, Melbourne, 2001; and *Aboriginal History* special issue on genocide, vol. 25, 2001; Colin Tatz, *With Intent to Destroy: Reflecting on Genocide*, Verso, London, 2003, chap. 4.

64. On genocide, see Henry Reynolds, *An Indelible Stain? The Question of Genocide in Australia's History*, Penguin, Melbourne, 2001; and *Aboriginal History* special issue on genocide, vol. 25, 2001; Colin Tatz, *With Intent to Destroy: Reflecting on Genocide*, Verso, London, 2003, chap. 4.

65. Quoted in Morrison, *Early Days*, p. 52.

66. Mackaness (ed.), *George Augustus Robinson's Journey into South-Eastern Australia, 1844*, p. 18.

67. See Nance for a discussion of this in 'The Level of Violence', pp. 537–9.

68. Nance, 'The Level of Violence', pp. 533, 540.

69. Robinson to William Thomas, 15 September 1839, *HRV*, vol. 2B, pp. 585–6.

70. Robinson to 'Select Committee on the Aborigines', 1845, p. 46.

71. Corris, *Aborigines and Europeans*, p. 59.

72. Geoffrey Blainey, *A Land Half Won*, Macmillan, Melbourne, 1980, p. 89.

73. Nance, 'The Level of Violence', p. 549.

74. See William McNeil, *Plagues and Peoples*, Doubleday, New York, 1976; Jared Diamond, *Guns, Germs and Steel. A Short History of Everybody for the Last 13,000 Years*, Vintage, London, 1998, chap. 11.

75. Campbell, *Invisible Invaders*, pp. 1–7.

76. See index *HRV*, vol. 2B; E.M. Curr, *Australian Race . . .*, Victorian Government Printer, Melbourne, 1886, vol. 1, p. 209; Beveridge, *The Aborigines of Victoria*, pp. 8–12; Campbell, *Invisible Invaders*, chap 1.

77. Morrison, *Early Days*, p. 42.

78. William Thomas to 'Select Committee on the Aborigines', 1845, p. 55.

79. Morrison, *Early Days*, p. 49.

80. Dr Watton to 'Select Committee on the Aborigines', 1845, p. 58; Corris, *Aborigines and Europeans*, p. 119.

81. On yaws being mistaken for syphilis see 'Yaws' in K.F. Kiple (ed.), *The Cambridge World History of Human Disease*, Cambridge University Press, Cambridge, 1993. For yaws offering protection from syphilis see Campbell, *Invisible Invaders*, p. 6.

82. William Thomas, 'Select Committee on the Aborigines', 1859, p. 58.

83. Henry Jones Report 1–31 August 1842, VPRS 4410, unit 2; Beveridge, *Aborigines of Victoria*, p. 17.

84. Dr Baylie to George Robinson 29 December 1841, VPRS 4410, unit 1.

85. 18 April 1839, Clark (ed.), *The Journals of George Augustus Robinson*, vol. I, p. 31.

86. For instance see Journal of William Thomas, 4 October, 19, 20 November 1839, *HRV*, vol. 2B, pp. 549–50, 563–4; Morrison, *Early Days*, p. 48.

87. Dr Baylie to George Robinson 31 January 1842, VPRS 4410, unit 1.

88. Dr John Watton, January 1843, Report for January Central Aboriginal Station, Loddon River, VPRS 4410 unit 1, item 16.

89. Dr Neil Campbell January 1844 Medical Report Goulburn River Station, ibid.

90. Noel Butlin, *Our Original Aggression: Aboriginal Populations of Southeastern Australia, 1788–1850*, Allen & Unwin, Sydney, 1983, passim, but p. 146 for the estimate.

91. See the discussion of western Victoria's pre-contact population in Ian Clark, *Aboriginal Languages and Clans: An Historical Atlas of Western and Central Victoria, 1800–1900*, Monash Publications in Geography, no. 37, 1990, pp. 16–17.

92. William Thomas, 'Select Committee on the Aborigines', 1859, p. 1.

93. Parker, *The Aborigines of Australia*, p. 14.

94. See Harry Lourandos, 'Change or Stability? Hydraulics, Hunter-gatherers and Population in Temperate Australia', in *World Archaeology*, vol. 11, no. 3, February 1980, pp. 245–64; Stephen Webb, 'Intensification, Population and Social Change in South-Eastern Australia; the Skeletal Evidence', *Aboriginal History*, vol. 8, 1984, pp. 154–72.

95. Beverley Blaskett, 'The Aboriginal Response to White Settlement in the Port Phillip District 1835–1850', MA Thesis, University of Melbourne, 1979, pp. 394–5.

96. Barwick, 'Changes in the Aboriginal Population', p. 301.

97. Parker, 'The Aborigines of Australia', p. 17; Thomas, 'Select Committee on the Aborigines', 1858, p. 1.

98. 'Reports on the Diseases of Aborigines', BPA, *Annual Report* 1st 1861, appendix 3, pp. 27–9.

99. See 'Syphilis' and 'Gonorrhea' in Kiple (ed.), *The Cambridge World History of Human Disease*.

100. 'Reports on the Diseases of Aborigines', BPA, *Annual Report* 1st 1861, appendix 3.

101. Ryan, 'Settler Massacres on the Port Phillip Frontier, 1836–1851', p. 270.

102. Alfred Crosby, *Germs, Seeds and Animals: Studies in Ecological History*, M.E. Sharpe, New York, 1994, p. 40.

103. Tony Barta, 'Relations of Genocide: Land and Lives in the Colonization of Australia', in I. Walliman and M. Dobkowski, *Genocide and the Modern Age: Etiology and Case Studies of Mass Death*, Greenwood Press, New York, 1987, pp. 238, 247–48.

104. Darwin, *Journal of Researchers* (1839), quoted in Barry W. Bucher, 'Darwinism, Social Darwinism and the Australian Aborigines: A Reevaluation', R. Macleod and P.H. Rehbock (eds), *Evolutionary Theory and Natural History in the Pacific*, University of Hawaii Press, Honolulu, 1994, p. 380.

6 Negotiating two worlds

1. W. Blandowski, 'Personal Observations Made in an Excursion Towards the Central Parts of Victoria, Including Mount Macedon, McIvor and Black Ranges', *Transactions of the Philosophical Society of Victoria*, 1855, p. 74.

2. William Westgarth, *The Colony of Victoria, Its History, Commerce, and Gold Mining, its Social and Political Institutions Down to the End of 1863*. Sampson, Low and Son, London, 1864, p. 226.

3. *Argus*, 25 October 1856.

4. Andrew Markus, *Race Relations in Australia*, Allen & Unwin, Sydney, 1994, chap. 1.

5. Hull, Select Committee 1859, A, Q.180.

6. Select Committee 1859, p. iv.

7. *Argus*, 8 November 1856.

8. *Argus*, 9 April 1861.

9. Central Board for the Aborigines (hereafter CBA), *Annual Report*, 1st 1861, p. 10.

10. For the Museum's early years see C. Rasmussen et al, *A Museum for the People. A History of Museum Victoria and its Predecessors, 1854–2000*, Scribe Books, Melbourne, 2001, pp. 10–72.

11. *Argus*, 5 December 1868.

12. *Argus*, 19 July 1861, 20 August 1861, 32 September 1865; *Riverine Herald*, 19, 22, 26, 29 July, 2 August 1865, 6 and 13 September 1865.

13. *Argus*, 23 September 1865.

14. See Robert Brough Smyth, *The Aborigines of Victoria: with notes relating to the habits of the natives of other parts of Australia and Tasmania*, Government Printer, Melbourne, 1878, vol. 2, p. 22. For Parliament's distribution see VPDLA, Session 1878, vol. 28, pp. 488, vol. 29, pp. 1331, 2186.

15. *Encyclopaedia Britannica*, 9th edition, Adam and Charles Black, Edinburgh, 1875, vol. 3, pp. 112–13.

16. *Argus*, 2 November 1866.

17. *Advocate*, 1 June 1872.

18. Ted Ryan, 'Wergaia Worlds. A Study of Indigenous–European Cultural Contact in the Mallee Region of North-west Victoria, 1870–1910, BA Hons thesis in History, La Trobe University, 1999, pp. 37–40.

19. For the deaths listed above see *Argus*, 5 December 1860, 14 January 1868; *Advocate*, 29 October 1870, 14 February 1880.

20. *Argus*, 14 January 1868.

21. Recited to the author in the early 1980s.

22. William Thomas, 'Succinct Sketch of the Aboriginal Language', in Select Committee 1859, appendix D.

23. William Thomas 4 March 1851, in weekly report 3–8 March 1851, VPRS 2893, unit 1, 1851/14.

24. ibid., 7 March 1851.

25. William Thomas 3 June 1851, weekly report 2–8 June 1851, VPRS 2893, unit 1, 1851/32.

26. William Thomas half-yearly report 5 July 1852, in *VPP* 1853–54, 'Aborigines', C no. 33a, p. 6.
27. William Thomas 25 April 1851, weekly report 14–20 April 1851, VRPS, 2893, unit 1, 1851/21.
28. William Thomas half-yearly report to 31 December 1852, *VPP*, 1853–54, 'Aborigines', C no 33a, p. 10.
29. T. Dingle, ' "The Truly Magnificent Thirst": An Historical Survey of Australian Drinking Habits', *Historical Studies*, vol. 19, no. 75, October 1980, pp. 227–49.
30. Hull, Select Committee 1859, p. 11.
31. William Thomas weekly report 25 November to 1 December 1850, VPRS 2893, unit 1, 1850/76.
32. William Thomas monthly report May 1851, VPRS 2893, unit 1, 1851/29.
33. William Thomas half-yearly report 5 July 1852, *VPP*, 1853–54, 'Aborigines', C no. 33a, p. 6.
34. William Thomas weekly report 5–11 May 1851, VPRS 2893, unit 1, 1851/26.
35. William Thomas 29 August 1850, weekly report 26 August–1 September 1850, VPRS 2893, unit 1, 1850/55.
36. William Thomas 21 September 1850, weekly report 16–22 September 1850, VPRS 2893, unit 1, 1850/58.
37. William Thomas monthly report August 1852, VPRS 2893, unit 1, 1850/56.
38. Thomas, Select Committee 1859, p. 2.
39. Half-yearly Special Return, Aborigines—Counties of Bourke, Mornington and Evelyn, 30 June 1853', *VPP*, 1853–54, 'Aborigines', C no. 33a, p. 16.
40. William Thomas to Surveyor General 19 January 1857, VPRS 44, box 639.
41. William Thomas 6 June 1851, weekly report 2–8 June 1851, VPRS 2893, unit 1, 1851/32.
42. Thomas half-yearly report 5 July 1852, VPP 1853–54, 'Aborigines', C no. 33a, p. 6 and Hull, Select Committee 1859, p. 11.
43. See Diane Barwick, 'Changes to the Aboriginal Population of Victoria, 1863–1966', pp. 300–3.
44. William Thomas letter to E. Bell, Superintendent's Office, 27 April 1851, VPRS 2893, unit 1, 1851/23.
45. ibid.
46. William Thomas monthly report April 1851, VPRS 2893, unit 1, 1851/24.
47. William Thomas to Charles La Trobe 14 September 1852, *VPP*, 1853–54 'Aborigines', C no. 33a, p. 17.
48. Thomas, Select Committee 1859, p. 68.
49. William Thomas in Bride (ed.), *Letters*, p. 417; see also 'Guardian of Aborigines Half-yearly Report, 5 July 1852', *VPP*, 1853–54 'Aborigines' C no. 33a, p. 5.
50. William Thomas weekly report 2 October 1857, VPRS 44, Box 639.
51. William Thomas weekly reports for 2 October 1857, VPRS 44, box 639.
52. William Thomas annual report 31 December 1856, VPRS 44, box 639; *Argus*, 3 January 1856.
53. *Ballarat Star* quoted in *Argus* 22 May 1860. See account from the *Ballarat Times* of an outdoor performance for money in 1857, *Argus*, 13 March 1857.

See also Michael Parsons, 'The Tourist Corroboree in South Australia to 1911', *Aboriginal History*, vol. 21, pp. 46–69.

54. William Thomas Half-yearly report to 31 December 1852, *VPP*, 1853–54, 'Aborigines', C no 33a, p. 10.

55. Thomas in CBA, *Annual Report* 1st 1861, p. 17.

56. Edward Bell, Commissioner of Crown Lands, Wimmera report, 10 January 1853, *VPP*, 1853–54 'Aborigines', C no. 33a, p. 28. See also reports in pp. 21–8.

57. Andrew McCrae, report on the Gippsland Aborigines, 15 March 1852, *VPP*, 1853–54 'Aborigines', C no. 33a, pp. 17–18.

58. Charles Tyers, report on the Gippsland Aborigines, 15 January 1853, *VPP*, 1853–54 'Aborigines', C no. 33a, pp. 19–20.

59. William Thomas Half-yearly report to 31 December 1852, *VPP*, 1853–54, 'Aborigines', C no 33a, p. 11.

60. William Thomas to Charles La Trobe 14 September 1852, *VPP*, 1853–54 'Aborigines', C no. 33a, p. 17.

61. Select Committee 1859, p. 20 and also appendix B.

62. Parker, Select Committee 1859, p.18.

63. Edward Parker 1 March 1853, *VPP*, 1853–54 'Aborigines', C no. 33a, p. 29 and Parker to Select Committee 1859, p. 19.

64. Franklingford farmers see Farmer, Green and Parker to Royal Commission, 1977, Q. 878–893; 565–581, 2251, respectively.

65. Edgar, *Among the Black Boys*, pp. 105–7.

66. William Thomas return of number being in school, *VPP*, 'Aborigines', 1853–54, C 33a, p. 33.

67. Hinkins, *Life Amongst the Native Race*, p. 60.

68. Inspector Geary 29 August 1857, VPRS 885, box 1, 57/1742; William Thomas 3 November 1857, VPRS 44, box 639.

69. CBA, 1st report 1861, pp. 8–9.

70. Hinkins, *Life Amongst the Native Race*, p. 68.

71. Hinkins, *Life Amongst the Native Race*, pp. 64–5, 72–3.

72. ibid., p. 71. For Thomas Bungaleen see also P. D. Gardner, 'A Melancholy Tale. Thomas Bungeleen, the Civilised Blackman', *Victorian Historical Journal*, vol. 52, no. 2, May 1981, pp. 101–12.

7 New communities

1. 'Report of the Select Committee of the Legislative Council on the Aborigines', 1859, *VPPLC*, 1858–59, Da, p. 68 (hereafter Select Committee 1859).

2. Select Committee 1859, p. 1.

3. Foxcroft, *Australian Native Policy*, pp. 78, 86, 90; Select Committee 1859, p. 31.

4. *Argus*, 2 July 1851, 3 April 1854.

5. Edward Stone Parker, *The Aborigines of Australia*, Melbourne, Hugh McColl, 1854, pp. 26, 31.

6. Spieseke and Hagenauer, Select Committee 1859, pp. 5–8.

7. Aldo Massola, *Aboriginal Mission Stations in Victoria*, Hawthorn Press, Melbourne, 1970, p. 28. For Yelta see pp. 13–30.

8. Fergus Farrow, 'McCombie, Thomas', *Australian Dictionary of Biography*, B. Nairn, G. Serle and R. Ward(general editors), Melbourne University Press, Melbourne, 1974, vol. 5, pp. 132–3.

9. *Argus*, 27 October 1858; *VPDLC*, 1858–59, vol. 4, pp. 110–11.

10. Select Committee 1859, p. iii.

11. Select Committee 1859, pp. iv-vi.

12. *VPDLC*, 1858–59, vol.4, pp. 747–9.

13. *Argus*, 3 February 1859.

14. See Diane Barwick, *Rebellion at Coranderrk*, L. E. Barwick and R. E. Barwick (eds), Aboriginal History Monograph 5, Canberra, 1998, pp. 39–40.

15. *Argus*, 8 March 1859.

16. *Argus*, 8 March 1859.

17. Barwick, *Rebellion at Coranderrk*, pp. 66–7. See also Jane Lydon, 'The Experimental 1860s: Charles Walter's Images of Coranderrk Aboriginal Station, Victoria', *Aboriginal History*, vol. 26, 2002, pp. 82–5.

18. Barwick, *Rebellion at Coranderrk*, p. 66. For the battles over a site see pp. 37–66.

19. Central Board for the Aborigines (CBA), *Annual Report* 4th 1864, p. 5.

20. *VPDLA*, 1859–1860, p. 1169.

21. Michael Hoard, 'Smyth, Robert Brough', *Australian Dictionary of Biography*, G. Serle and R. Ward (general editors), Melbourne University Press, Melbourne, 1976, vol. 6, pp. 161–3.

22. William Thomas quoted in Christie, *Aborigines in Colonial Victoria*, pp. 158–9.

23. Pepper and De Araugo, *The Kurnai of Gippsland*, pp. 121, 129.

24. See the important and useful works by Jan Critchett, *Our Land Till We Die. A History of the Framlingham Aborigines*, by the author, Warrnambool, 1980; Jan Critchett, *Untold Stories. Memories and Lives of Victorian Kooris*, Melbourne University Press, Melbourne, 1998; Phillip Pepper, *You Are What You Make Yourself To Be: The Story of a Victorian Aboriginal Family 1842–1980*, Hyland House, Melbourne, 1980; Pepper and De Araugo, *The Kurnai of Gippsland*; B. Attwood, *The Making of the Aborigines*, Allen & Unwin, Sydney, 1989; Diane Barwick, 'Coranderrk and Cumeroogunga. Pioneers and Policy', in T Scarlett Epstein and David H. Penny, *Opportunity and Response: Case Studies in Economic Development*, C. Hurst and Co., London, 1972, pp. 11–68; Ian D. Clark, *Aboriginal Languages and Clans: An Historical Atlas of Western and Central Victoria, 1800–1900*, Monash Publications in Geography, no. 37, Melbourne, 1990; Massola, *Aboriginal Mission Stations in Victoria*.

25. Christie, *Aborigines in Colonial Victoria*, pp. 205 and 172.

26. Attwood, *The Making of the Aborigines*, pp. 7–31.

27. Rene Maunier, *The Sociology of Colonies: An Introduction to the Study of Race Contact*, Routledge and Kegan Paul, London, 1949, vol. 1, p. 90.

28. ibid., pp. 1, 6, 29.

29. David Roberts, *Paternalism in Early Victorian England*, Rutgers University Press, New Brunswick, New Jersey, 1979, especially the introduction.

30. Hagenauer, 'Royal Commission on the Aborigines', *VPP*, 1877, no 76, Q. 984 (hereafter Royal Commission 1877)

31. Dawson, Royal Commission 1877, p. 100.
32. McLeod and Watson, Royal Commission 1877, pp. 108, 110.
33. Officer, Royal Commission 1877, p. 111.
34. Report, Royal Commission 1877, p. xvii.
35. Board for the Protection of the Aborigines (hereafter BPA), Annual Report, 4th 1864, p. 6.
36. CBA, *Annual Report* 2nd 1862, pp. 10–11.
37. *Argus*, 20 August 1869.
38. The 'Act to Provide for the Protection and Management of the Aboriginal Natives of Victoria', Victoriae Reginae, no. CCCXLIX, 33 Vic no. 349 and its regulations of 13 February 1871 and 6 March 1876, are found conveniently in Pepper and De Araugo, *The Kurnai of Gippsland*, pp. 270–5.
39. Sue Wesson, 'The Aborigines of East Victoria and Far South West New South Wales, 1830–1910. An Historical Geography', PhD Thesis, Monash University, 2002, pp. 259–60.
40. *Argus*, 3 June 1867.
41. Green, Royal Commission 1877, Q. 2172, see also, Q2139–2177.
42. Bulmer, Royal Commission 1877, Q. 1357.
43. For Lake Tyers, Framlingham and Lake Condah respectively see BPA, *Annual Report* 12th 1876, p. 12, Report, Royal Commission, 1877, p. viii; Critchett, *Our Land*, p. 25; and visitor quoted in BPA, *Annual Report* 8th 1872, p. 21.
44. Attwood, *The Making of the Aborigines*, pp. 10–12.
45. Alistair Campbell and Ron Vanderwal (eds), 'Victorian Aborigines. John Bulmer's Recollections 1855–1908', *Occasional Papers Anthropology & History, Museum of Victoria*, no. 1, 1994, p. 64.
46. Report, Royal Commission 1877, pp. vii–xi.
47. ibid., p. x.
48. Green written statement, Royal Commission 1877, p. 82.
49. Hagenauer, Royal Commission 1877, Q. 1190.
50. CBA, *Annual Report* 4th 1864, pp. 9–10.
51. BPA, *Annual Report* 9th 1873, p. 6.
52. Wandin, Coranderrk Inquiry Report, 1881–82, Q. 3849.
53. Kramer, Royal Commission 1877, Q 1661.
54. Mackie, Royal Commission 1877, Q. 1430.
55. Report, Royal Commission 1877, p. xiii.
56. Attwood, *The Making of the Aborigines*, p. 18.
57. Deans, Royal Commission 1877, Q. 2396.
58. Diane E. Barwick, 'And The Lubras are Ladies Now', in Fay Gale (ed.), *Woman's Role in Aboriginal Society*, Australian Institute of Aboriginal Studies, Canberra, 1974, p. 58.
59. Goodall, Royal Commission 1877, Q. 1816, 1836–37.
60. Robertson and Deans, Royal Commission 1877, Q. 2068 and Q. 2420, respectively.
61. Topp, Royal Commission 1877 p. 125. For the results see p. 115.
62. Kramer, Royal Commission 1877, Q. 1716–1734.

63. Bulmer, Royal Commission 1877, Q. 1172, 1180–82, 1030–32; Campbell and Vanderwal, 'John Bulmer's Recollections', p. 65.

64. H. Hahn to Secretary of Education Department 18 July 1889, VPRS 795, unit 559, file 11579.

65. Aboriginal parents of Ramahyuck to T. Broadribb, 29 February 1892, VPRS 640, unit 858, file 5252 and Aboriginal residents of Ramahyuck to Minister of Public Instruction, 22 April 1901, VPRS 795, unit 559, file 11579.

66. Letters for D. R. Morris to Education Department 1 April 1887, 30 March 1889, VPRS 640/P unit 882, school no. 1319. See also Alison Goding, *This Bold Venture. The Story of Lake Tyers House Place and People*, by the author, Melbourne, 1990, pp. 18, 25, 42.

67. Starr to Department of Education, 17 March 1891, VRPS 640/P Unit 882, School no. 1319.

68. Christie, *Aborigines in Colonial Victoria*, p. 171.

69. Critchett, *Untold Stories*, p. 85.

70. Pepper, *You Are What You Make Yourself to Be*, pp. 9–18; Kenny thesis passim.

71. Hagenauer, Royal Commission 1877, Q. 1063.

72. Mackie and Hamilton, Royal Commission 1877, Q. 1410, Q. 1992, respectively.

73. Green, Royal Commission 1877, Q. 2274.

74. Campbell and Vanderwal (eds), 'John Bulmer's Recollections', p. 60.

75. Stahle and Bulmer, Royal Commission 1877, Q. 376–86, and Q. 1250, respectively.

76. Letters reprinted in Pepper and De Araugo, *The Kurnai of Gippsland*, pp. 160–71.

77. Campbell and Vanderwal (eds), 'John Bulmer's Recollections', pp. 62–4.

78. 78. Barwick 'And the Lubras are Ladies Now', pp. 53–4; Campbell and Vanderwal (eds), 'John Bulmer's Recollections', p. 70.

79. Hagenauer, Royal Commission 1877, Q. 1126.

80. CBA, *Annual Report* 6th, p. 10.

81. BPA, *Annual Report* 8th, p. 5, 11th, p. 12.

82. Report, Royal Commission 1877, p. xv.

83. 'Number and Location of Aborigines, 26 February 1874' BPA, *Annual Report* 12th, appendix 23. See also Diane Barwick, 'Changes in the Aboriginal Population of Victoria, 1863–1966', pp. 291–3.

84. BPA, *Annual Report* 12th 1876, pp. 14–25.

85. Report and Correspondence Relative to the Mortality Amongst the Residents of the Aboriginal Stations of Victoria, etc', *VPP*, 1879, no. 86, p. 5.

86. Diane Barwick, 'Changes in the Aboriginal Population of Victoria, 1863–1966', pp. 292–5, 303–13.

87. Hamilton, 'Report of the Board Appointed to Enquire Into, and Report Upon, the Present Condition and Management of the Coranderrk Aboriginal Station, Together with the Minutes of Evidence', in *VPP*, 1882, no.5, (hereafter Coranderrk Inquiry Report, 1881–82, Q. 1518, p. 31.

88. Wylie, Coranderrk Inquiry Report, 1881–82, Q. 1797.

89. Matron Eleanor McKie, Coranderrk Inquiry Report, 1881–82, Q. 1838–43.

90. Williams, Coranderrk Inquiry Report, 1881–82, Q. 1881.

8 Country 'wanderers'

1. BPA, *Annual Report* 17th 1881, p. 10.
2. CBA, *Annual Report* 6th 1867, p. 16.
3. BPA, *Annual Report* 8th 1872, p. 5.
5. CBA, *Annual Report* 6th 1869, pp. 16 and 13.
6. Hamilton, Coranderrk Inquiry Report, 1881–82, Q. 1526–1535.
7. Ralston, Royal Commission 1877, p. 109.
8. CBA, *Annual Report* 6th 1867, p. 14.
9. *Argus*, 3 October 1866.
10. *Argus*, 26 July 1864.
11. *Argus*, 6 June 1865.
12. J. N. McLeod, Royal Commission 1877, p. 102.
13. Campbell and Vanderwal (eds), *John Bulmer's Recollections*, p. 67.
14. BPA, *Annual Report* 6th 1867, p. 16.
15. Clark, *Aboriginal Languages and Clans*, pp. 347, 349.
16. Jackson, Royal Commission 1877, p. 101.
17. Lists in BPA, *Annual Reports 8–11th* 1872–75.
18. *Argus*, 26 August 1862.
19. *Argus*, 11 October 1867, 29 October 1868.
20. Clarke's medal, A.M.A. Page to Goodall, 3 June 1886, NAA B 329, item 4; Royal Humane Society case list, no. 432–3.
21. Peter Pierce, *The Country of Lost Children. An Australian Anxiety*, Cambridge, Cambridge University Press, 1999, pp. 16–29. For Dick-adick's name see Clark, *Aboriginal Languages and Clans*, p. 250.
22. David Sampson, "'The Nature and Effects Thereof Were by Each of Them Understood": Aborigines, Agency, Law, and Power in the 1867 Gurnett Contract', *Labour History*, no. 74, May 1998, pp. 54–69.
23. For the history of the Aboriginal cricketers, see John Mulvaney and Rex Harcourt, *Cricket Walkabout. The Australian Aboriginal Cricketers on Tour 1867-8*, Melbourne University Press, Melbourne, second edition, 1988; Bernard Wimpress, *Passport to Nowhere, Aborigines in Australian Cricket 1850-1939*, Walla Walla Press, Sydney, 1999, pp. 67–130; Ashley Mallet, *The Black Lords of Summer. The Story of the 1868 Aboriginal Tour of England and Beyond*, University of Queensland Press, Brisbane, 2002; Roland Perry, *Captain Australia. A History of the Celebrated Captains of Australian Test Cricket*, Random House Australia, Sydney, 2000, pp. xxvii–li; Mark Whitaker, BBC radio documentary 2001; Geoffrey Burton and Elizabeth Izzard, 'A Fine Body of Gentlemen', television documentary, 2003. For the traditional names and origins of the cricketers see, Clark, *Aboriginal Languages and Clans*, pp. 249–50.
24. James Thomson to Cameron, BPA, 15 October 1885, E. M. Cameron to Captain Page, Secretary BPA, 3 February 1886, NAA B313/1 box 15 for respective quotes. See also Pepper and De Araugo, *The Kurnai of Gippsland*, pp. 199–200.
25. Royal Commission into Colonial and Indian Exhibition, 1886, p. 31, quoted in Lynette Russell, ' "Well Nigh Impossible to Describe': Dioramas, Displays

and Representations of Australian Aborigines', *Australian Aboriginal Studies*, 1999, no. 2, p. 39.

26. *Argus*, 2 September, 15 November 1864, 4 September 1865.
27. *Argus*, 24 November 1865.
28. *Argus*, 2 September 1865.
29. *Argus*, 27 August 1867.
30. *Argus*, 16 July 1861.
31. *Argus*, 18 December 1861, 19 January 1864.
32. *Argus*, 28 May 1868.
33. Critchett, *Untold Stories*, p. 32.
34. *Advocate*, 8 September 1888.
35. Officer, Royal Commission 1877, p. 103.
36. *Argus*, 2 June 1864.
37. Both matters were not cleared up until 1869 see *Argus*, 13 and 18 November 1869. For their tribal affiliation see Clark, *Aboriginal Languages and Clans*, p. 285.
38. *Argus*, 9 April 1867.
39. *Argus*, 9 April 1867.
40. *Argus*, 4 February 1861, 19 May 1862, 11 July 1866, 27 April 1868, and 6 February 1869.
41. Quoted in *Argus*, 27 July 1869.
42. *Argus*, 16 July 1860.
43. Bulmer BPA, *Annual Report* 5th 1866, p. 10; Parker, Royal Commission 1877, Q. 598.
44. BPA, *Annual Report* 8th 1872, p. 22.
45. Dennis, Royal Commission 1877, p. 107.
46. *Argus*, 11 July 1864.
47. Wimmera house and O'Rourke's BPA *Annual Report* 6th 1867, p. 30 and 12th 1876, p. 18 respectively.
48. Dennis, Royal Commission 1877, p. 106.
49. BPA, *Annual Report* 9th 1873, p.16; Dennis, Royal Commission 1877, p. 106; *Colac Herald*, 11 April 1879, 4 February 1890; Crough file, VPRS B337, item 196, memo 27 April 1922. See also a detailed account in Clark, *Aboriginal Languages and Clans*, pp. 223–32.
50. CBA, *Annual Report* 4th 1864, p. 10.
51. Critchett, *Untold Stories*, pp. 86–7; Edward Ryan, 'Wergaia Worlds. A Study of Indigenous/European Cultural Contact in the Mallee Region of north-west Victoria, 1870–1910', Ba Hons thesis La Trobe University, 1899, p. 47.
52. For Uncles see McLeod, Royal Commission 1877, p. 109; for Steward and Orr BPA, *Annual Report* 15th 1879, p. 11 and 21st 1885, p. 6, Ryan, 'Wergaia Worlds', pp. 46–7.
53. Pepper and De Araugo, *The Kurnai of Gippsland*, p. 179.
54. Attwood, *The Making of the Aborigines*, chap. 2; Diane E. Barwick, 'This Most Resolute Lady: A Biographical Puzzle', in D. E. Barwick, J. Beckett, Marie Reay (eds), *Metaphors of Interpretation. Essays in Honour of W. E. H. Stanner*, Australian National University Press, Canberra, 1985, chap. 8.

55. Campbell and Vanderwal (eds), 'John Bulmer's Recollections', p. 66. See also Pepper and De Araugo, *The Kurnai of Gippsland*, especially pp. 109, 193, 239.
56. Bain Attwood, 'Tarry Bobby. A Brataualung Man', *Aboriginal History*, vol. 11, pt 1, pp. 41–57; Critchett, *Untold Stories*, chap. 3.
57. BPA, *Annual Report* 9th 1873, p. 18.
58. BPA, *Annual Report* 11th 1875, p. 4.
59. Campbell and Vanderwal (eds), 'John Bulmer's Recollections', p. 46.
60. See Critchett, *Untold Stories*, for a discussion of his informants, chap. 8.
61. See Mary Howitt Walker, *Come Wind, Come Weather: A Biography of Alfred Howitt*, Melbourne University Press, Melbourne, 1971.
62. D. J. Mulvaney, 'The Anthropologist as Tribal Elder', *Mankind*, vol. 7, no. 3, pp. 205–17.
63. See Andrew Sayers, *Aboriginal Artists of the Nineteenth Century*, Oxford University Press, Melbourne, 1994, p. 20; and Pepper and De Araugo, *The Kurnai of Gippsland*, p. 209.
64. Sayers, *Aboriginal Artists of the Nineteenth Century*, chaps 1 and 2.
65. Bulmer, Royal Commission 1877, Q 1383.

9 'A miserable spadeful of ground'

1. See Shirley W. Wiencke, *When the Wattle Blooms Again. The Life and Times of William Barak, Last Chief of the Yarra Yarra Tribe*, by the author, Worri Yallock,1984; Andrew Sayers, 'Barak and the Affirmation of Tradition', in Andrew Sayers, *Aboriginal Artists of the Nineteenth Century*, Oxford University Press, Melbourne, 1994, pp. 13–26.
2. Green, Royal Commission 1877, Q. 2301.
3. Wandin, 'Coranderrk Aboriginal Station. Report of the Board Appointed to Inquire into, and Report upon, the Present Condition and Management of the Coranderrk Aboriginal Station, Together with the Minutes of Evidence', VPP, 1882, no. 5, (hereafter Coranderrk Inquiry Report, 1881–82).
4. Written statement by Michie, Coranderrk Inquiry Report, 1881–82, p. 8.
5. Quoted in Christie, *Aborigines in Colonial Victoria*, p. 167.
6. Green's Journal 1865–66 quoted in Royal Commission 1877, pp. 81–2.
7. Quoted by Green, Select Committee Report 1881, Q. 5217. See also the entirety of Green's evidence Royal Commission 1877, pp. 81–8, especially Q. 2248 and Coranderrk Inquiry Report, 1881–82, pp. 127–37.
8. For Green's dismissal see Green evidence to the Coranderrk Inquiry Report, 1881–82, Q. 5106–5128. For his later relationship see Q. 5077–80; Barwick, *Rebellion at Coranderrk*, chap. 7.
9. For Coranderrk's struggle see in particular Barwick, *Rebellion at Coranderrk*, passim; Christie, *Aborigines in Colonial Victoria*, chap. 8; Attwood, *The Making of the Aborigines*, chap. 4; Bain Attwood, *Rights for Aborigines*, Allen & Unwin, Sydney, 2003, chap. 1.
10. Quoted in Mackie, Coranderrk Inquiry Report, 1881–82, Q. 3960.
11. Christie, *Aborigines in Colonial Victoria*, p. 185; Susan Leitinger, 'The Board, the Parliament and the Aborigines', BA (Hons) thesis in History, La Trobe University, 1991, p. 30.

12. Godfrey, 29 February 1876, *VPDLA*, session 1875–76, vol. 23, p. 2331.

13. *VPDLA*, 24 August 1876, 1876, vol. 24, pp. 507–512; MacPherson, 4 October 1876, *VPD* Session 1876, vol. 25, pp. 974–5.

14. Godfrey, 4 October 1876, *VPDLA* Session 1876, vol. 25, pp. 978–9.

15. Duffy, 4 October 1876, *VPDLA*, Session 1876, vol. 25, p. 981. See also pp. 974–86.

16. Royal Commission 1877, pp. vii–xvii.

17. Zox, 21 December 1880, *VPDLA*, session 1880–81, vol. 35, pp. 1261.

18. Norris, Coranderrk Inquiry Report, 1881–82, Q. 4607–45.

19. For the Kulin deputations to Berry see, *Argus*, 30 March 1881 and to Grant reprinted in Coranderrk Inquiry Report, 1881–82, p. 58.

20. Quoted in Leitinger, 'The Board, the Parliament and the Aborigines', p. 45.

21. Jennings, Coranderrk Inquiry Report, 1881–82, Q. 1579.

22. Strickland, Coranderrk Inquiry Report, 1881–82, Q. 4176.

23. Aboriginal witnesses to Coranderrk Inquiry Report, 1881–82, pp. 8–28, 68, 98.

24. Strickland, Coranderrk Inquiry Report, 1881–82, Q. 4022.

25. For these two disputes see Coranderrk Inquiry Report, 1881–82, Wandin, Q. 3737–44, Strickland, Q. 4010–4017; Jackson, Q. 2535–2641, Strickland, Q. 2589–2641, Campbell and Davis, Q. 2642–2712.

26. Page, Coranderrk Inquiry Report, 1881–82, Q. 2184–2190.

27. Simpson, Coranderrk Inquiry Report, 1881–82, Q. 413.

28. Dunnolly, Coranderrk Inquiry Report, 1881–82, Q. 824.

29. See the evidence of Harris and Mackie, Coranderrk Inquiry Report, 1881–82, Q3561–68, 4007, respectively.

30. See John Hirst, *Convict Society and its Enemies*, Allen & Unwin, Sydney, 1983, chap. 2.

31. Barak, Coranderrk Inquiry Report, 1881–82, Q. 398.

32. Coranderrk Inquiry Report, 1881–82, p. 98.

33. For defiance at Lake Condah see Critchett, *Untold Stories*, chaps 6 and 8; for a strike at Ebenezer see BPA, *Annual Report* 19th 1884, p. 14; for other unrest see Christie, *Aborigines in Colonial Victoria*, p. 182.

34. See the three reports, Coranderrk Inquiry Report, 1881–82, pp. iii–vii.

35. Graeme Davison, 'Festivals of Nationhood', in F. R. Smith and S. L. Goldberg (eds), *Australian Cultural History*, Cambridge University Press, Melbourne, 1988, pp. 158–72.

36. *Age*, 17 May 1869; *Leader*, 14 August 1869; *Age*, 13 January 1881; *Age*, 11 January 1888, quoted in Andrew Markus (ed.), *From the Barrel of a Gun. The Oppression of the Aborigines, 1860–1900*, Victorian Historical Association, Melbourne, 1974, pp. 60–5.

37. Critchett, *Untold Stories*, pp. 220–8.

38. *Age*, 29 September 1896, quoted in Markus (ed.), *From the Barrel of a Gun*, p. 66.

39. Quoted in Geoffrey Serle, 'The Gold Generation', in *Victorian Historical Magazine*, vol. 41, no.1, February 1970, p. 270.

40. Ogilvie to F. R., Godfrey, 10 April 1877, reprinted in Royal Commission 1877, p. 2. See his testimony pp. 2–9.

41. Page to Chief Secretary 7 September 1881, quoted in Leitinger, 'The Board', p. 46.
42. BPA, *Annual Report* 17th 1881, p. 4.
43. Quoted in Bain Attwood, (ed.), *The Struggle for Aboriginal Rights*, Allen & Unwin, Sydney, 1999, p. 49.

10 Under the acts

1. *VPDLA*, Session 1886, vol. 53, 15 December 1886, pp. 2912–13, *VPDLC*, session 1896, vol. 53, 15 December 1886, p. 2882.
2. 'An Act to Amend an Act intitled "An Act to Provide for the Protection and Management of the Aboriginal Natives of Victoria"', No. DCCCXII, 16 December 1886, also reprinted in Pepper and De Araugo, *The Kurnai of Gippsland*, pp. 275-7.
3. Aborigines Act 1890, Regulations, *Government Gazette*, 12 September 1890. pp. 3719–22. Also reprinted in Pepper and De Araugo, *The Kurnai of Gippsland*, pp. 281-7.
4. For a discussion of genocide in Australia see Henry Reynolds, *An Indelible Stain? The Question of Genocide in Australia's History*, Viking, Melbourne, 2001; Colin Tatz, 'Australia: Defining and Interpreting Genocide', in his *With Intent to Destroy. Reflecting on Genocide*, Verso, London, 2003, chap. 4; and special issue of *Aboriginal History*, vol. 25, 2001.
5. BPA minutes, 5 September 1894, AA, B314.
6. BPA, *Annual Report* 24th 1888, p. 3.
7. Kate Ellinghaus, 'Regulating Koori Marriages: The 1886 Victorian Aborigines Protection Act', *Journal of Australian Studies*, no. 67, pp. 22–9, 208–10.
8. BPA, *Annual Report* 23rd 1887, p. 4.
9. For Bulmer rumours see Pepper and De Araugo, *The Kurnai of Gippsland*, p. 210; and Stahle to Hagenauer, 19 February 1890, VPRS 1694/P, unit 1.
10. Hagenauer Inspection Report of Framlingham, 31 May 1892, VPRS 1694/P, unit 1.
11. Quoted in Wilkinson, 'Fractured Families, Squatting and Poverty: the Impact of the 1886 "Half Caste" Act on the Framlingham Community', in I. Duncanson and D. Kirkby (eds), *Law and History in Australia*, vol. 2, La Trobe University, Melbourne, 1986, p. 12.
12. BPA, *Annual Report* 35th 1899, p. 10.
13. John Glasgow to BPA, 17 November 1890, VPRS 1694/P Unit 1.
14. Wilkinson, 'Fractured Families', p. 13.
15. BPA, *Annual Report* 28th 1892, p. 11.
16. P. Boglish to Hagenauer, 8 May 1894, Albert Coombes (Snr) file VPRS 337, item 171.
17. BPA, *Annual Report* 24th 1888, p. 4.
18. Shaw to Hagenauer, 16 July 1890, VPRS 1694/P Unit 1.
19. For the petition see Linda Wilkinson, 'Fractured Families', p. 11.
20. Hood to Stahle, 30 December 1889, VPRS 1694, unit 1.
21. C. Cooper and J. Urry, 'Art, Aborigines and Chinese: a Nineteenth Century Drawing by the Kwatkwat Artist Tommy McCrae', *Aboriginal History*, vol. 5, pt. 1, pp. 82–3; Sayers, *Aboriginal Artists of the Nineteenth Century*, p. 47.

22. *Victorian Government Gazette*, 27 November 1899.
23. BPA, *Annual Report* 36th 1900, p. 4.
24. Department of Neglected Children and Reformatory School, *Annual Report* 1900, p. 14.
25. D. McLeod to Commandant Booth, 8 August 1900, in Department of Neglected Children and Reformatory Schools, *Annual Report* 1900, p. 16.
26. Department of Neglected Children and Reformatory Schools, *Annual Report*, 1900 p. 16.
27. Quoted in Critchett, *Untold Stories*, p. 96.
28. Critchett, *Untold Stories*, pp. 97–101, 110–14.
29. BPA, *Annual Report* 32nd 1896, p. 4.
30. Victorian Census 1901, in *VPP* 1902–03, vol. 2, tables 2 and 10.
31. *Herald*, 22 March 1927; *Argus*, 23 March 1927.
32. Stahle in BPA, 36th *Annual Report*, 1900.
33. BPA, *Annual Report* 37th 1901.
34. BPA, *Annual Report* 38th 1902, p. 6.
35. BPA, *Annual Report* 41st 1905, p. 7.
36. BPA, *Annual Report* 38th 1902, pp. 11–12.
37. Pepper and De Araugo, *The Kurnai of Gippsland*, p. 232.
38. BPA, *Annual Report* 43rd 1907, p. 7.
39. BPA, *Annual Report* 38th 1903, p. 13.
40. BPA, *Annual Report* 43rd 1901, p.11.
41. BPA, *Annual Report*, 37th 1901, p. 11. For Mrs Saunders see BPA, *Annual Report* 44th 1909, p. 9.
42. Shaw to Hagenauer 30 October 1905 p. 98 in Crough file, AA B 337, item 196.
43. Material on Joseph and Elizabeth Crough see Crough file, AA B 337, item 196: Joseph Crough to BPA 1 June 1891, p. 103; Joseph Crough to Murray 8 May 1905, pp. 89–89a; Elizabeth Crough to Hagenauer July 1905, pp. 87–87a; Memo re Mrs Crow, Colac, p. 88; Joseph Crough to Hagenauer 24 October 1905, pp. 97–97a; Joseph Crough to A.E. Parker 20 May 1918, pp. 39–39a; Shire of Colac to BPA, 8 September 1933, p. 3; BPA to Shire of Colac 16 September 1933, p. 7. Crough file Colac and District Historical Society.
44. *Argus*, 8 December 1910, 21 December 1911.
45. Case File of Harriet King, NAA, B337, item 407, pp. 1–16.
46. Murray at Dimboola *Argus*, 14 September 1914; and to Anglican Church Missionary Association deputation *Argus*, 22 September 1915.
47. Murray, 8 September 1910, *VPDLA*, 1910, vol. 124, p. 1081. See Georgii Quinti Regis, no. 2255, 19 October 1910.
48. Reprinted in *Australian Christian Commonwealth*, 23 April 1920, reference courtesy of Walter Phillips.
49. Alick Jackomos and Derek Fowell, *Forgotten Heroes. Aborigines at War From the Somme to Vietnam*, Victoria Press, Melbourne, 1993, p.10 and BPA to Manager Lake Tyers, 23 February 1916, VPRS 10309.
50. Alick Jackomos, 'Sons of the Gournditch-Mara Tribe', typescript in author's possession.
51. Harry Gordon, *The Embarrassing Australian, The Story of an Aboriginal Warrior*, Lansdowne Press, Melbourne, 1962, pp. 36–7.

52.	The 1931 RSL survey is discussed in C. D. Clark, 'Aborigines in the First AIF', *Army Journal*, no. 286, 1973, pp. 21–6. For sources tallying thirty-seven, see Shire of Yarra Ranges, *Pride, Integrity and Honour. A Memorial Tribute to Indigenous Men and Women Who Served in Armed Forces and National Service Training*, April 1997, p. 1; Jackomos and Fowell, *Forgotten Heroes*, passim; C. D. Coulthard-Clark, 'Aboriginal Medal-Winners, *Sabretache*, vol. 18, October 1977, pp. 244–8; list of men who served supplied by Ronald Glen to Rutherford, 22 December 1938, Lake Tyers Correspondence, 1934–39, AA B356/2, item 17; Alick Jackomos, 'Sons of the Gournditch-Mara Tribe'; *Warrnambool Standard*, 3 August 1918; Phillip Pepper, *You Are What You Make Yourself to Be*, pp. 59–63. Aboriginal Case Files, AA, B337, item 98, pp. 333–4; item 197, p. 27, and item 39; 253, p. 31. The list by place which follows has been compiled from the above sources, Coranderrk: Albert Franklin, Walter Franklin, James Harris (KIA), Henry Patterson, George Terrick, James Wandin. Lake Condah: Alfred Lovett', Edward (Mick?) Lovett, Frederick Lovett, Herbert Lovett, Leonard Lovett, Chris Saunders, George Rose. Framlingham: William Rawlings (KIA), Herb Winters (KIA), Jack Winters, W A Egan (KIA). Lake Tyers: Harry Thorpe (KIA), Percy Pepper, G.T. H. Stephen, David Mullett, Walter McCreedie. Unknown Place of origin in Victoria: Jimmy McKinnon, James Arden, L. H. Booth, (KIA), Cornelius Coombes, W. F. Murray (KIA), H. C. Murray, John McLeod, Edwin O'Rourke, Alfred Stephen, Henry Thomas, Samuel Thomas, Laurie Young, John Rowan, Kenneth Crough, Joseph Crough, Alan McDonald, Robert Taylor, Malcolm Rivers, Chris Austin, Mickey McDonald (WWI?). These three also came from Cummeragunja just across the Murray: Arthur Nelson, Harry Nelson, Dan Cooper (KIA)

53.	The 1911 Census reveals there were 113 'half caste' and 364, 760 other males in Victoria between 15 and 45, while 42 Aboriginal and 112, 357 other males enlisted in Victoria, Michael McKernan, 'War', in *Australians. Historical Statistics*, Fairfax, Syme and Weldon, Sydney, 1987, p. 412.

54.	McKernan, 'War', pp. 412, 414.

55.	Alick Jackomos, 'Remembering Aboriginal Fitzroy', typescript of an interview by Steve Brown and Steve Avery of the Historic Places Section, Heritage Services Branch, Aboriginal Affairs Victoria, 31 July 1998, p. 26.

56.	NAA, B2455, George Terrick, item 4817823, Percy Pepper, item 4817819.

57.	Approximately 10,000 military medals were awarded in World War 1 to 416 809 who enlisted, a ratio of 1 to 41.6, see Australian War Memorial official website, encyclopedia/statistics page, and McKernan, 'War', p. 412.

58.	C. D. Coulthard-Clark, 'Aboriginal Medal-Winners, *Sabretache*, vol. 18, October 1977, pp. 245–6.

59.	Jackomos, 'Remembering Aboriginal Fitzroy', p. 15.

60.	Francis Stephens to O. C. Base Records, 25 October 1923 (?) NAA B2455, Harry Thorpe, item 4817817.

61.	Aborigines Act 1915, 6 George V, no. 2610, 6 September 1915.

62.	Aborigines Act 1915, Regulations, *Government Gazette*, 1916, vol. 3, pp. 3547–53.

63. Aborigines Act 1928, 19 Geo.V, 12 February 1929, no. 3631; Aborigines Act 1928 (no. 3631) Regulations, *Victorian Government Gazette*, 13 May 1931, pp. 1558–60.
64. Pepper, *You Are What You Make Yourself to Be*, p. 61.
65. For these Board decisions, see VPRS 10309, BPA letter book 1915–1916.
66. Elizabeth Jennings to Cameron 2 December 1915, Elsie Barrett case file, NAA, B337, item 56, p. 74.
67. Elsie Barrett to Parker BPA secretary rec'd 18 June 1921, NAA, B337, item 56, pp. 147–50.
68. Elsie Barrett to Parker rec'd 6 July 1921, NAA, B337, item 56, pp. 157–8.
69. Marriage and Death Indexes for Victoria did not contain details of Barrett or Carter.
70. *Argus*, 23 March 1916, 20 April 1916.
71. *Argus*, 6 June 1917.
72. BPA minutes 1917, p. 243 and BPA, *Annual Report* 49th 1922, p. 3.
73. McLeod, *VPDLA*, 18 December 1919, vol. 154, p. 3663.
74. Menzies, *VPDLA*, 18 December 1919, vol. 154, p. 3666.
75. Richard Broome interview with Valentine Leeper, East Melbourne, 25 October 1989.
76. See BPA, 36th—48th *Annual Reports*, 1900–12.
77. BPA, *Annual Report* 46th 1910, p. 6.
78. BPA, *Annual Report* 47th 1911, p. 6.
79. BPA, *Annual Report* 48th 1912, p. 6.
80. *Argus*, 3 August 1915.
81. Angeline Morgan in Alick Jackomos and Derek Fowell, *Living Aboriginal History in Victoria. Stories from the Oral Tradition*, Cambridge University Press, Melbourne, 1991, p. 98.
82. BPA, *Annual Report* 49th 1921.
83. *Argus*, 31 January 1922.
84. Quoted in Shire of Yarra Ranges, *Pride, Integrity and Honour*, p. 21.
85. *Argus*, 28 August 1923.
86. *Argus*, 29 January, 1 February 1924.
87. *Argus*, 9 April 1923, 23 March 1927.
88. For Maginnes see *Argus*, 18 March 1911; for Manton, *Argus*, 1 June 1929 and *Bairnsdale Advertiser*, 20 December 1927; for Pepper, *Herald*, 2 August 1937.
89. *Sunraysia Daily*, 12 and 13 November 1942.
90. *Herald*, 11 August 1932.
91. BPA, *Annual Report* 40th 1904, p. 5
92. *Argus*, 10 October 1931.
93. Letter to the editor, *Argus*, 14 November 1931.
94. See letters to the editor *Argus* 1931 from Hagenauer 18 November; Cameron 7 December; Bruce 26 November; Jones 25 November; Fraser 30 November; Hughes 4 December.
95. *Argus*, 28 November 1931.
96. *Argus*, 12 December 1931.
97. *Argus*, 21 November 1931.

98. *Argus*, 31 July and 4 August 1934.

99. A. H. Mitchell, *Argus*, 4 August 1934.

100. Quoted in letter to editor from 'Observer', *Argus*, 11 August 1934.

101. W. J. Dawbon to Anna White, 21 November 1946, SLV ms 9377, box 1726, V/3.

102. *Age*, 24 January 1955.

103. *Age*, 9 February 1934.

104. *Argus*, 29 February 1934.

105. *Herald*, 22 March 1934.

106. *Argus*, 2 March 1934.

107. Percy Learson, *The Last of the Victorian Aborigines*, p. 8.

108. Historical Sub-Committee of the Centenary Celebrations (C. Daley, A.W Grieg, A.S. Kenyon and C. R. Long), *Victoria. The First Centenary. A Historical Survey*, Robertson and Mullens, Melbourne, 1934, pp. 135–41, foreword.

109. Kathleen Ussher, *Hail Victoria*, Hodder and Stoughton, London, 1934, pp. 13, 52–3.

110. Ambrose Pratt, *The Centenary History of Victoria*, Robertson and Mullins, Melbourne, 1934, pp. 41, 74.

111. R. Broome, 'Historians, Aborigines and Australia. Writing the National Past' in B. Attwood (ed.), *In the Age of Mabo*, Allen & Unwin, Sydney, 1996, pp. 59–60.

112. Mimmo Cozzolino and Fysh Rutherford (eds), *Symbols of Australia*, Penguin, Melbourne, 1980, p. 47. See also pp. 45–8 for Aborigines in advertising.

113. Undated press clipping in Herald Fiche series, fiche 4, row f, frame 10.

114. BPA minutes 17 September 1941, NAA, B314/5 box 1, item 7.

115. BPA, 'Disposal of Aboriginal Reserves', 4 August 1943, NAA, B313/1, item 76, pp. 11–12.

116. *Warrnambool Standard*, 24 July 1942.

117. *Warrnambool Standard*, 4 February 1943.

118. *Herald*, 8, 10, 15 February, 17 March 1945.

119. BPA minutes 18 February 1948, NAA, B314/5 box 1, item 8.

120. Euphemia Day in Alick Jackomos and Derek Fowell (eds), *Living Aboriginal History in Victoria*, p. 138, 140; Jackomos and Fowell, *Forgotten Heroes*, p. 3 and Pastor R. W. Saunders in *Age*, 12 September 1956; Iris Lovett Gardiner, *Lady of the Lake*, Koorie Heritage Trust, Melbourne, 1997.

121. *Herald*, 11 June 1932.

122. L.R. Smith, Janet McCalman, Ian Anderson, Sandra Smith, Joanne Evans, Gavan McCarthy, Jane Beer, 'Fractional Identities: The Political Arithmetic of Aboriginal Victorians', *Journal of Interdisciplinary History*, vol. 38, no. 4, Spring 2008, p. 547.

11 'Old Lake Tyers'

1. Alick Jackomos, 'Speech at Lake Tyers 28 August 1991', in Alick Jackomos Private Papers.

2. See list of 34 women and girls' measurements, 8 February 1916 and list at VPRS BPA letter book 10309, no. 689.

3. Pepper and De Araugo, *The Kurnai of Gippsland*, chaps 37–8.

4. Pepper and De Araugo, *The Kurnai of Gippsland*, p. 248.

5. BPA to Lake Tyers' manager, 7 December 1914, 22 December 1915, VPRS 10309.

6. Majorie Pryor in *Sun News Pictorial*, 14 April 1926; *Bairnsdale Advertiser*, 1 February 1929.

7. Diane Barwick, 'Short History of Lake Tyers Farming Development' in Colin Tatz 'Report of the Lake Tyers Planning and Action Committee on Rehabilitation and Training for Aborigines at Lake Tyers Reserve', 1966, p. 36 in Alick Jackomos Private Papers.

8. Jack Green case file NAA, B337/0 item 278, pp. 1–2.

9. *Argus*, 1 July 1925.

10. Age, 21 October 1927.

11. *Herald*, 5 November 1927, 22 December 1927.

12. *Argus*, 24 April 1928.

13. Aborigines Act 1928 (no. 3631), Regulations, *Victorian Government Gazette*, 13 May 1931, pp. 1558–60.

14. *Herald*, 21 December 1928; *Argus*, 21 December 1928.

15. *Argus*, 23 January 1929; 20 February 1929, *Bairnsdale Advertiser*, 4 and 11 July 1930.

16. *Herald*, 3 October 1929, reprinted in *Bairnsdale Advertiser*, 5 October 1929.

17. *Herald*, 3 October 1929.

18. Dorothy Tonkin report 24 May 1915, Lake Tyers school file, PROV VPRS 640/P1, unit 1525, school no. 1319. See also the file 1900–1930, units 882, 1270, 1430. Harold Collen found it 'distasteful' and asked for a transfer, Collen to Education Department, 12 April 1923, unit 1624.

19. George Chapman, 'Manual Training at the Lake Tyers Aboriginal School with Special Reference to Woodwork, 19 April 1929', Lake Tyers school file , PROV VPRS 640/P1, unit 1783, school no. 1319.

20. *Bairnsdale Advertiser*, 9 November 1929.

21. *Bairnsdale Advertiser*, 29 November 1929.

22. *Sun Pictorial*, 23 March 1934.

23. Anna Vroland, 'Their Music Has Roots', Typescript, SLV, LTP 781.71 v96m 1951, p. 9.

24. *Bairnsdale Advertiser*, 30 April 1929.

25. *Argus*, 20 April 1929.

26. *Bairnsdale Advertiser*, 11 June, 2 August 1929.

27. Ronald Glen to Mr Vroland 29 October 1936 contains a list of sporting achievements, VAG papers SLV, ms 9212; Rev. M. F. Hancock to Amy Brown, 28 August 1939, SLV ms 9212 also said the footballers won a second year in a row.

28. *Argus*, 18 January 1936.

29. *Bairnsdale Advertiser*, 25 March 1930.

30. Ronald Glen to Mr Vroland 29 October 1936, list of sporting achievements, VAG papers SLV, ms 9212.

31. V. Glen to Amy Brown 27 June 1936, VAG papers, SLV ms 9212.

32. *Bairnsdale Advertiser*, 15 February 1929.
33. *Bairnsdale Advertiser*, 29 January 1930.
34. *Bairnsdale Advertiser*, 17 June 1930.
35. *Bairnsdale Advertiser*, 26 February 1929. For the Stratford case see 16 May 1930.
36. Reginald Thorpe to Lind, 28 July 1930, in Connolly case file, NAA B337/0, item 169, p. 34.
37. BPA Memo 'Light Coloured People on the Station', 21 March 1930, Connolly case file, NAA B337/0, item 169, p. 38.
38. Dora Green to Tunnecliffe 23 September 1930, Connolly case file, NAA B337/0, item 169, pp. 23–4.
39. A. Connolly to Lind, no date, Connolly case file, NAA B337/0, item 169, pp. 36–36A.
40. A. Connolly to Tunnecliffe, 30 September 1931, case file, NAA B337/0, item 169, pp. 39–40.
41. Diane Barwick, 'Short History of Lake Tyers Farming Development', Tatz Report, 1966, p. 36.
42. Interview with Albert Mullett, Bairnsdale, 2 September 2003.
43. Glen to Amy Brown 18 July 1933; W. Webster, Education Department to A.N. Brown, 8 August 1933; VAG resolution 21 September 1933, VAG papers, SLV ms 9212.
44. Notes of a visit, Lake Tyers Tues 23 April 1935', VAG papers, SLV ms 9212.
45. Educational Subcommittee—Victorian Aboriginal Group. 'Report on a Visit to Lake Tyers Station, September 26th and 27th 1936', SLV ms 9212.
46. *Argus*, 16 October 1935.
47. *Age* and *Argus* 17 October 1935; *Bairnsdale Advertiser*, 18 October 1935; *Argus*, 18 October 1935.
48. See *Argus*, 4 January, 11–14, 17, 20–22 February 1936.
49. 'Report of the Lake Tyers Investigating Committee, Baptist Union, 5 December 1936', typescript, WILPF papers, SLV ms 9377, box 1726, V/477.
50. *Argus*, 20 February 1936.
51. *Herald*, 20 August 1936.
52. *Age*, 20 February 1936.
53. W. Cooper to W. Gordon Sprigg, 22 February 1936, WILPF papers SLV ms 9377, box 1726, V/1.
54. 'Statement on Lake Tyers by Steward Hood' 20 February 1936 WILPF papers, SLV ms 9377, box 1726, V/477.
55. Alick Jackomos, 'Speech on Lake Tyers', Alick Jackomos family papers in private hands.
56. L. Chapman to VAG, 30 September 1942, VAG papers, SLV ms 9212.
57. Milliken to BPA 4 January 1946, Thomas Foster case file, NAA, B337/0, item 259, p. 14.
58. Milliken to Garnet, 29 January 1946, Thomas Foster case file, NAA, B337/0, item 259, p. 18.
59. Gillespie to W. Slater MLA 10 July 1946, Thomas Foster case file, NAA, B337/0, item 259, pp. 29–30.

60. J. T. Hawden, reference 25 July 1946, Thomas Foster case file, NAA, B337/0, item 259, p. 42.
61. Interview with Murray Bull, Sale, 2 September 2002.
62. 'Lake Tyers Aboriginal Station' June 1941, VAG papers, SLV ms 9212, 'Report on a Visit of WILPF Representatives to the Aboriginal Reserve at Lake Tyers, October 1951', WILPF papers SLV ms 9377.
63. Interview with Murray Bull, Sale, 2 September 2002; See Mavis Thorpe Clark, 'Ronald E. Bull. Aboriginal Landscape Painter', *Smoke Signals*, February–March 1967; *Age*, 18 April 1968; Sylvia Kleinert, 'Bull, Ronald', Sylia Kleinert and Margo Neale (eds), *The Oxford Companion to Aboriginal Art and Culture*, Oxford University Press, Melbourne, 2000, p. 551.
64. Cora Gilsenan to Anna Vroland 30 August 1953, WILPF papers, SLV ms 9377, box 1726, V/282.
65. Cora Gilsenan to Anna Vroland Thursday 27 ? 1953 (date obscured in original) WILPF papers SLV ms 9377, box 1726, V/365.

12 Fighting for Framlingham

1. W.W. Johnstone of Bushfield to John Murray 14 June 1910, NAA, B313/1 box 4, item 62, pp. 62–3.
2. 'Report of the Sub-Committee on Visit to Framlingham Reserve 5 April 1918', and Petition to Legislative Assembly both in NAA, B313/1 box 4, item 62, pp. 3–4 and 6–10.
3. Edna Brown, 'Framlingham' in *Now and Then*, Aboriginal History Programme, Melbourne, 1986, p. 10.
4. Egan to Bailey, October 1926, John Egan case file, NAA B337/0, item 237, p. 3.
5. BPA to Bailey, 23 October 1926, John Egan case file, NAA B337/0, item 237, p. 5.
6. Diane Barwick, 'Equity for Aborigines? The Framlingham Case', in Patrick N. Troy (ed.), *A Just Society? Essays on Equity in Australia*, Allen & Unwin, Sydney, 1981, pp. 190–2.
7. Interview with Ivan Couzens, Warrnambool, 3 October 2002.
8. *Star*, 27 December 1933.
9. *Star*, 2 January 1934.
10. Quoted in *Star*, 4 January 1934.
11. *Star*, 3 January 1934.
12. *Star*, 3 January 1934.
13. See lease document in NAA, B313/1, box 4, item 67, pp. 1–2, 12.
14. Egan was described in January 1934 as 'Age 63.I.P. 17/6. Here 60 years. No Legs. Sister Mrs Farcy half caste was for many years housekeeper on station. 4 room house and very clean and tidy. Two cows and gig. Record good.' Letter from the Board for the Protection of Aborigines to T. Isles, 18 January 1934, NAA, B313/1, box 4, item 67, p. 67. However, his case file with the Board for the Protection of Aborigines describes him as having one leg, Aboriginal case files, NAA B337/0 item 237, file of John Egan 1922–37.
15. *Star*, 6 January 1934.

16.   *Star*, 1 January 1934.

17.   *Warrnambool Standard*, 4 January 1934.

18.   *Warrnambool Standard*, 9 January 1934.

19.   Chief Secretary's Department statement, 10 January 1934, NAA, B313/1, box 4, item 67, p. 21.

20.   *Warrnambool Standard*, 13 January 1934.

21.   *Warrnambool Standard*, 13 January 1934; *Star*, 13 January 1934. 'Notes of a Deputation . . . 12 January 1934', NAA B 313/1, box 4, item 67, pp. 23–8.

22.   *Warrnambool Standard*, 25 January 1934.

23.   Letter for T. Isles to Parker, BPA, 16 January 1934, NAA, B313/1, box 4, item 67, pp. 35–6.

24.   Letter from the Board for the Protection of Aborigines to T. Isles, 18 January 1934, NAA, B313/1, Box 4, item 67, pp. 67–9.

25.   Farquharson to the Minister in Charge of Sustenance, 25 January 1934, NAA, B313/1, box 4, item 67, pp. 72–5.

26.   Clive Shields, Minister of Labour to I. Macfarlan, Chief Secretary, 5 February 1934, NAA, B313/1, box 4, item 67, p.76, also 77.

27.   A. W. Meadows report to the Director of Schools Warrnambool, 7 September 1936, VPRS 640/P/1, unit 2322, file 4532.

28.   *Star*, 14 July 1934.

29.   Reported in the *Star*, 30 May 1934, and by Ian Macfarlan in *VPD*, 13 September 1934, p. 1875.

30.   L. Chapman to I. Macfarlan, 4 July 1934, NAA, B313/1, box 4, item 67, pp. 104–5.

31.   Constable McNamara to Board, 13 October 1934, NAA, B313/1, box 4, item 67.

32.   Report by Constable Jas Forest to the Board, 16 February 1935, NAA, B313/1, box 4, item 68, pp. 8–13.

33.   L. Chapman memo 'Framlingham Reserve. Trespassing by Quadroons etc', 17 October 1934, NAA, B313/1, box 4, item 67, p. 117.

34.   *Warrnambool Standard*, 5 May 1938.

35.   *Warrnambool Standard*, 10 June 1938.

36.   G. H. Newnham to Chief Secretary H. S. Bailey, 3 July 1939, NAA, B313/1, item 72, p. 20.

37.   *Warrnambool Standard*, 24 June 1938.

38.   *Warrnambool Standard*, 17 August 1938; *Uplift*, vol. 1, no. 4, in VAG papers, SLV ms 9212.

39.   *Warrnambool Standard*, 28 November 1938.

40.   Interview with Ivan Couzens, Warrnambool, 3 October 2002.

41.   Local Guardian's report 19 January 1940, George Clarke case file NAA, B337/0, item 148, p. 8.

42.   First annual report of the FRBM, *Warrnambool Standard*, 28 June 1939, and BPA memos, NAA B313/1, item 72, pp. 22–4.

43.   *Warrnambool Standard*, 2 April 1940.

44.   Enquiry procedure and Report on the visit by W. H. Rutherford to Chief Secretary 3 May 1940, NAA, B313/1, item 73, pp. 25, 28–9 respectively.

45.   BPA Memo to Chief Secretary 2 May 1940, NAA B313/1, item 73, p. 22.

46. For the stories of Francis Hutchins, Albert Jackson, Gloria McHenry and Lloyd Clarke, see *Now and Then*, pp. 4–5, 12–17.
47. Gloria McHenry and Lloyd Clarke, see *Now and Then*, pp. 4–5, 12–17.
48. BPA to C. J. Hallowell, Secretary FRBM, 15 September 1942, NAA, B313/1, item 75, p. 7.
49. See the correspondence between the two at NAA B313/1, item 77, pp. 3–11.
50. BPA to C. J. Hallowell, 21 May 1845, NAA B313/1, item 78, p. 17.
51. WILPF Report on Framlingham November 1950, WILPF papers, ms 9377, box 1726, V/480.
52. Unsigned copies 12 December 1950 in WILPF papers, SLV 9377, box 1726, V/108, V/109.
53. Phyllis Dunnolly to Mary Clarke 19 [September] 1950, and 8 October 1950, WILPF papers ms 9377, box 1726, V/165 and V/170 respectively.
54. William Garnet, BPA secretary to Peter Dunnolly, 10 August 1950 and Keith Dodgshun, Chief Secretary to Anna Vroland, 27 September 1950, and WILPF papers SLV ms 9377, box 1726, V/? [file number obscured] and V/168 respectively.
55. Mary Clarke's claim is found in Mary Clarke, 'An Open Letter to Those Who Are Interested in Aborigines and their Descendants', Queen Victoria Hospital, 2 December 1951, in VAG papers, SLV ms 9212. It was also made to the author on 16 August 1978 during an interview with Mary and Ray Clarke at Framlingham. It was indirectly analysed by Diane Barwick in her exhaustively researched article on Louisa Briggs, 'This Most Resolute Lady: A Biographical Puzzle', in D.E. Barwick, J. Beckett and M. Reay (eds), *Metaphors of Interpretation. Essays in Honour of W. E. H. Stanner*, Australian National University Press, Canberra, 1985, pp. 185–239. A salient fact here besides Louisa's own claim in 1924 that she was not Truganini's descendant, was she was observed to have light blue eyes, a recessive gene, which depends on a genetic inheritance from both parents, meaning Louisa could not have been the daughter of a 'full blood' Tasmanian, Truganini or any one else, as blue eyes are not part of their genetic make-up.
56. Mary Clarke, 'An Open Letter to Those Who Are Interested in Aborigines and their Descendants', Queen Victoria Hospital, 2 December 1951, in VAG papers, SLV ms 9212.
57. Undated press clipping February 1951 in NAA B313/1, item 84, p. 78.
58. *Argus*, 23 February 1951.
59. A. Brown to G.H. Newnham 25 April 1955, VAG Papers SLV ms 9212.
60. Robert Lowe, *The Mish*, University of Queensland Press, Brisbane, 2002, pp. 34–5.
61. Percy Clarke, in Alick Jackomos and Derek Fowell (eds), *Living Aboriginal History of Victoria*. p. 124.
62. Lowe, *The Mish*, p. 5.
63. See Sketches of the early 1940s in NAA B313/1, item 75, pp. 9–10 and item 77, p. 15. See also Robert Lowe's map of the 1950s in Lowe, *The Mish*, p. v.
64. Walter Brice case file and George Clarke case file, NAA B337, items 78 and 148 respectively.

65. Interview with Brendan Edwards, Halls Gap, 4 July 2002.
66. Interview with Tim Chatfield, Halls Gap, 4 July 2002.
67. Interview with Brendan Edwards, Halls Gap, 4 July 2002.
68. Interview with Billy Primmer, Warrnambool, 15 August 1978.
69. Interview with 'Banjo' (Henry) Clarke, Warrnambool, 14–15 August 1978.
70. Interview with Eddie Gibbons, Warrnambool, 15 August 1978.
71. Interview with Noel Couzens, Geelong, 18 October 2002.
72. Interview with 'Banjo' (Henry) Clarke, Warrnambool, 14–15 August 1978.
73. Interview with 'Muscles' (Ray) Clarke, Framlingham, 16 August 1978.
74. Richard Broome with Alick Jackomos, *Sideshow Alley*, Allen & Unwin, Sydney, 1998. See also R. Broome, 'Theatres of Power: Tent Boxing 1910–1970', *Aboriginal History*, vol. 20, 1996, pp. 1–23.
75. *Warrnambool Standard*, 28 December 1948, 4 and 25 October 1949.
76. Interview with Noel Couzens, Geelong, 18 October 2002.
77. *Warrnambool Standard*, 8 April 1949.
78. Interview with Tim Chatfield, Halls Gap, 4 July 2002.

13 Country campers

1. Pastor Schulz, 'Aborigines at Antwerp, Victoria', *Uplift*, vol. 1, no. 5.
2. Interview with Betty Tournier, Geelong, 23 September 2002.
3. Interview with Betty Clements, Mildura, 23 August 2002.
4. Interview with Sandra Stewart, Mildura, 24 August 2002; interview with Myra Grinter, Mildura, 14 October 2002.
5. Interview with Betty Tournier, Geelong, 23 September 2002; Interview with Betty Clements, Mildura, 23 August 2002.
6. Interview with Myra Grinter, Mildura, 14 October 2002.
7. Interview with Albert Mullett, Bairnsdale, 2 September 2003.
8. The Maloga petition 1881, in B. Attwood and A. Markus (eds), *The Struggle for Aboriginal Rights. A Documentary History*, Allen & Unwin, Sydney, 1999, pp. 51–2.
9. ibid., p. 53.
10. Ronald Morgan, 'Cummeragunga and its Aboriginal People', Barmah, 1952, typescript; Diane Barwick, 'Coranderrk and Cumeroogunga. Pioneers and Policy' in T. Scarlett Epstein and D. H, Penny (eds), *Opportunity and Response: Case Studies in Economic Development*, C. Hurst and Co., London, 1972, pp. 11–68; Goodall, *Invasion to Embassy*, chap. 6 and pp. 123–34; Mavis Thorpe Clark, Pastor Doug, Rigby, Adelaide, 1972, pp. 30–42.
11. Bevan Nicholls and Merle Jackomos in Alick Jackomos and Derek Fowell (eds), *Living Aboriginal History*, pp. 106 and 168 respectively; see also Merle Jackomos, 'The History of Cummeragunga and Maloga', *Identity*, July 1972, pp. 29–32.
12. Barwick, 'Coranderrk and Cumeroogunga', pp. 51–64.
13. Doreen Barker Mooroopna parsonage to Amy Brown, 1 August 1939, VAG papers SLV, ms 9212.
14. *Shepparton News*, 27 February 1939; Helen Baillie to Minister for Sustenance 14 October 1939, VAG papers, SLV ms 9212.

15. Jack Horner, *Vote Ferguson for Aboriginal Freedom. A Biography*, Australian and New Zealand Book Company, Sydney, 1974, pp. 76–9; Goodall, *Invasion to Embassy*, chap. 18.

16. *Argus*, 7, 9, 27 February 1939, *Shepparton News*, 27 February 1939; see also Clark, *Pastor Doug*, chap. 11.

17. *Argus*, 11 March 1939.

18. *Argus*, 18 April 31, August 1939.

19. Quoted in Jackomos and Fowell (eds), *Living Aboriginal History*, p. 106.

20. Diane Barwick, 'A Little More than Kin. Regional Affiliation and Group Identity Among Aboriginal Migrants in Melbourne', PhD Thesis Department of Anthropology and Sociology, Australian National University, 1963, p. 195.

21. Nicholls in *Shepparton News*, 5 May 1941; Bailey in *Sun*, 5 May 1941; Wayne Atkinson in Jackomos and Fowell (eds), *Living Aboriginal History*, p. 182.

22. Quoted in Jackomos and Fowell (eds), *Living Aboriginal History*, p. 186.

23. Wayne Atkinson in Jackomos and Fowell (eds), *Living Aboriginal History*, p. 182; Hamill in *Shepparton News*, 18 July 1946.

24. *Herald*, 13 (or 15 or 18, date obscured in cutting) 1947.

25. Sergeant S. H. McGuffie, 'Conditions of the Aborigines Residing on the Goulburn River Flats Between Shepparton and Mooroopna', 16 September 1946, VPRS 242/P, unit 887, file C90480.

26. *Shepparton News*, 5 June 1944, See also 25 March 1943 and 17 March 1944 regarding this couple.

27. *Shepparton News*, 26 August 1948.

28. A. Vroland to Florence Grylls 18 February 1950, WILPF papers, SLV ms 9377, box 1726, V/117.

29. Barwick, 'A Little More than Kin', p. 176.

30. *Herald*, 4 June 1946; *Shepparton News*, 26 August 1946.

31. *Shepparton News*, 14 November 1946.

32. *Herald*, 3, 5, 6, 8 March 1947; *Shepparton News*, 24 November 1947.

33. *Shepparton News*, 13, 16 December 1948 for typhoid, 26 August 1948,

61. 23 June 1949 for demolitions.

34. *Shepparton News*, 'Observer' in 24 April 1950 and Fairchney, in 27 April 1950.

35. Shadrach James to William Slater, Chief Secretary 5 August 1946; James to Slater 19 September respectively, VPRS 242/P, unit 887, file C90480. See all ten letters in this file from 1946 to 1950. See also *Shepparton News* on these plans, especially 26 February, 10 June, 9 August 1948.

36. Quoted in Bain Attwood, Winifred Burrage, Alan Burrage, and Elsie Stoke, *A Life Together, A Life Apart*, Melbourne University Press, Melbourne, 1994, p. 121.

37. Paul Briggs quoted in Jackomos and Fowel (eds), *Living Aboriginal History*, p. 190.

38. For an account of his football career see Clark, *Pastor Doug*. pp. 57–67, 74–83, 104.

39. Interview with Merv Feenan, professional runner and trainer, East Malvern, 1 March 1978; Clark, *Pastor Doug*, pp. 41, 62–6; *Herald*, 10 February, 8 June 1948.

40. *Shepparton News*, 12 January 1950.
41. Interview with Jimmy Murray, Melbourne, 8 April 1997.
42. *Shepparton News*, 24, 25 September 1958, 28 August 1959.
43. Wayne Atkinson and Betty Lovett, quoted in Jackomos and Fowell (eds), *Living Aboriginal History*, pp. 182, 186 respectively.
44. *Shepparton News*, 4 October 1948.
45. McGuffie, 'Conditions of the Aborigines' 16 September 1946, VPRS 242/P, unit 887, file C90480.
46. Edwin Atkinson to Amy Brown, 3 June 1950, VAG Papers, SLV ms 9212.
47. *Sun*, 19 November 1946; *Age*, 24 August 1954; *Sun*, 24 August 1957.
48. Draft letter Cora Gilsenan to Chief Secretary, 1 March 1948, WILPF papers, SLV ms 9377, box 1726, V/39.
49. George Slaney to A. Brown, 2 July 1947, VAG papers, SLV ms 9212.
50. Interview with Albert Mullett, Bairnsdale, 2 September 2002.
51. *Herald*, 2 and 28 December 1942.
52. Quoted in Jackomos and Fowell (eds), *Living Aboriginal History*, p. 26.
53. Slaney to Brown, 3 June 1947, VAG papers, SLV ms 9212.
54. See Dr Eileen Fitzgerald in *Age*, 9 May 1944 and Rev. Green in *Age*, 5 May 1947.
55. Slaney to Brown, 11 March 1947, VAG papers, SLV ms 9212.
56. For the Committee's policy see Slaney to Brown 23 June 1947, VAG papers, SLV ms 9212.
57. Slaney to Brown, 3 June 1947, VAG papers, SLV ms 9212.
58. Slaney to Brown 28 January 1947, 3 June 1947, VAG papers, SLV ms 9212.
59. Slaney to Brown, 11 March 1947, VAG papers, SLV ms 9212.
60. Cora Gilsenan to Anna Vroland, 3 April 1951, WILPF papers, SLV ms 9377, box 1726, V/203.
61. Diane Barwick, 'Changes in Aboriginal Population of Victoria, 1863–1966', p. 313; *Victorian Year Book*, 1973 Centenary Edition, Commonwealth Bureau of Census and Statistics, Melbourne, 1973, pp. 1071–3.
62. 'Conditions of Dark Children in East Gippsland. Reports by Representatives of Women's International League for Peace and Freedom (Australian section)', June 1951, located in VAG papers, SLV ms 9212.
63. Four letters between WILPF and Dodgshun, 8, 17 August, 4 September 1951, WIPLF papers, SLV ms 9377, box 1726, V/213–5 and 219.
64. Quoted in WILPF to R. Holt, 11 September 1953 and referred to in WILPF to A. Lind, 22 October 1951, WILPF papers, SLV ms 9377, box 1726, V/284 and V/243 respectively.
65. WILPF to Holt, 11 September 1953, WILPF papers, SLV ms 9377, box 1726, V/284.
66. C. Gilsenan to A. Vroland, 8 January 1953, WILPF papers, SLV ms 9377, box 1726, V/271.
67. See Richard Harrison to R. Holt, 29 September 1953 and reply 5 October 1953 and A. Vroland to Premier John Cain, 30 November 1954 relating no progress, WILPF papers, SLV ms 9377, box 1726, V/287, and V/314 (a) respectively.

68. C. Gilsenan to ? no date (several pages missing) in WILPF papers, SLV 9377, box 1726, V/295.
69. For Elkin see Tigger Wise, *The Self-Made Anthropologist. A Life of P. Elkin*, Allen & Unwin, Sydney, 1985, chap. 13.
70. Constance S. Brown (nee Barling), 'An Account of Events and Lives of Aborigines in a Victorian Town', typescript lent by Renn Wortley of Hawthorn.
71. A. Vroland 'Their Music Has Roots', Melbourne, 1951, typescript in the SLV.
72. Vroland, 'Their Music Has Roots', p. 9; and one page typescript copy in VAG papers, SLV ms 9212; *Herald*, 12 September 1932.
73. Daryl Tonkin and Carolyn Landon, *Jackson's Track. Memoir of a Dreamtime Place*, Viking, Melbourne, 1999.
74. Graham in *Herald*, 30 July 1941; A. Burdeu 'Housing at Antwerp Aboriginal Camp. Report to Aborigines Uplift Society', no date, VAG papers, SLV ms 9212.
75. *Herald*, 1 August 1955; VAG report 'Aborigines on the Murray', 1957, VAG papers, SLV ms 9212, respectively.
76. Eva Marshall Hon. Sec. Swan Hill District Native Children's Recreation Centre to A. Brown, 29 April 1954 and 'Notes of a talk by Feldtmann to Ormond College, 8 September 19?' (date obscured). VAG papers, SLV ms 9212.
77. Brown (nee Barling), 'An Account of Events and Lives of Aborigines in a Victorian Town'.
78. Cora Gilsenan to Anna Vroland, 30 August 1953, in WILPF papers, SLV 9377, box 1726, V/282.
79. Alick Jackomos, 'Remembering Aboriginal Fitzroy', typescript of an interview by Steve Brown and Steve Avery of the Historic Places Section, Heritage Services Branch, Aboriginal Affairs Victoria, 31 July 1998, p. 43.
80. Minutes of Second Aboriginal Congress, 10–11 July 1965, in Alick Jackomos Private Papers.
81. A. H. Feldtmann, 'Survey of Aborigines at Various Centres in Victoria (Excluding Lake Tyers)', typescript in VAG papers, SLV ms 9212.

14 Melbourne and Aboriginal activism

1. *Sun*, 24 February 1951. See also *Herald*, 22 February 1951.
2. See *Herald*, 17 June 1954. See also *Herald*, 6 March 1953, 22 February 1951; for more on Bill Bull and gumleaf playing see Hugh Anderson, 'Lost in the Streets. A Gumleaf Requiem for Bill Bull', *Journal of Australian Studies*, no. 44, March 1995, pp. 22–37.
3. Both Barrett and the *Herald* quoted in Tony Birch, 'The Battle For Spatial Control in Fitzroy' in S. Ferber, C. Healey and C. McAuliffe (eds), *Beast of Suburbia. Reinterpreting Cultures in Australian Suburbs*, Melbourne University Press, Melbourne, 1994, pp. 20–1.
4. See Margaret Tucker, *If Everyone Cared. Autobiography of Margaret Tucker*, Ure Smith Sydney, 1977, chaps 13–14; Mavis Thorpe Clark, *Pastor Doug*, chaps 12–14.
5. Diane Barwick, 'A Little More Than Kin. Regional Affiliation and Group Identity Among Aboriginal Migrants in Melbourne', PhD Thesis Department of Anthropology and Sociology, Australian National University, 1963, p. 10.

6.   Barwick, 'A Little More Than Kin', p. 21.
7.   *Age*, 26 May 1952.
8.   A. Vroland to Professor Browne 4 October 1948, WILPF papers, SLV ms 9377, box 1726, V/68.
9.   Banjo Clarke as told to Camilla Chance, *Wisdom Man. The Compassionate Life and Beliefs of a Remarkable Aboriginal Elder*, Penguin/Viking Melbourne, 2003, p. 126.
10. Barwick, 'A Little More Than Kin', p. 49.
11. Barwick, 'A Little More Than Kin', p. xxiii.
12. Albert Mullett Interview, Bairnsdale, 2 September 2002.
13. Albert Mullett Interview, Bairnsdale, 2 September 2002.
14. Thorpe Clark, *Pastor Doug*, chaps 13–14.
15. Barwick, 'A Little More Than Kin', pp. 250–1.
16. Tucker, *If Everyone Cared*, p. 158.
17. Daphne Lowe Interview, Warrnambool, 4 October 2002.
18. Barwick, 'A Little More Than Kin', pp. 54–8, 267–72.
19. Clarke, *Wisdom Man*, p. 126.
20. *Truth*, 1 March 1941.
21. Alick Jackomos, 'Remembering Aboriginal Fitzroy', pp. 9–10.
22. Fitzroy Council Minutes, 3 March 1941, 490, p. 2, VPRS 0011086/p/0001, unit 17.
23. Fitzroy Council Minutes, 15 September 1941, 617, p. 3, VPRS 0011086/p/0001, unit 17.
24. Fitzroy Council Minutes, 8 December 1941, 668, pp. 2–3, VPRS 0011086/p/0001, unit 17.
25. *Herald*, 17 September 1941.
26. *Herald*, 17 September 1941.
27. *Argus*, 26 September 1941.
28. *Truth*, 18 January 1941.
29. Fitzroy Council Minutes, 29 September 1941, 652, p. 6, VPRS 0011086/p/0001, unit 17.
30. Jackomos, 'Remembering Aboriginal Fitzroy', pp. 10, 20, 24.
31. *Herald*, 17 September 1941.
32. Survey's major findings reported in *Age*, 9 December 1950.
33. *Age*, 6 December 1946; *Herald*, 11 June 1946.
34. Jackomos, 'Remembering Aboriginal Fitzroy', pp. 4–6, 21, 38; Alick Jackomos, editor of *Aboriginal News*, in 1964 reported seeing her recently, no. 4, March 1964, typescript.
35. See Helen Baillie to Goulburn Valley Branch World Council of Churches, 27 August 1951 and 'The Call of the Aboriginal' in *The Defender*, pp. 11–17 both found in VAG papers, SLV ms 9212.
36. Helen Baillie ASIO file, NAA A6126/XMO, item 23.
37. Interview with Valentine Leeper, East Melbourne, 24 October 1989.
38. Baillie to hon. sec. VAG, 13 June 1944, VAG papers, SLV ms 9212.
39. J. J. Clark to A. Brown, 22 February 1939, VAG papers, SLV ms 9212.

40. Helen Baillie to Shirley Andrews, 13 June 1956, SLV Council for Aboriginal Rights (CAR) papers, PA 222, 1540.
41. *Herald*, 6 March 1958. Clarke, *Wisdom Man*, pp. 127–9.
42. H. Baillie to V. Leeper, 14 October 1968, VAG papers, SLV ms 9212.
43. *Age*, 9 December 1950.
44. Tucker, *If Everyone Cared*, pp. 163–4.
45. *Herald*, 24 April 1948; *Age*, 26 April 1948, 18 April 1949.
46. *Argus*, 16, 30 January 1951; Thorpe Clark, *Pastor Doug*, pp. 153–7.
47. *Herald*, 4 April 1952.
48. William Onus, ASIO file, NAA, A6119/79, item 1063.
49. Quoted in Thorpe Clark, *Pastor Doug*, p. 157.
50. Eleanor Harding, 'Aboriginal Fitzroy', in *Fitzroy. Melbourne's First Suburb*, Melbourne University Press, Melbourne, 1991, pp. 287–98.
51. *Herald*, 15 December 1937.
52. See *Shepparton News*, 26 May 1947.
53. *Herald*, 24 March 1930 quoted in B. Attwood and A. Markus, *The Struggle for Aboriginal Rights. A Documentary History*, Allen & Unwin, Sydney, 1999, pp. 141–3.
54. See Bain Attwood, *Rights for Aborigines*, Allen & Unwin, Sydney, 2003, pp. 55–78; Andrew Markus, 'William Cooper and the 1937 Petition to the King', in *Aboriginal History*, vol. 7, pt 1, 1983, pp. 46–60; Bain Attwood and Andrew Markus, *Thinking Black. William Cooper and the Australian Aborigines' League*, Aboriginal Studies Press, Canberra, 2004.
55. *Argus*, 26 October 1937.
56. Letter to the *Argus*, 5 December 1934.
57. 'Notes of Deputation Representing Aboriginals and Various Associations interested in Aboriginal Welfare Work . . .', 23 January 1935, pp. 1–7 typescript; T. Paterson to W. Cooper 29 May 1935; Cooper to Paterson 24 June 1935; Cooper to Paterson June 1935; NAA A1/15, item 35/3951.
58. 'Australian Aborigines' League Annual Report 1936', VAG papers, SLV ms 9212, typescript.
59. *The Times*, 25 November 1937.
60. *Uplift*, vol. 1, no. 3, August 1938.
61. For the group's work see their magazine *Uplift* 1938–41.
62. *Uplift*, February 1941, pp. 10–12.
63. *Uplift*, vol. 1, no. 7.
64. See Fiona Paisley, 'Federalising the Aborigines? Constitutional Reform in the Late 1920s', *Australian Historical Studies*, no. 111, October 1998, pp. 248–66.
65. Interview with Valentine Leeper, East Melbourne, 25 October 1989.
66. Victorian Aboriginal Group and NAANR, 40th and Final Annual Report and History, 1971, VAG papers, SLV ms 9212.
67. Letter to the Editor, *Argus*, 1 August 1933.
68. Anne Bon to A. Brown 20 April 1934, VAG papers, SLV ms 9212.
69. For the VAG see their brief history of themselves 'The Victorian Aboriginal Group', April 1957 in VAG papers, SLV ms 9212, Attwood, *Rights for Aborigines*, pp. 81–101.

70. *Argus*, 13 November 1937.

71. *The Australian ABO CALL. The Voice of the Aborigines*, no. 1, April 1938.

72. ABO CALL, April 1938. Reprinted in Attwood and Markus (eds), *The Struggle for Aboriginal Rights*, 89–91.

73. Quoted in Attwood, *Rights for Aborigines*, p. 72. For another version of these events see R. McGregor, 'Protest and Progress. Aboriginal Activism in the 1930s', *Australian Historical Studies*, no. 101, October 1993, pp. 555–68.

74. Diane Barwick, 'William Cooper', *Australian Dictionary of Biography*, B. Nairn and G. Serle (general editors), Melbourne University Press, Melbourne, 1981, vol. 8, pp. 107–8.

75. Quoted in Robert A. Hall, *The Black Diggers: Aborigines and Torres Strait Islanders in the Second World War*, Allen & Unwin, Sydney, pp. 11–12.

76. *Argus*, 11 July 1940.

77. *Sun*, 17 January 1940; Pepper and de Araugo, *The Kurnai of Gippsland*, p. 256.

78. *Herald*, 5 July 1940.

79. Hall, *The Black Diggers*, chap. 2; for Lake Tyers men *Uplift*, vol. 2, no. 5.

80. *Herald*, 1 December 1944. See also his biography, Gordon, *An Embarrassing Australian. The Story of an Aboriginal Warrior*; 'Reg Saunders (1920–1991)', in Jackomos and Fowell (eds), *Forgotten Heroes*, pp. 19–22.

81. *Herald*, 15 March 1946; *Warrnambool Standard*, 13 February 1946.

82. Jackomos and Fowell list 207 Aboriginal Victorian service men and women in an appendix to their book *Forgotten Heroes. Aborigines at War from the Somme to Vietnam*, Victoria Press, Melbourne, 1993, but they do not distinguish those who served in WWII. However, as 42 fought in the Great War and about 10 in Korea and Vietnam, this leaves a figure of about 150 for WWII.

83. A. P. A. Burdeu hon. sec. Aborigines' Uplift Society to R. G. Menzies 30 June 1940 in NAA Series A406/62, item E1957/1pt1.

84. A. P. Elkin, 'Aborigines and the Franchise', NAA Series A406/62, item E1957/1pt1. For RSL see William Wannan letter to the editor, *Argus*, 25 March 1947; for Douglas, *Warrnambool Standard*, 12 March 1948; Hall, *The Black Diggers*, p. 39

85. Shadrach James to J. B. Chifley 21 February 1949, NAA Series A406/62, item E1957/1pt1. Deputation, *Herald*, 27 April, 26 May 1949.

86. Doug Nicholls to J. B. Chifley 6 August 1949, NAA Series A406/62, item E1957/1pt1.

87. *Shepparton News*, 21 February 1946.

88. *Argus*, 6 May 1947; for Onus' response *Shepparton News*, 26 May 1947.

89. 'Victorian State Program for Aborigines and Aborigines Castes. Campaign Objectives and Demands', September 1947, VAG papers, SLV ms 9212.

90. Sitarani Kerin, 'An Attitude of Respect', Anna Vroland and Aboriginal Rights 1947–1957, Monash Publications in History, no. 31, 1999.

91. *Warrnambool Standard*, 6 November 1948. Also A. W. R. Vroland Chairman NEF Statement 28 October 1948 and Agenda for NEF National Conference on Native Rights'; VAG papers, SLV ms 9212.

92. Vaughan Hulme, 'Working For: Working With Black Protest. The Council for Aboriginal Rights 1951–1968', BA (Hons) thesis La Trobe University, 1992.

93. See ASIO files, NAA A6126/XMO item 23, 1061, 1064, 1091, 292, and 1542/296 respectively.
94. *Argus*, 14 April 1949.
95. *Age*, 15 October 1952.
96. Anna Vroland to M. Healey of QLD TLC 18 February 1950, WILPF papers, SLV ms 9377, box 1726, V118.
97. Shirley Andrews to Ella Austin 29 September 1955, Council for Aboriginal Rights (CAR) papers, SLV PA 222, 1309.

15 Assimilation and its challengers

1. Quoted in Sharman Stone (ed.), *Aborigines in White Australia*, Heinemann, Melbourne, 1974, p. 192.
2. *Argus*, 21 August 1954.
3. *Sun*, 23 March 1955.
4. *Herald*, 19 October 1955; *Shepparton News*, 5 December 1956.
5. Quoted in the *Argus*, 11 November 1955.
6. Notes on a flyer for the meeting and letter from Irene Newton John to Valentine Leeper, 27 June, 29 July 1955, VAG papers, SLV ms 9212.
7. *Sun News Pictorial*, 8 April 1954. See also Corinne Manning, 'The McLean Report. Legitimising Victoria's New Assimilationism', *Aboriginal History*, vol. 26, 2002, p. 163.
8. Barwick, 'Changes in the Aboriginal Population of Victoria, 1863–1966', p. 300.
9. Manning, 'The McLean Report', pp. 168–70.
10. Charles McLean, 'Report Upon the Operation of the Aborigines Act 1928 and the Regulations and Orders made Thereunder', *VPP*, 1956, v. 2, n. 18, pp. 1–22.
11. McLean to Valentine Leeper, 12 April 1957, VAG papers, SLV ms 9212.
12. *Age*, 1 February 1957; Manning, 'The McLean Report', pp. 172–4.
13. *Sun*, 1 February 1957.
14. V. A. Leeper to McLean 12 April 1957, VAG papers, SLV ms 9212. A. Vroland, 'Comments on Mr Charles McLean's Report on the Operation of the Aborigines Act 1928 . . .' to Premier Bolte, 25 April 1957, WILPF Papers, SLV ms 9377, box 1726, V/490; CAR to Rylah, 3 April 1957, CAR Papers, SLV PA 222, 1727.
15. Lind and Doube, *VPD*, 1956–1958, vol. 282, pp. 1104 and 1106 respectively.
16. 'An Act Relating to Aboriginal Natives of Victoria and for other Purposes', (Aborigines Act 1957), no. 6086.
17. 'Aborigines Welfare Regulations 1958', *Victoria Gazette*, no. 680, 27 August 1958.
18. *Report of the Aborigines Welfare Board*, 1958, pp. 3, 5.
19. *Report of the Aborigines Welfare Board*, 1958, pp. 5, 9.
20. *Shepparton News*, 21 May, 2 July, 5 December 1956.
21. *Shepparton News*, 2 October 1957.
22. *Shepparton News*, 2, 14, 18, 25 October 1957.
23. *Herald*, 25 October 1957.

24. *Shepparton News*, 12 September 1960.
25. *Age*, 12 April 1958.
26. *Shepparton News*, 15 June 1959; *Herald*, 12 December 1960.
27. For the opening of both settlements see *Age*, 12 April 1958, 12 March 1960. See also Corinne Manning, ' "Humpies" to Houses: Victoria's Transitional Aboriginal Housing Policy 1957–1969', (revised edition), PhD thesis, La Trobe University, 2001, chaps 4–5.
28. Quoted in *Herald*, 12 December 1960, in Manning, ' "Humpies" to Houses', p. 134.
29. Florence Grylls, 'Aborigines' Welfare in Australia', in *The World's Children*, Autumn 1957, pp. 85–6.
30. Quoted in J. McQualter and E. Brady, *Rodney Recollections 1886–1986*, Shire of Rodney, Tatura, 1986, p. 120.
31. 'Mary Connor' and 'Michael Wilton', quoted in Manning, '"Humpies" to Houses', pp. 153, 156–7.
32. *Herald*, 3 September 1964.
33. *Sun*, 17 June 1966.
34. *Age*, 24 October 1959.
35. *Age*, 17 June 1966.
36. The two demands, *Age*, 28 March 1966; *Sun*, 20 July 1966.
37. *Herald*, 27 June 1969.
38. Manning, 'Humpies to Houses', pp. 237–9.
39. *Report of the Aborigines Welfare Board*, 1967, p. 17.
40. *Report of the Aborigines Welfare Board*, 1966, pp. 13–14.
41. *Age*, 17 August 1962.
42. *Herald*, 27 May 1961. See also *Sun*, 26 October 1959.
43. *Herald*, 5 May 1964.
44. Alick Jackomos, unpublished 'Memoirs', p. 59 in possession of the author.
45. Editor, *On Aboriginal Affairs*, no. 13, April 1965.
46. Lorna Lippman, *Words or Blows. Racial Attitudes in Australia*, Penguin, Melbourne, 1973.
47. Alick Jackomos, 'Speech at Lake Tyers Workshop 28 August 1991', in Alick Jackomos Private Papers.
48. Stan Davey, report of a visit to Traralgon-Morwell 28 August 1967, in *ABSCHOL Newsletter*, no. 20, July 1967. For evictions see *Age*, 21 November 1967, 7 July 1972.
49. *Herald*, 4 January 1963, 19 December 1964; Answer to Clyde Holding question in *VPDLA*, 43 session, 1965–66, vol. 281, pp. 2960–1.
50. Kym Thompson, 'A History of the Aboriginal People of East Gippsland', Report for the Land Conservation Council, Victoria, 1985, LT ms 11969, p. 65; the government listed 6 of 16 who left between 1963 and 1966 as not being in their own house, *VPDLA*, 43 session, 1965–66, vol. 281, pp. 2960–1.
51. *Report of the Aborigines Welfare Board*, 1966, pp. 9–11.
52. *Herald*, 28 April 1965.
53. *Herald*, 27 April, 12 May, 16 September 1965; *Age*, 23 June, 12 July, 20 September 1965.

54. Tonkin and Landon, *Jackson's Track*, pp. 247–62.
55. *Sun*, 24 September 1958; *Herald*, 25 September 1958.
56. *Sun*, 26 September 1958; *Herald*, 26 September 1958.
57. *Age*, 15 March 1960.
58. *Herald*, 16 March 1960.
59. *Sun*, 26 January 1966.
60. *Age*, 25 January 1966.
61. *Sun*, 26 January 1966.
62. *Sun*, 4 February 1966.
63. Interview with Daphne Lowe, Warrnambool, 4 October 2002.
64. Mark Harris, 'A "New Deal" for Victorian Aborigines 1957–68', MA thesis, Monash University, 1988, pp. 69, 112.
65. Diane Barwick estimated the population could be fifty per cent higher than the Board's estimation, Barwick, 'Changes in the Aboriginal Population of Victoria, 1866–1966', p. 300.
66. *Age*, 11 December 1963.
67. *Report of the Aborigines Welfare Board*, 1967, p. 24; Tom Roper National Director of ABSCHOL in *Age*, 30 June 1967.
68. *Age*, 24 June 1969; Zakia Ebrahim, '"Shaking the Commonwealth into Action". ABSCHOL 1952–1968', BA (Hons) History thesis, La Trobe University, 1990.
69. Diane Barwick, 'A Little More Than Kin', pp. 293–6.
70. *Age*, 5 December 1955; *Shepparton News*, 2 October 1957.
71. Alick Jackomos 'Statement in the Matter of Shane Kenneth Atkinson' taken by Kate Auty for Royal Commission Aboriginal Deaths in Custody, no date about 1990, Alick Jackomos family papers.
72. Interview with Daphne Lowe, Warrnambool, 4 October 2002.
73. Interviews with Glenda Austin and Daphne Lowe, Warrnambool, 3 and 4 October 2002 respectively.
74. Interview with Charlotte Jackson, Geelong, 23 September 2002.
75. *Herald*, 27 April, 15 May 1964; *Sun*, 20 January 1965.
76. *Herald*, 18 December 1967.
77. *Smoke Signals*, October 1959.
78. *Smoke Signals*, April and July 1960, October 1962.
79. Jackomos, 'Remembering Aboriginal Fitzroy', pp. 46–7.
80. Survey in *Smoke Signals*, December 1965.
81. Anon., *Victims or Victors? The Story of the Victorian Aborigines Advancement League*, Hyland House, Melbourne, 1985, chap. 4.
82. Interview with Myra Grinter, Mildura, 14 October 2002.
83. *Smoke Signals*, April 1960, April 1963. For Tanderra see *Herald*, 7 May 1962, 5 January 1963.
84. *Smoke Signals*, February–March 1967.
85. *Age*, 5 August 1957. See also 26 July 1957.
86. *Shepparton News*, 17 March 1958.
87. *Truth*, 20 June 1964; *Smoke Signals*, August–September 1965.
88. Alick Jackomos to Pauline Pickford, 14 December 1965, CAR papers, SLV PA 222, item 3646.

89. *Age*, 8 May 1967.
90. Fran Russell to Pauline Pickford 19 July 1964, CAR papers, SLV PA 222, item 3306.
91. Harris, 'A "New Deal" ', p. 74.
92. Petition reproduced in *VPDLA*, 1962–63, vol. 270, pp. 3943–4.
93. *Age*, 27 June 1963.
94. Aboriginal petition to parliament, *PPLA*, 1964–65, vol. 1, no. 38, 23 March 1965; to A. Rylah, 18 August 1964, copy, CAR papers, SLV PA 222, item 3323.
95. Harris, 'A "New Deal" ', chaps 5–7.
96. 'Aboriginal Policies of the Aborigines Welfare Board', in *Report of the Aborigines Welfare Board*, 1967, Appendix 1.
97. See *Herald*, 4, 6, 8, 17, 23 March 1967.
98. *Herald*, 11, 15 April 1967.
99. *Sun*, 20 March 1967.
100. For Roosevelt Brown's visit and reactions to it, see *Herald*, 28, 29 August 1969, *Age*, 30 August 1969.
101. *Herald*, 3 October 1969.
102. Interview with Myra Grinter, Mildura, 14 October 2002.
103. Jackomos, 'Remembering Aboriginal Fitzroy', pp. 27–8.
104. *Sun*, 7, 20 January 1969.

16 Seeking autonomy

1. *Herald*, 21 February 1968.
2. See *Sun*, 16 and 17 July 1969; *Age*, 17 July 1969; *Herald*, 15 and 16 July 1969.
3. Ministry of Aboriginal Affairs, *Annual Report* to June 1968, p. 9.
4. See the Ministry's annual reports, especially to June 1973.
5. *Age*, 10 June 1968.
6. See three reports of Worthy's speech in *Age*, *Sun* and *Herald* for 25 June 1968.
7. *Herald*, 25 June 1968.
8. *Sun*, 26 June 1968.
9. *Age*, 27 January 1969.
10. *Age*, 27–28 January 1969.
11. *Age*, 29 March 1972.
12. Reported in *Australian*, 3 June 1969 and *Sun*, 3 June 1969.
13. Michael Ryan, 'Boy off the Rubbish Tip Now a Tribal Wise Man', *Age*,
61. 25 January 1972.
14. Alan Stewart talks with Bruce McGuinness', *Herald*, 12 December 1970. For more on Bruce McGuinness see his homepage for images, press cuttings and some of his writings via <http://www.kooriweb.org/ indexb.html>. McGuinness died on 5 September 2003.
15. *Herald*, 13 April 1971.
16. *Sun*, 13 January 1972.
17. *Sun*, 16 December 1971. See also *Age*, 21 December 1971, *Sun*, 21 and 23 December 1971; *Sun*, 18 January 1972.
18. *Sun* and *Age*, 25 June 1968.
19. *Sun*, 7 July 1969; *Herald*, 22 July 1969, *Age*, 5 February 1970.

20. *Age*, 9 July 1969, 12 and 13 June 1972.

21. Quoted in Alick Jackomos, 'The History of Lake Tyers', *Identity*, October 1971, p. 8.

22. *Age, 1 April 1970, Sun*, 20 July 1971; Aboriginal Lands Act 1970, no. 8044.

23. For McGuinness' efforts see *Herald*, 25 July and 2 October 1970; *Age*, 3 and 9 October 1970.

24. *Herald*, 8 February 1971.

25. *Sun*, 15 February 1971. See also Sheryl Goodes, '"This Land is Ours!" Or Is It? The Struggle for Land of the Framlingham Aborigines', BA (Hons) thesis in History, La Trobe University, 2001.

26. *Herald*, 26 March 1971. See also John Larkin, 'In the Dark Forest Time to Dream and Time to Wait', *Age*, 6 March 1971.

27. *Sun*, 15 April 1971; *Age*, 15, 16, 17 April 1971.

28. *Sun*, 19 April 1971.

29. *Age*, 20 April 1971.

30. *Age*, 24 April 1971.

31. *Sun*, 1 December 1971.

32. *Herald*, 7 February 1972.

33. *Sun*, 4 February 1972. On the crisis see *Australian*, 6 February 1971, 27 July 1971; *Age* and *Herald*, 1 December 1971.

34. Ministry of Aboriginal Affairs, *Annual Report* to June 1971, p. 2; June 1974, pp. 3–4 respectively.

35. Ministry of Aboriginal Affairs, *Annual Report* to June 1973, p. 1.

36. *Sun*, 1 February 1974.

37. See the Aboriginal Affairs (Transfer of Functions) Act 1974, no. 8606.

38. *Melbourne Times*, 23 July 1976 and *Herald*, 7 October 1976.

39. *Age*, 21 April 1994, 11 March 1995; 10 April 1995; *Australian*, 6–7 April 1996.

40. VAHS Annual Report 1999–2000, also available on <http://www.koorie web. org/vahs/information.html> accessed February 2004.

41. Interview with Bessie Yarram, 12 August 2002, Sale.

42. 'Ramahyuck District Aboriginal Corporation Community Corporate Plan, 2002–2007', May 2002.

43. Interview with Charlotte Jackson, Geelong, 23 September 2002.

44. Interview with Robert Lowe, Warrnambool, 4 October 2002; Interview with Jenny Lowe, Coordinator, Worn Gundidj, Warrnambool, 6 February 2004.

45. Information from Julie Wilson, Coordinator, Budja Budja Cooperative, Halls Gap, 5 February 2004.

46. Interview with Bess Yarram, Sale, 12 August 2002.

47. Separate interviews with Bessie Yarram and Sandra Nelson, 12 August 2002, Sale.

48. Claire Williams and Bill Thorpe with Carolyn Chapman, *Aboriginal Workers and Managers. History, Emotional and Community Labour and Occupational Health and Safety in South Australia*, Digital, Adelaide, 2003, chap. 3.

49. Interview with Brendan Edwards, Hall's Gap, 4 July 2003.

50. Interview with Myra Grinter, Mildura, 4 October 2002.

51. Noel Couzens interview, Geelong, 18 October 2003.

52. *1994 National Aboriginal and Torres Strait Islander Surveys* for Ballarat and Wangaratta, ATSIC regions, 1996, p. 469 and p. 46, respectively. Advice from Reg Blow, indigenous employment consultant; Interview with Sandra Stewart, coordinator, Koori Business Network, Mildura, 24 August 2002.

53. Interview with Jamie Thomas, Warrnambool, 4 October 2002.

54. *Sun*, 29 December 1969.

55. *Australian*, 1 December 1976.

56. Interview with Sandra Stewart, coordinator, Indigenous Business Network, Mildura, 24 August 2002.

57. Information supplied by Esme Manahan and Brian Stevens of the Koori Business Network, Department of Innovation, Industry and Regional Development, 28 January 2004.

58. Ray Marks interview, Hall's Gap, 3 July 2002.

59. *Age*, 2, 5, October 1971; *Herald*, 6 October 1971; *Australian*, 12 October 1971.

60. *Australian*, 29 March 1973.

61. *Report of the Aborigines Welfare Board*, 1967, p. 4.

62. Barwick, 'Changes in the Aboriginal Population of Victoria, 1863–1866', p. 300.

63. *1994 National Aboriginal and Torres Strait Islander Surveys* for Ballarat and Wangaratta, ATSIC regions, 1996, p. 9 on both.

64. 'Statement in the Matter of Shane Kenneth Atkinson' by Alick Jackomos, no date, about 1990, in Alick Jackomos Private papers.

65. D. Barwick, 'The Aboriginal Family in South-eastern Australia', J. Krupinski and A. Stoller (eds), *The Family in Australia*, Pergamon Press, Sydney, 1978, p. 208.

66. 'Being Black and Together—That's Beautiful', *Women's Weekly*, 25 May 1977.

67. 'Introduction to VACCA' and 'Aboriginal Child Placement Principle', typescript VAACA, in possession of the author.

68. *Age*, 21 September 1989; and the video 'Savage Indictment' which follows the court case and appeal.

69. Copies of consent form 13 February 1963; social worker's report 22 February 1963; and adoption form 4 March 1963 signed by the Savages in Alick Jackomos Private Papers. *Age*, 19 May 1991.

70. *Age*, 19 November 1993, 30 January 1996.

71. *PDLA*, 54th Parliament, first session, vol. 4, p. 709.

72. See <http://www.vacca.org/about/objective/html> accessed February 2004.

73. *Age*, 15 July 1996.

74. *Age*, 22 January 2004.

75. *Age*, 9 May 2001.

76. Interview with the Coordinator, Albert Mullett, Bruthen, 12 February 2004.

77. *Age*, 20 September 2000.

78. *Age*, 14 June 2001.

79. *Age*, 8 May 2003, 14 February 2004.

80. *Age*, 5 December 2003, 28 August 2004.

81. *Age*, 10 December 2003.

82. 'Statement in the Matter of Shane Kenneth Atkinson' by Alick Jackomos, no date, about 1990, in Alick Jackomos Private papers.

83. E. Eggleston, *Fear, Favour or Affection?* Australian National University Press, Canberra, 1976; G. Lyons, 'Aboriginal Perceptions of Courts and Police: a Victorian Case Study', *Australian Aboriginal Studies*, 1983, no. 2, pp. 45–61.

84. *Age*, 20 October 1983.

85. *Age*, 7 August 1987; 13 April 1989; 6 November 1992.

86. Royal Commission into Aboriginal Deaths in Custody issued numerous volumes of evidence. See also Human Rights and Equal Opportunity Commission, *Racist Violence: A Report on the National Inquiry into Racist Violence in Australia*, AGPS, Canberra, 1991.

87. Sarah James, 'Policing and Victorian Aboriginal Offending', in ANZ Society of Criminology Conference, University of New South Wales, 1994, pp. 3–6.

88. Quoted in James, 'Policing and Victorian Aboriginal Offending', p. 6.

89. *Age*, 9 August 1996.

90. *Age*, 5 March 2003.

91. Interview with Lynette Bishop, Bairnsdale, 2 September 2002.

92. *Age*, 10 August 1993.

93. *Age*, 18 April 1993.

94. AFL brochure, 'One Game for All Australians. How Australian Football has Acted to Counteract Racial and Religious Abuse'.

95. Interview with Sandra Stewart, Mildura 24 August 2002; discussion with Karen Mudoo, Principal KODE School Mildura, 14 October 2002.

96. Notes taken by the author. See also the report in *Sunraysia Daily*, 24 August 2002.

17 Being Aboriginal

1. National Aboriginal and Torres Strait Islander Survey, Ballarat (Tumbukka) and Wangaratta (Binjiru) ATSIC Region, Australian Bureau of Statistics, Canberra, 1994, figure 1.4.

2. Interview with Sandra Neilson, Sale, 12 August 2002.

3. Interview with Sandra Neilson, Sale, 12 August 2002.

4. *PDLC & LA*, vol. 304, p. 2141; *Warrnambool Standard*, 13 August 1975.

5. *Canberra Times*, 22 May 1973; *Sydney Morning Herald*, 12 July 1974; The Minister for Planning and Environment E.H. Walker, estimated there were 8,000 Aboriginal artefacts in the Museum, 10 October 1984, *PDLC*, vol. 375, p. 620.

6. *Age*, 21 October 1983.

7. Jane Munday, 'Aboriginal Artifacts Pose Legal Dilemma', *Age*, 17 February 1984.

8. *Age*, 12, 18 April 1984.

9. *Age*, 26 May, 13 and 14 September 1984.

10. *Age*, 25 February 1982.

11. *Age*, 13 September 1984.

12. A. Xiberras and H. Du Cros, 'Aboriginal Involvement in Monitoring and Protecting Cultural Sites within the Wurundjeri's Tribal Boundaries,

Melbourne', in J. Buckhead et al (eds), *Aboriginal Involvement in Parks and Protected Areas*, Arcos, AIATSIS, Canberra, 1993, pp. 221–6.

13. *Age*, 16 August 1989; 22 August 1990; 18 January 1992. For new datings on Mungo woman by Jim Bowler see *Age*, 20 February 2003.

14. *Age*, 11 September and 6 November 2003.

15. *Herald*, 13 April 1971; *Collingwood Courier*, 23 June 1976; *Melbourne Times*, 23 June 1982; 'The Land Rights Fight: a National Scorecard', *Age*, 21 September 1982.

16. See R. Broome, *The Victorians. Arriving*, Fairfax, Syme and Weldon, Sydney, 1984, pp. 246–7.

17. Discussion with Daryl Rose, Chair, Lake Condah Sustainable Development Executive Committee, Warrnambool, 4 February 2004.

18. 'Mabo v Queensland', *The Australian Law Journal Reports*, vol. 66, January–December 1992, p. 429.

19. *Age*, 29 July 1993.

20. Sue Neales, 'Deep Social Ruts Appear in Land Claim', *Age*, 15 October 1994.

21. Richard Atkinson quoted in ibid.

22. *Age*, 8 December 1994.

23. Interview with Mark Matthews, Halls Gap, 3 July 2002; interview with Ivan Couzens, Warrnambool, 3 October 2002.

24. The Members of the Yorta Yorta Aboriginal Community v The State of Victoria & Ors (1998) 1606 FCA (18 December 1998), para 129. See also paras 1–5, 120–1.

25. *Age*, 7 February 2001.

26. *Age*, 13 December 2002.

27. *Age*, 1 May 2004.

28. Interview with Tim Chatfield, Halls Gap, 4 July 2002.

29. *Age*, 4 November 2002; 15 October and 21 November 2003.

30. H. Trevor-Roper, 'The Invention of Tradition: the Highland Tradition of Scotland', Eric Hobsbawm and Terence Ranger (eds), *The Invention of Tradition*, Cambridge University Press, Cambridge, 1983, pp. 15–42. See also the introduction, 'Inventing Traditions' by Eric Hobsbawm, pp. 1–14.

31. See Jocelyn Linnekin, 'On the Theory and Politics of Cultural Construction in the Pacific', in *Oceania*, vol. 62, 1992, pp. 250–1.

32. See Andrew Bolt, *Herald*, 22 and 23 November 2000.

33. Tiffany Shellam, 'Retelling Frontier Stories. The Presentation of Conflict on the Australian Frontier at the Melbourne Museum and the National Museum of Australia', BA (Hons) Thesis, La Trobe University, 2003, p. 75.

34. Interview with Ray Marks, Halls Gap, 3 July 2003.

35. See <http://www.loreoftheland.com.au/indigenous/gunditjmara> accessed December 2003.

36. Quoted in Michael Winkler, 'Elders of the Air', *Age*, 21 January 2004.

37. Margo Neale with Michael Eather et al (eds), *Urban Dingo. The Art and Life of Lin Onus 1948–1996*, Craftsman House, Brisbane, 2000.

38. For Worowa College's opening, see R. Broome, *The Victorians. Arriving*, pp. 244–5; See also *Age*, 30 November 2003.

39. Discussion with the Manager, Mark Edwards, Wathaurong Glass, North Geelong, 18 October 2002.
40. Interview with Lynette Bishop, Bairnsdale, 2 September 2002.
41. Interview with Sandra Neilson, Sale, 12 August 2002.
42. Interview with Lynette Bishop, Bairnsdale, 2 September 2002.
43. Interview with Tim Chatfield, Halls Gap, 4 July 2002.
44. Interview with Sandra Neilson, Sale, 12 August 2002.
45. Interview with Sandra Stewart, Mildura, 24 August 2002; Myra Grinter, Mildura, 14 October 2002.
46. Interview with Murray Bull, Sale, 2 September 2002.
47. National Aboriginal and Torres Strait Islander Survey, Ballarat (Tumbukka) and Wangaratta (Binjiru) ATSIC Region, Australian Bureau of Statistics, Canberra, 1994, figures 1.7–1.11.
48. Interview with Mark Matthews, Halls Gap, 3 July 2002.
49. Interview with Jamie Thomas, Warrnambool, 4 October 2002.

18 New day dawning?

1. Jessica Horton, 'Rewriting Political History: Letters from Aboriginal People in Victoria, 1886–1919', *History Australia*, vol. 9, no. 2, 2012, pp. 157–81.
2. Julie Andrews, 'Milestones of Aboriginal Women's Activism in Melbourne 1930s–1980s', *Victorian Historical Journal*, vol. 93, no. 2, December 2022, pp. 271–80.
3. Paul Strangio, 'Andrews' Titanic Legacy Assured', *The Age*, 9 February 2023.
4. See <www.abs.gov.au/articles/australia-aboriginal-and-torres-strait-islander-population-summary> accessed April 2023.
5. Nicholas Biddle, 'Indigenous and Non-Indigenous Marriage Partnerships', CAEPR Indigenous Population Project, 2011 Census Papers, Paper 15, CAEPR, Australian National University, Canberra 2013.
6. Janet McCalman, Rebecca Kippen, Len Smith and Sandra Silcot, 'Origins of "the gap": Perspectives on the Historical Demography of Aboriginal Victorians', *Journal of Population Research*, vol. 38, 2021, pp. 53–69. See also Janet McCalman and Len Smith, 'Family and Country: Accounting for Fractured Connections under Colonisation in Victoria, Australia', *Journal of Population Research*, vol. 33, 2016, pp. 51–65.
7. *ABC News*, 20 June 2008.
8. *The Australian*, 24 June 2011.
9. *The Age*, 19 March 2020.
10. *The Age*, 23 April 2021.
11. *The Age*, 4 July 2012.
12. Commonwealth of Australia, *Commonwealth Closing the Gap Annual Report*, 2018, p. 8.
13. *The Age*, 31 July 2020.
14. Commonwealth of Australia, *Commonwealth Closing the Gap Annual Report*, 2022, p. 5.
15. State Government of Victoria, *Victorian Aboriginal Affairs Framework, 2018–2023*, Department of Premier and Cabinet, 2018, p. 10.

16. State Government of Victoria, *Victorian Aboriginal Affairs Framework, 2018–2023*, pp. 6, 2 and 7.

17. E. Johnston, *National Report: Overview and Recommendations, Royal Commission into Aboriginal Deaths in Custody*, AGPS, Canberra, 1991, pp. 31–105.

18. *House of Representatives Standing Committee on Aboriginal and Torres Strait Islander Affairs, Justice under Scrutiny*, AGPS, Canberra, 1994; Human Rights and Equal Opportunity Commission, *Indigenous Deaths in Custody 1989 to 1996*, Canberra, AGPS, Canberra, pp. xxii–xxxi; *The Age*, 25 and 26 November 1996.

19. *The Age*, 19 April 2001.

20. See <www.aic.gov.au/statistics/deaths-custody-australia> accessed April 2023.

21. *The Age*, 20 September 2020.

22. *The Age*, 6 March 2023.

23. Australian Bureau of Statistics, *Prisoners in Australia, 2021*, cat. No. 4517.0, 2021.

24. Corrections Victoria, *Profile of Aboriginal People in Prison*, factsheet, July 2021.

25. *The Age*, 19 July 2021.

26. *The Age*, 16 May 2021.

27. *The Age*, 27 August 2020.

28. *The Age*, 30 January 2023.

29. *The Age*, 31 January and 1 February 2023.

30. *ABC Shepparton News*, 8 October 2022.

31. Ann-Claire Larsen and Peter Milnes, 'A Cautionary Note on Therapeutic Jurisprudence for Aboriginal Offenders', *eLaw Journal: Murdoch University Electronic Journal of Law*, vol. 18, no. 1, 2011, pp. 1–27.

32. See <www.mcv.vic.gov.au/about/koori-court> accessed April 2023.

33. See <www.countycourt.vic.gov.au/news-and-media/news-listing/2018-11-29-county-koori-court-reflects-10-years> accessed April 2023.

34. *ABC Shepparton News*, 8 October 2022.

35. *The Age*, 2 February 2023.

36. Reconciliation Australia, *2022 Australian Reconciliation Barometer*, Polity Research & Consulting, Sydney, 2022, p. 5.

37. Reconciliation Australia, *2022 Australian Reconciliation Barometer*, p. 5.

38. Australian Human Rights Commission, *Anti-Racism in 2018 and Beyond. A Report of the National Anti-Racism Strategy (2015–2018)*, pp. 7–9.

39. Colin Tatz, *Obstacle Race: Aborigines in Sport*, UNSW Press, Sydney, 1995, p. 341.

40. Tatz, *Obstacle Race*, chapter 8.

41. See <www.afl.com.au/news/866460/indigenous-and-multicultural-player-summit-returns-in-2022#:~:text=In%202022%2C%20there%20are%2010,come%20from%20culturally%20diverse%20backgrounds> accessed April 2023.

42. See <www.saints.com.au/our-yawa> accessed April 2023.

43. *The Age*, 3 May 2013.

44. *The Age*, 2 June 2015.

45. *The Age*, 2 February 2021.

46. *The Age*, 10 May 2022.

47. *The Age*, 23 August 2016.

48. *The Age*, 12 April 2017.

49. *The Age*, 19 April 2019.

50. *ABC News*, 4 April 2019.

51. Russell Jackson, 'The Persecution of Robert Muir is the Story Football Doesn't Want to Hear', *ABC News*, 23 August 2020.

52. *The Age*, 13 September 2021.

53. *ABC News*, 4 August 2022.

54. *The Age*, 6 February 2023.

55. Reconciliation Australia, *2022 Australian Reconciliation Barometer*, p. 9.

56. Department of Environment, Water and Planning, *Ancient Spirit & Lore of the Yarra*; Wurundjeri Woi Wurrung Cultural Heritage Aboriginal Corporation, *Towards Cultural and Environmental Renewal of Jacksons Creek*, 2021.

57. Victorian Traditional Owner Cultural Fire Knowledge Group, *The Victorian Traditional Cultural Fire Strategy*, Victorian Government, Melbourne, 2019.

58. Tony Birch, '"A Land So Inviting and Still Without Inhabitants": Erasing Koori Culture from (Post-) Colonial Landscapes', in Kate Darian-Smith, Elizabeth Gunner and Sarah Nuttall (eds), *Text, Theory, Space: Land, Literature and History in South Africa and Australia*, Routledge, London, 1996, pp. 173–88.

59. See <www.unesco.org/en/decades/indigenous-languages> accessed April 2023.

60. See <www.land.vic.gov.au/place-naming/place-naming-news/revitalising-aboriginal-languages-in-un-international-decade-of-indigenous-languages> accessed April 2023.

61. Gunditjmara People with Gib Wettenhall, *The People of Budj Bim: Engineers of Aquaculture, Builders of Stone House Settlements and Warriors Defending Country*, Em Press, 2010; *The Age*, 17 July 2019.

62. *The Age*, 15 December 2021.

63. *The Age*, 27 September 2022.

64. *Charter of Human Rights and Responsibilities Act 2006*, no. 43 of 2006, preamble and section 19, 1–2.

65. See <www.aboriginalheritagecouncil.vic.gov.au/our-logo> accessed April 2023.

66. See <www.aboriginalheritagecouncil.vic.gov.au/victorias-registered-aboriginal-parties> accessed April 2023.

67. Gavin Jennings, *Hansard*, 12 August 2010, Upper House, Second Reading Speech, pp. 4049, 4053–4.

68. Hon. Gabrielle Williams, Minister for Treaty and First Peoples, press release, 28 March 2023.

69. Lily D'Ambrosio, 'Historic Land Return to Traditional Owners', media release, 22 May 2022.

70. *The Age*, 10 December 2022.

71. *The Age*, 29 October 2020.
72. *ABC News*, 28 June 2022. For more on the controversy, see *The Age*, 25 August 2019, 4 and 28 October, 1 November and 4 December 2020.
73. *The Age*, 20 and 22 March 2019.
74. *The Age*, 10 December 2007; Richard Broome, 'Nicholls, Sir Douglas Ralph (Doug) (1906–1988)', <https://adb.anu.edu.au/biography/nicholls-sir-douglas-ralph-doug-14920> accessed April 2023.
75. See <https://monumentaustralia.org.au/themes/people/sport/display/90345-lionel-rose> accessed April 2023.
76. *The Australian*, 9 May 2011; *The Age*, 9 May 2011; *Herald Sun*, 9 May 2011.
77. https://www.firstpeoplesrelations.vic.gov.au/aboriginal-honour-roll
78. Quoted in Premier of Victoria, The Hon. Daniel Andrews, press release, 21 March 2023.
79. *The Age*, 1 August 2022.
80. *The Age*, 16 December 2022.
81. 'Statement from the Premier, Dan Andrews', media release, 26 September 2022; *ABC News*, 10 October 2022.
82. See <www.sbs.com.au/nitv/article/beloved-elder-uncle-jack-charles-passes-away/i8ir2x3zg> accessed April 2023.
83. *The Age*, 29 May 2016.
84. See <www.firstpeoplesvic.org/> accessed April 2023.
85. *The Age*, 1 November 2022.
86. See <www.firstpeoplesvic.org/news/victorian-parliament-passes-historic-treaty-legislation/> accessed April 2023.
87. See <www.facebook.com/firstpeoplesvic> accessed April 2023.
88. 20 October 2022, Agreement puts power back into Aboriginal hands—First Peoples' Assembly of Victoria (firstpeoplesvic.org).
89. *The Age*, 19 June 2023.
90. https://yoorrookjusticecommission.org.au/
91. Aunty Charmaine Clarke, *ABC Southwest Breakfast*, January 2023.

Index

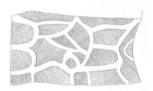

Note: page numbers in italics provide images to support the content; bolded page numbers indicate maps.

Aboriginal and Torres Strait Islander Commission (ATSIC) 356, 367–368, 386, 388, 390, 393
Aborigines' Progressive Association 266–267, 270, 304–305, 308–309
Aborigines Uplift Society 231–232, 245, 265–266, 281, 302–303
Aborigines Welfare Board
    Acts of Parliament 316–317, 336, 341
    aims 317–318
    assimilation 309, 316, 318, 323, 327, 335, 363
    and children 328
    criticisms of 327, 335
    house inspections 329
    housing 318–319, 323, 326, 327, 333–334, 335
    Lake Tyers 324, 333–334, 335
    Ministry of Aboriginal Affairs 341
    on racism 318
    reserve management 320–321
    Shadrach James 309
    see also Central Board for the Protection of Aborigines
Acts of Parliament
    1860 Act 398
    1869 Act 130–131, 134, 149, 161, 398
    1886 Act 185, 399
    1890 Act 185–186, 187, 192
    1903 Act 199, 201
    1910 Act 199
    1915 Act 202–203

1928 Act 203, 220–221, 239, 244, 258, 314
1949 Act 308
1957 Act 316
1965 Act 334
1967 Act 336, 341
1968 Act 342
1970 Act 346
1972 Act 376
1983 Act 377
1984 Act 364–365
1993 Act 383, 385
2006 Act 406, 412, 413, 414, 416
2010 Act 414
2018 Act 405, 419
2022 Act 419
agricultural techniques xix–xx
Alberts family 190, 236, 253–254, 329
alcohol 25–26, 96, 120, 158, 167–168, 258, 271, 352, 353, 357
Andrews government 399–400, 403, 411, 416, 419
Antwerp 121, 215, 258, 259, 281, 315
Apex 243, 245, 246, 323, 327, 335
archaeological findings xviii, xx–xxi, 376, 377, 385
arrests and imprisonment
    Aboriginal judicial proceedings 29
    alcohol related 104, 157–158, 225, 254, 266, 271, 286, 369, 404–406
    Bail Act, 2018 405
    begging 286
    Community Justice Panels 357, 369, 370
    deaths in custody 369, 404, 408
    'falls' 293, 405
    Koori Courts 406–407
    National Deaths in Custody Program 404

over-policing 293
Royal Commission, Deaths in Custody 365, 388
statistics 157, 326, 369, 370, 404
Victorian Aboriginal Justice Agreement, 2002 406
women 405
artefacts and relics 218–219, 354, 374, 376–378, 379, 386, 414, 416
artworks xix, 386–387, 389–390, 406, 417
assimilation
Aborigines Welfare Board 316, 318, 327, 335, 363
and Acts of Parliament 188, 189, 341, 398
definition 335
federal level xxiv–xxv
Framlingham 250
Gunai/Kurnai people 326–327
inter-marriage 318
McLean Report, 1957 315–316
models of 53, 359
Native Welfare Conference, 1937 312–313
Orbost 250
Protection Board 312
removal of children 328
review 314
Shadrach James 309
Sir Paul Hasluck xxiv–xxv, 24, 310, 313
United Nations on 423–424
Victorian Aboriginal Group 304, 316
Victorian Aborigines Advancement League 331
Welfare Board 309
William Thomas 114
Atkinson, Myra 260–261, 331, 336, 358, 392–393
Atkinson, Wayne 265, 271, 360, 384
Atkinson family 259, 260–262, 265, 271–272, 360, 362, 392–393
Austin family 193, 236, 250, 251, 253–254, 325–326, 361, 362, 396, 402
Australian Aborigines' League 263, 298, 299, 304, 309, 322, 332
Australian Natives Association 210, 239–240, 245, 246, 299, 306
Australian Security Intelligence Organisation (ASIO) 298, 310

Baillie, Helen 251, 252, 263–264, 295–297, 301, 304, 310
Ballarat xv, 109, 111, 158, 178, 248–249, 266, 328–329, 356, 361–362, 373, 412
Bangerang people 58, 62, 262, 299, 382, 419
Baptists 36–37, 47, 50, 220, 229
Barak, William 8, 38, 46, 125, 144, 164, 166, 168, 169, 175, 179, 207, 211, 212
Barrabool people 20, 45, 67, 92

Barwick, Diane (anthropologist) on
children 328
community and family 291
Coranderrk 169
death tolls 144
families 364
marriage patterns 288
movement patterns 289
population figures 315, 363
removal of children 228
traditional practices 141
women 136
Batman Treaty xxi, xxiii, 10, 11, 12, 13, 18, 26, 33, 166, 211, 346
Bendigo xv, xxi, 131, 158, 270, 373, 407
Berg, Jim 296, 352, 377, 386
Berry, Graham 169–170, 171, 180, 214
Beveridge, Peter 9, 22–23, 89, 100
Billibellary xxi, 13, 25–26, 32, 33, 44–45, 47, 49, 112, 123
Black, Neil 82, 83, 84
Blair, Harold 297, 310, 316, 330, 360
Blaskett, Beverley nee Nance 46, 80, 87, 92
Bon, Anne 144, 169, 210, 304
Boonwurrung people xxi, 3–4, 5–6, 19–20, 29–30, 31–32, 43, 104, 107, 109, 111, 114, 125, 382
Bourke, Sir Richard 14, 18, 36, 38
Bracks government 383–384, 399, 403, 412, 413
Briggs family 173, 265, 268–270, 334, 359, 389
Buckley, William (Murrangurk) 5, 7, 9, 11, 12, 66, 164
Bulmer, John 3, 120, 131, 133, 134, 137, 138, 140, 141, 142, 152, 163, 217, 218
Bungaleen, Thomas 'Tommy' 49–50, 115–116, 117, 117, 118
Bunurong Land Council 415
Bunurong people 416
Burdeu, Arthur 245, 281, 302–304, 307

camping and campers
Aggie's Swamp 159
Antwerp 258–259
assimilation 316
children 274
Daish's Paddock 264, 313, 319
Dimboola 258–259
Echuca 258
Edwards River 159
Goulburn River 264
Hamilton 281
Jackson's Track 258
living conditions 258, 265, 276, 313
local support 281
Mallee district 279

memories 265
mortality rate 276
Murray River 258
Nathalia 258
police report 271–272
population figures 285
religion 271–272
removal of children 276
and schools 274
Sherbrooke Forest 347–348
Swan Hill 258
'Wamba' (Murray Downs) 259
Welfare Board 278
cannibalism 11, 63–68, 80, 376
Central Board for the Protection of
  Aborigines
assimilation 192, 312
campers 278
controls and regulations 130, 150, 188,
  189, 199, 203, 205, 227, 244–245
conviction reports 157
criticisms of 174, 180, 231, 312
definition of Aboriginality 216
finances 189
forced movements 185–186, 204, 209, 244,
  252
on future of Aboriginal people 100, 177,
  185
housing 274
humane decisions 163–164
and John Green 169
land claims and proposals 161, 214
'living-off' reserves 276
on marriages 189
and members of Parliament 170
on military enlistment 201
mixed race people 184, 196–198, 227, 295
powers 146, 163, 202–203, 217, 219, 227
rations 174, 264
reform 311, 312
removal of children 134, 135, 192–193,
  228, 248, 263
reserve management xxiv, 125, 126, 131,
  132, 166, 170, 172, 180, 194–195, 243,
  244, 249, 252
and those 'living off' reserves 228
vocational training 194
see also Aborigines Welfare Board
Charles family 265, 320, 359, 362, 418
Chatfield, Tim 254, 256–257, 356, 385, 392
children
  1890 Act 187
  Aboriginal Legal Service 352
  adoptions 330, 343, 362, 365
  boarded-out and fostered 116, 171, 228,
    330, 343
  camping and campers 274

childhood memories 391–392
  and Christianity 48, 115
  Department of Neglected Children 187,
    188, 192
  Department of Social Welfare 364
  employment 148–149
  exploited 115, 330
  girls 331
  impact of diseases 88
  infant mortality 144, 373
  institutional care 61, 161–162, 192,
    204–205, 233, 248, 263, 330, 354,
    361–362, 363, 364, 402, 418
  literacy 96
  'men's business' camp 367
  of mixed race 186, 292
  population figures 92, 363
  punishments 173, 229–230
  on reserves 131–132, 170–171, 177, 233
  Stolen, Jane Harrison 365
  Swan Hill 329
  'Took the Children Away', Archie Roach
    365
  and tourists 219
  United Nations on 425
  Victorian Aboriginal Child Care Agency
    (VACCA) 364, 365–366
  Victorian Adoption Act, 1984 364–365
  vocational training 187, 192, 263
  see also removal of children
Christianity 24, 49, 50, 51, 57, 96, 120, 139,
  156
Clarke, Henry 'Banjo' 252, 255–256, 289,
  293, 388, 396
Clarke family 235, 236, 251–254, 256, 289,
  293, 296, 362
clothes
  Advancement League 331
  appeal of European clothing 50–52, 56,
    60–62, 156
  charitable support 327
  as compensation 42
  discrimination 258
  entitlements 129
  equality 317
  government supply 18, 196–199
  inadequate 266, 276
  local support 281, 295
  paternalism 218
  pride in 171
  purchasing 137
  rations 173–174, 186–187, 203–204,
    227–229
  as salary 16, 149
  self-sufficient 150, 160
  trade 4–5
  Uplift Society 302

Colac region xix, 36–37, 40, 67, 156, 160, 195–196, 198, 248
colonisation, impacts of xix–xx, 19, 21, 32, 79, 86, 88, 93, 96, 112–113, 119, 122
Community Justice Panels 357, 369, 370
Constitution, Australian 306, 308
Cooper, William 230, *242*, 262, 263, 270, 287, 300, *301*, 305–306
Cooper family 201, 265, 270–271, *284*
Cooperatives, Aboriginal
and employment 358
Geelong xii, 354, 357, 358
Gippsland 387
Halls Gap xii, 356, 358
Lake Condah 381
Melbourne 351
Mildura xii, 358, 366, 393
Robinvale 381
Sale xii
Warrnambool xii, xiii, 355–356, 358
Coranderrk reserve **xv**, *135*, *168*, *177*, *193*, *200*, *204*
Aboriginal selection 124
boarding house 136
cemetery 215
children 131–132, 136
Christianity 140
court 167
forced movements 209, 219
houses *128*, 143
management and moves to close 167, 169–174, 175–176, 180, 196, 207
mixed race people 196
permissions required 189, 203
population figures 215
rations 173–175
salaries 141–142
sanitary conditions 143
size 193
social activities 208
sports 167, 208
Temperance Society 207
Country Women's Association 243, 323, 327
Couzens, Ivan 237, 246, 382, 396
Couzens, John 237, 249–250, 252
Couzens, Nicholas *242*, *246*, 247, 249, 250, 253, 254
Couzens, Noel 250, 255–256, 358
Couzens family 236, 246, 249, 250, 253, 255
crime *see* arrests and imprisonment; law, the
Crough family (aka Crowe) 160–161, 196, 197–199
cultural heritage
Aboriginal Heritage Council 413
artefacts and relics xxi, 218–219, 354, 374, 376, 377–378, 379
renaissance 389–390, 393

sacred sites 69, 139, 378
Wurundjeri Woi Wurrung Cultural Heritage Aboriginal Corporation 411
cultural language groups xxi
Cummeragunja **xv**, 260, 262, 264, 268–270, 288, 332
Curr, Edward 15–16, 58, 62, 63, 383

Daish's Paddock 264, 267, 313, 318–320, 344
Daungwurrung people 12, 19–20, 28, 31–32, 63, 82, 105, 123, 125, 382
Dawson family xx, 129, 163, 177–178, 390
'Day of Mourning' 304–305
deaths
alcohol related 158
camping and campers 276
child mortality 275
Closing the Gap 402–403
in custody 369, 404, 408
diseases 91, 144
figures 79–80, 87
infant mortality 184
infanticide 11, 32–33, 63–65, 93
inter-se killings 159
life expectancy 373, 402
National Deaths in Custody Program 404
revenge killings 22
see also violence
demographics 146, 285
Depression, 1930s 198, 227, 237–238, 240, 243, 251, 264, 269, 278, 286, 288
Derrimut 5–6, 12–13, 25, 32–33, 74, 157
Dimboola 281, 282, 283, 285, 315, 323
discrimination 258, 315, 371, 392, 398, 408
diseases and illness 88, 91, 92, 93, 96, 143, 144
see also health and wellbeing
DjaDjawurrung people xxi, 41, 92, 112, 114, 124, 125, 379, 382, 384, **415**
domestic violence 21, 158, 271, 357, 373
Dredge, James 25, 28, 31–32, 67, 74, 78, 79
Dyer, Mollie 352, 359, 364, 388

Ebenezer Mission **xv**, 134, 139, 142, 147, 191, 195, 219
Echuca **xv**, 131, 155–157, 196, 258, 285, 315, 373, 396
Edgar family 46, 49–50, 52–53, 116
education
1890 Act 187
Aboriginal Education Consultative Group 351–352
attendance 259, 282, 313, 327, 328
bursaries and scholarships 327–328, 331, 342, 359
Citizens' Education Fellowship 303, 304
curriculum 290

Koori Open Door Education 372
level of 282, 327
memories 290
United Nations on 424
VCE, 'Indigenous Languages' 389
vocational training 187, 192, 194, 221, 222, 243–244, 245, 357
Edwards family 190, *191*, 225, 236–237, 265, 390
Elders 332, 406–407, 425
Elliminyt **xv**, 160, 195–196, 215
employment
  1890 Act 187
  Aboriginal Cooperatives 358
  Aborigines Act, 1957 317
  Aborigines Welfare Board 335
  and alcohol 105
  expectations and rules 317
  exploitation and discrimination 315
  gold rush years 111
  Metung 234
  on missions and reserves 38
  Mount Franklin *41*, 42
  salaries 39, 62, 112–113, 203
  Second World War era 232
  sexual services 18
  by shopkeepers 17
  United Nations on 424
  work ethic 148–149
equality and inequality 140, 245, 300, 303, 305, 309, 310, 317, 321, 322, 344, 348, 369, 373, 403, 423, 427
European artist's representations *13, 16, 19, 56, 59, 98*

family and families
  1886 Act 399
  Board for the Protection of Aborigines 189, 217
  children 192, 276
  core values 260–261, 391–392, 393
  Dimboola 279
  disputes between 85
  domestic violence 21, 158, 271, 357, 373
  drug and alcohol abuse 373
  extended kinship 324
  Fitzroy 291–292
  impacts on 366
  at Lake Condah 216
  population figures 32, 146
  Ramahyuck 135
  removal of children 315, 343
  on reserves 190–191, 203
  Save the Children Fund 279
  separated 50, 117, 136, 184, 185, 188, 195–196, 203, 205
  size 144, 148

stories xxv, 9
support 150
Victorian Aboriginal Child Care Agency (VACCA) 365–366
farming
  Bayswater Boys' Home 192
  Board for the Protection of Aborigines 191
  campers 275
  cattle farming 159
  Coranderrk 172, 207
  Cummeragunja 262, 332
  Framlingham 245, 249–250, 252
  historians on 127
  impacts on Aboriginal lives 20, 70–71, 96
  intercultural transactions 111, 112
  Kulin people 167
  Lake Condah 303
  Lake Tyers 159, 341
  living 'off reserves' 189
  Mount Franklin farmers *41*
  Protection Board support 196
  reserve lands 115, 120, 190, 209, 221, 252
  reserves 132, 168, 194
  salaries 129, 231, 240
  self-reliance 191, 197, 392–393
  thefts 75, 76–77, 83
  traditional xx, 54, 69, 412
  vocational training 192
  Woiwurrung people 111
financial support 149, 157, 178, 198, 227, 237, 240, 241–245, 247, 250, 264, 300–301, 303, 307
First People's Assembly 340, 419–421
Fitzroy *355*
  Archie Roach 417
  Christianity 290
  community and family 291–292
  Gore Street congregation *292*
  housing 294
  independent people 291
  Koorie Club 337
  police 293, 294, 369
  racism 295
  reputation 288
  Ruby Hunter 417
'Flat', the 267, 271, 318–319
food
  bush foods xxii, 19, 20–21, 42, 162, 258–259, 263, 281
  camping and campers 258
  fishing for xx, xxii, 19, 23, 60, 104, 162, 253, 263, 385, 412
  impacts on traditional 20
  rations 142, 162, 173–175, 204
  scarcity 20–21, 26
  supplied by government and settlers 16, 18, 21

swans' eggs 253, 260, 263
 theft of 20
forced movements 20, 124, 136, 161, 179,
  188, 189, 195, 209, 281, 319, 330, 418, 424
Framlingham **xv**, *253*
 Aboriginal trust 346, 356
 Aborigines Welfare Board 335
 assimilation 250
 attachments to 196, 236, 240, 252
 conditions 237, 247
 evictions 247, 249, 251
 farming 245, 248
 forced movements 209, 219
 houses 247
 land claims and proposals 235, 347, 381
 management 193, 245, 247–248
 memories 254, 257, 388
 migration to Melbourne 288, 289, 296
 mixed race people 191–192
 permissions required 196, 249
 population figures 215, 244, 249, 250,
  315
 Protection Board 244
 rations 142
 regulations and controls 250–251
 removal of children 248, 363
 Reserve Welfare Committee 250, 252
 salaries 142
 school 243
 Second World War 249
 sports 246, 254
 tensions 191–192
 Victorian Aboriginal Group 304
fringe dwellers *see* camping and campers
future, the
 Closing the Gap 402–403
 First Nations Knowledge Institute 411
 First People's Assembly 419
 Indigenous names 411–412
 Koori Courts 406–407
 Reconciliation Australia 408, 411
 Registered Aboriginal Parties (RAPS) 413,
  415, 416
 socio-economic targets 403
 United Nations 411–412, 420
 Victorian Traditional Owner Cultural Fire
  Knowledge Group 411
 Voice to Parliament 419

Geelong **xv**, xxi, 8–12, 30, 57, 61, 69, 74, 92,
  102, 109, 158, 248, 354
Gellibrand, Joseph 11–12, 14, 73–74
Gilsenan, Cora 234, 251, 272, 275–276, 278,
  281, 283–284, 289, 304, 310, 314, 328
Gippsland *277*
 Aboriginal guides 55
 Bairnsdale 387

 Elders Council 332
 employment 112–113
 families 391–392
 Gunai/Kurnai people xvii, 92, 125–126,
  163, 275, 325–326
 historians on 46
 Lake Tyers 217, 224–225
 local support 284
 Orbost 272
 population figures 80–83, 194
 trade routes 6
 violence 22, 69
gold rush xxii, xxiv, 46, 97, 104, 105, 108,
  149
Goulburn people 20, 53, 63, 103, 131
Goulburn region 8–9, 31, 40
Grampians region **xv**, xviii, xix, 45, 356
Green, John 125, 129, 131, 133, 134, 139,
  140, 141, 146, 152, 166–167, 168–169
Grinter, Myra nee Atkinson 260–261, 331,
  336–337, 358, 392–393
Guardians, local
 on alcohol 157
 Colac 160
 criticisms 247
 on racism 241
 rations 191
 reserves 171
 Stockyard Hill 162–163
 on unemployment 241
 see also Protectors
Gunai/Kurnai people
 Aboriginal and Torres Strait Islander
  Commission (ATSIC) 354
 Aboriginal Land Act, 1970 346
 assimilation 326–327
 at Brighton 109
 building homes 160
 Bung Yarnda (Lake Tyers) 126
 creation beliefs xvii
 cultural renaissance 393
 at Dandenong 109
 death tolls figures 83
 early European encounters 3
 Elders 367
 employment 112, 234
 entertainment 57
 and European explorers 55
 intermarriage 288(2)
 inter-se killings 161
 Jackson's Track 281
 and Kulin people 109
 Lake Wellington 126
 in Melbourne 109
 Orbost 272–273, 275
 population decline 92
 from Ramahyuck 154

trade routes 6
traditional lands 125–126
Traralgon 326
Gunditjmara people 6, 10, 73, 235, 256, 288, 384

Hagenauer, Friederich 121, 127, 128–129, 131, 133–134, 137, 138, 139, 152, 189–190
Harrison family 215, 225, 230, 272, 277, 278, 321, 322, 323
Hasluck, Sir Paul xxiv–xxv, 24, 310, 313
Healesville 34, 124, 126, 169, 172, 174, 208, 210, 212, 214, 346, 373, 389
health and wellbeing
  Aboriginal Health Service 351–353
  Budja Budja Aboriginal Cooperative, Halls Gap 356
  Closing the Gap 402–403
  Health and Public Works Committee 294
  life expectancy 373, 402
  malnutrition 7
  Protection Board 144
  statistics 366
  traditional medicines 26, 89–90
  Victorian Aboriginal Community Health Organisation 419
  Welfare Board 335
  Yarra camp 26
  see also diseases and illness
Hinkins family 53, 58–60, 63, 116
historians on
  Aborigines Welfare Board 327
  Christianity 139
  'Day of Mourning' 306
  death tolls figures 79–81, 82
  farming 127
  Gippsland 46
  inter se killings 87
  kings 102
  paternalism 127, 128
  population figures 91, 92
  Protection Board 157, 189
  reserves 126–127, 169, 334
  Richard Broome 81–82
  traditional land owners 213
  violent deaths 93
  William Cooper 300
holiday houses and programs 327, 330, 331–332, 343
housing xx, 160, 319, 320, 322, 323, 324, 326, 333, 335, 351–352, 374
Housing Commission 294, 299, 319, 323, 335, 342
Howitt, Richard xvii, 17, 24, 25, 28, 74, 80
Hull, William 32, 73, 99, 100, 105–106

imprisonment see arrests and imprisonment
infanticide 11, 32–33, 63–65, 93
interactions, Aboriginal and European
  1850s 104
  Aboriginal guides 57
  anecdotes 16, 58, 75, 103, 177–178, 254
  Corio Bay 5
  entertainment 57
  funerals 156
  hostile 2, 56
  intercultural transactions 110
  name exchanges 13
  peaceful 17–18, 56–57
  reciprocity 124–125
  school children 190
  trade 17, 23, 57–58
  Wilson's Promontory 6
investigations and reviews 14, 39, 41, 42, 79, 121, 314, 369, 404

Jackomos, Alick 231, 255, 284, 293, 307, 324, 328, 332, 388
Jackomos family 317
James, Shadrach 215, 266, 267, 271, 299, 301–302, 308, 309, 310
James, Thomas Shadrach 261–263, 264, 271, 287, 299
James family 262–263, 271, 308
Jika Jika see Billibellary

kings 102, 103, 111, 154, 156, 157, 158
Koorie Heritage Trust 386, 389, 397
Kulin people 179
  and alcohol 106
  and Batman's Treaty 10–11
  at Brighton 109
  criticisms of 170–171
  early European encounters 5, 10, 12–13, 30
  employment of 112
  expectations 18, 21
  and Gunai/Kurnai people 109
  impacts on traditions 29–30
  and impending attack 12
  judicial proceedings 29
  'Lettsom raid' 31–32, 41
  mainmet 85
  in Melbourne 104–105
  and Merri Creek School 49
  political movements xxiv
  population decline 114
  and reserves 125, 131, 175
  smallpox 7
  trade routes 6
  traditional lands 104, 106, 125–126

La Trobe, Charles Joseph 31–32, 38, 43, 79, 104, 120
Lake Boga **xv**, 120–121, 161, 285, 393
Lake Condah **xv**, 132, 154, 198, 208, *208*, 209, 215, 219, 381
Lake Tyers **xv**, *230, 233*
  Aboriginal Land Act, 1970 346
  Aborigines Welfare Board 333–334, 335
  Anglican Church 217
  attachments to 217
  Caleguine Bay *155*
  cattle farming 159
  Charles McLean on 315
  children 233
  Christianity 140
  conditions 220, 228–229, 231, 272
  criticisms of 228–229
  education 221, 222
  forced movements 205, 227, 232, 272, 324, 327
  Gunai/Kurnai people 126
  hand back *380*
  languages spoken 165
  layout 133
  management 205, 219, 221–222, 231, 232, 317, 324–325
  migration to Melbourne 288
  native court 221
  orphanage 161
  permissions required 201, 203–204, 224, 272, 288, 317
  population figures 219, 231, 232, 315
  Protection Board 217
  punishments 232–233
  rations 232, 272
  removal of children 233, 363
  salaries 142, 231
  'Save Lake Tyers Campaign' *337*
  school 222
  sports 221, 222, 224, 225
  tourism 218
  Victorian Aboriginal Group 304
land, traditional
  Boonwurrung people 382
  boundary disputes 382
  broader sense 380
  Buxton Committee Report, 1837 36
  Clifton Hill 380
  Daungwurrung people 382
  DjaDjawurrung people 382
  farms 20
  forced movements 20, 379
  impact of European colonisation xxiii
  and John Fawkner 13
  Kulin people 18
  meeting places xx, xxi–xxii
  Melbourne 15

  Murray River region xviii–xix
  patrilineal xxi
  respect for 379
  toll gate 102
  Welcome to Country ceremony *401*
  Woiwurrung people 382
  Wurundjeri xxi, 382
land claims and proposals
  Archaeological and Aboriginal Relics Preservation Act, 1972 376
  Bracks government 399
  Cain Government 267, 380
  Charter of Human Rights and Responsibilities Act, 2006 414
  Collingwood 380
  Crown land 347, 381
  Djap Wurrong people 384
  Fish Point 161
  Framlingham 381
  Gippsland *277*
  Gunditjmara people 384
  Heritage Protection Acts, 1984, 1987 378
  Hexham 161
  Indigenous Land Corporation 384
  Lake Boga 161
  Lake Condah 303, 381
  Lake Tyrell 161
  Liberal governments 380, 399
  Mabo, 1992 381
  Maloga 262
  Manatunga 381
  Metung 278
  militancy 345
  mineral resources 348, 381–382
  Mooroopna-Shepparton 313
  Mount William Creek 384
  Murray River 382
  native title 382–385, 393, 399, 412, 414
  Northcote 380
  press reporting 160
  Protection Board 161
  reserve lands 399
  sacred sites 69, 139, 377
  Sherbrooke Forest 347–348
  soldier settlement land 260
  Traditional Owner Settlement Act, 2010 414
  Trust for Nature 414
  United Nations on 425, 426
  Wik, 1996 381
  William Cooper 300
  Wotjobaluk people 385
  Wurundjeri Tribe Land and Compensation Cultural Heritage Council 378
  Yorta Yorta people 381–382, 385
language
  derogative names 138, 255, 275, 282, 283, 289, 344

Dictionary of Aboriginal Placenames of Victoria, 2002 390
Doug Nicholls on 289
pidgin 24
place names 2, 390, 411–412
traditional 138, 163, 165, 212, 280, 375, 389–390
United Nations Decade of Indigenous Languages 411
VCE, 'Indigenous Languages' 389
Victorian Aboriginal Corporation for Languages 389
law, the
alcohol 105, 120, 157, 406
firearms 14, 21
Koori Courts 406, *407*
mixed race people 241
movements of people 184, 219, 221
prejudices 84, 120, 368
respect for 367
see also arrests and imprisonment
law, traditional 29, 85, 386, 419–420
see also Community Justice Panels
Leeper, Valentine 207, 228, 303–304
Lowe, Robert 252, 253, 329, 355–356, 388, 396
Lowe family 252, 329

Macassan fisherman 7, 88, 91
Mackie, Alex 134, 140, 169, 301
Marks family *215*, 221, 361–362
Marmingorak *see* Parker, Edward Stone
marriage xxi, xxii, 12, 189, 204, 288, 291–293, 318, 400
massacres 81–82, 85, 93, 254
Maza, Bob 336, 343–344, 349, 418
McGuiness, Gilla 388–389
McGuinness, Bruce 323, 333, 336–337, 342, 344–345, 346, 347–348, 349, 350
McLean Report, 1957 315–316
Meagher, Ray 341–342, 343, 345, 347–348, 349
Melbourne **xv**
Aboriginal presence 15–17, 120, 286
appeals for Aboriginal people 18, 20
Barak bridge 417
Birrarung Marr 417
Collins Street *16*
European population figures 26
Government Mission 33, 36–40
Hospital 93
Kulin people 30
Mt Macedon people 20
population figures 315
proximity of reserves 126
Reconciliation Walk *397*
settler anecdotes 15, 17

smallpox 8–9
violence 394
Yarra camp 21, 25, 26
Merri Creek School 36, 47–50, 53, 116
Mildura **xv**, 285, 366, 369, 372
military service 199, 200, 201, 202, 215–216, 226, 232, 307
Ministry of Aboriginal Affairs 341, 342, 343, 349–350, 351
missionaries 54, 63, 99, 120, 125–127, 134, 138–139, 141–142, 145, 157, 171–172, 195, 248, 389
mixed race people xxiv, 184, 186, 187, 189, 191, 192, 194, 198, 203, 244, 272, 301
Mobourne family 225, 324, 326, 391
Monash University Koori Research Centre 370
Moore, Russell (James Savage) 365
Mooroopna **xv**, 264, *265*, 266, 268, 271–272, 313, 315, 318–319, 320, 323, 363
Moravians 120–122, 126, 195
Mount William **xv**, xxi–xxii, 384
Mullett, Albert 261, 273, 290, 367, *395*
Mullett family 209, 225, 228, 272, 280–281, *282*, 359
murders *see* massacres
Murray, John 3–4, 193, 198, 199
Murray, Stewart 342, 347, 349, 350, 369
Murray family 265, *274*
Murray people xxii, 9, 60, 66, *67*, 69, 80, 81, 92, 100, 121, 131, 155, 258
museums
Aboriginal artefacts 100, 379
American 377
Bairnsdale 387
disputes with 376
Museum Act 377
Museum Victoria 376–377, 379, 386–387
Museum Victoria collection *xviii*, 67, 90, *128, 135, 138, 142, 155, 159, 164, 173, 186, 193, 197, 200, 204, 208, 211, 220, 226, 230, 233, 235, 242, 265, 274, 277, 282, 284, 287, 292, 301, 308, 314, 317, 325, 333, 334, 337, 347*
National Museum 100, 237

Narre Narre Warren 31, 43, 45, 47
Narre Narre Warren reserve 32, 36, 40, 47, 52, 89
Native Police Corps 44
Billibellary 33
Billibellary's son 49
Boonwurrung people 43
Corporal Buckup 46
established 36–38
funding 120
impact of 76

killings 82, 85, 87
and mainmet (enemies or strangers)
    45–46
Merri Creek 45
Narre Narre Warren 43, 45
Queensland 155
role of 43
salaries 44
service reports 45
support of colonists 33
William Barak 46
Woiwurrung people 43
native title 381, 382, 383, 384, 385, 393, 399,
    412, 414
Neilson, Sandra 357, 375, 376, 391
Newman family 221, 223, 227, 280
Nicholls, Howard 'Dowie' 268–269,
    290–291
Nicholls, Lady Gladys 284, 290, 331, 417
Nicholls, Sir Doug 269, 284, 333
    Aboriginal trusts 346
    Aborigines Welfare Board 316, 333
    accolades 359, 417
    ASIO 310
    assimilation 323, 326
    Batman's treaty 345
    on Black Power 336
    Christianity 269, 272
    'Day of Mourning' 305
    Governor of South Australia 359
    housing 323
    on living conditions 264
    Maralinga people 330
    McLean Report, 1957 316
    'off reserves' 267, 294
    parliamentary representation 308
    reserves and missions 299, 321–322
    sports 268–269, 408
    Victorian Aborigines Advancement League
        331, 344, 349
    Victorian Council of Social Services 314
Nicholls family 264, 268–269, 284, 331
NSW Legislative Council 21, 41, 63–65, 66,
    79

'off reserves', living 147–148, 150, 157, 164,
    171, 189, 191, 204, 236, 294–295, 300
Olney, Justice 399
Onus, Bill 263, 267, 297, 298, 309, 310, 332,
    336, 337, 344–345, 360, 361
Onus, Eric 263, 273, 297–298, 342, 344, 359,
    360, 361
Onus, Lin 337, 347–348, 389
Onus family 263, 337, 360, 361
Orbost xv, 228, 250, 272–273, 275, 282, 283,
    285, 315, 323

Page, Captain 144, 174, 175, 180
parents and parenting
    access to children 47, 193
    bonds with children 241, 266, 276
    infanticide 64
    and John Green 134
    modelling for 366
    recovering children 49, 179
    removal of children 114, 131–132, 166,
        192, 248, 319
    and schools 39, 137–138, 243, 259, 328
Parker, Edward Stone
    on Aboriginal farmers 115
    on Aboriginal intellect 120–121
    and the DjaDjawurrung people 41–42
    employment of Aboriginal people 43, 114
    establishes a school 114
    on impact of diseases 88
    on infanticide 65
    Kolain, Aboriginal child 60–61
    Loddon station, Mount Franklin 41–43
    as patriarch 129
    population figures 92
    Protector of Aboriginals 41, 60, 71, 85, 88,
        92, 115
    removal of children 114–115
    on violent interactions 71
Parley 'Kitty' 49–50, 51, 53, 116
paternalism 50, 129, 177, 262, 284–285, 317,
    342, 344, 349
Pentridge (now Coburg) 43, 53, 116
performances
    Australian Aborigines' League 297
    displaying racism 409
    Gippsland 225
    Koori Open Door Education schools 372
    Lake Tyers 218
    Nindethana theatre 418
    radio 223, 388
    Stolen, Jane Harrison 365
    theatre 111
    'Took the Children Away', Archie Roach 365
    traditional practices 152, 153, 154,
        297–298, 394
    'Women of the Sun' 389
petitions 127, 169, 171, 172, 175, 191, 205,
    214, 262–263, 274, 290, 300–302, 304,
    306, 308, 327, 334, 347, 383, 412
police
    and Aboriginal Cooperatives 356
    and Aboriginal relations 368–369
    Community Justice Panels 357
    Fitzroy 294
    Human Rights and Equal Opportunity
        Commission 369
    Mounted Police 82, 85
    over-policing 369, 402

police-Aboriginal Liaison Committee 369
Protectors 368
racism 368, 369, 408
removal of children 134, 319, 328
Royal Commission on Aboriginal Deaths
    in Custody 408
Rumbalara 368
violence 369
see also Native Police Corps
policies
    assimilation xxv, 36, 53, 184, 245, 275, 304,
        309, 310, 312–313, 318, 323, 326–327,
        328, 331, 335, 337, 359, 363, 393, 398,
        400, 424
    centralisation and decentralization 114,
        119, 146, 179, 180, 184
    protection xxiii, 24, 37, 60, 122, 130–131,
        134, 146, 184, 187–188, 192, 198, 236,
        240, 264, 295, 304, 305, 312, 328, 341,
        377–378
population
    archaeological findings 92
    campers 285
    decline 91–92, 96, 97, 106, 143, 194, 209,
        398
    figures xxiv, 14, 19–20, 25, 29, 146, 258,
        285, 315, 341, 363, 373, 400
    increase 373
    'living off' reserves 147–148
    and low birth rates 93
    male to female ratio 71, 108
    reserves and missions 215, 261
    see also demographics
Port Fairy xix, 6, 37, 46, 61, 78, 256
Port Phillip District
    death tolls figures 80
    early interactions xxii, xxiv, 2, 5
    environment and landscape xviii–xix,
        xxiii–xxiv
    officially proclaimed 36
    Port Phillip Association 10, 11, 14
    Protectorate xxiii, 40, 90–91
    settlement 54
    smallpox 8–9
    violence 87
press reports
    Aboriginal and Torres Strait Islander
        Commission (ATSIC) 367–368
    alcohol 158, 226
    apprenticeships *357*
    assimilation 238, 316
    Daish's Paddock 313
    'Day of Mourning' 305
    Fitzroy 287, 294, *355*
    Framlingham 237
    future of Aboriginal people 99–100,
        176–177, 178, 209, 216, 245

on killing Aboriginal people 78
    land claims and proposals 102, *124*, 160,
        252, 348
    language use 78
    making comparisons 111
    McLean Report, 1957 316
    mixed race people 237–238
    performances 111
    police interactions 293
    racism 264
    rations 174
    removal of children 330
    reserves 176
    Royal Commission, Aboriginal Deaths in
        Custody 365
    sports *153*, 256
    violence *71*, 76–77, 86, 87, 367
    William Barak 211
Protection Board *see* Central Board for the
    Protection of Aborigines
Protectorates xxiii–xxiv, 18, 36–37, 40, *41*,
    42, 47, 78, 85, 86, 90–91, 104, 120
Protectors
    criticisms of 40, 78
    Edward Curr 63
    Edward Parker 41, 60, 71, 85, 88, 92, 115
    George Robinson xx–xxi, 18–19, 21, 30,
        40, 87, 383
    James Dredge 25, 31, 74, 78
    police as 368
    William Thomas 9, 19–20, 47, 66, 85, 88,
        390
    see also Guardians, local
protests 83, 123, 137–138, 175–176, 180,
    185, 193, 209, 215, 264, 298, 326, 333,
    346–348, 360, 377–378, 380, 416
punishments
    of children 173
    forced movements 186, 189, 196, 203,
        217–218, 219, 232
    ration cuts 38, 189, 190

racism 190, 199, 241, 254–255, 258, 264,
    268, 283, 295, 370, 371, 408–410
Ramahyuck **xv**, 132–133, 135, 137, 142, 193,
    194–195
rations
    Acts of Parliament 199, 239
    as inducements 107, 109, 141
    'off reserves' 180, 186
    Protection Board 162, 189–191, 196–198,
        204, 217, 237–240, 244, 264
    on reserves 38, 125–126, 142, 173–175,
        178, 187, 203, 220–221, 232–233, 272
    as salary 38, 62, 142, 240
    stations 40, 120, 148
    see also clothes

reconciliation 29, 356, *397*, 408, 411, 418, 419
referendums 308, 331, 341
Registered Aboriginal Parties (RAPS) 413, **415**, 416
removal of children
  1899 regulation 363
  1968 declaration 361
  Acts of Parliament 187, 191–192
  assimilation 328
  Bringing Them Home report, 1997 401
  camping and campers 276
  Charles McLean on 315
  Cummeragunja 260
  Framlingham 248
  legal action 362
  memories 259
  Protection Board 263, 266
  Reparations Steering Committee 402
  Royal Commission, Aboriginal Deaths in Custody 365
  statistics 363–364
reserves, 'living off' *see* 'off reserves', living
reserves and missions **xv**
  1890 Act 187, 189
  aims 130, 138
  attachments to 136, 180, 195, 196, 216, 236, 240, 252
  boarding houses 132, 133, 134, 135
  children 165
  demographics 147 *table*
  domestic violence 226–227
  early legislation xxiv
  forced movements 203, 209
  Goulburn River 40, 90, 91
  health and wellbeing 145
  land claims 235
  management 133–134, 141, 191, 203
  mixed race people 187, 190–192, 198, 203
  paternalism 128–129
  permissions required 38, 189–190, 196, 201, 203–204, 224, 227, 232–233, 391
  population figures 194, 208–209, 249
  salaries 141–142
  settler resentments of 40
  size 195
  sports 167, 208, 216
  women 161
  see also 'off reserves'
Returned Services League (RSL) 197, 201–202, 308
Roach family 254, 417–418
Robinson, George Augustus xix–xx, 21, 30, 40, 55, 67, 68, 87, 383
Robinvale **xv**, 282, 285, 315, 323
Rose, Lionel 281, *282*, 359, 416
Rose family *242*, 253–254, *282*, *284*

Royal Commission, 1877 115, 128, 129, 133, 142, 143, 157, 168, 171, 175
Royal Commission, 1988-1989 365
Royal Commission on Aboriginal Deaths in Custody 369, 388, 404, 408
Rumbalara 319, 320–322, 368

Sale xii, 162, 223, 225, 227, 234, 274, 353, 354, 371, 373
Salvation Army 192, 204–206, 291, 418
Saunders, Chris 200, *235*, 307, 332
Savage, James (Russell Moore) 88, 365
Save the Children Fund 279, 282, 321, 327, 359
Second World War 249, 306–307
  see also military service
Select Committees 35–36, 87, 88, 89, 99, 125, 157
sheep farming 20, 54, 55, 71
Shepparton 268, 270, 271, 282, 285, 313, 406
social media 410, 420
'Sorry Day' 365, *367*
sports 149, 152–153, 200, 224, 254–256, 268, 270–271, 281, 282, 289, *297*, 359, 371, 394, 408–410, 416
Stewart family 260, 270, 392–393
sustenance payments *see* financial support
Swan Hill **xv**, 285, 369, 372

Thomas, William
  Aboriginal advocate 104–105, 107, 120, 123
  Aboriginal justice 29
  and Aboriginal language 104, 390
  on alcohol 25–26, 105
  assimilation 114
  and Billibellary 26, 32–33
  on cannibalism 66
  and Charles Never 52
  firearms 21–22
  food rations 107
  on future of Aboriginal people 99, 114
  Guardian of the Aborigines 104
  and inducements 107, 109
  Inspector of reserves 125
  and Merri Creek School 48–49
  on Native Police Corps 44–45, 46
  as patriarch 129
  on the removal of children 114
  on reserves 122–123, 125
  on Samuel Lettsom's raid 32
  on schools 47, 114
  takes Aboriginal people to England 154
  on Tommy Bungaleen 117
  on treatment of Aboriginal people 20–21
  'Villiers Fighting' 83

Winberry *27*
on Woiwurrung employees 113
on the 'Yarra Camp' 30–31
Thorpe family 135, 161–162, 225, 227, *380*
tourism *200*, 218, 345
traditional beliefs and practices *164*, *413*
acceptance and recognition 335
Acts of Parliament 188
anecdotes xvii
aquaculture 412
artworks xix
attachments to country 375
boomerang xix
cannibalism 65
ceremonies 27–28, 63
and Christianity 139
corroborees 24, 28, 60, 109–111, 297
creation beliefs xvii
cultural renaissance 397
dances 396, *397*
death and mourning 26, 156, 376, 392
decision making 171
and elders 129
evidence of xix
fire *200*, 411
health and wellbeing 26–27
hunting xix
impacts of population decline 96
initiations 163
interment xix
killings 53, 86
kinship 40, 57, 249
Koori Open Door Education schools 372
and land 105, 383
language 212, 288–289
laws 28–29
marriage 141
medicines 89
meetings 109
names 13, 57
oral traditions xvii
performances 297–298, 372
protection of home 75
protocols 397
punishments 30–31
ritualistic killings 77, 85–86, 87
rubbing bodies with flesh 66–67
songlines 388
sorcery 67, 163
totemic animals 77
totemic division (moiety) xxi
and tourism 164
United Nations on 424, 426
VCE, 'Indigenous Languages' 389
warfare xxi
Welcome to Country *401*
see also cultural heritage

treaty *see* Batman Treaty
Tucker, Margaret 280, 287, 289, 294, 302,
308, 335, 342, 359, 389, *390*

United Nations 308, 334, 340, 347, 399, 400,
411, 412, 423–427

Victorian Aboriginal Group 228–229, 231,
246, 304, 316
Victorian Aborigines Advancement League
Aboriginal Girls Hostel Committee 331
Alick Jackomos 332
assimilation 331
Australian Aborigines' League 332
Doug Nicholls 349
'Doug Nicholls Centre' 332
Federal Council for Aboriginal
Advancement 331
finances 348–349
forced movements 330
funerals 352
housing 332
impact of Black Power movement 344
Lake Tyers 334
Onus, Bill 336
role 331
Stewart Murray 349
white membership 336
violence
access to land 70, 73–74
and alcohol 106, 158
anecdotes 22, 78, 293
Brodribb River 82
Convincing Ground 82
death tolls figures 79–82, 83
disputes over women 71
Fighting Hills 82
Gippsland 22, 69
inter-racial 81
inter-se killings 87, 159, 161
measured 75–76
Murdering Gully 82
Myall Creek 80
revenge 22, 26, 81–82
sealers 14
shepherds 14
Slaughterhouse Creek 82
Warrigal Creek 82
Wathaurong Aboriginal Cooperative,
Geelong 357
see also domestic violence
vocational training 187, 192, 243–244, 245,
263, *357*
voting rights 307–308
Vroland, Anna 251, 266, 280, 304, 310, 314,
316

Wandin, Robert 134, *135*, 167, 173, *179*, 207
Wandin family *135*, 207, 221
Wathaurong Aboriginal Cooperative, Geelong 354, 357, 358
Wathawurrung people xxi, 4–5, 11, 12, 74, 92, 125, 158
Western District xx, 46, 79, 80–82, 84, 87, 92, 244
Western Port people 20, 45, 107, 157
Westernport district xxi, 4, 6
Westgarth, William 64, 65, 66, 98
white people
  on Aboriginal deaths 82
  on Aboriginal intellect 100, 120–121, 222, 243
  Aboriginal perceptions of 57, 73, 74
  attitudes 28, 41, 61, 64, 72, 82, 300, 318
  compensation for losses 76
  at corroborees 110
  death tolls figures 79–80
  diversity of 54
  on future of Aboriginal people 94, 97–99, 100, 101, 122, 130, 143, 154, 176
  on inter-tribal skirmishes 86
  on killing Aboriginal people 78, 79, 83–84
  and land of the traditional owners 55, 63, 70, 74, 129–130, 177, 296
  Neerim South 326
  Nowa Nowa 326
  paternalism 128–129, 163, 177
  population figures 54
  rescued by Aboriginal people 151
  stock losses 78–79, 83, 84
  unwarranted violence 73
  Victorian Aborigines Advancement League 331
  voyeurism 163–164
Wimmera people 60, 147, 163, 346
Woiwurrung people
  arrests 31–32
  captured 5–6
  ceremonies 28
  clan xxi
  creation beliefs xvii
  demographics 29–30
  elders and alcohol 25
  in employment 111
  infanticide 64

intermarriage 288
land claims and proposals 382
in Melbourne 19–20, 105
Native Police Corps 43
ngurungaeta 32
and photographs 112
population decline 114
reserves and missions 38, 39, 125
school children 47
traditional beliefs and practices 26–27
at Warrandyte 107
women 6
  Aboriginal Girls Hostel Committee 331
  Acts of Parliament 187, 399
  and alcohol 158
  arrests and imprisonment 405
  death tolls 9
  domestic violence 21, 158, 271, 357, 373
  education 114, 301
  employment 62, 136, 148–149, 265
  independent 160–161
  and kinship 291
  Lady Gladys Nicholls Hostel for Girls *334*
  population figures 71, 108
  role in peacemaking 57
  salaries 148–149
  sexual assaults 366
  sexual services 58
  sexually transmitted diseases 88
  and smallpox 9
  traditional beliefs and practices 28–29, *164*
  United Nations on 425
  vocational training 136, 231, 263
Women's International League for Peace and Freedom 233, 251, 275–277, 310
Wonga, Simon 33–34, 112, 123, 125
Worthy, Reginald 343, 345, 350, 361, 362
Wotjobaluk people xvii, 9, 121, 149, 288, 385, 407
Wurundjeri Woi Wurrung Cultural Heritage Aboriginal Corporation 411–412, 413, **415**

Yarra camp 30–32, 34
Yarra River 38, 411
Yorta Yorta people xxiv, 262, 264, 288, 296, 347, 381–382, 383, 384, 385, 399, **415**